Morgan and Stedman on Computer Contracts

AUSTRALIA
LBC Information Services—Sydney

CANADA AND USA
Carswell—Toronto

NEW ZEALAND
Brooker's—Auckland

SINGAPORE AND MALAYSIA
Sweet & Maxwell Asia)
Singapore and Kuala Lumpur

Morgan and Stedman on Computer Contracts

Sixth Edition

Richard Morgan

MA, FBCS, FIInfSc

Kit Burden

Partner, Barlow Lyde and Gilbert

LONDON
SWEET & MAXWELL
2001

Published in 2001 by
Sweet & Maxwell Limited of
100 Avenue Road, London NW3 3PF
(http://www.sweetandmaxwell.co.uk)
Typeset by LBJ Typesetting Ltd of Kingsclere
Printed and Bound in Great Britain by
MPG Books Ltd, Bodmin, Cornwall.

First Published 1979
Sixth Edition 2001

Previous editions published as Computer Contracts,
authors Richard Morgan and Graham Stedman

No natural forests were destroyed to make this product;
only farmed timber was used and replanted

ISBN 0 421 742 50X

A CIP catalogue record for this book is available from
the British Library

The authors have in respect of this work aserted generally their
right of identification under the U.K. Copyright, Designs and Patents Act 1988.

©
SWEET & MAXWELL
2001

CONTENTS

PREFACE

Regular users of this book will have noticed a change of title. This is occasioned by the fact that Graham Stedman who was co-author of the second, third, fourth and fifth editions of this work, over a period of almost twenty years, has finally decided to bow out. We gratefully acknowledge the excellent work he did over that long period. The present standing of the book is largely due to his enthusiasm, legal skills and sense of structure.

This is not a book on the law contract as such. For that, the reader must be referred to the standard legal texts. Our purpose is twofold: to illuminate the computer content of agreements and to provide useable precedents. In writing this book, we have kept before us the picture of a company secretary or legal adviser with little experience of computers who is suddenly asked to look over "the computer contract" and comment on it. His problem in understanding the contract (let alone looking for pitfalls) arises chiefly from the computer aspects. This book may help him to understand the main types of computer contract and the provisions he may expect to find in them. We are also concerned with the lawyer or other person involved in drafting a contract and to that end have devised a set of precedents, one of the features of this book.

The main changes in this edition are in Part III on Computer Services. Two new chapters have been added: on outsourcing agreements. (Chapter 11), and one on Internet contracts (Chapter 12). The latter embraces both Internet service provider contracts (which by virtue of the Data Protection Act 1998 are required to be made or evidenced in writing) and website design agreements. These have resulted in corresponding new Precedents for an outsourcing agreement [S], website hosting agreements [T,U], and two website access agreements, one for business customers [V] and one for consumers [W].

In addition the whole text has been thoroughly revised. Since the last edition, there have been a sprinkling of new cases (most notably *South West Water Services Ltd v. International Computers Ltd* and *Mars UK Ltd v. Teknowledge*) but also a number of significant pieces of legislation, including, in particular, the Data Protection Act 1998, the Competition Act 1998, the Contracts (Rights of Third Parties) Act 1999 and the Electronic Communications Act 2000.

A word of explanation is required as to the examples of clauses which we have used in Chapters 1–13. We have been concerned to reflect the reality of computer contracts, warts and all. We have therefore consistently kept real contracts before us, and it seemed sensible to use some of these by way of illustration of the kind of thing to expect. They are to be distinguished from the precedents at the end of the book, and originate from a number of companies in the industry, though most clauses have been substantially rewritten to achieve some measure of uniformity. In one or two cases we have telescoped clauses from more than one source, or even devised our own. The originators of these clauses are in no way responsible for their clauses as they appear in this book, though we must take this opportunity of acknowledging help and co-operation from all sectors of the computer industry in contributing material.

The last chapter is primarily concerned with what to do when things go wrong. As this is not a book on the law of contract, we have generally avoided discussion of legal remedies and instead described a number of organisations to which the aggrieved party might turn. Needless to say that party must still consider his purely legal remedies as well.

The precedents are designed to give a standard form for practitioners to use in the majority of cases. Naturally there can be no attempt to cover every conceivable circumstance. In many instances, readers may have to use more than one precedent to satisfy all their needs. In particular, hardware contracts, unless they are for add-on equipment, almost invariably contain some software elements. Precedents are always potentially dangerous if followed slavishly and readers are reminded of the need to consider the circumstances of a transaction carefully before using any of the precedents in this book.

Clauses in precedents have a reference in square brackets to the point in the text at which such a clause is discussed. The reader should use this cross-reference to satisfy himself that the clause is fully relevant to his requirements and we would recommend the user to read Chapters 1–14 before using any of the precedents. In Chapters 1–13 there are also cross-references by which the reader can identify the precedent clauses which suggest deal with the matter in the text.

We wish to thank in particular our families for their patience and those of our colleagues who have taken the time to assist us with the process of reviewing and updating this latest edition.

July 2000   RSM
                                                             KB

TABLE OF CASES

---

[1] This report concentrates on only two aspects of this case: interim payments and leave to appeal. It is therefore more useful to consider the case as unreported so far as questions of liability in contract are concerned. The case was heard in QBD, Technology and Construction Court and judgment delivered July 5, 1999.

TABLE OF STATUTES

TABLE OF STATUTORY INSTRUMENTS

TABLE OF EUROPEAN LEGISLATION

CHAPTER 1

INTRODUCTION: THE IMPORTANCE OF CONTRACTS AND THE STRUCTURE OF THE INDUSTRY

1.0 INTRODUCTION

Computer people against Luddites is a hackneyed anti-thesis. Within the computer industry there are other less obvious antitheses: between the machinery and its programs; between buying a computer and buying the services of a computer; and between first time purchase and subsequent maintenance.

First some definitions: the machinery of a computer is loosely designated *hardware*. This applies to mainframe computers and PCs (personal computers) equally. The programs which run on this computer are equally generally called *software*. This is a fundamental distinction which must be grasped at the outset. No less important must be the realisation that both hardware and software are vital to the successful processing of any work on a computer.

1.1 THE IMPORTANCE OF CONTRACTS

Before considering the types of contract it is necessary to stress the importance of a written contract. The reasons for this will become obvious from further reading of this book, but it is worth mentioning at this point two cases where the supplier may be reluctant to provide detailed contracts. One is the field of PCs (dealt with in more detail below [1.4] and in Chapter 4), and the other is where the supplier gets from the customer a "letter of intent" which then (perhaps unexpectedly) proves to have contractual force as explained below.

Any purchase of computer or computer-related goods or services should be preceded by negotiations. Eventually there may be an exchange of letters (letters of intent) in which the customer will say that he is prepared to buy (rent or lease), subject to a formal contract being signed. The absence of the last phrase may well turn the letter of intent into a binding contract. Readers unfamiliar with computer contracts should accordingly read through the relevant sections of this book before signing any letter of intent, however contractually guarded.

Before ever reaching this stage a prospective purchaser will need to have thought not only about the contractual obligations he will be taking on, but also about those which he will want his supplier to undertake. In general it is highly desirable to see any supplier's standard contract early and to negotiate on its terms as part of the general negotiations, rather than to seek to change its terms after the main bargaining is complete, prices finalised, and the goods and services defined.

Particular areas which a customer should look to are:

(1) Confidentiality and the need for a non-disclosure agreement [Z];

(2) Acceptance criteria [2.3.6, 3.3];

(3) Disclaimers of responsibility and their enforceability under English law [2.3.8, 3.3.1];

(4) Title and intellectual property rights [2.8, 3.8].

Furthermore, we shall see also that under the Data Protection Act 1998 (Schedule 1, Part II, para. 12) what used to be known as bureau contracts will now have to be made and evidenced in writing [10.3.3] and that this applies to a large number of IT contracts which might not at first glance be thought to be bureau contracts [1.10, 6.2, 8.7.2, 11.3, 12.1.1]

Non-disclosure agreements [Z]

These are useful when details (particularly about software packages) are being sent to a prospective purchaser. The intention is to prevent the prospective purchaser (as far as possible) from cribbing your ideas for their own commercial benefit. Such contracts usually consist of an agreement to be signed by the user not to disclose the contents of documentation sent to him, to rivals or to any other third party; to limit data to authorised members of staff; and not to copy ideas. The examples in 10.6.3 cover these points. Another type of non-disclosure agreement, whereby a systems house and its staff undertake to safeguard a client's secrets, is discussed in Chapter 3 [3.7.2]. Non-disclosure is also particularly relevant to beta test agreements (see Chapter 6).

1.2 HARDWARE

Hardware is relatively straightforward. The companies which are generally thought of as "computer companies"—IBM, Compaq, Dell, Tiny, and so on—are all manufacturers and sellers of hardware. So too are a host of smaller companies which manufacture equipment to add to others' hardware. For example, in the field of screens/VDU's, there are large number of specialist manufacturers who must be thought of as hardware suppliers.

Hardware can be bought, rented or leased, the last sometimes being from specialised leasing companies rather than from the manufacturer (see Chapter 7). Hardware can also be bought from companies who do very little manufacturing, but whose primary purpose is to assemble equipment manufactured by others. In its extreme form this assembling of pre-manufactured parts is sometimes called "badge engineering". In these cases a purchaser will buy from a distributor [Chapter 5].

1.3 SOFTWARE

Software consists of programs, and programs are the instructions to the computer. Programs may be divided into two main categories: applications programs and systems software.

Applications programs are simply the programs to do the particular job required—payroll, order entry, stock control, etc. But the computer also requires an additional set of programs for more esoteric functions: operating systems, compilers, utility programs, etc. It may be useful to summarise these briefly. An *operating system* is a program present in the computer at all times which schedules the work being done, provides a log, allocates space and peripheral equipment, and so on. Windows, DOS, and Unix are all examples. *Compilers* are programs which convert instructions written by programmers into the machine code which alone can be read and used by the computer. *Utilities* are general programs to provide useful facilities which can be incorporated into applications programs (such as the ability to sort data into ascending or descending order), or which can be used as a general assistance to the computer department (for example, a program to detect computer viruses).

After this very brief discussion of what software is, an equally cursory glance at how software is produced may not be inappropriate. Software differs from hardware in its intangibility, in the near impossibility of defining precisely what is required. Although the user may have one computer, whether it is large or small, there is no limit to the potential number of programs it may require.

The analogy with books may be pursued. At first sight the vital feature of a book is its subject matter—what does it do? The same may be said of a program—what is the application? What function does it perform? But this is only the start. There are good books and bad books on the same topics, and there are good programs and bad programs to perform the same function. Programs may be crudely thought to be bad in the sense that they do not really fulfil the function at all. Here a package program (a program already written and available off-the-shelf to all comers) is like a book: if it doesn't do what you want, you shouldn't buy it. But many programs are written expressly for one particular user: if that program does not fulfil its function, where does the fault lie? It may of course be the programmer's fault—he didn't read his instructions, he doesn't understand the computer or its operating system or compiler, or simply he cannot write programs. In fact, the layman may be amazed to know that the actual *writing* of the program is in some ways the simplest part of the whole operation. What is more usually at fault is the specification of the client's requirements. This may be made clear if the stages in program production are considered.

First, there must be a perceived need by the client for the software, and this need must be unambiguously expressed. A document embodying this is usually called a *functional specification* and it may also include performance criteria [3.3.2].

Second, this functional specification must be translated into terms of the particular hardware and software which is going to do the job; this is sometimes called the *systems specification*.

Third, the systems specification must be reduced to a detailed analysis of each software component or program, called a *program specification*.

Fourth, the programs must be written, a time consuming and complicated process.

Fifth, they must be adequately tested. This is typically a two-stage operation: first each individual part of the program is tested alone (*program testing*); then the suite of the associated programs is tested as a whole (*systems testing*).

Sixth, each of these stages must be adequately documented both so that any residual "bugs" can easily be identified, and also to allow for future extensions and improvements—functions covered by the general term *software maintenance*.

The terminology to describe these stages may vary slightly from one systems house to another, and the distinction between the first three is slightly arbitrary and may be blurred. But—whatever names are used and whatever the number of stages—the elements of all six stages should be present if a piece of software is to be of any value. It follows that the neglect of any of these stages can bring disaster. The functional specification, for example, often becomes a contractual document incorporated by reference, and it is essential for a client to study it rigorously to ensure that it accurately and completely embodies all his requirements. The case of *MacKenzie Patten & Co. v. British Olivetti Limited* (unreported, decided January 11, 1984 (QBD)) in particular arose, at least in part, from the absence of a clear specification of what was required, with both sides apparently relying on nothing better than memory to help them decide what the purchaser had or had not asked the supplier to produce. Those who wish to study this cautionary tale should read G. Stedman: "The MacKenzie Patten Decision: Both Sides of the Coin" in *Computer Law & Practice* (January/February 1985), pp. 92–94 and G.M. Smith and D.W. Robinson: "MacKenzie Patten: The Defence View. *Caveat vendor*? Traps for Honest Salesman", *ibid.*, pp. 95–96.

Too many inexperienced purchasers of software look only as far as stage four, and ignore the possibility of testing and documentation. They do so at their peril, for—as the section on software acceptance [3.3] shows—the whole question of whether or not the program can be said to be complete, and therefore acceptable, can really be decided only by testing. Of course, a client should do his own testing, but a software house willing to carry out tests on his behalf, and show him the results of those tests (lists of each condition tested for and its result), is taking its job more seriously and is likely to inspire greater confidence.

All these things have to be paid for, and as a rough rule it may be said that a cut-price software job is likely to economise on testing first and documentation second. This means that any comparison of software quotations purely on price is apt to be misleading. A potential purchaser of software should check that all these stages are adequately covered. Similarly, where a software house has been held to a fixed-price quotation, if it is in any danger of exceeding its quotation it will be tempted to economise on stages five and six. For the client, a contract on which his software house is losing money is a difficult situation for he will have to make vigorous attempts to keep the work produced by all six stages up to the standard he requires.

New legislation which is likely to have significant effect on purchase and supply of software is the Contracts (Rights of Third Parties) Act 1999. The old English law principle of privity of contract whereby someone who was not a party to a contract has no rights under that contract has been turned on its head by this Act. The parties need to specify as such if it is the case that they wish to exclude third parties from having any rights under the contract. The general view of lawyers is that if the parties do not intend to exclude such third-party rights they would be advised to include them explicitly, probably in a Schedule. Obviously such third-party rights might arise in many guises and almost any type of contract, but one which is particularly relevant to IT contracts is the case of a software licence being granted by an organisation other than the one to whom the intellectual property rights belong. A classic instance of this was in the Scottish case of *Beta Computers (Europe) Ltd v. Adobe Systems (Europe) Ltd* [1996] F.S.R. 367. Software developed and owned by Oracle was being marketed (perfectly lawfully) by Beta, and Adobe sought to purchase a licence to use the software. Oracle were not party to the contract between Beta and Adobe, but the judge decided that Oracle's conditions were generally enforceable against the purchaser (Adobe). However, it is to be noted that Scots law never had the English privity of contract rule so there is not the same difficulty in positing the rights of a third party to the contract. In commenting on the nature of the third-party right the judge gave as an analogy:

> "a contract between a purchaser and a manufacturer of an object which could not be produced without making use of patented material, or used thereafter without a licence from the owner of the patent."

The analogy looks attractive, but as the whole principle of the Act is new to English law, it is as yet impossible to say how the Act will be used or what its effect will be; initial indications are, however, that contract draughtsmen are being assiduous in excluding its application!

For the moment it seems best to exclude or include the Act explicitly in all contracts and this approach has been followed throughout this book—not just in software contracts, though it is in these types of IT contract that the Act is expected to be most relevant [A37].

1.4 PCs

PCs and word processors and the associated software are best considered separately from other computers. Definitions of a PC are extremely difficult, but they certainly include all home computers, personal computers (hence PC) and word processors with only one screen—or indeed no screen at all (stand-alone word processors). Written contracts in some cases are very brief, or even non-existent, and there was at one time a general assumption that the purchaser of a PC or its software was an enthusiast rather than a business man. This has now changed, but the low cost of the goods and services associated with PCs means that suppliers and customers alike prefer a simplified contractual relationship [4, E].

1.4.1 Unsolicited disclosures

A particular problem which arises from the low cost of PC software is that of unsolicited disclosure to a company by a programmer.

In the field of computing as in any other type of technical or scientific development, the role of the amateur or freelance inventor is relevant. Stories in the press of teenage entrepreneurs who have made a fortune from a program or hardware development encourage amateurs to write in to computer companies or software houses with bright ideas.

Such unsolicited disclosures may pose grave problems if they relate to areas where the company receiving the disclosures is already at work, since there is a danger that the disclosure by the inventor may prompt the suggestion that the company has stolen his idea. Inventors should be discouraged from giving away too much about their inventions or software too readily, and equally companies receiving such disclosures must protect themselves as far as possible, and to this end we suggest a letter for such companies to use [AA].

1.5 DISTRIBUTION

We spoke above [1.2] about the arrangement whereby a manufacturer gets another company to sell his equipment to the customer. In fact many suppliers buy in part or all of their equipment from others. There is therefore a need for distribution agreements between the original manufacturer and his distributor.

This arrangement is frequently known as an *OEM* (Original Equipment Manufacturer) agreement and is extremely common. From the term "OEM agreement", the retailing supplier (distributor) is often—with a total lack of logic—called "the OEM". He is not actually the original equipment manufacturer at all.

Much the same arrangement is made for software, with the specialist software houses and even individuals producing software, though in this case it may be sub-licensed to the customer by the distributor under licence from the originator [5, G, H, I].

1.6 TEST AGREEMENTS

Suppliers both of hardware and of software are acutely aware that the equipment or software they wish to market must stand up to robust treatment by customers. The laboratory testing which the supplier provides, while essential, is no substitute for testing "in the field". The laboratory testing is usually referred to as *alpha testing*. Any test in the field is referred to as *beta testing*.

A supplier may therefore seek to release a version of his hardware or software early to a customer in return for information from the customer as to how the new product performs. In these circumstances, the customer is aware that he is taking something which is less than perfect and that he has obligations to provide additional information to the supplier. The pricing, warranty and liability structure will reflect this [6, J].

1.7 LEASES

In this kind of agreement, the supplier sells the equipment outright to a third party leasing company, which in turn hires it to the customer who intends to use it, usually so as to enable the customer to spread the cost of the hardware acquisition over a lengthy period.

Although in many respects leases replicate rental agreements [Chapter 2] they do present a number of difficulties peculiar to themselves and it therefore seems best to treat those aspects of leases separately from other hardware and software contracts [7].

1.8 HARDWARE MAINTENANCE

That the machinery you buy will need to be maintained in good working order will come as no surprise. The point to emphasise here is that you should be certain you know how it is to be maintained, and what level of service to expect, before you enter into any purchase agreement [8, K].

1.9 SOFTWARE MAINTENANCE

Software also requires maintenance in the sense that even the best designed and tested programs are liable to "cough" at totally unexpected data. Indeed, some of the best known and most widely used software is known to be subject to large numbers of bugs, albeit few which have a material impact on the overall operation of the software. There is a well-known fable in the industry about an American payroll package which worked well for years until two employees with identical names (it might have been Esmé Brown) decided to marry each other—a contingency which the system designer (not unreasonably) had not envisaged. It may be said that there is no such thing as an absolutely perfect program, any more than there is a perfectly healthy man. Having said this, it is obvious that there are adequately healthy men and obviously sick men, and there are eminently usable programs and appallingly unusable ones.

But for software maintenance, the correction of errors or bugs ought not to be a major anxiety unless the original program was very cursorily tested. The more important aspect is the ability to improve, enhance or extend a program to take account of second (and better) thoughts which are bound to occur to those who use the programs regularly or to reflect some external (usually legislative) requirement. It is no severe criticism of a program that it could be improved in a number of respects.

Granted that development and enhancement of programs are so important, anyone purchasing, or acquiring a licence to use, software should ensure that what he is acquiring can be improved as and when he requires it. He should therefore satisfy himself as to the standard of documentation and the facilities for software maintenance. This is a particularly acute problem for the small user who has no possibility of employing programmers full-time himself (still less providing them with a lifetime's career in his organisation), but who is having programs written specially to his requirements.

The above paragraphs are appropriate for bespoke software—i.e. software written to order. For standard software supplied with the machine, the important thing is to have support from the supplier or writer—usually in the form of telephone advice in the first instance—and access to the new versions of the software as and when they are made available. It is generally the case that the supplier will wish to limit the number of versions he has to support so that when a new version becomes available it means that an older one is likely to be withdrawn in the not too distant future, so as to obviate the need to maintain a pool of staff who need to keep familiar with the obsolete versions [9, L, M].

1.10 SERVICE CONTRACTS

The provision by one company of computer services for another is nothing new though the nature of the relationship is constantly changing. Historically bureau services whereby time was bought on someone else's computer were the norm. Now that no company is without a computer of its own, the nature of the services has changed and the usual types of service in this area comprise traditional bureau services, specialised bureau services, internal service level agreements, outsourced agreements and at least two types of Internet agreement: Internet service agreements and specific web-site access agreements [12, T, U, V, W].

All of these types of agreement are liable to be swept up into the new Data Protection Act 1998's definition of a *data processor* and as such need to have written contracts with particular security and other provisions to comply with the Act.

Bureau services

The work of processing data can be performed by someone other than the owner of the data. Traditional bureau services whereby paper records are transferred to the bureau, the bureau runs the data on its machine, and the resulting output—usually print out—is taken back to the customer are by no means dead, and there are also specialised services whereby the bureau contributes particular data to the customer's data. An example is where stock exchange prices are held on the bureau and users can obtain probate valuations of share holdings by entering the date of death and the holdings of shares [10, P, Q].

Service level agreements

The growth of corporate IT networks has led to a need for those using the network and those providing it to agree on precisely what is required and to what standard. Such network service agreements are effectively also types of bureau service [R].

Outsourcing agreements

A natural extension of this is to get an outside company to provide the IT services. For most companies this means getting rid of the existing IT Department and the obvious way of doing this is to hive it off to the outsource service company together with the computers and even the relevant premises. Special considerations such as TUPE (Transfer of Undertakings (Protection of Employment) Regulations)—which lie outside the scope of this book—apply here, but these contracts can be considered as extended service level agreements. Such contracts used to be called *facilities management contracts*, but the term *outsourcing* is now more generally used [11, S].

A different type of outsource agreement is the disaster recovery contract, *i.e.* a contract whereby a third-party agreement is provided a *duplicate* computer system so as to enable the customer to re-commence operating as soon as possible after a disaster such as a fire or flood, which renders its own computer facilities inoperable. Such contracts will normally oblige the disaster recovery supplier effectively to undertake to take on the role of an outsource service provider, as and when such a disaster strikes.

The internet

For most of us the Internet Service Provider's Agreement was something which flashed across our screens when we first set up as a user of a particular system. However, it is certainly a contract with a *data processor* within the Data Protection Act 1998 and to be evidenced in writing and treated as a type of bureau contract.

Some of these contracts are with the independent ISPs, but equally such an agreement might be with an in-house service centre or an outsource contractor, depending on the nature of the services being provided.

A variant is the web-site design agreement which may or may not be with the ISP, in-house centre or outsource company [12].

Data preparation

One specialised bureau service is data preparation. For the purposes of this book, *data* means the variable information given to a computer program to enable it to function. For example, in a sales ledger program the data might be the invoice information. Data traditionally has been fed into the computer in machine-readable form, in which case it will need to be prepared in advance of the running of the computer program to which it relates. This is what is normally meant by *data preparation*. When a computer is first installed in an organisation which previously has not had one, data preparation can be considerable.

For on-line services [10.1.2], the data may be input directly by the user through a terminal at the time when the program is running. The more usual term here is *data entry*. This again may be a bureau service.

An alternative to data preparation or data entry is the conversion of data from the form suitable for running on one machine to a form suitable for another. This is called *data transfer* or *data conversion*.

All the processes can be provided as a service and that service has the characteristics of other bureau service contracts. All the features relating to data [10.3] will be present though most other characteristics of bureau contracts will be attenuated or non-existent.

1.11 CONSULTANCY

Consultancy is required most usually in one or other of two cases: feasibility and procurement studies, or remedial work for a system which is unsatisfactory. Computer consultancy contracts are constituted on the same lines as many other special consultancy agreements. As soon as consultancy is concerned with the analysis of systems, the client is embarking on the first phase of software production and, as we make clear in Chapter 13, much of Chapter 3 becomes relevant—see especially [3.0.3]. The user must define his end product—usually a report—in the same way as he defines a program. He must also satisfy himself as to the impartiality of the consultant. Many "consultants" are also in the business of selling hardware, so it will not be surprising if they recommend that hardware. There is nothing immoral about this, provided the client is aware of it. But if he wants independent advice, he must insist on employing a consultant whose income is derived solely from consultancy.

1.12 COMBINED CONTRACTS

Turnkey agreements

Some users know little enough about computers and are happy to leave procurement of everything to someone else—hardware, software, data preparation/transfer, maintenance. The idea is that, at the end of the time specified in the agreement, the contractor (manufacturer or software house) offers the user the key to a sparkling new computer room and says "It's all installed; it all works; it's all yours"—hence the name "turnkey". The expression is said to originate from the building and furnishing industries. The main advantage of the turnkey contract is that the customer deals with only one supplier. Thus in the event of non-performance he does not have to decide whether the failure is one of hardware or of software. He simply turns to his supplier for a remedy. This contrasts with the situation where a customer has two contracts, one for hardware and one for software, and each supplier may be tempted to blame the other. These contracts, though important, do not merit a separate chapter since they are simply combinations of Chapters 2, 3, 8 and 9—or they should be [O]. Before entering into a turnkey agreement, the user should satisfy himself that these aspects will all be carried out.

Points to consider with combined hardware and software contracts include the following:

(1) The hardware will need to be fully installed and operational before the software is delivered. If the software is commissioned software the

hardware may also need to be installed before the development work can begin unless that work is being done elsewhere.

(2) Where commissioned software is being provided, it is usual for the client to withhold a substantial portion of the purchase price until final acceptance of the software so as to have some leverage against a failure by the systems house writing the software. However, as systems houses are not usually also manufacturers of hardware they often require the purchase price for the hardware to be paid at an early stage since they are themselves already out of pocket. To deal with this it is reasonable to have two payment profiles— one for hardware and one for software. A typical hardware payment profile is set out at 2.2.1. Where there are to be separate payment profiles for hardware and software, they can still take place on the occurrence of the same general milestones [3.2.1] which might typically be on signing the contract, on delivery of hardware and software, and on passing all acceptance tests [2.3.4, 3.3.1]. The delivery of hardware and software might well of course be at different times, though the final acceptance should be a single event so as to maximise the client's bargaining position and to reflect the ultimate requirement for them to be properly integrated. Thus we might have a payment pattern as follows:

Milestone event	Hardware proportion	Software proportion
Sign contract	50%	30%
Delivery of hardware	40%	0%
Delivery of software	0%	40%
Acceptance	10%	30%

(3) Where a contract goes wrong and the system does not work, questions of fitness for purpose may arise. The key legislation here is provided by the Sale of Goods Act 1979 and the Supply of Goods and Services Act 1982. Without going into detail it will be apparent that the obligations on suppliers of goods (*e.g.* hardware) are harder to discharge and different from the obligations of those who supply services (*e.g.* commissioned software). What happens if a contract is for both? This question has been answered in the case of *St Albans v. ICL* [1995] F.S.R. 698–699, where at first instance the judge followed an Australian precedent and concluded that in such combined contracts it was reasonable to treat software as goods. This point was also commented on in the Court of Appeal, where Sir Iain Glidewell was in no doubt that software constitutes goods, *i.e.* even in a contract for software alone (*St Albans v. ICL* [1997] F.S.R. 264–267), at least to the extent that the software is supplied on some form of physical medium, such as a CD, disk or magnetic tape. This view has been attacked and is only *obiter* (*i.e.* not fully binding) but the first instance decision that in a combined hardware and software contract the two together should be considered goods is on surer ground. It is in any event of less certain application in these days when software is increasingly downloaded directly from the Internet, *i.e.* without any physical medium.

1.13 Public Sector Contracts

Since our accession to the European Union, a steady stream of directives has been issued which define the rules for public sector procurements and hence have contractual implications. At the same time there are other aspects of public sector contracts which set them apart from all other contracts, mostly dictated by the greater need for accountability in public sector contracts.

These various requirements may affect all aspects of computer contracts and readers who have to deal with such contracts should study the relevant chapters about their *type* of contract first (hardware, software, maintenance, bureaux, consultancy, etc.) and then read the chapter on public sector contracts afterwards and modify their clauses and procedures accordingly [14].

PART 1

HARDWARE AND SOFTWARE ACQUISITION

CHAPTER 2

HARDWARE

2.0 INTRODUCTION

A book dealing with computer contracts must inevitably begin with contracts for the acquisition of the computer itself. The common industry term to cover all equipment is *hardware* and this term will be used in future in this book since it covers not only the physical computer equipment (including screens, PCs and servers) but also ancillary or peripheral equipment associated with the computer's performance.

Many contracts dealing with hardware will also cover programs (software), maintenance and other topics which are covered by separate chapters in this book. Anybody purchasing a computer would be advised to examine the other chapters and see whether they are not equally as appropriate as this chapter.

Hardware contracts may involve:

(1) complete computer systems;

(2) parts of, or additions to, computer systems.

The form of payment in such contracts may be:

(1) outright purchase;

(2) rental;

(3) rental with the option to purchase;

(4) lease.

12

The relation between the supplier and his customer may be:

(1) supplier to end user;

(2) contractor to a customer who will himself be a potential supplier to other end users (distributor, sometimes also known as a reseller). Distribution agreements are dealt with in more detail in Chapter 5;

(3) supplier to leasing company which will lease the equipment to the end user—see Chapter 7;

(4) supplier to the supplier of test facilities—see Chapter 6 and Precedent J.

It should be pointed out that most suppliers use more or less standard contract forms, and the prospective customer should not expect that they will necessarily be enthusiastic about re-writing their contract. It is therefore essential that he understands the nature of the contract he is being asked to sign, so that negotiation can focus on the areas where he has a good case to ask for specific changes. A formidable body of precedent is building up to show that the courts will in case of any dispute use the Unfair Contract Terms Act 1977 to assist customers who have been more or less forced to sign standard contracts whose terms are unreasonable (and the cases of *Salvage Association v. CAP* [1995] F.S.R. 654 and *St Albans v. ICL* [1995] F.S.R. 686 spring to mind, along with the more recent example of *South West Water v. ICL* [1999] B.L.R. 420). Nevertheless, the user must still be recommended to check the contract, rather than sign something blind. He should also not be afraid to negotiate since a modest amount of negotiation away from a standard contract will not, if the bargaining position of the parties remains the same, affect his ability to rely on the Unfair Contract Terms Act 1977. It also goes without saying that the larger the value of the transaction in question, the greater the likely latitude for making changes.

The standard form may be a contract explicitly or may be in the form of a proposal, quotation or tender which becomes a contract on acceptance and signing by the customer. The reader is advised not to accept a proposal and then hope to iron out the contractual difficulties later when all bargaining power has been eroded. The pages that follow should be taken as a guide to the implications of a contract rather than as an opportunity to question every clause in a standard form.

2.1 Equipment to be Supplied

2.1.1 Equipment [A1, A2, B1, B24, O2]

A computer hardware contract is an agreement for the delivery of goods. The description of the goods to be supplied will usually be determined by reference to the identifying codes devised by the supplier to describe each machine and model number. The exact description of the goods is therefore most usually set out in a schedule which is incorporated as follows:

"The Supplier agrees to sell and the Customer agrees to purchase the equipment listed in Schedule A hereof at the prices stated therein and upon the following terms and conditions."

In the schedule will usually be a list of pieces of equipment, giving for each:

(1) the quantity of such items;

(2) the manufacturer's description—usually in the form of a number and narrative, such as DEP 117X Disk Drive;

(3) the price.

The customer must satisfy himself first that the hardware is sufficient for his needs. By that we do not simply mean that the equipment must be capable of handling his volumes of data, but more fundamentally that the disk drive in the above example may be attached to a disk drive controller which must appear implicitly or explicitly in the list; and provision must also be made for the disk packs too. Failing to address this kind of deficiency can be likened to purchasing a car only to find out the wheels were extra! The customer must therefore check any such list extremely carefully with any orders or correspondence to ensure that it is complete and in doing so make sure that any appropriate technical input is obtained, either from in-house experts or external consultants, so as to be certain that the list is (a) complete, (b) intelligible and (c) agreed by both sides.

The equipment list does not usually include operating supplies or disposables, *e.g.* disk packs, toner cartridges, etc. One supplier explicitly excludes them:

"Operating supplies such as disk packs, stationery, printing cartridges and similar accessories are not supplied as part of the Equipment."

Even if no such clause appears, the customer should assume that he will have to order these separately, and he should seek his supplier's advice on the type, quality and quantity of such accessories as well as their price.

The list may well have some software (programs) added at the end. The most likely candidate is the operating system—the program described above [1.3] and supplied usually by the manufacturer and intended to schedule work on the computer and ensure the smooth and efficient utilisation of the peripheral devices such as disk drives, printers, and so forth. If this item is absent, the customer should ensure that it will be provided at some stage—perhaps in a second, related agreement for software. If it is present, the customer should be aware that he is purchasing a software package, and that the relevant provisions for a software contract should apply to that item at least [Chapter 3] though the price is usually "bundled" with that of the hardware. (The provision of hardware with embedded or integral software is discussed further in 2.8.3 below.)

It should also be observed that the supplier sometimes reserves to himself the right to substitute other equipment:

"The Supplier reserves the right to make substitutions and modifications in the Specifications of the Equipment designed by him provided that such substitutions or modifications will not materially adversely affect the functionality or performance of such Equipment in the intended application."

If this clause merely means that the supplier is constantly improving his equipment and wishes to incorporate such improvements, it cannot reasonably be objected to. But it is worth pointing out that performance [2.3.5] is not guaranteed in most contracts anyway. A cautious customer might ask for a list of such modifications and substitutions on delivery, but he should be warned that it will probably be both lengthy and technical. In practice, for most purchases of "standard" hardware from major suppliers, the customer will be able to do little about this clause, although the better he defines the performance level required in the application, the more secure his position will be.

In rental agreements there may be a limitation on the use of the hardware, since the supplier may be concerned to preserve some resale value in the equipment or possibly also to limit his maintenance obligation, in which case a clause such as the following, though unusual, may occur:

> "Payment by the Customer to the Supplier of the monthly charge as set out in *Clause X* hereof shall entitle the Customer to use of the Equipment for up to any *180* hours in each calendar month and to the benefit of maintenance in accordance with *Clause Y* hereof. Use beyond that limit shall be subject to an additional charge at the rate defined in *Schedule A* hereof.
>
> The Customer shall report to the Supplier at the end of each calendar month the total time of use of the Equipment during that month. Use of any part of the Equipment shall be deemed to be use of the Equipment. Any hours unused below *180* hours in any calendar month cannot be carried over into any subsequent month."

Alternatively, the hardware supplier may require that the equipment in question be kept severable from the customer's other hardware (albeit linked to it), so as to be easily identifiable (and therefore reclaimable) at the end of the rental period.

A word about second-hand equipment. Any proposing purchaser of second-hand equipment will not expect to find any manufacturer's warranties. There may also be difficulties about export control even though the vendor is in the same country as the purchaser [2.9.1]. If software (*e.g.* an operating system) is included there could also be serious problems in obtaining an assignment of (*i.e.* being able to transfer) the relevant licence, which are dealt with in 3.0.2, 7.6 and 11.6.3 below.

2.1.2 Location [A1, B1]

A hardware contract should specify precisely where the goods are to be installed, since this can affect delivery [2.3.1] and transport costs [2.3.3], and is also relevant to the customer's duty to prepare the site [2.6.3]. This is usually covered either by including an identification of the installation site in a schedule and referring to ". . . at the installation site described in the Third Schedule hereto" or else quite simply by saying in an ordinary clause: "The installation site is . . ."

Alternatively, if the supplier is to be responsible for installation (as may be the case where the supplier has taken on responsibility for a turnkey contract [1.12]), the supplier may be the one obliged to deal with installation, as follows:

> "The Supplier shall be responsible for preparing the Installation Site described in the *Third* Schedule. The Supplier shall use all reasonable endeavours to minimise any disruption to the Customer's business which may be occasioned thereby."

In appropriate circumstances, the supplier's obligations can be taken a step further by first requiring the supplier to confirm to the customer that the installation site is a suitable location for the installations of the hardware.

Sometimes—for instance for an OEM agreement on a cumulative discount basis [2.2.5, Chapter 5]—it is not possible to define the installation site(s) in advance, in which case a clause such as this is suitable:

"Delivery of each piece of Equipment shall be made to any address within the United Kingdom designated by the Customer in writing to the Supplier at least one month before the estimated date of delivery."

In a rental agreement it is usual to stipulate that the hirer cannot alter the equipment or move it to another location during the continuance of the agreement:

"No movement or alteration to the Equipment shall be made except with the Supplier's written consent which may be revoked if the performance or maintenance of the Equipment is thereby impaired. In the event of such revocation the Customer shall at his own expense relocate and reinstate the Equipment in its original position and to its original condition and standard of performance."

In practice, movement of equipment after installation (whether in a sale or rental agreement) is usually prohibited or limited in this way by a maintenance agreement [Chapter 8]. Any customer wishing to obtain equipment to move frequently (*e.g.* for demonstration purposes) should notify the supplier and maintenance contractor before signing any contracts. Different considerations of course apply to PCs and portables [8.1.1].

2.2 PAYMENT

2.2.1 Outright purchase [A3]

Sometimes hardware can be supplied "off-the-shelf" ("ex-works" may be the preferred term), in which case it is anticipated that delivery will follow shortly on the signing of the contract. An example clause to this effect reads as follows:

"The Supplier shall issue an invoice for the Equipment upon its shipment. Payment of such invoice shall be made in full within *ten* days of the issue of a certificate of test for the Equipment."

But see the section on Installation tests [2.3.4], since this example fails to deal with acceptance.

Occasionally, the hardware is a special piece of equipment, designed to the user's particular requirements and so will not be built until after the signing of the contract. In that case it is usual to make payment in two or more stages, the first being on signing the contract and the last usually on delivery and acceptance. For example:

"Invoices for payment of the Contract Price will be presented as follows:

   (i) *30* per cent on signature of this Agreement;

   (ii) *40* per cent on issue of a certificate by the Supplier that the manufacture of major items is complete;

   (iii) *30* per cent on delivery and acceptance in accordance with *Clause X* hereof."

It will be observed that the supplier has complete control over stage (ii) (by which time he has secured 70 per cent of the price), and that 'major' items are not defined. From the customer's perspective, it would obviously be preferable to delay as much of the contract payment as possible until acceptance [2.3.4]. However, where the contract is for both hardware and software, a different payment profile for the software may achieve much the same objective [1.12].

Where the purchase price is payable by instalments the parties should be careful to clarify whether any instalment is to be made by way of a part payment or a deposit. If an instalment is made by way of a deposit then it will not be recoverable by the customer if, in breach of contract, he does not perform his side of the bargain, even though the actual loss suffered by the supplier as a result of such breach is less than the amount of the deposit.

Chapter 6 on test agreements gives other examples of contracts for experimental or development work.

2.2.2 Rental [B1, B2, B13, B14]

The earliest computer contracts were almost all for a rental from the manufacturer, and for some people this is still the preferred method. It gives some protection against obsolescence and if an internal capital budget is exhausted equipment can be rented against a revenue budget. It may be particularly useful also where the project is of a research or experimental nature with the possibility of its being either abandoned or changed significantly on completion. However, some suppliers—particularly of peripheral equipment or of small systems—decline to consider rental agreements, so a customer should not assume this option is open to him. In the case of a rental, payment is usually monthly in advance.

Rental usually commences on the date of delivery, which is often not identified in the agreement. For small items at least, a common procedure is for the supplier to hand over a delivery note and the first invoice on delivery, and then date them. The customer should, however, seek to ensure that payment obligations run from the date that the hardware has actually been installed and is demonstrably ready for use, *e.g.* as follows:

> "The charges for the Equipment shall commence on the day following the day of issue by the Supplier of a certificate that the Equipment is or but for the Hirer's non-compliance with his obligations under this Agreement would have been installed and ready for use."

Rental is typically for an initial period of years with a proviso that it will be continued thereafter, terminable on an agreed number of months' written notice:

> "The period of rental under this Agreement shall continue for an initial period of *two* years from the date of commencement specified in *Clause X* above and will remain in force thereafter until terminated by at least *three* months' written notice given by either party to the other."

Alternatively, the agreement may be terminated at the end of the initial period (which will need to be defined) or at any time thereafter:

> "The period of rental under this Agreement shall continue for an initial period of *2* years from the date of commencement specified in *Clause X* above and will remain in force thereafter unless or until terminated by at least *3* months' written notice given by either party to the other expiring at the end of the said initial period or at any time thereafter."

An alternative might be to provide for termination within a set period before the anniversary date, failing which the agreement will automatically be renewed for a further year until the next anniversary date, and so on.

Agreements for one year are uncommon, and for less than one year almost unknown. For a longer rental period (three years or more), it is probably more advantageous to both sides to consider an outright purchase or leasing agreement [Chapter 7], since the rental price may well amount to the equivalent of purchase over three or four years.

In the case of a rental, where title to the equipment remains with the supplier, it is usual for the supplier to stipulate that the hirer must have the equipment maintained only by the supplier or supplier's nominee. Most rental agreements include the maintenance clauses in the same document and specify monthly payments of both rental and maintenance charges, but some have a separate but related maintenance agreement. For convenience, all maintenance clauses are dealt with in Chapter 8.

2.2.3 Rental with option to purchase [B33]

An agreement of this type may be particularly useful if the customer is not quite sure whether the equipment will be able to perform the particular functions he has in mind, and wishes to prove the equipment for a period. It will have all the clauses of an ordinary rental agreement and will in addition contain a clause such as:

"At any time after the expiry of *one* year from the date of commencement hereof the Hirer may upon giving *3* months' written notice purchase the Equipment at the price described in the *Second* Schedule hereto."

Then follow clauses appropriate to a purchase agreement, or alternatively:

"The Equipment shall be purchased by the Hirer on the Supplier's standard terms and conditions of sale for the time being in force."

The customer would, in such circumstances, do well to try to fix the purchase terms applicable as being those in existence on the date the agreement is entered into, to guard against the risk of (adverse) changes to the conditions in the period before the option to purchase is exercised.

In the case of such an agreement, the purchase price usually reflects some (but not all) of the payments made under the rental agreement. An alternative way of having a similar agreement is by terminating the rental and having a new rental-to-purchase agreement. Such an agreement defines the date of the rental-to-purchase purchase conversion, and then might proceed:

"The Supplier shall raise an invoice for the Equipment on the Rental-to-Purchase conversion date. Payment of such invoice shall be made in full by the Customer within *10* days of the date of the invoice."

2.2.4 Prices

These are often based on a published price list (almost invariably quoted exclusive of Value Added Tax), and will be taken from a proposal or quotation. As such, they are not likely to change except in the cases mentioned below.

Currency rates [A3 (2)]

Large numbers of manufacturers are based abroad, and in the past occasionally wildly fluctuating exchange rates for foreign currencies have had a damaging effect on the U.K. suppliers of goods manufactured abroad. This has prompted one supplier to add, in the days when the pound was falling against the dollar, the following clause in a rental agreement:

> "In the event that the prevailing exchange rate between the United States dollar and the English pound sterling has fluctuated in excess of two per cent from the time the quotation is tendered to the time payment is received the Supplier reserves the right in its sole discretion to adjust any prices or authorised quotations or price lists and to apply such adjusted prices or quotations or price lists to all customers of the same class and the customer agrees promtly to remit the amount of any such adjustment."

The basic intention is understandable, but we have to admit the drafting of this example is particularly poor. Two per cent of what? Is this two cents in the dollar or two pence in the pound? Then, too, "fluctuate" could mean an increase of 1 per cent followed by a decrease of 2 per cent, bringing the exchange back to 1 per cent below the starting price. The business of applying adjustments to other customers of the same class (and what is a class?) is of no interest in this agreement. Also, the adjustment is not geared to the changeability. And what if the rate goes up? Accordingly, a preferable form of words could be as follows:

> "The prices in this Agreement are based on an exchange rate between the United States dollar and the English pound sterling of $1.60 to £1. If from the date hereof to the date the last payment is received the pound shall fall 2¢ U.S. or more below that rate the Supplier reserves the right to increase any prices for equipment still unpaid proportionally to take account of the new exchange rates."

It is perfectly reasonable to quote an actual exchange rate in the agreement since presumably the original English price lists have been based on such a rate.

Price adjustments on long deliveries [A3 (3)]

Apart from quotation of exchange rates, the right to adjust a price is likely to figure in any contract for specially commissioned hardware which is not ex-works. This may reflect some uncertainty on the part of the supplier as to how exactly he is to construct the equipment, but more usually it is simply to protect him from the effects of inflation on his own suppliers:

> "At any time before the *three* months immediately preceding the Estimated Delivery Date the Supplier shall be entitled to vary this Agreement to accord with any changes in the Supplier's price list current from time to time and to give notice of such variation to the Purchaser. This Agreement shall be deemed to be varied accordingly by such notice of variation unless the purchaser shall within *14* days of receipt of such notice terminate this Agreement by giving notice to the Supplier."

This clause does not permit the supplier to increase his price beyond the date specified even though the actual delivery may be late, and it links any such increase to published price lists. As such it is quite a fair clause, though the option to terminate is not very realistic since the purchaser's preparations for receiving the equipment [2.6.3] will probably be so far advanced as to be irreversible.

2.2.5 Discounts

In a book of this sort it would be inappropriate to deal in detail with the different discount agreements. In general terms a discount of, say, 10 per cent is not unusual where the customer is buying (or enhancing) more than one machine; and sometimes much larger discounts are available when a customer is purchasing several machines either for himself or for customers of any computer-based service he provides. Some contracts have a complicated sliding scale based on the number of machines ordered within a particular year, and a provision for unearned discount (*i.e.* discount which has been allowed in expectation of a sales target for the year which has not been achieved) to be billed back to the customer. The benefit of such an agreement to the supplier is not simply that he enjoys greater turnover but also that, on the basis of such agreements, he can more accurately schedule the demand for and manufacture of his equipment. There are some manufacturers virtually all of whose output is available only under discount on OEM agreements [1.5], so that they have no interest in a purchaser of a single system. This is particularly true of the PC market.

2.3 DELIVERY AND ACCEPTANCE

2.3.1 Delivery

Most contracts expect payment on delivery of the equipment, although a customer will naturally not wish to make any payment until acceptance. In fact, "delivery" proves on examination to be a succession of different episodes each of which is necessary to establish the efficient functioning of the equipment in its new environment. The customer's obligation to prepare the site is dealt with below [2.6.3] and will not affect the delivery itself unless he has failed to complete his preparations (or unless that obligation has expressly been assigned to the supplier, *e.g.* in a turnkey contract [1.12]). The supplier, on the other hand, is required to assemble all the equipment, test it before it leaves the factory, arrange and effect transport and delivery to the customer's premises, assemble it there and do any further testing. Any software delivery and acceptance [3.3] takes place after this. The hardware stages deserve examination in detail and are set out below.

2.3.2 Pre-delivery tests [A7]

Once the supplier has assembled the equipment he will test it before delivery. Most manufacturers are happy to tell the customer precisely what these tests consist of, and may allow him or his representative to be present although this is not usually considered necessary unless there is something unusual or experimental about the hardware. A typical form of words might be as set out below:

> "(a) The Supplier shall submit the Equipment to his Standard Works Test ('the Test') before despatch to the Customer. The Supplier shall supply to the Customer on request copies of the Test Specification and certification that the Equipment has passed the Test.
> (b) If the Test is held in the presence of the Customer or his representatives the Customer will be charged therefor. In the event the Customer fails by the proposed time and date of the Test to confirm his intention to attend the Test upon being given not less than 7 days prior written notice the Supplier reserves the right to proceed with the Test and the Test will be deemed to have been

conducted in the presence of the Customer and the results thereof shall be deemed to have been accepted by the Customer."

Such tests are often called "diagnostic tests". Their purpose is to test the circuitry and all mechanical aspects of the equipment. For example, a test on a matrix printer will test the printing of each character in every print position so that if there is a defect either in the type itself or the print mechanism this can be identified. Engineers use the same or similar tests when checking equipment for maintenance. The customer is of course at liberty to ignore these tests (and save himself the cost of them), but by so doing he may possibly prejudice his ability at some future time to suggest that the equipment was in any way defective as at the date of delivery.

2.3.3 Packing and carriage [A8, A9, B5, B6]

Some suppliers themselves bear the costs of transportation, but some of the larger manufacturers will charge the customer:

"All costs of transportation within the United Kingdom and the Republic of Ireland and all delivery charges (including but not limited to heavy gang, handling and hoisting charges) and insurance costs until acceptance will be paid by the Customer."

The restriction of this clause to the U.K. and Ireland is not intended to benefit an export customer; rather it is because the supplier is American and is not charging separately for delivery from his factory to the U.K. but only from the airport to the customer's site.

Some manufacturers reserve the right to select the carrier, and at the same time exclude any liability for delay or loss by the carrier during delivery:

"(a) The Supplier shall select the Carrier but by so doing shall not thereby assume any liability in connection with shipment nor shall the Carrier in any way be construed as an agent of the Supplier.

(b) The Supplier shall not be liable for any damage for delay in delivery or failure to deliver when such delay is due to delays in transportation or any other cause beyond the Supplier's control."

If the supplier does not charge for delivery he will in fairness have the right to choose the carrier:

"The Contract Price includes the cost of all delivery charges to the Installation Site by any method of transport reasonably selected by the Supplier."

But even here "delivery" usually means only delivery to the door of the purchaser and not the actual putting of the equipment on to the site. The reason for this is simply that the cost of doing this will very enormously depending on the position of the site and whether hoists and other plant are necessary. An express provision to deal with this point might accordingly read as follows:

"The Supplier shall not be responsible for offloading the Equipment and moving it to the Installation Site."

Alternatively, the clause might read as follows:

"The Supplier shall deliver the Equipment to the Installation site, provided that the Customer shall be responsible for the installation of the Equipment at the Installation Site."

The packing materials, including polystyrene boxes and padded cases (called "muffs" in the trade), are often expensive since they will have been specifically built to the supplier's requirements. Some suppliers therefore ask for their return:

"All packing cases, skids, drums and other packing materials used for delivery of the Equipment to the Customer must be returned by the Customer to the Supplier's works in good condition and at the Customer's expense. The Supplier reserves the right to charge for any such packing cases and materials not so returned."

Because the equipment ceases to be under the supplier's physical control after delivery it is usual for risk, and hence the obligation to insure, to pass to the customer even though he has not yet accepted the equipment:

"Risk in the Equipment passes to the Customer upon delivery of the Equipment by the Supplier to the Installation site."

2.3.4 Installation tests [A11, B8, O12]

The results of the pre-delivery tests are not necessarily available to the customer and their purpose is primarily for the supplier. However, the prudent customer will seek to check that the equipment does indeed do what it is supposed to do, and is not defective or damaged. It is, in theory, open to the customer to devise any tests he thinks appropriate, and some customers will be capable of designing their own tests. If they do, they would be well advised to agree them with their supplier in advance, so that both sides can be clear that the tests are fair. But, for most commercial customers without specialist engineering and programming skills, it is simpler to use the existing diagnostic test packages which the supplier has himself used before delivery (and in certain circumstances the supplier will provide details of the proposed post-delivery, or installation tests). As the test is often the process which determines acceptance—and hence payment—it is in the supplier's interest that such tests should be commenced promptly:

"(a) Standard Tests on Installation ("the Tests") shall be performed by the Supplier in accordance with the Supplier's Standard Test Specifications within 7 days of the Supplier having given written notice of completion of the Supplier's installation of the Equipment at the Installation Site. If the Tests have not been performed completely within that 7-*day* period by reason of any action or omission of the Customer then the Tests will be deemed to have been performed correctly and the Customer to have accepted the Equipment.
(b) If any portion of the Equipment fails to pass the Tests on installation the Tests on the said portion of the Equipment shall, if required by the Customer, be repeated within a reasonable time and upon the same terms and conditions."

This last clause is bound up with the question of defects [2.3.8], but it is included here to point out that, before an installation can be considered complete and the equipment commissioned, each part of it must have passed (or be deemed to have passed) the acceptance tests. The clause above suggests that the customer has the option to reject the equipment immediately if it fails the installation tests, but some suppliers may seek at least one attempt to fix any identified problems before the customer can reject [A11 (2)].

It is important for the customer to ensure that the tests are carried out to his satisfaction. If he fails to carry the tests out at all, he may well be deemed to have accepted the equipment, either when he starts to use it or very soon afterwards. Failure to notify the supplier of defects may be deemed to constitute acceptance of the equipment. Indeed:

> " 'Commissioning Date' is the date on which the Supplier's standard tests on the Equipment have been satisfactorily completed at the Customer's premises or *one* month after operational use of the Equipment by the Customer begins, whichever is the sooner.
>
> Unless accepted earlier, the Equipment is deemed accepted by the Customer on the Commissioning Date."

In one example, the supplier, in stressing the importance of prompt payment, may not explicitly within the contract draw the customer's attention to his need to test the equipment. The relevant clauses say:

> "The Supplier will upon delivery and installation of the Equipment issue the Customer with a Commissioning Certificate certifying the date that the Equipment or any part thereof is ready for use.
>
> The Supplier shall issue an invoice for the Equipment upon its shipment, payment of such invoice to be made in full within *14* days of the date of the Commissioning Certificate. Interest on overdue amounts will become payable at a rate of *3* per cent per month or pro rata for parts of a month on invoices not fully paid."

The customer faced with such a clause should vigorously defend his right to have the equipment tested in his presence before acceptance can be said to have taken place and payment become due. In fact, both the parties need to be clear upon the procedure leading up to the issue of the Commissioning Certificate; the customer will want to be sure that this will only take place once the customer has agreed that the relevant acceptance tests have been successfully completed, whilst the supplier will for its part want to avoid any purely subjective measures which might enable the customer arbitrarily to delay the issue of a Commissioning Certificate, and so in turn delay payment.

2.3.5 Performance

Questions of performance—how many transactions the storage devices can hold, how quickly they can be processed, how many terminals can be handled, and what response time can be expected in a single transaction—all depend on the interaction of hardware and software. It is unlikely that there will have been any exactly analogous situation with which a proposed system can be compared. Any relatively small change in either hardware or software is liable completely to upset previous calculations. This matter is dealt with again under software [3.3.2], but it is worth repeating here that no respectable manufacturer is likely to allow performance to be a criterion of acceptance unless the opportunity is given (and paid for) to have very extensive performance tests on both hardware and software before delivery, and for any obligation to be made subject to various caveats and assumptions (*e.g.* as to the type of software to be run on it, the nature of the technical infrastructure to which it is to be connected, etc.). A clause such as the following is sometimes used:

> "The Supplier accepts no liability for failure to achieve any performance figures he or his servants may have given to the Customer unless:
>
> (a) the Supplier has specifically guaranteed them subject to specified tolerances in an agreed sum as liquidated damages; and
> (b) the environmental conditions specified in the Supplier's quotation are maintained.
>
> The payment by the Supplier of the said liquidated damages shall be in full satisfaction of any such liability for failure by the Supplier to attain such performance figures."

Even this form of words, however, may leave the supplier somewhat exposed (*e.g.* in relation to the number of batch programs as opposed to online transactions which the system is asked to deal with, etc.). One form of words we have encountered is as follows:

> "The measurement of performance will be taken at the database server level and will exclude the impact of the Customer's network (including its legacy systems). The measurement of performance will be based on responses for the top (*i.e.* fastest) *90* per cent of user dialogue transactions, and will exclude measurements taken whilst running large batch update processes which are designed to run out of office hours."

However, we are dubious whether any such wording is completely effective in removing potential areas of doubt. The customer may, in particular, be nervous of any formula which discounts the potential impact of its existing technical infrastructure and software systems. A better approach would therefore be to have the test depend on a test script agreed between the parties (which could therefore include the impact of the customer's software and which may be quite lengthy). Most importantly, the parties will also need to agree upon the actual or assumed volume of transactions which the tests are to based upon, as this will invariably be a key driver for the performance of the system.

In practice, performance figures are very rarely admitted as a part of the requirement for a commercial system, at least in relation to standard hardware sales. One attraction of outsourcing arrangements [1.10] is accordingly the possibility of negotiating such service levels, which may not have been obtainable directly from the hardware supplier.

With interactive or on-line systems where system response time [3.3.2] is important, it is of course incumbent on the customer to use telecommunications equipment at the right speed:

> "Where any data transmission speeds are given by the Supplier in relation to the Equipment, such speeds are at all times subject to conditions attached by the relevant telecommunications authority to the use of the relevant modem or other telecommunications equipment at the speeds indicated and to the capability of such modem or other telecommunications equipment to achieve such speeds."

2.3.6 Acceptance [A12, O15]

If we recapitulate the procedures for delivery so far, we see that a likely sequence of events might be:

(1) notice from supplier that the equipment is ready and invitation to customer to witness standard hardware tests at the supplier's premises;

(2) running of standard hardware tests at supplier's premises, sometimes with, more usually without the presence of the customer or his representative;

(3) delivery of equipment from a U.K. site to the customer's premises (using a carrier approved by the supplier)—sometimes involving an additional charge for delivery to the customer;

(4) offloading of equipment from the carrier's vehicles to the actual installation site on the customer's premises—usually at the customer's additional cost. Risk passes and the customer must insure;

(5) on-site running of standard hardware tests by the supplier's staff on the delivered equipment in the presence of the customer or his representative, following which the hardware is said to be commissioned.

It should be noted that:

(a) it is not always possible to examine both tests. In the case of equipment imported from abroad, the first one will usually be invisible to both the customer and the supplier's U.K. representative;

(b) the pre-delivery test may even be left to the supplier. This is particularly the case where a small peripheral device (as opposed to a whole computer) is involved;

(c) performance figures are unlikely to be accepted by the supplier as having any overriding relevance.

Acceptance by the customer of the equipment usually follows the successful completion of the last phase of this sequence: on-job running of the standard hardware tests; and, following such acceptance, the purchase price (or first rental payment) immediately becomes due. In the absence of any more specific directions in a contract (and it is amazing how vague some contracts are in these matters), it is reasonable to assume that the above procedure is what is involved.

At the end of stage (3) above (delivery to the customer's site), the carrier is likely to produce a delivery note to be signed when the equipment is handed over by him. The customer should satisfy himself that this delivery note is not, in fact, an acceptance form from the supplier.

Ignoring for the moment this unpleasant possibility, we may give as an example a payment clause implying acceptance:

"Payment for the Equipment shall be made by the Customer on acceptance of the Equipment by the Customer after completion of Tests in accordance with Clause X hereof.

Where part only of the Equipment has been tested delivered and accepted as aforesaid the sums required to be paid under this Clause shall be the relevant percentage of the part of the Contract Price which represents the price of the part of the Equipment which has been so tested delivered and accepted."

A more formal but basically similar approach is provided by a large manufacturer:

"After transporting the Equipment into position at the Installation Site the Customer will provide access to and the Supplier will undertake the installation and commissioning of the Equipment and will carry out the current Standard Hardware Test Programs details of which will have been given to the Customer prior to the start of such tests. This work will be done during normal working hours and will be at the Supplier's expense. When the Equipment or any item thereof is commissioned and the Standard Hardware Test Programs have been successfully completed the Supplier will issue a certificate to the effect as set out in Schedule C hereto (hereinafter referred to as the Commissioning Certificate).
. . . The Supplier shall issue an invoice for the Equipment on the day the Equipment is shipped from the Supplier's factory. Payment of such invoice by the Customer shall be made in full within 10 days after the date of the Commissioning Certificate."

At this point it is worth considering what significance formal acceptance will have (a point which recurs in the context of software and consultancy services) [3.3, 13.3]. It is unlikely, in the light of the court's decision in *Salvage Association v. CAP* [1995] F.S.R. 654, that acceptance will debar the customer from claiming damages in respect of to any subsequently discovered defects, but will probably bring to an end the rights of the customer to reject the equipment.

2.3.7 Liability for delay

Having considered what ought to happen, we must now examine the possible delays and hindrances which may occur in this process, and how the contracting parties may envisage dealing with them.

Supplier's delay in delivery [A10, O16]

The first delay may arise if the supplier has failed to assemble part or all of the equipment ready for delivery, or if—having assembled it—he finds it cannot pass his own standard hardware tests. When some or all of the hardware is imported, the chances of delay here can be considerable and, without accusing foreign manufacturers of negligence or any malfeasance, it is easy to see the opportunities for damage in shipment, hold-up in customs, and so on. Most manufacturers accordingly exclude liability for delay. One of the simplest and fairest such clauses is of a manufacturer who, after giving an estimated date of delivery, adds:

"The Supplier shall not be liable for any delay or for the consequences of any delay in performing any of its obligations under this Agreement if such delay is due to any industrial dispute or any cause whatsoever beyond its reasonable control and shall be entitled to a reasonable extension of the time for performing such obligation."

A customer should naturally look for a clear implementation schedule from the supplier for the performance of the contract. If delays are caused by an event outside the control of the supplier then the position is usually covered by a clause such as the example set out above—called a *force majeure* clause [A15]. This is not unreasonable, of course, but what happens if the delay is due to the default of the supplier? The customer's remedy will then depend on whether the time for performance was "of the essence" of the contract. If so, he will be entitled to cancel the contract, and recover damages. If not, his remedy will be confined to damages.

Time will be of the essence if there is an express provision to that effect in the contract. The same result may also be achieved in commercial contracts by simply specifying a date for performance, although this is less certain and a customer who has immovable time constraints should accordingly be explicit about this in the contract. However, even if time is not initially made of the essence, this does not mean that the customer has to wait forever for performance. If the supplier fails to complete by the agreed date, the customer may make time of the essence by serving notice on the supplier, requiring him to complete within a reasonable time. If the supplier fails to meet that deadline, the customer may then treat the contract as discharged and recover damages.

Some contracts do not mention a date for completion of the contract at all. Although this is unsatisfactory, it does not mean that the supplier may perform when he chooses, as the law will usually imply an obligation on the part of the supplier to complete within a reasonable time.

It is rare for a supplier to allow time to be of the essence in a contract, either by agreeing to an express provision or committing himself to a particular completion date. However, suppliers are sometimes prepared to give a firm date for completion if the customer agrees to confine his remedy to liquidated (*i.e.* estimated) damages in the event of a delay. Such an arrangement entails the parties' making a genuine pre-estimate of the loss likely to be suffered by the customer in the event of the supplier's delay. Such an estimate may in some cases be provided by costing a bureau service which the customer would need to use to tide him over the delay. The contract will then provide for the contract price to be reduced by a stated amount (reflecting the estimated damage) each week, or other period during which the delay continues, up to a stated maximum. The advantage to the supplier is that his overall liability is limited to the stated maximum. The customer may also benefit, because it will be possible to obtain a reduction in the price without resorting to litigation. An example is as follows:

> "(1) The Supplier shall complete this Agreement on or before *31 December 2002* ("the Completion Date").
>
> "(2) For the purposes of this Clause "complete this Agreement" means to deliver and install the System and to complete successfully the Supplier's standard tests in accordance with Clauses *X* and *Y* hereof.
>
> "(3) If the Supplier fails to complete this Agreement by the Completion Date then the Supplier shall pay to the Customer as and by way of liquidated damages for any loss or damage sustained by the Customer resulting from delay during the period from the Completion Date to the date on which the Supplier completes this Agreement the aggregate sum of *1* per cent of the total Contract Price for each week of such delay and pro rata for parts of a week up to a total maximum of *15* per cent of the total Contract Price. The payment of such sum shall be in full satisfaction of the Supplier's liability for delay in completing this Agreement. The payment of liquidated damages shall not relieve the Supplier from the obligation to deliver

the Equipment or from any other liability or obligation under this Agreement."

A word of warning, however, about such clauses. The pre-estimate of damage must not be penal (*i.e.* go beyond a genuine pre-estimate of the loss resulting from the delay), for otherwise the clause will be unenforceable. The customer should, therefore, resist any temptation to agree to an arbitrary figure, but instead be prepared to show that the pre-estimate was reached on a justifiable basis.

Customer's delay [A16]

It is of course possible for the customer to cause delay by failing to prepare his installation site. That obligation is dealt with below [2.6.3], but it is worth pointing out that any such delay will have serious consequences for the supplier since it will mean that he cannot proceed to commissioning, acceptance and payment; and also that he has to store and insure the equipment until it can be delivered. The same problem may also arise if the customer has failed to prepare test data in time [3.3.1, 10.3.2]. Accordingly, the clause on relief from the consequences of delay is often expressed in mutual terms:

"Neither the Supplier nor the Customer shall be liable for delay in performance or failure to perform their obligations if such delay or failure is caused by circumstances beyond the reasonable control of the party so delaying or failing."

However, this does not address the supplier's remedies if installation is delayed by reason of a failure on the part of the customer. The question of storage of equipment which cannot be delivered through the customer's fault is covered by:

"If by the Delivery Date the Supplier has not received from the Customer instructions sufficient to enable the Supplier to deliver the Equipment the Supplier shall be entitled to arrange storage of the Equipment on the Customer's behalf. All such storage charges insurance and other associated costs which may be incurred by the Supplier shall be discharged or repaid by the Customer and the risk of deterioration and damage to the Equipment so stored shall lie with the Customer."

The contract may also go on to provide for the compensation of the supplier generally:

"If the Supplier is unable to complete this Agreement by the Completion Date due to the neglect or default of the Customer then:
  (a) the Customer shall pay to the Supplier all reasonable costs, charges and losses of the Supplier attributable to such delay; and
  (b) notwithstanding the Supplier's inability to complete on the Completion Date the remaining balance of the Contract Price shall fall due to be paid by the Completion Date."

If payment is due on completion, the supplier would obviously be prejudiced if he could not complete due to the customer's default; hence the reason for the specific provision dealing with accelerated payment.

2.3.8 Defects [A19, O25]

Neither side would usually pretend that the on-site testing will discover every possible defect in the hardware. Many defects will become apparent only after extensive use. The usual procedure in the industry is for the supplier to guarantee the hardware for a limited period of either six or 12 months against faulty design, workmanship or materials, but to exclude all other conditions that may be implied in the customer's favour by law:

> "The Supplier will repair or at his option replace all defective parts which under proper use care and maintenance appear in the Equipment within *12* calendar months after the issue of the Commissioning Certificate and arise solely from faulty design materials or workmanship.
>
> Except as expressly provided in this Agreement, no warranty, condition, undertaking or term, express or implied, statutory or otherwise, as to condition, satisfactory quality, performance, durability or fitness for purpose of the Equipment is given or assumed by the Supplier and all such warranties, conditions, undertakings and terms are hereby excluded."

The warranty offered under clauses like this is often *off-site—i.e.* the customer must at his own expense return the faulty piece of equipment to the maintenance contractor or supplier. As an alternative, full maintenance contracts usually provide for *on-site* maintenance—*i.e.* the maintenance contractor comes to the customer's premises when equipment needs maintenance. So a warranty of this sort is rarely directly comparable to a full maintenance service.

Most contracts emphasise the proper use, care and maintenance aspects, and the customer who does not have a maintenance agreement [Chapter 8] with the supplier is obviously in a weaker position. It is also common for the contract to exclude from the warranty any equipment which has been modified by the customer:

> "This warranty is contingent upon proper use of the Equipment in the application for which the Equipment is intended and does not cover Equipment which has been modified without the Supplier's written approval or which has been subjected to unusual physical or electrical stress or on which the original identification marks have been removed or altered. Nor will this warranty apply if adjustment repair or parts replacement is required because of accident, hazard, misuse failure of electric power, air conditioning, humidity control, transportation or causes other than ordinary use."

The inclusion of transportation in this list is significant and not unusual. If insurance during transportation is the supplier's responsibility, the customer should satisfy himself that it covers defects caused by transportation but not apparent till later.

Electrical stress is a reminder of the damage power surges can cause and customers in any doubt about this should either endeavour to obtain a "clean" power supply and/or be prepared to fit a constant voltage transformer, "smoother" or uninterruptable power supply (UPS). These matters should be discussed in advance with the supplier.

The removal or defacement of identifications is primarily directed at OEM customers who purchase the equipment in order to sell it as a mixed configuration with their own or someone else's equipment. The practice of an OEM supplier affixing his own badge or identification to all the equipment he supplies is quite common; in its simplest form, where an OEM supplier does nothing but package disparate pieces of equipment under his own label, this practice is derogatively called "badge engineering". But it is natural that the supplier should want his own labels to be intact. Any customer purchasing a mixed configuration from an OEM should be on the watch for traces of defaced or removed labels, and should question his OEM as to his authority to do so—particularly if his maintenance is performed by somebody other than the OEM.

The customer may, of course, attempt to rely on his statutory rights and here the Unfair Contract Terms Act 1977 provides protection against unreasonable warranty exclusion or limitation clauses in supplier's standard contracts. This was demonstrated in both the case of *St Albans City and District Council v. International Computers Ltd* [1995] F.S.R. 686 (where it was held that a contractual limitation of £100,000 in a supplier's standard contract was unreasonable in the context of losses flowing from a defective computer system of £1,300,000—later reduced on appeal to £816,000 in [1997] F.S.R. 251, though the decision that the limitation was unreasonable was upheld) . . . and the more recent case of *South West Water v. ICL* [1999] B.L.R. 420 (where the courts ruled that a limitation clause of £250,000 in a supplier's standard contract originally for a supply of hardware and software worth £3,597,206 was similarly too restrictive and therefore unenforceable). Suppliers will now have to reassess their contracts in this area, and cannot assume that the same considerations will apply at all times and to every customer. Much is likely to turn on the relative strength and resources of the parties, the contract value, the insurance cover available to each party, the options available to the customer to seek a similar system elsewhere, any inducements offered to the customer to accept the limitations, as well as more nebulous public policy considerations. There has in the past been some doubt as to whether the Act (relating to the creation and transfer of intellectual property rights) would apply to software in every case but the courts have construed the relevant exemption in the Act in a fairly restrictive way such that customers for software should in most cases be able to rely on the Act's protection [3.3.3].

2.4 TERMINATION

2.4.1 Sale [A17, A18]

Many hardware contracts are curiously reticent about the possibility of termination. From the supplier's point of view, this is probably deliberate policy since he is concerned primarily in off-loading his equipment and claiming payments. Any attempt to fail to perform a contractual duty can be interpreted as a delay caused by the customer [2.3.7] rather than an attempt to terminate, and may even add to the cost [2.5]. To the extent that suppliers are very unwilling to vary their contracts, a customer should ensure that there is no possibility of his changing his mind before purchasing. If he is in any doubt he should seek a rental agreement which foresees an end to the agreement. Otherwise the price adjustment clause [2.2.4] provides an opportunity to terminate, or, of course, total failure of consideration may do so.

Nevertheless, a supplier with a full order book and long delays in delivery may find it worthwhile to include a termination clause which will enable him, if the customer wishes to cancel the order, to realise some money immediately from the customer and, by passing the equipment to another customer, bring forward the payment on that order also:

> "If the Customer wishes to terminate this Agreement in whole or in part at any time before the Delivery Date (other than for any breach by the Supplier

which would entitle the Customer to terminate this Agreement pursuant to Clause *X*) then the Supplier shall agree to the termination of this Agreement in respect of any equipment cancelled upon the Customer paying to the Supplier as agreed and as liquidated damages:

> (a) a sum equal to *6* per cent of the contract price of the Equipment cancelled; and
>
> (b) a sum equal to *12* per cent of the said contract price reduced by *1* per cent in respect of each complete calendar month unexpired between the date of termination and the Delivery Date."

As mentioned above [2.3.7], a contractual provision of this nature will be enforceable only if it represents a genuine pre-estimate of the loss likely to be suffered by the supplier. An alternative would be to provide for the payment of a deposit by the customer which would not then be returnable in the event of a cancellation by the customer [2.2.1].

2.4.2 Rental [B30]

Here termination is usually visualised either as a result of the customer's breach of an obligation (most usually to pay rent but also sometimes to maintain the equipment properly) or if his company commences to be wound up, and so on:

> "Without prejudice to any other remedy which may be available to the Supplier under this Agreement, the Supplier may by written notice to the Hirer forthwith determine this Agreement:
>
> (a) if the Hirer commits any breach of this Agreement which is not remedied within *30* days after the Supplier has given written notice thereof to the Hirer; or
>
> (b) if the Hirer, being an incorporated company, shall have a receiver, administrative receiver or liquidator appointed or shall pass a resolution for winding-up or a court shall make an order to that effect or being a partnership shall be dissolved or being an individual shall commit any act of bankruptcy or shall die or the Hirer (whether an incorporated company or not) shall enter into any voluntary arrangement with the Hirer's creditors."

A clause which deals with termination of rental begins with the same preamble as the example quoted above [2.4.1], and itemises the damages as given in that clause where the termination is before delivery. Where the termination is after delivery (by which time the equipment will no longer be new and thus cannot be delivered as new to another customer), the following may be appropriate:

> "Where the Customer wishes to terminate this Agreement at any time after delivery of the Equipment, there shall become payable by the Customer to the Supplier *75* per cent of the hire charges due for the balance of the minimum hire period, subject to a minimum payment equal to the full hire charges for a period of *six* months."

Again, such a clause may be unenforceable if it is considered to be penal, and a supplier should accordingly give thought as to how any such provision could be justified before inserting it into any standard form.

2.5 ALTERATIONS [B16, B25]

In the case of most standard hardware contracts the question of alterations should not arise except in so far as the supplier may himself improve, substitute or modify his own equipment [2.1.1]. However, sometimes the customer changes his mind about the nature or amount of equipment he requires, either because his own perception of his computing requirements has changed or because the supplier has offered an alternative new system. If the change to the requirements is substantial it is probably best to tear up the old contract and start again with new estimated delivery dates and time scales; but if the alterations are small the old contract may stand with appropriate modifications.

However, the customer should be aware of the likely effect of his change of plan. Each item of equipment requires a different length of time to prepare for dispatch, and a change of plan is likely to affect delivery periods. If the new equipment does not affect the viability of the previous configuration (*e.g.* a contract for two more terminals), the late delivery of these items causes very little problem. But if the equipment is fundamental (a larger or faster disk drive and controller to replace an older model), the entire delivery period and all that follows on that will have to be replanned. This might be interpreted as a delay by the customer [2.3.7] and the customer should clarify this point when he orders the new equipment. A clause visualising such a change runs:

"Should the Supplier incur extra cost owing to variation or suspension of the work by the Customer's instructions or lack of instructions or to interruptions, delays, overtime, unusual hours, mistakes or work for which the Supplier is not responsible all such extra cost shall be paid by the Customer."

The customer may balk at accepting all such liability and at least seek to limit it to such delays, work, etc., as have actually been caused by some act or omission on its part (*i.e.* as opposed to the acts of an unrelated third party). The *force majeure* clause will need careful scrutiny [A15].

If, in a rental agreement, new equipment is required which does not involve a complete replacement of existing equipment, but is simply in addition to that originally rented, the period of rental for the new equipment will probably be made to coincide with the unexpired portion of the existing rental agreement:

"The Customer may hire equipment (subject to the availability of such equipment) from the Supplier in addition to that listed in Schedule *A* hereof by written order to the Supplier referring to this Agreement, and by receipt of written acceptance of such order by the Supplier. The rental period for such additional equipment shall continue until the expiry of the rental period defined in Clause "*X*" hereof, unless the parties otherwise agree in writing. Monthly rentals initially payable for such additional equipment shall be those in effect when such additional equipment is delivered and accepted."

2.6 CUSTOMER'S DUTIES

The customer's duties, apart from the duty to pay the contract price or rental, include:

(1) providing information;

(2) maintaining confidentiality in respect of the supplier's information;

(3) preparing the site for installation of the equipment;

(4) care and maintenance;

(5) miscellaneous and general provisions.

These are addressed in turn below.

2.6.1 Providing information [A6]

This requirement is chiefly relevant where some feature is required in the system peculiar to the contract. In most commercial applications such features are provided by software [3.6.1] and to this extent a clause to this effect is not usually included in a hardware contract. Where it is relevant the clause might read:

"The Customer undertakes promptly to provide to the Supplier all necessary information that the Supplier may reasonably from time to time require to permit him to provide the Services. In the event that the Customer fails or delays in providing such information so that the Services are delayed or increased thereby the Supplier reserves the right to increase the Contract Price to cover the cost of such delay or increase."

2.6.2 Confidentiality [A21]

Obligations of confidentiality may be included in contracts which include some novel or unusual hardware feature which the supplier wishes to keep from his competitors, or in relation to aspects of the operating software or information in respect of the hardware's performance which may have been provided as part of the sales process. Confidentiality issues in relation to software generally are dealt with in more detail at 3.7.2. In the case of American companies, the early announcement of an enhancement or a new piece of equipment may even be interpreted as an unfair act under anti-trust laws, and it is therefore essential to the supplier that confidentiality shall be preserved until he is ready to make a public announcement. Sometimes also the customer may, wittingly or unwittingly, learn something of the supplier's other customers. In a tender, also, the unsuccessful tenderers do not want their ideas to be plagiarised by others. Such a clause as the following may therefore be appropriate:

"The Customer undertakes that he and his staff will keep confidential and not disclose to any third party without the Supplier's prior consent in writing any drawings, designs or information (whether of a commercial or technical nature) acquired from the Supplier in connection with the work the subject of this Agreement which is marked as confidential, which is notified to him as being confidential, or which may reasonably be inferred from its nature or contents to be confidential."

However, in the *Mars* case [3.3.3], it was held that the encryption of software was not in itself sufficient to enable a customer to infer that it was confidential. This decision seems somewhat odd as one would imagine that use of encryption would indicate a clear intention to maintain confidentiality. However, pending further clarification by the law in this regard, it would be prudent to put the issue beyond doubt by means of the contract terms.

2.6.3 Site preparation [A5]

Computers can be large pieces of equipment and some require special environments both for technical reasons (free of dust, with controlled temperature or humidity, and so on) and because of the sensitivity of the information they handle (requiring security checks, smart cards, and so forth). This can imply either a totally new building or a considerable refitting of an existing building. It is commonly the customer's duty to ensure that such an environment is ready before the equipment is to be delivered, and he cannot expect the supplier to bear the cost of any storage and/or insurance caused by delay due to his failure to have his computer room ready on time [2.3.7]. Accordingly, it is reasonable for a supplier to stipulate that:

> "The Customer shall at his own expense prepare and provide all proper accommodation and facilities (including proper environmental conditions) for the Equipment and its maintenance in accordance with the Supplier's specification, to be in place no later than one day before the Estimated Delivery Date. For this purpose the Supplier will make available to the Customer free of charge the advice of a site engineer."

This last point is a good one, for it means that the customer should get adequate on the spot advice from the supplier as to what is required. The customer can hardly be blamed for failing to prepare the site if the supplier has not advised him of what to do, nor checked that he has done it.

Another example of the same requirement, but also bringing in the question of supplier access, is comprised in the following:

> "To enable the Supplier expeditiously and properly to fulfill his obligations under this Agreement, the Customer shall provide the Supplier and his staff or agents with suitable access to and uninterrupted use of the Installation Site to prepare foundations and satisfactory environmental conditions for the Equipment, and shall provide any electrical power lighting hoisting equipment and all other facilities reasonably required by the Supplier for this purpose."

2.6.4 Care [A24, O21]

In a rental agreement the hirer undertakes to maintain the equipment [2.2.2], usually using the supplier or his approved maintenance contractor for the purpose:

> "The Customer hereby undertakes to enter into a Maintenance Agreement with the Supplier in the Supplier's standard form current at the date of this Agreement in respect of the Equipment."

In other circumstances, it will usually be prudent for the customer to make arrangements for the support and maintenance of the equipment [8, K].

2.6.5 Miscellaneous

These points, which need not be given in detail, include:

(1) undertakings not to assign or mortgage [A30];

(2) undertakings not to deface or remove badges or labels [2.3.8, A23];

(3) undertakings to insure [B17]; and

(4) undertakings not to jeopardise the insurance of the equipment.

2.6.6 Supplier's remedies

A customer who defaults on payment or fails to assume his other obligations may well not terminate the agreement but simply render himself liable to surrender the equipment to the supplier while still being fully liable for the contract price:

> "If after the date of this Agreement the Customer shall fail to perform any of his obligations under Clause X hereof the full amount of the Contract Price remaining to be paid by the Customer under this Agreement shall immediately and without notice become due and payable and the Supplier shall have the right to reposses the Equipment without notice on demand and without any let or hindrance on the part of the Customer."

Other breaches may give rise to claims in damages, or (in the case of a breach of the provisions of the operating software licence), revocation of that licence [3.4.2., 3.8.1].

2.7 SUPPLIER'S DUTIES

Aside from the primary duty to deliver the hardware in working order according to its specification, the supplier may have a number of further obligations, as set out below.

2.7.1 Confidentiality [A21]

This clause is common to both hardware and software agreements, but, since it is usually more relevant to software, it is dealt with in Chapter 3 [3.7.2].

2.7.2 VDUs and health [A19 (2)]

An obligation on a customer owed to his own staff should be supported by a duty on the supplier. Under E.C. Council Directive 90/270/EEC, as embodied in the Health and Safety (Display Screen Equipment) Regulations 1992 (S.I. 1992 No. 2792), employers have to comply with certain standards for staff who use display screens. Under Part 3, employers are obliged to analyse the workstations from a health and safety point of view and remedy the risks found. For all new workstations they should specify low radiation screens and each customer should ensure that the screens provided by the supplier comply with this. Therefore, a warranty from the supplier that the equipment complies would be an appropriate clause in a hardware contract.

For completeness we mention the customer's remaining obligations to his staff, though they do not need any change to the contract between the supplier and the customer. Regulation 4 requires that there must be breaks or changes in activity. Regulation 5 provides for eye tests. Regulations 6 and 7 require the customer to provide information and training to his staff.

These various requirements embody no more than good practice already put into operation in most responsible companies, but it should be noted that they are also backed by law.

2.7.3 Electromagnetic compatibility [A13]

The Electromagnetic Compatibility Regulations 1992 (S.I. 1992 No. 2372) (as amended by S.I. 1999, No. 1957; S.I. 1994, No. 3080 and S.I. 1995, No. 3180), implementing E.U. Directives 89/336/EEC, 91/263/EEC and 92/31/EEC, apply to nearly all electrical or electronic apparatus sold in EU states on or after October 28, 1992. Manufacturers and distributors are obliged to ensure their equipment meets certain standards of compatibility and this usually requires certification of compliance by the manufacturer or supplier. The legislation applies to assemblers (*i.e.* OEMs [1.5]) as well as manufacturers and applies when the apparatus is first put on sale as well as when it is first used and continues to be applicable thereafter. Exemptions are few—simple components such as integrated circuits, second-hand equipment and equipment which is or will be covered by other directives dealing with electromagnetic compatibility. The obligation continues even after installation. Apparatus which is suspected not to be compliant and whose sale is prohibited or suspended cannot be provided by a supplier and failure to observe this is an offence. There is no Crown immunity in the legislation.

It should be noted that there is a second statutory instrument on this topic (the Electromagnetic Compatibility (Wireless Telegraphy Apparatus) Certification and Examination Fees Regulations 1997 (S.I. 1997 No. 3051)). As its name suggests, it is confined to wireless telegraphy apparatus and in particular to such apparatus as is not covered in S.I. 1992 No. 2372 by defence, civil aviation or ordinary telecommunications through the BABT [2.7.4]. We doubt whether it can therefore apply to IT telecommunications apparatus and have therefore ignored it for the purposes of this book.

2.7.4 Telecommunications approval [A14]

No equipment can be connected to a telecommunications system which is, or is to be, connected to a public system in the U.K. unless it is approved by the Secretary of State for Trade and Industry (Telecommunications Act 1984, s. 22) on advice from the British Approvals Board for Telecommunications (BABT). The BABT is, in practice, responsible for inspecting and testing equipment which is proposed to be connected to a public telecommunication system and for recommending acceptance or rejection to the Secretary of State. Readers are no doubt familiar by now with the "BABT Approved" and "red triangle" stickers which are placed on telecommunications equipment pursuant to the Telecommunication Apparatus (Marking and Labelling) Order 1985 (S.I. 1985 No. 717) indicating either that they are or that they are not approved.

Despite the existence of such stickers there can be no harm in asking the supplier to warrant that his equipment is approved. The wording of such a warranty is likely to follow the wording on the sticker:

> "The Supplier warrants that at the date hereof the Equipment is approved for use with the telecommunication system run by [British Telecommunications plc] in accordance with the conditions in the instructions for use."

"Equipment" would include instruments, modems and other communications devices. There may also be a clause restricting the customer from modifying any approved equipment:

> "The Customer undertakes that he will make no modification to any part of the Equipment connected to any public telecommunication system without the prior written consent of the Supplier."

The supplier may also envisage the possibility that the Secretary of State may at some later stage alter the requirements, in which case he may be obliged to change his own equipment:

"If at any time the Secretary of State pursuant to the provisions of the Telecommunications Act 1984 requires the Supplier to modify or alter the Equipment or any part thereof as a condition of the Secretary of State's continued approval of the Equipment or part thereof then the Customer shall allow the Supplier from time to time to do so at the Customer's expense."

In practice, it is not likely to be a very onerous clause, since the possibility of it ever being invoked is remote.

Additionally, the supplier might seek to protect himself from inadvertently seeming to usurp the Secretary of State's authority:

"The Supplier does not warrant the continuation of the consent of the Secretary of State pursuant to the provisions of the Telecommunications Act 1984 to the connection of the Equipment to any public telecommunications system."

2.8 TITLE AND INTELLECTUAL PROPERTY RIGHTS [A4, A26, P16]

2.8.1 Title to the hardware

It is usual in a sale agreement for title to the hardware to pass to the customer after the final payment, but the insurable risk usually passes on delivery:

"Title to each item of the Equipment shall remain with the Supplier until the total Price for the item has been received by the Supplier. Risk shall pass to the Customer on delivery of the Equipment at the Installation Site."

This allows the supplier to repossess the equipment if full payment is not made. The customer should in turn take care to ensure that "the Price" referred to in any such clause is related solely to the equipment and not to any related consultancy, software (except for the operating system [1.3] which has no value divorced from its hardware) or support services. This is usually best done by checking the definition of "the Equipment".

This may also be followed by a warranty as to title:

"The Supplier warrants that upon the payment of the full Contract Price and any other charges payable under this Agreement the Customer shall acquire good clear title to the Equipment free from all liens or encumbrances."

Title remains with the supplier in a rental agreement [B15].

2.8.2 Intellectual property rights

A separate clause as to intellectual property rights, giving the customer an indemnity against any possible infringement of third-party intellectual property rights is also usual:

"The Supplier will indemnify the Customer against any claim for alleged infringement of any third-party intellectual property right by reason of the normal use or possession of the Equipment or any part thereof provided that the Supplier is given immediate and complete control of any such claim."

Often the clause seeks to cover all intellectual property rights together:

"Letters Patent, registered designs, design rights, trade marks or copyright."

This is particularly likely when the clause seeks to cover software rights as well as hardware rights, *e.g.* in relation to any accompanying documentation or operating system [1.3]. Increasingly, one also sees domain names included within the definition of intellectual property rights, although it may be argued that a domain name is a revocable licence (from ICANN or Nominet or other allocating body [12.1.2]) to use a name and not itself a form of intellectual property.

It is worth making the point that suppliers may reasonably seek to limit any intellectual property right indemnity they provide to breaches of U.K. intellectual property rights, by reason of the difficulties associated with predicting what rights (particularly trade marks) may subsist in other jurisdictions.

It should also be noted that indemnities of this nature are usually limited to the liabilities incurred by the customer to the third party and do not extend to compensating the customer for loss of use of the equipment. It is fairly common for the supplier to reserve the right to replace the infringing equipment with non-infringing equipment or, where this cannot be done, to buy back the infringing equipment at the original price paid by the customer less depreciation. Any such indemnities will also be subject to the usual caveats concerning the supplier's right to control any related litigation, etc. [A26].

2.8.3 Integral software [A4 (3–5)]

It is becoming increasingly common for computer equipment to be supplied to the customer with embedded or integral software or with software already loaded on to the hard disk. Typically, this would include operating systems and possibly applications software as well. Where the equipment is special equipment designed for a particular task, its functions may be controlled by a piece of specially formulated software which, because it is not likely to be changed, is embedded in the equipment in a board or in the form of a chip. Such software in hard form, known as *firmware*, is particularly common with computer games. The customer may be unaware that he is using such *firmware* and may not care as long as the machine performs the task he desires. In other cases, the supply of accompanying software will be a marketing feature and it is now commonplace for retailers of PCs and PC software to advertise "bundled" offers of a PC and a range of third party applications software for sale, often with a statement that the "normal" value of the bundled software is as much as the cost of the computer itself!

The contractual approach to integral or embedded software varies enormously. To take an everyday example, the "computer" contained in the modern motor vehicle is very unlikely to be accompanied by a licence agreement authorising the user to use it in a defined manner. It is embedded in the vehicle and commercial expediency dictates that a licensing agreement is impractical. The owner of the intellectual property rights in the firmware merely relies on his rights at law which, in that example, are probably perfectly adequate in relation to what is a relatively low value item. The law will imply a right in favour of the purchaser or user to use the embedded software for the purpose for which it is intended and nothing further is required. This is equally true of sophisticated computer equipment containing integral software of high value, but in that case the owner of the rights may be anxious at least to assert such rights by an acknowledgement from the customer that they exist and are protected and to go even further by incorporating express licence terms in any sale agreement. This may be the case particularly where the software owner is concerned that the embedded software may be extracted and used for a purpose other than the one which he intends, and in particular may be decompiled [3.8.1] by potential competitors for the purposes of producing their own software. The right to terminate any licence will give the owner added protection in that event. Where licence terms are incorporated the points raised in [3.8.1] will be relevant.

In theory, when the owner of a car with embedded firmware comes to sell the car, the question of how the software licence can be passed on to the new owner arises. This is treated in more detail in 7.6 where the problem is particularly acute. In the present instance, the owner of the intellectual property rights is likely to be the same as the manufacturer of the hardware and therefore there is an implied right for any subsequent purchaser of his car to use the software on the same terms as the original purchaser. On a car or washing machine where the presence of a computer is not generally understood, such a right might be more easily inferred; on a computer this seems less likely.

The ownership of the intellectual property rights in the integral software will help to determine the nature of the contractual documentation. Package software belonging to third parties which is supplied with hardware will often be accompanied with its own shrink-wrap licence agreement [4.3.1, 5.3.6.4]. It may be a term of any related distribution agreement that the distributor must take steps to draw to the customer's attention that he is required to abide by the terms of such licence agreement. Where the integral software is of high value, the owner (if not also the supplier of the software) may insist that the hardware supplier must require the customer to sign an express licence agreement before the software can be supplied as part of the equipment. In such a case, the sale agreement may include a term that the customer must execute the licence agreement before the equipment (including the integral software) will be delivered. If the software owner and the hardware supplier are one and the same, then the terms of any express licence may be incorporated in the sale agreement. In either case, the licence agreement may include a term requiring the purchaser to ensure that any subsequent purchaser agrees to abide by the terms of the licence.

2.8.4 Maintenance/Support

Increasingly now the hardware contract will also offer the customer the right to purchase hardware maintenance up-front. Sometimes the maintenance is free for a period (*e.g.* one year) and the charged maintenance starts after that. See also 4.2.2 as well as Chapter 8.

2.9 MISCELLANEOUS

2.9.1 Export control [A25]

Mainframes are generally supplied for use in one particular location. If the equipment is subsequently to be installed at a different location it is as well to advise the supplier, if only because otherwise maintenance agreements may be invalidated [8.5.1]. If the customer wishes to re-export the equipment, he will have not only to cover maintenance, but also comply with the necessary export regulations. These are the Dual-Use and Related Goods (Export Control) Regulations 1996 (S.I. 1996 No. 2721) (as extensively amended) (the "Regulations"). These Regulations empower the Secretary of State to grant licences for the export of certain dualuse products. Under this power the Secretary of State has granted the Open General Export Licence (Computers) (OGEL) dated

August 2, 1999. This licence permits the export of certain types of hardware to certain countries. In summary, the licence allows for the exportation to most countries of digital computers which are available to the public and which run standard commercial software. Equally relevant is the Export of Goods (Control) Order 1994 (S.I. 1994 No. 1191), as extensivley amended. Computers and software fall under Category 3 (Industrial Goods), especially sections 3 (Electronics), 4 (Computers) and 5 (Telecommunications and "Information Security") but users should use the Index to check all categories, and their re-export can be prohibited to certain countries.

But the export or re-export of computers was not always simply a U.K. matter. U.K. representatives met colleagues from other governments in a Co-ordinating Committee called CoCom. The governments in question comprised all the NATO states except Iceland but included Japan and Australia. The purpose of CoCom was to co-ordinate exports so as to prevent certain proscribed countries from obtaining technology which might have had a defence application. Each government agreed to give effect to the export bans through national legislation. As a result of the reforms in Eastern Europe considerable relaxations in the rules were implemented, particularly in relation to the export restrictions on computers. CoCom itself was finally disbanded by common consent of its members on March 31, 1994 because the strategic threat from the Eastern bloc had disappeared but all CoCom members agreed to maintain national export controls based on CoCom lists of goods and technologies.

Countries in the current list include states locked in civil war (*e.g.* Somalia, Sudan); countries involved in local wars (*e.g.* Armenia and Azerbaijan); Yugoslavia (Federal Republic of); and oppressive regimes such as Myanmar (formerly Burma). Intending exporters must apply to the Department of Trade and Industry for up-to-date information or consult the website at @www.dti.gov.uk/export.control. Further complications arise in equipment of American origin, or equipment which contains U.S. components or know-how. In the first edition of this book an example of such clauses was included from a contract with a U.S. manufacturer:

> "The Customer agrees that he will not resell, ship or otherwise dispose of the Equipment to the People's Republic of China, North Korea, Cuba, Uganda, Rhodesia or the USSR or any of the Soviet Bloc countries (as defined in the prevailing United States Export Regulations) without the prior written consent of the Supplier."

In the intervening years since that edition, the situation has become more complicated. The U.S. Government at the time of writing is very unlikely to grant any export orders to a number of countries including Communist and several Middle Eastern states, but now seeks to prohibit re-export of U.S. equipment to any country without a valid order from the Bureau of Export Administration in the U.S. Department of Commerce. Accordingly, such clauses as the following may be found in contracts for U.S. manufactured goods and/or goods being sold by U.S.-based manufacturers:

> "All Equipment, services and data provided pursuant to this contract are subject to U.S. export control and may also be subject to export and/or import restrictions in other countries. The Customer agrees to comply with all such laws, regulations and restrictions and to obtain all necessary licences

to export or import the Equipment following its delivery to the Customer by the Supplier."

There is also a requirement from some U.S. companies to non-U.S. OEMs that the U.S. manufacturer be allowed to audit the OEM's books to ensure that U.S. Department of Commerce regulations are being complied with. It has even been alleged that U.S. companies use such a clause to acquire full knowledge of the business of their foreign OEM and thus be in a good position to curb the OEM or take other commercial action against them.

2.9.2 Waste from Electrical and Electronic Equipment

It is also worth noting the current Proposal for an E.U. Directive on waste from electrical and electronic equipment, which would impose upon manufacturers and/or distributors duties to take back and recycle "end of life" electrical products.

It is, as yet, unclear whether the Proposal will ever make it through the E.U.'s processes so as to become a Directive, but its potential impact is such that its progress should be carefully monitored, especially as it would focus attention on the need to ensure that any data or software stored on hardware being submitted for recycling, had been duly erased [10.3.3].

CHAPTER 3

SOFTWARE

3.0 Introduction
3.1 Service to be Performed
3.2 Payment
3.3 Delivery and Acceptance
3.4 Termination
3.5 Alterations
3.6 Client's Duties
3.7 Systems House's Duties
3.8 Title

3.0 INTRODUCTION

3.0.1 Importance of software

When a computer is bought, the purchaser usually goes to a great deal of care in examining the contract for the machinery (hardware) itself, but may be tempted to examine the contract for programs (software) less critically. Yet software contracts are at least as important as hardware contracts because:

(1) the software may be tailor-made to your requirements and, if so, will involve estimates of future capabilities and hence uncertainty;

(2) the cost of software licences and, more particularly, the cost of implementing software packages or having them tailored to meet your requirements will usually far exceed the cost of any new hardware;

(3) hardware which proves unsuitable for your requirements will sometimes retain some capital value but unsuitable software which has been produced to meet your specific requirements is unsaleable: conversely, "good" software may prove to be a very valuable asset and can even turn into a new source of revenue if any bespoke elements are capable of being licensed to third parties;

(4) good software can get something useful out of poor or obsolescent hardware, whereas bad software can do nothing with even the finest hardware.

A further important aspect of software is that it may not be eligible for capital allowances. This point applies equally to contracts of purchase as to leases, but because of the other special aspects of leases it is dealt with in 7.6.

In speaking of tailor-made or *bespoke* software, we are dealing with programs written at the user's request, and not dealing with *packages*—the unlovely term used to describe standard programs where the user purchases merely a non-exclusive licence to use someone else's program which is in a generic form so as to be capable of use by multiple users. The first thing to establish, when purchasing software, is whether you are negotiating for a licence to packaged software, or whether you are embarked on the development of software written exclusively to your own requirements. A third possibility also exists—a package with a few modifications specifically asked for. In that case, the user has to consider the contract both in its package aspect and in its tailor-made context.

The distinction between packages and bespoke (or partially bespoke) software is an increasingly important one. Package software is becoming simply a commodity and as such marketed like hardware. This is particularly true of PC software [Chapter 4]. The development of bespoke software, however, is a service and so more akin to consultancy. Public sector rules seem to be tending towards treating package software as procurable under a supplies contract whereas bespoke software is more likely to come under a service contract [14.2.2].

3.0.2 Packages [C2, O2]

Package contracts are usually fairly straight-forward. The user should have had an opportunity to see and even test the package in advance of procuring it (although this will often depend on the size of the licence fee involved). Typically, package contracts will stress that the user is acquiring only a licence, which may be revoked in specific circumstances (*e.g.* a breach of the licence terms), is non-exclusive, and cannot be passed to a third party without the package owner's agreement or, alternatively, subject to the condition that the transferor must deliver the package and its documentation to the transferee on terms that the transferee agrees to abide by the package owner's licence. Often the package may not even be used on any other computer or in any other location than the one specified, even though the user may own more than one machine or may operate from multiple locations. Packages are often priced to provide a licence for use on an individual machine (*machine licence*). This maximises the licensor's fees but more importantly warns the customer that he cannot simply copy the package to another machine. When the customer has several appropriate machines, there may be economies of scale in seeking a *site licence* for all suitable machines to use copies of the package at a single site. Alternatively, the licence fee may be linked to the number of the licensee's staff who are to use the software. This is itself capable of being expressed in a variety of different ways; for example, the licence could be limited to the number of users of the software in the licensed organisation, a specific list of authorised users, or the maximum number of users able to access and use the software. There could also be different levels of usage each expressed at a different fee, for system managers at one rate and for ordinary users at another rate; or for users with authority to amend certain files at one rate and those with a bare licence to access and read but not to alter the files at a different rate. The package owner (licensor) reserves all title to the software and to its documentation (not only program lists, but also operating instructions, user manuals, etc., all of which are copyright material). There is often an installation charge and the amount of advice and instruction the user can expect from the package owner is defined, together with undertakings as to future maintenance of the package.

Sometimes, the user receives the full source listing of programs, which theoretically might enable him to alter or amend it himself. Some contracts expressly forbid him to do this, or allow him to do so only with the consent of the package owner. Whether or not he is allowed to do this, it is likely to have a serious effect on any maintenance contract for the software, which usually stipulates that the user cannot alter the package in any way. Sometimes, the user is not given the listing of the program at all, but only the program in a form ready to load and run—known as the *object code*; in this condition it is, for all practical purposes, impossible for all but the most expert user to amend (or even understand) the internal workings of the program.

Sometimes, the package may itself contain software written by a third party. Such software may be a file handler within a general system, for example. The user should satisfy himself that any package he buys is entirely the property of the purported owner and, if other software is involved, should enquire into the nature of the licence, any additional fee he may have to pay to the licensor of the original package, and the availability of instructions and maintenance (as required) for the package. He is justified in asking the software supplier for an indemnity against any future copyright infringement claim in respect of the package (or part of it) from a third party [C12].

When software is being purchased along with second-hand equipment (*e.g.* as part of an integrated system, or when it is the relevant hardware's operating system), there may be particular difficulties. For example, has the vendor the right to pass on his software licence to the purchaser? This problem arises acutely in the case of leases where a lessor attempts to resell the equipment and the arguments rehearsed in the chapter on leasing [7.6] appear equally to apply to any other second-hand purchase involving software. For a case in point, readers are referred to *Intergraph Corporation v. Solid Systems CAD Services Ltd* [1993] F.S.R 617.

Finally, it should be mentioned that the practice of "renting" software is becoming more widespread, especially in the context of Application Service Provision (ASP) contracts. By these arrangements customers gain access to software via the Internet or other dedicated communications link and will often have no independent licence right in respect of the software, but will instead simply be receiving a service, albeit one based on the functionality of such system. As with hardware rental [2.2.2], it is usual for the agreement also to encompass a maintenance agreement [9]. The term and termination clauses will not be that dissimilar to those for hardware rental [2.2.2, 2.4.2, B13, B30], though for the rest, the clauses in a software maintenance agreement will be used [9, L].

3.0.3 Bespoke software [D2, D4]

By this term is meant programs written expressly for a particular user. As noted above, such software is also referred to as *tailor-made* or *commissioned*; it involves considerations very different from those for the licence of package software, since whereas packages can be tested before purchase, in the case of bespoke software there must first be a contract to bring it into existence before it can be licensed.

This is likely to increase the cost, time-scale and risk. Most users will therefore prefer to purchase packaged software whenever possible, or at least to use a package solution as the basis from which a more limited set of bespoke modifications and additions can be made in order to meet specific requirements.

Companies who are able to undertake the writing of bespoke software for clients go by a number of names. The very largest companies also provide other services such as outsourcing [11] or consultancy [13], and these will usually be called *IT service companies*. More specialised suppliers of bespoke software may be called *software houses* or *systems houses*. Where companies specialise in tailoring an existing package to an individual client's requirement whether to fit with other software packages or to operate on a particular hardware configuration, the company may be called a *systems integrator*. In this chapter and in Precedent D, we have generally used the term "systems house" for all variants.

Bespoke software will usually be purchased under any of three main types of contract:

(1) time and materials;

(2) fixed price;

(3) estimated or capped maximum price.

Time and materials contracts

These are the simplest type of contracts, whereby the client promises to pay the systems house for all time spent and expenses incurred in the course of producing the required software. From the point of view of systems houses, providing they have adequately costed their staff's time, kept accurate time and expense records and (of course!) completed the required programming work satisfactorily, they run no risk of being out of pocket on the job. They will usually bill the client on a monthly basis, although different payment profiles are common, especially those which involve a delay of final invoices until the completion of the project, usually following satisfactory acceptance tests.

Contract programming (or *bodyshopping* as it is more usually and vulgarly known) is a primitive form of time and materials contract whereby the client hires the programmer from the systems house on a *per diem* basis. In this case, no actual program is specified, nor even mentioned: the sole requirement is that the programmer will be available to program at premises specified by the client on particular dates. The actual rates charged for each such programmer will depend upon a number of factors, including the type of skills required, the experience and qualifications of the programmer, and the size and reputation of the supplier itself. For smaller engagements where the programmer supplies his or her own services or is supplied via an agency, one should be wary of the possibility that they are "moonlighting" (*i.e.* still employed by Company A, but using spare time or even A's time to sell their services on their own account to earn extra money). This will almost certainly be in breach of his contract of employment with A, and will involve severe risks for the client, particularly if the programmer has misused any of A's confidential or proprietary materials in the course of providing the programming services. Whatever the status of the individual concerned, he should always be put under contract [Y].

A full time and materials contract (*i.e.* as opposed to one dealing solely with contract programming) will involve the systems house in taking on the responsibility of delivering a finished program (or suite of programs). "Materials" in this context may include the systems house's various expenses and costs incurred in providing the required services, including computer time, storage charges (for programs and test data on the computer)—unless, of course, the client can himself provide these. Although the cost is charged on the basis of time and materials, this should not preclude the supplier from giving as realistic an estimate as it can of the time and cost.

Such contracts (and indeed most IT-related delivery contracts) should specify any required *milestones*—*i.e.* particular stages in the work to be reached by particular dates [3.2.1]; and these, while primarily serving as a trigger for payment, give both parties a chance to monitor progress, and to review or even halt the proceedings if the original estimates seem to be too far astray. The client should also expect regular progress meetings to monitor development, at least once a month. The supplier should be obliged to provide the client with such reasonable information as may be required to enable the client properly to monitor progress.

Although a time and materials contract may seem a little vague for budgeting purposes, it is probably the commonest type of commissioned software contract in the computer industry and reflects the fact that the client itself will often not be able adequately to articulate its requirements at the outset of the development project. It depends on complete confidence between client and systems house, but then no software contract is worth making without such confidence.

Fixed price contract

A fixed price contract states that the systems house will write a program to perform certain functions at a particular price. The existence of such a contract (other than for packages) presupposes that a realistic price for the work can be estimated in advance, but, in practice, this is possible only after the systems house has done a good deal of investigative work. It is therefore common for a systems house to charge for such investigative or analysis work on a time and materials basis, and then set off all, or part, of the cost of this work against the fixed price for the programming. For example, C may ask S to write a program or a suite of programs, and insist that it be on a fixed price basis; S will say that the price can be fixed only after an investigation, and suggest an estimate of £8,000 for the investigation. At the end of it, he may say that the program could be written for £52,000, but allow the £8,000 already spent against this. Thus, if C accepts that estimate, he pays £8,000 now and a further £44,000 later; if C rejects the estimate, he simply pays £8,000 now and the work goes no further. It may sometimes be worth entering into more than one such agreement with shortlisted suppliers and rejecting all but one estimate at the end.

It is worth pointing out that many systems houses, including the most reputable, refuse to handle fixed price contracts at all unless the value of the work is trivial, or with substantial contingency built in, so as to make the fixed price appear very steep. The client who insists on such a contract is often inexperienced in software procurement, and accordingly inclined to be cautious and to insist on the certainty of a fixed price; such caution is understandable, particularly as in the early days of computing many time and materials contracts went completely out of control, and involved their hapless clients in hideous expenditure. Fortunately, the number and scale of such catastrophes have decreased. But the client will find that although a fixed price contract may give him peace of mind and budgetary certainty, it may not give him the best deal, since, as noted above, the contract price cannot be varied in the light of work done, the systems house must add on a contingency budget, which they expect never to have to use but which they need to protect themselves against a reasonable level of overrun in the estimates originally given. Furthermore, the definitions of milestones [3.2.1] and acceptance of the programs need to be stricter and the client is likely to find that the relationship with the systems house will generally be more formal and contractual in nature, as the systems house will need to be strict in defining and thereafter managing the scope of the work which is to be done for the fixed price agreed between the parties. If a client prematurely terminates a fixed price contract and allows the systems house to do any further work, he could find that he is faced with a time and materials contract in any case.

In an extreme case, the systems house may have failed to add on sufficient contingency. In this event, the systems house is obviously in dire trouble, but so too is the client. For the systems house, the most probable recourse will be to cut corners by using less experienced (and therefore less expensive) staff or, more likely in testing and documentation, with the result that the client will be asked to take delivery of software which may still contain serious bugs and has insufficient documentation to enable the bugs to be traced. Possible deficiencies of this sort illustrate clearly the dangers of comparing two software quotations, unless it is absolutely certain that the testing and documentation are to similar standards.

Estimated maximum/capped price contract

This type of contract is often used as an attempt to avoid the rigidity of the fixed price contract and the fluidity of the time and materials contract. The basis for the work is time and materials, but the systems house quotes an estimated maximum for their costs (though not always for their expenses), and agrees to warn the client as the costs approach the maximum and not to exceed it without the client's express authority. If the systems house does not reach the maximum the client pays only for the work performed. A contract for an investigation is often of this type.

Like the fixed price contract, the estimated maximum price contract will usually have a substantial contingency budget. Such a contingency could well be 25–50 per cent above any estimate, since it must take into account the worst possible combination of circumstances, and the systems house does not have the benefit of a potential "bonus" if it actually manages to deliver the required software with less time and effort than had been anticipated (as would be the case in a pure fixed price contract).

As with the time and materials contract, the systems house will submit records of time taken and disbursements and will expect to attend regular progress meetings.

3.1 Service to be Performed [D2, D4]

The systems house is presumably either writing a program or supplying a completed program, although the wording reflecting this is often terse and unhelpful. We have seen companies promising to "program a program" and even "do a program"! The more usual term is, of course, to "write a program". The simplest way of defining the purpose for which the program is written is by reference to an existing document which lists all functions in detail, *e.g.* "to write a program to perform all the functions more particularly described in the document entitled 'Bloggs Ltd . . . Stock Control-Functional Specification' and dated November 25, 1999 . . .". As noted at 1.3, such documents are commonly referred to as functional specifications, because they specify the functions which the software is to be able to carry out, once completed. In this way, the specification [1.3] becomes a part of the contract and both parties have greater certainty as to what is expected.

3.2 Payment [C3, D5]

Time and materials contracts, and estimated maximum price contracts, depend on the systems house keeping accurate and complete records as to the time spent by its staff in working on the client's project, and the client should satisfy himself on the adequacy of those records. He should also satisfy himself as to the records of expenses. The best opportunity to do this lies in regular progress meetings.

Under time and materials, and estimated maximum price contracts, accounts are usually rendered monthly. The alternative, which is the norm in the case of fixed price contracts, is for payment to be either once, on delivery—as also in a licence for an existing software package—or by instalments on reaching milestones.

3.2.1 Milestones [D5(1)]

A milestone is a defined stage in reaching the objective of a complete program. The first milestone is usually on signing the contract; the last is usually the client's acceptance of the software either as a result of formal acceptance tests and/or after an agreed period of live use of the programs in the client's business environment. Between those stages the definitions of what the milestones are, and how both sides will know when they are reached, are up to the two parties. A milestone could be the completion of part of the design phase—*e.g.* delivery of a system specification; or a successful demonstration of a particular part of the work. The problems of definition are analogous to the problem of defining acceptance [3.3.1].

On achieving a milestone, it is usual for a proportion of the total cost to fall due. It is thus essential for the client to satisfy himself as to the reasonableness and value of any milestones, and as to the ease (or otherwise) of saying whether or not they have been achieved. It may also be possible in certain circumstances for the client to have an option to terminate at a milestone (or if a specific milestone is not reached by a defined date). Any timetable for development should also allow the client sufficient time for examination and review at each milestone, so as to allow it to satisfy itself as to the progress being made.

3.2.2 Non-payment

A systems house may seek some mechanism to protect itself against the risk of non-payment by the client. A common one is to apply interest to all overdue invoices, although seeking to enforce this would jeopardise the relationship with the client. Another mechanism is the right for the systems house to suspend the provision of its services until the overdue monies are paid, which (provided there are further services for the systems house to perform on behalf of the client) can act as a powerful stimulant to the client to get the invoices paid!

A further possibility remains, the "logic bomb", where the systems house programs the software so that, after a period of time, it will become inoperable. The purpose of this is that if the customer fails to pay the supplier, the bomb can come into effect. If, however, payment is effected satisfactorily, the supplier can disable the bomb and allow the software to continue functioning. Apparently, at least one such case has been considered under the Computer Misuse Act 1990. Section 3 of the Act provides for an offence of unauthorised modification of computer material and is usually thought of as designed to deal with viruses. In a case heard by the Scunthorpe Magistrates' Court in 1993, the supplier of the software was convicted in that his software modified the contents of the computer on which it was running. It should be noted that the software supplied was apparently actually modified by the supplier at the time of installation and further that title to the software remained with the supplier until such time as the customer had paid for it. This case was unfortunately never appealed despite much expectation at the time that it would be (*The Computer Law and Security Report* (1994), p. 39; *PLC* December 1993 and reported in *IT Law Today* (1993), Vol. 1, Issue 8, and *Computer Weekly* on August 19, 1993. See also Rupert Battcock, "Prosecutions under the Computer Misuse Act", in *Computers & Law* (Feb./March 1996), N.S. vol. 6, Issue 6, p. 24, from which we learn that the defendant's name was Whitaker). The magistrate held that the modification was unauthorised, but had the supplier informed the customer contractually of the existence of the logic bomb, he might have been cleared. No case has yet come before the courts to test this assertion, but it would seem prudent for the supplier to include such a clause in the contract if he intends to use a logic bomb [D5(3)].

In some States of the U.S., the Uniform Computer Information Transactions Act (UCITA), among other provisions, by section 605 would appear to legitimise the use of logic bombs and other remote devices for disabling software if the supplier believes a breach of contract has occurred. In the Act such a device is called an "automatic restraint" and defined as:

> "a program, code, device, or similar electronic or physical limitation the intended purpose of which is to restrict the use of information."

As "information" is itself defined in the Act, s. 102, to include not only data, text images, etc., but also "computer programs", the effect of section 605 is very wide. However, before discussing the effect of this it is important to understand the validity or otherwise of the Act. In the U.S., there are Uniform Codes, drafted by the National Conference of Commissioners of Uniform State Laws, designed to promote uniformity of statute law in the various states. Such codes have no effect until they are formally adopted by one or more of the individual states. At the time of writing (early 2000), only two states have so far adopted UCITA (reported to be Maryland and Virginia), but this could obviously change very fast. If a state has adopted UCITA and a contract is expressed to be under the laws of that particular state it would seem that this would permit logic bombs as a contractual possibility. In that case it might be argued that the modification of computer material would not be considered unauthorised within the terms of the British Computer Misuse Act (see Margaret Harvey, "Software Licensing—Changes in U.S. Laws may Affect U.K. Practice" in *Computers & Law* (Dec. 1999/Jan. 2000), N.S. Vol. 10, Issue 5, pp. 26–27).

There are other even more disquieting aspects of the UCITA so far as clients are concerned, which will be dealt with below [3.3.4, 4.3.1]. Where one is dealing with a contract under the laws of a particular U.S. state it is at least prudent to check whether the UCITA has yet been adopted by that state and if possible exclude it. Exclusion by an express provision is made possible by section 104.

3.3 DELIVERY AND ACCEPTANCE [C4, D9, O13]

3.3.1 Acceptance tests [C6, D10, O15]

When the work is completed, the client may expect:

(1) delivery of the program in a usable form ready to load onto his computer, *e.g.* by disk or tape, or indeed actually loaded by the supplier, whether at the client's premises or (as is becoming increasingly common) over the Internet;

(2) evidence of adequate tests performed on the programs (though for a software package this may well have been done before the signing of the agreement);

(3) manuals necessary to use the software;

(4) commencement of training (see below, Staff training [3.7.3])—the schedule of training should already have been completed.

In the case of bespoke software, the programs ready to load, whether in source code or object code form will usually consist of:

(a) the source code. This is the actual programs as written and before compilation [1.3];

(b) flow charts and design documents and diagrams whether produced as part of the documentation or devised at the client's request to explain the overall design of the software;

(c) other documentation, possibly to an agreed standard; and possibly also

(d) the object code, *i.e.* the programs after compilation [1.3].

Items (a) and/or (b) will probably be in both computer-usable and paper format. These will be essential if anyone is to be able to maintain the program in the future [Chapter 9] and its safeguarding will help protect the client from piracy of his software [3.8]. Alternatively, where the title to the software is to remain with the systems house, the source code may be deposited in escrow with a third party from where the client can retrieve it in the event of the systems house going into liquidation, or failing to fulfil its obligations to maintain in cases where (as is usual) maintenance is carried out by the original supplier [9, N]

As mentioned above [3.2.1], the contract may also prescribe a period of live usage in the client's business environment before the system is accepted.

As with milestones, so *a fortiori* on completion of the program it is essential that there should be an agreed basis for deciding whether or not the programs are complete and perform their functions adequately. For example, one contract reads:

"*Acceptance by Licensee*

The Licensee's acceptance of delivery of the Software shall be conclusive evidence that the Licensee has examined the Software and found it to be complete, in accordance with the description in the Specification, in good order and condition, fit for any purpose for which it may be required and in every way satisfactory."

Such wording reflects the fact that, after acceptance of the software, it is difficult for the client/licensee to make complaints about the software's performance which he could have investigated before acceptance although not necessarily impossible; the court in *Salvage Association v. CAP* [1995] F.S.R. 654 made the point that non-technical clients could not be expected to pick up all potential errors, and so would not necessarily be debarred from bringing proceedings in respect of problems which became apparent at a later date; in such circumstances, 'acceptance' simply connotes confirmation that the software was in apparent conformance with its contractual specifications as at the date of testing, and should not be construed as waiving the right to make any future claims or complaints.

As there may be a number of minor bugs which remain undetected by acceptance tests, however, it is also common for systems houses to provide an additional warranty period after acceptance during which any bugs which may come to light and which were not picked up during acceptance testing will be corrected free of charge.

In the case of software packages, the prospective user can, of course, devise such tests of the packages as he thinks necessary before signing any contract and some systems houses offer short term demonstration/evaluation licences of their software (or part of it) for this purpose. Such short term licenses typically have a logic device which aborts the program either on a specific date or so many days after it has first been loaded. If the client has been notified of this in advance, it can be argued that this logic device does not infringe the Computer Misuse Act 1990 since it is authorised [3.2.2]. However, where bespoke programs are concerned, the nature and extent of the tests can be, and should be, defined in advance of the completion of the software. On the one hand, the tests must be agreed by both sides to be fair and reasonable: if they are not, then it would seem that the supplier has written a program other than the one the client required—perhaps the design specification was at fault? On the other hand, if the supplier knows the full nature and content of the tests before the programming is far advanced, the program may be designed too specifically for the expected data, failing to cope with the unexpected. In fact, this last problem is of a theoretical rather than practical nature, since the programming is defined by the specification, prepared in advance, rather than by the test data. Nevertheless, it follows that in many contracts three separate batches of test data are envisaged: test or control data delivered at an early stage by the client to the supplier and used to test the individual programs or parts of programs (program testing); further data to test the linkage of the various different programs which constitute the whole contract (systems testing or link testing); and acceptance test data prepared by the client and not shown to the supplier or made available until after the completion of the programs. If this test data is at all large—and it should be if it is to test the capacity of the system—it may well need to be prepared by someone other than the client (or, of course, the systems house), and the data preparation contract in 10.3 may be relevant. It should at the very least reflect realistic data which the system is expected to deal with and should ideally work systematically through the functionality as expressed in the Functional Specification.

The running of this acceptance test data through the programs must ideally be performed jointly by both client and systems house, since any error or unexpected result must be resolved by both sides; both must agree that the test is fair, that the condition the test reveals is an error, and that it is one which it is the systems house's duty to rectify. It will be observed that each of these terms is open to discussion, but, in practice, both sides will have an interest in completing acceptance tests successfully—the systems house so as to be able to invoice a satisfied customer and release staff for other assignments, and the representative of the client since the choice of systems house (and often many other aspects of the system) has been his own personal responsibility and he is usually anxious to demonstrate within his own organisation that he can obtain a satisfactory result in the notoriously hazardous business of software contracts. Accordingly, the success or failure of the acceptance tests should, as far as possible, be objectively ascertainable so that the interests of both parties can be balanced. Both parties should agree the tests after the software is delivered but before the tests start, to ensure that the tests mirror the Functional Specification. When the tests begin the results must be recorded and be replicable, so that the systems house can reproduce the effect of any discovered bug and search for its cause.

The test data itself will therefore have to include some description of the results to be expected, if the tests are to be at all meaningful. The preparation of test data and expected results can be an exceedingly laborious task, but will usually be a vital one. Both supplier and customer should be involved in this process, so as to ensure that the tests reflect as accurately as possible what the software has been commissioned to achieve.

This discussion of acceptance tests is by way of background to their relatively brief appearance in contracts, for it is most unusual to include a detailed description of the test data, even in a schedule. Instead, there is merely a brief acknowledgement of the existence of test data, usually included by the supplier as a way of defining acceptance. For example, in a licence agreement:

"The Client shall be responsible for providing the Supplier with suitable test data and proposed test scripts for the purposes of the Acceptance Tests. The

Supplier shall review such test data and test scripts and inform the Client of any proposed amendments within *10* days of receipt. Any disputes as to the test data and test scripts to be used in the Acceptance Tests shall be resolved pursuant to the dispute resolution procedure in Clause *X*. The Acceptance Tests shall thereafter be conducted in accordance with the procedure set out in Schedule/Clause *Y*."

The timing of the submission of such draft test data/scripts and the period within which they will have to be reviewed and approved will depend largely on the nature, size and urgency of the development project. It is also worth noting that the onus for the initial production of draft data and scripts can be (and quite frequently is) reversed, *i.e.* so as to require the systems house to produce the data and scripts for the client's staff to review and approve.

Finally, it should be pointed out that acceptance tests usually depend on the completion of training and if this is delayed or neglected [3.7.3], the whole timetable for acceptance may be endangered.

3.3.2 Performance

So far we have considered only the question of data input and expected results output. But there is a second, and more controversial, aspect to program testing, for, in addition to checking design logic, error checking, file maintenance, report generation, and so on, the licensee/client may be concerned with the throughput performance. In an operating system or other "pure" software, this may involve rigorous timing of the throughput (length of time taken to compile a program of x statements, length of time taken to link-edit y subroutines, etc.) or timing of performance (the execution time of a compiled program, etc.), or perhaps measurement of the program size after compilation.

Tests such as these are usually more appropriate to a software package which is to be compared against similar rival packages from other organisations, or even a simultaneous comparison of hardware and software of rival systems. For example, manufacturers A and B each claim to be able to supply a computer with a sort program and a compiler. The prospective customer devises a program with a sort phase. Program, sort phase and data for the program are all typical of the work the prospective customer hopes to use the computer for and the volumes of data are also realistic. Both manufacturers are given the program and are required to demonstrate the compilation. Following this, both manufacturers are given the data and required to demonstrate the execution of the program and the sort. All demonstrations must be performed in the customer's presence, and information is logged about timings, program size, disk area needed for the sort, and so on (*i.e.* so as to ensure that like is compared to like). The customer then compares the results and uses them to help him to decide between rival suppliers. Such *benchmark* tests are not usually mentioned in software contracts, but rather tend to be performed before the contractual stage is reached (*i.e.* as part of the tender/procurement process) since they are usually concerned with existing software packages.

For bespoke applications software, a client may also seek such guarantees of performance to a particular standard. It is fair to add that there is no area of computer performance so difficult to estimate as throughput (timing, program size, etc.), and few systems house would dare to give any guarantees in this area.

Performance may be included in the functional specification and in this way incorporated by reference in the contract. As mentioned when discussing hardware [2.3.5], performance depends on the interaction of hardware and software. It therefore follows that the functionality of the software, the exact configuration of the hardware on which it is to run and the expected volumes both of data and users will all need to be defined in advance. For the client able to look for such guarantees, the way ahead is extremely thorny. Performance criteria may include:

(1) Volume capacity in terms of

    (a) storage of data in terms of its rate of entry and the length of time it is stored;

    (b) throughput, *i.e.* speed of processing records;

    (c) storage and parallel processing of particular programs;

    (d) number of PCs, terminals and other active peripherals which can be linked to the system without degrading response time;

    (e) speed of individual components, *e.g.* telecommunications lines or printers.

(2) Response time, *i.e.* in an interactive system, the elapsed time between the depression of a message key and the appearance of a meaningful message on the screen, other than a wait message. This time will depend on the full interaction of hardware, software and telecommunications equipment and on the volumes of data and numbers of other simultaneous users. Any contractual provisions relating to response times are accordingly likely to be heavily caveated by the supplier (and indeed a failure by the supplier to insert such caveats may be a source of concern for the customer, as it may suggest that the supplier does not fully appreciate the nature of the customer's requirements).

(3) Maintenance and back-up cover [Chapter 9].

3.3.3 Error correction [C8, D11]

Software contracts are often reticent about the subject of error correction after acceptance, and for that reason the topic must be considered here, rather than as a systems house's duty [3.7]. If immediately upon acceptance of the software, the client enters into a software maintenance agreement with the original supplier, the absence of any mention of error correction in the software contract may not be so crucial, since any errors in the program which have not been discovered by acceptance tests can be put right under the maintenance contract (although there may still be an issue as to when a warranty period for the free correction of software faults will cease and support/maintenance fees become payable). Chapter 9 discusses such contracts and indeed the whole question of error correction and enhancement of software. It is suggested in that chapter, and repeated here, that anyone contemplating purchasing software should ensure that he knows how it will be maintained and by whom.

As mentioned above [3.3.1], usually there will be a period within which errors will be corrected. The length of the period varies (and may be dispensed with altogether if the supplier is also providing maintenance services), but 90 days is common. A sample form of words is as follows:

> "During a period of *90* days following the acceptance of the Software, the Supplier will correct any reported errors or defects in the operation of the Software free of charge."

However, if there is no maintenance contract and no specific provision in the procurement contract relating to error correction, the client can only fall back on the various statutory provisions loosely included in the term "consumer law", while being aware that his own acceptance tests (or lack of them) may be interpreted as affirmation of the contract (although as noted above [3.3.1], the case of *The Salvage Association v. CAP Financial Services Limited* [1995] F.S.R. 654 suggested that, for non-technically proficient clients at least, acceptance tests would constitute no more than confirmation of apparent conformance with the test criteria as at the date of the relevant tests, and not be construed as waiving rights in respect of defects discovered later). In practice, a reputable systems house may remedy small bugs which come to light quickly, as well as any major rewriting of the software which, for whatever reason, was not picked up during acceptance tests, or indeed before acceptance of the functional specification. This will be on the basis that this will be cheaper than having the client engage a different systems house to carry out such remedial work. Certainly, the "correction" cannot extend to anything which involves a change to the functional specification as this cannot be a fault in the delivered software. A practical difficulty which tends to delay the rectification of bugs is that the systems house will have redeployed the staff who wrote the original program(s) and so may have no one available to do the work without a considerable effort in studying the workings of the program first. In the absence of any maintenance agreement (and the client would do well to ask himself why there is no maintenance agreement) the client should look for some such clause as:

"Up to 6 months from the date of acceptance by the Client of the Software, the Supplier undertakes to rectify free of charge all faults and defects in the Software which the Client has notified to them in writing provided that:

(a) such reported faults or defects do not relate to changes required by the Client to the Functional Specification;

(b) the faults or defects have not resulted from any modifications to the Software not made by the Supplier or with the Supplier's written consent;

(c) the faults or defects do not arise from the Client's use of the software in any manner outside the scope of the Functional Specification; or

(d) the faults or defects could not reasonably have been discovered by the Client during the Acceptance Tests.

The Client shall provide the Supplier with reasonable details of the fault or defect and shall assist the Supplier in recreating such fault or defect and in the carrying out of any subsequent remedial work."

The time-scale of this undertaking (also frequently described as a *warranty period*) can of course vary from 6 months, but a systems house is unlikely to wish to enter into an open-ended contract which could suddenly be re-activated years later when the original programmers have long since left, and all knowledge of the application or machine is dim. Moreover, one might reasonably expect that any genuinely serious faults will have come to light relatively quickly.

In some cases a distinction may be made between significant and non-significant bugs:

"For the purposes of this Agreement, a 'Defect' shall mean a material divergence from the requirements of the Functional Specification, and should for the avoidance of doubt not include any divergences which are trivial or cosmetic or which do not impact to a material degree upon the use of the Software for the purposes of the Client's business."

It is not unreasonable for the supplier to protect himself from some perfectly frivolous fault, although there is room for debate as to whether any particular fault can be said to be material, or to have impacted upon the client's business. Frequently a fault can be managed by the client's staff "working round" it. However, if a work round involves either monetary cost to the client or loss of productivity then the argument that it impacts the client's business looks more plausible. In contrast a cosmetic fault might be where the pagination was in the lower left corner rather than the lower right, with no loss of data or clarity.

As mentioned above [2.3.8], the Unfair Contract Terms Act 1977 has been used to limit the effectiveness of contract terms which purport to exclude or limit liability for defects. However, the Unfair Contract Terms Act 1977, Sched. I, para. 1, provides for a number of exemptions from the provisions of sections 2–4 of the Act, including:

> "(c) Any contract so far as it relates to the creation or transfer of a right or interest in any patent, trade mark, copyright, registered design, technical or commercial information or other intellectual property, or relates to the termination of any such right or interest."

Software is clearly copyrightable [3.8]. However, Schedule 1, para. 1(c), gave rise to difficulties of interpretation; does it mean that exclusion clauses in software contracts (or even contracts with software elements) will never be affected by the Act or does it only affect provisions which themselves create, transfer or terminate intellectual property rights or interests thereby leaving the other clauses in the contract unaffected? Judicial guidance on this issue was received from Judge Thayne Forbes in *The Salvage Association v CAP Financial Services Limited* [1995] F.S.R. 662–664. In his view, the nugatory effect of paragraph 1(c) only concerned those clauses in an agreement that specifically dealt with the creation or transfer of a right or interest in an intellectual property right. It did not touch or concern terms which related to other matters such as the quality of the software, the competence and performance of the supplier's employees or liability for breaches of the agreement or in negligence which are still subject to the controls of sections 2–4 of the Act. In the context of software, this would seem to confine the operation of para 1(c) to the clause granting the right to use the software or assigning the copyright in the software to the customer, such that if there is some defect in the supplier's copyright ownership, the supplier could exclude his liability for such eventuality without being subject to the controls of sections 2–4. It is welcome that the court has adopted the narrower interpretation, for otherwise the provisions of the Act would easily be evaded by providing in a contract for the creation, transfer or termination of a relatively minor intellectual property right or interest. In any event, it is always safer for customers to treat exclusion clauses in software contracts (including also hardware [2.3.8] and turnkey [1.12] contracts with software elements) with care and to endeavour to negotiate appropriate relaxations if they are thought to be unduly onerous.

A different question arises as to the extent to which, in the absence of any express contractual provision, the client may be entitled to access and amend the source code of software in which it has acquired a licence right rather than ownership of copyright, when the purpose for doing so is to correct errors or bugs. In the case of *Saphena Computing Ltd v. Allied Collecting Agencies Ltd* [1995] F.S.R. 616, reported in *Computers & Law* (March 1989), N.S. Vol. 59, Issue 20, p. 21, although title to the software was in doubt (the facts of the case predated the present Copyright,

Designs and Patents Act) the defendants were still entitled to amend the software in order to eliminate bugs and make it usable (which it was not without the defendant's action). This was one of the points considered in the case of *Mars U.K. Ltd v. Teknowledge Ltd* [2000] F.S.R. 138. In this case, the copyright material worked and the point was whether the defendants had the right to change or adapt a working program as opposed simply to correcting bugs in the *Saphena* case. In the *Mars* case, it was argued by the defendant that copying and/or modification of software could, in appropriate circumstances, fall within the "right to repair" as established by the House of Lords in the case of *British Leyland v. Armstrong* [1986] A.C. 577 in relation to the creation of spare parts for cars. The court noted that the Copyright, Designs and Patents Act 1988 had largely superseded the *British Leyland* Case, and in particular, in relation to software, had provided in sections 50A to 50C for a number of permitted acts in relation to software, which did *not* include a right of repair [3.8.1]. The court accordingly concluded that there was no such right in respect of the software under English law.

If this line of reasoning is followed, it will further emphasise the need to ensure that there are appropriate source code escrow provisions [9.0, N] in the contract, so as to provide for a right to access and amend the relevant software in the event that the supplier fails to live up to its support and maintenance obligations. There must however be some doubt as to whether the decision will in fact be followed, at least insofar as the modifications are only required to correct defects in the original software and the *Saphena* decision (which seems not to have been considered by the judge in *Mars*) lends support to this.

3.3.4 Warranties

The client should carefully consider the scope of the warranties which it requires from the systems house; some are self-evident and mirror those which would be implied by the Supply of Goods and Services Act 1982 in any event, *e.g.* the obligation to use reasonable care and skill in the production of any bespoke software. Others are more specific to the requirements of the individual project, such as those relating to performance [3.3.2].

As a minimum, it is likely that the client will want a warranty in relation to any bespoke software that it will, upon completion, provide the functionality which was specified in the Functional Specification [3.1]. In the case of package software, the warranty will usually be linked to the provision of the functionality specified in its accompanying documentation.

In the run up to the year 2000, there was a considerable amount of attention focused upon the wording of warranties relating to the ability of the relevant software to cope with the advent of the Year 2000 and the associated date format changes that it entailed, variously called "Y2K", "the Year 2000 Problem" or "the Millennium Bug". In actual fact, the Millennium Bug ended up being something of a damp squib, and new software products will invariably now have been programmed in such a way as to cope with the millennium date change and the fact that the Year 2000 is a leap year without any impact upon performance or functionality, but there may still just be a case for clients to seek express warranties to this effect, especially for older software packages. In the U.K., the BSI definition of Year 2000 conformance, although not perfect, has become widely accepted, and a typical warranty clause based on the BSI definition would read as follows:

> "The Supplier warrants that the performance and functionality of the Software will not be adversely affected by the advent of the Year 2000 and that the

Software will be capable of accurately processing all date data between *January 1, 1999* and *December 31, 2099* all such dates within this period being a "valid date". In particular, the Supplier warrants:

(a) no current value of a valid date will cause any unintended interruption in the operation of the Software;

(b) all processing of date-related data will produce the correct results for all valid date values;

(c) if the date elements permit the century to be specified, all valid dates shall have the correct century specified for them so as to eliminate date ambiguity;

(d) where any valid date is specified without the century, the correct century shall be unambiguous for all processing involving the valid date;

(e) the Year 2000 shall be recognised as a leap year;

provided always that all hardware, software and other products which interact with the Software and which exchange date data with it are similarly Year 2000 compliant."

A more important practical consideration is the Euro [L5 (5)]. The issue is not just the representation of the Euro symbol which is primarily (but not exclusively) a software issue, but more importantly the conversion rules from one European currency to another and in particular the "triangularity" rule whereby in converting from (say) francs to deutschmarks the conversion has to be effected via the Euro and not directly. A suitable form of warranty wording for software which has to process currency-related data may be as follows:

"The Supplier warrants that the Software shall be capable of processing currency-related data involving the Euro in conformance with the applicable conversion and rounding requirements in E.C. Regulation 1103/97 without otherwise giving rise to any adverse effect upon the Software's performance and functionality."

Finally, the U.S. Uniform Computer Information Transactions Act, which has already been referred to [3.2.2] by sections 401(d) and 406, allows the supplier to disclaim statutory obligations as to correct functioning of the software. However, where the supplier has not disclaimed, section 401(c)(2) appears to mean that the warranties cannot apply in non-U.S. jurisdictions.

3.4 TERMINATION [C21, D26, D27]

An effect of the termination of a package program licence will probably be the delivery to the licensor or the destruction by the licensee of all copies of the software and its documentation [3.8.1]. In the case of bespoke software, the client will require copies of the software or specifications to date and in particular any source code to date [3.3.1].

3.4.1 Termination by performance

Many contracts specify that one of the means by which a contract can be terminated is by actual performance of the required services and/or obligations. "Termination" in this context is something of a misnomer; it refers to the end of the positive obligations to perform tasks, simply because they have all been satisfactorily completed. Satisfactory discharge of a software contract (thereby terminating it) will usually be by the delivery of the programs by the systems house, and acceptance and payment by the client. However, the contract will inevitably have to visualise less happy eventualities, and the possibility that the parties will have to call a premature halt to the software licence and any associated development work.

3.4.2 Termination or breach by the client

Voluntary termination

Like any other agreement, a software contract may provide for termination at the wish of either party. Logically (if not lawfully), a bespoke software contract can also be frustrated by the client-at least, in the earlier stages—since the systems house tends to be largely dependent on the client for information about his system, test data and often, of course, machine time and other facilities, though the clauses with regard to acceptance tests [3.3.1] mean that the client must take positive steps to reject any program the supplier produces. If a client wishes to terminate early, other than when the systems house is at fault (*i.e.* if the systems house has committed a material breach of contract) or is insolvent, the damage he can do to the supplier goes beyond mere monetary loss, since the supplier will have scheduled its future work on the basis of the staff for a particular project being gainfully occupied (and hence not available for other work) right up to the end of the project; it may not be able to find sufficient work at short notice if numbers of experienced staff are suddenly back on its hands. It may also have other expenses resulting from the early termination, if it has had to enter into its own supply or leasing contracts to perform its obligations to the client, and they cannot themselves be terminated at short notice. It is therefore not uncommon to specify a period of notice the length of which will probably take into account the number and experience of the staff working on the job, *e.g.* for a time and materials contract:

> "The Client shall be entitled to terminate this Agreement without cause upon having given the Supplier not less than *4 weeks* prior written notice. In the event of such termination, the Client shall pay the Supplier for all services provided up to the date of termination, and for all unavoidable expenses reasonably incurred by the Supplier in connection with this Agreement. Termination under this Clause X shall not otherwise affect the parties' accrued rights or liabilities under this Agreement."

The provisions relating to the payment of the full contract price are particularly important in a fixed-price contract where the stage payments made up to the date of termination may not fully reflect the value of the services provided up to that date— usually because the pattern of payments has a large amount held back until acceptance in order to provide the client with sufficient bargaining power in the event of non-performance; in such contracts, the reference to payment in the preceding example clause should be amended so as to refer to the supplier being paid all stage payments which have become payable as at the date of termination, plus a separate payment for all services provided since the last stage payment, on a time and materials basis. If this still does not fully reflect the value of the systems house's work, it may be necessary to agree a mechanism for determining the amount to be payable (possibly by reference to a third-party adjudicator).

Infringement of title

If the systems house reserves title to the software, either explicitly or implicitly, any act or attempted act calculated to interfere with or jeopardise that right is, in some contracts, deemed to be a condition justifying the systems house in terminating the contract, while still allowing it to pursue any other remedies that may be appropriate. This is especially likely to be the case in a licence for an existing piece of software:

> "If the Licensee shall do or allow to be done any act or thing which in the opinion of the Supplier may jeopardise the Supplier's rights in the Software or any part thereof and in particular but without prejudice to the generality of the foregoing if the Licensee shall make or allow to be made unauthorised copies of the Software or if the Licensee imparts or divulges the contents of the Software without the prior written consent of the Supplier, then in each and every such case the Supplier may by notice in writing sent to the Licensee at the Licensee's registered office forthwith or at any time thereafter and for all purposes terminate the rights granted to the Licensee under this Agreement and the licence thereby constituted, such termination to be without prejudice to the rights of the parties arising out of antecedent breaches and without prejudice to the Licensee's remaining and continuing obligations under this Agreement in relation to confidence and the Supplier's property in the Software."

A clause that relies purely on the system house's opinion seems gratuitously vague, and it is not easy to define "contents of Software". But the general intention is clear enough. From the point of view of a licensee, however, one would wish to impose a requirement for the system house's opinion to be a reasonable one.

Failure to pay

Similarly, failure to pay is likely to result in termination:

> "If the Licensee shall fail to pay any sum payable under this Agreement within 7 days of written demand made on or after the due date the Supplier may terminate this Agreement."

This is likely to be of particular relevance where the licence fee is an annual (rather than a one-off) payment. Licensees should however beware of a clause which might result in the termination of the licence if they fail to make payments of maintenance fees which become payable under a combined licence and support agreement, as the support services are properly severable from the grant of the licence. For example, if, in a contract like this, the licensee is minded to withhold some or all of the maintenance payments until the system house remedies some maintenance failure, a clause of this type might enable the systems house to terminate the licence, leaving the licensee with no software at all.

Client's incapacity

Clauses about death, bankruptcy, winding-up, etc., in software contracts do not differ from similar clauses in other contracts which permit termination.

3.4.3 Termination by the systems house

In the absence of fault on the part of the customer, clauses in this category are rare since termination by the systems house before completion of the contract leaves the client in an unsatisfactory position. In a very long and complicated development such a clause may be appropriate, provided it is firmly linked to milestones [3.2.1] which give the client some return on progress to date.

3.5 ALTERATIONS

3.5.1 Packages [C16]

For some standard software packages there will be a total ban on the client modifying the package, although, as mentioned in [3.3.3, 3.8.1], this may be ineffective to prevent the client lawfully making modifications to the extent necessary to allow interaction with other programs and, subject to what was said above in the context of the *Mars* and *Saphena* cases [3.3.3], possibly also for the purposes of error correction.

Nevertheless, the systems house may allow modification in some cases and many software packages are sold on the express assumption that this will be the case. The sample clause below assumes the client can also maintain the package himself:

"(1) The Licensee may modify the Package (other than . . .) and may merge the Package or parts thereof with other data and/or programs. This Licence applies to all parts of the resulting product which are or were the Package or part or parts thereof;

(2) The Licensee will notify the Licensor of all such modifications or mergers and without charge to the Licensor supply all necessary documentation of such changes including specifications and source code. This material will be used by the Licensor for the purpose of sub-clause (3) only;

(3) If the Package or any part or parts thereof so modified or merged by the Licensee are used on the Equipment and adversely affect it, then the Licensor will not be responsible for any resulting loss and may make an extra charge to the Licensee for any assistance the Licensor may provide at the request of the Licensee to investigate the Package so modified or its results."

Some agreements provide for ownership of the modifications to vest in the licensor and for copies to be provided to the licensor on expiry of the licence, or else for the copies to be destroyed and a certificate of such destruction to be given to the licensor. The agreement may well provide that the licensee include on all copies (including modifications) of the licensed software the licensor's copyright notice. The licensor's warranties and indemnities in relation to the infringement of third-party intellectual property rights are also likely to be invalidated by the making of such modifications, at least to the extent that the infringement claim results from a part of the software which has been so modified.

3.5.2 Commissioned software [D7]

An astonishingly large number of software contracts fail to cover the possibility of the client's wishing to modify his requirements after the systems house has already started on its task. In practice, this is an extremely common occurrence the effect of which on the work to date can range from trivial to catastrophic. The reason for its frequency is that, as the date of delivery approaches, the client thinks more and more deeply about the nature of what he has ordered, and how he has got to use it; as a result he has second, and better, thoughts about exactly what he wants. A competent systems house will endeavour to provide additional unused fields in record formats to cope with this, but even so relations are easily soured by the absence of any express provision to cover this—and, worst of all, the absence of any realisation or understanding by the client of quite how disruptive any change of mind may be. A clause such as the following can save a lot of trouble:

> "Any request by the Client for alteration to the Software shall be examined by the Supplier who shall, as soon as reasonably possible, provide an estimate of the costs which the Supplier would incur to effect the said alteration. Price modification of the Specification and delivery of any such alteration shall be agreed in writing between the Supplier and the Client before the Supplier commences work on the alteration."

Many contracts refuse to consider any alterations unless they have been submitted in writing by the client.

Whatever the contract may or may not say, it is very much in the client's interest that there is a clearly defined change management procedure, and in particular that:

(1) all such alterations are clearly specified;

(2) any such specifications have been notified to, and agreed with, the supplier at the earliest opportunity;

(3) any resultant variations, at least in the areas of price, timescale for delivery of the software and performance of the software, are fully discussed, agreed and documented.

Because of the frequency of clients requiring changes (modest or otherwise) after a system has been specified and agreed, less competent systems houses have sometimes agreed orally to changes, failed to discuss the implications of the change for the fulfilment of the contract, and then used the change as a "let-out" when they have been unable to deliver the software on time. It is nearly impossible for a client to gauge the truth of an assertion such as:

> "We could easily have finished the work by June 1, as originally agreed, but you asked us to implement changes and this upset our time schedules."

Correct documentation of both change and its effect on the contract is accordingly essential for both sides. An effective clause in the contract on the lines of that given above protects the client from the expensive and unsatisfactory results of an oral request by his staff (". . . just put this in, will you?"). Junior staff working for the client may easily be tempted to do this, and imagine they are furthering the client's interest, unaware that they may be doubling cost, timescale and complexity of the software, and even, in extreme cases, rendering it impossible to implement. An explicit requirement for requests for changes to be in writing (and possibly also for them to be made by specified individuals with an adequate level of authority) is very valuable, such as:

> "The Supplier shall not accept or implement any changes to the Software requested by the Client or his servants unless requests for such changes are made in writing and submitted in the manner prescribed in *Clause X* hereof."

Having said all this, it is not open to a contracting party unilaterally to alter an agreement and, in the absence of an agreed change control procedure embodied in the contract, a customer cannot compel the supplier to implement alterations.

3.6 CLIENT'S DUTIES

For an existing package the main client's duties relate to alterations [3.5.1] or title [3.8.1]; but in relation to a project for the creation of bespoke software it is essential that the client appreciates the extent of his duties. Even if they are not expressly set out in the contract, adequate input from the client will invariably be central to the success of the project.

3.6.1 Co-operation on systems design

Suppliers are dependent on the goodwill of their clients if they are to produce successful systems to fit their clients' requirements. A lawyer whose client withholds co-operation and confidence from him is at best at a grave disadvantage, and a systems house is in the same position. This goodwill can take a number of forms, including those set out below.

Liaison and nominees [D17]

The first requirement is for the client to nominate a member of his staff to supply information to the systems house. The original negotiations between the two sides will probably have included the client's directors or partners, or at least very senior management concerned with policy and contractual matters rather than detailed implementation. System design will usually require the participation of the IT staff, and a nominee should be as closely as possible concerned with the day-to-day working of the system. For instance:

> "The Client shall within *one week* of the date hereof nominate in writing to the Supplier the representative who will supply any information which may be needed by the Supplier to fulfil the provisions hereof. The Supplier cannot be held responsible for any delay caused by non-availability of such nominated representative."

The client's advantage from this will be that his nominee can control the progress of the project. A requirement to obtain a nominee's consent to any proposed alterations to the system [3.5.2] makes the role of a nominee particularly important.

Information [D19]

A systems house which is to perform a useful function needs a good deal of information about the client. Very often successful systems design depends not just on accurate knowledge of the particular application (*e.g.* stock control) performed in the client's business, but of the whole background of the client's work. Withholding of information can, therefore, seriously impair the systems house's effectiveness and disrupt schedules. Hence:

> "The Client shall provide all information and documentation reasonably requested by the Supplier in order to allow the Supplier to provide the Services. Such information and documentation shall be subject to the pro-visions of confidentiality contained in Clause *X* hereof. In the event that work is delayed or the extent of the work is increased by delay or failure in providing such information or documentation the Supplier reserves the right to amend the price and timescale of this Agreement to take account of any increased cost or timescale of the delivery of the Software caused by such delay or failure."

Office facilities [D23]

The nature of systems analysis and design usually requires that the systems house's staff will have to work on the client's premises. At least a desk per person is likely to be required, and many contracts cover provision of stationery and facilities like photocopying or even typing. It is customary for these to be provided free of charge:

> "Typing facilities equivalent to the services of one full-time copy typist shall be made available to the Supplier's team at the Client's premises in *Northtown* . . ."

Or, more succinctly:

> "The Client undertakes to provide to the staff of the Supplier such desks and office facilities as may be reasonably necessary to enable the Supplier to fulfil its obligations under this Agreement."

Computer facilities [D22]

With regard to machine time, if the client already has a suitable computer installed, the contract will usually require him to make it available for program development. This is usually free of charge:

> "The Client undertakes to provide the Supplier with all computer time reasonably necessary to write install and test the Software during normal working hours or at such other time or times as may be agreed, free of charge."

Sometimes, the machine time may be more precisely defined (". . . not less than n hours a day including x hours in prime shift . . .") and there may also be a minimum configuration defined:

> "Throughout this contract the Client shall provide at *Northtown* the machine time itemised below on an *ICBM* of the following specification:
> *16 Gigabytes* of memory
> printer
> etc . . ."

However, such detail is not usually necessary unless the work has an experimental (or at least unusual) character.

Alternatively, if the supplier is also procuring hardware for the client, it is likely to be required to complete the installation of the hardware first, and to thereafter utilise the new hardware for the purposes of the software development [1.12].

If a supplier is under particular pressure to complete a job quickly, it may seek to do so by increasing the number of staff on a project. It must be admitted that such a manoeuvre rarely has a beneficial effect unless introduced at a very early stage in the project; nevertheless, the client should be prepared to find that the use of his machine during the project will fluctuate wildly.

He should also be aware that failure to provide machine time, even though it is not his fault, may seriously increase costs and timescale.

If a client does not provide machine time this is usually either because he has not (yet) installed a suitable computer, or else because the computer is already too heavily used during ordinary daily operating, the time required for programming not being necessarily commensurate with the time required to run the completed program.

Occasionally, computer time is required on a different machine because the client's computer is too far from the supplier's staff, and providing remote access is for some reason not feasible, or the existing load on the machine does not allow the development work to take place on the same machine. In this situation, either the client can buy machine time elsewhere or, more usually, he deputes the supplier to do this for him, in which case any charges to be levied by the owner of the computer (if this is other than the supplier) must be defined and agreed in advance, and both sides should visualise the situation when a third party's computer is not available-through machine failure or some other reason. One would normally expect the client to bear the cost of any delay caused by the failure of a third party's computer, just as he would for failure of his own computer, but it is essential that this situation be considered at contract stage:

> "The Supplier shall not be held responsible for any delay or increase in costs caused by any failure in securing machine time for writing, installing and testing the Software."

Apart from machine time, the supplier will also, in theory, require storage space for stationery, floppy disks, and so on. This is often assumed as part of Office Facilities. Similarly, data preparation facilities may be required:

> "During the subsistence of this Agreement the Client will provide free of charge all such data preparation facilities as may be necessary for the staff of the Supplier to design write install and test the Software."

As with other clauses, there may be a rider spelling out the ghastly effects of delay or failure on the overall cost and timescale. With the growth of interactive or on-line systems, accessible directly through a keyboard, such facilities are becoming of less importance.

Expenses

If the supplier's staff are working away from home, the client is usually expected to bear the cost of their expenses (travel, accommodation, etc.). The definition of expenses varies and is often surprisingly vague. If in doubt, the client should negotiate with the supplier maximum figures or, if this is possible, himself provide accommodation. Many suppliers have a maximum scale which their staff must adhere to, and will be happy to make this available to the client. In the light of this, a clause such as that set out below may be appropriate:

> "Invoices for expenses properly incurred by the Supplier in fulfilment of this Agreement will be submitted to the Client monthly in arrears."

3.6.2 Poaching staff [D25]

At the end of a successfully completed project, a client may find that his confidence in the individual members of the systems house's staff has grown to the point where he would wish to employ them full-time. They probably know both his programs and his business rather better than any of his own staff and as full-time employees they would cost the client far less than the fees the client is paying to the systems house, since those fees contain the systems house's overheads and profits. From the systems house's point of view, such a loss of staff can be serious, since staff expertise is their sole asset. It is therefore quite common for a systems house to include a clause such as:

> "The Client accepts that the Supplier will suffer loss if a member of the Supplier's staff employed on work on the Client's behalf accepts an offer of permanent employment with the Client within *six* months of the termination of the work which is the subject of this Agreement. If such a member of the Supplier's staff accepts such offer of employment in such circumstances the Client agrees to pay to the Supplier the equivalent of *three* months' professional fees at the highest rate previously charged for that member of staff."

Systems houses do not necessarily charge any one member of staff out at a standard rate to all clients. Like many other professionals, they have to take into account factors other than the time expended and the salary of the individual concerned—in particular they will consider the degree to which highly specialist knowledge is a requisite for the task. This explains the reference to "at the highest rate" above.

The prohibition against poaching staff can also be expressed in terms mutual to the parties:

> "It is agreed that neither of the parties hereto shall approach employees of the other with offers of employment for the duration of this Agreement and for *six* months thereafter."

This is a little disingenuous, since the likelihood of the systems house wishing to employ the client's staff is usually minimal.

Clauses which purport to prevent poaching of staff are prima facie void and unenforceable as being in unreasonable restraint of trade (*Kores Manufacturing Co. Ltd v. Kolok Manufacturing Co. Ltd* [1957] 3 All E.R. 158 and *Hanover Insurance Brokers Ltd v. Shapiro* [1994] I.R.L.R. 82; *The Times*, November 17, 1993). However, they may be valid if two conditions are fulfilled. First, the restraint must be reasonable in extent and afford no more than adequate protection to the person seeking to rely on it. Second, it must not be against the public interest. A restraint of this nature will be against the public interest if it restricts an employee's freedom of choice of employment without constituting a fetter which the employer reasonably requires for his protection. The onus is on the person seeking to rely on the restriction to show that it is reasonable.

Such a restraint will stand more chance of being held valid if it is limited in duration and applies only to those staff which the systems house reasonably needs to protect against poaching. It would be unnecessary, for example, to apply such a restriction to unskilled manual workers. The restriction could be limited, say, to persons working on the project and either earning in excess of a stated salary level or above a certain seniority, or even to named individuals.

A systems house would be well advised to consider two restrictions, one prohibiting the client from soliciting his employees and one prohibiting their employment by the client. If the two restrictions are made severable then, in the event of one being found to be invalid, the courts will be able to apply what has become known as the "blue pencil" test and sever the offending restriction but enforce the other. The courts may be more sympathetic to a non-solicitation clause which prevents an employee from being head-hunted than to a non-employment covenant which could prevent an employee taking up employment as a result of a voluntary response to an advertisement. Indeed, larger systems houses are likely to insist upon a "non-solicit" rather than "do not employ" clause, owing to the difficulties of policing such provisions in multi-national companies who may at any time be running a series of general advertising campaigns.

In short, the systems house should only seek to impose restrictions which are necessary to protect it. The temptation to impose wider restraints should be resisted: the validity of the clause will be put at risk as a result. A suitable clause might be in the form of that contained in D25.

Restraint clauses like these, though common, are by no means universal.

There is a further point that to a large systems house hoping for repeat orders from a corporate client, the loss of a single member of staff in return for the placing of a member of staff trained in their methods into the heart of the client's business could be highly advantageous, since he will tend to think in terms of the skills and personalities of his old firm when new software is required.

3.7 SYSTEMS HOUSE'S DUTIES

In bespoke programming, many of the systems house's duties will correspond in essence or in form with the client's duties at [3.6] above, although they will naturally extend to cover the actual design, creation and delivery of the required software.

3.7.1 Staff

Nomination [D17, D20]

It is usual to allow the client to know who the individuals are who will be working for him. A good systems house is proud of its staff and anxious to show the client how relevant the individual members of staff's experience is to the work they will be doing for the client, and will invariably use the skill sets of key members of staff (usually by means of their CVs) as part of the sales process. It is also essential that the staff are personally acceptable to the client, since the success of the project depends on the client's confidence in those who are working for him. The client should therefore satisfy himself on this point and should expect to meet at least the more senior staff assigned to his project before starting the work. If the systems house's staff fail to inspire confidence at any stage of the project, the client should retain the right to reject them (albeit that the systems house may insist that this right only be exercised when there are "reasonable grounds" for the rejection, to prevent the project being run off the rails by arbitrary decisions). On the other hand, even in the absence of an express contractual right to require the removal of supplier's staff, it is likely that a supplier will seek to accommodate a client's request to remove staff who, for whatever reason, are not getting on with the client and/or its staff). At the same time, he should realise that the systems house's staff are not numerically inexhaustible and, like a counsel objecting to jurors, he should limit his fastidiousness—unless, of course, he loses confidence in the systems house as a whole, in which case (presuming the contract has still to be awarded) he should at once seek another.

This element of confidence cannot be overstressed. In certain cases, the client may be justified in insisting that only one or more named individuals should be considered competent to do the job; this can particularly happen with software evaluation and consultancy (rather than programming), where the named individuals have specialist knowledge.

In such circumstances the client should feel at liberty to insist on a clause requiring work to be carried out by specified individuals if he believes it necessary. Some such wording as this might be suitable:

"The Supplier agrees that the work more particularly described in Clause/ Schedule *X* hereof shall be performed by *Mr Fred Nurk* or such other person as may be approved by the Client in writing."

Dress and conformity [D24]

Some computer personnel have acquired a reputation for unconventionality in dress and appearance. It is possible that this is derived largely from visits to computer installations where the operators have been much in evidence. The antisocial hours many operators are obliged to work naturally require an individual who eschews the "9 to 5" image in dress as well as hours. Programmers are sometimes as unconventional, and the inspirational type (writing his programs, like Coleridge composing *Kubla Khan*, in some drug-induced trance in the early hours of the morning) is not quite extinct, though most software houses will avoid him like the plague. The majority of programmers from reputable software houses and suppliers such as the major IT consultancies are smartly or unimaginatively conventional in their dress. Nevertheless, fears still persist of computer staff showing large quantities of hair where skin should be, and large quantities of skin where clothing should be, and some clients require reassurance. It is, therefore, by no means unusual to find clauses like this:

"Whilst the Supplier's personnel are attending the Client's premises such personnel will conform to the Client's normal codes of staff practice."

It will be observed that such clauses also include implicitly time-keeping and less easily definable norms of behaviour on the client's premises, as well as dress and appearance. There is an implied duty on the client to advise the systems house of what those norms are.

There is, however, a more technical aspect of conformity. Many computer installations have rigid standards of procedure and documentation within their programming departments, designed to produce a uniformity of approach and design for all their software and hence a corresponding ease in updating and maintaining it. The documentation system referred to in 3.3.1 is relevant here. The introduction of contract programmers who do not know these standards and yet are experienced staff working on their own can give rise to problems. In extreme cases, some installations where there have been unpleasant experiences of this refuse to use contract programmers to supplement their own staff, and instead insist that each programming job must be done either entirely by in-house staff or entirely by an outside software house. Without going to this rigid position, it can be said that it is perfectly possible for a client to use a clause of this nature and notify the systems house well in advance:

(1) That he has such standards;

(2) That he will specify them to the contract programmers;

(3) That he will interpret this clause as requiring their conformity with his standards.

The client may also wish the systems house to confirm expressly that it will comply with any regulations or procedures which it has in place in relation to health and safety [2.7.2] and other regulations such as electromagnetic compatibility [2.7.3], and also any specific security procedures which it has in place in connection with the provision of access to its premises since it can be argued that the systems house in processing test data for the client is a data processor—*i.e.*—bureau—within the meaning of the Data Protection Act 1998 (for further detail on this see below [8.7.2, 10.3.3]). This leads us on to issues of confidentiality [3.7.2].

3.7.2 Confidentiality [C20, Z]

The duty of the client to furnish information about his business [3.6.1] must imply a like duty on the part of the systems house to respect the confidentiality of such information, which will often be properly describable as a trade secret. However, it is usual to include some statement of this duty explicitly in the contract, or in the example wording in the paragraph below:

> "The Supplier undertakes not to divulge or communicate to any person firm or company any confidential information acquired from the Client in respect of the Project and/or in respect of the Client's business without first obtaining the written consent of the Client.
>
> The Supplier shall ensure that all its employees and subcontractors are bound by the provisions of this clause."

In practice this may best be done by requiring all the supplier's relevant individual staff to sign a non-disclosure agreement, although this may be a little heavy handed if the systems house accepts responsibility for any breaches of confidentiality by such individuals and has the means to provide redress to the client, if necessary. However, in particularly sensitive situations, such individual agreements can be a useful means of bringing home the nature of the imposed obligations to the staff concerned.

There are certain widely accepted exceptions to the general obligations of confidentiality, as follows:

> "The obligations in this Clause X shall not apply to any information which:
>
> (a) comes into the public domain other than by reason of a breach of this Agreement;
> (b) is independently developed by the Supplier without any access or reference to the Client's confidential information; or
> (c) is received from an unaffiliated third party who is not connected with the Project and who is itself not in breach of any obligation of confidentiality in making such disclosure."

Another widely used group of exceptions relates to disclosures which are required by law, by the courts, or by regulatory or administrative bodies. In such circumstances, it may be prudent to require the party who is to make any such disclosure give notice to the other party (where possible), and thereafter to co-operate with the party whose confidential information is in issue in seeking to oppose or at least minimise any such required disclosure.

Since the coming into force of the Data Protection Act 1984 and its more recent replacement, the Data Protection Act 1998 (the Act), the parties will also need to consider the extent to which the supplier will require real data about real human beings. Some programs, of course, will not need the names of living identifiable individuals as data, and in such cases the Data Protection regime is not applicable. But in many cases, human beings will be identifiable, including projects involving software dealing with personal customers, employees, members of associations, and so forth. The special provisions of the Act in relation to what it calls "sensitive personal data" (which is defined in s2 to include racial, ethnic, political, religious, trades union, physical or mental health, sexual or data connected with an offence (actual or alleged) and the proceedings in connection with it) may also be applicable (see Sched 3 of the Act).

In all these cases involving data protection, the systems house may be acting as a bureau or data processor [10.3.3] and the clauses normally appropriate to a bureau and its customer—particularly by those concerned with security—may have to apply to the systems house and its client [L9].

Sometimes the work of the systems house may entail access not only to the client's confidential information but also to that of the client's own clients. A clause which recognises this can be helpful:

"The Supplier recognises that in the course of carrying out the Services it will have access to confidential information belonging to third parties including clients of the Client and that the Client is under a professional obligation of confidence towards its clients and such other third parties. The Supplier undertakes to the Client that it will treat all such information, including for emphasis only and not by way of limitation, the names and addresses of the clients of the Client, as confidential and secret and will not use or divulge any such information other than for the purposes of providing the Services. The Supplier further undertakes to draw the attention of all its directors, officers, employees, subcontractors and agents involved in carrying out any of the Services to the provisions of this clause and to ensure that each of them is also bound by obligations of confidence which are equivalent to it."

Finally, it should be noted that these confidentiality clauses are likely to continue to be effective after the contract's main provisions have been fully discharged. It is therefore necessary that both the systems house and its staff, agents and subcontractors fully understand that their obligation will continue not just after the end of the project but even after they have left the employ of the systems house or its subcontractor.

3.7.3 Staff training [C18, C19, D12, D13, O23, O24]

This area is often surprisingly neglected. Yet for a client whose staff are (as is often the case) new to the system and technically unsophisticated, adequate information on how to work the system is essential, and—even for a client who already possesses experienced computer staff—the exact workings of the new system (whatever it may be) must be learned in detail. We believe it to be one of the hallmarks of a good systems house that they pay special attention to the way that a particular client's staff will use the system, and bear in mind the staff's level of experience and the other pressures that work may put on them.

In practice, instruction is usually provided in two separate but related ways: (a) supply of operating manuals; and (b) staff instruction. Manuals may be either on paper, or on-line and accessible through a help command or similar, or both on paper and on-line. An on-line version is more likely to be included in the Functional Specification which should also deal with such questions as to how it is to be accessed and whether there is to be an on-line index to it. By contrast the paper copies are more likely to figure in the contract:

> "On acceptance of the Software, the Supplier undertakes to provide the Client with two fully-indexed paper copies of the Manual and Operating Instructions relating to the Software."

This allows the systems house to charge for additional copies should they be required. The client must ask himself how many copies of the manual he is likely to need, and also whether the operating manuals should themselves be subject to some sort of acceptance procedures (*i.e.* to establish that they are sufficiently comprehensive). On-line manuals which have been specified in the Functional Specification can of course be tested as part of the ordinary acceptance procedures. Paper manuals must usually be checked by other criteria: it would be reasonable to ensure, for example, that the workings of all functions of the new system as set out in the Functional Specification were described and fully indexed. This might be checked by having the manuals available at the time of staff training and checking for any items that came up under training and were not adequately covered by the manual. In any event it is desirable that manuals and training should be closely related.

Staff instruction varies. Some offer complicated arrangements allowing the client x course credits each worth one day's instruction for up to y members of staff. This may be difficult for the client to understand, and insufficiently sensitive to the fact that different systems (and different clients) require varying amounts of instruction. There are also more vague clauses like:

> "The Supplier undertakes to instruct the Client's employees and provide such technical advice as may be necessary in the use of the Software."

The difficulty with wording such as this is that it fails to meet either party's concerns; the client faces potential arguments as to whether further training can be said to be "necessary", whereas the supplier is faced with a potentially limitless obligation which is dependent in large part on the quality of the client's staff. Such arguments can often spill out later in bickering as to whether a help desk is dealing with frivolous matters or not [C, Schedule I].

In practice, once the software is complete the client has an interest in using it to its full potential, just as the systems house has an interest in satisfying his client and being paid. The best course is undoubtedly to draw up a detailed list of all staff likely to need any form of training and familiarisation, and incorporate a full training programme in a schedule (possibly including a specified minimum and maximum limit on the number of man- days to be provided by the supplier in carrying out such training sessions). Where possible a training course should train at the same time all staff performing similar functions. In practice this is limited, first by the fact that usually the client cannot spare all staff performing similar functions simultaneously, and secondly by the fact that any training involving a terminal cannot really be made available to more than two staff per terminal at any one time if they are to have adequate opportunity for hands-on experience.

It is desirable (a) that all staff be trained before the system is delivered, and (b) that use of their training be as soon after their training is completed as possible, *i.e.*

all training should be immediately before the software is delivered. If the drawing up of a full training schedule is neglected or delayed, it may be that there is no way of completing all the training without changing the date of delivery.

3.7.4 Maintenance

This is not the same as error correction [3.3.3] but means maintenance as defined in Chapter 9. As noted above [3.0.2], different kinds of support are often offered, depending on the clients needs and what it is willing to pay. For further details on the terms on which such support is then offered, see Chapter 9.

Package software is often offered with the option of support services from the software supplier. Some suppliers have different categories of software with different levels of support. The variations in support might cover such topics as:

(1) A guaranteed minimum time for which the package will be maintained (this might be Category I).

(2) A guarantee that the software will be compatible with any future releases of other software from the supplier, *e.g.* operating systems (this might be Categories I and II).

(3) A particular level of maintenance—or lack of it—depending on the amount of the support fee paid and the lifecycle of the package software itself; if the software supplier is producing new versions of the software which the user does not wish to take up, the software supplier will not want to have to maintain a support capability in respect of the older, obsolete version (Category III might have no maintenance). See 9.1 for a more detailed review of support provisions.

3.8 Title [C9, C11, P16]

This section touches on a crucial point all too often given limited treatment in software contracts. Who owns the software? What is the nature of the right to use it which appears to be conferred? The vexed question of whether software is copyright, patentable, or simply nothing more than a trade secret was solved so far as the United Kingdom was concerned by the Copyright (Computer Software) Amendment Act 1985. That Act, which came into force on September 1, 1986, declared that the owners of software are in the same position as regards copying as are the owners of literary works. The position has been reinforced by the Copyright, Designs and Patents Act 1988 and now, throughout the European Union, by the Council Directive of May 14, 1991 on the legal protection of computer programs (91/250) ("the Software Directive"). United Kingdom law to a large extent already complied with the Software Directive but its provisions were implemented in the United Kingdom by the Copyright (Computer Programs) Regulations 1992 (S.I. 1992 No. 3233) ("the United Kingdom Regulations").

However, as the law has provided better protection, suppliers have found the problems of enforcing the law are considerable. There are two suppliers' associations who provide advice and practical help on this: Federation Against Software Theft (FAST) and the Business Software Alliance (BSA). Their addresses and further details are to be found at 15.2.2 and 15.2.3.

In the case of a licence for an existing package, the licensor has potentially the most to lose by neglecting to protect his rights, for his customer may wittingly or unwittingly connive at proliferating the package (or the use of it) to other potential customers. In the case of bespoke software, the situation may be reversed, for the client is paying full price for new software which he hopes will give him a commercial edge over his competitors, and any attempt to make his package available to them at a reduced price (once it has been paid for) will harm him doubly. However, if the software is not of a kind to give him any commercial edge over his rivals for an appreciable period of time, there may be benefit in allowing the systems house to keep title since they may then increase the number of users of the package and thereby increase the viability of maintenance and software support facilities to be provided by the systems house [3.8.2]. In these circumstances, the client may be getting the bespoke software developed at a reduced price on the understanding that the supplier is either to own the rights in the new software or at least have a right to licence it (in certain defined circumstances) to third parties. Each project will accordingly need to be viewed on the basis of its own facts.

As with hardware (2.8.1), suppliers may wish to restrict any indemnities they grant in respect of intellectual property claims to such claims relating to UK intellectual property rights (*i.e.* to protect themselves against uncertainty regarding intellectual property regimes in other unfamiliar jurisdictions).

3.8.1 Licences [C9, C11, C12, C13, C14, C21, L7]

The unsatisfactory nature of legal protection as regards software before the passing of the Copyright (Computer Software) Amendment Act 1985 (now replaced by s3(1) of the Copyright, Designs and Patents Act 1988) led many suppliers to include a general clause such as:

> "Patent, copyright, and other intellectual property rights in the Package and its programs and any associated documentation shall be vested in the Licensor who reserves the right to give licences to use the Package to any other party or parties."

This would at the least have provided copyright in the manuals and so forth and it may still be appropriate for international contracts in dealing with countries which do not have adequate protection. The same contract continues:

> "The Licensee hereby agrees:
> (1) that the Package is the sole property of the Licensor and that the Licensee will take all reasonable precautions to maintain the confidentiality of the Package its programs and documentation;
> (2) that it will not assign transfer mortgage charge pledge or sublet any of its rights or obligations under this Agreement;
> (3) to make no copies of or duplicate the Package or any part or parts thereof by any means or for any purpose whatever (except as may be necessary for normal security storage) without the prior consent in writing of the Licensor;
> (4) that it will not modify, adapt, translate or decompile the Package or any part or parts thereof or attempt to analyse the Package in order to understand the ideas underlying any part or parts thereof;
> (5) to use the Package solely at the installation described in the Schedule hereto;
> (6) to instruct all its staff from time to time having access to the Package not to copy or duplicate the Package or any part or parts thereof or to make any disclosure relating thereto to any third party;

(7) to effect and maintain adequate security measures to safeguard the Package from theft or access by any person other than employees of the Licensee in the normal course of their employment;

(8) in the event that any of the programs comprising the Package or any part or parts of the associated documentation should come into the hands of a third party through the Licensee or any employee or former employee of the Licensee, the Licensee shall forthwith pay to the Licensor the price for the entire Package as would be charged to such third party for a Licence to use the Package as at the date of the Licensor's discovery of the possession of the Package by the relevant third party."

Notice that the mention of "former employee" in subclause (8) above stops up a loophole which is not otherwise dealt with, and effectively lays upon the licensee the duty to add a clause as to the security of this package to his contracts of employment with his employees. Yet it appears that the licensor is fully justified in this stricture, for cases have been known where a disreputable rival service bureau has recruited staff from a licensee expressly to learn about a licensor's package.

Sometimes the licensor is happy for the licensee to pass the package to third parties, provided he does so as the licensor's agent:

"The Licensee may act as agent for the Licensor in the grant of other Licences for the Package, provided that:

(1) The Licensee shall have no power express or implied to bind the Licensor in any way whatever;

(2) If such licence to a third party is granted through the efforts of the Licensee the Licensor shall be entitled to the full price for the time being of the Package from such third party and in the event of any default in such payment the Licensee hereby agrees to indemnify the Licensor for the full price for the time being of the Package;

(3) If such other licence is granted to a third party for a fee wholly through the efforts of the Licensee then upon the Licensor receiving the full price for the time being of the Package (whether from the third party or from the Licensee) the Licensee shall be paid by the Licensor a commission of x per cent of the price for the time being of the Package;

(4) The Package shall be supplied only by the Licensor and upon the terms and conditions contained herein and the Licensee has no authority express or implied to vary add alter or amend such terms and conditions in any way whatsoever."

However, care needs to be taken not inadvertently to fall foul of the Commercial Agents (Council Directive) Regulations 1993, (1993 No 3053) which might give rise to a right for the Licensee to claim compensation or an indemnity in the event that its agency is terminated (reg. 17). The Regulations are complicated, but one of the key elements of agency for the purposes of the application of the Regulations is the ability to negotiate prices and contract terms on behalf of the principal (*i.e.* the person on behalf of whom the agent acts), which should accordingly be avoided if one does not wish the Regulations to apply.

The licence will often be limited to running software on specified hardware (usually defined as "the Equipment"). Yet if the designated hardware becomes unusable for whatever reason, the client will probably seek to use a back-up machine [8.1.2], so although the client is usually prohibited from running the software on any but the designated hardware, the restriction may be relaxed:

> "If the Package cannot be used with the Equipment because the Equipment is not yet commissioned or because of any equipment failure as defined in Clause X hereof, this Licence will be deemed to be temporarily extended without additional charge to use with any other suitable equipment until installation of the Equipment or remedying of the failure."

Suppliers should be careful about insisting that the use of their software should be tied to the use of their own proprietary equipment; such provisions could well offend relevant competition law.

Other common forms of restriction on the scope of the licence being granted include usage at specific locations (although this is becoming less relevant as remote access becomes easier and more widely available to users), in specific territories or, most importantly, by reference to numbers or types of users—for example limiting the use of the software:

(a) to specific, named individuals;

(b) to a set number of users (calculated by reference to the licensee's staff who are likely to need to have access to the software);

(c) to a set number of concurrent users (based on a calculation of how many people might need to have access to the software simultaneously).

(b) and (c) above are frequently seen in licences for package software, and are usually tied in with the calculation of the licence fee, such that greater amounts of licence fees will become due if the licensee needs to increase its usage of the licensed software.

Less acceptable limitations on the licensee's usage may also be found, such that infringement means either moving up to a completely new scale of fees or the termination forthwith of the agreement, with the almost unavoidable implication that the licensee must enter into a new agreement with the software licensor at a higher rate. This practice, known in the IT business as *stiffing*, can include limitations on assignment of the contract (highly relevant if the licensee is thinking of moving his IT function to an outsource contractor [11.6.3]) and even limiting the use of the software to a machine of a particular speed which is usually expressed in Mips (*i.e.* millions of instructions per second). Thus if as is likely to happen the licensee moves his application to a new machine which naturally is of higher speed he finds his licence fees rise steeply.

Back up copies

The right for a licensee to make a back up copy has been given legal force by the Software Directive. In implementing the requirements of the directive, reg. 8 of the Copyright (Computer Programs) Regulations 1992 (S.I. 1992 No. 3233) inserts a new s 50A(1) in the Copyright, Designs and Patents Act 1988 ("the CDPA"):

> "50A(1) It is not an infringement of copyright for a lawful user of a copy of a computer program to make any back up copy of it which is necessary for him to have for the purposes of his lawful use."

This right is absolute. It may not be excluded by contract and any term which purports to do so is void. The language of the provision is somewhat curious, though. As mentioned above, it may be "desirable" or "sensible" to take a back up copy but can it always be said to be strictly "necessary" for the purposes of the lawful use of software? In many cases, quite possibly not. Quite how far this advances the rights of licensees remains unclear. One supplier who obviously cannot be bothered with such legal niceties simply gives his licensees the right:

> "Either (a) to make one copy of the Software solely for back up or archival purposes or (b) to transfer the Software to a single hard disk of a personal computer provided the Licensee keeps the original solely for back up or archival purposes."

Indeed, it is common for software owners expressly to permit licensees to make such back up copies, and thus to avoid potential legal debates on the meaning of section 50A(1).

It follows also on termination that all such copies must be accounted for, either by surrender to the licensor or by destruction:

> "Upon the termination of this Agreement the Licensee will return to the Licensor all such software and documentation including that modified by the Licensee and all copies thereof in whole or in part or, if requested by the Licensor, the Licensee will destroy all such software, documentation and copies and certify in writing that they have been destroyed."

Decompilation

The restriction on decompilation is more problematic. Generally speaking, the decompilation of software from its object code form to a higher level language such as COBOL or BASIC is a restricted act for copyright purposes and may not be carried out by a licensee without the software owner's permission. Nor is the decompilation of a program "fair dealing" for the purposes of the CDPA (see CDPA, s. 29(4) as introduced by regulation 7 of the U.K. regulations). However, the European Commission thought that a right to decompile for the limited purpose of achieving interoperability with other programs was something which a lawful user of software ought to be able to undertake.

This decompilation right was conferred by the Software Directive and is enshrined in U.K. law by section 50B of the CDPA (as introduced by reg. 8 of the U.K. Regulations). Section 50B provides that it is not an infringement of copyright for a lawful user of a copy of a computer program expressed in a low level language to convert it into a version expressed in a higher level language or, incidentally in the course of so converting the program, to copy it (*i.e.* to decompile it), provided two conditions are met. These conditions are first that it is necessary to decompile the program to obtain the information necessary to create an independent program which can be operated with the program decompiled or with another program (this is described as "the permitted objective"), and secondly that the information so obtained is not used for any purpose other than the permitted objective. However, these two necessary conditions are expressed not to be met in four situations:

(1) Where the lawful user has readily available to him the information necessary to achieve the permitted objective;

(2) Where he does not confine the decompiling to such acts as are necessary to achieve the permitted objective;

(3) Where he supplies the information obtained by the decompiling to any person to whom it is not necessary to supply it in order to achieve the permitted objective;

(4) Where he uses the information to create a program which is substantially similar in its expression to the program decompiled or to do any act restricted by copyright.

Again, this limited decompilation right is absolute. It may not be excluded by contract and any term purporting to do so is void.

The response from software owners has been varied. One, in its standard licence, simply refers to the statutory provision:

"Save to the extent and in the circumstances permitted by Section 50B of the Copyright, Designs and Patents Act 1988, the Customer must not decompile the Software (nor permit any third party to do so)."

Another, who obviously has found customers for his software in other countries of the European Union, stipulates that:

"You may not alter, merge, modify or adapt the Software in any way including disassembling or decompiling. This does not affect your rights under any legislation implementing the E.C. Council Directive on the Legal Protection of Computer Programs. If you seek interface information within the meaning of Article 6.1(b) of that Directive you should initially approach [Supplier's contact and address]."

To make available the necessary interface information might be one means of preventing licensees from decompiling programs. The argument will run that because a licensee has readily available to him the information necessary to achieve the permitted objective, the legislation does not permit him to decompile the software.

With this aim in mind one supplier provides:

"To the extent that local law grants you the right to decompile the Software in order to obtain information necessary to render the Software interoperable with other software, the Supplier hereby undertakes to make that information readily available to you. The Supplier has the right to impose reasonable conditions such as a reasonable fee for doing so. In order to ensure that you receive the appropriate information, you must first give the Supplier sufficient details of your objectives and the other software concerned. Requests for the appropriate information should be directed to [name and address]."

There seems to be no reason why this approach should not work; it is after all expressly envisaged by the legislation that the decompilation right should not apply where the licensee has the necessary interface information and, since the software owner is likely to be the only fruitful source of such information, an offer by the software owner to make it available seems to meet the desired objectives of the legislation. However, the information should be "readily" available and not subject to burdensome conditions. Whether the software owner is entitled to charge for the information is a moot point. A licensee may argue that it is not readily available if it is unreasonably expensive. If that argument is correct then the decompilation right will continue.

A question of timing also arises. A restrictive view of the legislation might be that information is not readily available unless it is available to the licensee at the same time as the program is supplied or, at least, at the same time as the licensee wishes to decompile the program for the permitted objective. A licensee who has to make a request to the software owner, provide information and then wait for a response may not be said to have the information readily available to him. In this context, a curious difference in wording appears between the language of the Software Directive and that of the U.K. Regulations. Article 6.1(b) stipulates that one of the conditions which must be met in order for the decompilation right to apply is "the information necessary to achieve interoperability has not previously been readily available to [the licensee]". The word "previously" was not imported into section 50B of the CDPA. Whether this means that the legislation will be construed restrictively as mentioned above remains unclear. It is to be hoped that common sense will prevail. By no means every licensee will wish to decompile the software licensed to it to achieve interoperability with other software. The mass circulation of interface information with software would seem an unwarranted expense. A genuine offer by a software owner to make interface information available in response to a licensee's request should, it is submitted, be sufficient to be construed as making that information "readily available" provided it is not subject to burdensome conditions. Certainly, no reasonable licensee ought to complain at such treatment. Whether this view will be adopted by the courts remains to be seen.

Analysing the ideas underlying software

The prohibition on the licensee's analysing the package in order to understand the ideas underlying the program also causes a problem. Generally speaking, copyright law protects the expression of an idea and not the idea itself and it should not therefore be offensive for a licensee to discover the ideas underlying the working of the program in his possession. As a consequence of the adoption of the Software Directive, a new section 296A was inserted in the CDPA by reg. 11 of the U.K. Regulations, which provides that any term or condition in an agreement shall be void in so far as it purports to prohibit or restrict the use of any device or means to observe, study or test the functioning of a program in order to understand the ideas and principles which underlie any element of that program. A term of a contract, such as the example given above, which attempts to prevent a licensee analysing software to discover its underlying ideas will consequently now be void and unenforceable. Licensees should be cautious, however, as this does not mean that the expression of those underlying ideas can be copied. This is recognised by the Software Directive and the U.K. Regulations, and new section 3(i)(c) of the CDPA (as inserted by regulation 3 of the U.K. Regulations) makes it clear that the "preparatory design material for a computer program" is itself protected by copyright as a literary work.

Copying and adapting software and correcting errors

Much debate has arisen as to whether the lawful user of a computer program has a legal right without the permission of the copyright owner to copy or adapt it in order to run the program, or in order to correct errors in it (in respect of which see the discussion regarding the *Saphena* and *Mars* cases in 3.3.3, above). Certainly, he now has the right to copy for back up purposes if that is necessary for his lawful use, as mentioned above. Certain copying of a program is necessary if it is to be used in the manner intended and this is usually expressly permitted by a software licence.

The position at law is governed by new s. 50C of the CDPA (as inserted by regulation 8 of the U.K. Regulations). This provides that it is not an infringement of copyright for a lawful user of a copy of a computer program to copy or adapt it, provided that the copying or adapting is necessary for his lawful use and is not prohibited under any terms of an agreement regulating the circumstances in which his use is lawful. The section goes on to say that it may, in particular, be necessary for the lawful use of a computer program to copy it or adapt it for the purpose of correcting errors in it.

The lawful user of a computer program who is not bound by an agreement governing its use, but instead is regulated only by copyright law, will consequently have the right to copy and adapt it where this is necessary for his lawful use, including for the purpose of correcting errors in it. This would certainly apply to the lawful acquirer of mass produced software where no separate agreement governing its use is applicable. Given the uncertainty surrounding the enforceability of shrink-wrap licences [4.3.1, 5.3.6.4], this position may also pertain even though the software owner purports to impose such a licence. Moreover, a "licence" may not always be an "agreement".

The opportunity for a software owner to restrict copying and adaptation in this fashion appears only to arise where there is a licence agreement between the owner and the licensee. It may at first sight seem perverse that a licensee with an agreement should have fewer rights, but presumably the law takes the view that it is open to a licensee with an agreement to negotiate the terms of that agreement as he sees fit and that if he wishes to accept restrictions that it is up to him. A licensee should nevertheless ensure that he is granted sufficient rights to permit him to use the software for its intended purpose and that the issue of future error correction, whether by a separate maintenance agreement or otherwise, is adequately addressed.

Unfortunately, the debate does not end there. There is an argument that the U.K. Regulations do not correctly implement the intention of the Software Directive and that the UK courts might need to have regard to the purpose of the directive in determining the rights of licensees. The source of the problem lies in art. 5(1) of the directive which reads:

> "In the absence of specific contractual provisions, the acts referred to in Article 4(a) and (b) shall not require authorisation by the right holder where they are necessary for the use of the computer program by the lawful acquirer in accordance with its intended purpose, including for error correction."

One interpretation of the phrase "in the absence of specific contractual provisions" is "in the absence of specific contractual prohibitions to the contrary" such that if an agreement specifically prohibits the licensee from copying or adapting the software that will be effective to exclude such rights. This seems to be the interpretation adopted by the draftsman of the U.K. Regulations. The other interpretation which could be put on the phrase is "in the absence of specific contractual provisions granting the necessary rights" such that, to the extent that a licence agreement does not expressly grant the necessary rights to copy and adapt for the use of the computer program by the lawful acquirer in accordance with its intended purpose including for error correction, then the directive fills in and grants such rights to the user. If the latter interpretation is correct, the question then arises as to whether a contractual provision which nevertheless prohibits copying or adaptation is effective. Regrettably, the directive is none too clear on the issue.

Article 9(1) renders void any contractual provision which attempts to exclude the rights conferred by the directive to make back up copies, to observe the underlying ideas of a program and to decompile for interoperability purposes but is silent about article 5(1), perhaps suggesting that a contractual prohibition would be valid. However, Recital 18 to the directive presents another view:

> "Whereas this means that the acts of loading and running necessary for the use of a copy of a program which has been lawfully acquired, and the act of correction of its errors may not be prohibited by contract."

Confused? So are we and, in the light of the *Mars* case [3.3.3], so are the courts and the legal profession. It seems a pity that this apparent inconsistency has been allowed to arise and, if Recital 18 reflects the intention of the directive, that the language of that recital was not expressly imported into the main body of the directive.

One software owner who obviously suffers from a headache over the whole thing, and wishes to save time and money on updating his licence terms in response to developing judicial interpretation, opts for simplicity:

> "Except as expressly permitted by this Agreement and save to the extent and in the circumstances expressly required to be permitted by law, the Licensee shall not rent, lease, sub-license, loan, copy, modify, adapt, merge, translate, reverse engineer, decompile, disassemble or create derivative works based on the whole or any part of the Software or use, reproduce or deal in the Software or any part thereof in any way."

Severability [A36]

Software owners concerned that some of their contractual terms could possibly be held to be void will not wish the illegality of one provision to infect the remainder of the contract:

> "Notwithstanding that the whole or any part of any provision of this Agreement may prove to be illegal or unenforceable the other provisions of this Agreement and the remainder of the provision in question shall remain in full force and effect."

Ownership of rights

The licensee should satisfy himself that the licensor is, in fact, the originator and owner of all parts of the package being sold, and it is not unreasonable for him to demand an indemnity in case of any future dispute, especially as increasingly software packages frequently include elements produced or provided by third parties:

> "The Licensor shall indemnify the Licensee against all claims demands costs charges and expenses arising from or incurred by any infringement of copyright, patent or other intellectual property right in respect of the Package or any part thereof provided that such infringement is not caused or contributed to by any unauthorised use of or modification to the Software by the Licensee, and provided further that the Licensee grants the Licensor sole

control of the defence of any such infringement claim and provides the Licensor with all reasonable assistance (at the expense of the Licensor) in the defence of the claim."

Regulation 6 of the Copyright (Computer Programs) Regulations 1992 (S.I. 1992 No 3233) amends section 27 of the Copyright, Designs and Patents Act 1988 and states that a copy of a computer program which has previously been sold in any other member state by or with the consent of the copyright owner, is not an infringing (*i.e.* illegal) copy. This has been argued to mean that if the copyright owner has sold a licence to use software, he (the copyright owner) cannot then charge again for that licence if it is subsequently sold on. It must be stressed that this has never been tested in the courts. In any event the Act speaks of the first sale being "in any other member state" which seems to imply that if this provision has the kind of interpretation being put upon it, that interpretation can only be accepted if the first sale and the second "sale" are in different member States of the EU. Until the courts clarify this issue we cannot recommend any reliance on this interpretation.

3.8.2 Bespoke software [D14, M7]

Under the Copyright, Designs and Patents Act 1988 (CDPA ss. 9(1) and 11(1)), title to bespoke software—unless the parties expressly stipulate otherwise—will belong to the person or organisation which wrote the software—that is to say the systems house—notwithstanding the fact that the client may have funded its creation (however, it may be possible to argue that the course of conduct by the systems house gave rise to an equitable assignment of copyright to the client; see *Lakeview Computers plc v. Steadman* (November 26, 1999) as summarised by Kit Burden in *Computer Law and Security Report*, vol. 16 no. 3, p. 190). For the systems house, parting with all rights in the software may limit its ability to profit from the programming skills (as opposed to the applications knowledge) which the systems house's staff may have acquired during the course of the work. One solution is simply to have no clause on title at all; in which case the systems house, as the author of the software, will retain the title, giving the client only a licence (subject to potential arguments regarding equitable assignments; on which see above). The downside to this is that the scope of the licence granted will be uncertain, and in particular will not have addressed any of the points made above concerning the rights to make back up copies, modifications or error corrections [3.8.1, 3.3.3]. It will accordingly invariably be preferable to set out explicitly the ownership and licence rights in the software (especially as the systems house may itself be utilising subcontractors and it would be preferable to ensure that all copyright issues are clarified in advance). In this regard, it should be noted that conceding ownership of the copyright in any bespoke software to the supplier is not necessarily a bad option for the client. He may indeed wish the systems house to retain title so as to encourage the systems house to continue to develop and maintain the software. In particular, there may be merit in the idea of the systems house selling the software to other users (provided they are not direct competitors of the client). In this way, the software will acquire a larger number of users, which, at the very least should ensure that its bugs are more readily found. There may even be opportunities for a user group to be created [15.6] and certainly maintenance spread over several users should work out cheaper for each particular user. The original user may even be able to negotiate a rebate on the price he paid, or the payment of a royalty, whenever the systems house effects another sale.

However, if the client insists on a clause formally passing title to him, the following example—allowing the systems house to retain and use the skills it has incidentally acquired, while passing title in the software to the client—seems appropriate:

"(1) Software is defined as programs written directly for the Client by the Supplier under this Agreement. Subject to any prior existing intellectual property rights, title to such Software passes to the Client immediately after its Acceptance in accordance with Clause X.

(2) Notwithstanding (1) above, the Supplier shall remain free to utilise any programming skills, knowledge of general application and skills used by the Supplier for the development of such Software."

Points remain to be defined in this example: "acceptance" must be defined [3.3.1]; "programming tools" are different from "skills". The former include actual coding—a sequence of instructions for handling a particular type of file, which has become standard within that systems house for work on that machine and in that language, for example. It is this sort of thing which may be relevant when considering "conformity", [3.7.1] above. "Skills" seem to be much wider and embrace not so much solutions to particular programming or design problems, as the approach to programming and design. "Software development" will presumably mean "work undertaken under the provisions of this Agreement", since it must include analysis and design, as well as programming.

The point about prior existing intellectual property rights is an important one, as bespoke software will frequently include elements which had previously been developed by the systems house for contracts with clients (although the systems house will have retained copyright in these (*e.g.* useful "short cut" subroutines etc) or which are being supplied by third parties. In these cases the systems house will be either unwilling or unable to assign copyright in these particular items. The licence provisions relating to such aspects of the bespoke software will need to be set out separately (probably in a schedule) and will presumably be linked to the extent that such elements need to be used in order to allow the client to make full use of the rest of the bespoke software for which the systems house can grant the client a clear title.

CHAPTER 4

PCs

4.1 Introduction
4.2 Hardware
4.3 Software

4.1 INTRODUCTION

Personal computers (PCs) are small computers for individuals to have on their desks. In this book we consider lap-tops as PCs and also all the personal computers whether or not they run such well-known operating systems as Windows, Linux or MacOS. This is because, contractually, Apple computers, for example, are not greatly different from other PCs and do not merit separate consideration.

Many of the first micros (predecessors of the PCs) were word processors, *i.e.* systems designed for only one application. Such systems still exist, though increasingly word processing is sold simply as a software licence, where the software runs on an existing PC which may or may not be used for other purposes.

In theory, there is no compelling reason why contracts for PCs (or word processors) should differ from any other hardware and software contracts. In individual cases some of the provisions of contracts for larger machines may be irrelevant: environmental conditions are less onerous, and heavy lifting tackle and hoists may not be needed. In general, however, the contracts in Chapters 2 and 3 are perfectly applicable. Some suppliers recognise this by using the same contracts for both large machines and small and to that extent it is a question whether the subject merits separate treatment in a chapter of its own. The bulk purchase of several PCs by a company is still likely to be under a formal agreement of the kind recommended in Chapter 2. Originally, it was because there were other companies whose contracts were inadequate or slipshod—even non-existent—that this chapter was needed. There then came into being a mass market of home computer enthusiasts. They were not primarily business users and they tended to purchase their equipment and software from High Street retailers rather than business equipment suppliers. They were not likely to let corporate lawyers loose on the fine print of contracts but instead trust to ordinary consumer protection law for redress in case of any contractual difficulty.

Suppliers responded to this new market and a great deal of hardware and software—particularly software—changed hands in a comparatively casual way in this market, and such methods have spilled over into business applications. This is especially the case with small software items designed for a mass market where the cost is low and not worth the scrutiny which lawyers and company secretaries and computer managers must give to mainframe installations costing hundreds of thousands of pounds.

The first and most important question is therefore as to whether there is a written contract at all. The intending purchaser of a word processing system is seeking to buy hardware [Chapter 2], software [Chapter 3] and maintenance [Chapters 8 and 9] and must satisfy himself that all these aspects are covered. The purchaser of a PC may be buying his software separately, though the chances are that there is some software with his hardware so that he too is buying a turnkey system [1.12]. He may also buy additional software alone and will need to consider Chapter 3. There is every reason to use the relevant chapters as a guide to the purchase of these smaller systems. However it has to be recognised that for purchases of single machines—especially from High Street retailers—lengthy negotiations are not appropriate. Orders for multiple machines, especially linked in networks, will give the parties much more reason and opportunity to examine contractual terms in the way set out in Chapters 2 and 3. Readers should bear these points in mind when using this chapter.

4.2 HARDWARE

4.2.1 Hardware purchase

Detailed examination of PC and word processor hardware contractual conditions has not uncovered any major surprises. Because of the low cost of the equipment, the margin for rental or leasing agreements is very small and such agreements are much less usual than with larger machines. One clause puts the onus on the customer to make his own leasing arrangements since the supplier cannot help.

"The Customer may enter into a leasing agreement with a third party acceptable to the Supplier provided that:

(a) the terms of such agreement do not adversely affect the obligation of the Customer owed to the Supplier hereunder;

(b) the Customer has notified the Supplier in advance of such intention; and

(c) the Supplier has notified the Customer in writing of the acceptability of the third party, such acceptance not to be unreasonably refused."

The hardware clauses in PC and word processor contracts tend to be vague about the customer's right to refuse to accept equipment which is not satisfactory. The last example given in the section on installation tests [2.3.4] is typical, although it is not in fact taken from a PC or word processing contract. The customer should of course point out to the supplier that he will accept the equipment only when he is satisfied.

Installation is usually left to the customer though he may obtain telephone help from the manufacturer (not the supplier) usually over a premium line in the same way as is increasingly used for software maintenance contracts [9]. If he really cannot manage on his own he will have to find someone else (and pay) for him to do the work.

4.2.2 Hardware maintenance

A significant change to PC hardware contracts over the past few years has been a recognition of the need to provide some sort of maintenance. This is provided by the manufacturer, not the retailer and can take a number of forms:

(a) warranty period of free maintenance—typically for a year;

(b) thereafter paid maintenance which may be purchased via the supplier at the same time as the initial purchase for a number of years in advance; or

(c) premium telephone calls for advice though no engineering work or other action in the same way as installation advice.

Where the purchaser has not opted to use one or other of these methods his options if any failure occurs are not attractive:

(a) a one-off call to the manufacturer (likely to be expensive); or

(b) no maintenance provision at all, *i.e.* the user will effect his own maintenance.

Within the manufacturer's maintenance option there is almost always a distinction between on-site and off-site maintenance. Off-site means that the equipment must be sent back to the manufacturer. This is usually cheaper but is subject to some very serious disadvantages:

(a) the user is without the machine while it is being repaired;

(b) the cost of postage or other delivery is expensive—still more so if he wants fast delivery;

(c) wrapping up the equipment to send it back is usually very difficult unless the purchaser has kept all the boxes etc in which the equipment was purchased—unlikely to be a practical option in an ordinary house or small office since the boxes are large.

The first year's free warranty is likely to be off-site though many purchasers feel that the chances of anything serious going wrong in that period are so slim that it is worth putting up with off-site maintenance for that period.

The alternative is on-site maintenance—that is to say an engineer comes to the customer's premises. The cost of this is high but it meets the objections to off-site maintenance.

4.3 SOFTWARE

Software on word processors and PCs usually means package software [3.0.2] for which the customer is granted a licence.

The most common deficiency in these contracts is a clear definition of what the software is supposed to do. Again this is a frequent fault in package software contracts generally and the remedy often involves incorporation of another document by reference ". . . more particularly defined in document entitled *Scrabble 200 Word Processor User's Manual Version 3.7*, March 14, 1999". In this way there should be no doubt as to whether or not the software includes a particular feature that the customer has asked for.

4.3.1 Shrink-wrap and Click-wrap licences

Software sold for personal computers in the rapidly increasing number of computer shops is usually sold under licence terms directly with the software owner in the form of a *shrink-wrap* licence [5.3.6.4, E]. A shrink-wrap licence is where the software container (box or package) is enclosed in a transparent shrink wrap. Prominently displayed will (or should be) a warning that opening the package will constitute acceptance of the terms of the licence. Those terms may or may not themselves be visible through the transparent shrink-wrap. If all those terms are so visible it seems likely that the purchaser who breaks the shrink wrap is indeed bound by those terms. However, where the actual terms are partially or totally obscured by the wrapping a decision in the Scottish Courts, while not binding on any court in England or Wales, sheds some light on the matter. In the case of *Beta Computers (Europe) Ltd v. Adobe Systems (Europe) Ltd* [1996] F.S.R. 367, the judge found that the purchasers could delay indefinitely their being bound by the conditions and therefore concluding the sale if they failed to open the package. This is hardly a satisfactory result from either the distributor's or the copyright owner's point of view though it still leaves the question of whether a person can be bound by conditions he cannot know. The US draft Uniform Computer Information Transactions Act (UCITA) [3.2.2, 3.3.4] is implied into all IT contracts of the States which adopt it (at the time of writing consisting of Maryland and Virginia). It specifies (s.608(a)(1)) a "right before payment or acceptance to inspect the copy at a reasonable place and time and in a reasonable manner to determine conformance to the contract" and then states (s.608(a)) that:

> "If a right to inspect exists. . . but the agreement is inconsistent with an opportunity to inspect before payment, the party does not have a right to inspect before payment."

Now that it has started to be adopted in individual States, the scope for U.S. companies to exploit this will be very difficult to avoid.

In the last few years, much software has been sold and then downloaded over the Internet. In place of the shrink-wrap licence, we now tend to see at an early stage during a set-up a "read-me" file which says words to the effect of "Please read the following licence agreement" and then contains the contractual provisions. At the end appear words such as:

> "Do you accept the above licence agreement? If you do, please press Yes. If you do not, please press No. Set up will only continue if you accept the agreement."

Thus, the only way to complete the set up is to click on "Yes". Such a contract is commonly termed a *click-wrap* agreement. In terms of legal certainty, it is certainly better than the shrink-wrap licence since the user now has an opportunity to read the conditions before becoming bound by them. However, it will be noted that the provisions of UCITA quoted above would apply equally if the act of acceptance were clicking on an acceptance without having had any opportunity to see all the conditions. In other words, it is open to a supplier whose contract is under the laws of a State which has adopted UCITA to withhold some or all of those conditions from the read-me file and still bind the user who accepts the conditions unseen.

However, although legally, in terms of its enforceability, the click-wrap licence offers advantages over the shrink wrap, there is another consideration. The practical defect of the click-wrap licence is that if the goods have to be returned, the copyright owner cannot be sure that the purchaser has not retained a copy of the software, whereas with the shrink-wrap he can be absolutely certain on this point.

4.3.2 Test software

An increasing trend is for licensors to provide a test version (sometimes called a *review copy*) of the software which enables the user to try out at least some of its functionality. The disk will have some or all of the functions available but will also have a time lock or logic bomb [3.2.2] which causes the software to cease to function—typically a month after it was first loaded on the customer's machine. A read-me file provides a limited click wrap licence [4.3.1] and tells the user how to obtain a proper (*i.e.* more permanent) licence for the software. A similar mechanism may be used with data files and some systems with a mix of software and data are made available in this way.

The observations as to the legality of logic bombs in 3.2.2 apply here, though it must be arguable that if the user is aware of the nature of his licence and that it is only for a limited period the "modification of the contents of a computer" (in the wording of section 3(1)(a) of the Computer Misuse Act 1990) which the time lock provides is authorised and hence the Act has not been infringed.

Test versions of software provided in this way are usually free of charge and so the click-wrap contract may not be valid in the first place (*i.e.* for want of consideration). However, they are also sometimes provided on the front of magazines and it may be that the charge for the magazine and test disk will be held to be sufficient to create a contract. It is therefore desirable that all such test disks be accompanied by information as to the terms on which they are made available and the presence of the time lock, with a mechanism for requiring the user's acceptance of these conditions before use.

4.3.3 Software title

A consideration for PC software is reservation of title and protection of that title [3.8.1]. Software sold on floppy disks, CDs or downloaded from the Internet can easily be copied, thereby infringing copyright [3.8]. People confidently assert that a piece of PC software is "in the public domain" and there is therefore no question of indemnity against infringement of title or payment of a licence fee. Public domain is appropriate to copyright material where 70 years have elapsed from the author's death. Although programs are now copyright, the newness of the computer business means that 70 years cannot yet have elapsed from the death of the author.

There is, therefore, at present no such thing as "software in the public domain" and rights, though dormant, unenforced and even untraceable, still exist (but see 3.8.1 for further arguments as to the effect of Regulation 6 of the Copyright (Computer Programs) Regulations 1992). However, increasingly copyright owners make their software available with a statement that it is "in the public domain" whereby they expressly waive any right to enforce their copyright. The user has no opportunity of knowing whether the person who makes the statement is indeed the copyright owner of all the software and of course there is no contract between the user and the person making the statement so there is no indemnity, actual or implied, to protect the user against any claim by a third party for copyright infringement.

It is also by no means clear whether the copyright owner having made such a statement of waiver is entitled to revoke it again at some future date and if so what would constitute notice to the user. Such "public domain" software or *freeware* is discussed further below.

An ordinary software licence for PCs allows the user to load the system on to his PC and use it there. In practice, he may well write it to the hard disk and leave it resident on the PC more or less permanently. He still has the original floppy disk from which he loaded it available to use as a back up.

In the case of software designed for virus protection, practice may vary as to how the software is to be used. For a company, it may well make sense to dedicate a single PC as a "quarantine" machine on to which all new software will be loaded and a virus protection program or series of programs run to check it, before the software is re-loaded on to its destination machine. The problems of "shrink-wrap licences" are discussed further at 4.3.2 and 5.3.6.4. In theory, such agreements assume that the software will only ever be loaded and used on one machine. The use of a "quarantine" machine means that in fact the software will be loaded first on to the "quarantine" machine and then on to its destination machine. Usually there is no specific wording in the "shrink-wrap licence" which prevents this and it follows, if that is the case, that the user can in fact move the software from one machine to another, provided it is available on no more than one machine at any time.

Where virus-protection software is sold to a company or individual with more than one machine but not able to dedicate a single machine as a "quarantine" machine, the user cannot, of course, simply copy the same software onto all his machines if he has licence only for a single machine. The simplest method of working will be for him to load the anti-virus software on to a machine immediately before other new software to be tested by it is loaded. Following the completion of the anti-virus test, he may well wish to eliminate the anti-virus software from his machine so as not to take up valuable memory. One software supplier who has fully grasped this has interesting wording to alert the user to his obligations as a licensee and at the same time recognises realistically how the software will actually be used. Consider the following:

> *"Licence*
>
> You have not become the owner of this software—you have purchased the right to use the software. You may make one copy of this software and you should keep that copy in a safe place; use the original write-protected disk as a working disk. You must not copy this manual. You must treat this software just like a book. You can use it in more than one place, but only at one place at a time. You may lend it to someone else, but if you do, you cannot use it at the same time, just like a book cannot be read by two people at different places at the same time. If you choose to install the programs on a hard disk, they may not be used on any other machine."

We regard this as both realistic and helpful. However, it has to be said that the enforcement of terms like this can only be left to the honesty and good sense of the licensee.

However, the flood of amateur producers of software—a sort of New Grub Street of schoolboys, hackers and home computer enthusiasts generally—means that copyright in software is frequently infringed and the culprit can rarely be traced. It is also true that a substantial number of the amateurs are not particularly interested in the money. Such people may wish to waive their copyright or at least dilute it by claiming that their software is *freeware* (*i.e.* copyright waived) or *honorware* or *shareware* (or some similar term) with a polite invitation to anyone into whose hands the software falls to experiment with the software free of charge, but if the user intends to keep the software on his system, he should send a fee to the originator of the software. In some cases, he will then be eligible for copies of future upgrades of the software. It may be suspected that not everyone is entirely scrupulous about honouring such an arrangement.

It must be admitted that "freeware" or "shareware", while drawing the user's attention to the existence of copyright in software, probably weakens the overall enforceability of software protection under the Copyright, Designs and Patents Act 1988. The Federation Against Software Theft (FAST) [15.2.2], an association of companies concerned about this, offers excellent practical advice to companies wishing to safeguard their software, including the clear incorporation of copyright notices, the placing of a "fingerprint" (*i.e.* some hidden notice or word readily identifiable by the owner but unlikely to have got there other than by the deliberate act of the copyright owner). The "fingerprint" may be either physically put onto the disk or other medium in some ineradicable form, or encoded, or both, the recording of serial numbers issued to authorised licensees (again put on the disk or other medium). This helps trace the source of any unauthorised copies, and the retention of manuals and documentation. Further details on these and other techniques may be obtained from FAST [15.2.2].

Most of the larger American software corporations use the American organisation Business Software Alliance to perform much the same function as FAST does in the U.K. and BSA's details are at 15.2.3.

An alternative way of limiting software licence infringement is to link the use of the software to its maintenance. Anti-virus software must constantly be upgraded if it is to continue to protect the system and the developers of such software analyse all the viruses they can find and then devise new ways of combating them. It is therefore not unreasonable to say that unless the upgrades are taken on as fast as they can be made available the software will very soon be more or less ineffective against the current types of virus. To do this the developers may provide an update service. It is not unlike the hardware warranty service we saw earlier. The purchaser of the software must register with the copyright owner and declare which machine the software will be loaded on, which must also be his Internet-linked machine. For the first year (typically) the upgrade service is free and once he has registered he can use the same machine to download upgrades from the copyright owner's website to that machine at no further cost during the first year. Thereafter, the service has to be paid for or the purchaser has to be encouraged to purchase a new version of the software.

Amateur software writers are not all as casual about software rights and there are some well-publicised stories of some who have made substantial sums from their ideas. To do this they will usually have to interest one of the larger software distributors, and this means hawking the idea round suitable companies to get the necessary backing for commercial exploitation of the idea. It is therefore not uncommon for software houses to receive unsolicited disclosures of allegedly new ideas from individual programmers.

Such disclosures can cause problems for the company receiving them. In the first place they must satisfy themselves that the programmer really does have full right to dispose of the idea. If it has been developed in his employer's time, or on his employer's equipment, then prima facie the rights in the software will belong to the employer and not the programmer [13.0.2]. The disclosure may also consist of ideas either already known to the company or readily discoverable by the company through its own efforts. If the company subsequently uses the ideas (even though both its knowledge of the ideas and its decision to use them are earlier in date than the disclosure by the programmer), the programmer will inevitably cry "Foul!" when he sees "his" ideas being exploited.

From the programmer's point of view, he must establish that the disclosure was for the sole purpose of enabling the company to assess the feasibility of entering into an arrangement with the programmer for the exploitation of his ideas. The courts, once they are satisfied that the programmer treated the information as confidential, will restrain the company's use of the material (the leading case is *Johnson v. Heat and Air Systems Ltd* [1941] 58 R.P.C. 229). The company's defence can only be if it can demonstrate that it already had possession of the information.

Faced with a letter offering unsolicited disclosures, a company should be extremely cautious about how it acts. At the risk of seeming bureaucratic, the safest course for both sides is an agreement, in the form of an exchange of letters, setting out the rights and obligations of both sides. In particular it should state that the company will treat the information as confidential only insofar as it is not already known to the company or is not independently developed by any of the company's employees who have not had access to the programmer's ideas. A sample of such a letter to a programmer is provided as Precedent AA.

CHAPTER 5

DISTRIBUTION AND MARKETING

5.0 INTRODUCTION

5.0.1 The need for distribution and marketing

So far in this book we have dealt almost entirely with contracts between the supplier of a product or service and the end-user. Behind that simple arrangement there may be many more complex ones which have led up to the supplier being in a position to supply the end-user. Crucial to the success of the supply chain are distribution and marketing arrangements, which are often of little concern to the end-user. He will acquire his product from one party and will be unaware of the agreements underlying the relationship between his supplier and the owner or manufacturer of the product. Occasionally, however, the end-user does become aware of a wider relationship. One example which springs to mind in relation to computer software is the end-user licence. Here, the end-user acquires his computer system from his supplier under a contract in the normal way but is also asked to enter into a licence agreement with the owner of the software whereby he undertakes directly with the owner to use the software in accordance with the licence terms. Of course, the end-user immediately becomes aware that the software is not owned by his supplier and this may lead him to question whether the supplier is in a position to provide appropriate software maintenance services or to arrange for a deposit of source code. This is particularly so in the case of leasing contracts.

While distribution and marketing arrangements can complicate matters contractually, they are in widespread use and reflect a growing need for manufacturers of products to appoint intermediaries to help them penetrate consumer markets. Even in these days of e-commerce (with the opportunities that it presents to advertise goods and services worldwide via a website), not every business has the resources both to manufacture the product and to market it effectively to the end-user. At one extreme, one might find an individual inventor who has no resources to manufacture or market his product but who, in return for a royalty, agrees that this should

90

be dealt with by a commercial organisation with the appropriate resources. At the other extreme a multinational company having almost limitless marketing resources may nevertheless find itself in a position where it has to appoint a distributor or agent in a particular territory in order to overcome local political or legal difficulties. Between these extremes there is scope for many different kinds of relationship but each reflects the need for one party to acquire the marketing and distribution skills of another.

Within the IT market the word *reseller* is frequently used to describe the distributor or agent, and the companies which specialise in this activity are often referred to as *channels*, *i.e.* channels of distribution.

5.0.2 Distributor or agent? [G2, G14, H2, H14, I2, I16]

Distributor

One of the first questions which will need to be answered is whether it is desired to appoint a distributor or an agent. In the former case, the relationship between the manufacturer and the distributor will be that of buyer and seller. The distributor buys from the manufacturer and sells on at a margin to his customers. There is no direct contract of sale between the manufacturer and the end-user. The distributor-ship agreement will include terms governing the sale of the products between the manufacturer and the distributor, but with the distributor being largely free to contract with his own customers as he sees fit. Distributorship agreements drafted from the seller's viewpoint often include the following provision:

> "Sales of the Products to the Distributor shall be governed by the Company's standard conditions of sale in force from time to time . . ."

Clearly, such a clause gives the seller of the products an opportunity to revise its standard conditions to the disadvantage of the distributor and will usually be resisted by the distributor for that reason. Being an independent contractor, the distributor assumes a greater degree of risk than an agent, particularly in respect of bad debts, carrying stock and liability to customers.

Agent

An agent, on the other hand, is in a very different position. He acts as the intermediary between his principal and the customer in return for a commission, and it is these latter two who are the contracting parties. The agent will not normally incur any personal responsibility under the contract and can expect to be indemnified by his principal for any loss which may arise which is not due to his neglect or default. Some agents (often referred to as *marketing agents*) merely procure orders for the products and then leave the principal to enter into a contract with the customer. Others (usually known as *sales agents*) are given authority to negotiate and enter into contracts on the principal's behalf. An essential part of an agency agreement is a clear statement of the authority (if any) given to the agent to contract on the principal's behalf. For example, if the agent is to have only a limited degree of authority, the relevant clause might read as follows:

> "Except as expressly provided in this Agreement the Agent has no authority to commit the Company to any obligation and shall indemnify the Company against any loss or damage which the Company may sustain or incur as a result of any unauthorised act of the Agent . . ."

An agent who exceeds his authority will be liable to his principal and in certain circumstances, the customer, for any loss suffered by either of them as a result. Precedents G and H illustrate some of the differences between an agent and a distributor, and provide examples of the types of obligations which commonly arise in order to avoid uncertainty regarding the status and capacity of the parties [G14, H2].

In the European Union, special legislation affords protection to commercial agents. This is dealt with in 5.9 below.

5.1 RESPONSIBILITIES OF THE PARTIES [G7, G8, H7, H8, I9, I10]

Distributorship or agency agreements usually do two main things. First, they establish the contractual relationship of the parties. For example, a distributorship agreement would stipulate that the relationship between the parties is that of buyer and seller, and would incorporate terms similar to those found in any contract of sale (*e.g.* retention of title, passing of risk, provisions for late payment, etc.). Secondly, they stipulate the responsibilities of the parties regarding the products themselves and their marketing to the end-user.

Commonly, a distribution agreement will need to stipulate who will be responsible for:

(1) *Manufacturing and packing the products.* The principal will normally manufacture, package and supply the products to the distributor. However, if this is to be done by the distributor, the agreement becomes more complicated, as the distributor will need to have in his possession all the necessary technical information to enable him to manufacture. The owner will be concerned to ensure that he has sufficient control over the distributor's activities in order to ensure compliance with specifications and quality control, to safeguard the confidentiality of the manufacturing processes and to protect his intellectual property rights.

(2) *Licensing.* If the product is software which is to be licensed to the end-user, the owner will need to decide whether to license the end-user direct [H4] or grant the distributor rights to sub-license the end-user [I4]. In the former case, the distributor will undertake to procure the end-user to enter into a standard form end-user licence with the software owner.

(3) *Maintenance and support of the products.* If this is to be undertaken by the distributor he will need to be provided with all the necessary information and spare parts to enable him to perform his obligations properly. Software maintenance can cause problems, and this is discussed in 5.3.6.6.

(4) *Compliance with local laws and regulations* [G7 (27), (28)]. Clearly, it is important that the products should comply with the laws and regulations of the territory in which they are to be sold and the responsibility for this is normally shared. The distributor advises the manufacturer of the local requirements and the manufacturer undertakes to manufacture them in accordance with those requirements.

(5) *Advertising.* It is obviously in both parties' interests to maximise sales in the territory in question, and advertising will be a key feature. The parties may agree elaborate provisions for determining who will be responsible for the costs of advertising or alternatively say nothing, leaving commercial

pressures to play their part. As a general rule, an exclusive distributor is more likely to be asked to commit resources to advertising, whereas a non-exclusive distributor, who is one of many in the territory, is more likely to look for a national strategy from the manufacturer. Obviously, joint websites and/or portals may be an option if various different jurisdictions and/or distributors are involved, though equally, precautions must be taken to ensure a global website does not fall foul of a particular jurisdiction's rules and regulations on advertising.

An example clause reads as follows:

"The parties shall cooperate in regard to the promotion and marketing of the Products. The Company undertakes to spend such reasonable sums on advertising and marketing activities as may be necessary sufficiently to promote the Products in the Territory."

5.2 Price and Payment [G1, G4, G16, H9, I11]

Distributor

Price and payment terms are a key aspect of any long-term purchasing arrangement and distribution agreements are no exception. Unlike a one-off sale, there must be a mechanism for establishing the price for each consignment of the products ordered. Commonly, the basic price is determined by reference to the seller's published prices from time to time, less an agreed discount whereby the distributor makes his margin. A distributor looking for price protection might be inclined to seek controls limiting price increases to demonstrated increases in costs of manufacture. However, prices can go down as well as up and sometimes it is as well to leave the seller to determine his prices freely; after all, it is not in the seller's interests to set prices which unduly restrict sales. In the case of a non-exclusive distributorship, the distributor is more likely to be concerned that he is being treated fairly in comparison with other distributors, particularly in his own market. If another distributor is being treated more favourably, this immediately undermines the distributor's position. A prudent distributor might therefore seek a "most favoured customer clause" whereby the seller undertakes that the prices charged to the distributor will be no more than those charged to the seller's other distributors purchasing similar volumes:

"The Company warrants and undertakes to the Distributor that the prices to be charged for the Products will be no greater than the lowest prices charged to the Company's other distributors in the Territory purchasing the Products in similar volumes."

In addition, a distributor may seek to limit the impact of price increases by requiring the seller to provide a minimum period of notice of price changes, and in extreme circumstances may even reserve the right to terminate the agreement if the distributor believes them to be more than the market will bear.

Volume discounts are a common feature of distribution arrangements. In addition to the basic discount on published prices, the distributor is given the opportunity to obtain additional discounts by achieving pre-determined sales targets. Such provisions require careful thought, however, and the seller should remember that in his effort to earn additional discounts the distributor may be inclined to spend fewer resources on such matters as after-sales support.

Pre-payment or prompt payment discounts also appear quite regularly in distributorship agreements. The seller offers an agreed discount for payment on order or within a short period after order, failing which the distributor has to pay the higher price. Cynics might argue that the seller merely adds on the amount of the discount to his "real" prices to ensure early payment and that late payment is really a bonus for the seller who receives something he did not otherwise expect to have! For his part, a distributor may want to delay his payment obligations (*i.e.* so as to account quarterly, or within a set period of time after receiving payment from the end customer) in order to improve his own cashflow.

The seller will invariably reserve the right to increase or reduce prices, usually by giving the distributor an agreed period of notice. The price is then expressed to be that prevailing at the time of delivery of the products to the distributor. This could work unfairly against the distributor if the seller deliberately withholds deliveries until a price increase becomes effective. This situation can be guarded against by a provision that if the distributor orders products with a requested delivery date prior to the effective date of the price increase, then the lower price will be charged notwithstanding that the products are actually delivered after the effective date. Similarly, price decrease protection can be given to the distributor by providing that if a delivery is made during the notice period of the price decrease the distributor will nevertheless be charged the lower price.

Agent

Unlike distributors, agents usually earn their living by charging a commission, often expressed as a percentage of the net sales price of the product. In these cases, the agent is perhaps more concerned in maintaining the price of the products lest his commission be reduced, although increasing volumes of sales will also increase his income. It will be important to establish exactly what the agent will apply his percentage to. Clearly, it will be in the seller's interests to express the agent's commission as a percentage of the net amount payable to the seller, and any definition of "net sales price" will normally exclude such items as VAT, customs duties and transport and insurance charges. A clause to this effect might read as follows:

> "For the purpose of this Clause 'Net Sales Price' means the price invoiced to the Company's customers excluding import duties and other levies, transport and insurance charges and Value Added Tax or other applicable sales tax."

Adjustments are sometimes made so that the agent is not entitled to his commission until payment is actually received by the seller or for the agent's commission to be paid in the same instalments as the purchase price is payable, (but see also 5.9 below).

Where prices are expressed in currency other than that in which the distributor sells the product, the currency rate considerations of 2.2.4 [A3(2)] may be relevant.

5.3 TYPES OF DISTRIBUTION SYSTEM

5.3.1 Territory or market sector [G13, H12, H13, I14, I15]

A distributor is normally employed for his marketing expertise either in a particular geographical territory or a particular market sector. The appointment will usually reflect that fact and will be limited to the area where the seller thinks that the distributor will have an impact. If the distributor has been over-optimistic in his ability to market the product, he may well find that the seller subsequently wishes to reduce the distributor's area of operations or terminate the contract.

5.3.2 Exclusive distribution [G2]

The most valuable agreement from a distributor's point of view is one which gives him the exclusive right to distribute the products in a particular area or market sector. This advantage may however be counterbalanced by the seller's insistence that minimum sales targets be achieved within a short period (which might be calculated on an annual basis) or alternatively that there be a short notice period for terminating the agreement. The right to sell may also be somewhat reduced if the seller retains its own rights to sell its products, without restrictions:

> "Notwithstanding the Distributor's exclusive appointment the Company reserves the right to sell the Products direct to end-user customers situated in the Territory."

Exclusive arrangements are inherently somewhat anti-competitive [5.10], but this does not mean that they are necessarily against the public interest. A distributor with exclusive rights may be inclined to put much greater resources into training, maintenance and after-sales support than one whose profit margins are continuously under attack from competitors dealing in the same products. However, for agreements which are of sufficient size as potentially to distort markets and/or competition within them, it would be prudent to seek specialist legal advice on any potential competition law pitfalls. It must be remembered in this regard that, since the advent of the Competition Act 1998, it may be sufficient for there to have been an anti-competitive effect in the U.K. alone (*i.e.* and not affecting intra-E.U. member state trade). It must also be noted that regardless of the size of a distributorship arrangement, certain types of severely anti-competitive restraints, such as minimum and fixed resale prices, would be likely to be unenforceable under current competition regulations.

5.3.3 Non-exclusive distribution [I2]

From the seller's point of view, the grant of non-exclusive rights to a number of distributors in a particular market has two advantages. First, the seller is not reliant on one distributor who may perform badly and, in contrast to an exclusive distributorship, the seller can himself sell directly to end-users if he wishes. Secondly, the existence of competition between distributors should ensure maximum sales effort. Excessive competition in a market can be counterproductive though, and may lead to the emergence of the "box-pusher" distributor who provides little service or support and could not care whether the end-user uses the computer as a computer or a door stop!

5.3.4 Selective distribution

In an effort to encourage competition yet keep out the discount stores, a number of manufacturers have put in place selective distribution systems. These systems work by requiring retailers who wish to become distributors or resellers to meet certain pre-determined qualitative criteria relating to such matters as the technical qualifications of their staff and the suitability of their premises and training and after-sales support. Once appointed, these qualified retailers are then permitted to purchase the products from one or more national distributors appointed by the manufacturer. Conversely, the distributors are only allowed to sell to those retailers who meet the qualitative criteria and who have been appointed as qualified dealers. In this way, the manufacturer can ensure that certain minimum standards of training and support are maintained. Attempts to restrict competition by quantitative criteria (*i.e.* by merely restricting the numbers of resellers of the product) are highly likely to offend relevant competition law [5.10] and even qualitative criteria must be applied fairly and uniformly so as not to exclude a dealer who can demonstrate that he meets them. This does not mean however that the manufacturer has to sell to anyone who meets the criteria; generally speaking, a manufacturer who is not in a dominant position in the market can sell to whom he chooses. What he cannot do is prevent his distributor from selling on to a retail dealer who meets the criteria, neither can he restrict cross-supplies between distributors within a selective distribution system.

5.3.5 Hardware distribution [G7 (8, 9, 19)]

In some respects hardware distribution hardly merits a separate mention as it is not markedly different from the distribution of any other product. If anything its distinguishing feature is the complexity of the product. In comparison with the domestic kettle, computers are difficult to use, and to many the term "user friendly" has yet to become a reality. An efficient distributor will be able to provide expert advice to his customers, helping them to make the appropriate choice and then ensuring that they receive effective after-sales support. It will be in the interests of the seller to ensure this happens by providing training courses for the distributor's personnel, spares for maintenance services and by monitoring the standard of service he provides.

5.3.6 Software distribution [G10, H4, I4]

The distribution of computer software presents a number of difficulties to the owner and it is important that these are considered before embarking on a distribution strategy.

5.3.6.1 Types of software

The practicalities of distributing software in a particular way often depend on the nature of the software (packages) to be distributed. Broadly speaking, one can identify three categories:

(1) specialist bespoke programs [3.0.3];

(2) general commercial software [3.0.2];

(3) mass marketed software [4.3].

It is fair to say that the first category of programs is unlikely to be relevant to distribution arrangements. They are usually developed for a particular customer and may not have a general application. The cost of producing them is therefore borne entirely by that customer, who will usually be unwilling to disclose even the existence of its proprietary software, much less share its benefits.

On the other hand, commercial programs with a general application are more ideally suited for distribution. The cost of development is, in effect, spread across a number of customers and once a user base is established, the producer can afford to spend additional resources on developing and enhancing the software. While the software may be used by a number of customers it may still be valuable enough to be worth protecting from general disclosure by the use of confidentiality undertakings and in these circumstances will be subject to a licence agreement governing its disclosure and use.

Mass marketed software presents the greatest number of difficulties, some of which have been mentioned in 4.3 [see also Chapter 9]. It is widely available and is probably not, for this reason, protected by the law of confidence (and in this regard see the case of *Mars U.K. Ltd v. Teknowledge Ltd* [2000] F.S.R 138) [2.6.2, 3.3.3], where the issue of software to users only in the form of encrypted object code (which might be thought to be advertising the software's confidential nature by the very reason of its being encrypted) was held not in itself to guarantee that the software is protected by confidentiality, unless its confidentiality has been explicitly advertised, the software has been disclosed only under the circumstances showing its confidentiality, and (to prove infringement) there has been unauthorised use to the detriment of the copyright owner. Mass market software has been subject to the same problem of unauthorised copying as has afflicted the music industry and the problem is likely to persist, particularly as it is almost impossible to keep track of every copy which is sold. As shown above [4.3.1], the move from shrink-wrap to click-wrap exacerbates this. Asking the purchaser of a £50 piece of software to sign and return a licence agreement governing its use is about as feasible as asking the purchaser of a compact disc to do the same (and this, of course, is the rationale behind the use of shrink-wrap, and more recently click wrap, software licence agreements for such mass-market software products).

5.3.6.2 Copyright protection [3.8, H10, I12]

Section 3(1) of the Copyright, Designs and Patents Act 1988 (the "1988 Act") confirms that computer programs are treated as "literary works" for the purposes of copyright law. Any copying of a program is therefore an infringing act unless the act is licensed by the copyright owner or it is specifically authorised by the 1988 Act. For instance, section 50A of the 1988 Act gives a lawful user of a program the right to make a back up copy which it is necessary for him to have for the purposes of his lawful use. Furthermore, section 50C stipulates that it is not an infringement of copyright for a lawful user of a program to copy or adapt it, provided that the copying or adapting is necessary for his lawful use (which may include copying or adapting for the purpose of error correction, but for this and especially the effect of the *Mars* Case, see 3.3.3) and is not prohibited under any term or condition of an agreement regulating the circumstances in which his use is lawful, although the possibility of the latter contractual opt-out may not be a correct implementation of the Software Directive [3.8.1]. Having said this, most programs are accompanied by an express licence permitting storage of the programs on a designated computer and also the taking of copies for security and back up purposes.

Given the existence of copyright protection, why do software owners still require end-users to enter into licence agreements? The answer to this is as follows:

(1) To impose an obligation of confidence on the user. However, as mentioned above, this is probably not applicable to software which is widely available to the public.

(2) To distinguish clearly between the warranties the software owner is prepared to give and those that it is not. The main warranty software

owners will give is that the software program will perform in accordance with its documentation; other warranties (especially implied warranties) will normally be expressly excluded [1.12, 3.3.4].

(3) To impose limitations and exclusions on the liability of the software owner for the program. A defective package costing £100 could result in consequential losses to the end-user considerably greater than the price of the program.

(4) To restrict the way in which the end-user may use the programs especially where the extent of any implied licence is unclear (*e.g.* to use the software on a designated computer and to use it for the end-user's internal purposes only and not for the purpose of operating a bureau service). Clearly, this is only necessary if the particular use is not restricted by copyright law.

(5) To permit acts which might otherwise be an infringement of copyright (*e.g.* to take a back up copy whether this is necessary for the purposes of lawful use or not).

(6) Specifically to draw to the attention of the end-user to the software owner's intellectual property rights and to underline the restrictions imposed by copyright law.

(7) To enable the software owner, in the event of a breach of the licence, to terminate the licence in accordance with its terms and enforce the remedies conferred by the licence agreement. This is in addition to the software owner's remedies of damages and injunctive relief for breach of copyright.

(8) to enable the software owner to sell maintenance/update arrangements to the end-user, which may be free for a period and then charged thereafter. A good example is up-dates for virus protection programs which can be downloaded by authorised users from the Internet.

5.3.6.3 Licensing [H4, I4]

The software owner who wishes to distribute his software through intermediaries and at the same time impose licence terms on the end-user has to face the problem that unless special arrangements are put in place, there will be no direct contractual nexus between the software owner and the end-user. However, see below [5.3.6.4] on the effects of the Contracts (Rights of Third Parties) Act 1999, which may soften the effect of this.

The software owner would prefer to receive direct covenants from the end-user as this ensures that the owner can enforce the licence terms himself rather than rely on an intermediary to do so. One method of achieving this is to appoint the intermediary as the agent of the software owner, authorised to enter into a standard form licence agreement with the end-user on the owner's behalf [I]. Alternatively, the agent can procure end-users to enter into a licence agreement which only comes into effect once it is submitted to and accepted by the owner [H]. The latter method gives the owner more control over who the software is licensed to while at the same time permitting more flexible negotiations between the owner and the end-user over the terms of the licence agreement.

The software owner's situation has, however, been considerably assisted by the enactment of the Contracts (Rights of Third Parties) Act 1999 [1.3] which is of particular relevance to shrink wrap licences (see 5.3.6.4 below).

5.3.6.4 "Shrink-wrap" licences [E, G10]

"Shrink-wrap" licences for mass-produced software have been described in detail at 4.3.1. For the purposes of this chapter we are concerned only with the relationship (if any can be established) between the purchaser who has a formal contract only with a distributor and the original software owner. This could be the case if a purchase downloads a piece of software from a distributor's Internet website.

Legal commentators have identified two main difficulties with shrink-wrap licences under English law:

(1) *The doctrine of privity of contract.* This provides that no one except a party to a contract can acquire rights under it and no one except a party can be subject to liabilities under it. Where the end-user purchases a package from a distributor the contract of sale is clearly between the distributor and the end- user (we say "sale" because the end-user will own the physical article, namely the media on which the program is recorded although equally the sale could be that of a licence to use the software downloaded from the Internet). The shrink- wrap licence is, however, expressed to be made between the software owner and the end-user. Every contract has to be supported by consideration, and it is difficult to see sometimes what benefit flows to the end-user from the software owner under most shrink-wrap licences which merely impose additional restrictions or limitations on liability.

(2) Incorporation of terms. Many shrink-wrap licences contain a condition to the effect that they are deemed to be accepted by the customer if he opens the package and breaks the wrapping. The difficulty that has been identified with this procedure is that in many cases the contract of sale will have been made before the act of acceptance has taken place. It is a clearly established principle of English law that all the terms of the contract have to be brought to the parties' attention before the contract is made otherwise those terms which are not will not be validly incorporated into the contract. Where the end-user purchases the package in a retail shop the contract is usually made at the till when the cashier accepts the customer's money, and there can be no guarantee that he will have read the licence terms prior to that time. Proving that he did is equally difficult. Alternatively—and this applies particularly to software downloaded from a distributor's website—a click-wrap agreement requires the user to read and click acceptance to contractual terms [4.3.1]. In this case the incorporation of terms is more straightforward since the purchaser can be assumed to have read the conditions and accepted them before by his action (clicking "Yes") he accepts the terms.

Another way of dealing with this is to provide the purchaser with a free registration mechanism, either via the Internet or by post. The purchaser reveals his identity to the copyright owner and may also be induced to enter into a contract for software maintenance/update arrangements [5.3.6.2]. However, it must remain the case that many users fail to register.

In the case of a mail-order transaction, the contract is probably made over the telephone (in the case of credit card transactions) or when the distributor commits some act of acceptance (*e.g.* cashing the customer's cheque or posting the goods to him) in response to the customer's written order. Mail-order-sales would appear to present particular difficulties in ensuring that the customer is aware of the licence terms before the contract is made.

How then does one circumvent these problems? The honest answer is probably with some difficulty. The relevant legal issues have been set out in the *Beta v. Adobe* Case [4.3.1], at least insofar as Scottish law is concerned. However, under the Contracts (Rights of Third Parties) Act 1999 [1.3] (the "1999 Act"), English law now recognises the concept of third-party beneficiary rights, which, in theory at least, significantly increase the chances of shrink-wrap licences being enforced and pave the way for English courts to follow the decision in *Beta Computers* (albeit that one will still need to show that the terms were effectively incorporated into the contract of sale). For the copyright-owner to ensure that his rights are enforceable against a purchaser who acquires his software via a distributor/retailer, the agreement between the purchaser and distributor/retailer will need to refer explicitly to the 1999 Act and identify the copyright-owner as an intended beneficiary of the rights and obligations created by the agreement.

In the absence of express judicial recognition of shrink-wrap and click-wrap licences under English law, software owners have traditionally sought to find the solution in copyright law rather than contract law, attempting to create a collateral copyright licence agreement between the software owner and the end-user which arises independently of the contract of sale and where it does not matter that the terms of that agreement are not communicated before the contract of sale is made. It is likely that given the opportunities presented by the 1999 Act, such arguments will become largely irrelevant, but we nonetheless set them out below for consideration in the event that the retailer's terms do not expressly purport to confer a direct benefit upon the software owner. Moreover, there will continue for some time to be much software sold under licences which predate the 1999 Act.

The argument has been run in the past that copying a computer program by storing it in any medium by electronic means (*e.g.* by loading it into the hard disk of a computer) is a restricted act for copyright purposes and may not be performed without the copyright owner's permission (see the Copyright, Designs and Patents Act 1988, s. 17(2)). So too, it was argued, was making a back up copy although, as mentioned above [3.8.1], a statutory right to make a back up copy is now conferred by section 50A of the Act. The software owner then sought to impose his licence terms on the end-user by pointing out these restrictions and granting him a licence permitting the requisite use subject to the other terms and conditions of the licence. The end-user was deemed to accept the terms by some act of acceptance, whether it be tearing off the wrapping or clicking acceptance in order to load the program onto the hard disk of a computer.

The hapless consumer who purchases his package software in a retail shop may complain with some indignation that, having paid his money and purchased his copy of the program from a reputable retailer who is presumably authorised to sell it, he should be entitled to use it for the purpose for which it is intended without any further restriction or limitation. The law, it seems, might agree with him in two ways.

The first is the argument that at common law, and without notice to the contrary, such a purchaser has an implied licence to use and copy the software for the purpose for which it is intended. Such an implied licence probably exists and it would therefore be necessary to bring to the purchaser's attention specifically the fact that the copyright owner does not intend such a licence to be granted but instead an express licence on the terms offered.

The second argument is even more problematic. As mentioned in 3.8.1 and 5.3.6.2, section 50C of the Copyright, Designs and Patents Act 1988, provided by the

Copyright (Computer Programs) Regulations 1992 (S.I. 1992 No. 3233), now provides that it is not an infringement of copyright for a lawful user of a program to copy or adapt it, provided that the copying or adapting is necessary for his lawful use and is not prohibited under any term or condition of an agreement regulating the circumstances in which his use is lawful. Rather unhelpfully, section 50A(2) defines a "lawful user" of a computer program as someone who has (whether under a licence to do any acts restricted by the copyright in the program or otherwise) a right to use the program. It is at least arguable that a person who buys a copy of a computer program legitimately is a lawful user particularly if it can be said that an implied licence arises in his favour at the time of purchase. Moreover, Article 5(1) of the Software Directive (91/250/EEC) which the regulations implement in fact refers to the lawful "acquirer" not "user", which is an altogether different concept. A person who purchases a copy of a program lawfully could be described as a lawful acquirer without having any licence, express or implied, to use the program. The U.K. courts may be compelled to interpret the expression "lawful user" in the light of the intention of the Directive as synonymous with "lawful acquirer". In fact, the draftsman of the U.K. legislation may have had the implied licence at common law in mind when using the expression lawful user and perhaps did not intend to deviate from the objective of the Directive. If, in fact, lawful acquirer and lawful user are synonymous for these purposes this means that a person who purchases a copy of a program lawfully (and does not sign or accept an agreement regulating his use beforehand or contemporaneously which prohibits copying or adapting) becomes entitled to copy and adapt it for his lawful use as a result of section 50C.

If either of these arguments is valid, it means that a person who purchases a copy of a computer program lawfully will already have the right to use it in accordance with its intended purpose. The offer of a licence from the software owner is therefore unnecessary and this casts doubt on whether an offer of a licence in return for restrictions and limitations in favour of the software owner is the basis for a valid agreement. Consideration must flow both ways, but if the purchaser already has the rights which the software owner is purporting to confer it is difficult to see what consideration flows in favour of the purchaser. In order to fall within section 50C, the instrument prohibiting the copying or adapting must be an "agreement" and not a mere "licence". Moreover, the agreement must be one "regulating the circumstances in which his use is lawful". If the purchaser already has the right to use the program lawfully it is perhaps difficult to argue that a subsequent agreement itself regulates his lawful use. One possible solution might be for the software owner to offer the user some additional benefit not conferred on him by law (perhaps an absolute right to make a back up copy or the offer of help-line support or updates) but there seems little compulsion on a user to accept this if it means agreeing to burdensome restrictions or limitations. Some software owners make the provision of help-line support conditional on the user signing and returning a registration card which includes a confirmation that the user agrees to be bound by the terms of the licence agreement. One further obstacle to the enforceability of the shrink-wrap licence is the argument, mentioned in 3.8.1, that section 50C is an incorrect implementation of the Software Directive in permitting the right to copy or adapt a computer program in order to use it for its intended purpose to be prohibited by a contract to the contrary at all.

One can see that the enforceability of the shrink-wrap or click-wrap licence does remain in some doubt, which will continue until there is judicial guidance on the issue. The trend appears to be in favour of the click-wrap or of a tear-off licence, with a physical act of acceptance (namely, the tearing open of the packet containing the disk) accompanied by an offer to refund the purchase price if the user does not accept the licence terms. It is a clearly established contractual principal that the terms of an offer can be accepted by a prescribed form of conduct provided the offeree is aware of the terms and he does the act with the intention of accepting the offer. Whether a lawful user of a program opens the packet containing the disk or clicks acceptance solely in order to use the program for its intended purpose or with the intention of also accepting the licence conditions will, we are sure, be a point which will be argued in any case attempting to establish the enforceability of such agreements.

The position is improved for the software owner where he is granting a site licence or multiple copy licence [5.3.6.5] and where there is some real additional benefit flowing from the software owner to the user. Such licences are often the subject of formal written agreements which avoid the need to rely on the device of the shrink-wrap agreement or, alternatively, confirm the user's agreement to be bound by the terms of the shrink-wrap agreement [F].

For those circumstances where it will still be of use (e.g. off-the-shelf purchases of package software, in respect of which the vendor, usually a retailer, will not have a written contract with the purchaser), a form of shrink-wrap licence agreement is offered in Precedent E. For reasons set out at 4.3.1, we think a click-wrap read-me file has greater chance of being enforceable than a shrink-wrap licence and we recommend that where possible the wording at Precedent E, be used as a read-me file with an obligation on the user to certify his having read it and click his agreement to it if he is to gain access to the software.

Where software is distributed, it should be made clear in the contract between the software owner and the distributor that it is the responsibility of the distributor to ensure that each copy of the package is sold with the accompanying shrink-wrap licence or that the distributor's contract clearly identifies the software owner as a third party beneficiary for the purposes of the Contracts (Rights of Third Parties) Act 1999. It is common to find distributors who, when demonstrating software to a potential customer, open up the package and throw away the shrink-wrap licence. This practice may be reduced by providing the distributor with a sufficient number of demonstration versions of the package [G5] or better still incorporating the terms of a click-wrap licence.

Shrink-wrap and click-wrap licences commonly permit the original licensee to sell the disk and transfer the licence to another user provided the user accepts the terms of the licence and the original licensee ceases to use the software. This is consistent with the exhaustion of distribution right contained in section 18(3) of the Copyright, Designs and Patents Act 1988 and such express transfer provisions will replace those implied by section 56(2) of the Act.

5.3.6.5 Networks and site licences [F, I Sched. 1]

Site licences have been introduced by the industry in response to two problems. First, the reluctance of multiple users of a program to pay the full price for each copy of the program they use. Second, the use of network systems where several processors are linked together and where the software can be resident at any time in any one of those processors.

The demand for multiple copies of a program can be met by bulk discounting. The more copies the customer purchases the less he pays for each individual copy. This requirement can quite easily be fulfilled by the distributor, who prices accordingly. However, it does not answer all the problems as it still means that the customer is required to purchase a series of single user licences. What may be preferred is a licence which enables the user to copy the program for use on all his computers without signing a separate licence for each copy [F]. A wider definition of "use" would be required and a change in pricing structure. Site licences need not be ruinous to the software owner and, indeed, may tempt business users with only one valid copy of a program to seek legitimacy by applying for a site licence.

A single user licence which permits use of the program on one processor only is clearly not appropriate for a network system. Again, the definition of "use" will need to be redrafted in a wider fashion while at the same time introducing an appropriate pricing structure.

Site licensing can be viewed as a specialist form of distribution. Because it entails redrafting the single user licence it is not something which the distributor can usually handle alone, unless the software owner has agreed upon a standard form of site licence (but even that may not cope with every situation). Larger corporate customers are increasingly going direct to the software owner to negotiate special arrangements for site licences. Their purchasing power may be such that the software owner cannot ignore them. In these circumstances distributors are likely to be left to service the smaller users unless they can negotiate exclusive distribution rights with the software owner, but even then the owner might reserve the right to supply end-user customers direct. The future is uncertain, but we doubt whether distributors are always going to view the introduction of the site licence with enthusiasm.

5.3.6.6 Support [G6, G8, H6, H8, I7, I8]

For a full discussion of maintenance readers are referred to Chapters 8 and 9. Maintenance of hardware by a distributor does not cause any particular difficulties. The distributor has to be trained, of course, but he can quite easily be supplied with a stock of spare parts, and this does not give him much more information than he could obtain by dismantling the machine.

Software maintenance is a different matter. If the distributor is to provide effective maintenance he will need access to the source code of the software and will need to employ skilled programmers to carry out the work. For this reason, one often finds that responsibility for software maintenance is retained by the software owner so that the distributor's duties are confined to supplying and installing the software and perhaps providing first line support (in this instance dealing with technical queries which do not require access to the source code in order to resolve). In this way the software owner protects his software by not revealing the source code.

It is only in cases where there is a great deal of commercial trust between the parties that the software owner will release his source code. This may arise, for example, where the software owner and distributor are parent and subsidiary or members of a joint venture.

5.4 TERMINATION [G3, G15, G17, H15, H16, I17, I18]

Like most term contracts, provisions giving one party the right to terminate in the event of the default or insolvency of the other are often incorporated in distributorship agreements. Additionally, one might find a right given to the seller to terminate if the distributor or agent fails to meet any agreed minimum sales targets.

The appointment of a distributor or agent is often considered as a personal relationship such that the distributor cannot assign or delegate his rights and obligations, as follows:

"The Distributor shall not be entitled to assign, sub-contract or delegate any of its rights or obligations under this Agreement."

A change in control of a corporate distributor might similarly be regarded as unacceptable by the seller (particularly if the new owner of the distributor is a competitor of the seller), and accordingly the contract might provide the seller with a right to terminate in that event.

Special obligations can arise on the termination of the appointment of a commercial agent. These are considered in 5.9.

5.5 ALTERATIONS [G8 (6), (7), H8, I7]

Alterations can occur in both the specification of the products and the range of products offered by the seller.

It is clearly in the seller's interests to ensure that the distributor is kept fully informed of all enhancements and changes to the products so that he can properly market and support them. To this end, the seller may offer the distributor's personnel a free training programme in respect of any major enhanced product.

It will be important to establish exactly what products will be sold by the seller to the distributor. The seller may not want to sell his entire product range through the distributor, as the latter may not have the necessary expertise to demonstrate and support the whole range. On the other hand, the distributor's position could be seriously affected if the seller is given the absolute right to discontinue selling products to the distributor. A compromise which is often agreed is that the seller will initially offer the distributor an agreed range of products which is identified in a schedule to the agreement. If the seller discontinues selling any of the products to the distributor then he must discontinue selling them altogether in the distributor's territory. If a new product is introduced which can reasonably be regarded as a successor to any existing product, then the distributor will be offered that successor product in lieu of the old one. (It will usually be in the seller's interest to discontinue sales of the obsolescent product as swiftly as possible.) Entirely new products are then left to be offered by the seller at his discretion.

Most sellers will wish to reserve the right to discontinue selling a product, not least to ensure that they can minimise the risk associated with product liability.

5.6 DISTRIBUTOR'S DUTIES [G7, H7, I9]

The distributor will usually undertake to:

(1) Use all reasonable endeavours to maximise sales in his territory;

(2) Achieve minimum sales volumes;

(3) Employ trained staff to demonstrate and support the products;

(4) Keep the seller advised of matters material to the exploitation of the products in the territory;

(5) Install and maintain the products;

(6) Provide training to end-users.

As regards (1) and (in particular) (2), the distributor will be cautious about agreeing to these if the seller reserves the right to refuse to accept the distributor's orders. Clearly, the distributor will not wish to be put in a position where he is deemed to be in breach of the agreement merely because his orders are not fulfilled by the seller.

5.7 SELLER'S DUTIES [G8, H8, I10]

The seller's obligations will normally include:

(1) Fulfilling the distributor's orders as soon as practicable;

(2) Training the distributor's personnel;

(3) Providing technical and commercial assistance;

(4) Keeping the distributor advised of technical changes to the products;

(5) Advising the distributor of any proposal to discontinue products or introduce new ones.

One of the main risks of dealing in high technology products is obsolescence. Entire ranges can dramatically decrease in value on the announcement of a successor product and a distributor can be faced with selling off large quantities of stock at a loss. It is vitally important, therefore, to the distributor that the seller agrees to keep the distributor informed of any new products proposed by the seller, thus allowing an orderly running-off of stocks.

5.8 LIABILITY [G18, I22]

Sellers will invariably seek the same type of limitations on liability as one would expect to see in any contract of sale [1.3, 3.3.3]. In particular, one often sees a limited one or two year warranty for defective products being offered in lieu of the statutory implied terms. The distributor should remember that he will be expected to extend similar warranties to his own customers and may find himself squeezed in the middle if the products have to be held in stock for a lengthy period of time. Some companies require their distributors to pass on the benefit of warranties:

"The Distributor shall offer to its customers a warranty in respect of the Products no less favourable then the warranty given to the Distributor by the Company under Clause *X* . . ."

More and more manufacturers are now offering "guarantees" direct to the end-user which tend in practice to absolve the intermediary from responsibility. Whilst these are not guarantees in the strict legal sense of the word, they are probably enforceable by the end-user as collateral agreements where it can be shown that the end-user was induced into the contract with the distributor because of the guarantee. If the manufacturer is also the copyright owner and the end-user has acquired a licence direct from him rather than from the distributor, this may possibly further strengthen the enforceability of the guarantee. Some contracts actively encourage distributors to arrange for defective products to be sent back to the manufacturer:

"The Distributor shall not attempt to repair any defective Products returned to it by its customers but instead shall assist them in completing the appropriate guarantee claim form and returning such Products direct to the Company . . ."

Other areas of liability that can arise are infringement of intellectual property rights and failure of the products to comply with local laws and regulations. Appropriate indemnities are usually taken.

An agent can usually expect a blanket indemnity from his principal, because the contract is not made with the agent but between the principal and the customer and is entirely transparent so far as the agent is concerned. However, where the agent has undertaken to the principal to perform certain of the principal's obligations under the contract, the agent may incur some liability to the principal against which he should not expect to be indemnified.

5.9 LEGAL PROTECTION FOR COMMERCIAL AGENTS

Special legal protection is afforded in Great Britain to commercial agents (as distinct from distributors) by the Commercial Agents (Council Directive) Regulations 1993 (S.I. 1993 No. 3053). These were implemented pursuant to the European Council Directive 86/653/EEC on Self-Employed Commercial Agents and came into force in Great Britain on January 1, 1994. Separate regulations cover Northern Ireland.

Prior to the regulations coming into effect, English law adopted a largely *laissez-faire* attitude towards the principal-agent relationship. The parties were mainly left to devise their own contractual relationship, subject to competition law, and very few terms were implied by law into an agency contract. This was in marked contrast to some other countries of the European Union where commercial agents were treated as more akin to employees with rights to compensation on termination (as under unfair dismissal and redundancy). The purpose of the directive was to harmonise the laws of the E.U. countries in this area.

The regulations give commercial agents important rights which cannot be excluded by contract. Chief among these are the right to a minimum period of termination notice, a right to commission on transactions concluded after the termination of the agency agreement where the transactions are mainly attributable to the efforts of the agent and a right to indemnification or compensation for any loss suffered as a consequence of the termination of the agency agreement by the principal. The regulations govern the relations between commercial agents and their principals in relation to the activities of commercial agents in Great Britain, but do not apply where the parties have agreed that the agency contract is to be governed by the law of another member state. It should be remembered, however, that there is similar implementing legislation in the other member states.

Readers should be aware of the following:

(1) The regulations only apply to commercial agents. A commercial agent is defined as a self-employed intermediary who has continuing authority to negotiate the sale or purchase of goods on behalf of another person ("the principal") or to negotiate and conclude the sale or purchase of goods on behalf of and in the name of the principal.

(2) It is generally believed that the regulations extend to agents which are corporations or partnerships as well as individuals.

(3) Contracts for the supply of services are not governed by the regulations. However, some of the other EU countries have extended their national legislation to cover supplies of services and consequently the local position should always be checked.

(4) Genuine distribution agreements where the distributor buys and sells goods on his own behalf are not affected by the regulations.

(5) Commercial agents do not include officers authorised to commit companies or associations, partners authorised to commit partnerships, insolvency practitioners acting as such, unpaid agents, commercial agents operating on commodity exchanges or markets, Crown agents for overseas governments or persons whose activities as commercial agents are secondary to some other primary purpose. Mail order catalogue agents for consumer goods and consumer credit agents are presumed, unless the contrary is established, not to be commercial agents for these purposes.

(6) A commercial agent and his principal are deemed to owe certain duties to each other which cannot be excluded by contract. A commercial agent must look after the interests of his principal, act dutifully and in good faith, make proper efforts to negotiate and, where appropriate, conclude the transactions he is instructed to take care of, communicate to his principal all the necessary information available to him and comply with reasonable instructions given by his principal.

(7) A principal must also act dutifully and in good faith, must provide his commercial agent with the necessary documentation relating to the goods, obtain for him the information necessary for the performance of the agency contract, notify him within a reasonable period once the principal anticipates that the volume of commercial transactions will be significantly lower than that which the agent could normally have expected and must inform him within a reasonable period of his acceptance or refusal of, and of any non-execution by him, of a commercial transaction which the agent has procured.

(8) Where the level of remuneration has not been agreed between the principal and agent (which is likely to be rare), the commercial agent is entitled to that customarily paid or, in the absence of a customary practice, reasonable remuneration.

(9) Where a commercial agent is remunerated, wholly or in part, by commission:

   (a) he is entitled to commission on commercial transactions concluded during the period covered by the agency agreement both where the transaction is concluded as a result of his action and where the transaction is concluded with a third party whom he has previously acquired as a customer for transactions of the same kind (ie repeat orders, even where the agent was not instrumental in obtaining them);

   (b) he is also entitled to commission on transactions concluded during his agency where he has an exclusive right to a specific geographical area or to a specific group of customers and where the transaction has been entered into with a customer belonging to that area or group (even where the customer was not procured by the agent). The directive, in fact, gave member states the other option of giving a commercial agent this right where he is "entrusted with a specific geographical area or group of customers", that is on a non-exclusive basis, and implementing legislation in other member states may cater for this possibility;

    (c) he is entitled to commission even after his agency contract has terminated in respect of a transaction concluded within a reasonable period following such termination if that transaction is mainly attributable to his efforts during his agency or where the order reaches the principal or the agent before the termination of the agency contract;

    (d) commission payable to him as mentioned in (c) above will not be shared with a successor agent unless it is equitable that this should be done;

    (e) he is entitled to his commission when one of the following events occurs, namely (i) the principal executes the transaction (presumably when he delivers the goods), (ii) the principal should, according to his agreement with the third party, have executed the transaction or, at the latest, when (iii) the third party executes the transaction (presumably when he pays for the goods) or should have done so if the principal had executed his part of the transaction as he should have. The commission must be paid by the last day of the month following the quarter in which it became due. These rights cannot be taken away by contract;

    (f) his right to commission can only be extinguished if it is established that the contract will not be executed and the principal is not to blame (*e.g.* the third party defaults or becomes insolvent or the contract is frustrated), in which case the commission must be returned. Again, the agent's rights cannot be diminished by contract;

    (g) he is given rights to be supplied with statements of the commission due to him and extracts from the principal's books in order to check the commission due to him. These rights may not be excluded by contract.

(10) The commercial agent and the principal may demand from each other a written document setting out the terms of the agency contract, including terms subsequently agreed. This right may not be excluded. The directive entitled member states to provide that an agency contract shall not be valid unless evidenced in writing. The U.K. did not adopt this option.

(11) Where the agency agreement is concluded for an indefinite period, either party may terminate it by giving certain minimum notice. This is one month for the first year of the contract, two months for the second year commenced and three months for the third year commenced and for the subsequent years. The parties may not agree on shorter periods of notice. Member states were given the option of fixing the notice period at four months for the fourth year, five months for the fifth year and six months for the sixth and subsequent years and to decide that the parties could not agree on shorter notice, but the U.K. did not take up that option. If the parties voluntarily agree to a longer period of notice, the period of notice to be observed by the principal must not be shorter than that to be observed by the commercial agent. Unless otherwise agreed, the end of the notice period must coincide with the end of a calendar month.

(12) An agency contract for a fixed period which continues to be performed by both parties after that period has expired is deemed to be converted into an agency contract for an indefinite period, with the consequence that the minimum periods of notice referred to above must be given (the earlier fixed period being taken into account in calculating the period of notice).

A party to an agency contract should therefore be careful not to perform it following the expiry of a fixed term if it is not intended to confer the entitlement to further notice.

(13) The regulations do not affect any statute or law which allows the immediate termination of an agency contract because of the default of one party or where exceptional circumstances arise.

(14) The directive stipulated that on the termination of an agency contract, member states were required to ensure that the commercial agent be entitled to either (i) an indemnity or (ii) compensation in prescribed circumstances. The following points should be noted:

(a) the agent is entitled to an indemnity if and to the extent that he has brought to the principal new customers or has significantly increased the volume of business with existing customers and the principal continues to derive substantial benefits from the business with such customers and the payment of the indemnity is equitable having regard to all the circumstances and, in particular, the commission lost by the agent on the business transacted with such customers. The amount of the indemnity may not exceed a figure equivalent to an indemnity for one year calculated from the commercial agent's average annual remuneration over the preceding five years and if the contract goes back less than five years the indemnity is calculated on the average for the period in question. The grant of an indemnity does not prevent the agent from seeking damages;

(b) the agent is entitled to compensation for the damage he suffers as a result of the termination of his relations with the principal. Such damage is deemed to occur particularly when the termination takes place in circumstances depriving the commercial agent of the commission which proper performance of the agency contract would have procured him while providing the principal with substantial benefits linked to the commercial agent's activities and/or which have not enabled the commercial agent to amortise the costs and expenses that he had incurred for the performance of the agency contract on the principal's advice;

(c) most member states have chosen to give commercial agents an indemnity. For the U.K., however, the regulations stipulate that the indemnity will only be payable where the agency contract provides and that consequently commercial agents will be entitled to compensation unless the parties have opted for the indemnity in the contract;

(d) while there is a maximum limit on the calculation of the indemnity, neither the directive nor the regulations stipulate how any compensation will be calculated and this is left to the national courts to assess;

(e) the agent must notify the principal of his claim for compensation or, as the case may be, indemnity within a year of the termination of the agency contract, otherwise the entitlement will be lost. This leaves the onus on the agent. If the claim, once notified, is not met the agent will have to pursue his entitlement in the national courts;

(f) there is no need to make any reference to compensation in the agency contract but if the parties wish to opt for the indemnity this must be provided for expressly;

(g) the parties may not derogate from the right to compensation or, as the case may be, indemnity before the agency contract expires. Any attempt to limit or exclude the amount of compensation or indemnity in the contract will therefore be ineffective. However, once the contract has expired there seems nothing to prevent the parties from reaching a binding settlement or, indeed, waiving the entitlement altogether;

(h) the entitlement to compensation or indemnity arises not only when the contract is expressly terminated but also where it terminates as a consequence of the death of the commercial agent;

(i) the entitlement to compensation or indemnity is lost if the principal terminates the contract because of the agent's default justifying immediate termination at law, if the agent himself terminates the contract (other than a justified termination as a consequence of circumstances attributable to the principal or other than on grounds of the age, infirmity or illness of the agent in consequence of which he cannot reasonably be required to continue his activities) or if the agent, by agreement with the principal, assigns his rights and duties under the contract to another person;

(j) it seems that the entitlement to compensation or indemnity may depend on who terminates the contract. For instance, the principal may terminate the contract for a breach which has arisen as a consequence of the incapacity of the agent. In such circumstances, no compensation or indemnity would seem payable. But if the agent terminates on grounds of infirmity or illness the entitlement will survive;

(k) although the right to compensation or indemnity cannot be excluded by contract, there seems to be no reason why the principal could not insist that the agent take out, at the agent's cost, life assurance and/or health insurance and assign the benefit of the policy to the principal to protect the principal against compensation or indemnity claims in the event of the death or illness of the agent.

(15) Finally, the regulations provide that a restraint of trade clause (that is, an agreement restricting the business activities of a commercial agent following termination of the agency contract) shall not be valid unless it is concluded in writing, relates to the geographical area or the group of customers and the geographical area entrusted to the commercial agent and to the kind of goods covered by his agency under the contract and does not exceed two years' duration. This is without prejudice to any statute or law which otherwise restricts the enforceability of such clauses.

The extent to which the regulations and the directive affect computer contracts depends on the products concerned and the nature of the relationship between the parties. There seems little doubt that hardware will be "goods" within the meaning of the regulations and that the regulations will apply to commercial agency agreements relating to such products. On the other hand, a genuine distributorship arrangement where the distributor buys and sells computer products on his own account, such as that envisaged by Precedent G, will not be caught by the regulations. Marketing of software by agents is more problematic. It raises the old argument as to whether software is "goods" for these or, indeed, other purposes. The authors' personal view is that it will be hard to deny that mass-produced package software which consumers are used to purchasing in retail outlets should be regarded as goods for these purposes; in *St Albans City and District Council v.*

International Computers Ltd [1997] F.S.R. 251, the judge remarked *obiter* that software could be regarded as goods for the purposes of the Sale of Goods Act 1979. It was stated that where media upon which software has been loaded is sold or hired, that sale or licence amounts to a supply of goods. A similar conclusion has been drawn by the U.S. Courts. However, the judge's opinion seems to be based on the fact that a physical object on which the software resides (*e.g.* a floppy disk) is passed to the purchaser. Where the software was acquired by downloading from the Internet and no physical object changed hands, it may be argued that software would not fall within the judge's definition of goods. Moreover, software which is furnished under a written copyright licence agreement, particularly where property in even the media on which the software is recorded is reserved to the copyright owner, should, it is submitted, not be regarded as a sale of goods for the purposes of the regulations and consequently outside the scope of the regulations which only apply to agency contracts relating to the sale or purchase of goods. Precedents H and I are examples of agreements to which the regulations may be said not to apply.

Software owners should be cautious, however, when dealing with commercial agents in other countries of the European Union where local law is to govern the contract. The local legislation should be checked to see whether the protection afforded to commercial agents extends beyond the sale and purchase of goods to services or other supplies, in which case even the marketing of copyright licences may be caught. Even English law may not be entirely clear cut in this area. It remains to be seen whether the courts draw a distinction between software media sold as goods and the provision of copyright licences where not even title in the media passes to the customer.

5.10 COMPETITION LAW

As illustrated by 5.3.2 and 5.3.4, distribution arrangements can give rise to anti-competitive practices by the parties and for this reason such arrangements have for a long time been subject to competition law designed to prevent such practices. Some systems of law are highly developed in this field (particularly in the U.S. and E.U.) and anyone who is considering entering into a distributorship agreement is strongly recommended to seek professional advice, especially in the light of the creation of a new competition regime in the U.K. by way of the Competition Act 1998, which may open up many domestic arrangements for scrutiny which previously fell outside the scope of the E.U. regime. Broadly speaking, parties to distributorship arrangements must pay careful attention to potentially anti-competitive provisions relating, in particular, to resale pricing, territorial restrictions and excessive non-compete obligations, which are some of the areas often focused on by competition regulators. However, it is not within the scope of this book to deal with competition law in the U.K. or elsewhere; for that the reader is referred to the standard legal texts dealing with the subject.

CHAPTER 6

TEST AGREEMENTS

6.1   Types of Test Agreements
6.2   Payment
6.3   Delivery and Acceptance
6.4   Termination
6.5   Alterations
6.6   Customer's Duties
6.7   Supplier's Duties

6.1 TYPES OF TEST AGREEMENTS [J]

As explained in 1.6 above, it is customary for both hardware and software to undergo two separate tests: the internal, or alpha, tests at the manufacturer's or systems house's premises; and field tests or "beta" tests, which allow the product/software to undergo testing by a real customer in circumstances as close as possible to the conditions to be encountered when in live use. The purpose of the testing is, of course, to provide the manufacturer or systems house with information about how the hardware or software performs, any bugs encountered, and how robust it is. In return, the company providing the beta tests may have the advantage of obtaining earlier than usual a new, and possibly more advanced, product. They may also expect some financial inducement such as a discount or even free use of the hardware or software for a period.

On many occasions the arrangements are informal, and may even be in the form of an exchange of letters, rather than a more formal contract. However, there are sufficient differences from ordinary purchase contracts (*e.g.* the date at which insurable risk passes) and issues of confidentiality and potential liability which make a formal agreement desirable.

In fact, a hardware test agreement is usually a special case of either a purchase contract with maintenance [A, K] or a rental [B] which may or may not have an option to purchase. For software it is a licence [C], usually limited as to duration, but with software support [L].

(Another form of test agreement has already been alluded to in the form of test versions (also called review copies or demonstration, or demo, licences) [4.3.2].

6.2 PAYMENT [J1, J3]

Beta test agreements differ from evaluation tests in that the test is primarily for the benefit of the supplier, rather than the customer. This means that the customer will pay a reduced fee or even none at all for the privilege of testing out the hardware or software. It also means that the supplier will wish to learn as soon as possible of any defects or problems with the equipment or software and will therefore expect to

112

provide a very high level of maintenance and support. It is usual for this maintenance or support to be provided at no further cost to the customer. In return, the customer is likely to be required to provide detailed information as to the performance of the hardware or software. This will be far more than simply reporting any glitches and may well involve the customer handing over his machine to the supplier's personnel, or even keeping it online to them, for detailed examination of the performance of the product. Where the product is software and the supplier's personnel are involved in its processing they will effectively become a sort of bureau for the customer with all the circumstances—particularly those for Data Protection—which that implies [10.3.3].

So far as evaluation versions of software packages are concerned, the benefit is entirely for the customer and although they are usually provided free of charge, the supplier will ensure that if this free test is abused he will automatically receive a full licence fee.

6.3 DELIVERY AND ACCEPTANCE [J2, J4, J9]

It is the nature of the beta test product or service that it almost certainly contains undetected errors or faults. The customer is well aware of this and takes the equipment "as is" and is in no way able to rely on its performance, robustness or anything else, though he should have taken reasonable steps to inform himself of its general condition beforehand. Full acceptance procedures are inappropriate here, particularly as the customer is not taking full title to the equipment or software but merely a limited licence. It is therefore reasonable for the agreement to begin from the date of delivery and to have no separate acceptance procedure. Another way of looking at it is to describe the evaluation itself as an extended acceptance procedure.

In some agreements—particularly those which tend more towards the software evaluation type—the customer is required at the end of the test period either to return the hardware or software being tested or to place an order. Failure to do either is deemed to mean that the customer is willing to place an order. Consider the following:

> "The Customer is expected within 7 days of the expiry of the Test period either to return the Product to the Company or to place an order for its procurement. If the Customer fails to do this after a further 14 days' written notice from the Company to the Customer requiring it so to do the Customer shall be deemed to have agreed to purchase the Product. The terms and conditions applicable to the procurement of the Product, howsoever invoked, shall be the Company's then current commercial 'Hardware Agreement' terms in relation to the supply of the same or similar products."

Although under English law it is not usually possible to infer acceptance from silence, the fact that such a provision is itself embodied in an agreed contract is likely to make it enforceable.

A particular point to notice is that in the case of test hardware (unlike ordinary hardware contracts [2.3.3]) the insurable risk may well remain with the supplier since title does not pass to the customer and indeed the customer is providing a form of service to the supplier in testing the hardware at all. There remains, nevertheless, an obligation on the customer to take all reasonable steps to ensure that the hardware is safeguarded against obvious hazards, and the supplier will need to impose a duty of care on the customer to ensure that such safeguards are in fact in place (and potentially also impose an obligation upon the customer to insure, perhaps to a value specified by the supplier).

6.4 TERMINATION [J6]

Almost all agreements of this type have a definite termination period that could of course be extended if the parties agree. In the preceding section we have already considered the possibility that on termination the product tested must be either returned or purchased. As the period is very short premature termination is not usually a problem and need not be considered here.

When a product is ready to launch on the market it is unlikely that the supplier will wish to leave any beta test versions in the hands of third parties. Accordingly a right is often reserved to recall test versions when the final product launch is imminent. Alternatively, a logic bomb [6.7, 3.2.2] may be used to destroy or disable the software.

6.5 ALTERATIONS [J7]

Again, the short period of the trial means that changes are not very likely. Sometimes, the agreement may be for a range of products to be tested either in succession or simultaneously but this does not usually constitute a change to the arrangement once it has been signed. In a longer-term arrangement the parties may anticipate an improved beta test version becoming available and the supplier may reserve the right to substitute this for an existing version to get the full benefit of the customer's evaluation.

6.6 CUSTOMER'S DUTIES [J5]

The first duty will of course be to test the hardware or software. It is important from the supplier's point of view that this test begins as soon as possible and to this extent the test is somewhat similar in character to an acceptance test following delivery. Failure by the customer to make proper use of the hardware or software would be of no use to either side.

A related requirement is for the customer to report as rapidly as possible to the manufacturer any defects or problems which he may encounter with the product. As he can anticipate a high level of response from the supplier this should operate in the interests of both sides.

It is the nature of beta tests that they relate to new products or software and confidentiality will therefore be very important. The supplier will wish to keep secret from its competitors not only the functions and capabilities of the new product but also its very existence. The premature announcement of a new product can have a dramatic impact on sales of existing products and may significantly reduce the value of stocks held by the supplier and its distributors. There may therefore be far stricter and higher levels of confidentiality exacted from the customer than would normally be the case (which will in particular extend to the results of the tests themselves, which the supplier will be anxious to keep to itself).

Some agreements seek to limit the use of the hardware or software to evaluation purposes only. This may not be entirely sensible since it is the nature of the tests that they should be as realistic as possible and the only way to do this is with real data. It is therefore reasonable for the customer to wish to process genuine workloads and have the benefit of such processing. However, this may give rise to a risk of the loss or corruption of live data, and accordingly needs to be carefully considered. In particular, the supplier will not expect to take any responsibility for faulty or lost processing of what is admitted to be an immature product. The customer's risk in doing this has already been compensated for by the supplier in letting him begin to use the product early, obtain it at an advantageous price, and enjoy a much higher level of support.

When dealing with an evaluation version of a software package, it will be particularly important for the customer to ensure that it does not fall into other hands and if he allows it so to do, he may find himself deemed to have acted as an agent for the original supplying company and obliged to provide them with an appropriate fee.

6.7 SUPPLIER'S DUTIES [J2, J8]

These include delivery of the product, its insurance while still on the customer's premises, and the provision of a high level of support and maintenance.

There will not usually be any liability on the supplier for the experimental hardware or software in terms of its performance, capacity, or even fitness for purpose. However, there may need to be a provision on liability to deal with any period of time during which the hardware or software is in live use, even if this is set out at a lower level than normal.

The supplier will of course retain all title to the product right to the end of the test period and after, unless the customer then purchases it (or, in the case of software, acquires a "full" licence in respect of it). The supplier will therefore require the customer to deliver up the product, destroy copies (if for software), or purchase it outright, as appropriate or (with the customer's agreement) he will use the logic bomb [6.4, 3.2.2] to destroy or disable it.

Intellectual property rights will be relevant in a testing context and the customer should insist on the usual indemnity against claims by third parties that their intellectual property rights have been infringed. However, the customer will not otherwise acquire any rights in respect of any changes, modifications, or alterations made to the products during the evaluation period.

CHAPTER 7

LEASES

7.1 Introduction
7.2 Accounting Treatment of Leases
7.3 Tax Treatment of Leases
7.4 Advantages of Leasing
7.5 Lessee's Enforcement of Warranties
7.6 Software Licensing

7.1 INTRODUCTION

Leasing is a relatively simple method for an organisation to obtain the right to use or acquire computer equipment, where the leasing company (called the *lessor*) retains ownership of the asset and grants the lessee, or organisation seeking to acquire the equipment, a right to use/purchase it over the term of the lease in return for the payment of a fixed sum at regular intervals. Under a third-party lease, the equipment is purchased from the supplier by a third-party leasing company (*lessor*), which then hires it to the customer who intends to use it (*lessee*). Usually, it will differ from a rental agreement principally in that the lessor will be a separate entity from the supplier of the equipment.

Under a lease, title to the asset normally remains with the lessor. This fact presents a key advantage to the lessor of leasing computer equipment, namely the ability to claim capital allowances against tax, which are available to the owner of the equipment. However, this fact also means that the lessee may be able to upgrade the leased equipment or software without the need for new capital outlay. For both lessor and lessee, the decision to lease computer equipment will have accounting, tax and risk implications. This chapter discusses these three factors and their impact on lessor and lessee.

Leases of hardware and software are, of course, subject to the general provisions of hardware and software contracts [Chapters 2 and 3]. This chapter presupposes knowledge of those chapters and assumes that the kinds of clauses described in those chapters are, where relevant, incorporated. As leases give rise to types of problems different to those of outright purchase, the structure of this chapter necessarily differs from that of the previous chapters in order to focus on those differences. In view of the size of this topic and the relatively small proportion of IT law we also do not think it worth providing a precedent.

7.2 ACCOUNTING TREATMENT OF LEASES

In the U.K., the accounting requirements for leases are governed by the Standard Statement of Accounting Practice 21 (SSAP 21), "Accounting for leases and hire purchase contracts", where a lease is defined as "a contract between the lessor and the lessee for the hire of a specific asset". This definition also catches hire purchase contracts, which are treated as leases for accounting, but not for tax, purposes [7.3]. Under SSAP 21, leasing agreements can be classified into two types, with a different accounting treatment of each type. One is simply an arrangement enabling the lessee to enjoy the use of the equipment (*operating lease*) whilst the other is primarily a source of finance (*finance lease*). An operating lease is one under which the majority of the risks and rewards of ownership of the asset remain with the lessor, whereas a finance lease is one which "transfers substantially all the risks and rewards of ownership of an asset to the lessee". This is deemed to occur where the minimum lease payments amount to substantially all (normally 90 per cent or more) of the value of the leased equipment. Although all leases normally transfer some of the risks and rewards of ownership of the leased asset to the lessee, whether a particular lease is an operating or a finance lease will generally be evident from its terms.

7.2.1 Operating lease

This type of lease either runs for a short fixed period or is subject to termination by the lessee on short notice at any time (or after a stated initial period).

The lessor will charge a rent fixed by market rates and, as it expects to re-lease the equipment to other customers before the end of the equipment's useful life, will allow for the asset's depreciation (usually on a straight line basis) over the period of the lease. The leased property is an asset of the lessor, who accounts for the rental income (after deducting maintenance and insurance charges) in the profit and loss account. The lessee simply treats the rental payments as an expense.

Operating leases are popular where there is a buoyant second-hand market for the equipment. The lessee may prefer an operating lease where the equipment is subject to rapid changes in technology, as the lessee may, in these circumstances, not want it for the whole of its useful life. The lessor will normally purchase the equipment before being approached by the lessee and will usually be experienced in its technology. He will also bear the burdens and risks of ownership and will usually maintain and insure the equipment. The risk of obsolescence of the equipment will clearly be reflected in the lease rentals but where the lessor is associated with the manufacturer he may be better informed than the user about anticipated obsolescence and will be able to price accordingly.

Operating leases are similar in many respects to rental agreements [2.2.2], and are therefore not dealt with separately further in this chapter, although the problem of software licence transfer [7.6] applies equally to them.

7.2.2 Finance lease

The finance lease, as its name suggests, is essentially a source of medium to long-term finance and provides the customer with an alternative to borrowing on an outright purchase. It runs for a minimum fixed period which reflects the estimated useful life of the equipment so that there will be only one lessee. In contrast to the operating lease, where the lessor is effectively providing a service to the lessee and under which the lessor's profits are calculated from income for the provision of the service over the term of the lease, under a finance lease the lessor is providing a financial service (provision of funding for the asset) and the lessor's profits are therefore calculated on the basis of the cost to the lessor of purchasing the equipment plus his desired return on capital, after taking account of such variables as the lessor's entitlement to capital allowances and grants (and the delay between incurring the expenditure on the equipment and receiving the benefit of such allowances and grants) and rental cash flow. Under SSAP 21, a finance lease is required to be shown in the balance sheet of the lessee as an asset with the obligation to pay future lease payments being shown as a liability.

The lessor will purchase, own and eventually sell the equipment. In practice, however, it is the lessee who accepts the burdens and risks of ownership (such as obsolescence, defects and loss). The lessee usually initiates the transaction by choosing the equipment and the supplier, and by arranging for the lessor to buy the equipment and then lease it to him. The lessee will normally also be responsible for negotiating the sale contract with the supplier.

7.2.3 Future developments in accounting for leases

The Accounting Standards Board is currently reviewing the distinction between accounting for the two types of lease (see the ASB Discussion Paper "Leases: Implementation of a New Approach", December 1999). At the time of printing, their proposed standard to replace SSAP 21 removes the distinction between finance and operating leases and instead requires lessors and lessees to account for their rights and obligations under all leases. At the beginning of the lease, the lessee would account for the fair value of the rights and obligations under the lease (normally the present value of the minimum rental payments required under the lease plus other liabilities incurred). In subsequent years, the leased asset would be shown in the accounts in accordance with the normal principles for fixed assets and debt. The lessor would account for financial assets (payments receivable from the lessee) and the residual interest in the asset as separate assets.

7.3 TAX TREATMENT OF LEASES

In contrast to accounting, the tax treatment of a lease is dependent on its legal form, not on the effective economic ownership of the asset. In particular, under a hire purchase contract, the customer "owns" the asset for tax purposes, whereas for leases, ownership rests with the lessee.

7.3.1 Tax issues for lessors

One particular tax issue which affects lessors is capital allowances. As discussed in paragraph 7.2.2 above, the lessor will normally set the lease rentals on the basis that he is entitled to receive capital allowances which can be deducted from trading profits when computing corporation tax. There are three basic conditions which must be met before the lessor can claim the allowance: he must incur capital expenditure, the machinery or plant (or software—see below) must belong or have belonged to the lessor as a consequence of his incurring that expenditure and the expenditure must have been incurred for the purposes of the lessor's trade or deemed trade. Particular care is needed when drafting finance leases, under which substantially all of the risks and rewards of ownership pass to the lessee, as the lessor must have legal title to the asset as a prerequisite to claiming capital allowances.

Capital allowances are not calculated on assets individually. Instead, expenditure on machinery and plant assets is "pooled". There is no apparent difficulty in classifying expenditure on hardware as machinery and plant. The position in relation to software was defined in the Finance (No. 2) Act 1992, s. 68, which introduced the right for the lessor to claim an allowance on capital expenditure on a right to use or otherwise deal with computer software. The expenditure will be treated as having been incurred on machinery or plant for the purposes of the lessor's trade and, so long as the lessor is entitled to this right, the software will be treated as his (see Capital Allowances Act 1990, s. 67A). The term "computer software" is not defined by the Capital Allowances Act 1990. It is understood that the Inland Revenue considers that the term includes both programs and data.

Where capital expenditure is incurred on software which is not machinery or plant (*e.g.* where the software is acquired by electronic means), it is nevertheless treated as such for capital allowance purposes. In relation to the lease of licensed software, a lump sum payment for the licence will be capital expenditure if the licence is of a sufficiently enduring nature to be considered a capital asset in the context of the lessor's trade. Equally, the benefit may be transitory (and the expenditure revenue) even though the licence is for an indefinite period. Inspectors of Taxes will in any event accept that expenditure is on revenue account where the software has a useful economic life of less than two years, the timing of the deduction again depending on normal accountancy practice.

This two-year-rule raises a potential problem with regard to software versions since it is usual for commercial software to be reissued (and a new licence granted) about once a year. In theory, therefore, a licence to use a piece of software could be purchased in year 1 (version 1) and by year 3 the licensee could have abandoned use of that licence and be using a completely new version (version 2) of the software under a new licence granted to him in the intervening period. Much will presumably depend on whether he has *purchased* a new licence as such, or whether the new version is made available to him under a general maintenance contract which also doubtless provides "patches" for intermediate versions as well as general mainte-nance advice. In this latter case, the expenditure on version 1 may or may not be capital but that on version 2 is clearly on the revenue account since the licensee has primarily contracted for a service. If, however, the licensee has actually paid for a new version as if buying a new piece of software, it seems arguable that it could be considered capital expenditure if for more than two years. Otherwise, it must be revenue. On balance then, it may be quite difficult to establish that software licence expenditure is capital, though this is most likely to be the case if it is for the first version of that software which the licensee has purchased.

Expenditure on a package containing both hardware and a licence to use software must be apportioned before these principles are applied. Currently, capital allowances on expenditure on plant and machinery is available as an annual writing down allowance of 25 per cent on a reducing balance basis. This has resulted in an increase in the effective rate of interest payable under leasing agreements. This notional interest rate is greater for short-term leases where the writing down allowances do not absorb the full purchase price of the equipment. The popularity of finance leasing diminished as a result of the abolition of first year capital allowances with effect from March 31, 1986 and the reduction in the rate of corporation tax over recent years. Although these were reintroduced in the first Labour Budget in 1997 for small and medium sized businesses, expenditure on plant and machinery for leasing is excluded. Until the abolition of first year allowances, the finance lease compared favourably with alternative forms of finance. The lessor was, in effect, able to give away a large percentage of the tax saved as a result of the first year allowance by passing this on to the lessee in the form of reduced rentals. Finance leases are not dead and one still finds lessors willing to give away at least some of their writing down allowances to lessees in order to offer reduced rental payments. Because of the reducing nature of writing down allowances, it is unlikely that lessors will enter into leases for more than five years, as by that time 76 per cent has been written down and it is unlikely to be cost-effective to continue thereafter.

If the equipment is likely to be scrapped or sold for nominal value within five years of first use then it may be advantageous to the lessor to elect for the equipment to be treated as a "short life asset" (Capital Allowances Act 1990, s. 37). The residue of expenditure not written down at sale or scrapping can be deducted as a balancing allowance as opposed to remaining in the "pool" of expenditure being written down at 25 per cent per annum. However, the penalty is that every piece of equipment must form a separate calculation in the capital allowance computation and increased administration costs will be incurred. Expenditure on software qualifying for capital allowances by virtue of the Capital Allowances Act 1990, s. 67A, may also qualify for the special treatment for expenditure on "short life assets".

7.3.2 Tax issues for lessees

For the lessee, regular payments such as operating lease rentals will usually be a fully deductible expense for tax purposes for the year in which they are payable. Finance lease rentals will also be a tax deductible expense as they are charged to the accounts in accordance with the normal principles of commercial accountancy under SSAP 21 (see *Gallagher v. Jones: Threlfall v. Jones* [1993] S.T.C. 537).

7.4 ADVANTAGES OF LEASING

In view of the reduced advantages of the finance lease, the user of equipment will now need to consider carefully whether he should lease or buy his equipment either outright or under a hire purchase contract. Capital allowances arising on a purchase will not be of immediate benefit where the lessee is currently carrying on business at a loss and it may be advantageous to lease the equipment, permitting the lessor to claim these in exchange for his passing some of the benefit on to the lessee in the shape of reduced rentals. If a company does wish to purchase but at the same time ease its cash flow, hire purchase may be the answer. The hirer is entitled to writing down allowances on the full cost of the equipment. If a company does purchase its equipment outright any interest paid on borrowings will be tax deductible. Generally speaking, where the lease term equates with the useful life of the equipment it is more advantageous to lease than it is to borrow. Rental payments are lower because the lessor has the residual value of the equipment and can also afford to give away some of his writing down allowances. However, the lessee should remember that when he commits to a leasing agreement the "notional interest rate" is fixed, whereas by borrowing (especially where he foresees a fall in interest rates) the lessee may be able to take advantage of loan finance at variable interest rates.

Unlike hire purchase or bank borrowings, leasing companies can sometimes offer more flexible payment terms. In addition, lessors are less inclined to seek guarantees or other security for their contracts.

When acquiring computer equipment obsolescence can be a key factor in determining whether the user opts to buy or lease, or indeed whether to take a finance or an operating lease. If a significant change in technology does take place, the lessee who holds his equipment under an operating lease can quickly change his old computer for a new one at a marginally increased rental. This may override all other considerations.

It should not be forgotten that the finance lease is essentially not a short-term arrangement. There will be few opportunities to terminate before the contractual term and even then the lessor will usually look to be compensated for the rentals he has forgone. Rental increases are also a possibility. Because the lessor's return can be affected by such matters as changes in the law relating to capital allowances, leases often provide for a variation in rentals to compensate for any loss caused to the lessor in such circumstances.

7.5 LESSEE'S ENFORCEMENT OF WARRANTIES

In circumstances where the lessor is not involved in the selection of the equipment or the supplier and relies on the lessee to use his own skill and judgement, the lessor will not usually give the lessee any warranties in relation to the equipment and will attempt to exclude any implied in the lessee's favour by law. The effectiveness of such an exclusion will be subject to the Unfair Contract Terms Act 1977. It might be thought that because the lessor has little responsibility for or control over defects in the equipment the courts will regard such exclusions as reasonable. However, this appears not to be the case for in *Lease Management Services Limited v. Purnell* [1994] 13 Tr.L. 337, the court held that an exclusion clause is not rendered reasonable because it is imposed by a finance company rather than the original equipment supplier. This case has not been discussed following the implementation of the Contracts (Rights of Third Parties) Act 1999 (see below and [1.3]) but if the lessee has rights to bring a claim directly against the supplier for breach of warranty, the imposition of an exclusion clause in the lease seems likely to now be considered reasonable under the Unfair Contract Terms Act 1977.

Under the Contracts (Rights of Third Parties) Act 1999, the lessee may be able to take advantage of any warranties given by the supplier to the lessor in the sale contract. The lessee will be able to enforce these warranties directly if it is identified in the contract either by name, or simply as a "lessee" (s. 3). In addition, the term containing the relevant warranty must be expressly stated to be enforceable by the lessee (s 1(1)(a)), or must purport to benefit the lessee and the contract must not indicate that the supplier and the lessor did not intend the warranty to be enforceable by the lessee (ss. 1(1)(b) and (2)).

The right of the lessee to recover for the supplier's breach of warranty will be subject to any exclusion or limitation clauses contained in the sale contract (s. 1(4)), and the supplier will be protected from liability to both the lessor and lessee in respect of the same breach of warranty by section 5 of the Act.

A prudent lessor will attempt to identify the lessee by name or as a "lessee" in his contract with the supplier, and obtain warranties that are expressly stated to be for the benefit of the lessee, as the lessee is likely to require the right to enforce these directly against the supplier. This will be particularly important if the lessor intends to lease the equipment under a finance lease, where the lessee assumes the risks of ownership of the equipment and will wish to bring claims directly against the supplier for breach of warranty.

The lessor usually acquires title to the equipment in one of three ways:

(1) by himself entering into a contract with the supplier;

(2) by appointing the lessee as his agent to contract with the supplier;

(3) by taking over the contract already entered into by the lessee with the supplier by means of a contract called a novation agreement between the supplier, the lessor and the lessee.

In its simplest form the novation agreement provides for the supplier and the lessee to be released from their respective obligations and for the lessor to purchase the equipment from the supplier in the lessee's place. An alternative is for the three parties to enter into a hybrid of the novation agreement. Such an agreement provides for the lessor to take over the lessee's obligation to pay for the equipment (and consequently for the lessor to acquire title) in return for the lessee agreeing to lease the equipment from the lessor. In other respects, the sale agreement remains intact. The lessee is entitled to the benefits of the sale agreement (including warranties and delivery and installation obligations) subject to his complying with its burdens. This type of agreement has the important practical advantage of resulting in relatively little disturbance of standard documentation. All the obligations to be performed will be the same as in any ordinary sale agreement and will be performed by the same parties (namely the supplier and the lessee). The lessor's involvement is minimal—he simply has to pay the price and take title in accordance with the terms of the sale agreement once the equipment has been accepted. The lease will also be simplified because all the lessor need do is to impose an obligation on the lessee to comply with the terms of the modified sale agreement, rather than set out the lessee's obligations (as to preparation of installation site, taking of delivery, acceptance testing, etc.) in detail.

In entering into a novation agreement the parties should ensure that title to the equipment has not already passed to the lessee (this is unlikely as most contracts provide for title to pass only on payment of the purchase price in full) and that the contract is wholly unperformed. Failure to do this may have adverse tax consequences. Needless to say, the lessee must ensure, prior to his signing the contract of sale, that the supplier and the lessor will enter into the novation agreement.

7.6 SOFTWARE LICENSING

Special arrangements will have to be made regarding the licensing of software in a leasing transaction.

The lessee will, of course, require a right to use the software during the continuance of the lease but the lessor will also wish to acquire rights. The lessor's need is not so much a right to use the software as a need to protect his investment. If the lessee defaults on rental payments the lessor will usually hope to recover his investment by proceeding against the lessee for the rental payments due in respect of the remainder of the lease (suitably discounted) or, if there is one, by claiming under a third party guarantee. If, however, the lessee is insolvent or there is no guarantee, then, in order to recover as much of his investment as possible, the lessor has one of three options:

(1) sell the equipment back to the supplier; or

(2) sell the equipment to a third party; or

(3) re-lease the equipment to a third party.

The first option does not cause a problem but the effectiveness of the other two may depend on the lessor being able to license the purchaser or subsequent lessee to use the software, as the equipment may be virtually useless without the software. If the lessor cannot grant such a licence then the purchaser or subsequent lessee will have to acquire a licence direct from the supplier at a fee. This would mean that the lessor would be unable to recover his investment on software, which could be serious if software represents a significant part of the value of the system.

The lessor will therefore need to negotiate an appropriate arrangement with the supplier to protect himself. One means of achieving this would be for the supplier to grant to the lessor a licence to use the software, together with rights (a) to grant sub-licences to lessees; and (b) to assign the benefit of his licence to a purchaser (but so that the licence in the hands of the purchaser will not be assignable) during a period equal to the minimum period of the first lease. In this way the lessor can recover his investment in full.

A supplier may argue that a purchaser or subsequent lessee should pay an additional licence fee. However, the lessor can point out with some justification that if the supplier sold the equipment direct to the customer he would not reasonably expect to obtain more than one licence fee during the useful working life of the equipment.

A lessee will also be concerned to see that a purchaser can be licensed to use the software, so that on a voluntary termination of the lease by the lessee prior to the expiry of the minimum period, the resale value of the equipment will be as high as possible, thus ensuring the maximum set-off against the termination payment due under the lease. However, in these circumstances the supplier may argue more forcibly that an additional licence fee should be paid.

PART II

MAINTENANCE

CHAPTER 8

HARDWARE MAINTENANCE

8.0 Introduction
8.1 Services to be Performed
8.2 Payment
8.3 Limitations and Exceptions
8.4 Termination
8.5 Variation
8.6 Customer's Duties
8.7 Supplier's Duties

8.0 INTRODUCTION

In Chapter 2 on hardware we have seen that it is usual in a rental agreement for the supplier to require the customer to maintain the equipment in good order [2.6.4]. In the case of a lease, the supplier or third party leasing company usually specifies who shall perform this maintenance. Generally, it is the supplier himself. In this chapter, we consider such a hardware maintenance agreement; in the next, we examine the more nebulous concept of software maintenance.

For convenience, we refer to the company performing the maintenance as "the supplier" since in many cases the supplier is the sole maintainer. The alternative where this is not so (the "mixed shop") is discussed below [8.5.1].

PC maintenance for a company with a number of machines to support is not necessarily different from other kinds of hardware maintenance. For the rather different case of the maintenance of a single home PC, see 4.2.2.

8.1 SERVICES TO BE PERFORMED

8.1.1 Equipment and Location [K1]

These are usually defined in exactly the same way as in a hardware contract [2.1.1, 2.1.2]. For PCs and laptops, the concept of a location is slightly difficult. It is the nature of a laptop that it is moved around. This may also be true of some PCs.

This inherently exposes the laptop to additional risks, and the best that can be arranged here is either that laptops (which are basically fairly reliable machines) are supported only on a call-out basis—*i.e.* the user pays separately each time he requires an engineer to attend—or at best the equipment is only maintained at a

124

single location, which means that the user must bring his laptop back to base—*i.e.* the location identified in the contract—before the maintenance contractor can deal with it.

8.1.2 Service

Maintenance is usually concerned with two separate types of engineer service:

(a) preventive maintenance; and

(b) corrective maintenance.

Preventive maintenance [K2 (1)]

Preventive maintenance is concerned with the regular testing and treating of the equipment. This includes the running of the diagnostic programs (which will probably be the same as those used for pre- and post-delivery tests [2.3.2, 2.3.4]), the adjusting of those features which may through use have got out of tune (for example, on an impact printer the tension of the paper is critical: if it is too taut the type will pierce it; if it is too slack the impression will be unclear or smudged and the paper may not feed properly), the checking of disk-head alignment, and generally advising the customer of the condition of the equipment, including the likelihood of his requiring replacements. On this basis, the installation site will be visited regularly (say every six months) by a suitable engineer. For example:

> "The Supplier shall make visits for the periodic servicing of the Equipment to test the functions thereof and make any adjustments the Supplier deems necessary to keep it in good working order. Such visits shall be on Mondays to Fridays (public holidays excluded) between the hours of *9 a.m.* and *5 p.m.*."

Notice first that the definition of "servicing" means that the customer's ideas of how the equipment should work are irrelevant unless shared by the supplier. The customer should agree in advance criteria to define working. Secondly, the supplier stipulates that the maintenance shall be during ordinary working hours. For a machine which will be worked round the clock, this may present problems, and any scheduling should take account of engineers' visits. In practice, this is unlikely to be too serious a problem, since it will often be possible to run the engineer's diagnostic test programs at the same time as other programs—providing either that they use different peripheral devices or that slightly slower running of the customer's application programs is possible. In practice, a supplier will, as far as possible, fit in with a customer's schedules.

Corrective maintenance [K2 (2)]

Corrective maintenance means the remedying of defects or mechanical faults which arise. Visits for this kind of maintenance are usually in response to a service call from the customer to say that some particular piece of equipment does not work:

> "The Supplier shall make emergency service available on request on Mondays to Fridays (public holidays excepted) each week throughout the year between the hours of *9 a.m.* and *5 p.m.* to rectify a breakdown or malfunction of the Equipment and on receipt of such a request from the Customer shall send an engineer to the Installation Site as soon as reasonably practicable at the said times to test adjust or repair the Equipment as may seem to him appropriate."

Notice again the emphasis on ordinary working hours. If the customer is likely to be performing time-critical work outside ordinary working hours, he should take this up with his supplier. If it is merely a question of running the payroll program on Thursday nights, the supplier will probably point out that, even if the agreement allowed the customer to telephone for an engineer at 2 a.m., there would inevitably be a delay of some hours before the engineer arrived, and more time would elapse before the problem was cured; in other words, the customer would do better to replan his schedules to envisage the possibility of interruption or delay. The most likely candidates for truly time-critical programs are real-time applications—for instance, a traffic flow system controlling the use of traffic lights in a large city. In this case, the stand- by facilities are likely to be very much more copious than in ordinary commercial processing, and might include a duplication of part or all of the system. The time taken by a supplier from receipt of the customer's request for corrective maintenance to having an engineer on the customer's premises is called *response time*—a term to be distinguished from system's response time defined above [3.3.2].

Should a customer have an application like the traffic flow system and have taken the supplier's advice about duplicating part or all of his system in the interests of stand-by facilities, he must then seek to negotiate with the supplier for a special maintenance agreement. He may also seek a back-up agreement with the owner of another installation similar to his own and geographically near it. It is usual for two users of similar configurations of equipment to enter into mutual back-up agreements, whereby in certain circumstances each undertakes to provide spare capacity on his machine to the other. Such agreements are in effect bureau agreements [Chapter 10] and must:

(1) define the circumstances;

(2) define the configuration and capacity available;

(3) define any timescale or other limitations on the use of the service;

(4) specify personnel and define access to the premises;

(5) specify price (if any—in mutual agreements there may be no price).

Both sides should try the arrangements out rather than await the disaster which will make them necessary. Compatibility of the two systems is essential. In practice such agreements are difficult to set up, unless the alternative machine is very lightly used and can easily accommodate the new load as well as its existing load. There are now specialist disaster recovery contractors available to provide these services on a paid (as opposed to mutual) basis. As to how to find an appropriate installation, see below on User Groups [15.6].

In other cases, the agreement is often more specific about the speed with which an engineer will arrive at the installation. This will in fact depend on the distance the installation site is from the supplier's nearest service area, but a typical example might be:

"In this Agreement 'Working Hours' means the time between 9 *a.m.* and 5 *p.m.* on all Mondays to Fridays except public holidays . . .

The Supplier shall make emergency service available to the Customer who requests such service within Working Hours and on receipt of such request will despatch an engineer to assist at the Installation Site within the next *eight* Working Hours after such request was received . . ."

In other words, if a customer telephones for an engineer at 3 p.m. on a Tuesday afternoon, the engineer may turn up at any time between 3 p.m. and 5 p.m. on Tuesday, or 9 a.m. and 2 p.m. on Wednesday. This kind of agreement is extremely common, and is what is usually meant by an "eight-hour maintenance agreement" ("four-hour" maintenance agreements are also common). It does not mean that the engineer will arrive within eight elapsed hours after the call is put in if any of those hours are outside working hours. Still less does it mean that the fault will be rectified in eight hours—or, indeed, in any particular number of hours. However, an escalation procedure [8.7.1] will at least ensure that the customer can vent his frustration against a more senior member of the supplier's staff than the luckless engineer.

The supplier will need to schedule his maintenance services by priority (four-hour response before eight-hour, for example). This means that customers with no formal agreement who simply pay on a call-out basis often receive a poor response time.

When the customer first contacts his supplier he will usually be given a call number—*i.e.* a serial number uniquely identifying that particular call. Any future enquiries must be referenced by that same number. The software at the supplier's end will then call up that call number and display the current state of the call. It is accordingly essential that the customer's staff understand the system and have procedures which fit in with those of the supplier, so as to be able to make full use of the support services on offer and track the progress being made by the supplier.

In many instances, on-line diagnostics are used, whereby the customer's machine can be linked by telecommunications to diagnostic programs and equipment on the supplier's premises. In this way the fault can often be pinpointed by telephone and it may even be possible to cure the fault by telephone in some instances. Sometimes the supplier is prepared to provide the modem free of charge to facilitate this. The customer should ensure that the use of the modem is entirely under his control so that the supplier can eavesdrop on the customer's system only when the customer authorises it (which should be only when a fault has been reported) and that once the fault has been satisfactorily dealt with, the on-line link to the supplier is broken. To do otherwise will undermine the customer's security arrangements and almost certainly fall foul of the security-related requirements of the Data Protection Act 1998. As a precaution the customer should notify this possible disclosure of personal data to the Data Protection Commissioner, and receive an indemnity from the supplier in respect of any unauthorised disclosure or use of personal data [8.7.2].

Furthermore, it may be argued that the supplier in these circumstances becomes a bureau ("data processor") for the customer and the precautions as to security etc which are required for bureaux handling personal data are no less applicable here [10.3.3, K15 (2)].

Nevertheless, the clauses described above guaranteeing response time should still appear in the contract, as a safeguard.

Spares

The question of what spare parts may reasonably be kept, and who will keep them, must be considered. Sometimes, the supplier will look after this:

> "The Supplier will keep a stock of spare parts at his Service Centre nearest to the Installation Site."

Sometimes, the supplier will require the customer to keep spares. A clause to this effect is described below [8.6.4]. There we notice that the purpose of the clause is probably to reduce the service charge to the customer; it may also reflect the distance of the customer from the nearest service centre.

A word about the location of suppliers' service areas: when negotiating with his supplier, the customer should always enquire where the nearest service area is. In practice, the supplier may offer to open a new service area (*i.e.* take on a new engineer) specially for one particular customer, if the customer's business is big enough. At any rate, if the service area seems uncommonly distant, this will be a good reason for the customer to query the credibility of the maintenance service being offered.

8.2 PAYMENT [B14, K4]

Payment for both preventive and corrective maintenance is usually by a single annual charge spread over monthly or quarterly payments in advance. The annual charge varies, but may typically be at or near 12 per cent of the purchase price of main frames. However, such a figure cannot necessarily be maintained in the future [8.5.2]. Obsolescence and technological advance may reduce the list price of the equipment, but the effect of this will probably be to increase the maintenance cost since spares will probably be produced in smaller quantities and it will be less worthwhile for the supplier to train and maintain engineers who can repair equipment at only one or two installations.

A typical payment clause reads:

> "The Customer will pay to the Supplier monthly in advance the sum of £x charge for the Service the first such payment falling due promptly on the commencement of this Agreement."

8.3 LIMITATIONS AND EXCEPTIONS [K5]

The maintenance service provided by the supplier is subject to numerous limitations and exceptions. Many of these are breaches of the customer's duties which are more particularly described below [8.6]—*e.g.* failure to use and care for the equipment properly. Others (like *force majeure*) are common to all agreements. But some may be considered here.

8.3.1 Frivolous calls [K7]

Most agreements have a clause preventing the customer from summoning an engineer on a frivolous pretext:

> "If the Customer requests the Supplier's service without good reason the Customer will be liable to pay to the Supplier in accordance with the Supplier's then subsisting scale of charges for such calls such charges being in addition to any other moneys due under this or any other agreement from the Customer to the Supplier."

Most examples of such clauses omit to define "good reason" or say in whose judgment a reason may be "good". Other clauses will be more specific, *e.g.* by listing specific types of circumstances which will be deemed to be outside the scope of reasonable maintenance, including call-outs due to problems caused by equipment other than that being supported, "phantom" problems which cannot be replicated, etc.

8.3.2 Out-of-hours maintenance [K7]

Despite what has been said relating to service [8.1.2], a customer may have an ordinary "four-hour maintenance" agreement and still wish on a particular occasion to have a service call out of hours. Many agreements cover this by adding a clause:

> "If the Customer requires to make a Service Request out of Working Hours he shall become liable to pay to the Supplier such charge as may be in force for the time being for such service calls in addition to any other charges due under this Agreement."

The customer may in turn wish to set a pre-defined table of rates to apply to such work.

8.3.3 Amount of usage

The contract is for a particular period, but it may be that the user wishes to use the equipment so heavily that signs of wear will show early. (Purchasers of cars will recognise that mileage, as well as age, is relevant to the car's reliability.) For example:

> "Maintenance under this Agreement does not cover any reconditioning required after a period equal or equivalent to 5 years' single shift usage."

With increasing hardware reliability, the less reliable elements of a system become more conspicuous and it is reasonable to assume that such elements will become still less dependable with age. Accordingly, some agreements stipulate that equipment over a particular age which contains moving or mechanical parts will not be maintained under the same agreement as that for the rest of the system, but will either attract a higher premium, or be maintained only on a "call-out" basis—*i.e.* the supplier charges separately for each call, rather than on a fixed price basis monthly, quarterly or even annually in advance.

The cost of maintenance to the supplier has been worked out on the basis of the mean time between failures (MTBF to engineers—or, as a slightly mealy-mouthed alternative, mean time between systems incidents (MTBSI))—for each separate piece of equipment. After a long period the MTBF could be alarmingly short: the supplier is therefore protecting himself. But notice that this limitation may sometimes be based on single-shift working—that is, working in ordinary office hours (or the equivalent). Some machines are worked on a double or even treble shift system and in those cases the agreement would for all practical purposes expire after two years and six months or one year eight months. If you expect to use your equipment as heavily as this, and your manufacturer includes a clause of this nature, you should seek clarification from him. If you think the above clause is hard, consider this variant:

> "When in the Supplier's opinion reconditioning of any part of the Equipment is considered necessary the Supplier will submit to the Customer a cost estimate for such reconditioning such costs being in addition to any charges within this Agreement. If the Customer declines to accept this cost estimate then the Supplier reserves the right to cancel this Agreement forthwith so far as it relates to that piece of Equipment or to terminate this Agreement forthwith if in the Supplier's opinion failure to recondition that piece of Equipment impairs the satisfactory operation of the whole of the Equipment."

The MTBF tells you the number of times, on average, that a piece of equipment is out of action, but not for how long it is out of action. This is dealt with by another set of initials—MTTR or mean time to repair.

8.3.4 Delays [K18]

Most suppliers will do their best to keep to the timescales within which they expect to be able to respond to a call for emergency maintenance for a customer. Nevertheless a supplier is likely to seek to exclude at least some of the responsibility for his failure to do so:

"The Supplier shall not be liable for any delay or the consequences thereof in performing any of his duties under this Agreement if such delay is due to any industrial dispute or any cause whatsoever beyond his reasonable control."

In this particular case the exclusion is not unreasonable.

8.4 TERMINATION [K14]

8.4.1 Term

Normally a maintenance agreement will be for a particular period; three years is common, though other periods often occur—66 months occurs in one clause. We have already seen [8.3.3] that the equipment is likely to need more maintenance as it gets older, so this is one reason for a time limitation. But many agreements visualise the supplier increasing the charges [8.5.2] and therefore that is not necessarily the whole story. The truth is that where the company effecting the maintenance is the manufacturer or supplier, they will not wish to have to commit engineers to the task of maintaining obsolete equipment for perhaps a handful of customers—particularly as the supplier hopes by then to have a newer (and more easily maintained) machine available.

Many agreements are not for a fixed term but for a minimum term with the agreement continuing from month to month or year to year thereafter until determined by one or other party [8.4.2].

In the case of linked rental and maintenance agreements, maintenance will terminate at the same time as the rental.

8.4.2 Termination by notice

This may be after a minimum term, in the form:

"Subsequent to the Minimum Period either party shall be entitled to terminate this Agreement by giving to the other not less than 3 months' written notice to expire on the last day of a calendar month."

Three months' notice is easily the commonest notice period. For example, a supplier will sooner or later wish to terminate when the equipment is completely obsolete. The last provision in the example (for termination at the end of a full month) is to avoid apportionment of the charge for part months, but this is not so common. If an annual charge is paid the customer might expect reimbursement of part if the contract terminates otherwise than on the anniversary, but many contracts are silent on the point.

From the customer's point of view such notice from the supplier faces him with a dilemma: within, say, three months he must decide either to find an alternative maintenance contractor, which may be impossible if the one who is giving him notice is the manufacturer; or to upgrade to the manufacturer's more recent equipment. He should always be alive to the possibility that the manufacturer will not wish to maintain obsolescent equipment for ever and accordingly, if the equipment is getting obsolete it will be probably be better not to wait until he receives the three months' notice from the supplier, but instead well before that carry out an evaluation of the manufacturer's more recent equipment at the same time as alternative equipment from another supplier. In this way he will be purchasing competitively and give himself time to change suppliers or equipment.

8.4.3 Other terminations

An agreement can also be determined by breach of the customer's duties [8.6], or in some cases by failure of the customer to allow the supplier to recondition equipment (see the second example in 8.3.3), or to increase charges [8.5.2].

8.5 VARIATION

8.5.1 Variation of equipment [K1, K6]

The standard arrangement is that the agreement excludes any change in the equipment as defined (usually in the schedule). In practice, however, provided the equipment comes from the original supplier and maintenance charges have been negotiated in advance, it is generally possible to vary the charges and the list of the equipment. The dangerous situation from the point of view of the customer arises when new equipment is to be added which comes from a different supplier. An innocent-looking clause, *e.g.* "The Customer shall not make any movement of or alteration addition or attachment to the Equipment except with the Supplier's written consent" is designed to cover a complex situation. Obviously,

(a) it is very much easier and more efficient for a supplier to maintain equipment which is well-known to his staff; but

(b) it is in the supplier's interest to lock the customer into an agreement whereby the customer can buy his equipment only from the supplier.

Nevertheless, a flourishing market has grown up of suppliers whose equipment is fully compatible with, and designed to look like, that of major suppliers. Such equipment is often marketed by companies whose level of support and profit margins are lower than those of the main manufacturers, with the result that they can be offered at prices which are much lower than those of the manufacturers they are imitating. The big manufacturer's maintenance agreement with his customers is his most powerful weapon in keeping out the "plug-compatible" equipment. Any customer who wishes to take advantage of plug-compatible low prices must first decide how he is to cope with maintenance in an installation which becomes, in the jargon expression, a *mixed shop*. The solution is basically either to do all maintenance himself—and for some large customers it is practical for them to have their own engineers and maintenance staff; or to give the work to a third party maintenance company who may be the supplier of the plug-compatible equipment or who may be a separate maintenance company. No customer should consider the possibility of a mixed shop unless he can deal with the question of maintenance.

Another aspect of variation is the way in which many maintenance suppliers "swap out" equipment. The principle works like this: a customer contacts the supplier to ask for an engineer to call. The engineer does so, and either diagnoses a major fault or is unable with certainty to diagnose the precise fault at all. He exchanges the equipment for another one more or less identical while he takes the faulty one away for more detailed examination. The advantage of swapping out is that the customer has the fault cured very quickly while the supplier's engineer, instead of working under pressure, has all the time in the world to examine and correct the fault, and he can also more readily compare this fault with other faults in similar pieces of equipment which he is dealing with. However, the contractual aspect of this can be fairly serious and deserves careful thought.

In the first place, if the equipment list identifies each particular item of equipment by serial number, the supplier may actually be in breach in swapping out.

Secondly, at the very least the supplier may be exchanging a new piece of equipment for an old one and in some cases exchanging equipment for something which is not quite the same—e.g. an earlier model of the same piece of equipment or one whose performance is in some way more limited.

Thirdly, it may prove very difficult to decide at any one time who owns what. In an extreme case where a receiver is called in for a supplier's business, the receiver could require the customer to surrender part or all of his equipment to him.

Fourthly, if the equipment contains any data it will be necessary to make sure that this data cannot fall into anyone else's hands. This is especially important for personal data of any kind and letting it fall into other hands would be a breach of the Data Protection Act 1998. This is particularly likely to be the case with PCs where data in cache memory and on the disk can be retrieved fairly easily. Steps must be taken to erase data.

Fifthly, a different but similar problem arises with software. If a customer leaves software on equipment which he disposes of he will, at best, be being careless about the software owner's property since it will be possible for the person into whose hands the equipment falls, physically, albeit illegally, to use the software without a licence. The software owner could bring an action against him for the full value of the licence fee and possibly more. Again all software should be erased.

The matter is not helped by the proposed E.U. Waste from Electrical and Electronic Equipment Directive which if and when adopted in the U.K. will mean that all equipment must be recycled, and that customers should negotiate with suppliers to have equipment refurbished for others' use. The purpose behind all this is to benefit schools and charities by making sure that equipment which may not be the latest but is perfectly usable is not wasted—all very laudable, but the practical problems are considerable and there is much to be said for simply hitting the machine with something heavy.

Enough has been said to show that swapping out, whether of whole pieces of equipment or of their components, may have practical advantages, but is something of a contractual minefield, and while it is reasonable for the supplier to require (as in the sample clause above) that the customer should not alter his equipment, it seems no less reasonable that the customer should have the same safeguard against the supplier altering his equipment for the worse. The problem of ownership can be fairly readily dealt with by an appropriate clause [K6], but even with this safeguard the customer may still wish to think before agreeing to swap out.

Where the agreement is to maintain a number of PCs it is probably the case that the owner of the machines is constantly adding to their number, replacing older machines by more modern ones or increasing machines' memory or other features. There is thus not a fixed list of the equipment to be incorporated into a schedule. Clearly, the parties must as far as possible be agreed as to how many machines there are and of what type, but inevitably sooner or later a new machine will have been acquired which is not on the list and requires urgent maintenance attention.

The most helpful way for this to be dealt with is for the maintenance contractor to treat it as a valid machine to be maintained and sort the details out later. The customer is thus expected to advise the contractor after the maintenance has been effected when he acquired the machine so that the relevant maintenance charge for that machine can be backdated [K4 (3)].

8.5.2 Variation of charges [K4 (4)]

Many agreements visualise the possibility of varying charges. As the equipment becomes older and obsolescent, the number of staff the supplier will wish to use for its maintenance is likely to drop, and consequently the cost may rise. Inflation may also ensure that what was (say) 8.5 per cent of the list price last year may not be so high a percentage at next year's prices for the same equipment. Some such clause as this may appear:

> "The maintenance charges specified in the *xth* Schedule hereto are based on the Supplier's Scale of Charges in force at the date hereof. After the initial period of this Agreement all maintenance charges may be adjusted on *one month's* written notice by the Supplier to the Customer to correspond to the Supplier's Scale of Charges then in force."

To prevent the supplier from simply forcing the customer to terminate by quoting excessive new maintenance rates, in some long-term maintenance contracts the parties agree that the maintenance charges shall be increased by reference to the Retail Prices Index. The following is an example:

> "After the initial period of this Agreement has expired the Supplier shall be entitled to increase the maintenance charges at any time and from time to time by giving to the Customer not less than *one month's* notice in writing but any such increase shall not exceed a percentage equal to the percentage increase in the Retail Prices Index for the relevant period plus 3 per cent."

It should be noted that no definition of the "relevant period" is given and that there is no limit on the number of times that the Supplier may increase the charges.

Such clauses are of course appropriate in any contracts involving regular payments, but are particularly suitable in hardware maintenance agreements where the lifetime of the contract may be many years. It may also happen that the customer is dilatory in purchasing (and paying for the maintenance of) the original equipment. A manufacturer may therefore state:

> "At any time before the *x* months immediately preceding the date of commencement of the term of this Agreement the Supplier reserves the right to vary the charges to correspond to the Supplier's Scale of Charges then in force by written notice to the Customer. If the Customer does not accept these charges he may treat the Agreement as discharged by giving to the Supplier *one month's* notice in writing within 2 weeks of receiving the notice of variation of the charges."

This clause is usually of little effect unless there is an unusually long lead time.

8.6 CUSTOMER'S DUTIES

Many of these—such as the duty to pay [8.2] and not to attach other equipment [8.5.1]—have already been dealt with. However, there remain others which, while related to the last, are best considered here.

8.6.1 Use and care of the equipment [K9 (1)–(8)]

In addition to promising not to add to the equipment, the customer is also likely to be required to maintain the electricity supply and/or any environment, and to use the equipment properly. The first of these may be phrased negatively:

"Such repair or replacement shall be free of additional charge to the Customer unless caused by fluctuation in the electricity supply."

Power surges can be extremely damaging. Lifts which involve intermittent heavy use of electricity are the principal culprits, and customers would be well advised to obtain a power supply separate from that used by the rest of the building. Even when the power supply has been isolated in this way, it is still good practice to install equipment to inhibit the effect of any surges, and ensure that in the event of a power interruption or "brown out", the power for the hardware is either not interrupted at all, or at least for any fairly lengthy period, or is able to allow the system to shut down slowly while performing all necessary checks and completing any tasks.

In general, a customer is likely to be required to undertake:

"to maintain in good order the accommodation of the Equipment the cables and fittings associated therewith and the electrical supply thereto"

and he must also expect to be required:

"to keep and operate the Equipment in a prudent and proper manner in accordance with the Operator's Manual issued by the Supplier with the Equipment"

and:

"to use for the operation and servicing of the Equipment only those materials and supplies approved by the Supplier and listed in the Operator's Manual."

This is primarily concerned with print cartridges, stationery and so on. It follows also that he will:

"not allow the Equipment to be repaired serviced or otherwise attended to except by the Supplier's staff or by the Customer's own staff working according to the Supplier's Operator's Manual."

Finally, the customer may not move his computer [8.5.1].

8.6.2 Access [K9 (9)–(12)]

The next group of clauses refer to facilities to be provided by the customer to the supplier's staff. The first is obviously access and accommodation usually described as "full and fit" but the agreement may more specifically ask for:

"adequate working space around the Equipment for use of the Supplier's staff and adequate facilities for storage and safekeeping of test equipment and spares."

If the customer has had his site inspected by the supplier before delivery [2.6.3] and the supplier is, as is usually the case, the maintenance contractor, this should present no difficulty.

The agreement may also specify:

"a suitable vehicle parking facility which is free of any legal restrictions and immediately close to the Installation;"

or in certain cases:

"handling or lifting tackle scaffolding together with any labour required to move plant and equipment."

A further sensible precaution might be the following:

"In the interests of health and safety the Customer shall ensure that the Supplier's personnel whilst on the Customer's premises for the purposes of this Agreement are accompanied at all times by a member of the Customer's staff familiar with the Customer's premises and safety procedures."

This places the onus on the customer to ensure that the supplier's maintenance engineers are properly supervised and do not inadvertently cause damage by being ignorant of safety procedures. If damage does arise as a result of an engineer not being properly supervised then the blame will attach to the customer not the supplier.

8.6.3 Notification [K9 (13)–(17)]

An important requirement is usually that the customer will:

"promptly notify the Supplier if the Equipment needs maintenance or is not working correctly.

Failure by the Customer to notify the Supplier within 6 months of becoming aware of any such need for maintenance or any such failure to work correctly shall free the Supplier from all liability to investigate such need for maintenance or correct such fault."

This is designed to prevent the customer relying on some such vague complaint as that the equipment "has never worked".

A further aspect of notification is that the supplier will reasonably wish to know how the equipment has been used. As it is usual to keep a log of all usage the customer may find this embodied as an obligation on him. This is particularly likely where the equipment does not belong to the customer—e.g. in rental and leasing agreements [2.6.4]:

"The Customer will at all times keep a record of the use of the Equipment in a form to be approved by the Supplier and at the Supplier's request provide the Supplier with copies of the entries and allow the Supplier to inspect such record at all reasonable times."

This is in any event a sound precaution and will enable the customer to check on the speed with which the supplier deals with matters. It is usual for the supplier's engineer to leave a copy of a form for each visit which records the date and time of notification of the fault, of the engineer's arrival, the type of fault, its cure and any action taken by the engineer, and the time of the engineer's departure. It is in the customer's interest to reconcile this with his own log and notify the supplier of discrepancies, if possible before the engineer has left.

For third-party maintenance of PCs the contractor will require the customer to advise him as soon as possible of the date of acquisition or at least installation at the customer's premises of new machines [K9 (17)].

8.6.4 Spares [K10]

Some agreements require the customer to keep spares; this is usually feasible only on sites which are either very large or very distant from the supplier's depot—or both:

> "(a) The Customer shall purchase from the Supplier and hold available to the Supplier such spare parts as the Supplier shall recommend, such spare parts to be supplied at the Supplier's List Prices then in force.
>
> (b) The Supplier may draw on this stock of spare parts for maintenance and repair of the Equipment. The Supplier shall not be liable for any delay in performing maintenance or repairs under this Agreement if any such spare parts as are recommended to be held are not available and shall be entitled to charge the Customer for all additional expenses and costs incurred by the Supplier as a result of such delay.
>
> (c) Any spare parts which are not in the recommended list shall be supplied by the Supplier at the then current List Price."

A maintenance agreement like this is not particularly common. The advantage to the customer lies partly in his maintenance being quicker and more reliable, and partly in the lower charges.

An alternative system allows for the supplier to hold all spares, but:

> "the Customer will if so required by the Supplier provide storage space at the Installation Site for a reasonable stock of spare parts."

8.6.5 Miscellaneous [B24, K6, K9 (18)]

If the customer holds spares, then it may well be that:

> "Any parts removed from the Equipment by the Supplier in pursuance of maintenance or repair shall be the property of the Customer."

Otherwise, more usually:

> "When replacement parts are fitted the parts removed shall become the Supplier's property."

This of course refers to the practice of "swapping out" [8.5.1] with all the difficulties that gives rise to. With systems involving telecommunications apparatus supplied by British Telecom or some other telecommunications supplier it may not be possible to test the computer supplier's equipment without also using some telecommunications apparatus. We therefore find a clause like the following:

"The Customer will at his own expense provide such telecommunications facilities as are reasonably required by the Supplier for testing and diagnostic purposes and will bear the charge for the use of such facilities by the Supplier for such purpose."

8.7 SUPPLIER'S DUTIES

8.7.1 Escalation [K2 (4), Sched. I]

We have seen in the discussion about response time [8.1.2], that a four-hour response does not mean that the problem will be fixed within four hours. Naturally, suppliers are reluctant to commit themselves to completing an undefined piece of work in any particular time. No less logically, customers are increasingly reluctant to pay for a service with no time scale at all. The compromise is to establish escalation procedures, whereby the longer a reported fault is uncured the more the senior the staff of the supplier need to be involved. Thus if a fault is still uncured (say) three hours after the supplier's engineer has arrived at the customer's premises, the engineer's supervisor is told about the problem with the implication that if the engineer needs additional resources to solve the problem, a more senior manager can provide those resources. By the same token, if, for example, the problem is still uncured one day after the engineer first arrived, the escalation procedure turns the ratchet further and the supplier's head of maintenance services is involved, with possibly a further turn of the ratchet to involve the supplier's Managing Director after two days. The implication is that not only will the additional resources (if appropriate) be provided, but if an engineer is simply not up to the job, the supplier has every opportunity of finding out and removing him. It must also be the case that the customer's senior staff will similarly wish to be involved if their system is out of action for so long.

One should also consider the imposition of financial penalties in the event that target response times are not met, *e.g.*, in the manner of the service credit regimes described in Precedent S, Sched. 4.

All this can be embodied in an appropriate clause with details of the escalation in a Schedule.

8.7.2 Data protection [K15 (2)]

We have seen how making one's system available to a supplier for maintenance purposes may have data protection implications [8.1.2] and details of the effect of treating the supplier as a bureau for this purpose are set out at 10.3.3. It follows that the customer will require an indemnity from the supplier in respect of compliance with the Data Protection Act.

CHAPTER 9

SOFTWARE MAINTENANCE

9.0 Introduction
9.1 Services to be Performed
9.2 Payment
9.3 Limitations and Exceptions
9.4 Termination
9.5 Variation
9.6 User's Duties
9.7 Supplier's Duties

9.0. INTRODUCTION

Any computer program which is being used regularly will inevitably put its user in mind of ways in which it can be improved and enhanced. A program which is never expanded in this way will quickly become a fossil. Users will inevitably think of better ways of doing things and these (possibly communicated to the supplier through a user group [15.6]) may be incorporated in future versions of the software. Software maintenance is therefore to be directed at least in part to the business of improvements and enhancements.

Aside from ongoing improvement, maintenance services will also need to address the remediation of any software bugs or errors which are discovered. This is most likely to occur in bespoke software or in package software which is at the beginning of its commercial life and so immature in the sense that it has not yet been exposed to very heavy usage.

A third reason for software to need modification is because of external circumstances. The most common such reason is legislative. For example, a decision to adopt the Euro would result in substantial modification of a huge range of software, both bespoke and package [3.3.4, L5 (5)]. But even without a change as substantial as this quite modest legislative changes can involve substantial rewriting of software.

In the case of an off-the-peg package, the series of improved versions will usually be known as *Releases* or *Versions* and numbered sequentially. *Releases* are distinct from *Updates* or *Patches* which are more in the nature of limited issues of a small part of the code to deal with one or more specific identified bugs. Thus the sequential numbering system for a new Release or Version might typically refer to V3.2, which would signify version 3 of the Software, but incorporating a number of updates so that it may be seen as being the second edition or update of version 2.

Alternatively, the software being maintained may be a bespoke system which the user is unwilling or unable to maintain himself: a small company with a few programs to maintain, and few opportunities for promotion or for working on interesting new projects, will experience the utmost difficulty in recruiting or retaining good programming staff, since maintenance has acquired a reputation of being a salt mine of the software industry and programmers can, and do, change employers to avoid what is seen to be dreary work. In these circumstances a company will probably turn to the supplier who designed the program and ask him to provide the maintenance.

Whether or not the maintenance of bespoke software is performed by the systems house which wrote it, the source code (*i.e.* the form in which the program is written) is essential to effect the maintenance services. As mentioned in 3.3.1, the customer may well wish to ensure that in the event of any failure by the software maintenance contractor (whether failure of capacity—*e.g.* liquidation—or a failure to fulfil the terms of the contract), the current version of the source code can be recovered. For standard software, one method is to have each version of the source code deposited with a third party who then is placed under an obligation to deliver it to the client if any disaster overtakes the maintenance contractor or if the maintenance contractor is unable or unwilling to perform its contractual obligations. For his part, the customer will probably be required to agree not to attempt to resell the source code or make it available to anyone else or otherwise exploit it, but simply to use it to maintain his system [N].

For software available through a distributor, there are particular difficulties in leaving the maintenance aspects to the distributor [G8, H8]. If the distributor is to provide effective maintenance he will need access to the source code of the software and will need to employ skilled programmers to carry out the work. Without this access to the source code, it is impossible for the software to be properly maintained which in turn may damage the reputation of the software and hence sales on which the distributor depends. For this reason, one often finds that responsibility for software maintenance is retained by the software owner so that the distributor's duties are confined to supplying and installing the software. In this way the software owner protects, first, his proprietary interest in the software by not revealing the source code and, secondly, the software's reputation by ensuring its proper maintenance is in his own hands.

For PCs, software maintenance contracts *per se* are rare. The customer who buys his software over the counter of a home computer shop or other retailer is likely to have no rights to software maintenance at all. In general, this is due to the fact that the low initial cost of the product must inevitably mean that maintenance is relatively expensive. However, maintenance can often be provided in the form of new releases or upgrades which are becoming more usual—and suppliers can use this as a further weapon in their fight against "piracy" (copyright infringement). The user can obtain information about maintenance and new upgrades by completion of a simple form and sending a remittance. The transaction (the completion of the form, the downloading of the software version or patch, and the sending of the remittance) can often now be performed entirely over the Internet. A variant of this is where the original software is provided in the first instance over the Internet and the user pays for the licence fee in the same way (and usually at the same time) as for the maintenance. It will be noted that this is applicable to shareware [4.3.3] and software generally which changes hands by methods other than ordinary purchase from an authorised dealer. It is also, of course, a chance for the user to regularise his position on copyright infringement. However, much of the software concerned is American and the opportunity to obtain maintenance information by transatlantic telephone call or over the Internet will not always be appropriate.

In general, when offered a new version of software, the customer must satisfy himself that new or updated manuals or on-line help facility will be provided where relevant, and either that the new release requires no new training or that it will be provided, either free of charge or at a reasonable price by the supplier (unless the user thinks he is capable of training himself or his staff).

For the question of levels of support in different software categories from the same supplier and for possible changes in the levels of support, see above at 3.7.4.

Increasingly for PC software, although there is no formal maintenance contract as such, suppliers will provide technical support via hotlines at a premium rate of (say) 50p per minute so as to provide an income for the supplier to cover the cost of the support and at the same time discourage frivolous calls. A further benefit to the supplier lies in the feedback on usage of the software. An alternative method is to provide support via e-mail in the same way as patches and updates can be provided. Usually this is not really a matter of maintenance, since the majority of the enquiries will not be reporting a bug, but simply asking for help in the use of the software. In theory, the enquiries could have been dealt with by the user finding the relevant place in the manual or invoking the on-line (often supposedly "context sensitive") help facilities, but in fact both manuals and on-line help facilities are notoriously unhelpful. Initially, some software houses provided this service free but increasingly now (with the use of PCs in companies rather than purely by the home market) this is a charged service.

Contractually, it may or may not be greatly different from traditional software maintenance services and may still contain "bug-fixing" provisions, but the main service will be the manning of a helpdesk between particular hours and the provision of information over the phone. For this aspect of the work, a network service level precedent agreement [R] may be appropriate.

9.1. Services to be Performed [L5]

The service will be limited to one or more particular pieces of software (usually defined in a schedule) and also in the case of non-PC software, to one or more particular installations. In part, this last feature is dictated by the fact that the maintainer of a software package is usually a licensor who may be anxious to prevent the user from making use of the software on more than one machine without taking out a second licence (depending on the type of licence and how its fee has been calculated [3.8.1]). But it is also dictated by the physical distance between supplier and user, and the desire to be certain about any minor variant versions which may be in use, since each additional site may have differences of configuration which may require different versions.

Beware of a clause like the following:

> "The Supplier's Maintenance Service for Software includes the installation of the Software and subsequent Software Releases in accordance with the Supplier's usual procedures."

This may be the first and last mention of software maintenance in the entire contract, as opposed to any other clauses referring to the licence. The supplier is not committed either to producing new versions or to supplying them to the customer; on the other hand, the correction of faults and bugs should be covered elsewhere in the contract [Chapter 3].

9.1.1 New releases

The release of new versions is important because the supplier of the software will wish to keep as much uniformity as possible in the versions in use. This will mean that he is not maintaining too many different versions, and that the effect of any changes can be gauged on all versions then in use. He will therefore put pressure on all customers to use the new releases as soon as they are available, by telling them that, after a certain time, old version(s) will no longer be maintained or that maintenance will continue to be provided for no more than the current release and the immediately preceding one (or two) versions. Alternatively, he may give notice (typically two years) that a release will cease to be maintained on a particular date. Sometimes a new release is found to be so defective that a customer declines to change to it from an older release; in these circumstances he would be well advised to contact all other users (perhaps through a user group [15.6], so as to present a united front to the supplier. In any event, it would be prudent for any customer faced with such a defective version to make further enquiries of the supplier so as to ascertain exactly how onerous it may be in practice to stay with the old but workable version; key matters to clarify are the supplier's release strategy (*e.g.* is it one a year, or one every six months?), the likely overhead in implementing new releases, and whether any charge is made for them.

Where a manufacturer's standard package is to be maintained by someone other than the manufacturer, the customer will also need to satisfy himself that the maintenance contractor can get hold of the new versions of the software as soon as they are available and learn enough about them to be able to provide a credible service.

A more detailed clause to cover the provision of new releases is:

"The Supplier shall make available to the Customer [without additional charge] such improvements and modifications to the standard version of the Software as the Supplier shall make and release from time to time and which are compatible with the version installed for the Customer. The Supplier shall install and integrate such new release(s) [on the Supplier's standard scale of charges in force from time to time/at a charge to be determined pursuant to the provisions of Schedule *X*]."

"Without additional charge" does not mean that the provision of the new releases will be free of charge, simply that it will already have been covered by the relevant support and maintenance charges. This clause also visualises the possibility that the customer may already have a version which is not in every respects standard, and therefore a new release may be inappropriate (*e.g.* if it has been substantially modified at the customer's request). In such circumstances, the customer and the supplier will need to agree in advance upon the nature and extent of the maintenance obligations in the future; it is not unreasonable to expect the supplier to provide such maintenance, but it may be justified in charging an increased fee in doing so, owing to the need to ensure that any new releases are brought into line with the previous modifications to the standard version. The standard version will usually be described in a schedule. Reference to a standard scale of charges will be an essential protection for the customer against being effectively held to ransom, if he wishes to have access to the expert implementation skills available to the supplier. Sometimes, the supplier will charge for installation of the new releases rather than charging for providing them in the first place.

9.1.2 Statutory requirements [L5 (4), M5 (2), Q13]

Some software packages reflect legal requirements and could be affected by statutory changes. Alterations of the standard rate of VAT, for instance, may require changes to software which calculate currency data. An intelligently designed program will be able to cope with this without the need for the release of a new version (*e.g.* allowing the current rate of VAT to be a reconfigurable parameter, under the user's control), but it is possible to imagine more far reaching changes which might involve software modification. This is especially true of payroll programs, and it is therefore usual to include in any agreements for the maintenance of such programs a clause such as:

"The Supplier will modify the Software so that it conforms to any change of legislation or new legal requirements."

This clause places no time limit on the speed with which such a modification would be required, and the speed with which such changes can be published and made effective by a Chancellor makes it impossible for any maintenance provider to wish to give any firm undertaking in this respect, (although it would be reasonable for the maintenance provider to commit to providing the modifications within a reasonable period of time). It is to be hoped that by now all governments are aware of the time that must be taken to design, produce and test software in order to implement changes, although the *St Albans v. ICL* case shows the pressure St Albans was under due to the extremely tight time table for introducing the Community Charge. The Euro [3.3.4, L5 (5)] will doubtless be a test of this.

9.1.3 Error detection and correction [L5 (1), M5 (1)]

Another side to maintenance obligations is the correction of reported errors in the software which has been supplied: bug-fixing. The supplier will need to investigate and correct errors, and this is usually covered any some such clause as:

"The Supplier shall correct any faults in the Software provided such faults do not result from:

(a) defects or errors resulting from any modifications of the Software made by any person other than the Supplier;

(b) incorrect use of the Software or operator error; or

(c) any fault in the Equipment or in the *XYZ* operating system referred to in the Functional Specification or in any other software used by the Customer in conjunction with the Software."

This is of course much the same as the clause on error correction during the warranty period in a software contract [3.3.3] but extends the period of free correction for the duration of the maintenance contract.

The supplier may also reserve to himself the incorporation of enhancements at his own discretion; this could be necessary because the package incorporated some obsolescent facility or is written in a version of the computer language which is no longer in common use, or runs under an obsolete version of the operating system:

"The Supplier may at his own discretion [and with prior notice to the Customer] introduce into the Software such enhancements as he shall from time to time consider necessary, provided that such enhancements shall not adversely affect either the performance, functionality or ease of use of the Software."

The only anxiety from the user's point of view should be that he is informed of such changes, and that his documentation is brought fully up to date. Documentation may be covered by:

"The Supplier shall supply to the Customer such documentation as may be reasonably necessary to reflect all changes to the Software."

A clause of this nature is essential if the user is to be able to keep track of all changes to the system—whether introduced by the supplier or the user's own staff or contractors.

9.1.4 Advice and information [L5 (3), M5 (3)]

The writing of bespoke software involves a good deal of consultancy and giving of advice by the software supplier to the client, and this is reflected in such clauses in software contracts as seen in 3.6.1. Even after the software has been accepted, this giving of advice is often liable to continue. As stated at the outset of our discussion of software maintenance, a regular user of the software package will inevitably think up ways of improving the package and, when he has done so, he will need technical advice to see whether his ideas are technically and commercially feasible:

(a) Can this improvement be done at all? Will it fit within the confines of the existing software?

(b) How will it affect that software and the rest of the client's work?

(c) How much will it cost, and how long will it take?

(d) How valuable are the expected benefits?

The client faced with these questions will inevitably turn to the supplier/ manufacturer. Satisfying these questions is likely to take a good deal of time for it may require a lot of investigation to determine the precise effect of them. This is particularly so if a proposed change is liable (as they frequently are) to change the client's clerical or other non-computer procedures, since this will involve visiting the client's own premises and interviewing relevant staff. For this reason a software maintenance contract will often provide only for giving advice by telephone—or at least not attending the client in person. It will often be up to specified limits in terms of time before such advice becomes separately chargeable. If a client insists on an investigation which involves anything more than this, then this would be considered by the software supplier as a proposal for a new study contract.

Such advice on the use of or potential changes to the software ("technical advice", as opposed to error correction) is also usually limited in scope to elucidating the use or worth of the existing package:

"The Supplier will provide the User with such technical advice by telephone, fax, e-mail or mail as is reasonably necessary to resolve the User's difficulties and queries using the software."

As noted above, this technical assistance can be further limited to a few days per annum:

"The Supplier will provide technical assistance to the User at the Installation Site for a maximum of 5 man-days per annum during the continuance of this Agreement."

If the user does not take all his days' worth of what is in effect pre-paid consultancy in any one year, there is usually no facility for crediting this to any succeeding year. Conversely, if he uses more time, he will find himself paying for it, over and above the maintenance charges, at the supplier's standard rates.

9.1.5 Enhancements [M5 (3)]

The boundary between advice, whether on site or not, and proposals for enhancements is a narrow one, and the clauses in the last section might equally as appropriately have been considered under the present head. However, a clause like the following may also be included:

> "The Supplier will undertake at the Supplier's sole discretion the study and/or implementation of enhancements to the Software for the User."

"Sole discretion" is a phrase to raise hackles and blood pressure, but it is difficult to devise a valid alternative, given that it would be unreasonable to expect a supplier to be obliged to assess any enhancements the user may care to suggest. The supplier could limit his involvement to a particular number of days, or to a particular cost value of work, but as the assessing of the number or days or the cost value of doing some work for the user must perforce be almost under the supplier's control, the milder form of words does not correspond to any reality more favourable to the user.

9.1.6 Response time

Response time—*i.e.* the speed with which a manufacturer starts to rectify an error of which he has been notified—was discussed above [8.1.2]. The concept is becoming increasingly common in software maintenance contracts which were previously often silent on the rapidity with which the work or correction/ enhancement would begin, despite the fact that an obligation to correct errors is largely meaningless without some idea as to how soon this will be done. The user will infer—correctly, no doubt—that the maintenance function does not have particular staff associated with it, but is done by anyone on the supplier's staff who happens to be around and can spare the time to bone up on the user's software. A clause which takes this point seriously and implies that staff are permanently assigned to the maintenance function is therefore very refreshing:

> "Upon receipt of the User's request for support or rectification of a defect the Supplier shall subject to its then current commitments normally begin work on such support or defects not later that the *first* working day thereafter and shall diligently continue the work during the normal working hours or at such times as may be mutually agreed until the work is accepted by the User as completed satisfactorily. If the User requests support in an emergency the Supplier shall use all reasonable efforts to fulfil the request as quickly as possible."

Depending upon the value and complexity of the software, more complicated clauses may be required. For example, they could categorise reported errors into different degrees of seriousness, each with its own required response time and deadlines for resolution [9.2]. Acceptance has been dealt with [3.3], and need not be re-examined here. Indeed, it is not normally recapitulated in any software maintenance contract, though is obviously relevant. Ideally such contracts should cover it, for example by setting out the manner in which bug fixes will be tested.

9.2 PAYMENT [L3]

Payment for software maintenance can be extremely simple in the case of a manufacturer's standard package software, and rather more complicated for bespoke software.

To deal with the manufacturer's package software first, the position will depend on the size and complexity of the software. For smaller, off-the-shelf software, for which the only maintenance service offered is access to technical support, it is usual for the licence charge to include such software maintenance as is provided [3.2], though there may be a charge for the installation and the magnetic media on which new releases are sent to the customer.

However, for bespoke software and for more complicated and/or expensive package software—especially those which are critical to the customer's organisation's operation (all cases for which there are likely to be more significant support and maintenance obligations), the payment will usually be monthly or quarterly, and will often represent an annual percentage of the original software cost (say 10 per cent):

> "The Supplier shall charge and the User shall pay the Standard Maintenance Charge due monthly in advance."

So far, so good. But if the maintenance obligation is to provide a predefined input of x days, some contracts will also specify the rates for work over and above the standard maintenance charge. Where this is so, the software maintenance provider may further distinguish between ordinary office hours and overtime:

> "The Supplier shall charge and the User shall pay fees at the standard or overtime rates specified in the Schedule hereto in respect of all time spent by the Supplier's Staff in initial familiarisation work and in other work required by the User under this agreement over and above 5 man-days consultancy per annum."

Such clauses may also be appropriate where the maintenance provider is asked for support but discovers that the root cause of the perceived bug is not, in fact, an error in the software. For maintenance provided by the software supplier who wrote the original system, the familiarisation period should be negligible (or even non-existent). For the other work, the software supplier is in effect contracting on a different basis from ordinary software contracts in that it does not give an overall estimate of the cost of the work. A maintenance contract of this sort is then a hybrid between a pure maintenance contract and software contract, and Chapter 3 should be consulted for many of the terms and conditions which it will contain—including expenses, the ability to vary the charges and so on.

Many maintenance contracts also link payment with the rectification of reported errors, for example by setting target resolution times for different categories of errors and by providing that the customer will accrue service credits or rebates if such targets are not met. A sample clause to that effect might read as follows:

> "on each occasion that the Supplier fails to rectify a reported Error within the Target Resolution Time specified in Clause X, the Customer shall be entitled to a Service Credit amounting to $y\%$ of the Maintenance Fee."

In this context, a service credit means a pre-set reduction in the amount which would otherwise have been payable to the supplier which is intended to act as an incentive to the supplier to maintain high levels of service. If a large number of target times are missed, more service credits will accrue, and the maintenance fee will be reduced accordingly. Care must be taken, however, to ensure that the service credits are not set at too onerous a level, as it has not been confirmed that such clauses are immune from attack as a form of liquidated damages clause, in which case the amounts incurred would need to represent a genuine pre-estimate of loss.

9.3 LIMITATIONS AND EXCEPTIONS

9.3.1 Scope of maintenance [L5 (1), M5 (1)]

As with hardware maintenance contracts, the supplier often specifies what is not covered by the service. This will include breaches of the user's duties, *e.g.*:

> "The Supplier's maintenance Service for Software excludes service in respect of:
>
> a) failure caused by equipment or software not supplied by the Supplier;
> b) failures resulting for the Customer's unauthorised modifications of the Software;
> c) mis-use of the Software or operator error;
> d) errors arising in software releases earlier than the Supplier's then current release;
> e) tests and checks requested and specified by the Customer which are outside the Supplier's normal test specifications and procedures."

In (d), in place of the reference to the then current release we might alternatively expect a reference to releases earlier than those specifically stated to be subject to provision of maintenance services.

9.3.2 Performance

Whether the maintenance contractor has or has not written the program to be maintained, the question of the performance and/or results to be achieved from the use of that program (even after amendments made under the maintenance agreement) is liable to be excluded:

> "The Supplier disclaims all liability for the results to be achieved by the User's use of the Software, the usefulness of the results produced or its possible effect on the User's business."

Unless the Supplier has also been involved in the provision of the hardware and operating system he is also likely to disclaim responsibility for the performance of the software. Even then there would have to be clear assumptions as to equipment, volumes, etc., upon which any performance obligations are based.

9.3.3 Loss and consequential loss [L14, M14]

It is usual for contracts of this type to limit (so far as the law will allow) loss and consequential loss. These clauses are usually very general and do not differ in form or enforceability from such clauses in other contracts for services.

9.4 TERMINATION [L10, M11]

Many software maintenance contracts remain in force until revoked, a situation which would become embarrassing to a supplier who has no adequate clause to increase his charges [9.5] since he would then be under the necessity of revoking it himself simply to increase his fees, when a combination of inflation and obsolescence of the hardware made a price rise inevitable.

Most contracts provide for termination on notice by either party. The minimum notice period is likely to be at least a month. Whether this is sufficient must be carefully considered by the customer. The issue must be how quickly he can put in place an alternative arrangement. If the system is absolutely standard this may not be difficult. If it presents novel features, it may be nearly impossible.

We shall see in 9.5 that charges can often be reviewed and altered—usually annually. When this happens it is common for the customer to be given an opportunity to accept or reject the new figure. In the event that he rejects it the contract is terminated.

Apart from this, most contracts allow termination for the user's non-payment or incapacity, or when either party is in material breach of contract. Again, these clauses are not any different from similar clauses in other contracts for services.

However, as with hardware where new equipment replaces obsolete equipment, so also with software packages, the supplier may reserve the right to terminate the maintenance agreement in order to encourage the customer to use new software. This should of course be distinguished from the case where the supplier is encouraging the customer to use a latest version of an existing package [9.1.1]

9.5 VARIATION [L3 (3)]

None of the contracts we have examined visualises the possibility of any change in the identity of the software. This is hardly surprising, though the fact that they also fail to envisage any change in the location of the computer on which the software is to run is perhaps more unexpected. In practice, of course, this will usually be covered in the software licence [3.5].

The charges are a different matter. Some clauses are virtually the same as those for hardware maintenance [8.5.2]; a more complex clause provides in effect for annual negotiation:

> "Any alteration to the charges shall be subject to negotiation between the parties hereto commencing not later than x days and ending not later than y days prior to the anniversary date in each year. Failing agreement the Supplier shall specify the alteration to the User and give written notice thereof not less than 2 days prior to the anniversary date. Such alterations shall become effective for the year beginning with the anniversary date."

Alternatively, many contracts are renewable annually, providing the maintenance contractor with the opportunity to increase charges by agreement with the user. From the point of view of the user, it would be likely to be preferable to link such increases to an agreed index so as to provide certainty in the future. Such indices might either be national ones measuring inflation, or industry-based ones measuring increases in IT service charges. Where users have made significant investments in licensing and implementing specific systems, they have, in our experience, sought commitments from their suppliers for longer support periods—say a minimum of three years instead of just consecutive annual periods. The Computing Services and Software Association [15.2.1] can provide details of commonly applied indexes.

9.6 USER'S DUTIES [L6]

As with a contract for software development [3.6, D17, D19, D22, D23] or consultancy [13.6, X6], the user will have some responsibilities of his own to fulfil in order to receive maintenance services.

9.6.1 Not to alter [L6 (4)]

One of the key concerns of the maintenance provider is to ensure that the program is not tampered with by anyone other than its own staff, on the basis that any change to the software about which it does not know will not be reflected in its documentation and so will make its task harder if not impossible. It is accordingly common to see clauses providing that any alteration, however trivial, will automatically invalidate the contract:

> "The User will not permit anyone other than the authorised representatives of the Supplier to change the Software, its operating instructions or manuals."

This is the standard view, though it is occasionally relaxed by the licensor to the extent of requiring authorisation for any changes.

> "The User may with the Supplier's prior written consent modify the Software or its documentation at its own expense and on his own responsibility provided that all relevant intellectual property rights in any such changes shall vest in the Supplier and the User shall ensure that the Supplier's copyright notices are incorporated in all modifications and accompanying documentation. The User agrees that the Supplier will have the right to charge for all services resulting from the User's modification of the Software and documentation. The User shall have a licence to use the modifications on the same basis as it is licensed to use the Software."

9.6.2 Use current release [L6 (1)]

The question of the issue of releases is discussed above [9.1.1]. A manufacturer will normally seek to impose uniformity on his customers. An extreme form of words is as follows:

> "The User shall use only the current release of the Software. Without prejudice to the Supplier's other remedies the User agrees that Supplier will have the right to charge for all services resulting from the User's failure to use the current Software release."

9.6.3 Notification [L6 (7)]

The user is usually obliged to notify any defect to the maintenance provider in the same way as for hardware defects [8.6.3], especially if this is to be linked to target resolution times [9.1.6, 9.2] etc:

> "The User will give written notice to the Supplier of any defect in the Software within *seven* days of such defect becoming apparent."

9.6.4 Information and services [L6 (7)–(9)]

Finally, the user is likely to be expected to provide information, office and computer facilities in order to enable the maintenance provider to address any reported errors. This may include the provision of screen dumps or other printouts and will frequently extend to a requirement to provide remote access to the user's system for the maintenance provider's staff. For security reasons, the user will be reluctant to allow the maintenance provider continuous and unfettered access to the system so any such access must at all times be under the user's control but when a suspected fault occurs the user's staff will have the power, temporarily, to allow the maintenance provider access:

> "The User shall make available free of charge to the Supplier all information facilities and service reasonably required by the Supplier for the purpose of the fulfilment of its obligations under this Agreement including but not limited to computer-runs, print outs, discussion with User's staff, data preparation, office accommodation, typing and photocopying. The User shall in addition provide the Supplier with a means of remote access to its system so as to enable it to analyse the reported error."

This is a comprehensive list but no more than required in software contracts. In addition, users will usually be asked to provide sufficient information to enable the reported error to be recreated by the maintenance provider.

> "The User shall provide the Supplier with a means of remote access to the Equipment so as to enable the Supplier to examine any error reported to it by the User. The Supplier agrees that this means of remote access to the Equipment shall be at all timers under the sole control of the User. In the event that the User does not provide the Supplier with this link when requested to do so for the examination of an error reported to it by the User, the Supplier shall take no responsibility for such reported error and its obligations under this Agreement in respect of such reported error shall be fully discharged."

The question of information may be amplified by clauses relating to nomination of representatives, exactly as in ordinary software contracts [3.6.1, 3.7.1].

In limited circumstances, users are required to maintain separate copies of the configured software (mirror images of the working system, but not for live use) so as to facilitate the replication of reported problems with the working system. However, as the cost and overheads of such duplicate systems are high, such an obligation is very rare and only likely to be used for very critical systems where the duplicate system may also act as a back-up system in the event that the main system is unavailable.

9.7 SUPPLIER'S DUTIES [L8, L9]

These are identical in intention (if not in form) to corresponding clauses in a software contract, and will relate to liaison and nomination [3.7.1, 9.6.4]; conformity and dress [3.7.1] and confidentiality [3.7.2]. Confidentiality requires a further example since under a maintenance agreement the software, and therefore its documentation, are already in existence at the time the contract comes into force and belong to the user:

> "The Supplier shall be entitled to retain a copy of all appropriate documenta-tion of the Software on its premises for the duration of this Agreement. Such documentation shall be held in confidence and only for the purposes of this Agreement and returned to the User at the expiry of this Agreement."

Staff poaching [3.6.2] is less likely in a maintenance situation and is not often included.

Staff training [3.7.3] is not relevant unless the modifications are very substantial, in which case the modifications will probably be part of a new software contract (as opposed to a software maintenance contract).

As the supplier may need to process the user's data for diagnostic purposes and the data may be or include personal data thereby constituting the supplier a data processor under the Data Protection Act 1998, the supplier should (as does a hardware maintenance contractor in similar circumstances [8.7.2]) give the usual undertakings to comply with the Act [L9].

PART III

COMPUTER SERVICES

Chapter 10

SERVICE CONTRACTS: BUREAUX

10.0 Introduction
10.1 Nature of the Service
10.2 Payment
10.3 Data
10.4 Termination
10.5 Variation
10.6 Customer's Duties
10.7 Bureau's Duties and Liabilities

10.0 Introduction

Some years ago, a company selling computer bureau services ran an advertisement with the slogan: "You don't need to buy a cow if all you want is a pint of milk". This is the essence of the bureau business: that a company with computer resources makes them available to others in return for payment. Within this broad concept, a number of distinctions is possible of which two main types seem to us interesting from a contractual point of view. The first type of distinction is between a generalised bureau which is not particularly interested in what is done on its equipment, the customer simply providing his own programs and data, and a specialised bureau providing a specific service, where the fact that a computer is used may well not be the most important aspect. The second distinction is between a batch bureau and an on-line one [10.1.2]. The first of these distinctions affects the application: the second is technical and thus these two types of distinction may interact with each other producing batch general services, on-line general services (sometimes called "time-sharing bureaux"), batch specialised services and on-line specialised services. Networks and the Internet are both different forms of bureau service, and network service agreements or Internet Service Provider (ISP) agreements are really only particular kinds of on-line bureau services. Recent months have also seen an explosion of interest in Application Service Provision (ASP) contracts, whereby the use of software applications is rented via the Internet. Although the manner of delivery and payment profiles for such ASP arrangements may be novel, in essence these contracts retain the essential features of a bureau contract [3.0.2].

10.1 Nature of the Service

10.1.1 Batch bureaux [Q2, Q8]

Batch bureau agreements are in sharp decline but not yet finally extinct, and are therefore included in this book for completeness. At the risk of slight boredom, the reader may find it easier to consider batch bureau contracts first where the physical separation of the bureau and customer makes the issues clear, before examining on-line and network agreements.

Most agreements have proved amazingly vague as to exactly what is being provided:

> "The Bureau shall perform such services for the Customer as are expressly agreed between the Bureau and the Customer."

—agreed when? In what form? Does "expressly" mean "in writing"? Does this clause permit the agreement to be varied in the future after it has come into force?

> "The Bureau shall provide computing services in accordance with its current literature . . ."

This is surely better in that it refers to an identifiable document (although again the question of variation is relevant), but then this example is from a specialised bureau whose precise service may be expected to be defined in some detail in its current literature. The simple answer to this problem must be a schedule, and in the schedule the following might be relevant, at least for a specialised service:

(a) commencement date of service;

(b) general content and form of customer's data (*e.g.* standard forms as prescribed by bureau/DAT tape containing customer's accounting information/mailing list/etc.);

(c) processing by bureau defined either by result (to produce payslips and other payroll information for the customer) or run such programs as the customer shall deliver to the bureau, etc.;

(d) timescales—of delivery, of processing, of re-delivery—expressed both as to days of the week or month and as to times of day.

For the casual bureau user, who does not want a regular service but simply the opportunity to run program X now and again, other considerations apply. In this case he usually knows the performance of his program well, and simply wants to read Y records or print Z pages. Provided the charging structure is based on some such criteria as this, a vaguer clause is possible:

> "The Bureau shall make available to the Customer the facility of running the programs more particularly described in the Schedule hereto on the Bureau's computer upon the charges hereinafter described."

It should also be noted that the bureau may well wish to charge for time booked and not used:

> "A charge of *25* per cent of the standard rate will be made for computer time booked and not used (whether because the Customer has failed to ensure that his data is delivered on time or otherwise) unless the Customer has given to the Bureau at least *12* hours' notice of cancellation."

10.1.2 On-line bureaux [P2, P3]

The basis of an on-line or time-sharing bureau is that the customer has access to the bureau on-line, either through a terminal specially supplied by the bureau (as is usual for specialised services) or through any suitable terminal or PC (a common arrangement with general time-sharing bureaux). Very occasionally, the customer may even take his data to the bureau's premises and there input it through the bureau's own terminal, although this is not much different contractually from a batch bureau.

The generalised clause suggested in the previous section is suitable here, but the charging structure will be concerned not with physical records or pages but with the concepts of data stored, connect time, CPU time, etc.—these concepts are explained below [10.2].

Terminals [P1, P6]

If the customer provides his own terminal, the bureau may well not be too concerned as to its precise nature. A clause requiring the customer to use only equipment which has been BABT approved would not be inappropriate and could follow the pattern of those in ordinary hardware contracts [2.7.4, A14].

Apart from this, the bureau will be concerned only with the customers' correctly using their terminals, see 10.6.2 below.

Sometimes, however, the customer also hires a terminal from the bureau; this is usually optional in a generalised contract, but for a special contract it is more common. This is usually because a specialised service may well have a specialised terminal with functions peculiar to that application shown on the keyboard. A contract of this sort must therefore have a hardware hire component containing some of the elements of contracts in Chapter 2. In particular, it will probably allow for hire, installation, restriction on use, and return by the customer on termination. The last two of these may be dealt with under customer's duties [10.6]; the first two are considered as part of the bureau's duties [10.7.4].

It will be noticed that the bureau will usually be responsible for maintaining the terminal [10.7.4]: terminals are generally reliable devices but the on-line bureau services contract may well have elements of a hardware maintenance contract.

If it is a PC the only questions of interest will be the operating system (Windows, Unix, MacOS, etc.) and its speed and capacity.

10.1.3 Network service level agreements [R]

A network service level agreement is really only a form of on-line agreement, whereby the bureau services to be provided will be those usual in networks such as electronic mail, certain retrieval services, perhaps a fax service, virus protection service, etc. The terminal is usually the user's own PC with hardware or software items added to it to enable it to gain access to the network. The user will probably be heavily dependent on the network and will therefore be looking for a high level of availability. He will also typically expect to have training provided by the network provider, as well as a helpdesk which he can contact by telephone if he has any difficulties or queries.

10.1.4 Volumes [Q15]

Remarkably, very few contracts specify any limitation on volume. Some allow a sliding scale of charges to benefit the high volume user, or at least discourage very small volumes, but few seem to envisage the predicament when the customer gives them a larger volume than they can cope with. The following clause is therefore interesting:

"All the work (provided that it does not exceed in volume the Customer's specified maximum volumes as set out in Schedule 3 hereto) shall be performed by the Bureau in accordance with Schedule *1* hereto. Any work in excess of the maximum volume or volumes set out in Schedule *3* hereto shall be performed by the Bureau as soon as is reasonably practical for the Bureau having regard to the other commitments of the Bureau."

A clause like this is obviously vital if the bureau gives any indications as to speed of processing or delivery.

10.2 PAYMENT

Payment is usually monthly. In this section no sample clauses are given since the charging systems vary widely and are usually incorporated in a schedule.

10.2.1 General bureaux: batch [Q3]

The basis on which charges are calculated can vary a good deal. Originally, machines were available to a single user who was charged purely on time, regardless of how much of the machine or its facilities he used. With more sophisticated machines it was based on both time and peripheral usage. The operating system gave the time used by each program on a printed log and also after each printout on the line printer, and this was generally taken as evidence of the time taken. Peripheral usage was usually expressed in a measure appropriate to that peripheral (*e.g.* £x per 1,000 records read, £4 per page) or simply per number of characters transferred—whether to disk, tape, printer or other peripheral. Data preparation or transfer (if any) would also be charged for [10.3]. Sometimes a bureau would also charge for consumables (paper used, etc.); it was of course up to the customer to provide these himself for use on the computer.

10.2.2 General bureaux: on-line [P4]

These bureaux customarily charge on some mix of three main bases: data stored (and sometimes other peripheral usage), connect time, and CPU time.

Data stored and other peripheral usage

This is the easiest basis for charging and should therefore be dealt with first. The customer is charged for all the data he stores on disk or tape. It is usually measured in bytes (*i.e.* characters) or words (a longer unit whose relation to bytes/characters varies from machine to machine), and is sold in units of so many "K", "M" or "G". "K" stands for "kilo" and means, loosely, 1,000: more precisely, 1,024 (binary 2^{10} for those who are interested). "M" stands for "mega" and means 1,000,000. "G" is "giga", *i.e.* 1,000,000,000 (American billion). It is also measured per day (or per working day). Sometimes, charging may also be by other peripheral usage—usually the printer, although if the terminal has (or can have) a printer attachment this may more easily be monitored there. If the main computer's printer is used, this is essentially a batch function and some time-sharing bureaux prefer to have a separate scale of charges for batch work. These will, of course, be charged like other batch services, see 10.2.1 above.

Time

"Time" on the computer may be simply the elapsed time taken to run the program (elapsed or, for on-line systems, connect time). Alternatively, it may be the actual fraction of the elapsed time during which the computer actually executed the customer's program (CPU time). A brief explanation may clarify the last concept: an on-line bureau may be running programs for three customers, A, B and C, simultaneously. What is actually happening is that the Central Processing Unit is switching rapidly between A's, B's and C's programs. The time spent on each will not be exactly even, since the computer will take advantage of delays in the various peripheral devices to service other programs. It follows, therefore, that, in a single minute, the CPU may have executed A's program for 21 seconds, B's for 27 seconds and C's for 12 seconds. A charging system based on elapsed or connect time would charge all three customers for 1 minute; a charging system based on CPU time would charge A for 21 seconds, B for 27 seconds, and C for 12 seconds.

A further complication is the question of program size. Under older operating systems each user was allocated a single partition and all partitions were of the same size. This saved the bureau needing to differentiate between programs of differing size. For other bureaux whose operating systems allocate program space on a more flexible basis depending on the size of programs to be run, the scale of charges will be by CPU time for so many "K" or "M" words or bytes of memory. It is also possible that the operating system may obligingly work out some combination of CPU time and program size to produce a new unit of x seconds per y "K".

10.2.3 Specialised bureaux

In specialised bureaux, it is generally easier to charge in terms of the transactions handled. A payroll service might be on the basis of the number of employees in any run (weekly or monthly) and the number of additions, changes and deletions. An accounts program might be charged per 1,000 postings.

Joining fees are also usual in this kind of service. In the case of an on-line service, the joining fee will also cover the cost of installing the terminal. There may also be a charge structure for taking on the customer's data before the system can operate. There may also be delivery charges.

Frequently, there is a minimum charge. In the case of an on-line system, this minimum charge will include (but not necessarily comprise) terminal rental.

Finally, the contract may specify a charge for "dumping" the customer's file. "Dumping" is an inelegant term of art meaning the reproduction on an appropriate peripheral of a file. This is likely to become relevant if the customer wishes to leave the service, since he will not necessarily automatically have the right to transfer his data in computer-usable form. Whether or not the bureau can withhold his data from him is discussed below, but in many cases it is perfectly legitimate for them simply to give the departing customer a printout (charged at normal printout rates) of all his data, which he must then go to the expense (and delay) of preparing afresh for a new service with another bureau. If, on the other hand, the bureau are prepared to dump his file on magnetic tape or some other computer-usable medium, the customer should expect that the charge may well be on the high side so as to discourage him from leaving the service. This is a point which a customer should consider not only when contemplating terminating the service [10.4], but also before beginning.

10.3 DATA

A point to be clear about is whether data means that which goes from the customer to the bureau, that which is stored and processed by the bureau, and/or that which the bureau sends to the customer. A contract will need to differentiate.

This section must consider the data handling separately for batch programs and on-line. With a batch system the data actually leaves the customer's premises, is held by the bureau for the purpose of inputting it, and then may or may not be returned to the customer; in an online system no physical document leaves the customer's premises, and the contract will be concerned solely with the data in its computer-usable form [10.2.2].

Contracts purely for data preparation or data transfer [1.10] with no other processing element are also relevant here. The batch system described in 10.3.1 is of course far less common than it used to be, but it may arise when new hardware and/ or software are being purchased and the customer wishes to get a backlog of data on the system quickly, so that he can begin acceptance testing as soon as possible after delivery.

10.3.1 Batch systems

In a batch system, the usual procedure is for the customer to deliver his data to the bureau's premises; for the bureau to input it to the computer; and then for the bureau to send the results, and sometimes also the data, back to the customer. This part of a bureau's work is virtually indistinguishable from an ordinary data preparation bureau's work, except that in the latter case the results will consist of some computer-readable medium rather than a printout.

Delivery [Q7]

Delivery is typically effected by the customer himself, by post, or by a courier service. If the customer performs the delivery himself, the contract is often silent on the question of delivery—though it is to be noticed that failure by the customer to deliver data could seriously disrupt the bureau's operation. For such a clause see 10.1.1 above, or this general clause on frustration:

> "If this Contract or any part thereof shall become impossible of performance or otherwise frustrated the Bureau shall be entitled to reasonable remuneration for any work done or prepared to be done by the Bureau."

This last phrase is designed to cover, at least in part, time booked on a machine, the payment of overtime to operators and so on. The clause also covers poor quality of data [10.6.1]. However, the customer's failure to deliver data might also be covered by the service being on a minimum charge basis. It is also to be noted that silence on this point, and an apparently tolerant attitude to this point, facilitate a bureau's exclusion of liability for any delay in processing the data—usually within a more general exclusion clause such as:

> "The Bureau will not accept any responsibility for loss or damage or delay, etc."

Some contracts deal with delivery in the more general context of incidental expenses:

> "The cost of transporting data or supplies necessary to the performance of this Contract . . . shall be borne by the Customer."

Safe-keeping

It is quite common for a bureau to exclude any responsibility for the safe-keeping of data while on their premises:

"The Bureau shall not be responsible for the loss of or damage (howsoever arising) to any documents or data supplied by the Customer while on the Bureau's premises nor for any consequential loss arising therefrom."

At first sight, this seems gratuitously harsh, but it might serve to remind a customer that he will usually need to be able to check that the data he supplied is the data which was used, and in his own interests he should keep a duplicate copy of that data. Otherwise, should any dispute arise as to what data was actually run, he has no evidence on his side. The reader should bear this in mind when considering return of data (see below).

In this regard, it will usually be prudent to specify the intervals at which the bureau will be required to undertake a general back-up of the customer's data (especially for ASP arrangements, where the totality of the customer's system will be located at the bureau's premises).

Return of data [Q8]

It is by no means usual for data to be returned to the customer. If data is to be returned, this should be expressly provided for:

"After completion of the processing all Data and documents supplied by the Customer to the Bureau shall be returned to the Customer."

In this connection, the case of *Re Kingsley (dec'd)* (1978) 122 S.J. 458 is important. It concerned a firm of solicitors using a specialised bureau for their time-recording records. They had claimed costs in respect of 815.5 hours' work but the bill was taxed (*i.e.* assessed for allowable costs) for only 777.5. After processing on the bureau's machine the original records had been destroyed. Payne J. suggested that all the data (including the non-computer data such as attendances) should be kept intact until after taxation or any review of taxation. This is a case which all bureau users should study.

Retention of data [P8]

So far we have considered data only in its tangible form as human-readable or computer-readable material delivered from the customer to the bureau (and sometimes returned after use). But of course the processing usually involves the bureau storing the data in some different form such as disk on their computer. This storage has been considered in its cost aspects above [10.2.2], but there is also an ownership aspect:

"The data held by the Bureau on computer files as a result of a service provided by the Bureau to the Customer shall become the property of the Customer only upon payment of all the Bureau's invoices in full."

This clause is of course designed to prevent a customer's leaving a bureau without paying. The transfer of ownership will of course have a strange effect on the Data Protection principles [10.3.3]. The clause continues:

"The Bureau shall at its normal charges for the time being make all reasonable facilities available for the transfer of the data as the Customer may desire."

In other words, if a customer leaves the service (and has paid his bills), the bureau will provide print-outs, tapes or whatever of the data to facilitate its transfer elsewhere, but reserves the right to charge for it—a not unreasonable precaution; and this cost is one which any customer contemplating changing bureaux must consider, as well as the cost of re-inputting the data with the new bureau.

It will always be prudent from a customer's point of view to take and keep copies of the total data file from time to time. If there is a dispute the bureau may unreasonably withhold the master tape which would leave the customer in a very difficult position.

10.3.2 Data transfer

If a customer is moving from one type of hardware and/or software to another he may need to have his existing data transferred to the new system. To do this he will need to test that the transfer can be done successfully by sending a test sample of his existing data to his supplier or other data transfer contractor and asking him to produce data in the form for the new system which must then be run successfully on that new system. Only after a careful and accurate test of this sort should the customer negotiate a data transfer agreement.

Having satisfied himself that the transfer is feasible and that the contractor can actually perform it, the customer will need to define the service contractually. Usually the contract envisages the customer's real data leaving his premises (probably in tape or disk form), being taken to the contractor's premises, the transfer being effected, and the original data together with its new format being returned, or just possibly being kept for further processing. The types of clause described in 10.3.1 for delivery [Q7], safe-keeping, return [Q8] and retention of data [P8, Q9] are likely to be relevant here.

10.3.3 Data protection [P15 (2)]

The Data Protection Act 1984 (now repealed) had much to say about bureaux and one of the Data Protection Principles in that Act (Principle 8) was specially created to deal with the inherent risks of one organisation or person processing someone else's personal data. By contrast, the Data Protection Act 1998 does not use the word "bureau" but talks of a "data processor" which is defined in section 1(1) as:

> "in relation to personal data, . . . any person (other than an employee of the data controller) who processes the data on behalf of the data controller."

The data controller is the person who "determines the purposes for which and the manner in which any personal data are, or are to be, processed" (also section 1 (1) of the Act), and is thus usually the 'owner' in a business sense of the data. This wide definition embraces a large number of contracts including traditional bureau contracts but also service level agreements, outsourcing and even Internet Service Agreements and contracts for the creation of website designs [11.3.1, 12.2.1].

This wider definition of a data processor is also liable to bring within its orbit maintenance contracts, as where a bug is suspected the contractor may well wish to conduct some of the customer's processing in order to replicate the symptoms which have been reported. If that processing requires personal data to be processed it is difficult to resist the conclusion that the contractor is (albeit temporarily) operating as a data processor under the Act. [8.7.2, K15 (2)]

All these contracts involving a data processor are subject to particular provisions under the Data Protection Act 1998 if they involve personal data—*i.e.* data about an identifiable living person. Under section 4(4) of the Act, the data controller must comply with the Data Protection Principles set out in Schedule I, Part I, of the Act, interpreting them in accordance with Part II of Schedule 1 (s.4(2)). Indemnities against potential losses stemming from infringements of the Principles would accordingly seem appropriate.

However, two Principles call for further elaboration in bureau and other service contacts, as follows.

The Seventh Principle

"Appropriate technical and organisational measures shall be taken against unauthorised or unlawful processing of personal data and against accidental loss or destruction, or damage to, personal data."

Of the Seventh Principle, the interpretation in Part II says:

"12. Where processing of personal data is carried out by a data processor on behalf of a data controller, the data controller is not regarded as complying with the seventh principle unless:

(a) the processing is carried out under a contract:

(i) which is made or evidenced in writing, and

(ii) under which the data processor is to act only on instructions from the data controller, and

(b) the contract requires the data processor to comply with the obligations equivalent to those imposed on a data controller by the seventh principle."

The provisions of the Seventh Principle are suspended until October 24, 2001 for personal data on which processing was already under way before October 24, 1998 (s.39 and Sched. 8, Pt 1, para. 1 and Pt II, para. 3(2)). The effect of this is that all personal data whose bureau processing was *not* under way by October 24, 1998 has been bound by the Seventh Principle since March 1, 2000 when the main provisions of the Act came into force.

So, to comply with the Seventh Principle, the contract must be made in writing, and must have an explicit clause requiring the data processor (*i.e.* the bureau) to act at all times only on instructions from the data controller.

Furthermore, the data processor/bureau must comply with the obligations imposed on the data controller by this Principle. Those are defined in the same Part II of Schedule 1 as requiring a level of security which balances technological development and cost against the harm which might result from unauthorised or unlawful processing or accidental loss, destruction or damage (para. 9) and taking reasonable steps to ensure the reliability of any employees who have access to the personal data (para 10).

Paragraph 11 of the same Part II of Schedule 1 also requires the data processor to provide to the data controller sufficient guarantees in respect of technical and organisational security measures governing the processing; and the data controller must himself take steps to comply with those measures. Thus the first of these is an obligation on the bureau/processor and the second on the controller.

It has been argued that compliance with BS7799 for information security management might be good evidence of compliance. This has obvious attractions, but cannot be regarded as a certainty, especially for highly sensitive and/or confidential personal information.

It should be noted that where the data is not personal—*i.e.* not about identifiable living persons—these provisions to not apply. There is also a limited number of exemptions to the Act set out in sections 27–39, including such matters as national security, crime, taxation, etc. Thus, for example, a specialised bureau providing stock market values for the purposes of probate will be exempt since the only personal data will refer to a dead person. But general bureaux of all kinds and especially on-line ones, which have no direct control over the data input by the data controller, should comply with these provisions.

The Eighth Principle

> "Personal data shall not be transferred to a country or territory outside the European Economic Area unless that country or territory ensures an adequate level of protection for the rights and freedoms of data subjects in relation to the processing of personal data."

The European Economic Area consists of the European Union plus Iceland, Norway and Liechtenstein. Within all these states there are reckoned to be sufficient data protection safeguards for personal data to circulate freely. The Data Protection Commissioners of the various European Union states may produce "findings" as to other countries outside the EEA with sufficient safeguards and if they do these countries also may receive personal data as well as those on the EEA list (Sched. 1, Pt II, para. 15). But outside that area, safeguards need to be sought in accordance with the other provisions of Schedule 1, Pt II, paras 13–14. For interpretation, the guidance of the Data Protection Commissioner at **www.dataprotection.gov.uk/transbord.htm** is essential. The most important part of her advice is a distinction between transit of data and transfer. This means that data which passes through a state without being processed at all—and processing includes disclosure (s.1(1))—is simply in transit and does not need to comply with provisions for transfer. Furthermore, in accordance with the Data Protection Directive (95/46/E.C., Arts 25–26) with which the Act expresses U.K. compliance, the difficulties of transborder flows may be circumvented by contract. The Commissioner's advice in general lies outside the scope of this book but indemnities against unauthorised transborder flows would seem to be vital, and where a transborder flow to a third country (*i.e.* non-EEA) is visualised, appropriate contractual terms must be in place to cover it.

An analogous consideration to data protection is the need for a prohibition on defamatory and obscene material. Some of this might also fall foul of the Data Protection Act but even if it does not the bureau will wish for an indemnity from the customer in respect of it [P14]. The case of *Godfrey v. Demon Internet* is a salutary warning here [12.3.1].

10.4 TERMINATION [P19]

Termination of bureau services is usually a fairly simple matter, being triggered either by incapacity (*e.g.* receivership), effluxion of time, by notice or by breach. The first two need hardly detain us: a typical clause on notice might read:

> "Either party to this Agreement may at any time after the date of commencement by giving *three* months' written notice to the other terminate the service period under this Agreement."

In contrast, a clause allowing termination for breach:

"The Bureau shall be entitled to terminate the service period under this Agreement by notice in writing to the Customer in the event of the Customer's being in arrear for a period of *30* days after any payment to be made hereunder has become due or if the Customer shall commit or allow to be committed a breach of any of the terms of this Agreement and shall fail to remedy such breach within *30* days of notice by the Bureau requiring such breach to be remedied or if the Customer shall become bankrupt or insolvent."

Sometimes, a contract may also permit a customer to terminate if he refuses an increase in charges (for the increase itself see 10.5.1 below):

"If the Bureau shall give to the Customer notice to alter any charges in accordance with Clause *X* hereof the Customer may within the period of *one month* commencing on the date of such notice give to the Bureau notice in writing of the Customer's refusal to agree to such alteration and the Bureau's notice shall then be deemed to be notice to terminate this Agreement to take effect *3* months after the Bureau's notice."

Termination may also sometimes be triggered by the customer reducing his volume of work by more than a certain amount.

"Any notice given by the Customer to the Bureau under Clause *X* hereof which seeks to reduce the specified minimum volume of work by more than *30* per cent of the volumes specified in Schedule *Y* hereof shall be deemed to terminate this Agreement."

10.5 VARIATION

10.5.1 Variation of charges [P4 (4)]

One form of words for the variation of charges is as follows:

"The Bureau reserves the right to vary any of the charges due under this Agreement upon giving to the Customer not less than *3* months' notice in writing of such alteration."

This is a fairly standard clause and merits no special analysis, though it should be noted that sometimes the contract allows the customer to terminate the contract if he refuses to accept the alteration in the charges [10.4].

10.5.2 Variation of service

The disparate nature of the services which can be the subject of a bureau contract means that a variation of almost any clause is at least conceivable. In practice, there is often no variation clause as such, since it is simpler for one party or the other to give notice and negotiate a fresh contract. However, the following example is an interesting attempt to allow for this, while allowing the customer to terminate if the alterations are unacceptable:

"Any change in any element of the services the subject of this Agreement may necessitate other changes to the Bureau's charges or otherwise whether such change of an element is made under the following clause or otherwise agreed between the parties hereto."

This clause is followed by:

"The Customer may request the Bureau to vary any element in the service the subject of this Agreement by giving 3 months' notice in writing to the Bureau specifying the variation required provided that if the Bureau consider that such variation is not technically practicable or desirable or ambiguously or inadequately specified the Bureau may within 10 working days of such notice give further notice to the Customer to that effect whereupon the notice given by the Customer shall be cancelled."

This clause does not, of course, spell out the cost of implementing the alterations which is not necessarily the same as the cost of performing the alteration. In other words, the customer's request might well require a software alteration which would need specifying in writing. Finally, if the alteration reduced the volume of data below a particular point, this might be construed as termination [10.4].

10.6 CUSTOMER'S DUTIES

Customer's duties may be divided into three classes:

(a) batch service duties (mostly concerned with the submission of data);

(b) on-line service duties (mostly concerned with the usage and abuse of the terminal); and

(c) general duties.

10.6.1 Batch services: data

This section should be considered closely with section 10.3.

Provision of data

We have already considered [10.3.1, 10.1.1] the effect of a customer's failing to deliver data. The point is reinforced in some contracts by imposing on the customer a direct obligation to provide data and the programs to be run if they in fact are the customer's:

"The Customer shall provide the Bureau with all programs operating instructions and data necessary to enable the Bureau to perform its services under this Agreement."

Quality of data [Q7]

It also follows that the programs and data must be of adequate quality. Strictly speaking, the customer's duties extend only to the provision of data sufficient to enable the bureau to execute its side of the bargain; in practice, this is usually expressed negatively with the bureau excluding liability for faulty or illegible or otherwise defective data:

"The Bureau does not accept responsibility for loss or damage arising from or consequential upon the Customer's act or default in relation to errors in the coding of information, illegible information or documents, faulty damaged incompatible or incorrectly encoded computer media supplied to the Bureau, the late arrival or non-arrival of data, incorrect data, data out of sequence or in the wrong form, variations in data from that originally agreed to be supplied. The Bureau reserves the right to charge for any additional work needed to be run as a result of any of the faults listed in this clause."

This is a formidable and alarming list, and one which is well worth considering in detail, if only because these considerations apply to all data preparation contracts.

Errors in the coding of information includes illegible information: data preparation costs are based on assumptions as to the number of keystrokes an hour which can be performed by an operator. This obviously depends on the physical speed and dexterity of the operator, and also on the quality of the data. The customer should insist on the bureau seeing representative samples of the data at its worst before the contract is signed, so that the bureau are aware of what they will be receiving. However, if the data actually submitted after the contract is noticeably worse in quality (illegible, badly laid out, etc.), the bureau's operator is likely to produce results which are not only unsatisfactory (in terms of characters misread and so forth) but also more expensive since the operator will have had to spend more time wondering whether the figure is a 0 or a 6. The correct analogy here is with typesetting where a printer will charge extra for the setting of "bad copy"—a term of art which for some reason has not permeated to the computer industry.

Faulty, damaged, incompatible or incorrectly encoded computer media: whereas the previous problems were concerned with data written on sheets, these words are concerned with data on computer media. The problems which can arise here are complex, technical, and often highly intractable. "Faulty" media are the easiest to consider. A magnetic tape has on it magnetised particles arranged in a pattern. If the tape drive which produced it failed to reproduce the code correctly, it obviously cannot be read. "Damaged" is also straightforward. "Do not fold staple or mutilate" used to be a common litany when punch cards were used. Cards which had been folded, stapled or mutilated could not be read. "Incompatible" is more complicated. The codes which represent each character are not always identical for each machine and nor is the density in which the codes are packed. The customer who intends to supply data in computer-usable form should satisfy himself that his data will run on the bureau's machine, and the simplest way to do this is to ask the bureau to let him have a trial run with a fair sample of the data. For late arrival and non-arrival, see 10.3.1 above. "Incorrect" data—Is the stuff which is being delivered to the bureau the right data for the run of which the customer expects to receive the results? Data "out of sequence" applied chiefly to punched cards where the recurring nightmare had always been the box of cards tipped on the floor. The remaining categories (wrong form, variations of data) are blanket definitions to cover any other imaginable forms of defective data.

10.6.2 On-line services: terminals and modems

With on-line services where the customer has a terminal, the quality of the data does not really arise since, if the customer inputs rubbish, only he knows and only he is involved. Nor is the provision of data really relevant since charging is not usually dependent on booking computer time at a particular time [10.2.2].

Limitation of terminal use [P6]

If the customer provides his own terminal for the service, the rest of this section is irrelevant. If, however, the terminal is provided by the bureau, the bureau is in effect hiring a terminal to the customer, and many of the clauses will come straight from a hardware hiring contract covering the correct use of the terminal, duty to insure it, and so on [2.6]. However, in addition to these duties, the customer may be restricted from attempting to gain access to the system by any other terminal:

> "The Customer shall not utilise or attempt to utilise any equipment other than that provided by the Bureau under the terms of this Agreement for the purpose of using the services of the Bureau."

The reason for this clause may be complex. At its crudest, the clause may do no more than reflect the profit the bureau makes on hiring terminals. But there are other more justifiable reasons: the bureau may wish all users to have a standard terminal so as to simplify maintenance and staff training among the customer's employees. These considerations apply particularly where the customer lacks deep experience of computer applications, and needs a good deal of both support and training. The design of standard operating instructions (which may be enshrined in a manual or on-line help facility) becomes very difficult if terminals vary.

Limitation of service availability

In a similar way, most bureaux will seek to prevent their customers from using the terminal for services provided by other bureaux:

> "The Customer shall use the terminal equipment solely for the purpose of the service provided by the Bureau under the terms of this Agreement."

The purpose of this clause is straightforward: no bureau providing a terminal to enable customers to use their service is likely to be enthusiastic about that terminal being used to give his customer access to a rival system, and, in practice, pretty well the only way to seek to stop it is by contract. It is also designed to prevent the customer from gaining access to the bureau's other services and data.

This problem arises because the bureau cannot actually see what is done with the terminal, or who uses it. So a bureau may also seek to use the contract to prevent the customer from using the service on behalf of someone else. This is particularly likely to be so when the charging structure has a joining fee, specialised terminal charge, or other charging basis apart from machine usage and storage charges:

> "The Customer shall not use the service provided by the Bureau under the terms of this Agreement for the benefit of any person or organisation other than the Customer."

This clause is a little difficult to define without becoming too specific about the service, and perhaps the most satisfactory way to define it is in those terms. For example, a bureau providing a sales ledger service might draft the following:

> "The Customer shall use the Sales Ledger service provided under the terms of this Agreement solely for his own sales ledger and shall not use it for the sales ledger of any other company organisation or body whatsoever."

Another clause designed to deal with a related problem is the following:

> "The Customer shall not sell lease assign transfer or otherwise make available for any purpose whether gratuitously or for a valuable consideration the System

or any part thereof or any information with respect thereof to any person firm or company (other than his own employees for the sole purpose of enabling the Customer to use this service within the terms of this Agreement)."

This clause deals not only with the customer effectively running the service as if he were a bureau for others, but also with the mischief which could arise where a customer revealed information about the system to someone else which enabled this third party to gain access to the system. On-line systems are usually accessed by telephoning the correct number of the computer (thereby setting up the communication line) and the inputting of user name and code word to identify the particular user. It follows that an unauthorised person, obtaining these three pieces of information (telephone number, user number and code word), and already possessing a terminal or PC and modem, could get into the system. For an ordinary on-line bureau, where each user builds up his own files on the computer, this is bad enough, though at least, in theory, it is detectable when the customer whose number has been used without authorisation identifies files as not being his own. But for a retrieval system where the customer is not building up data files, the danger is even greater since it is virtually undetectable. Failure to guard against this may in some circumstances be a breach of the Data Protection Act 1998. The damage to be guarded against is twofold: unauthorised access ("hacking"); and damage to data or programs ("virus"). Both these activities are criminal offences, under sections 1, 2 and 3, respectively, of the Computer Misuse Act 1990 [R3 (7)].

Incidentally, this clause provides the bureau with further protection for his software [3.8], a point which is considered below [10.6.3].

Modems and network cards [R6]

On a network a customer is likely to wish to attach a PC and the mechanism for this if the customer's machine cannot be directly cabled to the network is by modem— "modulator/demodulator"—which converts data signals to voice signals for transmission over the public switched telephone system and then converts them back to data on receipt after transmission.

Modems are usually integral to a PC but there may still be occasional cases in older systems where a modem will need to be hired with the cost. It is impossible for a bureau or network provider to know what the modem is used for and as it has no moving parts it cannot be said to be harmed by being used for other services. So restrictions on terminal use described in the preceding section are not usual with modems. However, the contract will need to ensure that on termination the modem is surrendered or that the customer pays for the modem's retention.

If the customer's PC can be directly cabled to the network (this usually arises when customer and network provider are part of the same group of companies), there will probably be a network card to be installed in the customer's PC. Again, there will probably be no separate rental for this, no restriction on its use, but procedures for its return to the network provider on termination of the contract.

10.6.3 General duties [P13, Q19]

Protection of the system

Software protection [3.8] is often relevant to bureau services since it has been known for a bureau's customer to hand over as much information as he can gather about the service program (operating manuals, forms, print-outs of runs, and so on) to a third party in order to get them to write a program for him to run on his own machine. Therefore, the clauses considered in Chapter 3 [3.8] are relevant here. A variant of this to cover the situation for an accounting program may be of interest:

> "(a) The Bureau is the sole owner of all rights in connection with the programs to provide the Services and the Customer shall not pass information about such programs or the Services to any person or body except the Customer's own staff, auditors, HM Inspector of Taxes, HM Customs & Excise and similar persons and bodies having a right duty or obligation to know the business of the Customer and then only in pursuance of such right duty or obligation.
>
> (b) The Customer shall not at any time hereafter (whether or not the Services are still being used by the Customer) pass any information about the Programs and Services their working methods structure nature or content to any computer service company software house bureau consultant or to any other person except as mentioned in (a) of this clause without the written permission of the Bureau and upon such terms and conditions as the Bureau may specify."

Like most such clauses it is not perhaps completely watertight. A customer with considerable ingenuity and dishonesty could probably get round these clauses, though after notice like this he would have to admit that he was warned.

In view of this situation, an indemnity clause is not inappropriate:

> "The Customer hereby agrees to indemnify the Bureau in respect of any breach by the Customer or any of its employees servants or agents of any terms or conditions of this Agreement resulting in any loss damage liability costs or expenses which the Bureau may suffer."

The clause itself is usual enough in all kinds of contracts for services, and in no way peculiar to computers, but—considered in conjunction with the preceding clauses—it adds up to a formidable attempt by a bureau to protect its property.

Communications software

A network provider may also supply software for the customer to run on his PC to facilitate communications. Contractually this is not much different from providing applications software for the customer to run on a bureau's equipment, except that the software once installed on the customer's PC is no longer directly under the control of the bureau. However, the licensed software continues to belong to the bureau (network provider), and so must be either surrendered or destroyed on termination of the contract.

Data protection

The obligations under the Data Protection Act 1998 are binding on both the bureau and the user and each will need to indemnify the other against failure to comply with the Act. Details have already been set out in 10.3.3.

Duty to pay

This duty is virtually indistinguishable from such clauses in other contracts. It is usual to bill customers monthly in arrears for payment in 30 days:

> "The Customer shall pay to the Bureau all charges due under this Agreement within *30* days of the last day of the month in which the Service was performed."

Report of defects

We shall be considering below [10.7.3] the circumstances in which the bureau may be obliged to re-run work. For this to be remotely practicable, it is essential that the customer report any defects, faults or imperfect runs as soon as possible:

> "Full charges shall be payable by the Customer for time used if the Customer shall not have reported any machine errors within 2 days of the Customer's receipt of the data produced by the run in which such machine errors are alleged to have occurred."

Leaving aside for the moment the question of whether machine errors could possibly include operator errors or other malfunctionings within the control of the bureau, we see that this clause, in effect, seeks to impose on the customer a duty to check all his results within two days. It is therefore essential that he keeps records (duplicate entry forms?) of all data he submits, and that the service prints out an audit trail of all data it has received (whether or not it has been able to process it successfully [10.3]).

This situation is usually covered by a very general clause excluding the bureau's liability in the event of *force majeure* (and thereby admitting it in cases of negligence and the like on the bureau's part) or even by a more explicit offer to replace or reprocess data negligently handled [10.7.3], provided it is in a reasonable time. We feel a more explicit clause is desirable to impress on the customer a duty to report errors, faults and mishandlings, with a like explicit clause requiring the bureau to reprocess in such an event. For instance:

> "The Customer shall notify the Bureau within 7 days of all claims in respect of replacement or reprocessing made necessary whether as a direct result of the negligence of the Bureau their servants agents or sub-contractors in the performance of the Service or otherwise."

Do the seven days flow from the date of occurrence of the error, or from the customer's becoming aware of it? For the bureau's clause, see 10.7.3 below.

10.7 BUREAU'S DUTIES AND LIABILITIES

10.7.1 Confidentiality [P13, Q17]

Many of the bureau's duties in specialised services mirror a software house's duties [3.7], including confidentiality [3.7.2], and need not be recapitulated here.

An aspect of this confidentiality is the obligation alluded to above [10.3.1] on return of the data after processing. A further aspect is Data Protection [10.3.3].

10.7.2 Helpdesk and training [R2 and Schedule 1]

A network agreement will frequently include a helpdesk facility. The helpdesk will be manned—usually not for the full time the network is available since many networks are available 24 hours a day, 365 days a year. Instead, a helpdesk may be manned during ordinary business hours. The staff on the helpdesk will provide telephone advice to the customer's users trying to gain access to the network and use its services. The staff will keep records of all reported faults and difficulties which can provide valuable analysis as to how satisfied the users are with the network.

Training is a related service; see 3.7.3, which provides information about staff training which is equally appropriate to network training.

10.7.3 Replacement and reprocessing [Q14, Q16]

This has already been mentioned above in discussing the customer's obligation to report errors and defects [10.6.3]. Many contracts are altogether silent about even the possibility of replacement of data which has been faultily prepared, or the reprocessing of runs lost through machine malfunction or operator error. Nevertheless, there is a well recognised custom that negligence or fault of this kind should be rectified by replacement or re-run:

> "If the results produced by the Bureau for the Customer are incorrect by reason of a fault occurring in the computer or of a mistake due to negligence or inadvertence of the Bureau or their servants agents or sub-contractors then the Bureau shall reprocess the data to produce correct results without further charge to the Customer but the Bureau shall not be under any further liability to the Customer in respect of the said incorrect results or their consequences."

This is the usual form of this obligation, and it allows reprocessing for only two types of error: machine malfunction (*e.g.* a printer fault preventing the data from appearing legibly), or negligence and inadvertence (*e.g.* operator mishandling or loss or damage of the results). This clause is appropriate only where the bureau owns the program since, if they do not, the error may have been due to programming error in a piece of software supplied by the customer. It follows, of course, as has already been emphasised, that the customer must keep his data (or accurate records of it) and secure his audit trail in order to be able to prove his point. It should be noted that:

(1) Reprocessing is limited to these situations, and most bureaux exclude *force majeure*;

(2) It is up to the customer to complain promptly of any faults [10.6.3];

(3) Most contracts seek to limit the obligation to reprocessing, and decline to entertain any further claims for consequential loss.

In this last connection, it is clear that consequential loss is likely to increase rather than decrease the longer the error remains undetected, and this again reinforces the customer's interest in complaining as soon as possible. A comprehensive clause in this area runs:

> "(a) The Bureau will replace free of charge and as soon as is practicable having regard to the Bureau's other commitments any materials spoilt destroyed or lost as a direct consequence of the negligence of the Bureau its servants or agents or subcontractors in the performance of the Service.
> (b) The Bureau will correct free of charge and as soon as is practicable having regard to the Bureau's other commitments any errors in results produced by them solely through their negligence provided that such errors are notified to the Bureau in writing by the Customer within *2* days of the Customer's receipt of such results.
> (c) Save as expressly provided in *x(a)* and *x(b)* above the Bureau shall be under no liability whatsoever in respect of any loss damage or delay of any nature

whatsoever and however caused whether direct or consequential and whether or not caused by the negligence of the Bureau its servants agents or subcontractors."

10.7.4 Maintenance [P6, P11]

Maintenance of the terminal or modem (if hire is involved, see 10.1.2) and of the software is covered in Chapters 8 and 9.

10.7.5 Performance and availability

Guarantees as to performance of an ordinary bureau are extremely rare, but the checklist of points at 3.3.2 may be equally applicable to bureau contracts. To those should be added availability—*i.e.* a measure of the times of day when the system must fulfil the minimum performance criteria.

In networks, performance criteria are rather more usual. The users of the network will want a guarantee that the electronic mail messages will reach their destination in a reasonable period of time, that faxes initiated on the network will be sent at the specified time and that if there is to be any delay or a fax cannot be delivered (*e.g.* a non-existent fax number), they will be notified swiftly. Most of all they will want a guarantee that the network will be up at specified hours, which often means in practice 24 hours a day, 365 days a year, and if there has to be any downtime they are notified of it well in advance. They will also want a guarantee that the helpdesk is available within specified hours (not usually the same hours as the network [10.7.2]).

CHAPTER 11

OUTSOURCING AGREEMENTS

11.0 Introduction
11.1 Services to be Performed
11.2 Payment
11.3 Data
11.4 Termination
11.5 Variation
11.6 Customer's Duties
11.7 Outsource Contractor's Duties

11.0 INTRODUCTION

The service level agreement described in the previous chapter [10.1.3, R] is common where cost-centre accounting is used in an organisation, as it enables the users to see exactly what the information services in their organisation cost. It is a small step from this to the process of putting all these services to an outside company—a mechanism formerly known as *Facilities Management* but now more usually called *Outsourcing*. Outsourcing is, accordingly, a shorthand means of describing those arrangements whereby the activities of an in-house service department (for example, the IT Department) are transferred to a third party, who in turn uses the assets and people who had previously worked within that service department for the purpose of providing the same services back to the client.

It follows that the outsource agreement will have within it the sort of definition of service levels which the in-house agreement has, but in addition there are likely to be detailed requirements for the outsource contractor to take over the customer's premises, hardware, software and staff which were formerly used to provide the services in-house. Each of these has important implications for the customer. An additional important consideration is what happens at the end of the contract. Too few outsource contracts consider the possibilities of either switching outsource contractor, or even taking the service back in-house, and indeed after an outsourced contract has been operational for several years, it is not at all easy to change back again. If on the other hand, the relationship between the parties breaks down, arrangements must be fair to both sides and manage the "divorce" as amicably as possible.

11.1 SERVICES TO BE PERFORMED [S2]

These are usually the services that might be described in a Service Level Agreement [10.1.3, R2], but because the agreement is between two companies at arms' length, they need to be much more precisely defined—usually in a Schedule which may build on an existing service level agreement. However, unlike an internal Service

Level Agreement, the parties must define not just the services but also be more rigorous about the level to be attained in each. As with any software contract, the customer needs to distinguish clearly between things which are essential to his business' functioning and things which however attractive are minor or peripheral (as this will inevitably impact on the price which he will ultimately have to pay).

If the services are (as is usually the case) substantial, there may be a plan (incorporated in a Schedule) for an orderly transfer from the customer to the contractor, with different services being taken on at different times. Acceptance and payments should be linked to the plan.

Performance standards should be established much as for Service Level Agreements [10.1.3, R, Sched. 3]. These will be used both for monitoring the standard of services provided at the regular review meetings [11.7.4] and for any claw back of fees or other agreed penalty for failure to maintain the standards [11.2]. They may even be used in certain circumstances to permit early termination of the contract but for difficulties in making use of this see 11.4 below.

11.2 PAYMENT [S4, S13]

Ways of pricing the services to be performed under the contract include calculations based upon the number of full-time-equivalent customer staff whose roles have been extinguished by the contractor, and calculations based upon the actual costs incurred by the contractor in providing the services (plus an element of profit). Nevertheless, the most common payment mechanism usually involves a fixed fee, so as to give the customer a degree of financial certainty about the cost of the services to be provided.

However, the nature of outsource agreements is such that there inevitably needs to be a degree of flexibility over payment provisions. In particular:

(a) for longer term contracts, the contractor may wish to vary the amount of any annual fixed fee to reflect wage inflation or other related costs. The customer will wish to be protected from the risk of being blackmailed by the contractor part-way into a long term arrangement. Accordingly, if such increases are to be allowed at all, it would be usual to see them linked to a pre-agreed index, such as the retail price index:

"On April 1 of each year, the annual fee payable in respect of the Services as specified in *Schedule X* shall be varied in line with the increase in the Retail Price Index during the preceding 12 month period."

(b) IT outsource contracts often involve *technology refresh* provisions, whereby the contractor takes on an obligation to keep up to date the IT infrastructure being used for the provision of the services. For example, the contract may require that the main processor and operating system should be upgraded in the fourth year of the contract. Such obligations may be subsumed within the overall fixed price, but may equally be priced separately, depending on the nature and extent of the updating required. It is essential that the customer understands the extent of the contractor's obligations in this regard, or he may find himself inheriting outdated equipment at the end of the contract.

(c) Changes to the nature of the customer's business and its service requirements are inevitable; accordingly, as with software development and consultancy contract [3.5, 13.5], detailed change control provisions are essential so as to reflect any required changes to the costs to the outsourcer and consequently, the charges to be levied to the customer. This is discussed in more detail in 11.5 below.

Most outsource contracts include a claw-back clause whereby if the contractor fails to provide the level of service required, the customer can withhold money. For example, if one aspect of the required performance has been defined as having the network up and available 98 per cent of the time between 8.30 a.m. and 6.30 p.m. each working day, then for each hour or part hour below this in any one calendar month, the customer can withhold 5 per cent of the fee for a month's services. Such clauses, often known as *service credit regimes*, need to be checked very carefully. Although 98 per cent sounds a high level of service, the 2 per cent latitude in the above example results in the contractor being allowed to have the system down four hours a month during this prime time. Is that acceptable? Similarly, how much will 5 per cent withheld per month amount to? Is this sufficient incentive to the outsource company? On the other hand, is the money withheld liquidated damages or does it look like a penalty?

Many outsource contracts also have incentive clauses linked to more subjective measures, such as the levels of user satisfaction with the services being provided. Although this satisfaction will often be a more accurate measure of the apparent success or failure of the outsource arrangement, the contractor will legitimately be wary of placing significant amounts at risk from purely subjective measures. However, if the amounts in issue are modest, it can be an acceptable way reflecting the all round co-operation which is required for the success of any outsourcing arrangements.

11.3 DATA

The usual provisions as to an indemnity against data which is defamatory or obscene must apply here [P14]. The contractor will also seek protection against the financial consequences to it should any data supplied by the customer and upon which it relies in providing the services turn out to be incorrect and so cause the supplier a loss [S10].

11.3.1 Data Protection Act 1998

Whereas a Service Level Agreement is often between two parts of the same organisation, an outsourcing agreement is explicitly between two separate organisations. Accordingly, the provisions of the Data Protection Act 1998 for data processors/bureaux will apply with clauses requiring the outsource contractor to provide the level of security, guarantee the reliability of its employees, etc. [10.3.3, L9].

All this is in addition to the usual requirements for both sides to observe the provisions of the Act and the Data Protection Principles, and particularly to give undertakings about transborder data flows.

11.4 TERMINATION [S14, SCHEDULE 5]

The contract will typically be for a term of years, probably with an option to renew. Such a renewal may be automatic unless the customer gives notice. The point about the term of years is that it must on the one hand be long enough for the relationship between the parties to stabilise—a period which is usually considered a probationary one. Once this has passed the contract must last long enough to enable the contractor who will have amortised costs to be recovered over a period to start to enjoy the economies of scale and benefits from the contract. Thus for the contractor a longer period will be more attractive and enable him to offer a better service to the customer at a lower price. However, for the customer there must be a mechanism for him to end the contract if the service deteriorates to a defined point and a chance for him either to change contractors then or after the initial period, or even to take the services back in-house. Either finding a new contractor or taking the services in-house would take a considerable amount of time and effort. It is probably not realistic to imagine that such an exercise can be completed easily in less than two years. So a six-month notice period from the contractor is only viable for the customer if he is somehow able to start his search for an alternative to the present contractor well before he receives the notice.

So far as termination for breach is concerned, we have already seen that if the service deteriorates below a certain point the customer may have the right to claw back part of the fees otherwise payable. A point below which the contract can be terminated is also desirable. However, as we have seen in the preceding paragraph such notice must be on such terms as to allow the customer time to find an alternative supplier for the services. A termination for breach which visualises having to continue with the defaulting contractor for a further two years whilst a new tender process is being carried out is hardly realistic, so the claw back is a more realistic mechanism for ensuring the standard of the services. If the service is so bad that the customer exercises the claw back nearly all the time, the value of the contract to the contractor will be so negligible that it should be possible for the parties mutually to agree to terminate the contract early.

Upon either termination or expiry, the customer will wish to ensure that it has in place such terms as will be sufficient to enable it to transfer the provision of the services to either an alternative supplier or in-house but at the same time ensuring continuity of service. Such provisions are often grouped together under the heading *exit provisions* [S, Sched. 5].

One essential aspect of termination is the customer's continuing right to use the licences and infrastructure associated with the services, either on his own account or through the services of a third party, so as to try to maintain the operation of the underlying business whilst a re-tender of the outsourcing contract is arranged. The termination provisions will accordingly need to provide for the customer to have a continuing licence in respect of these aspects of the supplier's Intellectual Property Rights (IPRs) which are necessary for the continuation of the outsource operations, as well as an option to acquire any associated hardware or technical infrastructure [S, Sched. 5, clause 3].

For its part, the contractor will want to ensure that any licence of its IPRs goes no wider than is necessary (and in particular is restricted *vis-à-vis* any use by its competitors) and also that it is only obliged to transfer ownership in dedicated equipment and infrastructure (*i.e.* equipment which is used solely for the customer, and not as part of a shared service centre simultaneously serving the needs of other customers). A simple clause (with reference each to a more detailed explanation in one of the accompanying schedules) might accordingly read as follows:

"Upon the termination or expiry of the Contract, the Customer shall have the option to:

(a) require the Contractor to transfer all the Contractor's rights, title and interests in the Equipment [specified in *Schedule X*] in consideration of the payment of the Transfer Sum [specified in *Schedule Y*];

(b) require the Contractor to assign or novate in favour of the Customer or any replacement supplier nominated by the Customer (at no additional premium) any equipment or hardware leases, software licence and related support agreements so as to ensure that the Customer negotiates the terms of such agreements so as to enable it to comply with this provision); and

(c) require the Contractor to grant to it or any replacement supplier nominated by the Customer a non-exclusive, perpetual licence to use the Supplier Software utilised in connection with the Services, such licence to extend to the use, modification and amendment of such Supplier Software for the Customer's internal business purposes only. In the event that the licence is to be granted to a replacement supplier, it shall be a precondition to the exercise of this option that the replacement supplier agrees to enter into a confidentiality and non-disclosure agreement with the Contractor in the form set out in *Schedule Z*."

Any costs associated with reassigning the licenses at the end of the contract should if possible be explored and defined with the licensors at the same time as the cost of transferring them is being defined before the start of the contract [11.6.3].

On termination, however caused, the usual provisions should be in place for returning the customer's data [10.2.3]. More importantly there must be a mechanism for the contractor to provide necessary information to any new contractor about the service (although allowance may need to be made for information which can genuinely be said to be confidential to the supplier, such as that which relates to its internal processes, rather than the detail of the services provided). Whether anything else is returned—premises, hardware, software, or staff—is a matter for the parties to consider at the time that they draft the contract.

There may also be a mechanism for arbitration or other dispute resolution. If the parties fall out the effects will be considerable for both, the contractor losing a substantial and profitable contract and the customer probably losing a mission-critical service. The Civil Procedure Rules 1998 (Part 1.4(2)(e)) encourage the parties to use an *alternative dispute resolution* procedure, which the Rules define in the Glossary as:

"Collective description of methods of resolving disputes otherwise than through the normal trial process."

This is a definition sufficiently wide to encompass arbitration but also other mechanisms whereby a third party endeavours to persuade the parties to compromise without going to court [S28]. Possible arbitrators or other intermediaries for this are suggested in Chapter 15.

11.5 VARIATION [S3]

No business process stands still and nor does information technology. There must be a mechanism for amending or altering the existing services and adding new services after transfer. All such changes (like any other software or hardware changes) must be agreed between the parties in writing, showing for each proposed change the agreed cost, time scale for implementation, any additional resources required, training implications, and the impact on the existing services. Resources might include new hardware, new software, new staff (including staff to man the helpdesk). However, as the length of such contracts means that the customer will, to a large extent, be dependent upon the contractor to agree to changes which may be critical to reflect changes in the needs of its business, it is usual for there to be a pre-agreed tariff for the fee notes to be applied to the calculation of any requested change, and occasionally also a provision for a reference to an independent expert in the event that the parties do not agree on the amount of effort required. The observations on arbitration or alternative dispute resolution at the end of 11.4 apply equally here.

Training for the customer's staff which is required for some enhancement or change of the services should also include manuals and other documentation.

The impact might deal with the running speed of existing services, or for very large runs limitations on the time of day or day of the week when these can be run. This may need detailed discussion between the parties, as altering such arrangements will frequently impact upon any performance and/or availability obligations which the supplier may have taken on.

So far we have spoken only of changes to the services since these are what the customer really wants. Technical changes to the system taken over by the contractor to enable him to fulfil those services are usually left to him. For example, it will probably be left to the contractor as to how he upgrades or replaces the hardware, provided the level of service is maintained if not improved. If third-party software is used the contractor will probably also have the responsibility of seeking, commissioning where necessary and installing the new versions, again provided always the service level is maintained.

However, if the software includes any items where the customer retains title there must be agreement as to whether the contractor can amend them and if so how title to these amendments is to be handled.

It is sometimes the case that the contractor's duties include an obligation to upgrade the relevant systems over the course of the contract period, especially when this is to be for five years or more. Such obligations are often referred to as *technology refreshers*. The relevant provisions need to be carefully set out so that the contractor can be certain of what it is to do (and can plan accordingly), and the customer can clearly see the mechanism by which it will be asked to pay for the new technology.

The contract may well have a clause allowing the contractor in certain circumstances to increase the charges after a time. Although such clauses usually have a proviso that the customer can terminate the contract if he is not prepared to pay the increased fees, as we saw under Termination [11.4], it is likely to take the customer at least a couple of years to find an alternative supplier. In practice, therefore, it will be difficult for him to terminate and he should instead look to some limitation in the possible increases unless they are linked to some inflation measure and some increased value of service, as suggested for hardware maintenance contracts [8.5.2, K3 (4) Version B].

11.6 CUSTOMER'S DUTIES [S11, S10]

In particular, the customer will usually be responsible for ensuring that all relevant assets can be transferred to the outsource contractor (although this could equally well be dealt with as a joint responsibility during the pre-contract due diligence process) and will need to indemnify the contractor against all past claims arising out of premises, hardware, software licences, and staff which have been transferred.

Some of the customer's likely key responsibilities are set out in more detail below.

11.6.1 Premises

There will invariably be a Schedule describing any premises to be handed over. The premises may be part of a building otherwise retained by the customer, or they may be complete building or group of buildings. Either way, it may seem appropriate from the customer's point of view to offer the contractor a lease. However, it will not be easy to persuade the contractor that it should be for the duration of the contract, to be terminated at the same time and in the same circumstances as the outsource contract, if the contractor hopes within that time to consolidate the system, premises, hardware, etc., with some other system which he already owns, or to use the premises provided to institute a shared service centre of some kind, so as to be able to provide services to clients other than just to customer.

It may well be convenient to the parties to have the actual transfer carried out in associated contract, in which case care must be taken to ensure that all of the usual formalities and investigations associated with the sale and purchase of such properties are undertaken [S, Recital C]. As this is not a book on the Law of Property details of how this might be effected are inappropriate here.

If the premises are part of a building otherwise retained by the customer, rights of access, etc may need to be defined.

The contractor may seek some form of warranty that they are in a fit and proper state:

> "The Customer warrants that the Premises will be made available for use by the Contractor [on the terms of this lease/licence in *Appendix X*] by *January 1, 2002*, and that they are in a fit and proper state for the provision of the Services."

However, it is more likely that the contractor will, as part of the due diligence process, be required to satisfy itself of the suitability of the premises. A sample clause to this effect is at 11.7.1.

11.6.2 Equipment

If a wholly owned subsidiary company is being transferred in its entirety from the customer to the contractor, the equipment to be used for the services can be easily described. Alternatively, the transfer of equipment may be only part of the hardware assets owned by the customer and will need to be carefully defined to provide the services reserving to the customer whatever he needs or else allowing for disposal elsewhere of the untransferred assets. If, however, the transfer is not of a complete company, but is instead simply a transfer of relevant equipment to the contractor, the possibility of a ban on the onwards sale of the hardware from an American company [2.9.1] should be borne in mind and the customer's original hardware purchase contract examined to see if it applies. As problems may also arise in the matter of software licences [11.6.3], there may even be a case for creating a subsidiary company first for the services to be transferred with ownership of all the hardware, licences and other assets, so as to facilitate the transfer.

The parties must also consider whether a lease of such equipment is appropriate to terminate with the rest of the outsource contract. The argument here is different from that for premises, since the premises are likely to have a good residual value, whereas the hardware at the end of (say) five years will be nearly valueless, and indeed as noted above [11.5], it may well be a provision of the contract that the contractor will upgrade or replace the hardware as may be necessary.

11.6.3 Software [S7]

Where the software has been developed in-house by the customer and he owns all the property rights in the software, the customer can grant a licence to the contractor for the use of the software on his (the customer's) behalf. However, where the rights in the software belong to a third party, the matter is less straightforward, since the licence to use such software is not usually transferable [7.6]. In these circumstances, unless a wholly owned company to whom and in whose name the original licence was granted is transferred in its entirety to the contractor, it will usually be necessary to involve the licensor and get him to grant a new licence to the contractor. Do not expect in those circumstances that the licensor will be eager to credit the customer for the unexpired remainder of his licence, or to agree to an assignment of the licence to the contractor without charging a premium.

It is essential that all such software is identified by a complete software audit during the due diligence process, the extent of any rights to assign/novate to licence assessed, and the licensors approached as necessary to ascertain the total cost of effecting any required assignments. This cost will ordinarily be borne by the customer, but could in certain circumstances be shared. This is also the time to ascertain from the licensor(s) the likely cost of reassigning the licences at the end of the contract.

We have spoken above [3.8.1] of the practice rudely called "stiffing" whereby a software supplier can increase charges on the occurrence of quite ordinary business events. One of these may be assignment and the customer's original software should be examined to ensure that with any assignment additional charges will not be incurred. If necessary the software copyright owner may need to be brought in: it may be preferable for the contractor to embark on a new direct contractual relationship with the copyright owner to enable him to fulfil the contract.

11.6.4 Staff [S12]

The impact on employees in an outsourcing agreement is usually governed by the Transfer of Undertakings (Protection of Employees) Regulations 1981 (S.I. 1981 No. 1794) amended by 1987 and 1995 Regulations (S.I. 1987 No. 442 and S.I. 1995 No. 2587) and the Trade Union Reform and Employment Rights Act 1993. This body of law is collectively known as *Tupe*. The general purpose of Tupe is to safeguard the rights and conditions of the transferred staff so that they will be no worse off under their new employer (the outsource contractor) than they were under their old employer (the organisation outsourcing). Tupe is a complex and fast-changing area of law and a detailed consideration of it lies outside the scope of the present work. The reader is referred to the *Outsourcing Practice Manual* (John Angel ed., Sweet & Maxwell) for a detailed discussion of this topic.

Tupe will apply to most outsourcing arrangements although recent decisions of the courts have shown it will not apply to every case. Tupe may apply to an outsourcing arrangement at three different stages:

(a) on the initial outsourcing by the customer to a third party (usually called the contractor);

(b) when the outsourcing contract ends and the customer decides to switch contractors; or

(c) when the outsourcing contract ends and the customer decides to take the outsourced activity back in-house.

If Tupe applies, it has the following principal effects:

(a) all employees working in the service before the transfer will automatically become employed by the new contractor;

(b) the new contractor is obliged to employ such staff on their existing terms and conditions and it cannot change these terms and conditions if the reason for the change is the business transfer;

(c) dismissals in connection with the transfer will automatically be deemed unfair, unless they take place for an economic, technical or organisational reason entailing changes in the work force;

(d) both the customer and the contractor will have an obligation to inform and consult with recognised trades unions (if they exist) and/or with employee representatives; and

(e) the new contractor will assume most of the same employment liabilities to the employees as the old employer.

The customer will usually want to ensure that Tupe applies so that all of the employees will be transferred automatically to the contractor (although it will first wish to evaluate which of such staff it may wish to retain, *i.e.* by transferring them to other parts of its business). The contractor will need to be aware of this process so that it makes allowances for the potential disappearance of "key" staff from the operation it inherits.

If the contractor is not willing to take on some or all of the employees, the customer will need to make arrangements for either deploying the employees elsewhere within his organisation or making them redundant. As it is possible that the customer will re-inherit the employees at the end of the contract, it may wish to retain some control over the employees during the period of the outsourcing contract.

The customer should think about what will happen at the end of the contract. For example, it may re-inherit the employees, or may have to provide information on the employees to a second contractor who will take over provision of the service. The customer is therefore likely to seek to impose an obligation on the part of the contractor to provide information on the numbers of employees and a summary of their terms and conditions.

There will also be more general staff-related provisions other than those relating directly to Tupe. For example, in much the same manner as for software development contracts [3.6.1, D17] it is essential that the customer nominates liaison staff to co-operate with the contractor's named staff and provide information to the contractor as appropriate of the customer's requirement [3.6.1, D19]. Regular review meetings should be held and minuted to monitor the working of the contract, decide on whether any failures have occurred within the contract's definition and if so operate the resulting claw back or other penalty [11.1, 11.2, S13], and co-operate on any development or upgrade of hardware or software.

The usual provision about either the contractor poaching further staff from the customer or the customer trying to get back the staff he has handed over are likely to figure in the contract and be subject to the usual difficulties of enforcement [3.6.2, D25].

11.7 OUTSOURCE CONTRACTOR'S DUTIES [S7 (5), S9]

In general, the contractor will need to indemnify the customer against all future claims arising out of premises, hardware, software licences, and staff which have been transferred, as the contractor will then have control of them. An exception will, however, apply in case of claims which go back to the period before the transfer, where the indemnity will go the other way [11.6]. Good examples would be IPR infringement claims arising from customer software which is either licensed or assigned to the contractor, or employee claims dating back to the period before the outsourcing of the relevant services.

11.7.1 Premises

If the contract is for some kind of lease, the usual provisions for delivery up of the premises will be required. Where the obligation is laid on the contractor to inspect the premises before transfer [11.6.1], some such clause as the following may be used:

> "Prior to the Commencement of Service Date, the Contractor will inspect the Premises and shall notify the Customer of any aspect of the Premises which may adversely impact the provision of the Services."

In particular also, the customer will usually want to insist upon adherence to its relevant health and security policies:

> "The Customer shall provide the Supplier with such access to the Premises as it may reasonably require for the purposes of providing the Services, including access out of normal office hours where necessary. The Supplier shall give the Customer as much notice as is reasonably practicable of any requirement to attend the Premises outside of normal office hours. The Supplier shall adhere to all of the Customer's health, safety and security procedures relevant to the Premises."

11.7.2 Equipment

The contractor may need to give undertakings as to providing suitable hardware for the services for the future. In the case of longer-term contracts with a "technology refresh" element [11.5], it will be probable that during the lifetime of the contract, the contractor will need not just to upgrade the hardware but completely to replace it. In doing this he may find it advantageous to combine his hardware for this contract with this required for some other contract and provided the level of service is maintained the customer should accept this, although recognising that this has an impact upon the ultimate exit provisions [11.4] as it may then be impossible to take the infrastructure back in-house or transfer it to another contractor.

11.7.3 Software [S7 (5)]

If the software is from a third party, the customer will require the usual indemnities from the contractor as to infringing intellectual property rights. There will also need to be the usual undertakings as to obtaining and installing new releases as and when they are available from the software supplier and it is usually in the customer's interest to include an obligation upon the contractor to upgrade [S15]. In addition, the customer may need to warrant that it can transfer or sub-license the contractor to use the software.

Where the customer is not in some sense transferring the software but instead the licence for the software for the service is being provided from the contractor (whether because the contractor is the copyright owner, because the contractor already has a licence from the third party copyright owner or because the contractor undertakes to obtain such a licence), indemnities will be required from the contractor against infringing intellectual property.

11.7.4 Staff [S, Sched. 5, clause 7]

For a brief discussion about the impact of Tupe on the employees in an outsourcing arrangement, see 11.6.4 above.

Contractors will have different concerns from the customer. For a start, a contractor should discover the extent of the liabilities it is taking on. Contractors should also bear in mind that they are likely to be responsible for any dismissals they ask the customer to make prior to the transfer and that such dismissals are likely to be construed as in connection with the transfer and therefore automatically unfair.

A contractor will often wish to harmonise the terms and conditions of the employees it has inherited from an outsourcing contract with those of its existing employees. Recent cases suggest this will be extremely difficult and changes to employees' terms and conditions following Tupe will often be invalid. It is sometimes possible to effect changes by dismissing employees and rehiring them on new terms and conditions, but this course of action is likely to trigger claims for unfair and wrongful dismissal and require substantial redundancy payments.

The contractor will also wish to ensure that the outsourcing contract includes terms that deal with the position at the end of the contract. The contractor may not wish to be left with the employees when the contract ends and should therefore consider asking for an indemnity from the customer in respect of redundancy costs which may be incurred at the end of the contract. Alternatively, the contractor could require the customer either to offer employment to the employees or to obtain agreement that any incoming contractor does so.

If Tupe applies, the contractor must give the necessary undertakings to safeguard the rights of the staff transferred [S9 (1)(c)].

In much the same manner as for software development contracts, it is essential that the contractor also nominate liaison staff [3.6.1, D17]. In particular, they will attend the regular review meetings which should be held and minuted to monitor the working of the contract, decide on any failures and resulting claw back or other penalty, and co-operate on any development of new software or hardware [11.6.4, S8].

Again, the usual provision about poaching staff may be included in a mutual form, binding on both parties. In practice, the contractor will have more to lose if staff go back to the customer taking with them their understanding of the customer's business (especially if they have been engaged in a shared service centre, and are therefore also providing services to other clients), and it will be more likely that the customer will be the one who wishes to poach staff if he finds that the contract is not satisfactory and he wishes either to find a new contractor or even take the service back in-house. For that reason he may also be asked by the contractor not to facilitate the movement of staff to any third party who might be groomed by the customer to take over the contract from the contractor.

In any event, such clauses are subject to the usual difficulties of enforcement [3.6.2, D25].

CHAPTER 12

SERVICE CONTRACTS: THE INTERNET

12.0 INTRODUCTION

It is to be hoped that the Internet will not need to be described in detail to readers of this book. However, it may be worth noting that the Internet has basically three characteristics: the ability to search and/or manipulate another organisation's data on-line; the ability to put up one's own data for others to search and/or manipulate; and electronic mail (e-mail). There are a number of contractual relationships involved in the way these Internet services are provided which deserve consideration (and in this regard we are not referring to the general practice electronic commerce (e-commerce) *per se*, whereby goods or services can be purchased over the Internet) but for the purposes of this book we examine certain specific contractual issues—*i.e.* the kinds of IT service contract which can arise in relation to the ordinary functioning of the Internet, and the types of contract terms required in relation to the provision of access to particular websites.

Internet Service Provider (ISP)

For most of us using the Internet, the most obvious contractual relationship is that with our Internet Service Provider (ISP). This organisation provides a raft of services including access to the Internet, an addressing system whereby we can receive electronic mail (e-mail), information, possibly discounted telecommunications charges and so forth. Many ISPs provide their services free of charge to the user. Under English Law a valid contract cannot exist where no consideration (money, goods or services) flow from one party to the other and vice versa (save in the case of agreements formed by way of a deed). In other words, a truly free gift from A to B does not constitute a contract. However, free ISPs make their money usually in a combination of three ways:

(a) by paid advertising on their web home page which the customer is bound to see whenever he encounters the home page;

(b) by taking a percentage from the telecommunications provider on all telephone calls accessing the Internet through the ISP; and

(c) by charging a premium on all calls from the customer to the ISP's Internet support facilities—typically 50p per minute.

On the basis of this last item at least, it can therefore be argued that there is a valid contract since the user who signs up with an ISP is holding himself out as prepared to use the telephone services and pay for them. An alternative agreement may be to the effect that agreeing to undertake the commitments and obligations set out in the ISP's contract itself constitutes a form of consideration (although this is, at best, a doubtful proposition [T, U]).

Website design

A different type of Internet service contract arises where an organisation or individual is commissioned to set up an Internet website. There is often also a requirement for the website to be maintained by the company setting it up and they may also provide additional services such as recording and passing back to the owner of the website information about the number of "hits" recorded on that website. These website set-up and hosting agreements contain, as we shall see elements of the ISP agreement, but with some additional matters.

Terms for accessing websites [V, W]

Finally (at least for the purposes of this chapter), there will be the contract terms and disclaimers which will apply whenever one accesses a website (often regardless of whether an actual transaction is undertaken as a result).

One must not ignore the need to ensure that each website properly incorporates the terms governing its use, as well as any "standard" contract terms usually applicable to the particular goods and/or services which are being sold across the Internet.

Some of the terms will simply reflect some of the points made earlier in this chapter (*e.g.* relating to getting positive "opt in" by the customers to the use of personal data, imposing prohibitions on the transfer of the obscene or defamatory comments to the website, etc. [W A3]). However, others will relate specifically to the medium of communication between the parties, *i.e.* via the relevant website. Specific provisions will therefore be required so as to address:

(a) the extent to which the user is licensed to download and utilise material from the website;

(b) disclaimers of responsibility for the contents of any third party websites to which a hypertext link may be provided [W A3 (6)];

(c) required information/terms (*e.g.* by reason of the Distance Selling Regulations (Consumer Protection (Distance Selling) Regulation 2000 (S.I. 2000 No. 2334)) *vis-à-vis* the right of customers to cancel any contracts formed solely via the Internet) [W B5].

As E.U. law imposes an additional level of protection for consumer (as opposed to business-to-business) transactions, we have prepared two separate precedents as a basis for such website contracts, *i.e.* for use in relation to website advertising/selling goods or services aimed at consumers and businesses. Respectively the business to business version is Precedent V, and the consumer version is Precedent W.

All these contracts are service contracts and in particular have some elements of bureau services in them. The rest of this Chapter considers them in that light.

12.1 SERVICES TO BE PERFORMED

12.1.1 ISP [U1]

The contract between a user and an ISP is clearly a type of service contract. The services to be provided by the ISP include some or all of the following types of services and obligations:

(a) providing access software;

(b) granting access to the Internet whenever the user needs it;

(c) either providing a search engine whereby the user can look for data or giving access to somebody else's search engine;

(d) enabling the user to download and/or print the results of searches on the Internet;

(e) providing information. This is usually in the form of certain "key" pages. In the case of "free" ISPs, the pages usually consist of paid advertising. In the case of other ISPs, more substantial benefits may be conferred, such as a news and sports service or chat services;

(f) providing a certain amount of web space dedicated to the user;

(g) enabling the user to keep records of certain web pages off-line ("favourites");

(h) providing a unique Internet address by means of which the user can receive e-mail;

(i) advising the user when incoming e-mail has been received;

(j) sending the user's e-mail to other hosts;

(k) advising the user when an item of his outgoing e-mail has been returned as undeliverable—or at least as undelivered;

(l) enabling the user to keep his e-mail files and distinguish between different categories of e-mails (*e.g.* opened and unopened; "sent" and "out"—*i.e.* those which have been put out ready for sending and those which have actually been sent on to their destinations);

(m) providing an address book facility for the user whereby shorter addresses can be stored to give access to full e-mail addresses;

(n) maintaining confidentiality in respect of the user's data;

(o) providing a telephone help service;

(p) providing a discounted telephone call service. The proceeds of this may be kept by the ISP in the case of "free" Internet services or passed on in part to the user;

(q) providing a virus protection service by scanning e-mails.

(r) providing a (usually fairly basic) screening service to protect the user's children from downloading the more unpleasant pages;

(s) providing a mechanism to prevent "spamming"—*i.e.* the sending of a single message to an enormous number of e-mail recipients;

(t) providing a discount to the user for his telecommunications—*i.e.* not all calls are charged at full telecommunications rates.

Not all ISPs provide all these services. No doubt this list could be extended but it gives a flavour of what is available. Many of these services involve processing data on behalf of the user (*e.g.* in directing e-mail to him) and are therefore likely to be construed as a form of bureau services.

In practice, the contracts governing the provision of such services are usually in the form of a read-me file similar to those for much PC software [4.3.1]. The conditions are presented on screen to the user who is not allowed to progress further in the matter until he has clicked on a button (generally at the end of the conditions) to say that he has read them and is prepared to abide by them. How many users actually read the conditions apart from entering their name and address must be a matter for speculation, and surely only very few of those actually retain any of what they have read.

In addition to the read-me file there is probably also a CD with printed on the sleeve what in effect are more contractual conditions. For example, there will be some instructions on it as to the minimum configuration of PC which can support the system, with the implication that if your machine complies with this the ISP will be prepared to provide the service. There may also be instructions as to how to load the system, how to obtain the telephone support, etc. Other printed provisions include:

(a) that the software is protected by copyright and/or (in the case of U.S. or Japanese software especially) patent;

(b) that the user must pay any charges to the ISP;

(c) that the user is responsible for the premium charges for the telephone support, and any other charges incurred; and

(d) that if the account is inactive for a period (say 90 days) the address and all data associated with it (including incoming e-mails) will be deleted.

Clearly, the incorporation of these provisions into the final contract between the ISP and the customer may be in doubt, unless the terms of the read-me file are carefully drafted so as to expressly include them.

Data protection [T10]

It has to be recognised that any use of Internet services is likely sooner or later to require processing of data about identifiable live persons (*i.e.* personal data) and hence involve the Data Protection Act 1998. The more services that an ISP offers to its customers, the greater the likelihood will be that it is gathering data from them which will be subject to the provisions of the 1998 Act.

Under the Data Protection Act 1998, s.1(1):

(a) a "data controller" is defined as "a person who (either alone or jointly with other persons) determines the purposes for which and the manner in which any personal data are, or are to be, processed";

(b) a "data processor" is defined as "any person (other than an employee of the data controller) who processes the data on behalf of the data controller"; and finally

(c) "processing" includes "retrieval . . . disclosure of the information or data by transmission, dissemination or otherwise making available".

From this clutch of definitions it is possible to argue that:

(a) use of the Internet for retrieval or e-mail is "processing" under the Act;

(b) a user of Internet services is a data controller under the Act; and

(c) the ISP is a data processor under the Act (insofar as it fulfils instructions from users, or provides some of the "value add" services described above, which involve the manipulation of personal data).

A further point is that the definition of a data processor describes precisely the relationship in a bureau service [10]. Indeed, this definition replaces the definition in the now repealed 1984 Data Protection Act, s.1(6), which describes a "computer bureau".

If then it is the case that the ISP is a data processor or bureau processing personal data on behalf of the customer/data controller, then a number of consequences flow most of which are explored in 12.3.1 and 12.7.1 below. The initial point to make is that, as we have shown at 10.3.3, a contract enabling a data processor to process personal data on behalf of data controller must be "made or evidenced in writing" (Data Protection Act 1998, Sched. 1, Pt II, para. 12(a)(i)).

Clearly, the text printed on the sleeve of the CD is in writing. But is the read-me file made or evidenced in "writing"? It is certainly possible—even probable—since the text can at any time be printed out by the customer and this appears to be the intent of both the Electronic Communications Act 2000 and the draft E-Commerce Directives working their way through the European Parliament. But it is not certain, as the issue so far has not come before the Courts.

12.1.2 Website design

The considerations as to whether those who design the website for a client are independent contractors or employees are relevant here and are set out below when considering consultants [13.0.2]. For the purposes of this chapter we have assumed the website designer is an independent contractor.

Domain address

Establishing a brand on the Internet (and preferably one which is in keeping with any existing name or mark used by your business) is crucial. Before embarking on the design of the site, the client will therefore need to ensure that he has obtained the necessary address or get the website designer to obtain it for him. Already there is a wealth of case law on this, dealing with so-called "cybersquatting" (see *British Telecommunications PLC v. One in a Million Ltd and others* [1999] F.S.R. 1) whereby a third party attempts to register the name of an organisation before the rightful owner of that name, so as to hold the owner up to ransom, seeking to get him to purchase the domain name from the squatter. A number of widely publicised cases have shown that provided the name which the cybersquatter seeks to pre-empt is a trademark, there is usually adequate protection for the victim's name and the cybersquatter can be evicted, *i.e.* made to relinquish this registration of the domain name.

However, where the name is not a trademark there is no such automatic protection. It may therefore be desirable to register a trademark first before embarking on obtaining (or evicting others from) the domain name.

An alternative approach is provided by using the World Intellectual Property Organisation's Arbitration and Mediation Center in Geneva [15.3.3]. If the parties agree to use the Center it can resolve disputes about (*inter alia*) domain names—a notable decision is *Jeanette Winterson v. Mark Hogarth* (Case No. D2000–0235 at **www.arbiter.wipo.int/domains/decision.../d2000–0235**) where the agreement between the defendant and ICANN (Internet Corporation for Assigned Names and Numbers, which controls .com, .net and .org registrations) evidently obliged the defendant to use the Center and it was decided that an author has the right to use her own name for a website, despite the facts that there was no trade mark of that name and that someone else had already registered .com, .net and .org websites of that name. Other domain name registries (such as Nominet in the U.K.) have also established dispute resolution procedures for dealing with conflicting claims to particular names.

The Internet domain names are usually allocated on a country basis with the country-less ".com" names (at least in theory) being reserved for companies of international standing. It is therefore the case that what is registered in one country may not mean that there is a monopoly of use in another—or rather the name may be allocated to someone else, so the xyzco.co.uk will not prevent someone else registering the domain name xyzco.co.fr in France. This can cause particular difficulties when the same or similar domain names are registered by companies who may enjoy trade mark protection for them in their countries of origin, especially as their "competing" websites will be accessible worldwide.

Design services

The design stage is really a form of consultancy with elements of programming. The design may simply concern itself with the home page—*i.e.* the first page which users encounter when they first gain access to that site. The home page should be welcoming, state clearly the ownership of the site, and facilitate access to other pages.

The client will require the designer to keep in mind certain objectives:

(a) the site must be welcoming;

(b) the site must be easy to use and to navigate around;

(c) the site must fit in with the client's corporate image, correctly using logos, trademarks, typefaces and corporate colours;

(d) the site must identify specified items of the client's products or services;

(e) links may need to be provided to other of the client's sites and possibly also to sites outside the client's business.

So far as the links with other sites are concerned the obvious step would be to seek the permission of those other sites. Where permission as not been sought, the Scottish case *Shetland Times Ltd v. Wills* S.C. [1997] 316 may be relevant. The case concerned two newspapers—*the Shetland Times* and *the Shetland News*. The *News* set up links on its own home page to pages of the *Shetland Times* thereby enabling users to bypass the latter's home page (with all its paid for advertising). This linkage was done by repeating on the *Shetland News* pages text from the *Shetland Times* pages (which, whilst identifiable as coming from the *Shetland Times*, were "framed" by material from the *Shetland News*). This was held to breach the *Shetland Times* copyright. However, this is a Scottish case and so not binding in English Courts. Moreover, it has been persuasively argued that provided the links do not involve actually lifting copyright text (*i.e.* if they are simply hypertext links to the other websites) and also do not pass off the linked site as belonging to the organisation owning the site linking to it, the Courts could probably not restrain the provision of the links to another organisation's website (see Richard Harrison, "Unacceptable Linking . . . is *Shetland* relevant?" in *Computers & Law* (April/May 1999), N.S. Vol. 10, Issue 1, p.32).

As with other work by a contractor for a client [3.8.2, D14] the law will imply (in the absence of any express provision in the contract) a provision that the copyright belongs to the contractor. However, in the case of anything so fundamental to a business as its website, it is likely that the client will wish to acquire all intellectual property rights and it will accordingly be essential to ensure that the development contract contains a term to this effect. As the material used to construct the site is presumably based on his (the client's) data, any other arrangement would be messy, even though the contractor may continue to maintain the site [T3].

Website maintenance [T2, T5]

A separate aspect of these contracts is the matter of website maintenance. Sometimes, an organisation will commission a website design and then hope to maintain it in-house. However, it must be admitted that website maintenance can be quite a substantial job, especially if it is intended to be interactive and updated on a regular basis and it may well be appropriate for the organisation that set up the website to maintain it.

As with software maintenance [9], it is not always easy to quantify in advance the amount of work that may be needed. Some of it will be entirely within the control of the client and in response to information furnished by the client, as it alters its marketing objectives, changes its corporate image, produces new goods or services, and so forth. But some also will be dictated by external factors such as changes to telephone numbers, changes in any linked pages on other websites, etc., Moreover, occasional bugs with any software package are to be anticipated, and it would be prudent to ensure the availability of specialist support, if required.

It is obviously simplest if the website contractor handles all alterations to the website. However, this may not be always feasible. Unlike in the case of software maintenance, it may well be essential that the client's staff amend the website in at least some respects—*e.g.* for unexpected changes in prices of goods advertised on the site—without funnelling all changes through the contractors. If this is the case the boundaries of which side does what will need careful definition. There will also need to be a mechanism to enable the website design contractor to work on the website off-line but see and have full access to any other changes to it introduced by the client.

12.2 PAYMENT

12.2.1 ISP [T7, U5]

Payment may be of the following kinds:

(a) payment for the service (*e.g.* provision of access to the Internet, etc. as set out in 12.1.1 above);

(b) payment to the ISP of some or all telecommunications charges associated with the service;

(c) payment for any support services.

Some ISPs are, as we have seen, "free" in relation to at least the first of the above. Where access is not free it may be charged directly according to the customer's timed usage, or on the basis of a single charge monthly for some usage with the rest charged by timed usage, or a single charge monthly for all usage, and so forth.

The mechanisms for charging mobile telephones have also influenced the ways in which Internet services are charged. Normally, telecommunications charges will continue to be paid by the customer to his usual telecommunications provider and not the ISP. Where the ISP is able to offer free or discounted telecommunications services for its Internet customers, it will generally make the arrangement directly with the telecommunications provider, requiring the Internet customer to pay the ISP solely for access.

The use of the Internet by the customer may also result in payments by the customer to other third parties, for accessing particular websites or for purchasing goods or services over the Internet. These will of course be the sole responsibility of the customer and will not usually go via the ISP.

12.2.2 Website design

The usual options for payment in creative IT contracts are relevant here—fixed price, estimated price, capped price, or on a time and materials basis [3.0.3, 13.2]. Again the intelligent use of milestones [3.2.1] with time built into the contract to give the client an opportunity to review progress at each stage will be essential. Such milestones may include:

(a) securing the domain address;

(b) designing the general structure of the home page;

(c) design of each of the other pages;

(d) approval of the designs and their live display on the web.

12.3 DATA

12.3.1 ISP [T10, U4]

ISP's will usually seek to protect themselves against claims which may arise by reason of the type of information transmitted by its customers by way of the Internet services it provides. Conditions in the read-me file might include:

(a) a prohibition on defamatory material;

(b) a prohibition on obscene material;

(c) a prohibition on data contrary to the Data Protection Act 1998.

If this list looks familiar it is because we have already encountered it in dealing with bureau contracts [10.3], and as we have seen in 12.1 above, Internet services appear to be bureau services.

In at least one instance there has been a decision in the English Courts on defamation over the Internet. In the case of *Godfrey v Demon* (see Kit Burden, "Fallen Angel: Demon Faces Defamation Claim" in *Computers & Law* (June/July 1999), N.S. Vol. 10, Issue 2, p.31), the plaintiff alleged that an ISP who carried material which was defamatory of him failed to remove it immediately he pointed out the libel to them. Despite initially contesting the action, the ISP was eventually compelled to settle the claim for a total of £400,000 (albeit that the vast majority of this was apportioned to legal costs), after the English courts ruled that a failure to remove material of a defamatory nature after it had been notified of it rendered the ISP a "publisher" for the purposes of the Defamation Act 1996.

Two lessons in particular can be drawn from this case: first it will be noted that the plaintiff's action was only in respect of the period after the ISP became aware that the material was defamatory. Whether an ISP is also liable in respect of a libel of which it is not aware is another matter about which there have so far been no decided cases in the U.K. ISPs naturally will protest in these circumstances that they are common carriers like the telecommunications companies or the Royal Mail with no possibility of checking the contents of all the material they carry, and it is impossible not to sympathise with them. In this regard, it is to be noted that in cases involving child pornography on the Internet the police have not acted against the ISPs through whom the data was downloaded. However, where the ISP knows of a libel there is no such excuse and what is more the very world-wide quality of the web means that actions in those circumstance can and evidently do lie against an ISP in several jurisdictions. Indeed, in Germany recent case law suggests that the courts are taking a different line from that adopted by the U.K. and are imposing an objective test, *i.e.* not just material that the ISP knew about but what it *ought* to have known about.

12.3.2 Website design [T10]

As noted in 12.1.1, it is highly likely that the Data Protection Act 1998 will apply to ISPs, but it may not so obviously apply to website design companies. The issue is simply whether or not data will be processed which relates to "a living individual who can be identified from the data alone or with other information" (1998 Act, s.1(1)). If so, the Act will apply (and, in particular, it may be necessary to ensure that the website contractor provides its services so as to ensure that the website complies with the provisions of the 1998 Act, *e.g.* in relation to securing it against unauthorised access.

12.4 TERMINATION

12.4.1 ISP [T12, U6]

A customer who has his service terminated by failure to use the service or by breach is liable to find not only that he no longer has the service available, but also that he has lost the storage space allocated to him, any data there has been erased (including any e-mails), and that all future e-mails addressed to him at this address will be returned to sender.

Anonymous customer [U3]

A contract can also be terminated by fundamental breach by the customer. When he first installs the Internet access software and registers to use the services provided by the ISP, he is generally required to identify himself with name and address and in the case of charged ISP services this is the name and address which will be charged.

In the case of free ISPs, there is a risk that the customer fails to identify himself properly to the ISP. This must be particularly likely in the case of those intending to commit some kind of crime over the Internet. The telephone charges will after all be charged to the telephone number, and there is no practical necessity for the ISP to know the identity of the user. Nevertheless, the ISP will for its own protection wish to know who the user is so that it can remove the service from him in the case of any crime. If it gains part of the revenue from the telecommunications provider it will have an additional reason for wishing to identify the user. It will therefore have a registration process whereby the user identifies himself by name and address. This does not physically prevent the user from giving a fictitious name and/or address, but it will be fundamental breach of the contract if he has been found to do so and the contract will than be terminated and the provision of services suspended.

Spamming [U4 (5)]

Another condition with which the customer must comply may include spamming [12.1.1]. Many ISPs impose a condition that a customer who initiates spamming will be held to be in fundamental breach of the contract. The problem here is to arrive at a universally acceptable definition of spamming, as one man's junk mail is another man's vital information.

There may also be a requirement on the Customer to report spamming by others—especially other customers of the same ISP, though failure to report such spamming is not usually a fundamental breach.

Other termination [U4 (4)]

Finally the customer will be liable to have the service terminated if he is found to be using the service for a criminal activity—fraud, for example, or the transmission of pornography.

12.4.2 Website design

The termination conditions for consultancy contracts apply here [13.4]. The point about the website designer surrendering all papers is equally relevant. It will also be important to ensure that even if the contract terminates early the intellectual property rights in the site belong to the client [12.2.2].

12.5 VARIATION

12.5.1 ISP [U7]

Many ISPs tell their customers of proposed changes to the service by means of e-mails. It has to be said that this is a less than satisfactory mechanism. We have argued above [12.1.1] that the contract with the ISP must be made or evidenced in writing and it is not certain that an e-mail is sufficient for this. There are also practical objections. For example, since some customers delete such messages unread—the fear of viruses feeds this—and some only look for e-mails when they expect a message. It is accordingly unclear whether this is a valid way of informing the customer. If the ISP can be reasonably sure that the customer has given a valid address the proposed changes would be better posted (*i.e.* in a letter with a stamp on it) to the customer. Most ISPs would of course object that e-mail is not only faster but also much cheaper. Their best recourse is to include in their contract with the customer a provision that e-mail will be the way proposed changes are brought to the customer's attention with an obligation on the customer to check his mail for this. However to insist on daily checking would be unreasonable—perhaps weekly is a more acceptable frequency. Even then this may not be sufficient [12.1.1].

12.5.2 Website design

The same need for rigorous change control applies to website design contracts as it does for consulting and/or commissioned software contracts [3.5, 13.5].

12.6 Customer's Duties

12.6.1 ISP [T6, U4, U5]

As we have seen [12.4] there is likely to be a prohibition on using the Internet for any criminal purpose (such as fraud or child pornography). A clear undertaking by the customer as to this is reasonable.

The customer may have a duty not only to refrain from spamming [12.1.1, 12.5.1] but also to report all occurrences of spamming to the ISP—or at least all those that originate from a customer of the ISP.

The customer will also be required to give an undertaking that any charges he incurs with third parties in the use of the service will be paid for by him and will not be the responsibility of the ISP. These include charges for telecommunications (where these are not charged by the ISP), access to chargeable websites, and any purchase by the customer of goods or services over the Internet (e-commerce).

12.6.2 Website design

These will be broadly similar to those for consultancy and commissioned software [3.6, 13.6]. In particular, as with other contracts of design and consultancy, it is essential that the client provide adequate information to the website designer. For example, all house style (logos, type faces, use of colour, etc.) must be well understood by the contractor, The nomination of suitable liaison staff will probably be the easiest way of providing this [3.6.1, D17].

For the maintenance aspects, this will continue to be important. Someone in the client's organisation must decide when a change is required in the website and in general terms what kind of change that must be.

12.7 Service Provider's Duties

12.7.1 ISP

Security

In a contract between an ISP and its customer, as we have seen [10.3.3, 12.3.1], the Seventh Data Protection Principle requires the contract to be made or evidenced in writing and the data controller (customer) has to require the data processor (ISP) to comply with the Seventh Principle which states in Schedule 1, Pt I, para. 7;

> "Appropriate technical and organisational measures shall be taken against unauthorised or unlawful processing of personal data and against accidental loss or destruction of, or damage to, personal data."

paras 9 and 10 of Schedule 1, Pt II, set out what is needed:

"9. Having regard to the state of technological development and the cost of implementing any measures, the measures must ensure a level of security appropriate to:

   (a) the harm which might result from such unauthorised or unlawful processing or accidental loss, destruction or damage as are mentioned in the seventh principle; and
   (b) the nature of the data to be protected.

10. The data controller must take reasonable steps to ensure the reliability of any employees of his who have access to the personal data."

A clause in the ISP's contract obliging the data processor (ISP) to comply with these requirements would seem essential [K15 (2)].

Confidentiality

A related question to that of security is confidentiality. The ISP should undertake to keep the customer's data confidential [3.7.2, 13.7.2]. Such an undertaking should survive termination (for whatever reason) of the agreement though in practice if the ISP deletes the customer's data on termination this may not be of so much practical importance.

Release of data to third parties [U3 (3)]

A condition of the contract is likely to be that users who do not wish to receive mailing from third parties can opt out. ISPs as we have seen above make some of their money by advertising [12.0], and therefore are likely to have close links with organisations interested in exploiting the marketing information which the customers represent so the ISPs may be reluctant to give much prominence to a provision requiring the customer to state explicitly whether or not he or she is content for his/her data (data about him/her or even originating from him/her) to be passed to others, but the law gives no choice in this regard. It is likely that if the data the ISPs pass on to third parties includes (as no doubt it will do) personal data, this will infringe the Second Data Protection Principle which is concerned with data not being processed in a manner incompatible with its original purpose. A series of cases before the Data Protection Tribunal (*e.g. British Gas v. Data Protection Registrar* [1998] Info. T.L.R. 393) make clear that a customer must positively opt in to further use of data about him/her, not simply fail to tick an opt-out box. The case was brought under the 1984 Act but it seems hard to escape the conclusion that the 1998 Act can safely be observed only by the positive opt-in.

Transborder flows

Again in our discussion of bureaux [10.3.3], we emphasised the problems which the Eighth Data Protection Principle gives rise to in the matter of transfer of personal data to countries outside the European Economic Area (EEA). The ISP must accordingly ensure that, if such transborder data transfers are to be made, it can be sure of complying with the requirements of the Eighth Principle.

Filtering services [U1]

An ISP which provides filtering services whether for viruses or to screen out unpleasant material from children will recognise that neither of these services can be performed infallibly. Virus-protection as we have seen is only as good as the latest type of virus to have been guarded against. No virus protection system can guarantee that it will give protection against a hitherto unknown types of virus.

Similarly, systems which screen data for children—or any one else for that matter—can only do so on the basis of the occurrence of particular words. It is easy to compile a list of words which are unacceptable, and no less easy to see first that not one of them occurs in say *Fanny Hill*, which carefully uses words which do not in themselves carry sexual connotations; and that a large amount of material will be trapped which may be entirely innocent. In an overseas English-speaking country, a friend of one of the authors found his system was programmed to seek to deny access when it encountered an address containing the word "Essex". As with the viruses, though for different reasons, there can be no guarantee that the system will always hit the right target. It is therefore reasonable that the ISP make clear to the customer that its system is not infallible.

Similarly with undertakings to reduce spamming [12.1.1], some ISPs require the customer to undertake that it will not initiate spamming and make any such action a fundamental breach [12.5.1]. But the ISP may also go further and seek to intercept spamming from outside. Again only on the most mechanistic definition of spamming can it hope to succeed in this.

12.7.2 Website design [T2]

Confidentiality is likely to be of much more importance in website agreements since the contractor will need to know a lot about the client in order to construct and/or maintain a website. The considerations in writing bespoke software or consultancy apply here [3.7.2, 13.7.2] and such provisions should survive the agreement. In extreme cases there may also be a requirement for individual confidentiality agreements with the staff who work on the project.

As with consultancy there may also be a requirement for the website design contractor to undertake that it will do no similar work for a rival organisation. Consideration of restraint of trade are relevant [3.6.2, 13.7.2].

CONSULTANCY

13.0 INTRODUCTION

13.0.1 The nature of consultancy

Consultancy—the calling in of expert advice on a short-term basis—can happen in almost any conceivable type of commercial or professional matter. On the one hand, it can be far wider than computers, covering scientific process, marketing, personnel, asset realisation and thousands of other activities. On the other hand, it can be argued that bespoke programming by a software house or other IT consultancy organisation is itself a form of consultancy, and it is certainly a fact that much of what has been said in Chapter 3 about the development of bespoke software is directly applicable to consultancy generally. The problems, therefore, of defining computer consultancy for the readers of this book are formidable.

Nevertheless, it can be argued that as a minimum it should embrace the use of consultants to assist the client or organisation in choosing a system which will meet its particular requirements, and this is the aspect we have concentrated on in this chapter and in precedent W.

There are numerous unkind jokes about consultants, such as the one about their being the people who are paid to borrow your watch in order to tell you what the time is. In fairness to consultants it can be suggested that if all the client employing the consultant wanted was to find out the time, the consultant's response was perfectly correct. Properly used, consultants can undoubtedly add significant value, and bring to bear their wider experience of best practice and the merits and potential of various different forms of software, hardware and third party suppliers. However, there is a danger of assuming their omniscience, and the client should remember that the most successful consultancy contracts are usually those which succeed in fostering a "partnership" approach to the requirements of the client's project.

> "In classical drama, the problems that arise in this world were sometimes depicted as being solved by divine intervention. Many modern managers, faced with technological perplexities, look for divine help and the modern *deus ex machina* is the consultant—an omniscient being who is above this mortal world. After his brief intervention all should come right and even if it does not the blame can safely be laid at the door of somebody else other than the manager."

195

(Richard Morgan and Brian Wood, *Word Processing* (2nd ed., Pitman Publishing Limited, 1985.)

However, choosing a consultant must be largely on the same basis as choosing a good employee—namely by looking for the right combination of experience (relevant to your work), knowledge (of the wider and more technical aspects of your problem), skill (particularly in management) and temperament (the consultant's sensitivity to the character and ethos of your organisation).

13.0.2 Consultant or employee? [X21]

There are a number of significant legal differences between independent contractors (including consultants and freelance programmers [Y]) and employees which are worth emphasising:

(1) Generally speaking, the intellectual property rights in any work produced by the consultant will vest in the consultant unless the contract specifically provides otherwise, (in this respect the copyright in a consultant's report is not different from the copyright in bespoke software [3.8.2] or web design [12.1.2], notwithstanding the fact that the client may have funded its creation (although it may be possible to argue that there was a course of conduct by the consultant which gave rise to an equitable assignment of copyright; see *Lakeview Computers plc v. Steadman*, November 26, 1999)). In the case of an employee such rights usually vest in the employer.

(2) A duty of confidentiality on the part of the employee is implied into the employer/employee relationship. While the circumstances surrounding a consultancy may give rise to such a duty it is usual to incorporate an express provision in the contract so as to be clear on both the nature and extent of the relevant obligations [X11].

(3) Unlike the employee, the consultant does not owe a duty of fidelity to the person engaging him unless the contract so stipulates. This may give rise to a number of express provisions in the consultancy contract, covering such matters as working for competitors, accounting for commissions and secret profits and publicity [X12].

(4) An employee is able to be directed by the client in the manner in which he performs his services; a consultant will usually follow his own methodologies and ways of working.

In view of these differences it is essential to establish the relationship of the parties before a contract is entered into. In many instances the position will be clear and this will be particularly so in cases where the independent contractor is other than an individual, thus ruling out an employment relationship.

Companies are more likely to run into difficulties where they engage a "regular casual" contractor who is an individual; in these cases the distinction between an employee and an independent contractor can become blurred and legal advice should be sought as to whether the individual concerned should be regarded as one or the other. Apart from the matters referred to above, employees are entitled to certain employment rights (such as those relating to unfair dismissal and redundancy) and the employer is liable to deduct PAYE. The independent contractor, on the other hand, makes a taxable supply for VAT purposes and where he is registered for VAT he should add this to his fee.

13.0.3 Independence [X5]

The independence of the consultant will usually need to be established. Some "consultancy" is provided by organisations which have a financial interest in the equipment they recommend. This does not necessarily mean that the client is not getting "best advice", but the client should at least be aware of any such relationships.

Clauses in the contract whereby the consultant warrants his independence of suppliers and agrees not to accept commissions from them may sometimes be appropriate [X5].

13.0.4 Contract or letter?

A large number of consultancies are undertaken on the basis of an exchange of letters rather than a full-blown contract. As it is the nature of consultancy not only that the relationship between the parties is short-term but also that the information to be discovered by the consultant is required in a hurry; major management decisions are sometimes held up until the consultancy is complete. There may be nothing wrong with doing business in this way (*i.e.* by exchange of letters), provided all the essential contractual points are covered in the letters and the description of the services to be provided is sufficiently clear.

However, it can equally cogently be argued that almost all contracts can be replaced by an exchange of letters. Why have formal contracts at all? The answer must of course be that to cover all essential points the letter would usually need to be inordinately long (especially for larger or more complicated projects), that much of what needs to be included is standard to other types of contract (*e.g.* [A28, A29]) and—most important of all—the structure of a good contract provides a checklist and discipline to ensure that all essentials have indeed been covered.

Nevertheless, if a reader wishes to use this chapter and precedent X simply as a checklist for an exchange of letters there is nothing to prevent him from doing so.

13.1 SERVICES TO BE PERFORMED [X4, X5]

The very first requirement is for the client employing the consultant to define precisely what he wants the consultant to do. A clear statement of the terms of reference will help the consultant to use his time efficiently and should also assist the client in setting realistic objectives for the consultant and not expecting the impossible. It also provides a useful means for both the client and the consultant to track the cost of the services being provided (*i.e.* without the consultant arguing that original estimates are no longer valid because the nature of the original requirements has changed).

All that was said in Chapters 1 and 3 [1.3, 3.1, D4] about the need for a functional specification is relevant here, at least in relation to software-related projects.

The first thing, therefore, to decide is the end-result of the consultancy. In the example we consider primarily in this chapter, it is the acquisition of a computer system, though it is essential to say what the system is to do. Computers are not an end in themselves for business, but a tool to enable an organisation to achieve particular objectives of speed, efficiency, comprehensiveness, and so forth [X, Sched. 1].

An alternative type of consultancy is the feasibility study to decide whether a computer is of value at all for a particular application, and such a study usually goes on to ask the consultant to say in general terms what the characteristics of such a system should be if the answer to the first question is yes.

Such terms of reference might therefore include:

> "To report on the value of a computer to the Client in carrying out its functions of mail order (or distribution, or production of proposals for clients, or making up to date financial information available to its branch offices, or whatever it may be) as set out in . . ."

Again, the end objective in computerising must be clearly identified, and it will be almost essential to set this out in more detail either in a Schedule or by reference to an identified existing document. In this document all the questions the client needs answers to should be fully set out. The main way of deciding whether the consultant has done his job will be to see whether he has given full answers to all such questions [13.3].

If tangible outputs ("deliverables") are to be produced (*e.g.* a feasibility study report, some pilot software program, etc.), each should be clearly identified, and any relevant acceptance criteria clearly set out unambiguously [13.3].

The timetable for the performance of the services is often a cause for debate. If the project is truly time critical, it may be appropriate to make time "of the essence" [2.3.7]—*i.e.* such as to place the consultant in breach of contract if the required delivery/completion date is not achieved. However, in practice, the scope of the consultants' task will often be exploratory with the result that the size of the project will not be clear or the consultants will be dependant to a large degree upon input from the client's staff, making such onerous conditions inappropriate. An alternative means of speeding up the consultant's work may be to link its payment to the date of delivery, *e.g.* such that the consultants get a bonus for delivering early, but can only recover reduced fees if they deliver late, or to provide for the payment of liquidated damages in the event of delay. Care must however be taken in setting the tariff for the payment of liquidated damages, which must represent a reasonable pre-estimate of the client's likely loss by reason of the delay [2.3.7].

13.2 PAYMENT [X9]

The options for payment are likely to be the same as we have already considered for bespoke software in Chapter 3; *i.e.* time and materials, fixed price, or estimated capped maximum price [3.0.3]—and for the same reasons. It is the nature of consultancy even more than for software that there is often uncertainty as to the amount of work involved. The consultant therefore normally quotes for his time at so much per hour or per day. The contrary pressure will also be felt, of a company wishing to be sure that the consultancy will not end up costing more than the system it is designed to help procure.

Again, the same point must be made that if a client insists on a fixed price contract he must not be surprised if the consultant protects himself against underestimating by putting a fairly substantial "contingency" into his quotation, and imposing clear obligations upon the client to make sure the client performs his own side of the bargain and does not seek to offload tasks onto the consultant tasks which his own staff should be doing.

Like the commissioned software contract, the consultancy contract may, if the work is at all lengthy, require milestones [3.2.1, D5 (1)] giving both sides a chance to assess how the work is going before proceeding to a later phase.

At such milestones it may be that the nature of the work will change and that different skills or expertise will be required with some consequential change in the size and composition of the consultancy team. Separate phases will need to be identified in the contract-possibly in a Schedule or by reference to a separate document. As noted in 13.1 above, such milestones can also be used as a trigger for potential bonus/penalty payments, depending on whether the relevant targets are hit or not.

It can also be that at the outset the precise nature of the skills or expertise required for later phases cannot be known, in which case the consultant may need to make provision for a change in the future hourly charge-out rates to cover this. Equally, for longer term assignments there may be a need for the parties to agree upon a mechanism for agreeing annual variations to the consultant's charge out rates, so as to protect the client against unforeseen "hikes" in the rates whilst also allowing the consultant to counter the effects of wage inflation.

There may equally be an opportunity for the client to redefine, at least in part, the objectives or terms of reference for future phases [13.5]. A clear change control mechanism will accordingly be required in order to ensure that both parties have an opportunity to assess any suggested changes to the nature or scope of the project, and to agree upon any consequent alterations to the price, timescales or other aspects of the contract. This is considered in further detail in section 13.5 below.

In the unlikely event that the parties forget to deal with payment, the law will imply an obligation on the client to pay a reasonable charge to the consultant (Supply of Goods and Services Act 1982, s. 15).

In the case of *The Salvage Association v. CAP Financial Services Ltd* [1995] F.S.R. 654, a feasibility study was followed by a contract for the production of bespoke software from the same company. When the software was found to be useless, the plaintiff recovered not only the costs of the software but also the costs of the original feasibility study, even though it had been accepted at the time by the plaintiff. The precise reasons for this are not clear from the law report and doubtless turn on the facts of the individual case, but from the supplier's point of view the two contracts will need to be kept as separate as possible and from the client's point of view they will need to be as closely linked as possible.

13.3 COMPLETION OF THE CONSULTANCY SERVICES [X3, X10]

In some instances a consultancy will be indefinite in time, continuing until such time as either of the parties chooses to give notice of termination, but it is usually preferable for the project to have a definite point of completion. Having a clear definition of the service to be performed [13.1] should assist in deciding this.

If the contract is for the production of a feasibility study alone, it will terminate on the delivery by the consultant to the client of a report or rather on the presentation of the report with an opportunity for the client to question the consultant on the report [13.7.1]. The importance (mentioned in 13.1) of listing all the questions to which the client needs answers will be apparent here, and it must be the case that the more detail the client can go into in defining them, the better will be the result. Woolly terms of reference all too often result in a woolly report.

As a general rule, the more detailed the outputs required from the consultant become, the greater will be the need for defined acceptance procedures and criteria, so as to provide an objective basis upon which an assessment can be made of the consultant's work. For example, in the case of a consultancy project leading to the acquisition of a system, it will usually be appropriate to set out a process to test the finished result, provided that the consultant is retained until full acceptance of the system has been achieved [2.3, 3.3, A11, A12, D10]. This will also have the further advantages of encouraging the consultants to get on with the procurement and also taking the burden of procurement and even testing of the system off the client's shoulders. Another technique for the consultant which may be used in addition to or instead of defined acceptance criteria is some system of retainer or refresher payments to continue during the life of the contract even though the client is not actually obtaining consultancy advice from the consultant all the time. This in effect means that the consultant is on hand to give such advice at once when requested. The obvious danger to the client from this approach is that the project may drag on indefinitely, through circumstances beyond his control (*e.g.* a supplier's late delivery), and he must ensure that he himself acts promptly on such matters as preparing his machine room, which are within his own control [2.3.7, A15].

If the nature of the consultancy services is such that it is difficult to set out detailed acceptance criteria (as may well be the case where a single report is being produced), the approval process need not be left unaddressed; both parties benefit from an understanding of when and to whom the deliverables will be delivered for approval. Many contracts refer to approval being subject to the "satisfaction" of the client. This is clearly a subjective standard which is likely to favour the client, who can require the consultant to carry out potentially unlimited amounts of rework. Accordingly, one often sees caveats in acceptance provisions to the effect that acceptances/approvals will not in any event be unreasonably withheld [X10].

If the parties do not fix a time for performing the consultancy services in the contract, there is an implied term that the consultant will, if acting in the course of a business, carry out the services within a reasonable time (Supply of Goods and Services Act 1982, s. 14). Even if the parties do not agree upon a specific term making time "of the essence" [13.1], it would in any event be normal for consultants to agree to perform their obligations using reasonable skill and care and within a reasonable period of time. The question of when a delay has become so long as to constitute a breach of contract will then be one for the courts to assess on the facts of each individual case. See *The Salvage Association v. CAP Financial Services Ltd* [1995] F.S.R. 654 and *South West Water v. ICL* [1999] B.L.R. 420.

13.4 TERMINATION [X3, X8, X14]

The usual types of termination clause considered for other contracts will be applicable here.

Like most professionals, the consultant will not usually expect to be able to terminate the contract before it is completed unless there is good cause. On the other hand, consultants will recognise that any professional relationship is based on the trust of the client and once that trust is gone there is little to be gained from insisting on the contract being allowed to run until completion; the relationship is only likely to get worse rather than better. However, in a long consultancy, or one involving many consultancy staff, or both, there may be a period of notice for termination sufficient to allow the consultant time to redeploy productively what may be a significant proportion of his staff [3.4.2].

The effects of termination are often not expressly dealt with in consultancy contracts (or indeed in other forms of contract). In the event of "no fault" termination (*e.g.* where the client has simply lost faith in the consultant without being able to show that the consultant is in material breach of contract or has decided to discontinue the project for reasons unconnected with the consultant's performance), the consultant will usually expect to be paid for all services rendered by him up to the date of termination, and to be compensated for any reasonable expenses incurred by him as a result of such termination. The client may in turn require the consultant to mitigate such expenses, and may, in particular, impose an express obligation upon the consultant to ensure that all relevant subcontracts can be terminated within the same period that it can terminate the consultant's contract—see *South West Water v. ICL* [1999] B.L.R. 420 for the dire effects of a main contract not having a back-to-back subcontract.

Regardless of the reason for the termination, the client will usually want to have all deliverables (however incomplete) produced to date to be handed over to him, and for the intellectual property rights in them also to pass to the client subject to any pre-existing or third party rights, in respect of which the client will usually obtain only a licence. It is also common to see a clause requiring each party to return any confidential information of the other party which is then in its possession. This is a reasonable provision (after all, if the project is coming to an end there should be no on-going need to utilise such information) but may need to be qualified by a right to retain copies to the extent required for professional, regulatory or audit purposes, including the purposes of prosecuting or defending any legal proceedings resulting from the termination of the contract. Any retained information should, however, continue to be subject to the obligations of confidentiality set out in the relevant contract.

13.5 ALTERATIONS [D7, X4 (4)]

As noted above [13.2], the fact that consultancy from its nature deals with matters which contain an element of the unknown (at least for the client) means that the probability of future alteration of the terms of reference must often be allowed for—particularly in larger consultancy tasks. It helps both parties considerably not only to insist that all such changes are properly defined and agreed in writing with full consideration of the effect in terms of cost and duration of the project as a whole [3.5.2, D7, X4 (4)], but also to limit the times when they can take place to completion of defined phases or milestones [13.2]. This in turn means that the timetable for the various phases must allow sufficient time between one phase and the next for an adequate review by both sides before the next phase can commence.

Additional issues for the parties to consider in this regard include whether changes can be requested only by specific client staff (which may be necessary in order to maintain project discipline and control of the overall budget) and whether the consultant is to be entitled to make any charges for assessing changes requested by the client; the rationale for *not* allowing charges is that the process of assessing changes is akin to proposal costs, for which the consultant would not normally charge. The counter-argument is that the consultant will not usually have a choice as to whether or not to assess a particular change request, and so should at least be able to recover the cost of assessing potential changes, which may take a number of man-days properly to analyse.

13.6 CLIENT'S DUTIES [X6]

These must draw largely on those appropriate for commissioned software [3.6], although they will inevitably be amended so as to reflect the precise nature of the project in question.

13.7 CONSULTANT'S DUTIES [X4]

13.7.1 The report

Chapter 3 is again relevant [3.7], but in addition the consultant will probably be required to deliver up any report or deliverable(s) in a particular form and in a specified number of copies. The need for clarity in defining the matters the consultant should address has been stressed more than once [13.1, 13.3, 13.4]. Such points are probably best dealt with in a Schedule.

"*SCHEDULE X*

The Consultant shall upon Completion of the Project provide *five (5)* copies of the Report to the Client.
The Report shall be divided into sections as follows:

- Introduction;
- Terms of Reference;
- Statement of present system;
- Summary of areas where information technology may help;
- Consideration in detail of each such area;
- Description of proposed system;
- Proposed system suppliers;
- Proposed system environmental considerations;
- Proposed system training needs;
- Timetable of proposed system implementation;
- Costs of proposed system;
- Summary of recommendations."

It will almost certainly be necessary for the consultant to attend at least one meeting following the completion of his report so as to present the report and answer questions about it, which will form part of the acceptance process by allowing the client an opportunity to confirm that the work done meets its requirements.

If necessary, this also can be incorporated into a definition of completion of the project:

" 'Completion of the Project' means the acceptance by the Client of the Report following the attendance by the Consultant's Team at the Client's premises to present the Report and reply to questions from the Client's directors and staff about it. Acceptance by the Client shall not be unreasonably withheld."

13.7.2 Confidentiality [X5, X11, X12]

In addition to the points made in 3.7.2, it is perhaps worth stating that any report produced by the consultant will itself usually need to remain confidential; the consultant may require assurances from the client that it will not be passed to third parties without his consent and/or an indemnity from the client against any third party claims which result from unauthorised disclosures. Copyright in the report should pass on acceptance and payment to the client, and this may also go for a draft report on premature termination of the contract [13.4]. Such transfer of copyright will not, however, include any of the consultant's pre-existing materials or third party products or materials. For these, the client should ensure that it is being granted a suitable licence, extending to its group companies if necessary.

In certain cases, a client may seek to insist that the consultant does no similar work for rival companies. Such a condition would amount to a restraint of trade but would ordinarily be enforceable if it is reasonable in its scope and necessary to protect the legitimate interests of the client. Clearly, a consultant advising on the implementation of an accounts package is not nearly so likely to be asked to agree to such a restriction as one who has advised on a specialist program which only the client's direct competitors could benefit from. The key issue is inevitably the balancing of the legitimate expectations of the client and the consultant; it may, for example, be sufficient for only certain of the consultant's staff to be constrained from working for specified competitors of the client, and for a limited period, that is, sufficient time for the client to derive substantial advantage from the services provided.

13.7.3 Quality of service

The quality of the service which the consultant is to provide is obviously a key concern for the client. It is perhaps therefore at first sight alarming to find out how many consultancy contracts avoid the issue altogether. The reason for this may often lie in the fact that where a consultant acts in the course of a business, section 13 of the Supply of Goods and Services Act 1982 implies a term that the consultant will carry out his services with reasonable skill and care. However, such implied terms can be and are often excluded by the consultant's proposed contract terms, and so the client should take care to ensure that the contract wording properly reflects his expectations. If the terms are to be excluded, the exclusion must specifically *negative* the terms—it is not enough for the terms to be restated in somewhat different words (*The Salvage Association v. CAP Financial Services Ltd* [1995] F.S.R. 654).

In many cases, reliance on the Supply of Goods and Services Act may be perfectly adequate and nothing more is required. What is reasonable in this context will depend on the circumstances and, in particular, upon the standards generally observed in the industry as good practice. The codes of practice of bodies in the industry representing consultants may therefore become relevant [Chapter 15]. The type of work undertaken will also be relevant. For instance, one would expect the standards of skill and care to be applied by a surgeon to be somewhat higher than those of a car mechanic. This somewhat obvious and stark comparison may be applied in a more refined way when considering different types of consultancy. A client who is concerned that his consultant should provide a particular quality of service would be well advised to specify this in the contract. A consultant who sells his services on the basis that he abides by a particular code of practice may expect to have to restate this as a term of the contract.

The case of *Stephenson Blake (Holdings) Ltd v. Streets Heaver Limited* in *Computers and Law* (Aug./Sept. 1999), N.S. Vol. 10, Issue 3, p.38) appears to be the only reported case on an IT consultancy. The consultant's task was to recommend a suitable system for the client. The court found six implied duties binding on the consultant:

1. To ensure that the system conformed to the specification and if not, or it was impossible to recommend such a system, to warn the purchaser (*i.e.* the client) in plain terms of the fact and its likely consequences. Checking the supplier's claims for his system was to be done by talking to other users, or testing the software.

2. To use due care and skill to ensure that the system recommended would carry out the functions for which it was required efficiently and would have an acceptable minimum of operational faults or bugs. In the alternative, if no supplier was capable of meeting these standards, the consultant's duty was to advise to that effect.

3. To use due care and skill to ensure that the hardware recommended would perform in conjunction with the recommended software in such a way that

the purchaser's computer operations could be carried out with reasonable speed.

4. To use due care and skill to ensure that the suppliers recommended had the requisite skilled staff and could reasonably be expected to show the necessary stability, both financial and organisational, to maintain and support the system over a substantial period.

5. To use skill and care to ensure that the supplier recommended was in a position to deliver the required system in accordance with the purchaser's requirement.

6. To advise or warn about the impact, if any, of financial constraints on the purchaser's requirements.

The majority of these duties require the consultant to make an independent assessment of claims by the supplier and advise the client of any difficulties and their impact.

PART IV

PUBLIC SECTOR CONTRACTS

Chapter 14

PUBLIC SECTOR CONTRACTS

14.0 Introduction
14.1 Cultural Differences
14.2 E.C. Rules
14.3 U.K. Government Advice and Assistance

14.0 Introduction

Public sector contracts differ from private sector contracts in four main respects. First there is the cultural difference between the two. For example, quantifying lost benefits in the event of late completion and/or defective work can pose particular problems for public sector bodies who cannot point to any loss in profits in the event of their contractor failing to supply what is required. Secondly, there are clauses in contracts which are appropriate only to the public sector, such as those dealing with the Official Secrets Act. Thirdly, there is a large amount of law and procedure enjoined on public sector bodies by the E.C. Rules which have been implemented in this country by various regulations, and which also implement the provisions of the World Trade Organisation Government Procurement Agreement (GPA). Finally, there are specific rules imposed on contractors by British Government policy. These overlay and amplify the E.C. international obligations.

There are several government organisations to assist public sector bodies and their contractors in complying with the necessary rules and procedures. So far as IT contracts are concerned those most relevant are described in more detail in 15.4.

14.1 Cultural Differences

It is difficult to be exhaustive about the cultural differences. The following is therefore a selection of points.

One area in which public sector contracts are likely to differ from private sector contracts is in the overall timescale for implementation. The E.C. Rules will be considered in detail below, but the time which must elapse between each stage means that inevitably contracts above a certain size will take anything from six months to one year (or even more) to implement.

Several results flow from this. In the first case, it is more likely that a contract with such a long gestation will probably result in a change in the requirement during the course of the negotiation. Such a change may come about as a result of technical advances, or as a result of better understanding of the requirement, or both. This means that the contractor will need to be prepared to negotiate for the whole of this period and recognise that it will be expensive for him to do so. Inevitably, this tends to rule out the smaller contractors for the larger jobs (unless bidding as part of a larger consortium, which is increasingly common). It also means that the change control procedure [3.5.2] must be rigorous and that there must be a clear mechanism for documenting any possible changes to the requirement since it was first defined, and ensuring that the implications of such changes (in terms not only of cost but also of timescale and performance) must be fully clarified and agreed by both sides.

One possible solution is to have a phase of technical design to be let as a sort of pre-contract to a number of interested suppliers before the main contract is proceeded with. For a contract with a good deal of development work this may be appropriate, but for other contracts it may be less useful.

A lengthy timescale also implies a lengthy acceptance procedure [3.3.1]. There is nothing to prevent private sector contracts from having a full acceptance procedure though in many cases this is curtailed simply because the purchaser of the goods or services is in a hurry to obtain the benefits they represent. The dangers of this are obvious. However, with a full acceptance procedure lasting at least a month or longer, it inevitably means that the contractor must wait longer for his money. Early part payment of the value of the contract is a possibility but it must be made clear that these payments do not pre-empt the acceptance process and in particular do not imply an acceptance that has not yet been completed. Thus, if a system fails the acceptance tests, any moneys paid in advance should be recoverable.

Public sector contracts are usually let following a competition. The rules for this for the larger contracts are set out below in discussion of the E.C. Rules, but even for small contracts it is typical for there to be several competitors. A short list of three is often considered the optimum. This protects the officers letting the contract from any suspicion of favouritism and enables them to show a clear understanding of competitive costs for the goods or services. Each supplier has to be held at arm's length during the negotiation process, and the exact selection process has to be well documented showing, at least for the senior officers in the public sector body, the criteria used for selection, any weighting given to those criteria, and the relative performances of the various suppliers against this.

Another effect of the sheer difficulty in putting in place public sector contracts is that they tend to last for longer. Once everyone has gone through the gruelling process of acquiring a system, it is inevitable that neither the public sector body nor contractors themselves can lightly face a rerun. There is therefore a reluctance to terminate such contracts early. The length of time a public sector contract may run obviously varies but five or even seven years are not untypical. It follows from this that a public sector body may be held to ransom by a contractor who has managed to find some inequitable clause in his favour in the contract since he knows that the public sector body cannot easily switch to an alternative supplier, or if they do it will take them at least six months to a year to complete that switch. On the other hand, suppliers who find themselves tied to a "bad" deal can face mounting losses over the course of the contract, knowing that any attempt to terminate the contract would precipitate a major damages claim.

To try to protect themselves over the length of such a contract, many public sector bodies seek to insert various "incentivising" provisions, such as defined service levels (with service credits accruing if the levels are not met) and/or milestone dates tied to the payment of liquidated damages. To amplify the matter of liquidated damages, the point here is that such damages should be easily calculable and represent a clear estimate of the loss to the organisation in question. For a commercial company, a loss in profits would be an obvious criterion. For a public sector body, there may be a loss in some cash saving which was to have been realised and if this is the case calculation may not be too difficult. It may be that additional staff will need to be brought in on a contract basis and their exact cost can again be calculated. Alternatively, it may be that some diminution in a service to the public; for example, the failure of the library system run by a local authority may result in an extreme case in the borrowers being unable to take any books out at all or in a less extreme case that there are excessive queues for borrowers taking books out and that the tracking of books and collecting fines may not be up to standard. Here the calculation of liquidated damages is virtually impossible.

Another area is publicity. Whereas most commercial organisations may be perfectly content that both they and others with whom they do business should be entitled to publicity and their only concern is likely to be how factual it is and what if any effect it has on them, for a public sector body there is usually no particular advantage in publicity of this kind. Indeed, on occasion it may be positively harmful (as shown by the large amount of adverse publicity for the Passport Agency in 1999 when its new computer system created lengthy delays in the issuing of new passports). The public sector body is therefore likely to require strict control on publicity and even ban it altogether.

However, if a contract goes wrong, and bearing in mind the difficulties mentioned above about liquidated damages, it may well be that the most powerful weapon the public sector body holds over the defaulting contractor is that of publicity. Inevitably, any failure in a public sector contract receives far more publicity than would a corresponding failure in a private sector contract. This is not to suggest that public sector bodies welcome the publicity so generated, especially as some sections of the press particularly delight in investigating public sector bodies in these circumstances. Nevertheless, it must be recognised that the failure is likely to be even more damaging to the contractor and may well result in a considerable loss in business once the failure of the system is known. This may be so even when the case is first set down for hearing. It is thus in the interests of the contractor to avoid this state of affairs and having a dispute resolution provision which provides for arbitration (*i.e.* as opposed to litigation in the Courts) may be one way in which he is tempted to do this. Arbitration will at the very least buy time and no publicity about the failure will usually be possible during this time, although the public sector body may only agree to have an arbitration clause in the contract if it is also free to use the threat of adverse publicity as an aid to enforcement.

Another difference from private sector contracts is that whatever is being done is more likely to be unique. The Passport Agency project mentioned above is a good example; although systems involving the issuing of documentation to the public are not uncommon, few (if any) will also involve the levels of authentication and time constraints required in relation to the issue of a passport.

Yet another aspect is that unlike in the private sector, the changes in business methods which result from computerisation often cannot be implemented except by means of legislation. Sometimes, such legislation cannot be pursued with the result that the system is "skewed" to avoid the business change.

We propose to say nothing in detail about the clauses specific to public sector contracts such as the Official Secrets Act, certain clauses about corrupt gifts or the right to use land. Such clauses are typical of all public sector contracts and not just of ones involving computers and information technology and the wording is purely "boiler plate".

14.2 E.C. RULES

Strictly speaking the E.C. Rules and the GPA Rules are separate, although in practice they apply to the same bodies and the E.C. Rules have incorporated the

GPA Rules anyway, in order that E.C. suppliers and service providers are treated no less favourably than suppliers from GPA countries. It is therefore appropriate to confine discussion to the E.C. Rules as implemented into the national law. The general philosophy behind these rules is the encouragement of open and competitive tendering and the prohibition of protectionist policies in the public sector.

The Rules provide for various methods of procurement, with timetables and certain obligations as to advertising and the information that should be contained in such advertisements. The Rules are directed at public sector bodies seeking to let contracts, rather than at the contractors themselves. However, the contractors will need to be aware of the rules which affect both the procurement process and the contract itself so that they know what behaviour by the awarding authority and themselves is acceptable. It will be seen that the main concern of the contractor will be to make a bid in accordance with the terms of the contract notice which will have been published in the *Official Journal of the European Communities*. Therefore, the contractor must have an awareness of time limits, criteria for making awards and potential remedies. Needless to say preference for a company because of its nationality is outlawed by the E.C. Rules. The recent case of *Harmon CFEM Facades (U.K.) Ltd v. The Corporate Officer of the House of Commons* (see Professor Sue Arrowsmith, "E.C. Procurement Rules in the U.K. Courts: An analysis of the *Harmon* Case: Part I" in [2000] 9 P.P.L.R Issue 3, 120) is not an IT case but was concerned with windows for the new House of Commons building where a contract was apparently awarded to a company because it was British. There seems no reason for believing the principle does not apply equally to IT procurements.

The public contracts directives, and their implementing regulations, divide into the following main classes:

(a) goods and supplies;

(b) services;

(c) works;

(d) utilities;

(e) compliance and remedies.

"Works" is concerned with building works (the Public Works Contracts Regulations 1991, Sched. 1 (S.I. 1991 No. 2680)) and can be ignored from the point of view of IT.

14.2.1 Supplies

The Supplies Directive goes back to 1976–77 (77/62/EEC) which was originally embodied in the Public Supply Contracts Regulations 1991 (S.I. 1991 No. 2679), but the 1993 Directive (93/36/EEC), embodied in the Public Supply Contracts Regulations 1995 (S.I. 1995 No. 201) supersedes this. This part therefore refers to the 1995 Regulations. Regulation 2 contains the definitions and in particular defines a "contracting authority" (which is elaborated in Regulation 3). Regulation 2 also defines a "public supply contract", where it can be seen that supplies are simply referred to as "goods" but goes on to include "siting and installation of those goods". Regulation 6 sets out contracts which are exempted from the regulations— in particular, contracts which are secret or where the delivery of the goods involves special security measures. Such exempted contracts will still have to comply with the E.C. Treaty obligations.

On a *de minimis* basis, the regulations apply only to contracts whose value is over a certain threshold. Again, the fundamental principles of the E.C. Treaty, such as non-discrimination on the grounds of nationality and state of establishment, will still apply to contracts which fall below the threshold. The current thresholds for all the regulations implementing the E.C. Directives were set for January 1, 2000 and will apply until December 31, 2001, when new thresholds will be set. For supply contracts being procured by central government bodies which are subject to the WTO GPA (and which are listed in Schedule 1 to the Public Supply Contract Regulations), the threshold is currently £93,896, (130,000 Special Drawing Rights (SDR); 139,312 Euros). The threshold for all other contracting authorities is £144,456 (SDR 200,000; 214,326 Euros).

The value of the contract is taken to be the value of the consideration. Regulation 7(6) provides for how the value of the consideration is to be estimated where there is a series of contracts or a renewable contract. Where there are regular contracts or contracts which are renewed within a given time, the value is either:

(a) the actual aggregate value of similar contracts for goods of the same type concluded over the previous physical year of 12 months; or

(b) the estimated aggregated value of similar contracts for goods of the same type anticipated for the 12 months following first delivery; or

(c) where there is a definite period greater than 12 months, the estimated aggregated value of similar contracts for goods of the same type for the term of the contract (Regulation 7(6)).

Where a contract is for an indefinite period, it is assumed to last at least four years and thus the anticipated monthly consideration must be multiplied by 48 (Regulation 7(8)). Where the procurement is for a single requirement of goods implemented by a number of contracts, their values must be aggregated (Regulation 7(4)). In other words, it is not possible to split a contract in order to avoid the thresholds (Regulation 7(10)).

There are three types of procedure available: open, restricted or negotiated. An *open procedure* is one whereby all interested suppliers may submit tenders. A *restricted procedure* limits tenders to those suppliers who have actually been invited to submit. A *negotiated procedure* allows the contracting authority to consult with suppliers of their choice and then negotiate the terms of the contract with one or more of them. The general rule is that either the open or restricted procedure must be used. However, in exceptional circumstances, the negotiated procedure can be used. These are specified in Regulation 10, but the most important of these for IT purposes is where there are technical or artistic reasons, or the goods are to be manufactured purely for research and development purposes, or where the use of the open or restricted procedure has failed. In such circumstances, not only can the negotiated procedure be used, but also, the awarding body does not need to comply with the advertising and time-limit requirements.

The timetable for each procedure is set out in Regulations 11, 12 and 13. As soon as possible after the beginning of each financial year, contracting authorities must publish an indicative notice (a Prior Information Notice in the form set out in Part A of Schedule 3) for contracts to be awarded that year that are expected to be valued above £505,500 (750,000 Euros)—see Regulation 9. For all contracts to which the regulations apply, the body awarding the contract must advertise its intention in a notice in the *Official Journal*, which has to be drawn up in a form set out in Schedule 3, Pt B. It should be published in the *Official Journal* 12 days after despatch. It cannot be published elsewhere until the *Official Journal* has published it. The notice should specify the time limits for the various stages of the procurement. At least 52 days must elapse between the date of despatch of the notice and the deadline for receipt of tenders in the open procedure. Where the negotiated or restricted procedures are used, at least 37 days must be allowed from date of despatch to the deadline for receipt of requests to participate in the tender selection. At least 40 days must elapse before those who have been invited to participate are required to submit their tenders. In practice, a sifting process is usually necessary to ensure that everyone is agreed who the contractors are. Once a decision has been made as to whom the contract has been awarded to, it will also be necessary to give reasons within 15 days of a request for reasons. An award notice must then be despatched to the *Official Journal* no more than 48 days after the award.

Regulation 8 raises the question of technical specifications in contract documents. Generally, where a European standard exists, it should normally be specified in the offer documentation and adhered to in a contract. The principle is that specifications should not be drawn up so that their effect is that it is more difficult for firms in other member states to meet than domestic firms. British standards which implement European standards are included as being European standards. If no European standard exists then an international standard should be used. The CCTA [15.4.1] established a series of interlocking standards which were originally known as GOSIP (Government Open Systems Implementation Profile). Subsequently, these have been superseded, after negotiation with other European countries, by the EPHOS (European Procurement Handbook for Open Systems) Standards. EPHOS still exists for the purposes of backwards compatibility—*i.e.* were a new requirement must interface with an existing system—but in most cases the *de jure* standards imposed by the Internet are considered sufficient.

Awarding the contract

Before tenders reach the bid evaluation stage, they can only be rejected on certain grounds. These grounds are where a bidder does not fulfil criteria as to economic and financial standing (Regulation 15), or technical capability (Regulation 16), or where other factors are present, such as where the supplier has been convicted of a criminal offence (Regulation 14). Of these, technical capability is in practice the most important. Typically, the contractors will be bidding against a detailed requirement. Where a contractor cannot fulfil a fundamental requirement of the system, his bid cannot be considered. The important thing is to distinguish between such fundamental requirements, and other requirements which however desirable, cannot be said to be fundamental. For the avoidance of doubt, a well drafted specification will label each requirement mandatory or desirable.

Contracts have to be awarded to either the supplier which offers the lowest price or whose bid is the "most economically advantageous". A common way of expressing this is to judge on the most cost-effective solution over the lifetime of the project. Thus if the new system has a projected lifetime of seven years the value over those years can be set out and totalled, making clear whether a project with a high first year cost and low running costs is to be preferred to one with a low up-front cost but higher running costs. At one time when inflation was more significant it was usual to discount money to be spent later in the project as against money earlier in the project, but more recently this practice seems to have been abandoned. No doubt it could be revived if inflation rises. It will be seen from this that contractors who wish to win should cost all aspects of their bid realistically. Woolly costing makes it difficult for the evaluation team to assess the project and they may even be forced to guess costs which have been omitted. The criteria for determining which is the most economically advantageous offer are set out in Regulation 21, although the list is not exhaustive. The general purpose behind the rules is to prevent the award of a contract on frivolous grounds. Regulation 21(7) requires the contracting body to enquire more closely into an abnormally low tender. A very low tender may be a loss leader by the company who is anxious to do business with the contracting authority; it is more likely because the company has totally failed to understand the scope, size or complexity of what is required.

14.2.2 Services

Services are defined in Schedule 1 of the Public Services Contracts Regulations 1993 (S.I. 1993 No. 3228) which implement Directive 92/50/EEC. Services include computers and related services (Part A, Category 7).

We have gone into the supply contract regulations in some detail and broadly, the Public Services Contracts Regulations have the same principles, so here we touch on areas that either differ or otherwise should be specifically highlighted in the context of computer contracts. The threshold is currently the same as for public supply contracts.

The aggregation rule whereby like contracts can be considered jointly to see whether they have reached the threshold is particularly important with services contracts, since it seems that contracts for broadly similar services must be so aggregated. The most likely candidate here is consultancy, and public sector bodies are being advised to lump together all IT consultancy contracts for aggregation purposes. Clearly, a threshold of £144,456 is easily reached, let alone £93,896. The way to deal with this must be for the public sector body to procure by full open tender one or more contractors who can provide the services after a competition. It will then be possible for the public sector body to call off days or weeks for particular projects for consultancy from these contractors as required. A *framework arrangement* (whereby suppliers of a particular type have been chosen—usually by open procedure—to provide a range of call-off services so that public sector users can immediately call off those services from them with no further procurement) which falls well short of a contract may be equally valid provided it had been procured by full open tender in this way. The effect of this is to procure letters of intent which can then be converted into contracts at a later stage. [15.4.3]

One of the exceptional circumstances in which the negotiated procedure can be used with supply contracts is where the nature of the services is such that it is not possible to draw up specifications with sufficient precision to enable the contracting authority to use the open or restricted procedure. This may be important in relation to IT services, as often the specifications at the outset will need to be developed through negotiation, in many cases permitting use of the negotiated procedure.

In addition to the open, restricted and negotiated procedures used in the supplies contracts, the services contract also has design contests (Regulation 24). This enables a jury to select a particular design (typically in the field of architecture but it could also apply to IT) following a full open procedure which has selected a number of candidates.

Where contracts are for a mixture of goods and services the rule is basically that the contract is treated as a services or as a supply contract depending solely on which of the two components is the larger. In practice, since service contracts tend to have a longer life than supply contracts, it is often the case that the balance is more easily tipped towards service contracts than supply contracts.

14.2.3 Utilities

A utility is a public sector body in such fields as water, energy, transport and telecommunications performing its relevant activity. For example, a public rail network procuring a traffic control system for itself would be a utility. Privatisation of the old utilities does not affect the applicability of the Utilities Directive to the private sector companies who now handle utilities except in the case of telecommunications.

The original Utilities Directive 90/531/EEC which was implemented by the Utilities Supply and Works Contracts Regulations 1992 (S.I. 1992 No. 3279) was amended by the Utilities Supply and Works Contracts (Amendment) Regulations 1993 (S.I. 1993 No. 3227) only to the extent that certain exemptions for utilities operating in the oil and gas, and other solid fuel sectors were considered. However, the original directive and the regulations are now superseded by Directive 93/38/EEC, which lists in its annexes the various utilities affected in the U.K. and elsewhere in Europe. The thresholds are currently £288,912 (SDR 400,000; 428,653 Euros) for the water, electricity, urban transport and ports sectors; £269,600 (400,000 Euros) for the oil, gas, coal and railway sectors. In other respects, the regulations are broadly similar to the supplies and services regulations, at least so far as IT contracts are likely to be concerned.

14.2.4 Compliance and remedies

Under Regulation 30 of the Utilities Supply and Works Contracts Regulations 1992 (S.I. 1992 No. 3279), Regulation 32 of the Public Services Contracts Regulations 1993 (S.I. 1993 No. 3328) and Regulation 29 of the Public Supply Contracts Regulations 1995 (S.I. 1995 No. 201), remedies are available in the U.K. courts. Remedies are also available before the European Court of Justice. An action in either of these, if successful, may result in an injunction or damages. However, for an injunction to be successful the contract will need not yet to have been let. In practice there is usually insufficient time for this. Damages also are time limited to within three months of the contract being let.

An alternative strategy is for the company not to raise an action itself but simply to notify the Commission who may itself take the necessary action against the defaulting country. The problem here is that the Commission has acquired the reputation of being reluctant to take action unless the case is a particularly gross one. It is also the case that there will be considerable delay. A further point is that it is unlikely to result in any useful result for the aggrieved company, beyond seeing humiliation of their rival.

14.3 U.K. GOVERNMENT ADVICE AND ASSISTANCE

The Government has a number of organisations to assist public sector users in the task of procuring IT and IT-related goods and services. Within the Treasury for example, is the Office of Government Commerce (OGC) which brings together old purchasing organisations, including, in particular so far as this book is concerned, the CCTA (Central Computer and Telecommunications Agency) [15.4.1]. Another part of the Treasury houses PUK (Partnerships U.K.) which focuses on Private Finance Initiative (PFI) projects, now more usually called public/private partnerships. Meanwhile, within the Cabinet Office is to be found CITU, the Central IT Unit, which is more concerned with high-level questions of strategy and policy than with procurement for individual projects.

The Private Finance Initiative (PFI) began under the previous Conservative Government and has continued under the present Labour administration. It is a mechanism for financing large infrastructure projects (of which IT furnishes plenty of examples), whereby the private sector assumes an element of the risk for the project while value for money is demonstrated in the public sector. As such it fits well with the commercial culture of outsourcing [Chapter 11]. Thus private capital finances a project and takes the risk (or at least such of the risk as can properly be passed to it, as opposed to being retained by the public sector) but in return will expect a share of the financial benefits when the project goes live. Such financial benefit may take a number of forms: from alternative revenue streams (*e.g.* by marketing the data or services to others), additional markets for the software, or by selling off excess capacity (a classic side-benefit of outsourcing). Thus the private sector body can look for any of the following advantages: greater control of the project, greater reward commensurate with the risk, optimising assets, more predictable revenue and improved profitability. The benefits to the public sector have been said to be better services, better value for money, to move public services "away from being a provider to an enabler and facilitator of public services", increased investment, a speeding up of the delivery of IT, a reduction in risk and the development of a private sector partnership. However, it must also be noted that some high profile IT PFI projects have run into difficulties in recent years, which calls into question whether IT projects are as well suited to PFI as might have been thought. PFI projects are now usually referred to as PPP (public/private partnerships). However, the principle has changed little.

Partnerships UK comprises the old projects division of the Treasury Taskforce and was set up to support PFI, so that a "best practice" for the contracting of such projects could evolve and the processes could be streamlined. This is clearly important in terms of Government procurement and the Taskforce produced some guidance on the standardisation of PFI contracts, and accompanying guidance specifically for IT contracts. However, it now appears that this guidance will be superseded by guidelines promulgated by the Office of Government Commerce (OGC), who may not take a similar line. Accordingly, those involved with Government projects would be well advised to keep a close eye out for the pronouncements and guidance from the OGC—see above.

Local Government has an additional advisory body which works with PUK: Public Private Partnerships Programme (4ps). This is a centre for advice for local authorities on all kinds of public private partnerships and is not restricted to PFI [15.4.5].

14.3.1 CCTA catalogues

Provided a proper public sector procurement has been carried out with all appropriate evaluation procedures, a contract can be set in place for the calling off of items as and when they are required. As mentioned above [14.2.2], such contracts are called *framework contracts*. These are now generally used for most IT procurements below the GATT thresholds. The Central Computer and Telecommunications Agency (CCTA—also part of OGC—see 15.4.1) has put in place such framework agreements with a large number of suppliers of goods and services and summarised the framework agreements with the relevant suppliers in a series of catalogues. The effect of this is that Government Departments can use these catalogues without needing to go through a full public sector procurement, relying on the framework contracts already evaluated and entered into on the Government's behalf by the CCTA. There are three catalogues:

(1) GCat (Government Catalogue) for IT products and services such as hardware, software, training, consumables, maintenance and project implementation, telephony;

(2) S-CAT (Services Catalogue) for services such as strategy development, programme and project management, IT, architecture design, specification, acceptance and implementation, support services, advice and consultancy; and

(3) GTC (Government Telecommunications Contracts) for network and telecommunications services.

As the suppliers of these services have already been identified through procedures fully compliant with E.C. procurement rules, public sector bodies to whom the rules can apply can safely do business directly with the suppliers within the catalogues.[1]

In addition, the CCTA continues to provide general IT services for Government such as the application of Best Practice, the use of model contracts, establishing methodologies for procurement such as PRINCE and SSADM for systems analysis and design. It also represents the U.K. Government on appropriate international bodies.

---

[1] As this book goes to press, the validity of framework agreements is being questioned. Revised framework arrangements to meet any objections are likely and readers should check with the CCTA.

PART V

SOURCES OF ADVICE

CHAPTER 15

SOURCES OF ADVICE

15.0 Introduction
15.1 Professional Bodies
15.2 Trade Associations
15.3 Other Bodies
15.4 Public Sector Bodies
15.5 Special Interest Groups
15.6 User Groups

15.0 INTRODUCTION

Computing in all its forms is an open profession in the sense that anyone can call himself a programmer or analyst, or run a bureau service, without requiring any particular qualifications for the task. Nevertheless, those involved in the IT industry have from the outset been anxious to police their own profession(s) and have established professional bodies to institute standards of conduct and expertise in the hope that the lay public in time may come to rely on the qualifications of these bodies as a guarantee of excellence. A guarantee implies an indemnity in the sense that any falling short of the professional standards must be subject to a sanction.

This section considers two purely professional bodies—the British Computer Society and the Institute of Management of Information Systems—some trade associations, and three other bodies (Oftel, NCC and WIPO). It also considers special interest groups, particularly the Society for Computers and Law which provides a forum for those further interested in computer law. There will, however, be other groups who will be of potential influence but who we feel are beyond the scope of this book (for example, the Institute of Chartered Accountants of England and Wales, who have a regulatory function in relation to some of the big audit-linked consultancy firms)

The heads of these various organisations might be considered as suitable persons to be named in an arbitration clause for the purpose of nominating an arbitrator in the event that the parties cannot agree on the appointment of an appropriate person.

Finally, a brief word is included about user groups, as a possible forum for dealing with complaints and common problems.

15.1 PROFESSIONAL BODIES

There are two principal professional bodies for computer personnel in Britain: the British Computer Society, and the Institute of Management of Information Systems.

215

15.1.1 British Computer Society (BCS)

This is the oldest professional body for computer people in Britain, and one of the oldest in the world, being founded in 1957. The Society's entrance is now by examination. It has 36,000 members which probably represents between one-and two-thirds of the profession (depending on definitions of the profession: is a manager whose job includes computer responsibilities but with no day-to-day involvement, a member of the profession?).

The British Computer Society has two codes for its members—a *Code of Practice*, and a *Code of Conduct*. The *Code of Practice* is a document far too little known and used. It takes a step-by-step approach to computer operations and provides a valuable checklist of points to look for. Unfortunately, it is a little abbreviated in its attempt to cover a very wide field, and it may be said that the information will not always be easily understood by the non-expert. So far as a previous (1972) version of the *Code of Good Practice*'s legal status is concerned, Article 9 (p. 15) was explicit:

> "Relevance to Law: The Code has no relevance to law. But the Code may be quoted by an expert witness giving his assessment of whether certain conduct was good practice. Or a supplier may be asked to comment if, in his view, his product is in accordance with the Code. There is no way in which the Code as at present written can be quoted in a contract and enforced."

See also *Johnson v. Bingley & others*, The Times, February 28, 1995, where it was held that breach of a professional code of conduct was not *ipso facto* negligence.

However, a new BCS *Code of Practice* has been published which no longer incorporates this limitation and it is the hope of the Professional Panel of the BCS that the Code may be incorporated by reference into contracts as providing a standard to be invoked in case of dispute.

The *Code of Conduct* is a much shorter document, but more immediately comprehensible. It is binding on all members of the British Computer Society.

Copies of up-to-date versions of both codes are available from:
The Chief Executive
The British Computer Society
1 Sanford Street
Swindon
Wilts SN1 1HJ
Tel: 01793–417417
Fax: 01793–480270
01793–417473
Website: www.bcs.org.uk
E-mail: bcshq@bsc.org.uk

If anyone having work done for them by a member of the BCS feels that the work does not measure up to this Code of Conduct, they should immediately contact the BCS. It must be emphasised that in the past there has not been extensive use of this disciplinary procedure—a fact which may reflect either the probity of BCS members or the ignorance of the public. However, it is the case that the BCS has been successful in encouraging members to resign whose activity is liable to bring the Society into disrepute.

The BCS also keeps a register of consultants, and another of expert witnesses for the benefit of solicitors and others who need advice in disputes involving computer contracts and technology.

Finally, arbitration clauses in computer contracts have not been discussed in detail in this book since their format is indistinguishable from any other arbitration clauses. However, it is worth pointing out that the President of The Law Society may be thought, without being unkind or patronising, to be a less appropriate appointor of an arbitrator in computer contracts than the President of the British Computer Society. Anyone wishing to do this is requested to use the BCS's approved clause which is as follows:

"In the event of any dispute or difference under or arising out of this Agreement either party may give notice thereof in writing to the other and the same shall be referred to the Arbitration of a person agreed upon or failing agreement within 14 days of the date of such notice of some person appointed by the President for the time being of the British Computer Society. Such Arbitration shall be in accordance with the provision of the Arbitration Act 1950 or any statutory modification or re-enactment thereof."

Anyone wishing to make use of this facility should contact either the Registrar or the Chief Executive of the BCS first.

15.1.2 Institute of Management of Information Systems (IMIS)

Previously known as the Institute of Data Processing Management, this body is an amalgamation of two professional bodies—the Data Processing Management Association (founded in 1966) and the Institute for Data Processing (founded in 1967). It now numbers 11,000 members.

The IMIS introduced in July 1989 a *Code of Professional Conduct*. The IMIS' present address is:

Institute of Management of Information Systems
5 Kingfisher House
New Mill Road
Orpington
Kent BR5 3QG
Tel: 0700–0023456
Fax: 0700–0023023
Website: www.imis.org.uk
E-mail: central@imis.org.uk

The President of the Institute of Management of Information Systems could also be suggested as a potential nominator of an arbitrator in the appropriate clauses of computer contracts. He would, of course, be an alternative to the President of the British Computer Society.

15.2 TRADE ASSOCIATIONS

15.2.1 Computing Services and Software Association

The Computing Services and Software Association was formed in 1975 as an amalgamation of two older associations. It has only corporate members (unlike the BCS and IMIS, both of which have personal membership). A condition of membership is adherence to a *Code of Conduct* (the newest edition is January 2000). Complaints of any infringement by a CSSA member should be addressed to:

The Director General
Computer Services and Software Association Ltd

20 Red Lion Street
London WC1R 4QN
Tel: 020–7395 6700
Fax: 020–7404 4119
Website: www.cssa.co.uk
E-mail: csssa@cssa.co.uk

The Association has powers to invoke sanctions against any member found to be infringing the code, though to date all fully investigated complaints have been more or less contractual misunderstandings.

The Association's consultancy, facilities management, contingency planning, education and training, bureau, and marketing groups have Codes of Practice and the third-party maintenance group is in the process of producing one.

15.2.2 Federation against Software Theft (FAST)

The Federation Against Software Theft was formed in 1984. Its members are generally companies who produce or market software and, perhaps not surprisingly, it has accordingly been prominent in the battle against software piracy and copyright infringement.

Further information is available from:

Chief Executive
Federation Against Software Theft
1 Kingfisher Court
Farnham Road
Slough
Berks SL2 1JF
Tel: 01753–527999
Fax: 01753–532100
Website: www.fast.org.uk
E-mail: fast@fast.org

15.2.3 Business Software Alliance

The Business Software Alliance represents software houses with Government etc. but in particular it has a role similar to FAST in assisting software suppliers in protecting their copyright. However, it is more international in flavour, and its members include many of the largest American software corporations.

Further information is available from:

Regional Manager, Northern Europe,
Business Software Alliance,
79 Knightsbridge
London SW1X 7RB
Tel: 020–7245 0304
Fax: 020–7245 0310
Website: www.bsa.org
E-mail: europe@bsa.org

15.3 OTHER BODIES

15.3.1 Office of Telecommunications (Oftel)

Under the Telecommunications Act of 1984, the Office of Telecommunications (Oftel) was established under a Director General of Telecommunications and Parts II and III of the Act describe his functions. These include in particular:

(1) Investigating complaints about the provision of telecommunications services and the supply of apparatus (s. 49);

(2) Exercising powers under the Fair Trading Act 1973 and the Competition Act 1980 concurrently with the Director of Fair Trading in relation to monopoly situations and anti-competitive practices in telecommunications (s. 50);

(3) Monitoring and enforcing conditions in telecommunications licences (s.16).

On the March 1, 2000, the Fair Trading Act 1973 and the Competition Act 1980 were superseded by the Competition Act 1998. The effects of the new Act on the telecommunications sector are set out in a consultation paper available from Oftel's website.

The majority of Oftel's functions are concerned with competition in the telecommunications industry, but obviously at least the three functions listed above and possibly others also have consumer aspects. Anyone with grievances on telecommunications matters should first try to resolve their complaint with the supplier of the service. However, if this does not produce a satisfactory solution, customers may well think it worthwhile contacting Oftel. They should note that the Director General has no responsibilities for any other aspects of computing except telecommunications. There are separate Advisory Committees on telecommunications for England, Scotland, Wales and Northern Ireland, but Oftel's Headquarters are to be found at:

Office of Telecommunications (Oftel)
Export House
50 Ludgate Hill
London EC4M 7JJ
Tel: 020–7634 8700
Fax: 020–7634 8943
Website: www.offtel.gov.uk

15.3.2 National Computing Centre (NCC)

The National Computing Centre was established in 1966, with the primary objective of "promoting an increased and more effective use of computers in every field of national and commercial activity".

The Centre is a non-profit-distributing organisation with revenue derived from members' subscriptions, government contracts for projects and sales of products and services. Many of the NCC's activities lie outside the scope of this book but readers may wish to be aware of three: (i) a conciliation service, (ii) the escrow service and (iii) the NCC Legal Group. These are all run by NCC Services Ltd which is the trading subsidiary of the NCC.

(a) *Conciliation*: The staff of the NCC will, when invited to do so, see both sides in a dispute, all on a without-prejudice basis, and consider the legal, commercial and technical issues. It is an informal procedure, leading to pragmatic solutions;

(b) *Escrow*: The NCC provides what is probably the largest escrow arrangement in the world with about 4,500 software products in their safekeeping [3.3.1, 9.0, N];

(c) *NCC Legal Group*: see 15.5.3 below.

Anyone interested in any of these activities can contact the NCC at:

The National Computing Centre Ltd
Oxford Road
Manchester M1 7ED
Tel: 0161–2286333
Fax: 0161–242 2400
Website: www.nccglobal.com

For the escrow department, contact NCC Escrow International Ltd at the same address.

Tel: 0161–242 2324
Fax: 0161–242 2275
E-mail: escrow@nccglobal.com

15.3.3 The World Intellectual Property Organisation (WIPO) Arbitration and Mediation Center

The World Intellectual Property Organisation at Geneva has an Arbitration and Mediation Center which was established in 1994 for the resolution of international commercial intellectual property disputes between private parties. A speciality of the Center is disputes over domain names and it can be nominated contractually as an arbitrator—in particular it is so nominated by ICANN [12.1.2].

Dispute resolution is on the basis that both sides accept WIPO's role as Arbiter or Mediator, as the case may be, and this may be best effected by an arbitration/mediation clause naming the Center. Standard clauses for this are available from the Center.

The Center can be contacted at:
Arbitration and Mediation Center
World Intellectual Property Organisation
34 chemin des Colombettes
P.O. Box 18
1211 Geneva 20
Switzerland
Tel: (41–22) 338 9111
Fax: (41–22) 740 3700
Website: www.arbiter.wipo.int
E-mail: arbiter.mail@wipo.int

15.4 PUBLIC SECTOR BODIES

15.4.1 CCTA

The CCTA is the Government Centre for Information Systems responsible for stimulating and promoting the effective use of information systems in support of the efficient delivery of business objectives and improved quality of services by the public sector. It is part of the Office of Government Commerce [15.4.2] under HM Treasury. Its customers are government departments, executive agencies and certain non-Crown bodies and for these organisations it provides a number of services including model agreements, assistance in procurement and legal advice including advice on contracts. It also has a commercial intelligence service and another of its roles is advice on standards.

Its address is:

CCTA
Rosebery Court
St Andrews Business Park
Norwich NR7 0HS
Tel: 01603–704704
Fax: 01603–704817
Website: www.ccta.open.gov.uk
E-mail: info@ccta.gov.uk

15.4.2 Office of Government Commerce (OGC)

The Office of Government Commerce includes CCTA and also the Buying Agency.
It is the policy arm of Government procurement and is preparing a revision of
government advice.

Its address is:

Office of Government Commerce
Fleet Bank House
Salisbury Square
Blackfriars
London EC4Y 8AE
Tel: 020–7211 1323
Fax: 020 211 1345
Website: www.ogc.gov.uk

15.4.3 Partnerships UK (PUK)

HM Treasury has had a number of initiatives to assist in the public sector in its
procurement, the general purpose being both to raise standards and to build up
expertise in this (to some) esoteric area. The Central Unit on Procurement gave
way to the Treasury Taskforce and this in turn has given way so far as projects are
concerned to Partnerships UK, known as PUK, which is dedicated to assisting
public/private partnerships (PPPs) including Private Finance Initiative (PFI). PUK
is funded largely by the private sector with minority public sector investment. It
offers advice on a charge-out basis and is further described in 14.3.

Further details can be obtained from:

Partnerships UK
10 Great George Street
London SW1P 3AE
Tel: 020 7273 8383
Fax: 020 7273 8367/8
Website: www.partnershipsuk.org.uk

15.4.4 Society for Information Technology Managers (SOCITM)

Three organisations particularly serving the needs of local government may also be
mentioned. The first is the Society of Information Technology Management. As its
title suggests the organisation is not confined to local authority needs but much of
its original focus was on public utilities and with liberalisation/privatisation it has
increasingly turned its attention to local government. It is a professional organisation for officers responsible for recommending corporate IT policy and it serves "to
provide a focal point for IT and related issues, share experiences, promote the
recognition of IT and influence legislation". The society operates through regional

branches co-ordinated by a national committee. It has local meetings on IT and a twice-yearly conference.

Its address is:

National Secretary,
SOCITM Office,
PO Box 121
Northampton NN4 6TG
Tel & Fax: 01604–674800
Website: www.socitm.gov.uk

15.4.5 The Audit Commission

The Audit Commission for Local Authorities and the National Health Service in England and Wales is charged under section 33 of the Audit Commission Act 1998 with carrying out studies designed to improve the economy, efficiency and effectiveness of local government. It can provide informal advice on contracts and it has produced a number of reports some of which deal with contractual issues.

It can be contacted at:

Director of Audit Support
The Audit Commission
1 Vincent Square
London SW1P 2PN
Tel: 020–7828 1212
Fax: 020–7976 6187
Website: www.audit-commission.gov.uk

15.4.6 Public Private Partnerships Programme (4ps)

Public Private Partnerships Programme, known as 4ps, is a consultancy set up to help local authorities develop and deliver Private Finance Initiative (PFI) schemes. As such it is roughly a counterpart in local government to central government's PUK [15.4.3]. However, it differs from PUK in that is funded largely by government grant.

Further information from:

The Chief Executive
Public Private Partnerships Programme
6th Floor
83 Victoria Street
London SW1H 0HW
Tel: 020–7472 1550 or 020–7472 1560
Website: www.4ps.co.uk
E-mail: firstname.surname@4ps.co.uk

15.5 Special Interest Groups

15.5.1 Society for Computers and Law

This Society was founded in 1973 and now has nearly 2,800 members. It exists to encourage and develop both IT for lawyers and IT-related law. Hence it is interested in such topics as data protection and software ownership as well as computer contracts. It publishes a journal called *Computers and Law* which includes articles on contracts as well as reports of leading IT cases and it sponsors talks and seminars (including branch meetings) on these topics.

Those interested in the Society should contact:

The Administrative Secretary
Society for Computers and Law
10 Hurle Crescent
Clifton
Bristol BS8 2TA
Tel: 0117–923 7393
Fax: 0117–923 9305
Website: www.scl.org

15.5.2 BCS' Special Interest Groups

An aspect of the British Computer Society we have not touched on is its special interest groups. These bodies vary in size, scope and vigour, but usually provide a forum for talks and discussion. These groups include a word processing group, data protection group and a law group. Details of their activities are available from the British Computer Society [15.1.1].

15.5.3 NCC Legal Group

This is part of the NCC [15.3.2]. It provides informed comment to NCC members and issues a useful series of guidance notes on a number of IT contractual issues. It also provides first-line support on legal issues to its members, as well as briefings and seminars on legal matters.

15.6 USER GROUPS

All the main manufacturers of hardware, many of the smaller ones, many specialised bureaux and even some of the package software suppliers, have user groups. Their purpose is twofold: first, to provide a common front to the manufacturer/supplier when joint action is required, and generally to safeguard their members' interests; secondly, to act as a forum for the manufacturer/supplier when he wishes to announce improvements, new ranges of equipment or software, and so forth. It will be seen that these two activities can easily be in conflict, and it must be said that some user groups incline more to one aspect than the other. Some, for instance, are, in effect, the manufacturer's poodle, having an annual beano at the manufacturer's expense when they receive a pep-talk as to why their manufacturer's equipment is the best. Others have been formed from a common sense of frustration at the dilatoriness or inability of the manufacturer to put right genuine grievances. But even at their most docile they provide an insurance to their users. If you have equipment that is faulty, or package software which is unreliable (even though hitherto your supplier's record has been good), the user group gives you an opportunity to compare your experiences with others and, if you think the supplier is at fault, to present a common front.

Again, if you are looking for mutual back-up facilities [8.1.2], your first requirement will be another user of the same equipment or package as near as possible to you geographically. A user group meeting will enable you to canvass a number of possible firms (though, to be fair, manufacturers are usually very willing to put their users in touch with each other for this purpose anyway).

Enhancements are also often fostered through user groups. You may wish for some particular additional feature in a software package; you cannot put it in yourself either because you have no source language form of the package or because you are debarred from doing so contractually. But if you can find other like-minded users, your chances of persuading the supplier to include that feature as a standard option in the package are greatly enhanced.

Or perhaps it isn't a question of software, but rather some hardware enhancement. Your manufacturer A, forces all his users to have disks of a certain size, or printers of a certain speed, and you are aware that manufacturer B (whose hardware is comparable and compatible) has equipment of the type you need. Your hardware maintenance contract debars you from attaching B's disks or printers to A's processor. But a joint simultaneous revolt by all A's users might force A either to introduce peripherals of the type required, or even to sanction direct interfacing of B's peripherals. Users contemplating a mixed shop [8.5.1] would do well to consider this possibility and make discreet enquiries among their fellow users before going off on their own.

And finally, there is the opportunity of banding together in the face of disaster. Hardware manufacturers and suppliers of packaged software have gone out of business before now. This is not a common event, but when it does happen their wretched users are in an unenviable position because they are virtually stripped of all maintenance cover. Individually, there is usually little they can do, but as a group they may be able to find someone to take over at least the maintenance aspects, and possibly even part of the manufacturing or software function. In extreme cases they may even raise the finance to take over some of the sinking company themselves.

If the disaster is solely on the software side, it may be possible to identify the individual programmers who worked on the programs for the now defunct software house and offer them the business of software maintenance. Again such an offer from a user group will be very much more effective than an individual user trying this on his own.

This situation, involving the total collapse of a supplier or manufacturer, is mercifully rare. But the user group can still find itself faced with very similar problems without such a dramatic failure. This can arise when a manufacturer decides he no longer wishes to support (*i.e.* maintain) a particular piece of hardware or software. This usually goes through a number of stages, of which the first is likely to be an announcement by the manufacturer that he is no longer making or supplying the particular piece of hardware or software, though he has no plans to phase out its maintenance. Nevertheless, in this situation, no manufacturer wishes to keep large numbers of staff working on obsolete equipment—indeed, the staff themselves do not like it and, in a highly mobile industry, this will be sufficient to cause some of them to seek employment elsewhere. Since the user base of the equipment is being reduced, the manufacturer will be under pressure to redeploy his staff, both for financial and personnel reasons.

A user faced with this situation usually has about a couple of years before facing the total loss of manufacturer's support. His first question must be to see what the manufacturer is offering instead; perhaps this is the right moment for him to change to a new machine—or even another manufacturer. Perhaps what is being withdrawn is software and the supplier is offering a very much better alternative. The user must see whether this better alternative is compatible with his requirement and his other software; if it is, he will probably be well advised to change. Users who have changes of this nature forced upon them by the manufacturer will be in a good bargaining position (if they can present a united front through their user group) to negotiate special terms for existing users—perhaps a healthy discount, or some other hardware or software provided or maintained free—since it will very much suit the manufacturer to have all his users abandon the obsolete equipment at the same time as he does. If, on the other hand, the alternatives offered do not look attractive, the user group can either try to force the manufacturer to make them more attractive (perhaps by keeping some aspect of compatibility), or can even, in extreme cases, refuse to change and at the same time obtain a good deal of publicity for their case.

The power that user groups wield should not be exaggerated. No manufacturer will automatically fulfil all user group demands. But equally, manufacturers are highly sensitive to criticism from their user groups, if only because such criticism is likely, if well publicised, to impair their future sales. The situation produces an uneasy ambivalent relationship between manufacturers and their user groups which must be exploited by both sides with care, reserving confrontation for really important issues, and proceeding in a spirit of give-and-take on smaller issues.

With this in mind, it is recommended that all purchasers of hardware and package software (and bureau users)—particularly those using specialised services—enquire from their manufacturer/supplier about the relevant user group, and join at the first opportunity. If there is no user group, they should think seriously of forming one—neither so as to be the manufacturer's poodle nor his hornet (for both extremes are to be avoided) but so as to exchange ideas and provide mutual assistance.

INTRODUCTION TO PRECEDENTS

PRECEDENTS

The drafting of a good precedent is comparable to the writing of good software. We have endeavoured to think through all the error conditions likely and unlikely, but cannot guarantee to have eliminated all bugs anymore than a software house can.

The precedents follow the general structure of the book, except that PCs seem not to merit separate treatment apart from shrink wrap and click wrap licences (Chapter 4) and (as we point out in Chapter 7) new finance leases are less frequent than before and while the points in Chapter 7 may prove helpful in interpreting finance leases, a precedent for such a lease in lengthy and likely to be of limited value.

The rest of the precedents are, we hope, straightforward though we should point out that we have included a set of hardware maintenance clauses in the Rental Agreement (B) since in our experience separate maintenance agreements on rental are rare.

At the risk of repeating what was said in the preface, we must point out that readers should study the relevant sections of the text of this book before using any precedent. To assist the reader we have in many instances provided cross-reference numbers in square brackets after the clause titles to identify the sections of the text. Readers should also bear in mind that any attempt to be exhaustive would have tripled the length of this book. We have therefore been selective in the circumstances covered by the precedents. In many cases more than one precedent is required and the Turnkey Precedent (O) is an attempt to show how in one instance this might be done and when the reader is referred back to clauses in earlier precedents he may have to alter the titles of the parties and make some other minor amendments in order to apply the clause.

We have used square brackets to indicate alternatives [either this clause] [or that] or to indicate material which may be omitted.

Notes and commentary on the precedents are contained within square brackets and can be recognised by the smaller type size. Words or numbers which are examples, and which the user will doubtless wish to vary, *e.g.* "within *14* days", have been indicated with the use of italics.

HARDWARE SALE AND INSTALLATION AGREEMENT

THIS AGREEMENT is made the   day of   20

PARTIES:

(1) COMPUTER COMPANY [LIMITED] [PLC] whose registered office is at
("the Supplier")

(2) CUSTOMER [LIMITED] [PLC] whose registered office is at
("the Customer")

RECITAL:

The Supplier has agreed to supply and install certain computer equipment for the Customer upon the terms and conditions hereinafter contained

NOW IT IS HEREBY AGREED as follows:

1 Definitions

In this Agreement, unless the context otherwise requires, the following expressions have the following meanings:

"business day"	means a day other than a Saturday, Sunday or a public holiday [in the country, state or territory in which the Off-Loading Point is situated].
"the Commissioning Date" [2.3.4]	means the date on which the Equipment is accepted by the Customer pursuant to Clause 12 or *one month* after operational use by the Customer of the Equipment has begun, whichever shall be the earlier.

[Note: The definition of "the Commissioning Date" is designed to protect the supplier from the situation where the customer unreasonably refuses to accept the equipment yet brings it into operational use. In those circumstances the balance of the price will be payable after the expiry of one month—see clause 3(1).]

"Confidential Information"	means all information obtained by one party from the other pursuant to this Agreement which is expressly marked as confidential or which is manifestly of a confidential nature or which is confirmed in writing to be confidential within 7 days of its disclosure.
"the Delivery Date" [2.3.7]	means the delivery date specified in the Schedule or such extended date as may be granted pursuant to clause 15.
"the Equipment" [2.1.1]	means the computer equipment specified in the Schedule and any replacement equipment and/or parts provided pursuant to clauses 2, 19 or 26 [and the Integral Software] as the context admits or the case may require.

["the Equipment Price"   means that part of the Price payable in respect of
                               the Equipment as specified in the Schedule.]

[**Note**: The definition of "the Equipment Price" will only be required if clause 3(2) is used (currency rate fluctuation).]

["the Integral Software"   means the computer software embedded in or form-
[2.8.3]   ing an integral part of the Equipment as specified in
                               the Schedule.]

"the Location" [2.1.2]   means the Customer's computer room in which the
                               Equipment is to be installed as specified in the
                               Schedule.

"the Off-Loading Point"   means the Customer's off-loading point specified in
                               the Schedule.

"the Price"   means the price for the Equipment and the services
                               to be provided hereunder as specified in the Sched-
                               ule.

2 Products and services to be provided [2.1.1]

(1) The Supplier hereby agrees to:

(a) sell the Equipment to the Customer free from any encumbrances;

(b) deliver the Equipment to [and install it at] the Location on the Delivery
    Date;

[(c) provide a licence for the Customer to use the Integral Software;] and

(d) provide the other services hereinafter described,

upon the terms and conditions hereinafter contained.

[(2) The Supplier reserves the right prior to delivery of the Equipment to substitute
an alternative item of equipment for any item of equipment agreed to be supplied
hereunder provided that such substitution will not materially affect the performance
of such equipment and will not result in any increase in the Price.]

[**Note**: If the customer is unhappy about allowing substitutions he should delete this sub-clause. Any substitutions will then have to be agreed to in writing by the customer—see clause 29.]

(3) Operating supplies such as disk packs, stationery, printing cartridges and similar
accessories are not supplied as part of the Equipment.

3 Price and payment [2.2.1]

(1) The Price shall be paid by the Customer as to *15* per cent upon the signing of
this Agreement [(by way of a deposit)] [(by way of a part payment)] and as to the
balance upon the Commissioning Date.

[*Currency rate* [2.2.4]]

(2) (a) The Equipment Price is based on an exchange rate between the United States dollar and the United Kingdom pound sterling of *$1.61* to *£1* ("the Contract Rate"). If on the [Commissioning Date] [the date on which the Supplier pays its supplier for the Equipment ("the Payment Date")] the dollar value of the pound shall have fallen by *2* cents or more below the Contract Rate then the Supplier shall be entitled to increase the Equipment Price to compensate the Supplier for such fall in the dollar value of the pound but not further or otherwise. The amount of such increase shall be paid by the Customer on the Commissioning Date.

(b) For the purposes of paragraph (a) above the value of the pound on [the Commissioning Date] [the Payment Date] shall be taken as the arithmetic average of the buying and selling dollar prices of the pound quoted by *ABC Bank plc* as their closing prices on the business day immediately preceding the Payment Date]

[**Note**: The use of sub-clause (2) should be examined critically by the customer who should consider the following:

(1) The clause assumes that the supplier will be purchasing with dollars and selling in pounds. If the supplier is purchasing in pounds then the clause is unnecessary.

(2) Strictly speaking, any adjustment to the price should be crystallised on the date on which the supplier buys his dollars not when he pays for the equipment. However, if a supplier is constantly purchasing dollars this date might be difficult to establish. It is therefore suggested that the date of payment be used; although this does to some extent leave the situation open to manipulation by the supplier who could choose a payment date (within the constraints of its contractual arrangements with its own supplier) when the dollar value of the pound is low and then pay with dollars already purchased at a more favourable rate. An alternative is therefore to link the formula to the Commissioning Date, assuming that some or all of the payment for the Equipment has been differed until then, as proposed by para. (1) above.

(3) It should be noted that the clause does not provide for the price to be reduced in the event of a rise in the value of the pound. Also, some of the equipment may not be purchased in the U.S. (or not in dollars) in which case any increase should only apply to the equipment which is.

(4) There may be more than one U.S. manufacturer delivering to the Supplier on different dates.]

[Price adjustment on long deliveries [2.2.4]]

(3) The Price and any additional charges payable under this Agreement are in accordance with the Supplier's standard scale of charges in force on the date of this Agreement. The Supplier shall be entitled at any time before the period of *30* days immediately preceding the Delivery Date to vary the Price and any additional charges payable under this Agreement to accord with any changes in the Supplier's standard scale of charges and to give written notice of such variation to the Customer. This Agreement shall be deemed to be varied accordingly by such notice of variation unless the Customer shall within *14* days of the receipt of such notice terminate this Agreement by giving notice in writing to the Supplier in which event neither party shall have any liability to the other in respect of such termination.

(4) The Price and any additional charges payable under this Agreement are exclusive of Value Added Tax which shall be paid by the Customer at the rate and in the manner for the time being prescribed by law.

(5) Any charges payable by the Customer under this Agreement in addition to the Price shall be paid on the Commissioning Date.

(6) If any sum payable under this Agreement is not paid within *7* days after the due date then (without prejudice to the Supplier's other rights and remedies) the

Supplier reserves the right to charge interest on such sum on a day to day basis (as well after as before any judgment) from the date or last date for payment thereof to the date of actual payment (both dates inclusive) at the rate of 2 per cent above the base rate of *ABC* Bank plc (or such other London Clearing Bank as the Supplier may nominate) from time to time in force compounded quarterly. Such interest shall be paid by the Customer on demand by the Supplier.

4 Title and risk [2.8.1, 2.8.3]

(1) The legal and beneficial ownership of the Equipment shall pass to the Customer on payment in full and in cleared funds of the Price and any other sums which may then be due under this Agreement.

(2) Risk in the Equipment shall pass to the Customer on delivery of the Equipment to [the Off-Loading Point] [the Location] and accordingly the Customer shall be responsible for insuring the Equipment against all normal risks with effect from the time risk passes.

[(3) In relation to each item of Integral Software the copyright, design right or other intellectual property rights in which are owned by a third party ("the software owner") as identified in the Schedule:

   (a) the performance by the Supplier of its obligations under this Agreement is in all respects conditional upon the Customer entering into on the date of this Agreement an end-user licence agreement with the software owner or (as the case may be) a sub-licence agreement with the Supplier (in either case a "Licence Agreement") governing the use by the Customer of that item of Integral Software as may be required by the software owner in the form annexed to this Agreement; and

   (b) the Customer agrees with the Supplier as a term of this Agreement to be bound and abide by the terms and conditions of each such Licence Agreement.]

[(4) In relation to each item of Integral Software the copyright, design right or other intellectual property rights in which are owned by the Supplier as identified in the Schedule:

   (a) the Customer is purchasing the media on which such Integral Software is recorded or embedded only;

   (b) nothing contained in this Agreement shall be construed as an assignment or transfer of any copyright, design right or other intellectual property rights in such Integral Software, all of which rights are reserved by the Supplier;

   (c) the Supplier hereby grants to the Customer a non-exclusive and (except as provided in paragraph (e) below) non-transferable licence to use such Integral Software in the form in which it is embedded in or integrated into the Equipment at the time of delivery to the Customer as an integral part of the Equipment for use in conjunction with the remainder of the Equipment but subject to the condition that the Equipment is used only for its intended purpose and for the Customer's internal business purposes only;

(d) except as expressly permitted by this sub-clause (4) and save to the extent and in the circumstances expressly required to be permitted by law, the Customer shall not rent, lease, sub-license, loan, copy, modify, adapt, merge, translate, reverse engineer, decompile, disassemble or create derivative works based on the whole or any part of such Integral Software or use, reproduce or deal in such Integral Software or any part thereof in any way. In respect of any such activities claimed to be made permissible by law, the Customer undertakes first to make a prior written statement to the Supplier identifying the activity and stating why the Customer believes it to be permissible, and to refrain from commencing any such activity until the Supplier shall have had a reasonable opportunity to consider and thereafter give a response to the Customer in respect of each statement;

(e) the Customer shall be entitled to transfer the benefit of the licence granted pursuant to paragraph (c) ("the Licence") and the right to transfer the Licence in terms of this paragraph (e) to any purchaser of the Equipment provided the purchaser agrees before making such purchase to be bound by the terms of this sub-clause (4) including the provisions of this paragraph (e). If the purchaser does not accept such terms then the Licence shall automatically and immediately terminate;

(f) the Licence shall remain effective without limit in time until it is terminated in accordance with paragraph (e) or until the Customer shall terminate it by erasing or destroying such Integral Software. The Licence shall also terminate automatically and immediately if the Customer shall fail to abide by the terms of this sub-clause (4). Upon termination of the Licence, for whatever reason, the Customer shall deliver up to the Supplier the media on which such Integral Software is recorded or embedded (and all copies thereof (if any) in the Customer's possession) or, at the Supplier's option, shall erase or otherwise destroy such Integral Software (and all copies thereof (if any) in the Customer's possession) and shall certify to the Supplier that the same has been done.]

[(5) The Price includes the right for the Customer to use the Integral Software in terms of sub-clauses (3) and (4).]

5 Location preparation [2.6.3]

The Supplier shall supply to the Customer in reasonable time before delivery of the Equipment such information [and assistance] as may be reasonably necessary to enable the Customer to prepare the Location for the installation of the Equipment and to provide proper environmental and operational conditions for the efficient working and maintenance of the Equipment [and for this purpose the Supplier will make available to the Customer free of charge the advice of a suitably qualified engineer]. The Customer shall at its own expense prepare the Location and provide such environmental and operational conditions prior to delivery.

[Note: It will be in the interests of the customer to require the supplier to provide the necessary advice in writing. This may avoid arguments at a later stage if it is alleged that the customer failed to prepare the location properly. The supplier may seek to charge for any such assistance, either as a fixed fee or on a time and materials basis.]

6 Information and access [2.6.1]

(1) The Customer undertakes to provide the Supplier promptly with any information which the Supplier may reasonably require from time to time to enable the Supplier to proceed with the performance of this Agreement without undue delay or impediment.

(2) The Customer shall, for the purposes of this Agreement, afford to the authorised personnel of the Supplier during normal working hours reasonable access to the Location and shall provide adequate free working space and such other facilities as may be reasonably necessary for the installation of the Equipment. The Supplier's personnel shall comply with all health and safety procedures in effect at the Location.

[Note: If the proposed location is particularly sensitive then the customer may wish to restrict access to the supplier's named personnel only. The customer may also wish to reserve a right to refuse to admit persons who are in its reasonable opinion unfit to be on its premises.]

[7 Pre-delivery tests [2.3.2]

(1) The Supplier shall submit the Equipment to its standard works tests ("the Works Tests") before delivery to the Customer. The Supplier shall promptly supply to the Customer on request copies of the specification of the Works Tests and a certificate that the Equipment has passed the same.

(2) The Customer or its authorised representative may attend the Works Tests. [If the Works Tests are held in the presence of the Customer or its authorised representative, the Supplier will charge the Customer its standard fee therefor]. The Supplier shall give the Customer at least 7 days' written notice of the date and time at which the Supplier proposes to carry out the Works Tests. In the event of any delay or failure by the Customer or its authorised representative in attending the Works Tests at such time, the Supplier reserves the right to proceed with the Works Tests without the Customer.]

[Note: the parties will need to agree whether the customer should pay for the carrying out of the Works Tests.]

8 Delivery [2.3.3]

EITHER:

[(1) On the Delivery Date the Supplier shall deliver the Equipment to the Off-Loading Point but shall not be responsible for off-loading the Equipment or moving it to the Location which shall be undertaken by the Customer at its own expense.]

OR:

[(1)(a) On the Delivery Date the Supplier shall deliver the Equipment to the Off-Loading Point and be responsible for its transportation thereafter to the Location;

(b) The Supplier shall not carry out or be responsible for the removal of doors, widening of entrances or any other structural work of any description for the purpose of moving the Equipment from the Off-Loading Point to the Location, which work shall be undertaken by the Customer at its own expense prior to delivery;

(c) The Customer shall be responsible for all reasonable costs incurred by the Supplier in providing any special equipment, personnel or works reasonably necessary to move the Equipment from the Off-Loading Point to the Location. Such costs shall be paid by the Customer in addition to the Price.]

EITHER:

[(2) [Save for the special delivery costs referred to in sub-clause (1)(c)] the Price includes the cost of delivery of the Equipment to the [Off-Loading Point] [the Location] by any method of transport selected by the Supplier.]

OR:

[(2) The Price does not include the cost of transportation of the Equipment [from the Supplier's premises] [within the United Kingdom] or any other delivery costs, which shall be paid by the Customer in addition to the Price.]

[(3) All packing cases, skids, drums and other packing materials used for delivery of the Equipment to the Location must be returned by the Customer to the Supplier in good condition and at the Customer's expense. The Supplier reserves the right to charge for any such cases and materials not so returned.]

9 Installation [2.3.3]

(1) The Supplier shall install the Equipment at the Location on the Delivery Date.

(2) If in the reasonable opinion of the Supplier it is reasonably necessary to remove or otherwise disconnect any of the Customer's existing equipment at the Location in order to carry out the installation of the Equipment, then the Customer shall permit, and obtain all necessary consents for, such removal and/or disconnection and shall give the Supplier all necessary assistance to enable such work to be carried out.

10 Time [not] of the essence

The time of delivery and installation of the Equipment shall [not] be of the essence of this Agreement [provided always that the Supplier shall use all reasonable endeavours to complete the delivery and installation as soon as reasonably possible thereafter].

[Notes:

(1) Time of delivery and installation may arguably be of the essence in this agreement simply by virtue of the fact that a delivery date is specified (although it avoids argument to incorporate an express provision to that effect). If the supplier wishes to avoid the consequences of this he should incorporate this clause specifying that time will *not* be of the essence. Where time is not of the essence and the supplier does not deliver by the delivery date then, unless the supplier quickly remedies its default, the customer should serve notice on the supplier requiring him to complete the delivery and/or installation within a reasonable time:

"The time for delivery and installation of the equipment under the above-mentioned agreement has passed. We now require you to deliver and install the equipment no later than *December 31, 2001*, and time shall be of the essence in this regard. Failure to complete the delivery and installation within this further period will entitle us to terminate the agreement and, whether or not we terminate, to recover from you all damages and costs resulting from such failure."

Any revised delivery date must be reasonable if time is to be made "of the essence". One means of stipulating a "reasonable" revised delivery date would be to obtain a new estimate from the supplier. It would then be difficult for the supplier to argue that the time allowed was unreasonable.

(2) It should be remembered that even if time is made of the essence, the supplier will be allowed an extension of time for performance in the circumstances specified in clause 15.

(3) The supplier may only agree to a specific delivery date if its liability for delay is confined to liquidated damages.]

11 Installation Tests [2.3.4]

(1) The Supplier shall, within *14* days after the Equipment has been installed, submit the Equipment to the Supplier's standard installation tests ("the Installation

Tests") to ensure that the Equipment and every part thereof is in full working order. The Supplier shall supply to the Customer copies of the Installation Tests' scripts applicable to the Equipment and results of the Installation Tests.

(2) If the Equipment or any part of the Equipment fails to pass the Installation Tests then, if requested by the Customer, the Installation Test or Tests for the Equipment or for such part or parts of the Equipment as have failed the Installation Test or Tests shall be repeated within a reasonable time thereafter up to a maximum of 3 such repeated tests for the Equipment as a whole or for any one part of the Equipment as may be substituted by the Supplier pursuant to clauses 2, 19 or 26 hereof.

[**Note**: The failure may be of part of the system or of the system as a whole. The supplier may wish to reserve the right to try to rectify any problems (including the chance to substitute equipment if necessary) and have the equipment resubmitted for Installation Tests at least once. Equally, the customer will wish to limit these tests.]

(3) The Customer or its authorised representative may attend the Installation Tests. The Supplier shall give the Customer at least 3 days' written notice of the date and time at which the Supplier proposes to carry out the Installation Tests. In the event of any delay or failure by the Customer or its authorised representative in attending the Installation Tests at such time the Supplier reserves the right to proceed with the Installation Tests which will then be deemed to have been carried out in the presence of the Customer and the results thereof accepted by the Customer.

[**Note**: Three days' notice is probably sufficient, as the tests will be carried out on the customer's premises. However, if the customer requires the tests to be carried out in the presence of his consultant a longer period of notice may have to be negotiated. In practice, it will be difficult for the supplier to carry out tests in the absence of the customer as they will have to be carried out on the customer's premises.]

12 Acceptance [2.3.6]

(1) Once the Equipment and every part thereof has successfully passed the Installation Tests the Equipment shall be accepted by the Customer and the Customer shall, if required by the Supplier, sign a commissioning certificate in the form annexed hereto acknowledging such acceptance.

(2) If the Equipment or any part thereof has failed to pass the Installation Tests (including any repeat Installation Tests authorised by the Customer pursuant to clause 11(2)), the Customer may reject the Equipment and terminate this Agreement for breach.

13 Electromagnetic compatibility [2.7.3]

(1) In this clause the expression "Electromagnetic Equipment" means any part or parts of the Equipment which are electric or electronic and covered by the Electromagnetic Compatibility Regulations 1992, as amended.

(2) The Supplier warrants to the Customer that at the date hereof all the Electromagnetic Equipment complies fully with the Electromagnetic Compatibility Regulations 1992, as amended.

(3) The Customer undertakes to the Supplier that it will not make any modification to the Electromagnetic Equipment without the prior written consent of the Supplier.

[14 Telecommunications [2.7.4]

(1) In this clause the expression "Relevant Equipment" means any part of the Equipment which is intended to be connected to any telecommunication system which is, or is to be connected to, a public telecommunication system.

(2) The Supplier warrants to the Customer that at the date hereof the Relevant Equipment is approved by the Secretary of State for Trade and Industry for connection to the telecommunication systems specified in the instructions for use of the Relevant Equipment subject to the conditions set out therein but does not warrant the continuance of any such approval.

(3) If after the date hereof the Secretary of State for Trade and Industry or any person to whom he has delegated his powers requires the Relevant Equipment or any part thereof to be modified as a condition of the continuance of any such approval the Supplier reserves the right to make such modification at the Customer's expense.

(4) If the Customer connects the Relevant Equipment to any telecommunication system the Customer shall be responsible for obtaining the consent of the owner of that system (if necessary) to such connection and for complying with all conditions relating thereto.

(5) The Customer undertakes to the Supplier that it will not make any modification to the Relevant Equipment without the prior written consent of the Supplier.

(6) Where any data transmission speeds are given by the Supplier in relation to the Equipment, such speeds are at all times subject to any conditions attached to the use of the relevant modem, cabling or telecommunication equipment at the speeds indicated and to the capability of such modem, cabling or other telecommunication equipment to achieve such speeds.]

15 *Force majeure*

Notwithstanding anything else contained in this Agreement, neither party shall be liable for any delay in performing its obligations hereunder if such delay is caused by circumstances beyond its reasonable control (including without limitation any delay caused by any act or omission of the other party) provided however that any delay by a sub-contractor or supplier of the party so delaying shall not relieve that party from liability for delay except where such delay is beyond the reasonable control of the sub-contractor or supplier concerned. Subject to the party so delaying promptly notifying the other party in writing of the reasons for the delay (and the likely duration of the delay), the performance of such party's obligations shall be suspended during the period that the said circumstances persist and such party shall be granted an extension of time for performance equal to the period of the delay. Save where such delay is caused by the act or omission of the other party (in which event the rights, remedies and liabilities of the parties shall be those conferred and imposed by the other terms of this Agreement and by law):

(1) any costs arising from such delay shall be borne by the party incurring the same;

(2) either party may, if such delay continues for more than 5 weeks, terminate this Agreement forthwith on giving notice in writing to the other in which event neither

party shall be liable to the other by reason of such termination [save that the Customer shall pay the Supplier a reasonable sum in respect of any work carried out by it prior to such termination and for that purpose the Supplier may deduct such sum from any amounts previously paid by the Customer under this Agreement (the balance (if any) of which shall be refunded to the Customer whether paid by way of a deposit or otherwise)];

(3) both parties will in any event use all reasonable endeavours to mitigate the impact of any event of *force majeure* and to recommence performance of their obligations under this Agreement as soon as reasonably possible.

[**Notes**:

    (1) Even if time is made of the essence in relation to a particular obligation this clause will override that provision to give the delaying party an extension of time for performance without incurring any liability for the delay.

    (2) A frequent problem with a clause of this nature is that the delaying party is inclined to seek its protection even if the delay is due to its own default. This can be avoided to some extent by requiring the delaying party promptly to notify the reason for the delay (which can then be investigated) and by providing the other party with an opportunity to terminate the agreement if the delay continues for an unreasonable period.

    (3) Many customers will refuse to entertain a clause of this nature if it excuses defaults by sub-contractors or suppliers. Customers will argue, perhaps rightly so, that it is up to the supplier to ensure that his sub-contractors and suppliers are reliable.

    (4) Where a delay does occur it will be in the interests of both parties to ensure that a proper record of the period of the delay is kept and that the extended date for performance is confirmed in writing.]

16 Customer's default [2.3.7]

If the Supplier is prevented or delayed from performing its obligations under this Agreement by reason of any act or omission of the Customer (other than a delay by the Customer for which the Customer is excused under clause 15) then the Customer will pay to the Supplier all reasonable costs, charges and losses sustained or incurred by the Supplier as a result (including without limitation the cost of storage and insurance of the Equipment), subject always to the limits on liability in clause 27. The Supplier shall promptly notify the Customer in writing of any claim which it may have under this Clause giving such particulars thereof as it is then able to provide.

17 Cancellation [2.4.1]

(1) If the Customer wishes to cancel this Agreement in respect of all or any part of the Equipment (other than for any breach of this Agreement by the Supplier as would entitle the Customer to terminate) then the Customer shall be entitled so to do at any time up to *14* days prior to the Delivery Date upon giving written notice to the Supplier and upon paying to the Supplier as agreed and liquidated cancellation charges:

    (a) a sum equal to *6* per cent of the elements of the Price relating to the Equipment (or such part or parts of it as have been cancelled); and

    (b) a sum equal to *12* per cent of such elements of the Price, reduced by *1* per cent in respect of each complete calendar month unexpired between the date of cancellation and the Delivery Date.

[(2) In the event that the Customer cancels this Agreement [within *30* days before Delivery Date] then such deposit as shall have been paid by the Customer to the

Supplier under clause 3(1) hereof shall be forfeited to the Supplier and not be recoverable by the Customer from the Supplier.]

[(3) The amount of the Customer's deposit paid under clause 3(1), if forfeited to the Supplier, shall be deducted from the cancellation charges payable under sub-clause (1).

(4) Until the Supplier shall have received such payment, the Customer's notice of termination shall be of no effect and the Supplier may treat this Agreement as subsisting.]

[Note: If a deposit has been taken, the supplier may be content simply to keep that sum on a cancellation, in which case this clause will be unnecessary. In such cases, it should expressly be stated that the deposit will be forfeited in the case of cancellation.]

18 Termination [2.4.1]

(1) This Agreement may be terminated forthwith by either party on giving notice in writing to the other if the other party shall have a receiver or administrative receiver appointed or shall pass a resolution for winding-up (otherwise than for the purpose of a bona fide scheme of solvent amalgamation or reconstruction) or a court of competent jurisdiction shall make an order to that effect or if the other party shall become subject to an administration order or shall enter into any voluntary arrangement with its creditors or shall cease or threaten to cease to carry on business.

(2) This Agreement may also be terminated forthwith by either party on giving notice to the other if the other party is in material breach of the terms of this Agreement and has failed to rectify such breach (in the case of a breach capable of being remedied) within *30* days of receiving a written notice requiring it to do so.

(3) Any termination under sub-clauses (1) or (2) shall discharge the parties from any liability for further performance of this Agreement and in the case of a termination by the Supplier shall entitle the Supplier to enter any of the Customer's premises and recover any equipment and materials the property of the Supplier (and so that the Customer hereby irrevocably licenses the Supplier, its employees and agents to enter any such premises for that purpose) and also to be paid a reasonable sum for any work carried out by it prior to such termination, and in the case of a termination by the Customer shall entitle the Customer to be repaid forthwith any sums previously paid under this Agreement (whether paid by way of a deposit or otherwise) and to recover from the Supplier the amount of any direct loss or damage sustained or incurred by the Customer as a consequence of such termination.

(4) Any termination of this Agreement (howsoever occasioned) shall not affect any accrued rights or liabilities of either party nor shall it affect the coming into force or the continuance in force of any provision hereof which is expressly or by implication intended to come into or continue in force on or after such termination.

19 Warranties [and performance] [2.3.8]

(1) (a) The Supplier warrants that the Equipment will be free from defects in materials, workmanship and installation for a period of *12* months after the Commissioning Date ("the Warranty Period").

(b) If the Supplier receives written notice from the Customer of any breach of the said warranty then the Supplier shall at its own expense and within a reasonable time after receiving such notice, repair or, at its option, replace the Equipment or such parts of it as are defective or otherwise remedy such defect, provided that the Supplier shall have no liability or obligations under the said warranty unless it shall have received written notice of the defect in question no later than the expiry of the Warranty Period. The legal and beneficial ownership of the Equipment or any defective parts shall revert to the Supplier upon the replacement of the Equipment or such defective parts (as the case may be), whereupon the legal and beneficial ownership of the replacement Equipment or parts shall vest in the Customer.

[Note: Some warranty provisions provide that replacement parts will themselves be subject to a 12 months' warranty period with effect from the date of replacement.]

(c) The Supplier shall have no liability or obligations under the said warranty other than to remedy breaches thereof by the provision of materials and services within a reasonable time and without charge to the Customer, save that if the Supplier shall fail to comply with such obligations within a reasonable time, it shall be liable in damages to the Customer provided that its liability for such failure shall be limited to a sum equal to the Price. The foregoing states the entire liability of the Supplier, whether in contract or tort, for defects in the Equipment notified to it after the Commissioning Date other than liability assumed under clause 27.

(d) The said warranty is contingent upon the proper use of the Equipment by the Customer and does not cover any part of the Equipment which has been modified without the Supplier's prior written consent or which has been subjected to unusual physical or electrical stress or on which the original identification marks have been removed or altered. Nor will such warranty apply if repair or parts replacement is required as a result of causes other than ordinary use including without limitation accident, hazard, misuse or failure or fluctuation of electric power, air conditioning, humidity control or other environmental conditions.

[Note: A warranty of this nature will be of less importance if the customer immediately takes out a maintenance contract with the supplier. However, where the supplier has built a contingency element into the price to cover his warranty obligations the customer will wish to ensure that such contingency is taken into account when assessing the first year's maintenance charges.]

(2) The Supplier warrants to the Customer that the Equipment complies fully as to noise heat radiation and all other characteristics with the requirements in the Health and Safety (Display Screen Equipment) Regulations 1992 and in particular that the display screens and keyboards comply fully with the said Regulations.

(3) The Supplier does not give any warranty that the Equipment is fit for any particular purpose unless that purpose is specifically advised to the Supplier in writing by the Customer and the Supplier confirms in writing that the Equipment can fulfil that particular purpose.

[(4) The Supplier does not warrant that the Equipment will achieve any particular performance criteria unless:

(a) the Supplier has specifically guaranteed such criteria in writing, subject to specified tolerances in an agreed sum as liquidated damages; and

(b) the environmental conditions specified by the Supplier are maintained.

The payment by the Supplier of such liquidated damages shall be in full satisfaction of any liability of the Supplier in respect of the Equipment failing to achieve such performance criteria.]

(5) The express terms of this Agreement are in lieu of all warranties, conditions, terms, undertakings and obligations implied by statute, common law, custom, trade usage, course of dealing or otherwise, all of which are hereby excluded to the fullest extent permitted by law.

20 Customer's warranty

The Customer hereby warrants to the Supplier that the Customer has not been induced to enter into this Agreement by any prior representations or warranties, whether oral or in writing, except as specifically contained in this Agreement and the Customer hereby irrevocably and unconditionally waives any right it may have to claim damages for any misrepresentation not contained in this Agreement or for breach of any warranty not contained herein (unless such misrepresentation or warranty was made fraudulently and was relied upon by the Customer) and/or to rescind this Agreement.

[Note: At first sight this may appear harsh on the customer, but it will be in the best interests of the customer to incorporate important representations into the agreement by specific reference, rather than rely on oral promises or general descriptions. It will probably not be possible to bind the customer to waive damages for fraudulent misrepresentation.]

21 Confidentiality [2.6.2, 2.7.1]

Each party shall treat as confidential all Confidential Information and shall not divulge such Confidential Information to any person (except to such party's own employees and then only to those employees who need to know the same) without the other party's prior written consent provided that this clause shall not extend to information which was rightfully in the possession of such party prior to the commencement of the negotiations leading to this Agreement, which is already public knowledge or becomes so at a future date (otherwise than as a result of a breach of this clause) or which is trivial or obvious. Each party shall ensure that its employees are aware of and comply with the provisions of this clause. If the Supplier shall appoint any sub-contractor then the Supplier may disclose Confidential Information to such sub-contractor subject to such sub-contractor giving the Customer an undertaking in similar terms to the provisions of this clause, and the Supplier shall in any event be responsible for any breach of the obligations of confidentiality contained in this clause 21 by such sub-contractor. The foregoing obligations as to confidentiality shall survive any termination of this Agreement.

[Note: Pre-contract disclosures should, of course, be covered by a separate confidentiality undertaking—see Precedent Z.]

22 Operating manuals [and training]

(1) The Supplier shall provide the Customer with 2 copies of a set of operating manuals containing reasonably sufficient information for the proper operation of

the Equipment. If the Customer requires further copies of such operating manuals then these will be provided by the Supplier in accordance with its standard scale of charges from time to time in force.

[(2) The Supplier shall provide training in the use of the Equipment for the Customer's staff as set out in the Schedule. Any additional training required by the Customer shall be provided by the Supplier in accordance with its standard scale of charges from time to time in force and at such times and to such extents as may be agreed between the parties.]

[Note: clause 22(2) only required if such training is in fact to be provided].

23 Removal of labels [2.6.5]

The Customer shall not change, remove or obscure any labels, plates, insignia, lettering or other markings which are on the Equipment at the time of installation thereof.

[24 Maintenance [2.6.4]

The parties undertake to enter into a maintenance agreement on the Commissioning Date in respect of the Equipment in the form of the draft annexed hereto.]

[Note: Alternatively, the parties could enter into a maintenance agreement at the same time as this agreement, such agreement to commence on the Commissioning Date or perhaps on the expiry of the warranty period under clause 19. Or the customer may elect to acquire maintenance services only from the end of the relevant warranty period.]

[25 Export control [2.9.1]

The Equipment is subject to Export Control imposed by the Department of Commerce of the United States of America and is restricted to resale in the United Kingdom.]

[Note: This clause will apply only to equipment of United States origin.]

26 Intellectual property rights indemnity [2.8.2]

(1) The Supplier will indemnify the Customer and keep the Customer fully and effectively indemnified on demand against all costs, claims, demands, expenses and liabilities of whatsoever nature arising out of or in connection with any claim that the normal use or possession of the Equipment infringes the [U.K.] intellectual property rights (including without limitation any patent, copyright, registered design, design right or trademark) of any unaffiliated third party, subject to the following conditions:

    (a) the Customer shall promptly notify the Supplier in writing of any allegations of infringement of which it has notice and will not make any admissions without the Supplier's prior written consent nor take any step (or omit to take any step) which would prejudice the Supplier's defence of the claim;

    (b) the Customer, at the Supplier's request and expense, shall allow the Supplier [(subject to paragraph (c) below)] to conduct and/or settle all negotiations and litigation resulting from any such claim;

    [(c) the conduct by the Supplier of any such negotiations or litigation shall be conditional upon the Supplier:

(i) giving to the Customer such reasonable security as shall from time to time be required by the Customer to cover the amount ascertained or agreed or estimated, as the case may be, of any compensation, damages, expenses and costs for which the Customer may become liable; and

(ii) taking over such conduct within a reasonable time after being notified of the claim in question;]

(d) the Customer shall, at the request of the Supplier, afford all reasonable assistance with such negotiations or litigation, and shall be reimbursed by the Supplier for any reasonable out of pocket expenses incurred in so doing.

(2) The indemnity given under sub-clause (1) above will not apply to infringement arising out of the use of the Equipment or any part thereof in combination with any equipment [and/or computer programs] not supplied or approved by the Supplier for use with the Equipment or by reason of any modification or alteration made to the equipment other than by the Supplier or with the Supplier's prior written consent.

(3) If the Customer's normal use or possession of the Equipment is held by a court of competent jurisdiction to constitute an infringement of a third party's intellectual property rights or if the Supplier is advised by legal counsel that such use or possession is likely to constitute such an infringement then the Supplier shall promptly and at its own expense:

(a) procure for the Customer the right to continue using and possessing the Equipment; or

(b) modify or replace the Equipment (without detracting from its overall performance) so as to avoid the infringement (in which event the Supplier shall compensate the Customer for the amount of any direct loss and/or damage sustained or incurred by the Customer by reason of such modification or replacement); or

(c) if (a) or (b) cannot be accomplished on reasonable terms, remove the Equipment from the Location and refund the Price to the Customer.

[Note: Some contracts provide for the price to be refunded less depreciation. This may be inadequate if the customer has to purchase new equipment at much greater cost.]

(4) The foregoing states the Supplier's entire liability to the Customer in respect of the infringement of the intellectual property rights of any third party.

27 Liability [2.3.8]

(1) The Supplier shall indemnify the Customer and keep the Customer fully and effectively indemnified on demand against any loss of or damage to any property or injury to or death of any person caused by any negligent act or omission or breach of this Agreement by the Supplier, its employees, agents or sub-contractors or by any defect in the design or workmanship of the Equipment.

(2) The Customer shall indemnify the Supplier and keep the Supplier fully and effectively indemnified on demand against any loss of or damage to any property or

injury to or death of any person caused by any negligent act or omission or breach of this Agreement by the Customer, its employees, agents or sub-contractors.

(3) Except in respect of injury to or death of any person or any other liability which cannot be limited or excluded by law (for which no limit applies), the respective liability of the Supplier and the Customer under sub-clauses (1) and (2) in respect of each event or series of connected events shall not exceed £*500,000*.

[Note: Some contracts specifically require the parties to back up their indemnities with insurance. An alternative approach to sub-clause (3) would also be to have an aggregate cap applied to all liabilities incurred under the Agreement, regardless of the number of claims made.]

[(4) Notwithstanding anything else contained in this Agreement the Supplier shall not be liable to the Customer for loss of profits or contracts, loss of goodwill or other special, indirect or consequential loss whether arising from negligence, breach of contract or howsoever.]

(5) The Supplier shall not be liable to the Customer for any loss arising out of (and to the extent caused by) any failure by the Customer to keep full and up-to-date security copies of the computer programs and data it uses in accordance with best computing practice.

28 Waiver of remedies

No forbearance, delay or indulgence by either party in enforcing the provisions of this Agreement shall prejudice or restrict the rights of that party nor shall any waiver of its rights operate as a waiver of any subsequent breach and no right, power or remedy herein conferred upon or reserved for either party is exclusive of any other right, power or remedy available to that party and each such right, power or remedy shall be cumulative.

29 Entire agreement

This Agreement supersedes all prior agreements, arrangements and understandings between the parties and constitutes the entire agreement between the parties relating to the subject matter hereof (save that neither party seeks to exclude liability for any fraudulent precontractual misrepresentation upon which the other party can be shown to have relied). No addition to or modification of any provision of this Agreement (including for the avoidance of doubt any substitution of the Equipment or any part of it pursuant to clauses 2, 19 and 26) shall be binding upon the parties unless made by a written instrument signed by a duly authorised representative of each of the parties.

[Note: This clause may have to be amended in the light of any side letters or collateral agreements.]

30 Assignment [2.6.5]

Save as expressly provided in this Agreement, neither party shall assign or otherwise transfer this Agreement or any of its rights and obligations hereunder whether in whole or in part without the prior written consent of the other (such consent not to be unreasonably withheld or delayed).

31 Sub-contracts

The Supplier shall not, without the prior written consent of the Customer (which shall not be unreasonably withheld or delayed), enter into any sub-contract with any person for the performance of any part of this Agreement provided that this provision shall not apply to:

(a) the purchase by the Supplier of equipment and materials; and

(b) the sub-contract(s) (if any) specified in the Schedule.

The Supplier shall not be relieved from any of its obligations hereunder by entering into any sub-contract for the performance of any part of this Agreement. If requested by the Customer, the Supplier shall promptly provide the Customer with copies of any sub-contracts.

32 Notices

All notices which are required to be given hereunder shall be in writing and shall be sent to the address of the recipient set out in this Agreement or such other address in England as the recipient may designate by notice given in accordance with the provisions of this Clause. Any such notice may be delivered personally or by first class pre-paid letter or facsimile transmission and shall be deemed to have been served if by hand when delivered, if by first class post 48 hours after posting and if by facsimile transmission when despatched.

[**Note**: if notices are also to be accepted by email, the procedure by which they will be sent and verified also needs to be set out.]

33 Interpretation

In this Agreement:

(1) reference to any statute or statutory provision includes a reference to that statute or statutory provision as from time to time amended, extended or re-enacted;

(2) words importing the singular include the plural, words importing any gender include every gender and words importing persons include bodies corporate and unincorporate; and (in each case) vice versa;

(3) any reference to a party to this Agreement includes a reference to his successors in title and permitted assigns;

(4) the headings to the Clauses are for ease of reference only and shall not affect the interpretation or construction of this Agreement.

34 Law

[(1) This Agreement shall be governed by and construed in accordance with the laws of England and Wales.]

[(2) The provisions of United States Uniform Computer Information Transactions Act shall not apply to this Agreement.]

[**Note**: For UCITA see 3.2.2, 3.3.4 and 4.3.1.]

35 Disputes

Any dispute which may arise between the parties concerning this Agreement shall be determined by the English Courts and the parties hereby submit to the exclusive jurisdiction of the English Courts for such purpose.

[Note: An alternative is to provide for an expert or an arbitrator to resolve disputes—see clause 37 of Precedent D or the standard provisions provided by the centre for Dispute Resolutions.]

36 Severability

Notwithstanding that the whole or any part of any provision of this Agreement may prove to be illegal or unenforceable the other provisions of this Agreement and the remainder of the provision in question shall remain in full force and effect.

37 Third parties [1.3]

EITHER (VERSION A Contracts (Rights of Third Parties) Act does not apply):

[The parties confirm their intent not to confer any rights on any third parties by virtue of this Agreement and accordingly the Contracts (Rights of Third parties) Act 1999 shall not apply to this Agreement.]

OR (VERSION B Contracts (Rights of Third Parties) Act does apply):

[The parties confirm their intent not to confer any rights on any third parties by virtue of this Agreement except for the third-party rights (the 'Third-Party Rights') set out in the Schedule and accordingly the Contracts (Rights of Third Parties) Act 1999 shall apply to this Agreement only in respect of the Third-Party Rights.]

EXECUTED under hand in two originals the day and year first before written

SIGNED for and on behalf of
COMPUTER COMPANY [LIMITED] [PLC]

By

Signature

Title

Witness

SIGNED for and on behalf of
CUSTOMER [LIMITED] [PLC]

By

Signature

Title

Witness

THE SCHEDULE

A THE EQUIPMENT

[Note: The Schedule should show a full description of each item, the number of such items and the price per item. The description should have both the manufacturer's reference number and enough English narrative to define the equipment uniquely from other equipment from the same manufacturer—*e.g.* "Disk drive" is not enough. It should state the capacity of the disks—"149 Gbyte Disk Drive".]

[B THE INTEGRAL SOFTWARE

Owned by third parties:

Owned by the Supplier:]

C THE PRICE

[THE EQUIPMENT PRICE]

D THE OFF-LOADING POINT

E THE LOCATION

F THE DELIVERY DATE

[G TRAINING]

[H SUB-CONTRACTS]

[I THIRD-PARTY RIGHTS]

COMMISSIONING CERTIFICATE

TO: COMPUTER COMPANY [LIMITED] [PLC]
FROM: CUSTOMER [LIMITED] [PLC]

Date: 20

Dear Sirs,

We refer to the agreement between our respective companies dated
20 ("the Agreement") relating to the sale and installation of certain computer
equipment ("the Equipment") and confirm the following:

1 We have today accepted the Equipment.

2 We have inspected the Equipment and confirm that the same conforms to the
description contained in the Agreement and that the same has been installed and
set up to our satisfaction at the Location (as defined in the Agreement).

3 The Equipment has passed the Installation Tests (as defined in the Agreement),
the results of which are annexed hereto and signed by us for the purpose of
identification.

SIGNED for and on behalf of
CUSTOMER [LIMITED] [PLC]

By

Signature

Title

Witness

RENTAL MAINTENANCE AGREEMENT

[**Note**: At the risk of repeating material from Precedent K we have included maintenance obligations in this agreement since this is a common practice.]

THIS AGREEMENT is made the   day of   20

PARTIES:

(1) RENTAL COMPANY [LIMITED] [PLC] whose registered office is at

("the Supplier")

(2) CUSTOMER [LIMITED] [PLC] whose registered office is at

("the Hirer")

RECITAL:

The Supplier has agreed to install and let on hire to the Hirer certain computer equipment and to maintain the same upon the terms and conditions hereinafter contained

NOW IT IS HEREBY AGREED as follows:

1 Definitions

In this Agreement, unless the context otherwise requires, the following expressions have the following meanings:

"the Acceptance Date"	means the date on which the Equipment is accepted by the Hirer pursuant to clause 9.
"Confidential Information"	means all information which is obtained by one party from the other pursuant to this Agreement expressly marked as confidential or which is manifestly of a confidential nature or which is confirmed in writing to be confidential within 7 days of its disclosure.
"the Delivery Charge"	means the charge for the delivery and installation of the Equipment as specified in the Schedule.
"the Delivery Date" [2.3.7]	means the delivery date specified in the Schedule or such extended date as may be granted pursuant to clause 36.
"the Emergency Maintenance Services"	means the emergency maintenance services to be provided by the Supplier pursuant to clause 20.

249

"the Equipment" [2.1.1]	means the computer equipment specified in the Schedule and any replacements or renewals of the whole or any part thereof provided by the Supplier from time to time.
"the Initial Period"	means the initial period of the Rental Period as specified in the Schedule.
"the Location" [2.1.2]	means the Hirer's computer room in which the Equipment is to be installed as specified in the Schedule.
"the Maintenance charges"	means the charges payable in respect of the provision of the Schedule Maintenance Services, as specified in the Schedule.
"Maintenance Hours"	means the hours between 9.00 a.m. and 5.00 p.m. each day in the United Kingdom excluding Saturdays, Sundays and U.K. public holidays.
"the Maintenance Services"	means, collectively the Scheduled Maintenance Services and the Emergency Maintenance Services.
"the Off-Loading Point"	means the Hirer's off-loading point specified in the Schedule.
"the Rental Charges"	means the rental charges payable by the Hirer during the Rental Period, as specified in the Schedule.
"the Rental Period" [2.2.2]	means the period during which the letting and hiring of the Equipment under this Agreement shall continue and during which the Maintenance Services shall be provided.
"the Scheduled Maintenance Services"	means the maintenance services to be provided by the Supplier pursuant to clause 19.

2 Products and services to be provided [2.2.2]

(1) The Supplier hereby agrees to:

    (a) deliver the Equipment and install it at the Location on the Delivery Date;

    (b) let the Equipment on hire to the Hirer for the Rental Period;

    (c) provide the Maintenance Services;

upon the terms and conditions hereinafter contained.

(2) The Hirer agrees to take or hire the Equipment for the Rental Period upon the terms and conditions hereinafter contained.

[(3) The Supplier reserves the right prior to delivery of the Equipment to substitute an alternative item of equipment for any item comprising part of the Equipment agreed to be supplied hereunder provided that such substitution will not materially affect the performance of the Equipment as a whole and will not result in any increase in the rentals or the charges for the Scheduled Maintenance Services.]

(4) Operating supplies such as disk packs, stationery, printing cartridges and similar accessories are not supplied as part of the Equipment.

3 Location preparation [2.6.3]

See clause 5 of Precedent A.

4 Information and access [2.6.1]

See clause 6 of Precedent A.

5 Delivery [2.3.3]

(1) On the Delivery Date the Supplier shall deliver the Equipment to the Off-Loading Point and be responsible for its transportation to the Location.

(2) The Supplier shall not carry out or be responsible for the removal of doors, widening of entrances or any other structural work of any description for the purpose of moving the Equipment from the Off-Loading Point to the Location, which work shall be undertaken by the Hirer at its own expense prior to delivery.

(3) The Hirer shall be responsible for all reasonable costs incurred by the Supplier in providing special equipment, personnel or works necessary to move the Equipment from the Off-Loading Point to the Location. Such costs shall be paid by the Hirer in addition to the Delivery Charge.

[(4) All packing cases, skids, drums and other packing materials used for delivery of the Equipment must be returned by the Hirer to the Supplier in good condition and at the Hirer's expense. The Supplier reserves the right to charge for any such cases and materials not so returned]

[Note: In the case of a rental agreement where title to the equipment remains with the supplier, the supplier will usually wish to assume full control over the delivery and installation of the equipment.]

6 Installation [2.3.3]

See clause 9 of Precedent A.

7 Time [not] of the essence [2.3.7]

See clause 10 of Precedent A.

8 Installation testsFS [2.3.4]

See clause 11 of Precedent A.

9 Acceptance [2.3.6]

Adapt clause 12 of Precedent A.

10 Hirer's default [2.3.7]

If the Supplier is prevented or delayed from performing its obligations under this Agreement by reason of any act or omission of the Hirer (other than a delay by the

Hirer for which the Hirer is excused under clause 36) then the Hirer will pay to the Supplier all reasonable costs, charges and losses sustained or incurred by the Supplier as a result (including without limitation the cost of storage and insurance of the Equipment) subject always to the limits on liability in clause 37. The Supplier shall promptly notify the Hirer in writing of any claim which it may have under this clause giving such particulars thereof as it is then able to provide.

[11 Supplier's warranties [2.3.8]

(1) The Supplier warrants to the Hirer that the Equipment complies fully as to noise heat radiation and all other characteristics with the requirements in the Health and Safety (Display Equipment) Regulations 1992 and in particular that the display screens and keyboards comply fully with the said Regulations.

(2) The Supplier does not give any warranty that the Equipment is fit for any particular purpose unless that purpose is specifically advised to the Supplier in writing by the Hirer and the Supplier confirms in writing that the Equipment can fulfil that particular purpose.

[(3) The Supplier does not warrant that the Equipment will achieve any particular performance criteria unless:

  (a) the Supplier has specifically guaranteed such criteria in writing, subject to specified tolerances in an agreed sum as liquidated damages; and

  (b) the environmental conditions specified by the Supplier are maintained.

The payment by the Supplier of such liquidated damages shall be in full satisfaction of any liability of the Supplier in respect of the Equipment failing to achieve such performance criteria.]

(4) The express terms of this Agreement are in lieu of all warranties, conditions, terms, undertakings and obligations implied by statute, common law, custom, trade usage, course of dealing or otherwise, all of which are hereby excluded to the fullest extent permitted by law.]

12 Hirer's warranty

See clause 20 of Precedent A.

13 Rental Period [2.2, 8.2]

The Rental Period shall commence on the Acceptance Date, shall continue for the Initial Period and shall remain in force thereafter [unless and] until terminated by either party giving to the other not less than 6 months' written notice of termination [given on] [expiring on] the last day of the Initial Period or at any time thereafter but shall be subject to earlier termination as hereinafter provided.

[**Note:** Delete the first and third bracketed phrases if the agreement is to be for a minimum period equal to the Initial Period plus the notice period. Delete the second bracketed phrase if the agreement is to be for a minimum period equal to the Initial Period.]

14 Charges and payment [2.2, 8.2]

(1) The Delivery Charge and any additional charges payable by the Hirer under clause 5(3) shall be paid on the Acceptance Date.

(2) During the Rental Period the Hirer shall pay to the Supplier the Rental Charges and the Maintenance Charges specified in the Schedule periodically in advance as stated therein. Such Rental Charges and Maintenance Charges shall be paid without prior demand and no payment shall be considered made until it is received by the Supplier in cleared funds. All such payments shall be made in the manner specified in the Schedule.

(3) Any charges payable by the Hirer under this Agreement in addition to those specified in sub-clauses (1) and (2) above shall be paid within *14* days after the receipt by the Hirer of the Supplier's invoice therefor.

(4) The Supplier shall be entitled at any time and from time to time after the expiry of the [Initial Period] [the period of *one* year after the Acceptance Date] to vary the Rental Charges and/or the Maintenance Charges to accord with any change in the Supplier's standard scale of charges by giving to the Hirer not less than *90* days' prior written notice. Where and whenever such notice is given, the Hirer shall have the right to terminate this Agreement as from the date on which such notice expires by giving to the Supplier written notice of termination not less than *30* days before such date.

[**Note**: For a clause limiting the increase by reference to the Retail Prices Index—see the second alternative clause 3(4) of Precedent K.]

(5) All charges payable under this Agreement are exclusive of Value Added Tax which shall be paid by the Hirer at the rate and in the manner for the time being prescribed by law.

(6) If any sum payable under this Agreement is not paid within *7* days after the due date then (without prejudice to the Supplier's other rights and remedies) the Supplier reserves the right to charge interest on such sum on a day to day basis (as well after as before any judgment) from the date or last date for payment thereof to the date of actual payment (both dates inclusive) at the rate of *2* per cent above the base rate of *ABC* Bank plc (or such other London Clearing Bank as the Supplier may nominate) from time to time in force compounded quarterly. Such interest shall be paid on demand by the Supplier.

[**Note**: Where reliability is an important factor for the hirer the downtime clause (clause 13 of Precedent K) may be appropriate.]

15 Ownership and risk [2.8.1]

The Equipment shall at all times remain the sole and exclusive property of the Supplier and the Hirer shall have no right or interest in the Equipment except for quiet possession and the right to use the Equipment upon the terms and conditions contained in this Agreement. Notwithstanding the foregoing, risk in the Equipment shall pass to the Hirer on delivery of the Equipment to [the Off Loading Point] [the Location].

16 Replacements and renewals

The provisions of this Agreement shall apply to all replacements and renewals of the Equipment or any part thereof made by the Supplier during the continuance of this Agreement.

17 Insurance [2.6.5]

(1) The Hirer shall from (and including) the date on which the Equipment is delivered to the Location effect (if not previously effected) and maintain thereafter

until the Equipment has been re-delivered to the Supplier with insurers acceptable to the Supplier:

(a) insurance covering the Equipment against all usual risks relating to loss or damage from whatever cause arising (other than exclusions agreed in writing by the Supplier). Such insurance shall:

    (i) be in the joint names of the Supplier and the Hirer;

    (ii) cover the Equipment for its full replacement value;

    (iii) specify the Supplier as loss payee;

    (iv) be free from restriction or excess (save as may be agreed in writing by the Supplier);

    (v) not be capable of cancellation or variation other than by the insurers giving to the Supplier not less than *30* days' prior written notice (in which event the Hirer shall be responsible for procuring new cover with insurers acceptable to the Supplier, in accordance with the provisions of this clause).

(b) insurance for an amount not less than £*500,000* against claims from any persons whatsoever (including, without limitation, employees, agents and sub-contractors of the Hirer) who may suffer damage to or loss of property on death or bodily injury arising directly or indirectly out of the presence, control or use of the Equipment. Such insurance shall:

    (i) be in the joint names of the Supplier and the Hirer;

    (ii) provide that any payment made thereunder pursuant to any claim shall be applied directly in or towards satisfaction of the claim in respect of which such payment is made;

    (iii) not be capable of cancellation or variation other than by the insurers giving to the Supplier not less than *30* days' prior written notice (in which event the Hirer shall be responsible for procuring new cover with insurers acceptable to the Supplier, in accordance with the provisions of this clause).

(2) The Hirer shall:

(a) prior to the delivery of the Equipment and thereafter on demand produce to the Supplier the policies relating to the aforesaid insurances and the receipts for premiums;

(b) forthwith notify the Supplier in writing in the event of any loss of or damage to the Equipment;

(c) punctually pay all premiums payable under the said insurance policies, do everything necessary to maintain the said insurance policies in full force and effect and not do anything whereby they will or may be vitiated either in whole or in part;

(d) not effect any other insurance relating to the Equipment if a claim under such insurance would result in the operation of any average clause in the policies maintained in compliance with sub-clause (1).

(3) The Hirer shall be responsible for and shall indemnify the Supplier against any loss or damage to the Equipment insofar as such loss or damage is not covered by insurance (other than loss or damage caused by the negligence or wilful misconduct of the Supplier, its employees, agents or sub-contractors)

[**Note**: The alternative is for the supplier to insure and recover the premiums by way of increased rental charges.]

18 Application of insurance moneys

(1) If the Equipment shall be damaged and in the opinion of the insurers it is economic that such damage be made good (as opposed to procuring replacement equipment) then all insurance moneys payable under the insurance policy mentioned in clause 17(1)(a) shall be applied in making good such damage

(2) If the Equipment shall be lost, stolen, destroyed or damaged to such an extent as to be in the opinion of the insurers incapable of economic repair then the said insurance moneys shall at the option of the Supplier:

(a) be applied in replacing the Equipment with equipment having capabilities at least equivalent to that of the Equipment, in which event the replacement equipment shall at all times remain the sole and exclusive property of the Supplier and shall be held by the Hirer upon the terms of this Agreement and the Hirer shall continue to be liable to pay the Rental Charges and Maintenance Charges hereunder as if such loss had not taken place. The Hirer shall be liable to pay to the Supplier a sum equivalent to any amount deducted by the insurers by way of excess or in respect of damage caused to the Equipment prior to the date of total loss; or

(b) be paid to the Supplier to the extent necessary to discharge the Hirer's liability to the Supplier at the date of such payment and to compensate the Supplier for the loss, theft or destruction of or damage to the Equipment, any surplus to be paid to the Hirer. If the insurance moneys paid to the Supplier are insufficient to discharge such liability and to compensate the Supplier as aforesaid the amount of the deficiency shall be paid by the Hirer to the Supplier forthwith. Upon all payments being made as aforesaid, this Agreement shall automatically terminate.

19 Scheduled maintenance services

During the Rental Period the Supplier shall provide the following maintenance services in respect of the Equipment:

(1) *Preventive maintenance*

The Supplier shall make visits to the Location [at such intervals as the Supplier shall reasonably determine to be required for the Equipment] [every 6 months] to test the functions of the Equipment and make such adjustments as shall be reasonably necessary to keep the Equipment in working order in accordance with its accompanying specifications. Such visits shall be made during Maintenance Hours by prior appointment with the Hirer. If it is expedient in the opinion of the Supplier so to do, such maintenance may be carried out at the same time as corrective maintenance.

(2) *Corrective maintenance*

Upon receipt of notification from the Hirer that the Equipment has failed to perform in accordance with its accompanying specification to a material degree the Supplier shall during Maintenance Hours make such repairs and adjustments to and replace such parts of the Equipment as may be reasonably necessary to restore the Equipment to operation in accordance with its accompanying specification.

(3) *Response time*

On receipt of a request for corrective maintenance the Supplier undertakes [to use its reasonable endeavours] to despatch a suitably qualified service engineer to the Location within *4* Maintenance Hours [but such response time is an estimate only and shall not be contractually binding on the Supplier].

[**Note**: The time of arrival of the service engineer at the location will depend upon how far he has to travel. Some suppliers may set out different priority levels depending upon the severity of the reported problems, with different response times applying to each one.]

20 Emergency maintenance services [8.3.2]

See clause 4 of Precedent K.

21 Exceptions to the maintenance services [8.3]

See clause 5 of Precedent K.

22 Replacement parts [8.3.1, 8.3.2]

Any replacement parts provided by the Supplier hereunder and any parts removed from the Equipment shall remain the property of the Supplier.

23 Service visits outside the maintenance services [2.1.1]

The Supplier shall make an additional charge, in accordance with its standard scale of charges from time to time in force, for service visits made at the request of the Hirer by reason of any fault in the Equipment due to causes not covered by the Maintenance Services or which relate to matters not falling within the scope of the Maintenance Services as set out in clauses 19 to 21.

[24 Replacement equipment

The Supplier shall on giving to the Hirer *30* days' prior written notice be entitled if it considers it reasonably necessary or desirable to replace the Equipment with equipment having capabilities at least equivalent to that of the Equipment. Where the Supplier avails itself of this right, it shall be responsible for all the costs of replacing the Equipment, but the Hirer shall provide the Supplier with all facilities and assistance reasonably required by the Supplier for the purpose of effecting such replacement.]

[25 Additional equipment [2.5]

The Hirer may hire additional equipment (subject to the availability thereof) from the Supplier by the Hirer's written order to the Supplier referring to this Agreement, and by receipt of a written acceptance of such order from the Supplier. The period of hire for such additional equipment shall continue until the expiry of the Rental Period unless otherwise agreed. Any charges initially payable for such additional equipment shall be those in effect when such additional equipment is accepted and shall thereafter be added to and form part of the Rental Charges or Maintenance Charges as appropriate. Subject to the foregoing such additional equipment shall be hired on the same terms and conditions as provided in this Agreement (insofar as the same are applicable).]

26 Hirer's obligations [2.6]

Rental

(1) The Hirer shall:

    (a) not sell, assign, sub-let, pledge or part with possession or control of or otherwise deal with the Equipment or any interest therein nor purport to do any of such things nor create or allow to be created any mortgage, charge, lien or other encumbrance on the Equipment;

    (b) not change, remove or obscure any labels, plates, insignia, lettering or other markings which are on the Equipment at the time of installation thereof or which may thereafter be placed on the Equipment by the Supplier or by any person authorised by the Supplier;

    (c) do all things reasonably necessary to protect and defend the Supplier's title to the Equipment against all persons claiming against or through the Hirer and shall use all reasonable endeavours to keep the Equipment free from distress, execution or any other legal process, and shall forthwith give to the Supplier notice of any claim or threatened claim to the Equipment by any third party;

    (d) not cause or permit the Equipment or any part thereof to be attached or affixed to any land or building so as to become a fixture;

    (e) not make any movement of the Equipment or move the Equipment from the Location without the Supplier's prior written consent;

    (f) permit the Supplier and any person authorised by it at all reasonable times to have access to the Location (or such other place where the Equipment may be situated) for the purpose of inspecting and examining the condition of the Equipment;

    (g) not sell, assign, demise, sub-let, mortgage, charge or otherwise dispose of any land or building on or in which the Equipment is kept or enter into any contract to do any of such things without giving the Supplier at least 2 months' prior written notice. The Hirer shall in any event procure that any such sale, assignment, demise, sub-lease, mortgage, charge or other disposition is made subject to the right of the Supplier to repossess the Equipment at any time and for that purpose to enter upon any such land or building;

    (h) pay to the Supplier all costs and expenses (including legal costs on a full indemnity basis) incurred by or on behalf of the Supplier in ascertaining the whereabouts of the Equipment or repossessing it by reason of a breach by the Hirer of any term of this Agreement and of any legal proceedings taken by or on behalf of the Supplier to enforce any provision of this Agreement;

    (i) obtain all necessary licences, permits and permissions for the use of the Equipment and not use the Equipment or permit the same to be used contrary to any law or any regulation or bye-law in force from time to time;

    (j) indemnify the Supplier against all claims and demands made upon the Supplier (so far as the same are not covered by insurance) by reason of any loss, injury or damage suffered by any person arising directly or indirectly out of the presence, control or use of the Equipment save where such damage loss or injury arises from the negligence or breach of contract of the Supplier, its employees, agents or sub-contractors or by reason of any failure of the Equipment to operate in accordance with its accompanying specifications other than by reason of one of the causes set out in clause 21(1) (a) to (f);

(k) at all times keep a record of the use of the Equipment in a form to be approved by the Supplier and shall at the Supplier's request provide the Supplier with copies of the entries and allow the Supplier to inspect such record at all reasonable times.

Use and care of the equipment [8.6.1]

See sub-clauses (1) to (8) of clause 9 of Precedent K.

Access [8.6.2]

See sub-clauses (9) to (12) of clause 9 of Precedent K.

Notification and information [8.6.3]

See sub-clauses (13) to (17) of clause 9 of Precedent K.

Miscellaneous [8.6.5]

See sub-clauses (18) to (19) of clause 9 of Precedent K.

27 Electromagnetic compatibility [2.7.2]

See clause 13 of Precedent A.

[28 Telecommunications [2.7.4]

See sub-clauses (1) to (4) of clause 14 of Precedent A.

(5) The Hirer undertakes to the Supplier that it will not make any modification to the Relevant Equipment or connect the Relevant Equipment to any telecommunications equipment [except such telecommunications equipment as is set out in the Schedule] without the prior written consent of the Supplier [such consent not to be unreasonably withheld.]

[(6) Where any data transmission speeds are given by the Supplier in relation to the Equipment, such speeds are at all times subject to any conditions attached to the use of the relevant modem, cabling or telecommunication equipment at the speeds indicated and to the capability of such modem, cabling or other telecommunication equipment to achieve such speeds.]

29 Operating manuals [and training]

See clause 22 of Precedent A.

30 Termination [2.4.2]

(1) Notwithstanding anything else contained in this Agreement, this Agreement may be terminated at any time on or after the Acceptance Date:

(a) by the Supplier forthwith on giving notice in writing to the Hirer if the Hirer shall fail to pay any sum due under the terms of this Agreement (otherwise than as a consequence of any default on the part of the Supplier) and such sum remains unpaid for *14* days after written notice from the Supplier requiring such sum to be paid and referring to this clause 30(1)(a); or

(b) by either party forthwith on giving notice in writing to the other if:

    (i) the other commits any material breach of any term of this Agreement (other than any failure by the Hirer to make any payment in which event the provisions of paragraph (a) above shall apply) and (in the case of a breach capable of being remedied) shall have failed to have remedied such, within *30* days of receiving a written notice requiring it to do so; or

    (ii) the other party shall have a receiver or administrative receiver appointed of it or over any part of its undertaking or assets or shall pass a resolution for winding-up (otherwise than for the purpose of a bona fide scheme of solvent amalgamation or reconstruction) or a court of competent jurisdiction shall make an order to that effect or if the other party shall become subject to an administration order or shall enter into any voluntary arrangement with its creditors or shall cease or threaten to cease to carry on business.

[**Note**: This agreement can be separated into two distinct stages; the first being the period up to the Acceptance Date (dealing with delivery, installation, acceptance etc) and the second being the period after acceptance (dealing with rental and maintenance). The parties should always make it clear to which stage any express termination provisions apply. For example, if sub-clause (1)(b) applied to the first period it could, in effect, make time of the essence by giving the innocent party an immediate right to terminate in the event of a breach incapable of remedy, ie if a required delivery date was not met. However, the "innocent" party should beware of making any precipitate decision that a breach is incapable of remedy; save in the clearest of cases, the breaching party should be allowed the 30 day period to rectify the breach.]

(2) The Supplier shall be entitled to terminate this Agreement in any of the events mentioned in sub-clause (1) notwithstanding any subsequent acceptance of Rental Charges.

(3) In the event of a termination by the Supplier pursuant to sub-clause (1):

(a) the Hirer shall relinquish any claim to possession of the Equipment and the Supplier may without notice repossess the Equipment and may for that purpose without notice enter any of the Hirer's premises in which the Equipment or any part thereof is or is reasonably believed by the Supplier to be situated (and the Hirer hereby irrevocably licenses the Supplier, its employees and agents to enter upon any such premises for such purpose);

(b) the Hirer shall not be entitled to the repayment of any sums previously paid by it to the Supplier under the terms of this Agreement nor to any credit or allowance in respect of any such payments.

(4) Any termination of this Agreement (howsoever occasioned) shall not affect any accrued rights or liabilities of either party nor shall it affect the coming into force or the continuance in force of any provision hereof which is expressly or by implication intended to come into or continue in force on or after such termination.

(5) Without prejudice to the provisions of clause 31, as from the date of termination of this Agreement until such time as the Equipment shall be returned to the

Supplier the Hirer will pay by way of compensation for the continued use of the Equipment a monthly sum (payable in arrears) at the same rate as the Rental Charges previously due in respect thereof. This sub-clause shall not, however, confer on the Hirer any right to the continued use or possession of the Equipment.

31 Return of the equipment

(1) Upon termination of the Hirer's right to hire the Equipment (for any reason), the Hirer shall forthwith re-deliver possession of the Equipment in good order, repair and condition to the Supplier who shall for the purpose have access to the Location or any other place where the Equipment may be situated (and the Hirer hereby irrevocably licences the Supplier, its employees and agents to enter upon any such premises for such purpose).

(2) Except in the case of a termination by the Supplier pursuant to clause 30(1) (in which case the costs of removal and re-delivery shall be borne by the Hirer), normal costs of removal of the Equipment and of re-delivery shall be borne by the Supplier [provided that all reasonable costs incurred by the Supplier in providing special equipment, personnel or works necessary to transport the Equipment from the Location (or such other place where the Equipment may be situated) to the Supplier's vehicle shall be borne by the Hirer. The Hirer shall reimburse such costs to the Supplier within *30* days after the receipt of an invoice from the Supplier].

32 Intervention by the supplier

If the Hirer fails to comply with any of its obligations hereunder, the Supplier may, without being obliged to do so, or responsible for so doing, and without prejudice to its other rights and remedies, effect compliance on behalf of the Hirer, whereupon the Hirer shall become liable to pay forthwith any moneys expended by the Supplier together with all costs and expenses (including legal costs on a full indemnity basis) in connection therewith.

[33 Option to purchase [2.2.3]

On termination of the hiring of the Equipment (other than by termination by the Supplier pursuant to clause 30(1)), the Hirer shall have the option to buy the Equipment at a price to be agreed with the Supplier and on the Supplier's standard terms and conditions of sale in force from time to time.]

[Note: We have included this clause as an example of the type of provision commonly encountered in rental agreements. It should be noted that as the price is still to be negotiated, it is merely an "agreement to agree" and is therefore unlikely to be binding on the supplier. In order for the option to have contractual force the price must be ascertainable in advance and not be left to the parties to negotiate at a later stage.]

34 Intellectual property rights indemnity [2.8.1, 3.8.1]

See clause 26 of Precedent A or clause 12 of Precedent C.

[Note: The terms of clause 12 of Precedent C will be relevant where software (*e.g.* an operating system) forms part of the Equipment.]

35 Confidentiality [2.6.1, 2.7.1]

See clause 21 of Precedent A.

36 *Force majeure*

Neither party shall be liable for any delay in performing any of its obligations hereunder if such delay is caused by circumstances beyond the reasonable control of the party so delaying and such party shall be entitled to a reasonable extension of time for the performance of such obligations.

[Note: this is a "short form" *force majeure* clause: a longer form of words is that in clause 15 of Precedent A.]

37 Liability

See clause 18 of Precedent K.

38 Waiver of remedies

See clause 28 of Precedent A.

39 Entire agreement

See clause 29 of Precedent A.

40 Assignment

See clause 30 of Precedent A.

41 Sub-contracts

See clause 31 of Precedent A.

42 Notices

See clause 32 of Precedent A.

43 Interpretation

See clause 33 of Precedent A.

44 Law

See clause 34 of Precedent A.

45 Disputes

See clause 35 of Precedent A.

46 Severability

See clause 36 of Precedent A.

47 Third parties

See clause 37 of Precedent A.

EXECUTED under hand in two originals the day and year first before written

SIGNED for and on behalf of
RENTAL COMPANY [LIMITED] [PLC]

By

Signature

Title

Witness

**SIGNED for and on behalf of
CUSTOMER [LIMITED] [PLC]**

By

Signature

Title

Witness

The Schedule

A THE EQUIPMENT

B THE DELIVERY CHARGE

C THE OFF-LOADING POINT

D THE LOCATION

E THE DELIVERY DATE

F THE INITIAL PERIOD

G CHARGES AND METHOD OF PAYMENT

Rental Charges

£[   ] for each [month] [quarter] [year], payable in advance
First Rental Charge payment due on: [the Acceptance Date]
Subsequent Rental Charges payable on the first working day of each [month] [quarter] [year] thereafter

Maintenance Charges

£[   ] for each [month] [quarter] [year], payable in advance
First Maintenance Charge payment due on: [the Acceptance Date]
Subsequent Maintenance Charges payable on the first working day of each [month] [quarter] [year] thereafter

Method of payment

By standing order to [   ] Bank PLC

(Rental Company's Account No [   ])

[H THE TELECOMMUNICATIONS EQUIPMENT]

[I TRAINING]

[J SUB-CONTRACTS]

[K THIRD-PARTY RIGHTS]

Commissioning Certificate

TO: RENTAL COMPANY [LIMITED] [PLC]

FROM: CUSTOMER [LIMITED] [PLC]

                                                    Date: 20

Dear Sirs,

We refer to the agreement between our respective companies dated   20
("the Agreement") relating to the rental and maintenance of certain computer equipment ("the Equipment") and confirm the following:

1 We have today accepted the Equipment.

2 We have inspected the Equipment and confirm that the same conforms to the description contained in the Agreement and that the same has been installed and set up to our satisfaction at the Location (as defined in the Agreement).

3 The Equipment has passed the Installation Tests (as defined in the Agreement), the results of which are annexed hereto and signed by us for the purpose of identification.

SIGNED for and on behalf of
CUSTOMER [LIMITED] [PLC]

By

Signature

Title

Witness

SOFTWARE LICENCE AGREEMENT

[**Note**: This agreement covers not only the use of computer programs but also associated documentation such as user manuals. Such agreements frequently include software maintenance—see Precedent L. Alternative Software Licence and Support Agreements for end-users are set out in Schedule 1 of Precedent H and Schedule 1 of Precedent I.]

THIS AGREEMENT is made the   day of   20

PARTIES:

(1) SUPPLIER [LIMITED] [PLC] whose registered office is at

("the Licensor")

(2) CUSTOMER [LIMITED] [PLC] whose registered office is at

("the Licensee")

RECITAL:

The Licensor has agreed to deliver to the Licensee and install on the Licensee's computer certain computer programs and to grant the Licensee a non-exclusive licence to use such programs and their associated documentation upon the terms and conditions hereinafter contained

NOW IT IS HEREBY AGREED as follows:

1 Definitions

In this Agreement, unless the context otherwise requires, the following expressions have the following meanings:

"the Acceptance Date"   means the date on which the Licensed Programs are accepted (or deemed to be accepted) by the Licensee pursuant to clause 6.

"Confidential Informa-   means all information which is expressly marked as
tion"   confidential or which is manifestly of a confidential nature or which is confirmed in writing to be confidential within 7 days of its disclosure.

"the Delivery Date"   means the delivery date specified in the Schedule or such extended date as may be agreed by the Licensee pursuant to clause 23.

"the Equipment"   means the Licensee's computer hardware and associated peripherals in respect of which the Licence is granted, specified by type and serial number in the Schedule [and using the *XYZ* operating system].

"the Licence"   means the licence granted by the Licensor pursuant
                                to clause 9(1).

"the Licence Fee"   means the fee for the Licence and the services to be
                                provided under this Agreement as specified in the
                                Schedule.

"the Licensed Program   means the Licensed Programs, the Program Docu-
Materials"   mentation and the Media.

"the Licensed Programs"   means the [systems] [and] [applications] computer
                                programs of the Licensor specified in the Schedule.

"the Location"   means the Licensee's computer room where the
                                Equipment is [located] [to be installed] as specified
                                in the Schedule.

"the Media"   means the media on which the Licensed Programs
                                and the Program Documentation are recorded or
                                printed as provided to the Licensee by the Licensor.

"the Program Documen-   means the operating manuals, user instructions,
tation"   technical literature, on-line help and other docu-
                                mentation and all other related materials in eye-
                                readable form supplied to the Licensee by the
                                Licensor for aiding the use by the Licensee of the
                                Licensed Programs.

"the Specification"   means the specification of the Licensed Programs
                                describing the facilities and functions thereof, a
                                copy of which is [annexed hereto] [contained in the
                                Program Documentation].

[Note: Where the Licensed Programs are applications programs intended for use with the licensee's
existing systems programs then this should be made clear in the specification. It should also be made
clear that such use will not affect the licensor's obligations and liabilities under this agreement.]

"Use"   means (as appropriate) either the reading and pos-
                                session of the Program Documentation, or the
                                loading and subsequent processing of the Licensed
                                Programs on the Equipment, and the possession of
                                the Media in accordance with the terms of this
                                Agreement.

2 Products and services to be provided [3.0.2]

The Licensor hereby agrees to:

(1) grant to the Licensee a non-exclusive licence to Use the Licensed Program
    Materials;

(2) deliver the Licensed Programs to the Licensee and install them on the
    Equipment;

(3) provide training and operating manuals to the Licensee;

(4) provide the other services hereinafter described

upon the terms and conditions hereinafter contained.

3 Payment [3.2]

(1) The Licence Fee shall be due to be paid by the Licensee on or before the Acceptance Date.

(2) The Licence Fee and any additional charges payable under this Agreement are exclusive of Value Added Tax which shall be paid by the Licensee at the rate and in the manner for the time being prescribed by law.

(3) Any charges payable by the Licensee hereunder in addition to the Licence Fee shall be due to be paid within *30* days after the receipt by the Licensee of the Licensor's invoice therefor.

(4) If any sum payable under this Agreement is not paid within 7 days after the due date then (without prejudice to the Licensor's other rights and remedies) the Licensor reserves the right to charge interest on such sum on a day to day basis (as well after as before any judgment) from the date or last date for payment thereof to the date of actual payment (both dates inclusive) at the rate of *2* per cent above the base rate of *ABC* Bank plc (or such other London Clearing Bank as the Supplier may nominate) from time to time in force compounded quarterly. Such interest shall be paid on demand by the Licensor. For the avoidance of doubt, any failure to make payment within 7 days after the due date shall constitute a material breach of contract for the purposes of clause 21(2).

4 Delivery and installation [3.3]

EITHER

[On the Delivery Date the Licensor shall deliver the Licensed Programs to the Licensee and install the same on the Equipment at the Location. Time shall be of the essence in this regard.]

OR

[The Licensor shall use all reasonable endeavours to deliver the Licensed Programs to the Licensee [and to install them on the Equipment at the Location] on or before the Delivery Date. [Time shall not be of the essence in this regard, [save that if delivery [and installation] of the Licensed Programs has not taken place within 7 days of the Delivery Date, the Licensee may serve written notice on the Licensor requiring delivery [and installation] to be completed within a further 7 days, in respect of which time shall be of the essence.]] The Licensed Programs shall consist of one copy of the object code of the Licensed Programs in machine-readable form only, on the storage media specified in the Schedule.]

5 Risk

Risk in the Media shall pass to the Licensee on delivery. If any part of the Media shall thereafter be lost, destroyed or damaged the Licensor shall at the request of the Licensee replace the same promptly (embodying the relevant part of the Licensed Programs or Program Documentation) subject to the Licensee paying the reasonable cost of such replacement.

6 Testing and acceptance [3.5.1]

(1) The Licensee shall supply to the Licensor [as soon as reasonably possible after installation of the Licensed Programs] test data which in the reasonable opinion of the Licensee is suitable to test whether the Licensed Programs are in accordance with the Specification together with the results expected to be achieved by processing such test data using the Licensed Programs. The Licensor shall not be entitled to object to such test data or expected results unless the Licensor can demonstrate to the Licensee that they are not suitable for testing the Licensed Programs as aforesaid, in which event the Licensee shall make any reasonable amendments to such test data and expected results as the Licensor may request. Subject to the receipt of such test data and expected results, the Licensor shall process such data, in the presence of the Licensee or its authorised representative, on the Equipment using the Licensed Programs by way of acceptance testing within 7 days after such receipt at a time mutually convenient to both parties.

[**Note**: this clause is less likely to be applicable to lower value package software]

(2) The Licensee shall accept the Licensed Programs immediately after the Licensor has demonstrated that the Licensed Programs have correctly processed the test data by achieving the expected results. The Licensee shall not unreasonably withhold or delay its acceptance. The Licensee shall, if required by the Licensor, sign an acceptance certificate in the form annexed hereto acknowledging such acceptance. If the Licensed Programs shall fail to correctly process the test data so as to achieve the expected results, [the Licensee shall be entitled to reject the Licensed Programs and to be repaid all sums paid by it to the Licensor] [the Licensor shall, within a period of *14* days of the completion of the acceptance tests, correct the Licensed Programs so as to enable them to correctly process the test data and achieve the expected results].

[**Note**: the second option is only likely to be applicable where there has been an element of bespoke programming; licensors of package software are unlikely to make amendments to reflect the requirements of individual licensees.]

(3) If the Licensee shall not supply any test data as aforesaid or shall fail to make itself available to attend acceptance tests within the said period of 7 days then the Licensee shall be deemed to have accepted the Licensed Programs.

(4) The Licensed Programs shall not be deemed to have incorrectly processed such test data by reason of any failure to provide any facility or function not specified in the Specification.

[7 The Equipment

The Licensee shall be responsible for ensuring that the Equipment is installed and fully operational at the Location on the Delivery Date. If the Licensor is delayed from performing its obligations under clauses 4 and 6 by reason of any failure by the Licensee to ensure the same, then the Licensee will pay to the Licensor all reasonable costs, charges and losses attributable to such delay.]

[**Note**: This clause will be appropriate where the equipment has not yet been installed and is to be supplied by a third party.]

8 Warranty

(1) (a) The Licensor warrants that the Licensed Programs will after acceptance by the Licensee provide the facilities and functions set out in the Specification when properly used on the Equipment and that the Program Documentation [and the Licensed Programs] will provide adequate instruction to enable the Licensee to make proper use of such facilities and functions;

[**Note**: The Licensed Programs may also contain "help" functions to assist the user.]

(b) If the Licensor receives written notice from the Licensee after the Acceptance Date of any breach of the said warranty then the Licensor shall at its own expense and within a reasonable time after receiving such notice remedy the defect or error in question provided that the Licensor shall have no liability or obligations under the said warranty unless it shall have received written notice of the defect or error in question no later than the expiry of 6 months after the Acceptance Date;

(c) The said warranty shall be subject to the Licensee complying with its obligations hereunder and to there having been made no alterations to the Licensed Programs by any person other than the Licensor;

[**Note**: an alternative form of words would be to provide that the warranty will only be ruled inapplicable to a particular fault if it *results* from the breach of obligation/unauthorised alteration. However, the licensor is likely to insist upon the provisions as drafted as a more powerful deterrent.]

(d) When notifying a defect or error the Licensee shall (so far as it is able) provide the Licensor with a documented example of such defect or error;

(e) The Licensor shall have no liability or obligations under the said warranty other than to remedy breaches thereof by the provision of materials and services within a reasonable time and without charge to the Licensee save that if the Licensor shall fail to comply with such obligations, its liability for such failure shall be limited to a sum equal to the Licence Fee. The foregoing states the entire liability of the Licensor, whether in contract or tort, for defects and errors in the Licensed Program Materials which are notified to the Licensor after the Acceptance Date.

[**Note**: Where a maintenance agreement is entered into (see clause 17) sub-clause (1) will need to be amended—follow clause 25 of Precedent O.]

(2) The Licensee acknowledges that the Licensed Programs have not been prepared to meet the Licensee's individual requirements and that it is therefore the responsibility of the Licensee to ensure that the facilities and functions described in the Specification meet its requirements. The Licensor shall not be liable for any failure of the Licensed Programs to provide any facility or function not specified in the Specification.

[**Note**: This is reasonable, of course, in the case of a package. If the licensee requires modifications to the package to meet its individual requirements then these would have to be paid for in addition and this clause will not then be appropriate in this form.]

(3) The express terms of this Agreement are in lieu of all warranties, conditions, terms, undertakings and obligations implied by statute, common law, custom, trade usage, course of dealing or otherwise, all of which are hereby excluded to the fullest extent permitted by law.

9 Licence [3.8]

(1) The Licensor hereby grants to the Licensee a non-exclusive licence to Use the Licensed Program Materials subject to the terms and conditions contained in this Agreement.

(2) The Licensee shall Use the Licensed Program Materials for processing its own data for its own internal business purposes only. The Licensee shall not permit any third party to use the Licensed Program Materials nor use the Licensed Program

Materials on behalf of or for the benefit of any third party in any way whatever (including, without limitation, using the Licensed Program Materials for the purpose of operating a bureau service).

[**Note**: Sub-clause (2) will have to be altered if mutual back-up arrangements with another user are envisaged.]

(3) The use of the Licensed Program Materials is restricted to use on and in conjunction with the Equipment save that:

(a) if the Licensed Program Materials cannot be used with the Equipment because it is inoperable for any reason then the Licence shall be temporarily extended without additional charge to use with any other equipment until such failure has been remedied, provided that such equipment is under the direct control of the Licensee. The Licensee shall promptly notify the Licensor of such temporary use and of the commencement and cessation thereof;

(b) the Licensee may with the prior written consent of the Licensor (such consent not to be unreasonably withheld or delayed) Use the Licensed Program Materials on and in conjunction with any suitable replacement equipment (to be specified by type and serial number) if the use of the Licensed Program Materials on and in conjunction with the Equipment is permanently discontinued. Upon such consent being given the replacement equipment shall become the Equipment for the purposes of the Licence.

The use of the Licensed Program Materials on and in conjunction with such temporary or replacement equipment shall be at the sole risk and responsibility of the Licensee who shall indemnify the Licensor against any loss or damage sustained or incurred by the Licensor as a result. Without prejudice to the generality of the foregoing the Licensor shall not (unless otherwise agreed in writing by the Licensor) have any liability under Clauses 8 and 12 hereof in connection with such use.

[(4) The Licensee shall not without the prior written consent of the Licensor Use the Licensed Program Materials in any country except the countries specified in the Schedule.]

[**Note**: Some licences restrict use to a designated location, particularly if there are any applicable export restrictions.]

(5) The Licence shall not be deemed to extend to any programs or materials of the Licensor other than the Licensed Program Materials unless specifically agreed to in writing by the Licensor.

(6) The Licensee hereby acknowledges that it is licensed to use the Licensed Program Materials only in accordance with the express terms of this Agreement and not further or otherwise.

10 Duration of Licence

The Licence shall commence on the Acceptance Date and shall continue until terminated in accordance with clause 21 or as otherwise provided in this Agreement.

11 Proprietary rights [3.8]

(1) The Licensed Program Materials and the copyright and other intellectual property rights of whatever nature in the Licensed Programs Materials (including

any modifications made thereto) are and shall remain the property of the Licensor and the Licensor reserves the right to grant licences to use the Licensed Programs and/or the Program Documentation to third parties.

(2) The Licensee shall notify the Licensor immediately if the Licensee becomes aware of any unauthorised use of the whole or any part of the Licensed Program Materials by any person.

(3) The Licensee will permit the Licensor to check the use of the Licensed Program Materials by the Licensee at all reasonable times and for that purpose the Licensor shall be entitled to enter any of the Licensee's premises upon reasonable prior notice (and so that the Licensee hereby irrevocably licenses the Licensor, its employees and agents to enter any such premises for such purpose).

[Note: if the licensor suspects widespread abuse of its software, it may need to conduct a "dawn raid" with little if any notice to the licensee. It is arguable that, in such circumstances, "reasonable" notice may mean no notice at all.]

12 Intellectual property rights indemnity [3.8.1]

The Licensor shall indemnify the Licensee against any claim that the normal use or possession of the Licensed Program Materials infringes the [U.K] intellectual property rights of any third party provided that the Licensor is notified promptly in writing of any claim that the Licensor is given immediate and complete control of such claim, that the Licensee does not prejudice the Licensor's defence of such claim, that the Licensee gives the Licensor all reasonable assistance with such claim (at the cost of the Licensor) and that the claim does not arise as a result of the use of the Licensed Program Materials in combination with any equipment (other than the Equipment) [or programs] not supplied or approved by the Licensor or by reason of any alteration or modification which was not made by the Licensor or with its prior written consent. The Licensor shall have the right to replace or change all or any part of the Licensed Program Materials in order to avoid any infringement. The foregoing states the entire liability of the Licensor to the Licensee in respect of the infringement of the intellectual property rights of any third party.

[Note: Alternatively, use clause 26 of Precedent A appropriately amended. Sub-clause (3)(c) will read:
    "(c) if (a) or (b) cannot be accomplished on reasonable terms, refund the Licence Fee whereupon the Licence shall terminate".]

13 Confidentiality of Licensed Program Materials [3.8.1]

(1) The Licensee undertakes to treat as confidential and keep secret all Confidential Information contained or embodied in the Licensed Program Materials and the Specification and all Confidential Information conveyed to the Licensee by training (hereinafter collectively referred to as "the Information"), provided that this clause shall not extend to information which was rightfully in the possession of the Licensee prior to the Commencement of the negotiations leading to this Agreement, which is already public knowledge or becomes so at a future date (otherwise than as a result of a breach of this Clause) or which is trivial or obvious.

(2) The Licensee shall not without the prior written consent of the Licensor divulge any part of the Information to any person except:

  (a) the Licensee's own employees and then only to those employees who reasonably have a need to know the same;

(b) the Licensee's auditors, HM Inspector of Taxes, HM Customs & Excise and any other persons or bodies having a right duty or obligation to know the business of the Licensee and then only in pursuance of such right duty or obligation;

(c) any person who is from time to time appointed by the Licensee to maintain any equipment on which the Licensed Programs are being used (in accordance with the terms of the Licence) and then only to the extent necessary to enable such person properly to maintain such equipment.

(3) The Licensee undertakes to ensure that the persons and bodies mentioned in paragraphs (a), (b) and (c) of sub-clause (2) are made aware prior to the disclosure of any part of the Information that the same is confidential and that they owe a duty of confidence to the Licensor. The Licensee shall indemnify the Licensor against any loss or damage which the Licensor may sustain or incur as a result of the Licensee failing to comply with such undertaking.

[Note: In practice the licensee should obtain written acknowledgements from such persons. The licensee will then be able to demonstrate that he has complied with his undertaking.]

(4) The Licensee shall promptly notify the Licensor if it becomes aware of any breach of confidence by any person to whom the Licensee divulges all or any part of the Information and shall give the Licensor all reasonable assistance in connection with any proceedings which the Licensor may institute against such person for breach of confidence.

(5) The foregoing obligations as to confidentiality shall remain in full force and effect notwithstanding any termination of the Licence or this Agreement.

14 Copying [3.8.1]

(1) The Licensee may make only so many copies of the Licensed Programs as are reasonably necessary for operational security and for the Licensee's operational security at the location or for the use of the Licensed Programs. Such copies and the media on which they are stored shall be the property of the Licensor and the Licensee shall ensure that all such copies bear the Licensor's proprietary notices. The Licence shall apply to all such copies as it applies to the Licensed Programs.

(2) No copies may be made of the Program Documentation without the prior written consent of the Licensor.

15 Security and control

The Licensee shall during the continuance of the Licence:

(1) effect and maintain adequate security measures to safeguard the Licensed Program Materials from access or use by any unauthorised person;

(2) retain the Licensed Program Materials and all copies thereof under the Licensee's effective control;

(3) maintain a full and accurate record of the Licensee's copying and disclosure of the Licensed Program Materials and shall produce such record to the Licensor on request from time to time.

16 Alterations [3.5.1, 3.8.1]

EITHER

[(1) Except to the extent and in the circumstances expressly required to be permitted by the Licensor by law, the Licensee shall not alter, modify, adapt or translate the whole or any part of the Licensed Program Materials in any way whatsoever nor permit the whole or any part of the Licensed Programs to be combined with or become incorporated in any other computer programs nor decompile, disassemble or reverse engineer the same nor attempt to do any of such things.

(2) To the extent that [the law in the Licensee's jurisdiction] [local law] grants the Licensee the right to decompile the Licensed Programs in order to obtain information necessary to render the Licensed Programs interoperable with other computer programs used by the Licensee, the Licensor hereby undertakes to make that information readily available to the Licensee and the Licensee agrees to make such request of the Licensor before attempting to decompile the Licensed Programs. The Licensor shall have the right to impose reasonable conditions such as a reasonable fee for doing so. In order to ensure that the Licensee receives the appropriate information, the Licensee must first give the Licensor sufficient details of the Licensee's objectives and the other software concerned. Requests for the appropriate information should be given by notice to the Licensor in accordance with this Agreement.]

OR:

[(1) (a) The Licensee may modify the Licensed Program Materials at its own expense and responsibility. The Licensee shall indemnify the Licensor against any claim that such modifications infringe the intellectual property rights of any third party;

   (b) The copyright and other intellectual property rights of whatever nature in such modifications shall vest in the Licensor and the Licensee shall ensure that all such modifications bear the Licensor's proprietary notice. The Licensee hereby assigns (by way of future assignment) all such rights to the Licensor. The Licensee shall be entitled without further charge to use such modifications upon the same terms and conditions as the Licensed Program Materials but not further or otherwise. The Licence shall be extended accordingly;

   (c) The Licensee shall promptly notify the Licensor of all such modifications and shall supply to the Licensor without charge copies of all documentation relating to such modifications including specifications and source codes.

(2) The Licensee may combine, at its own expense and responsibility, the Licensed Programs with other programs to form a combined work. Any of the Licensed Programs included in the combined work shall continue to be subject to the terms and conditions contained herein. Where such other programs are the property of a third party the Licensee shall be responsible for obtaining all necessary consents to their use with the Licensed Programs. The Licensee shall indemnify the Licensor against any claim that the use of the Licensed Programs in combination with such

other programs infringes the intellectual property rights of any third party. Upon termination of the Licence, the Licensee shall completely remove the Licensed Programs from such combined work before returning or destroying the same in accordance with clause 21(4).

(3) The Licensor shall not be responsible for any error in the Licensed Programs or failure of the Licensed Programs to fulfil the Specification insofar as such error or failure occurs in or is caused by any part of the Licensed Programs being modified or combined by the Licensee with other programs as aforesaid.]

17 Software maintenance [9.1]

[The parties undertake to enter into a maintenance agreement on the Acceptance Date in respect of the Licensed Program Materials in the form of the draft annexed hereto.]

[Note: See Precedent L.]

ALTERNATIVELY

[Unless the Licensee enters into a software maintenance agreement with the Licensor on or before the Acceptance Date (on terms to be agreed between the parties) the Licensor will not provide any maintenance in respect of the Licensed Program Materials. If at a later date the Licensee wishes to receive the then current release of the Licensed Program Materials or maintenance therefor then the Licensor may at its option provide the same subject to the Licensee entering into a new licence agreement in respect of such release (and paying the Licensor's then current charge therefor) and (if applicable) entering into the Licensor's standard software maintenance agreement then in force.]

18 Operating manuals [3.7.3]

The Licensor shall provide the Licensee with 2 copies of a set of operating manuals for the Licensed Programs containing sufficient information to enable the Licensee to make use of all the facilities and functions set out in the Specification. If the Licensee requires further copies of such operating manuals then these may be obtained under licence from the Licensor in accordance with its standard scale of charges from time to time in force.

19 Training [3.7.3]

(1) The Licensor undertakes to provide training in the use of the Licensed Programs for the staff of the Licensee as set out in the Schedule.

(2) Any additional training required by the Licensee beyond the scope of that set out in the Schedule shall be provided by the Licensor in accordance with its standard scale of charges from time to time in force.

20 Licensee's confidential information [3.7.2]

The Licensor shall treat as confidential all Confidential Information supplied by the Licensee under this Agreement provided that this clause shall not extend to any information which was rightfully in the possession of the Licensor prior to the commencement of the negotiations leading to this Agreement or which is already public knowledge or becomes so at a future date (otherwise than as a result of a breach of this clause). The Licensor shall not divulge any of the Licensee's Confidential Information to any person except to its own employees and then only to those employees who need to know the same. The Licensor shall ensure that its employees are aware of and comply with the provisions of this clause. The foregoing obligations shall survive any termination of the Licence or this Agreement.

[**Note**: If real personal data is involved the bureau Data Protection clause [9] may also be relevant.]

21 Termination [3.4]

(1) The Licensee may terminate the Licence at any time by giving at least *30* days' prior written notice to the Licensor.

(2) The Licensor may terminate the Licence forthwith on giving notice in writing to the Licensee if:

(a) the Licensee commits any material breach of any term of this Agreement and (in the case of a breach capable of being remedied) shall have failed, within *30* days after the receipt of a request in writing from the Licensor so to do, to remedy the breach; or

(b) the Licensee shall have a receiver or administrative receiver appointed of it or over any part of its undertaking or assets or shall pass a resolution for winding up (otherwise than for the purpose of a bona fide scheme of solvent amalgamation or reconstruction) or a court of competent jurisdiction shall make an order to that effect or if the Licensee shall enter into any voluntary arrangement with its creditors or shall become subject to an administration order or shall cease to carry on business.

(3) Save as expressly provided in clause 21(2) or elsewhere in this Agreement, the Licence may not be terminated.

(4) Forthwith upon the termination of the Licence the Licensee shall return to the Licensor the Licensed Program Materials [including any modifications thereof made by the Licensee] and all copies of the whole or any part thereof or, if requested by the Licensor, shall destroy the same (in the case of the Licensed Programs by erasing them from the magnetic media on which they are stored) and certify in writing to the Licensor that they have been destroyed. The Licensee shall also cause the Licensed Programs to be erased from the Equipment and shall certify to the Licensor that the same has been done.

(5) Any termination of the Licence or this Agreement (howsoever occasioned) shall not affect any accrued rights or liabilities of either party nor shall it affect the coming into force or the continuance in force of any provision hereof which is expressly or by implication intended to come into or continue in force on or after such termination. For the avoidance of doubt, there shall be no refund of any element of the Licence Fee by reason of any termination by the Licensee.

22 Assignment

The Licensee shall not be entitled to assign, sub-license or otherwise transfer the Licence whether in whole or in part [save that the Licensee shall be entitled to assign the entire benefit of the Licence (but not part thereof) with the prior written consent of the Licensor (not to be unreasonably withheld or delayed) to any company which is from time to time a holding company or a subsidiary of the Licensee or a subsidiary of any such holding company (as those expressions are defined in section 736 of the Companies Act 1985) subject to such company first entering into a legally binding covenant with the Licensor undertaking to comply with the terms and conditions hereof and provided that at the time of such assignment such company shall be entitled to the exclusive possession of the Equipment (or such substituted equipment as is permitted under clause 9(3)(b)) for its own use and benefit].

[Note: The exception in brackets is designed to facilitate group reconstructions. However, outsourcing [11] is another matter. If the licensee is contemplating outsourcing it should raise this issue with the licensor before signing the agreement. The licensee may also wish to negotiate a right to assign to a purchaser of its business. The purchase of a corporate licensee's shares will not cause a problem as the identity of the licensee will not change. The licensor may however wish to reserve a right to consent to any proposed assignment etc so as to guard against the possibility of the software falling into the hands of a party likely to abuse it.]

23 *Force majeure*

See clause 15 of Precedent A.

24 Licensee's warranty

See clause 20 of Precedent A.

25 Liability

See clause 27 of Precedent A.

26 Waiver of remedies

See clause 28 of Precedent A.

27 Entire agreement

See clause 29 of Precedent A.

28 Notices

See clause 32 of Precedent A.

29 Interpretation

See clause 33 of Precedent A.

30 Law

See clause 34 of Precedent A.

[Note: If the governing law is changed to that of any of the States of the U.S., the Choice of Law clause should expressly exclude the application of the Uniform Computer Information Transactions Act.]

31 Disputes

See clause 35 of Precedent A or clause 37 of Precedent D.

32 Severability

See clause 36 of Precedent A.

33 Third Parties

See clause 37 of Precedent A.

EXECUTED under hand in two originals the day and year first before written

SIGNED for and on behalf of
SUPPLIER [LIMITED] [PLC]

By

Signature

Title

Witness

SIGNED for and on behalf of
CUSTOMER [LIMITED] [PLC]

By

Signature

Title

Witness

THE SCHEDULE

A THE EQUIPMENT

B LICENSED PROGRAMS

C LICENCE FEE

D DELIVERY DATE

E LOCATION

F STORAGE MEDIA

G COUNTRIES

H TRAINING

[**Note**: This section should identify for each operational function:
   (i) how many staff are to be trained in total;
  (ii) how many can be trained at one time;
 (iii) how many days' training is required for each person and function;
 (iv) where and when training is to take place;
  (v) who is to be responsible for subsistence and travelling expenses.]

ACCEPTANCE CERTIFICATE

TO: SOFTWARE HOUSE [LIMITED] [PLC]

FROM: CUSTOMER [LIMITED] [PLC]

Date: 20

Dear Sirs,

We refer to the agreement between our respective companies dated [   ] ("the Agreement") relating to the installation and licensing of certain computer programs ("the Licensed Programs") and confirm the following:

1 We have today accepted the Licensed Programs.

2 We have inspected the Licensed Programs and confirm that the same conform to the description contained in the Agreement and that the same have been installed on the Equipment (as defined in the Agreement) to our satisfaction.

3 The Licensed Programs have correctly processed the test data referred to in clause 6 of the Agreement. Copies of such data and the results of such tests are annexed hereto and signed by us for the purpose of identification.

SIGNED for and on behalf of
CUSTOMER [LIMITED] [PLC]

By

Signature

Title

Witness

COMMISSIONED SOFTWARE AGREEMENT

[**Note**: This agreement assumes that the client has commissioned and paid for a feasibility study by the systems house and that a detailed functional specification has been prepared and agreed.]

THIS AGREEMENT is made the   day of   20

PARTIES:

(1) SUPPLIER [LIMITED] [PLC] whose registered office is at

("the Systems House")

(2) CLIENT [LIMITED] [PLC] whose registered office is at

("the Client")

RECITAL:

The Systems House has agreed to write certain computer programs for the Client and to provide the other services hereinafter described upon the terms and conditions hereinafter contained

NOW IT IS HEREBY AGREED as follows:

1 Definitions

In this Agreement, unless the context otherwise requires, the following expressions have the following meanings:

"the Acceptance Date"   means the date on which the Programs are accepted (or deemed to be accepted) by the Client pursuant to clause 10.

"the Completion Date"   means the date specified in the Implementation Plan by which the Systems House is to provide the Programs Ready for Use, or such extended date as may be set pursuant to any provision of this Agreement.

[**Note**: When fixing the Completion Date the parties should allow sufficient time for acceptance testing.]

"Confidential Informa-   means all information obtained by one party from
tion"   the other pursuant to this Agreement which is expressly marked as confidential or which is manifestly of a confidential nature or which is confirmed in writing to be confidential within 7 days of its disclosure.

"the Equipment"   means the Client's computer hardware and associated peripherals equipment specified in Schedule 1 or such other equipment as may be agreed between the parties.

280

[**Note**: If performance criteria are relevant then any change in the configuration of the equipment ought to be agreed between the parties.]

"the Functional Specification"	means the functional specification [dated *July 31, 2000*] in accordance with which the Programs are to be written [a copy of which is annexed hereto].

[**Note**: For a document such as a functional specification which goes through several drafts, the date may serve to identify the relevant version. Alternatively, a specific version number can be referred to.]

"the Implementation Plan"	means the time schedule for the completion of the stages of preparation and delivery of the Programs as specified in Schedule 2.
["the Maximum Cost"	means the sum specified in Schedule 4.]

[**Note**: The definition of "the Maximum Cost" will only be required in the case of a time and materials contract, for which a limit has been agreed.]

"the Operating Manuals"	means the operating manuals to be prepared by the Systems House pursuant to clause 12.
["the Performance Criteria"	means the performance criteria which it is intended the Programs shall fulfil as specified in the Functional Specification subject to the tolerances, limitations and exceptions stated therein.]

[**Note**: See 3.3.2 of the text for suggested performance criteria.]

["the Price"	means the price to be paid by the Client for the Services as specified in Schedule 4.]

[**Note**: The definition of "the Price" will only be required in the case of a fixed price contract.]

"the Programs"	means the [applications] computer programs to be written by the Systems House pursuant to clause 4.
"Ready for Use"	means fully installed, and tested and accepted in accordance with clause 10.
"the Services"	means the services to be provided by the Systems House under this Agreement.
"the Staff"	has the meaning attributed thereto in clause 20.
"Stage"	means a stage of the Implementation Plan.
"the Training Plan"	means the training in the use of the Programs to be provided by the Systems House for the Client's staff the details of which are set out in Schedule 5.

2 Services to be provided [3.0.3, 3.1]

The Systems House hereby agrees to:

(1) write the Programs;

(2) successfully install the Programs on the Equipment;

(3) provide the Programs Ready for Use by the Completion Date; and

(4) provide Operating Manuals and training;

upon the terms and conditions hereinafter contained.

3 Systems House's acknowledgement

The Systems House acknowledges that the Programs are to be used by the Client in conjunction with the Equipment and [version X of] the client's existing *XYZ* operating system. The Systems House also acknowledges that it has been supplied with sufficient information about the Equipment and the said operating system to enable it to write the Programs in accordance with the Functional Specification for use with the Equipment and the said operating system. The Systems House shall not be entitled to any additional payment nor excused from any liability under this Agreement as a consequence of any misinterpretation by the Systems House of any matter or fact relating to the functions, facilities and capabilities of the Equipment or the said operating system.

[Note: if the system house is specifically relying upon the accuracy or adequacy of any client-provided information on materials, this should be specifically set out.]

4 Writing of programs [3.1]

The Systems House shall write a series of applications programs in [C language] [operating under [version V of] the Z database management system] which shall provide the facilities and functions set out in the Functional Specification [and shall fulfil the Performance Criteria]

[Note: It will be a sensible precaution to specify the language in which the programs are to be written; otherwise they may be written in an esoteric language which may be difficult for anyone else to understand and therefore to maintain and/or modify on the client's behalf. It may also be necessary to identify the database management system or other middleware, and even its version—especially if performance is an issue.]

5 Payment and expenses [3.0.3, 3.2]

EITHER (VERSION A Fixed price—payment by milestones):

[(1) The Price shall be paid as to *10* per cent upon the signing of this Agreement [(by way of a deposit)] [(by way of a part payment)] as to *x* per cent upon the completion of each Stage (by way of part payments) and as to *10* per cent on the Acceptance Date.]

[Note: Where payment is linked to stages the criteria for deciding when each stage is completed should be made clear in the Implementation Plan.]

OR (VERSION B Time and materials—subject to maximum price and retention):

(1)(a) The Client shall pay the Systems House for the time properly spent (which for the purposes of this Agreement [shall] [shall not] include any travelling time spent necessarily by the Staff in the course of providing the Services other than time spent travelling between the registered office of the Systems House and the registered office of the Client) and the materials [and computer time] properly used by the Staff in providing the Services on the terms and conditions set out below provided that the total amount payable to the Systems House for the Services shall not (save as expressly provided elsewhere in this Agreement) exceed the Maximum Cost;

[Note: Computer time is now less frequently chargeable as a separate item. Also, if the registered offices are not the relevant premises the premsies will need to be defined.]

(b) The time spent by the Staff in providing the Services shall be charged at the hourly rates specified in Schedule 6. Parts of an hour shall be charged on a pro-rata basis. [The Systems House shall ensure that those Staff engaged in providing any part of the Services shall not be unduly over-qualified or under-qualified to provide the same].

[Note: This clause assumes that the hourly charge out rates for the Staff include the cost of ancillary staff and overheads and a profit element. Other possibilities include daily rates, in which case it will be necessary to specify how many hours are included in a normal working day, and whether overtime will be chargeable in addition.]

(c) The rates of charge for materials [and computer time] shall be those specified in Schedule 6;

[(d) The Systems House shall be entitled at any time and from time to time to vary any or all of the rates referred to in paragraphs (b) and (c) above to accord with any change in its standard scale rates by giving to the Client not less than 30 days' prior written notice];

[Note: The systems house may also wish to reserve a right to adjust the Maximum Cost accordingly.]

(e) The Systems House shall maintain full and accurate records of the time spent and materials [and computer time] used by the Staff in providing the Services in a form to be approved in writing by the Client. The Systems House shall produce such records to the Client for inspection at all reasonable times on request;

(f) The Systems House shall render itemised invoices to the Client in respect of the said charges monthly in arrears. Each invoice shall specify the time spent by each member of the Staff and shall give a breakdown of the charges for materials [and computer time];

(g) Each invoice will be subject to a 10 per cent retention by the Client up to a maximum cumulative retention amount equal to 10 per cent of the Maximum Cost. The cumulative retention moneys shall be paid to the Systems House on the Acceptance Date.]

[Note: this assumes that the programs will all be subject to testing in one go; further splits may be required if there is to be a phased implementation.]

(2) If it shall be necessary for any of the Staff to visit the Client's premises or make any other journeys in the course of providing the Services, then the Client shall reimburse the Systems House for all reasonable travelling and subsistence expenses properly incurred in so doing. Apart from minor out-of-pocket expenses, claims for reimbursement of expenses shall be paid by the Client only if accompanied by the relevant receipts.

[(3) The Systems House advises the Client and the Client accepts that at the Completion Date the Programs will contain special software which will deny the Client the use of the Programs or part of the Programs in the event that the Client fails full to comply with sub-clause (1) of this clause. The Systems House undertakes to the Client immediately and completely to disable and remove such special software as soon as the Client complies fully with sub-clause (1) of this clause.]

[Note: For the validity of so-called logic bombs for non-payment, see 3.2.2.]

(4) All charges payable by the Client under this Agreement [other than the payments mentioned in sub-clause (1)] shall be due to be paid within *30* days after the receipt by the Client of the Systems House's invoice therefor.

[Note: Delete the bracketed phrase in sub-clause (4) if the time and materials basis is used.]

(5) All charges payable under this Agreement are exclusive of Value Added Tax which shall be paid by the Client at the rate and in the manner for the time being prescribed by law.

(6) If any sum payable under this Agreement is not paid within 7 days after the due date then (without prejudice to the Systems House's other rights and remedies) the Systems House reserves the right to charge interest on such sum on a day to day basis (as well after as before any judgment) from the date or last date for payment thereof to the date of actual payment (both dates inclusive) at the rate of *2* per cent above the base rate of *ABC* Bank plc (or such other London Clearing Bank as the Systems House may nominate) from time to time in force compounded quarterly. Such interest shall be paid on demand by the Systems House.

6 Implementation Plan and delays [3.2.1]

[Note:

(1) If a delay arises due to the fault of the systems house then the client should consider the payment terms of the agreement carefully. Where a fixed sum is payable in instalments linked to milestones, the client will not have to make any payment until the relevant milestone is reached. Where, however, payment is to be made on a time and materials basis the systems house will be entitled to payment for services performed during the period of the delay unless the agreement provides otherwise. If the systems house does cause a delay in breach of the agreement then the client will in any event be entitled to damages in relation to any loss which it can show has been caused, even if it does not seek to terminate the agreement. In order to create a degree of certainty, many clients seek to impose a regime of liquidated damages so as to make clear its entitlement to claim in the event of delay; see the variants of sub clause 6(2)(b), below.

(2) If a delay arises due to the fault of the client then in the case of a fixed price contract payable in instalments linked to milestones the systems house should seek a provision that payments should be made on the scheduled dates for completion even though actual completion is delayed. The systems house should also seek compensation for any other costs and losses arising out of the client's default including any additional time spent on rectifying errors caused by the client. Where payment is on a time and materials basis, work performed during the period of the delay will automatically be rewarded (subject to any maximum) but the systems house should make it clear that payment will be made for additional time spent on rectifying errors caused by the client.

(3) Where a delay is caused by *force majeure*, clause 28 will be brought into operation. In the event of *force majeure* the parties must decide whether payment is still to be linked to milestones or whether any additional or accelerated payment should be made or, if payment is on a time and materials basis what payment, if any, should be made for idle time. This is a difficult area of course because neither party is at fault. Clause 28 is drawn on the assumption that both parties will incur costs as a result of the delay and therefore provides that each party will bear its own costs. However, clause 28 gives either party a right to terminate in the event of a prolonged delay; the possibility of a termination should encourage the parties to reach a sensible compromise if they wish to continue with the contract. Clients should bear in mind that slippage at the beginning of a project is extremely rarely recovered before the end of the project.]

EITHER (VERSION A Fixed Price):

[(1) The Systems House undertakes to use its reasonable endeavours to complete each Stage by the date specified in the Implementation Plan but time shall not be of the essence in relation to such obligations.

[**Note**: The client will, of course, be primarily interested in the date on which the programs are finally completed and ready for operational use. However, a timetable for each stage of preparation will give the client an indication of how matters are progressing during the course of the contract.]

Systems House's default

(2) (a) The Systems House shall provide the Programs Ready for Use on or before the Completion Date;

(b) If the Systems House shall fail to provide the Programs Ready for Use by the Completion Date then the Systems House shall pay to the Client as and by way of liquidated damages for any loss or damage sustained by the Client resulting from delay during the period from the Completion Date to the date on which the Systems House provides the Programs Ready for Use the sum of £*500* for each week of such delay and pro rata for parts of a week up to a total maximum of £*5,000*. Subject to the provisions of paragraph (c) below, the payment of such sums shall be in full satisfaction of the Systems House's liability for loss suffered by the Client during such period of delay. The payment of liquidated damages shall not relieve the Systems House from its obligation to provide the Programs Ready for Use or from any other liability or obligation under this Agreement;

(c) If the Systems House shall fail to provide the Programs Ready for Use within *10* weeks after the Completion Date then, notwithstanding anything else contained in this Agreement, the Client shall be entitled to terminate this Agreement forthwith on giving written notice to the Systems House and to recover from the Systems House the amount of all [direct] damages and loss suffered by the Client resulting from such failure (provided that the Client shall give credit for all sums received by it pursuant to clause 6(2)(b), above). Upon such termination the Systems House shall (without prejudice to the Client's right to recover the amount of such damages and loss as aforesaid) forthwith refund to the Client all moneys previously paid to the Systems House under this Agreement.

[**Note**: refunds of sums previously paid may be contentious, as the client may still have received substantial benefit from the services performed, even if the programs were not completed on time.]

Client's default

(3) If the Systems House shall be prevented, hindered or delayed from performing any of its obligations under this Agreement by reason of any act or omission of the Client (other than a delay by the Client for which the Client is excused under clause 28) then, notwithstanding anything else contained in this Agreement:

(a) if as a result any Stage is not completed by the date specified in the Implementation Plan (or by any extended date granted pursuant to any provision of this Agreement) then the part payment due to be paid on the completion of that Stage shall be paid on the scheduled date for such completion (taking into account any extension of time granted pursuant to any provision of this Agreement) as distinct from the actual date of completion;

(b) the Client shall pay to the Systems House a reasonable sum in respect of any additional time spent and materials [and computer time] used by the Staff in rectifying any errors in the Programs or the Operating manuals and/or in providing the Services caused by such act or omission of the Client including without limitation the provision of any incorrect or inadequate information or data by the Client; and

(c) the Client shall pay to the Systems House all other reasonable costs, charges and losses sustained or incurred by the Systems House as a result of such act or omission (and for which the Systems House is not compensated pursuant to paragraph (a) and (b) above), and which can reasonably be substantiated by the Systems House.

The Systems House shall promptly notify the Client in writing of any claim which it may have under this sub-clause giving such particulars thereof as it is then able to provide.]

OR *(VERSION B Time and materials):*

[(1) *See sub-clause (1) of Version A.*

Systems House's default

(2) (a) The Systems House shall provide the Programs Ready for Use on or before the Completion Date;

(b) If the Systems House shall fail to provide the Programs Ready for Use by the Completion Date then the Systems House shall pay to the Client as and by way of liquidated damages for any loss or damage sustained by the Client resulting from delay during the period from the Completion Date to the date on which the Systems House provides the Programs Ready for Use the sum of £*500* for each week of such delay and pro rata for parts of a week up to a total maximum of £*5,000*. Subject to the provisions of paragraph (c) below, the payment of such sums shall be in full satisfaction of the Systems House's liability for loss suffered by the Client during such period of delay. The payment of liquidated damages shall not relieve the Systems House from its obligation to provide the Programs Ready for Use or from any other liability or obligation under this Agreement;

(c) If the Systems House shall fail to provide the Programs Ready for Use within [*10*] weeks after the Completion Date then notwithstanding anything else contained in this Agreement the Client shall be entitled to terminate this Agreement forthwith on giving written notice to the Systems House and to recover from the Systems House the amount of all [direct] damages and loss suffered by the Client resulting from such failure. [Upon such termination the Systems House shall (without prejudice to the Client's right to recover the amount of such damages and loss as aforesaid) forthwith refund to the Client all moneys previously paid to the Systems House under this Agreement.

[**Note**: refunds of sums previously paid may be contentious, as the client may still have received substantial benefit from the services performed, even if the programs were not completed on time.]

(3) If the Systems House shall fail to provide the Programs Ready for Use by the Completion Date then notwithstanding anything else contained in this Agreement

the Systems House shall not be entitled to any payment for the time spent and materials [and computer time] used by the Staff in providing any part of the Services after the Completion Date.

Client's default

(4) If the Systems House shall be prevented, hindered or delayed from performing any of its obligations under this Agreement by reason of any act or omission of the Client (other than a delay by the Client for which the Client is excused under clause 28) then, notwithstanding anything else contained in this Agreement:

(a) the Client shall pay the Systems House (at the rates specified in Schedule 6) for any additional time spent and materials [and computer time] used by the Staff in rectifying any errors in the Programs or the Operating Manuals caused by such act or omission of the Client including without limitation the provision of any incorrect or inadequate information or data by the Client; and

(b) the Client shall pay to the Systems House all other reasonable costs, charges and losses sustained or incurred by the Systems House which are attributable to such act or omission.

Any payments due under paragraphs (a) and (b) shall be paid notwithstanding that, when added to the other payments due under this Agreement, the resultant sum exceeds the Maximum Cost.

The Systems House shall promptly notify the Client in writing of any claim which it may have under this sub-clause giving such particulars thereof as it is then reasonably able to provide.]

7 Alterations [3.5.2]

(1) If at any time [before the completion of Stage *X*] the Client wishes to alter all or any part of the Programs then the Client shall provide the Systems House with full written particulars of such alterations and with such further information as the Systems House may reasonably require in connection with such proposed alterations.

[Note: Alterations which result in a significant reduction in the price may not be acceptable to the systems house which may require some control over such reductions.]

(2) The Systems House shall then submit to the Client as soon as reasonably practicable a full written quotation for such alterations specifying what changes (if any) will be required to [the Price] [the Maximum Cost] the Completion Date and the Implementation Plan and what adjustments will be required to the Functional Specification, [the Performance Criteria] the Operating Manuals and the Training Plan.

(3) Upon receipt of such quotation the Client may elect either:

(a) to accept such quotation, in which case this Agreement shall be amended in accordance therewith; or

(b) to withdraw the proposed alterations in which case this Agreement shall continue in force unchanged (subject to sub-clause (4) below).

(4) The Systems House shall be entitled to make a reasonable charge for considering such alterations and preparing the said quotation and if the Client's request for such alterations is subsequently withdrawn but results in a delay in the performance of the Services then the Systems House shall not be liable for such delay and shall be entitled to an extension of time for performing its obligations equal to the period of the delay.

(5) The Systems House shall not be obliged to consider or make any alterations to the Programs save in accordance with the aforesaid procedure. Pending agreement on any proposed alterations, both parties shall remain bound to comply with their obligations under the latest agreed version of this Agreement.

8 Changes to the Functional Specification and Operating Manuals

If any alterations are made to the Programs pursuant to clause 7 then the Systems House shall make appropriate modifications to the Functional Specification, the Operating Manuals and the Training Plan to reflect such alterations. The provisions of this Agreement shall then apply to the Functional Specification, the Operating Manuals and the Training Plan as so modified. The cost of such modifications shall be included in the quotation given under clause 7.

9 Delivery and installation [3.3]

The Systems House shall at the agreed Stage:

(1) deliver to the Client:

   (a) one copy of the object code of the Programs in machine-readable form on the storage media specified in Schedule 7;
   (b) certified copies of the test data and results of tests carried out by the Systems House on all parts of the Programs prior to delivery;
   (c) the Operating Manuals.

(2) successfully install the Programs on the Equipment.

10 Testing and acceptance [3.3.1]

(1) On or before the completion of Stage P the Client shall submit to the Systems House test data which in the reasonable opinion of the Client is suitable to test whether the Programs are in accordance with the Functional Specification [and the Performance Criteria] together with the results expected to be achieved by processing such test data on the Equipment using the Programs and [version X of] the Client's *XYZ* operating system. The Systems House shall not be entitled to object to such test data or expected results unless the Systems House can demonstrate to the Client that they are not in accordance with the Functional Specification [and/or the Performance Criteria], in which event the Client shall make such amendments to such test data and expected results as may be necessary for them to conform to the Functional Specification [and the Performance Criteria].

(2) After the Programs have been successfully installed on the Equipment, the Systems House shall give to the Client at least 7 days' prior written notice (or such shorter notice as may be agreed between the parties) of the date ("the Testing Date') on which the Systems House will be ready to attend acceptance tests at the Client's premises. The Client and the Systems House shall attend such tests on the

Testing Date and shall provide all necessary facilities to enable such tests to be carried out.

(3) On the Testing Date the Client shall process, in the presence of the authorised representatives of the Systems House, the said test data on the Equipment using the Programs and the said *XYZ* operating system. The Systems House shall if required by the Client give the Client's personnel all reasonable assistance in processing such test data.

(4) The Client shall accept the Programs immediately after the Programs have correctly processed such test data by achieving the expected results.

(5) The Programs shall not be deemed to have incorrectly processed such test data by reason of any failure to provide any facility or function not specified in the Functional Specification.

(6) If the Programs shall fail to process such test data correctly then repeat tests shall be carried out on the same terms and conditions within a reasonable time thereafter but in any event no later than *14* days thereafter. [The Systems House shall not be entitled to make any charge for attending such repeat tests.]

[**Note**: The words in brackets will be needed only in the case of a time and materials contract.]

(7) If such repeat tests demonstrate that the Programs are still not in accordance with the Functional Specification [or the Performance Criteria] then the Client may by written notice to the Systems House elect at its sole option:

(a) to fix (without prejudice to its other rights and remedies) a new date for carrying out further tests on the Programs on the same terms and conditions as the repeat tests (save that all reasonable costs which the Client may incur as a result of carrying out such tests shall be reimbursed by the Systems House). If the Programs shall fail such further tests then the Client shall be entitled to proceed under paragraph (b) or (c) below; or

(b) to accept the Programs subject to an abatement of [the Price] [the total consideration payable hereunder] such abatement to be such amount as, taking into account the circumstances, is reasonable. In the absence of written agreement as to abatement within *14* days after the date of such notice the Client shall be entitled to reject the Programs in accordance with paragraph (c) below; or

(c) to reject the Programs as not being in conformity with this Agreement in which event this Agreement shall automatically terminate [and the Systems House shall (without prejudice to the Client's other rights and remedies) forthwith refund to the Client all sums previously paid to the Systems House under this Agreement].

[**Note**: As previously stated, a refund of all monies paid may not be appropriate if notwithstanding termination, the client has acquired benefit from the services previously provided. Clause 6(2)(c).]

(8) Notwithstanding anything else contained in this Clause, the Systems House shall be entitled (provided it has complied with its obligations under this Clause) at any time and from time to time after the Testing Date to serve written notice on the Client requiring the Client to identify any part of the Functional Specification [or

the Performance Criteria] which the Programs do not fulfil. If the Client shall fail to identify in writing to the Systems House within *14* days after the receipt of such notice any part of the Functional Specification [or the Performance Criteria] which the Programs do not fulfil then the Client shall be deemed to have accepted the Programs.

(9) If at any time the Client shall commence live running of the whole or any part of the Programs (as distinct from acceptance testing) then the Client shall be deemed to have accepted the Programs.

(10) For the avoidance of doubt, "acceptance' shall denote that, at the relevant date, the Programs were in apparent compliance with the Functional Specification [and the Performance Criteria] but shall not operate as a form of waiver of any claim which either party may have against the other.

[**Notes**: (1) Sub-clauses (8) and (9) are designed to protect the systems house in the event that the customer unreasonably refuses to accept the programs.

(2) In a complicated development, testing and acceptance will be undertaken in stages with a final contractual acceptance at the end.

(3) The systems house may seek relief in relation to failures of acceptance tests which can be shown to result directly from user input in relation to the interpretation of functional or user requirements. Such instances however, will be rare, and the customer will usually resist such a clause on the basis that the systems house may seek to use it as a general "get out".]

11 Warranty [3.3.3]

(1) (a) The Systems House warrants that the Programs will after acceptance by the Client provide the facilities and functions set out in the Functional Specification [and will fulfil the Performance Criteria] when properly used with the Equipment and [version *X* of] the said Client's *XYZ* operating system and that the Operating Manuals and the Training Plan will provide adequate instruction to enable the Client to make full and proper use of the Programs in conjunction with the Equipment and the said operating system without the need for reference to any other person or document;

(b) If the Systems House receives written notice from the Client after the Acceptance Date of any breach of the said warranty then the Systems House shall at its own expense and within a reasonable time after receiving such notice remedy the defect or error in question provided that the Systems House shall have no liability or obligations under the said warranty unless it shall have received written notice of the defect or error in question no later than the expiry of *12* months after the Acceptance Date;

(c) The Systems House's primary obligation under the said warranty is to remedy breaches thereof by the provision of materials and services within a reasonable time and without charge to the Client, provided that the Systems House shall fail to comply with such obligations its liability for such failure shall be limited to [a sum equal to the Price] [£   ]. The foregoing states the entire liability of the Systems House, whether in contract, tort or howsoever for defects and errors in the Programs and the Operating Manuals which are notified to the Systems House after the Acceptance Date.

[**Note**: Where a maintenance agreement is entered into (see clause 16) sub-clause (1) will need to be amended—follow clause 25 of Precedent O.]

(2) See Clause 19(5) of Precedent A.

12 Operating Manuals [3.7.3]

The Systems House shall prepare and provide the Client with *2* copies of a set of operating manuals containing sufficient information to enable the Client to make full and proper use of the Programs in conjunction with the Equipment and the Client's *XYZ* operating system. [If the Client requires further copies of the Operating Manuals then these will be supplied by the Systems House under licence at a reasonable charge.]

[Note: If copyright in the operating manuals is to pass to the client then the bracketed sentence will not be required.]

13 Training [3.7.3]

(1) The Systems House undertakes to provide training in the use of the Programs for the Client's staff in accordance with the Training Plan.

(2) Any additional training required by the Client shall be provided by the Systems House upon reasonable notice in accordance with its standard scale of charges from time to time in force.

14 Proprietary rights [3.8.2]

EITHER (VERSION A Rights retained by the Systems House):

[(1) The copyright and all other intellectual property rights of whatever nature in the Programs, the Operating Manuals, the Functional Specification and in all other specifications and documentation relating to the Programs (other than in any pre-existing materials provided by the Client) shall be and shall remain vested in the Systems House.

(2) The Systems House hereby grants to the Client with effect from the Acceptance Date a non-exclusive and non-transferable licence to use and copy the Programs and the Operating Manuals for its own internal business purposes but for no other purpose whatsoever. The Client shall not be entitled to sub-license the use of the whole or any part of the Programs or the Operating Manuals.

[Notes:

    (1) The client may wish to reserve a right to assign the licence to another member of its group of companies—see clause 22 of Precedent C.

    (2) The systems house may wish to impose a more restricted right to use the programs in which case incorporate all relevant clauses of Precedent C.

    (3) The client may accept a non-exclusive licence in return for the systems house undertaking to refrain from making the programs available to any of the client's competitors.]

(3) The Systems House and the Client shall enter into a source code deposit agreement on the Acceptance Date in respect of the Programs in the form of the draft annexed hereto and the Systems House shall procure that the third party named therein shall enter into such agreement.

[Notes:

    (1) Adapt Precedent N for use with a single user.

    (2) The alternative would be for the source codes to be made available to the client immediately against an undertaking only to use them for the purposes of maintenance, but this may entail a loss of control for the systems house.]

(4) (a) The Client undertakes to treat as confidential and keep secret all information contained or embodied in the Programs, the Operating Manuals, the Functional Specification and in all other specifications and documentation relating to the Programs and all information conveyed to the Client by training (hereinafter collectively referred to as "the Information").

(b) The Client shall not without the prior written consent of the Systems House divulge any part of the Information to any person except:

(i) the Client's own employees and then only to those employees who need to know the same;

(ii) the Client's auditors, HM Inspector of Taxes, HM Customs & Excise and any other persons or bodies having a right, duty or obligation to know the business of the Client and then only in pursuance of such right duty or obligation;

(iii) any person who is from time to time appointed by the Client to maintain any equipment on which the Programs are being used (in accordance with the terms of the licence granted pursuant to sub-clause (2)) and then only to the extent necessary to enable such person properly to maintain such equipment;

(iv) any professional adviser of the Client in connection with a dispute arising from this Agreement or the Client's use of the Programs.

(c) The Client undertakes to ensure that the persons and bodies mentioned in sub-paragraphs (i), (ii), (iii) and (iv) of paragraph (b) are made aware prior to the disclosure of any part of the Information that the same is confidential and that they owe a duty of confidence to the Systems House. The Client shall indemnify the Systems House against any loss or damage which the Systems House may sustain or incur as a result of the Client failing to comply with such undertaking.

[**Note**: In practice the client should obtain written acknowledgements from such persons. The client will then be able to demonstrate that he has complied with his undertaking.]

(d) The Client shall promptly notify the Systems House if it becomes aware of any breach of confidence by any person to whom the Client divulges all or any part of the Information and shall give the Systems House all reasonable assistance in connection with any proceedings which the Systems House may institute against such person for breach of confidence.

(e) The foregoing obligations as to confidentiality shall remain in full force and effect notwithstanding any termination of the licence granted pursuant to sub-clause (2) or this Agreement.]

OR (VERSION B Rights to vest in the Client):

[(1) Subject to any intellectual property rights subsisting in any materials whether provided by the Systems House or by any third party licensor which said materials are used by the Systems House in order to fulfil the Services ("the Special Materials"), the copyright and all other intellectual property rights of whatever nature in the Programs, the Operating Manuals, the Functional Specification and in all other specifications and documentation relating to the Programs shall pass to the Client on the Acceptance Date. If any Special Materials are provided in conjunction with the Programs, the Operating Manuals and/or the Functional Specification, they shall be licensed to the Client, such licence being to such extent as is necessary to enable the Client to make the envisaged use of the Programs, the Operating Manuals and/or the Functional Specification.

[**Note**: The effect of sub-clause (1) will be to make this agreement an agreement for the sale of copyright thereby attracting *ad valorem* stamp duty under section 59 of the Stamp Act 1891. Where appropriate a certificate of value should be incorporated.]

[(2) Notwithstanding sub-clause (1), the Systems House reserves the right to use in any way it thinks fit any programming tools, skills and techniques acquired or used by the Systems House in the performance of this Agreement.]

(3) The Systems House shall treat as Confidential Information all information contained or embodied in the Programs (and in any documentation relating thereto, including source code), the Operating Manuals and the Functional Specification and shall not disclose the whole or any part of such information to any third party without the prior written consent of the Client. The Systems House shall ensure that its employees comply with the provisions of this sub-clause. The foregoing obligations shall survive any termination of this Agreement, but shall not extend to the Special Materials.

(4) The Systems House shall deliver to the Client on the Acceptance Date:

(a) the source code of the Programs in the form both of printed listings and magnetic [tape] [disk];

(b) the Operating Manuals;

(c) all other materials necessary to enable a reasonably skilled programmer to correct, modify and enhance the Programs without reference to any other person or document.]

[**Note**: If the systems house is to maintain the programs then it will need to retain copies of the source code for maintenance purposes.]

15 Indemnity

(1) The Client will indemnify the Systems House against all costs, claims, demands, expenses and liabilities of whatsoever nature arising out of or in connection with any claim that the use by the Systems House of any information or material supplied by the Client for the purpose of enabling the Systems House to prepare and write the Programs and/or the Operating Manuals infringes the intellectual property rights (of whatever nature) of any third party. Subject to the foregoing, the Systems House shall likewise indemnify the Client against all costs, claims, demands, expenses and liabilities of whatsoever nature arising out of or in connection with any claim that the Services provided by the Systems House infringe the intellectual property rights (of whatever nature) of any third party.

EITHER (VERSION A Rights Retained by the Systems House):

[(2) The indemnities granted pursuant to this clause 15 shall be subject to the indemnifying party being granted immediate and complete control of such claim, the indemnified party not prejudicing the indemnifying party's defence of the claim, the indemnified party giving the indemnifying party all reasonable assistance with such claim (at the expense of the indemnifying party) and, in the case of the indemnity granted by the Systems House, to the claim not arising as a result of any alteration or modification to the Programs, the Operating Manuals, the functional Specification or other materials provided by the Systems House which was not made or expressly approved in writing by the Systems House.]

OR (VERSION B Rights to vest in the Client):

(2) The indemnities granted pursuant to this clause 15 shall be subject to the indemnifying party being granted immediate and complete control of such claim, the indemnified party not prejudicing the indemnifying party's defence of the claim, and the indemnified party giving the indemnifying party all reasonable assistance with such claim (at the expense of the indemnifying party).]

[16 Maintenance [9.1]

The parties undertake to enter into a maintenance agreement on the Acceptance Date in respect of the Programs and the Operating Manuals in the form of the draft annexed hereto.]

[Note: See Precedent M.]

17 Representatives [3.6.1, 3.7.1]

Each party shall nominate in writing upon the signing of this Agreement the person who will act as its representative for the purposes of this Agreement and who will be responsible for providing any information which may be required by the other party to perform its obligations hereunder.

18 Progress meetings

The parties shall procure that their respective representatives will meet at least once a month between the date hereof and the Acceptance Date to discuss and minute the progress of the Services.

[Note: Minute taking is a laborious but useful exercise especially if a dispute arises. More extensive meeting obligations (*e.g.* of steering groups, project boards, etc) may be required for larger projects.]

19 Client's Responsibilities to provide Information [3.6.1]

(1) Without prejudice to the provisions of clause 3 the Client shall provide all information and documentation reasonably requested by the Systems House to enable the Systems House to prepare and write the Programs and the Operating Manuals. Such information and documentation shall be subject to the provisions of confidentiality contained in clause 21.

(2) The Client shall ensure that it provides the Systems House with such access to its staff as may be reasonably required for the purposes of the provision of the Services.

20 The Staff [3.7.1]

The Services shall be provided by the employees of the Systems House named in Schedule 3 or such other persons as may be approved by the Client in writing from time to time ("the Staff"), such approval not to be unreasonably withheld or delayed.

[Note: If particular systems house staff are seen as being crucial to the success of the project, the client may seek commitments that they will work full time on the project and/or not be removed from it without the client's consent.]

21 Confidentiality [3.7.2]

(1) Each party shall treat as confidential all Information obtained from the other pursuant to this Agreement and shall not divulge such Confidential Information to any person (except to such party's own employees and then only to those employees who need to know the same) without the other party's prior written consent provided that this clause shall not extend to information which was rightfully in the possession of such party prior to the commencement of the negotiations leading to this Agreement, which is already public knowledge or becomes so at a future date (otherwise than as a result of a breach of this clause) or which is trivial or obvious. Each party shall ensure that its employees are aware of and comply with the provisions of this clause. If the Systems House shall appoint any sub-contractor then the Systems House may disclose Confidential Information to such sub-contractor subject to such sub-contractor giving the Client an undertaking in similar terms to the provisions of this clause. The foregoing obligations as to confidentiality shall survive any termination of this Agreement.

[**Note**: Pre-contract disclosures should, of course, be covered by a separate confidentiality—undertaking—see Precedent Z.]

(2) The Systems House will establish and maintain such security measures and procedures as are reasonably practicable to provide for the safe custody of the Client's Confidential Information and data in its possession and to prevent unauthorised access thereto or use thereof.

[**Note**: If real personal data is involved, the bureau Data Protection Clause [P15] may also be relevant.]

[22 Computer facilities [3.6.1]

The Client agrees to provide the Systems House free of charge during the Client's normal working hours (or during such other times as the Client may agree in writing) with such reasonable computer facilities (including computer consumables, storage and data preparation facilities) and time on the Equipment as may be necessary to enable the Systems House to prepare, write, test and install the Programs]

[**Notes:**

   (1) This will be an alternative to the systems house using its own facilities.

   (2) The client may wish to insure against the possibility of failure of its equipment giving rise to a delay in completing the work.]

[23 Office facilities [3.6.1]

The Client undertakes to provide the Staff with such desks, word processing, copying and other office facilities at the Client's premises as may be reasonably necessary to enable the Systems House to fulfil its obligations under this Agreement.]

[24 Dress and conformity [3.7.1]

While the Staff attend at the Client's premises they will conform to the Client's normal codes of staff, health and safety and security practice.]

[25 Poaching staff [3.6.2]

The Client shall not without the prior written consent of the Systems House (and so that each of sub-clauses (1) and (2) below shall be deemed to constitute a separate agreement and shall be construed independently of the other):

(1) at any time during the period from the date hereof to the expiry of six months after the Acceptance Date or the date of termination of this Agreement (as the case may be) solicit or endeavour to entice away from or discourage from being employed by the Systems House any person who is, or shall at any time between the date hereof and the Acceptance Date or the date of such termination be, one of the Systems House's employees engaged in providing the Services provided however that this provision shall not apply to any person employed by the Systems House whose rate of gross basic contractual remuneration payable by the Systems House as at the date of this Agreement (or as at the date of commencement of such person's employment if such employment shall commence after the date of this Agreement) is less than £25,000 per annum;

(2) at any time during the period from the date hereof to the expiry of six months after the Acceptance Date or the date of termination of this Agreement (as the case may be) employ or attempt to employ any person who is, or shall at any time between the date hereof and the Acceptance Date or the date of such termination be, one of the Systems House's employees engaged in providing the Services provided however that this provision shall not apply to any person employed by the Systems House whose rate of gross basic contractual remuneration payable by the Systems House as at the date of this Agreement (or as at the date of commencement of such person's employment if such employment shall commence after the date of this Agreement) is less than £25,000 per annum.]

26 Termination [3.4]

Notwithstanding anything else contained herein, this Agreement may be terminated:

(1) by the Systems House forthwith on giving notice in writing to the Client if the Client shall fail to pay any sum due under the terms of this Agreement (otherwise than as a consequence of any default on the part of the Systems House) and such sum remains unpaid for *14* days after written notice from the Systems House that such sum has not been paid (such notice to contain a warning of the Systems House's intention to terminate); or

(2) by either party forthwith on giving notice in writing to the other if the other commits any [material] [serious] breach of any term of this Agreement (other than any failure by the Client to make any payment hereunder in which event the provisions of sub-clause (1) above shall apply) and (in the case of a breach capable of being remedied) shall have failed, within *30* days after the receipt of a request in writing from the other party so to do, to remedy the breach (such request to contain a warning of such party's intention to terminate); or

(3) by either party forthwith on giving notice in writing to the other if the other party shall have a receiver or administrative receiver appointed of it or over any part of its undertaking or assets or shall pass a resolution for winding-up (otherwise than for the purpose of a bona fide scheme of solvent amalgamation or reconstruction) or a court of competent jurisdiction shall make an order to that effect or if the other party shall become subject to an administration order or shall enter into any voluntary

arrangement with its creditors or shall cease or threaten to cease to carry on business; or

(4) by the Client by giving to the Systems House not less than *30* days' written notice of termination to expire on the scheduled date for completion of any Stage (taking into account any extensions of time granted pursuant to any provision hereof). Upon such termination the Client shall immediately pay to the Systems House all sums accrued due to the Systems House hereunder and any reasonable costs or expenses incurred by it by reason of such early termination (provided always) that the Systems House will use all reasonable endeavours to avoid or mitigate such costs or expenses.

27 Effects of termination

(1) Any termination of this Agreement (howsoever occasioned) shall not affect any accrued rights or liabilities of either party nor shall it affect the coming into force or the continuance in force of any provision hereof which is expressly or by implication intended to come into or continue in force on or after such termination.

(2) Upon any termination of this Agreement by the Client pursuant to clause 26(2) or 26(3) the Systems House shall forthwith deliver to the Client all specifications, programs (including source codes) and other documentation relating to the preparation and writing of the Programs and the Operating Manuals existing at the date of such termination whether or not the same shall be complete. In the event of such termination the copyright and other intellectual property rights in and ownership of all such material shall forthwith automatically pass to the Client [(subject always to the reservation of rights and licence granted in respect of Special Materials, as provided in clause 14)] who shall be entitled to enter any premises of the Systems House for the purpose of taking possession of such material (and so that the Systems House hereby irrevocably licenses the Client, its employees and agents to enter any such premises for such purpose).

[**Note**: If the systems house defaults or goes into liquidation the client will usually wish to terminate the agreement and appoint another systems house to complete the work as quickly as possible. This clause enables the client to obtain all documentation relating to the programs and to hand it to the new systems house for the purpose of completing the work.]

(3) Upon any termination of this Agreement (howsoever occasioned) the Systems House shall forthwith deliver up to the Client all copies of any information and data supplied to the Systems House by the Client for the purposes of this Agreement and shall certify to the Client that no copies of such information or data have been retained, save that the Systems House may retain one copy of any material upon which its services were based for audit purposes, provided that such material remains subject to the obligations of confidentiality contained in clause 21 of this Agreement.

28 *Force majeure*

See clause 15 of Precedent A.

(2) In the event of any extension of time being granted pursuant to sub-clause (1) the Implementation Plan shall be amended accordingly.

[29 Further assurance

The parties shall execute and do all such further deeds, documents and things as may be necessary to carry the provisions of this Agreement into full force and effect.]

[**Note**: This clause should be incorporated where Version B of clause 14(1) is used. The client will then be able to require the systems house to execute any further documents which may be necessary fully to vest the proprietary rights to the programs in the client.]

30 Liability

(1) The Systems House shall indemnify the Client and keep the Client fully and effectively indemnified on demand against any loss of or damage to any property or injury to or death of any person caused by any negligent act or omission or wilful misconduct of the Systems House, its employees, agents or sub-contractors.

(2) The Client shall indemnify the Systems House and keep the Systems House fully and effectively indemnified on demand against any loss of or damage to any property or injury to or death of any person caused by any negligent act or omission or wilful misconduct of the Client, its employees, agents or sub-contractors.

(3) Except in respect of injury to or death of any person (for which no limit applies), and/or in relation to any claim to which the limitation set out in clause 11(1)(c) applies the respective liability of the Systems House and the Client under sub-clauses (1) and (2) in respect of each event or series of connected events shall not exceed £500,000.

[**Note**: Some contracts specifically require the parties to back up their indemnities and/or prospective liabilities with insurance. Others seek to link the limit on liability with the value of the contract, although the effectiveness of this approach for the purposes of the Unfair Contract Terms Act 1977 has not been proved.]

[(4) Notwithstanding anything else contained in this Agreement the Systems House shall not be liable to the Client for loss of profits or contracts or other indirect or consequential loss whether arising from negligence, breach of contract or howsoever.]

(5) The Systems House shall not be liable to the Client for any loss arising out of any failure by the Client to keep full and up-to-date security copies of the computer programs and data it uses in accordance with best computing practice.

31 Waiver of remedies

See clause 28 of Precedent A.

32 Entire agreement

See clause 29 of Precedent A.

33 Sub-contracts

See clause 31 of Precedent A.

34 Notices

See clause 32 of Precedent A.

35 Interpretation

See clause 33 of Precedent A.

36 Law

See clause 34 of Precedent A.

37 Disputes

Any dispute which may arise between the parties concerning this Agreement shall be determined as follows:

(1) if the dispute shall be of a technical nature concerning the interpretation of the Functional Specification or relating to the functions or capabilities of the Programs or any similar or related matter then such dispute shall be referred for final settlement to an expert nominated jointly by the parties or, failing such nomination with *14* days after either party's request to the other therefor, nominated at the request of either party by the President from time to time of the British Computer Society. Such expert shall be deemed to act as an expert and not as an arbitrator. His decision shall (in the absence of clerical or manifest error) be final and binding on the parties and his fees for so acting shall be borne by the parties in equal shares unless he determines that the conduct of either party is such that such party should bear all of such fees;

(2) in any other case the dispute shall be determined by the High Court of Justice in England and the parties hereby submit to the exclusive jurisdiction of that court for such purpose.

38 Severability

See clause 36 of Precedent A.

39 Third Parties [1.3]

See clause 37 of Precedent A.

EXECUTED under hand in two originals the day and year first before written

SIGNED for and on behalf of SUPPLIER
[LIMITED] [PLC]

By

Signature

Title

Witness

SIGNED for and on behalf of
CLIENT [LIMITED] [PLC]

By

Signature

Title

Witness

SCHEDULE 1

THE EQUIPMENT

SCHEDULE 2

IMPLEMENTATION PLAN

[Note: This Schedule should show each stage of the preparation of the Programs and the scheduled completion date for each stage. Each stage should be as detailed as possible and should specify what will happen and what will be produced on the completion thereof.]

SCHEDULE 3

SYSTEMS HOUSE'S PERSONNEL

SCHEDULE 4

[THE PRICE] [THE MAXIMUM COST]

SCHEDULE 5

TRAINING PLAN

[Note: This schedule should identify for each operational function:
    (i) how many staff are to be trained in total;

    (ii) how many can be trained at one time;

    (iii) how many days' training is required for each person and function;

    (iv) where and when training is to take place;

    (v) who is to be responsible for subsistence and travelling expenses.]

SCHEDULE 6

CHARGING RATES

[Note: The Client should agree the following with the Systems House:
    (a) Hourly rate for each individual or staff category;

    (b) Rates of charge for materials and computer time.

If charging by the day the number of hours in a working day should be specified.]

SCHEDULE 7

STORAGE MEDIA

SCHEDULE 8

SUB-CONTRACTS

[SCHEDULE 9

THIRD-PARTY RIGHTS]

"SHRINK-WRAP"/"CLICK-WRAP" LICENCE
[4.3.1, 5.3.6.4]

LICENCE AGREEMENT

EITHER (VERSION A Shrink-wrap):

The copyright and other intellectual property rights in this software ("the Software") and its associated documentation are owned by [   ] ("the Owner"). By opening this package you (an individual or legal entity) agree with the Owner to be bound by the terms of this Agreement which will govern your use of the Software. If you do not accept these terms you may within *14* days of purchase return the Software, its packaging and documentation unused and intact to your supplier together with proof of purchase for a full refund.

[**Note**: This text should be put under the shrink-wrap transparent cover but in such a way as to be visible.]

OR (VERSION B Click-wrap):

The copyright and other intellectual property rights in this software ("the Software") and its associated documentation are owned by [   ] ("the Owner"). Please read through the following licence conditions. If you agree to be bound by them please click YES at the end of the conditions at which point the software will be loaded onto your computer. If you do not agree to be bound by these terms the software will not be loaded onto your computer. Please then return the disk, packaging and documentation to your supplier for a refund of any Licence fee paid, provided that the supplier reserves the right to withhold some or all of the refund if such disk, packaging or documentation has been damaged in any way.

[**Note**: This text should be a read-me file visible to the user as soon as he attempts to load the software.]

1. Licence

You are permitted to:

    (1) load the Software into and use it on a single computer which is under your control and which meets the specifications referred to in the front of the packaging containing the Software;

    (2) transfer the Software from one computer to another provided it is used on only one computer at any one time;

    (3) use the Software on a computer network provided you have purchased such number of copies of the Software equal to the maximum number of copies of the Software in use on that network at any one time;

    (4) make up to *3* copies of the Software for back-up purposes only in support of the permitted use. The copies must reproduce and include the Owner's

copyright notice. Such copies and the media on which they are stored shall be the property of the Owner and this Agreement shall apply to all such copies as it applies to the Software;

[**Note**: This may not be possible if the software is "copy protected".]

(5) transfer the Software (complete with all its associated documentation) and the benefit of this Agreement to another person provided he has agreed to accept the terms of this Agreement and you contemporaneously transfer all copies of the Software you have made to that person or destroy all copies not transferred. If any transferee does not accept such terms then this Agreement shall automatically terminate. The transferor does not retain any rights under this Agreement in respect of the transferred Software.

You are not permitted:

(a) to load the Software on to a network server for the purposes of distribution to one or more other computer(s) on that network or to effect such distribution (such use requiring a separate licence);

(b) except as expressly permitted by this Agreement and save to the extent and in the circumstances expressly permitted by law, to rent, lease, sub-license, loan, copy, modify, adapt, merge, translate, reverse engineer, decompile, disassemble or create derivative works based on the whole or any part of the Software or its associated documentation or use, reproduce or deal in the Software or any part thereof in any way.

[To the extent that local law gives you the right to decompile the Software in order to obtain information necessary to render the Software interoperable with other computer programs, the Owner hereby undertakes to make that information readily available to you. The Owner shall have the right to impose reasonable conditions such as a reasonable fee for doing so. In order to ensure that you receive the appropriate information, you must first give the Owner sufficient details of your objectives and the other software concerned. Requests for the appropriate information should be made to [   ].]

2. Term

This Agreement is effective until you terminate it by destroying the Software and its documentation together with all copies. It will also terminate if you fail to abide by its terms. Upon termination you agree to destroy all copies of the Software and its documentation including any Software stored on the hard disk of any computer under your control. The media on which such copies resided will after destruction of the copies residing on them revert to you.

3. Ownership

You own only the diskette (or authorised replacement) on which the Software is recorded. You may retain the diskette on termination of this Agreement provided the Software has been erased. The Owner shall at all times retain ownership of the Software as recorded on the original diskette and all subsequent copies thereof regardless of form. This Agreement applies to the grant of the licence contained herein only and not to the contract of sale of the diskette. The Owner's warranties and telephone support service under this Agreement are available only to the original registered user (being the person who has signed and returned duly completed the enclosed Licence Registration Form to the Owner within *30* days after the date of original purchase).

4. Warranties

The Owner warrants that the diskette on which the Software is supplied will be free from defects in materials and workmanship under normal use for a period of *90* days after the date of original purchase ("the Warranty Period"). If a defect in the diskette shall occur during the Warranty Period it may be returned with proof of purchase and (so far as you are able) a documented example of such defect or error to the Owner who will replace it free of charge.

The Owner warrants that the Software will perform substantially in accordance with its accompanying documentation (provided that the Software is properly used on the computer and with the operating system for which it was designed) and that the documentation correctly describes the operation of the Software in all material respects. If the Owner is notified of significant errors during the Warranty Period it will correct any such demonstrable errors in the Software or its documentation within a reasonable time or (at its option) provide or authorise a refund (against return of the Software and its documentation).

[**Note:** The computer (minimum configuration) and operating system (version) must be specified and visible in either the licence agreement or on the packaging before the diskette package is opened.]

The above represent your sole remedies for any breach of the Owner's warranties, which are given only to the original registered user.

The express terms of this Agreement are in lieu of all warranties, conditions, undertakings, terms and obligations implied by statute, common law, trade usage, course of dealing or otherwise all of which are hereby excluded to the fullest extent permitted by law.

The Owner does not warrant that the Software will meet your requirements or that the operation of the Software will be uninterrupted or error-free or that defects in the Software will be corrected. You shall load and use the Software at your own risk and in no event will the Owner be liable to you for any indirect or special loss or damage of any kind (except personal injury or death resulting from the Owner's negligence or breach of this Agreement) including any form of lost profits or consequential loss arising from your use of or inability to use the Software or from errors or deficiencies in it whether caused by negligence or otherwise. The Owner shall also not be liable for any failure by the Software to provide any functions not specified in its associated documentation. In respect of any other claim, in no event shall the Owner's liability exceed the amount paid by you for the Software.

5. Support

The Owner's technical support staff will endeavour to answer by telephone any technical queries the original registered user may have regarding the use of the Software or its application for a period of *60* days after the first support service call, which must be made within the Warranty Period. For telephone support please call [   ] between the hours of [   ] and [   ] [Monday] to [Friday] inclusive.

[Please note that calls to the above number are charged at a premium rate (currently 50p per minute, but the owner reserves the right to increase the rate form time to time)].

6. Waiver of remedies

See clause 28 of Precedent A.

7. Third parties

See clause 37 of Precedent A (Version A).

8. Law

See clause 34 of Precedent A.

If you have any questions concerning this Agreement please write to [   ].

Click-wrap version only

If you agree to be bound by the above conditions please click YES at which point the software will be loaded onto your computer. If you do not agree click NO. The software will then not be loaded onto your computer.

I agree to be bound by the above conditions for the use   YES   NO
of the Software

[**Notes:** It is recommended that in conjunction with the Licence Agreement you observe the following guidelines:

(1) The usual copyright notice should appear prominently on the diskette, the packaging and the user manual as well as being encoded in the Software:

© [Owner] 2001

(2) The following notice should appear on the front of the packaging:

IMPORTANT NOTICE: This software and its associated documentation are the copyright of [   ]. The use of this software is governed by the Licence Agreement accompanying this package.

This package requires an *ABC* computer with a minimum of *YM* of memory and the *XYZ* operating system version Z.

(3) A copy of the Licence Agreement should appear in the user manual.

Shrink-wrap only:

(4) The following first screen display should be encoded in the Software to appear each time the Software is loaded:

© **[Owner] 2001**

IMPORTANT NOTICE: This software is the copyright of [   ] and its use is governed by the terms of the Licence Agreement accompanying this package a copy of which is set out in the user manual. If you cannot locate the Licence Agreement please write to the owner at [ADDRESS] for a copy. If you accept the terms of the Licence Agreement, enter "AGREED".

(5) The accompanying Licence Registration Form entitling the original registered user to technical support should contain a form of confirmation for signature to the effect that the user agrees to be bound by the Licence Agreement.

(6) As well as describing the use of the software the user manual should:

    (a) identify the software;
    (b) describe its purpose;
    (c) say what equipment (minimum configuration) and operating system (version) the software is suitable for;
    (d) give the name and address of the owner;
    (e) describe the software and the documentation as being copyright;
    (f) give the telephone number for service calls and say between what hours, and on what days and on what terms, the lines are open.]

MULTIPLE COPY SOFTWARE LICENCE AGREEMENT
[5.3.6.5]

[**Note**: This agreement is designed for use by a supplier in relation to a large corporate user which wishes to have the freedom to use multiple copies of package software either on a stand alone basis, or distributed via host computers to personal computers or workstations on a network, both for its own use and the use of other companies within its group.]

THIS AGREEMENT is made the   day of   20

PARTIES:

(1) SUPPLIER [LIMITED] [PLC] whose registered office is at

                               ("the Supplier")

(2) CUSTOMER [LIMITED] [PLC] whose registered office is at

                               ("the Customer")

RECITALS:

(A) [The Supplier is the owner of various computer software products and their associated documentation] [The Supplier is authorised by [   ], a company incorporated in [   ] ("the Owner"), to distribute and sub-license various computer software products and their associated documentation which are owned by the Owner]

(B) The Customer wishes to have for its own benefit [and for the benefit of its Associates (as hereinafter defined)] a non-exclusive licence to possess and reproduce multiple copies of certain of such software products (and any additional software products as may be mutually agreed) for internal use by its employees [and those of its Associates] on one or more computers owned or lawfully used by the Customer [or its Associates] and the Supplier has agreed to grant such licence on the terms of this Agreement

[**Note**: Grants of licence rights throughout a corporate group are not uncommon, and the remainder of this precedent assumes that this is the approach adopted. However, care needs to be taken to ensure that this does not expose the supplier to greater liabilities than it would have had directly to the customer itself.]

NOW IT IS HEREBY AGREED as follows:

1 Definitions

In this Agreement, unless the context otherwise requires, the following expressions have the following meanings:

"Associate"   means, in relation to the Customer, another person, firm or company which directly or indirectly controls, is controlled by or is under common control with the Customer (and the expression "control" shall mean the power to direct or cause the direction of the general management and policies of the person, firm or company in question) but only (i) so long as such control exists, and (ii) if that person, firm or company is approved in writing by the Supplier.

"Authorised Computers"   means (i) the Hosts and (ii) the personal computers and workstations specified in Schedule 2 and/or such other personal computers and workstations as the Customer may notify the Supplier in Customer Reports from time to time and which, in each such case, [are located at the Premises and] are owned or lawfully used by one of the Users, but excluding, in any such case, any Hosts, personal computers or workstations which cease to be Authorised Computers in accordance with clause 6(6) or clause 14(3).

[**Note**: If laptops or other PCs are used at home or elsewhere than in the premises omit the words in square brackets]

"Confidential Information"   means all information which is expressly marked as confidential or which is manifestly of a confidential nature or which is confirmed in writing to be confidential within 7 days of its disclosure.

"Copies"   means Electronic Copies and Stand Alone Copies.

"Credit"   has the meaning ascribed thereto in clause 6(6).

"Customer Report"   means a report from the Customer to the Supplier in the form set out in Schedule 4 or in such other form as the Supplier and the Customer may agree in writing from time to time and which is certified as true and complete by a *director* of the Customer.

"Electronic Copies"   means copies of the Software which the Users may make from time to time pursuant to clause 2(1)(c).

"End User Licence Agreement"   means, in relation to each item of Software, the relevant end-user licence agreement routinely provided with Stand Alone Copies thereof or otherwise supplied in connection with the use of such Software by the [Supplier] [Owner] to end-users in the United Kingdom from time to time and a copy of which has been supplied to the Customer either annexed hereto (in respect of the Original Software) or pursuant to clause 2(2)(e).

[**Note**: the form of the End User Licence Agreement can take different forms: see **Note** at end of this Precedent.]

"the Hosts"	means the mainframe computers, mini computers and/or file servers specified in Schedule 2 and/or such other mainframe computers, mini computers and/or file servers as the Customer may notify to the Supplier in Customer Reports from time to time which are located at the Premises and which are, in each such case, owned or lawfully used by one of the Users.
"the Master Copies"	means the master copies of the Software to be supplied by the Supplier pursuant to this Agreement.
"the Original Software"	means the computer software which the Supplier has agreed to supply to the Customer hereunder as specified in Schedule 1.
["the Premises"	means those premises [located in the United Kingdom] specified in Schedule 2 and/or such other premises [located in the United Kingdom] as the Customer may notify to the Supplier in Customer Reports from time to time].
"Products"	means the Software, the Master Copies, the Copies, the Software Documentation and the Stand Alone Products.
"Software"	means all or any items of Original Software and/or Supplemental Software as the context admits or the case may require.
"the Software Documentation"	means, in relation to each item of Software, the operating manuals and other literature routinely provided from time to time as part of the Stand Alone Product in respect of such Software by the [Supplier] [Owner] or in conjunction with any modification, enhancement or upgrade of such Software.
"Stand Alone Copies"	means copies of the Software comprised in Stand Alone Products.
"Stand Alone Product"	means, in relation to each item of Software, the boxed software product routinely provided by the [Supplier] [Owner] to end-users in [the United Kingdom] from time to time which is designed for use by an end-user [on and in conjunction with a single personal computer or workstation] and which comprises, *inter alia*, a diskette with that Software recorded on it, a copy of the operating manuals and other literature, an End User Licence Agreement and its associated packaging.

"Supplemental Software"	means any software additional to the Original Software which the Supplier may agree in writing to license pursuant to this Agreement from time to time and which shall be accepted by the Customer and, in relation to the Original Software and such additional software, all modifications, enhancements, upgrades and replacements thereof and additions thereto as may be provided by the Supplier pursuant to this Agreement from time to time and accepted by the Customer.
"United Kingdom"	means the United Kingdom of Great Britain and Northern Ireland.
"Users"	means the Customer and its Associates, who shall be deemed to be third parties upon whom express benefits and rights are to be bestowed pursuant and subject to the terms of this Agreement for the purposes of the Contracts (Rights of Third Parties) Act 1999.

2 Grant of licence

(1) Subject to the terms and conditions of this Agreement and to the relevant End User Licence Agreements, the Supplier hereby grants to each of the Users a non-exclusive right:

(a) for the User's employees to use the Software in accordance with the Software Documentation for the User's own internal business purposes on Authorised Computers;

(b) to install the Software on the Hosts using the Master Copies;

(c) to reproduce the Software for use in accordance with clause 2(1)(a) either by downloading copies of the Software electronically from the Hosts to the hard disks of other Authorised Computers or by installing the Software directly on to the hard disks of such other Authorised Computers using the Master Copies;

(d) to install each Stand Alone Copy which may be supplied pursuant to this Agreement on the hard disk of an Authorised Computer for use in accordance with clause 2(1)(a).

(2) For the purposes of this Agreement, the Supplier shall supply to the Customer:

(a) two Master Copies of the Original Software (in a form suitable for reproduction of Electronic Copies) on appropriate electronic media within *14* days of the date of this Agreement;

(b) in respect of the Original Software, such number of copies of the Software Documentation and Stand Alone Products as are specified in Schedule 3 within *14* days of the date of this Agreement;

(c) two Master Copies of any Supplemental Software (in a form suitable for reproduction of Electronic Copies) on appropriate electronic media at such time or times as may be separately agreed between the Supplier and the Customer;

(d) such new or additional copies of the Software Documentation and Stand Alone Products at such time or times as may be separately agreed between the Supplier and the Customer;

(e) a copy of the version of the End User Licence Agreement applicable to each item of Software provided to Users pursuant to this Agreement.

(3) No User shall be entitled to copy or reproduce any Stand Alone Copies (except for back-up copies permitted by the relevant End User Licence Agreement or by law) or the Software Documentation either in whole or in part.

(4) The use of each of the Copies made available under this Agreement shall be governed by the terms and conditions of the End User Licence Agreement relevant to such Copy and the Users shall be subject to the obligations and shall be granted the rights specified therein except insofar as the terms and conditions thereof are inconsistent with the terms and conditions of this Agreement in which case the latter shall prevail. Each of the Users covenants and agrees with the Supplier that during the term of this Agreement such User will observe, perform and be bound by all the terms of such End User Licence Agreements as modified by this Agreement.

(5) Save as expressly provided in this Agreement or in the relevant End User Licence Agreement as modified by this Agreement, and save to the extent and in the circumstances expressly required to be permitted by law, none of the Users shall:

(a) rent, lease, sub-license, loan, copy, modify, adapt, merge, translate, reverse engineer, decompile, disassemble or create derivative works based on the whole or any part of the Products;

(b) use, reproduce or deal in the Products or any part thereof in any way.

[(6) No User shall be entitled to use the Software on any Authorised Computer which is located at premises outside the United Kingdom.]

[**Note**: The territorial restriction should correspond to those jurisdictions in which the governing law of the end user agreements is considered to be effective. If the supplier is not the owner there may also be a territorial restriction in the distributorship agreement between the supplier and owner.]

(7) The Supplier will make the Software available to the Customer in object code form only.

(8) Each User shall effect and maintain adequate security measures to safeguard the Products from access or use by any unauthorised person and shall retain all copies thereof made available to it under this Agreement under its effective control.

(9) Each User shall duplicate the [Supplier's] [Owner's] copyright and other proprietary notices on each copy of the Software within its possession or control both within the program and on any diskette (or other media) labels.

(10) The provision of each Stand Alone Product pursuant to this Agreement shall be deemed to be a contract of sale of the tangible property comprised therein (but not the copyright or other intellectual property rights therein) between the Supplier

and the Customer and/or its Associates (as the case may be). All copies of the other Products are and shall remain the property of the Supplier and are made available under this Agreement by way of a non-exclusive licence to possess the same for use in accordance with this Agreement and may not be sold or otherwise disposed of to any third party except the Users.

(11) This Agreement, and all or any of the rights or obligations hereunder, shall not be assigned or sub-licensed by any User without the prior written approval of the Supplier.

3 Guarantee and indemnity

(1) Each of the Users ("the Guarantor") hereby (a) guarantees to the Supplier the due and punctual performance and observance by each of the other Users of all such other User's obligations under this Agreement (by virtue of its execution of this Agreement or a Deed of Adherence) and (b) undertakes to hold the Supplier fully and completely indemnified on demand against any loss, damage and liability occasioned by any failure of any of the other Users so to perform or observe any of its obligations under this Agreement.

(2) The liability of the Guarantor under this Clause 3 shall be as primary obligor and not merely as surety and shall not be affected, impaired or discharged by reason of any act, omission, matter or thing which but for this provision might operate to release or otherwise exonerate the Guarantor from its obligations under this clause 3 including without limitation any time or other indulgence granted by the Supplier to any of the other Users or any variation of the terms of this Agreement or any End User Licence Agreement or any new or revised End User Licence Agreement becoming applicable to the use of any Software in terms of this Agreement.

(3) Where more than one User is liable under this clause 3 their liability shall be joint and several.

(4) The provisions of this clause 3 shall survive the termination of this Agreement.

4 Duration

This Agreement shall commence on [the date hereof] for an initial period of 2 years and shall continue thereafter unless or until terminated by either the Supplier or the Customer giving to the other not less than 6 months' written notice expiring on the last day of the said initial period or at any time thereafter, but shall be subject to earlier termination as provided in clause 12.

5 Prices and payment

(1) The Customer shall pay the charges specified in Schedule 3 for:

(a) the supply hereunder by the Supplier of the Master Copies of the Original Software;

(b) the supply hereunder by the Supplier of the Master Copies of any Supplemental Software;

(c) the number of Electronic Copies of the Software which the Users wish to make;

(d) in relation to the Original Software, the number of copies of the Software Documentation to be supplied by the Supplier hereunder as specified in Schedule 3;

(e) in relation to the Original Software, the number of Stand Alone Products to be supplied by the Supplier hereunder as specified in Schedule 3;

(f) any new or additional copies of the Software Documentation and Stand Alone Products supplied hereunder by the Supplier from time to time.

(2) The charges for the items mentioned in clauses 5(1)(a), 5(1)(d) and 5(1)(e) shall be paid forthwith upon the execution of this Agreement. The charges for the Electronic Copies mentioned in clause 5(1)(c) made in a particular calendar month shall be paid at the same time as the submission of the Customer Report immediately following the making of such Electronic Copies (or, if such submission is late, the date on which such Customer Report should have been submitted in accordance with this Agreement). The charges for each of the items mentioned in clauses 5(1)(b) and/or 5(1)(f) shall be invoiced to the Customer on delivery of such item to the Customer and shall be paid within *30* days after the delivery of such invoice.

(3) Any charges payable by the Customer hereunder in addition to those mentioned in this clause 5 shall be due to be paid within *30* days after the receipt by the Customer of the Supplier's invoice therefor.

(4) All charges payable under this Agreement are exclusive of Value Added Tax which shall be paid by the Customer at the rate and in the manner from time to time prescribed by law.

(5) If the Customer fails to make any payment to the Supplier under this Agreement on the due date then, without prejudice to any other right or remedy available to the Supplier, the Supplier shall be entitled to:

(a) suspend (by notice in writing to the Users) the rights granted to the Users pursuant to clause 2(1) of this Agreement until payment of the unpaid sum is made in full (and the Users shall so comply with such suspension); and/or

(b) charge the Customer interest on the amount outstanding on a day-to-day basis (as well after as before any judgement) from the date or last date for payment thereof to the date of actual payment (both dates inclusive) at the rate of *2* per cent above the base rate of *ABC* Bank plc (or such other London Clearing Bank as the Supplier may nominate) from time to time in force compounded quarterly. Such interest shall be paid on demand by the Supplier. For the avoidance of doubt, any failure to make payment within *7* days of the due date shall constitute a material breach of contract for the purposes of clause 12(3).

(6) The Supplier's standard retail price list in force from time to time as referred to in Schedule 3 shall be made available by the Supplier to the Customer promptly after written request therefor by the Customer at any time during the term of this Agreement

6 Customer Reports

(1) The Customer agrees to record the exact number of Electronic Copies made by Users during each calendar month of the term of this Agreement and to report that

information in Customer Reports together with the other information required by such Customer Reports.

(2) The Customer shall provide a Customer Report to the Supplier within *30* days after the end of every calendar month of the term of this Agreement (commencing with the calendar month in which this Agreement is executed) containing the information required thereby in respect of, and accurate as at the last day of, such calendar month.

(3) If no Electronic Copies are made during a calendar month, the Customer shall state this in the Customer Report.

(4) References in this clause 6 to a calendar month shall include, where appropriate, references to the unexpired part of the calendar month in which this Agreement is executed and to the expired part of the calendar month in which this Agreement is terminated.

(5) If during any calendar month of the term of this Agreement any Authorised Computer shall no longer be used for the purposes of running any Software then the Customer shall state this in the next Customer Report and shall prior to the submission of such Customer Report procure that all Software is erased from such Authorised Computer. Upon the submission of such Customer Report that Authorised Computer shall cease to be an Authorised Computer for the purposes of this Agreement.

(6) If during any calendar month of the term of this Agreement any of the Users shall cease to use any Electronic Copy on an Authorised Computer then the Customer shall state this and specify the Authorised Computer concerned in the next Customer Report and shall prior to the submission of such Customer Report procure that the relevant Software is erased from such Authorised Computer. Upon the submission of such Customer Report the Customer shall be given a credit in respect of that item of Software ("Credit") which shall entitle a User to use one Electronic Copy of that item of Software (but only that item and not any other version thereof) on another Authorised Computer free of any additional charge under this Agreement. Such Credit and, where applicable, such use shall be reported in the relevant Customer Report. A Credit shall not entitle the Customer to any cash refund or any other benefit.

(7) The Supplier reserves the right at any time to change the name and/or address of the person to whom Customer Reports and the associated payments should be despatched by the Customer (as appearing in the Customer Report from time to time) by notice in writing to the Customer, and the Customer shall thereafter comply with such instructions.

7 Implementation, training and help line services

(1) At the request of the Customer and subject to the reasonable availability of the Supplier's staff, the Supplier agrees to provide:

    (a) assistance to all or any of the Users with the installation and implementation of any item of Software;

    (b) training in the use of any item of Software for employees of all or any of the Users; and

(c) access for the Users' technical personnel to the Supplier's telephone help line for the purpose of assisting in the resolution of the Users' difficulties and queries in using the Software.

(2) The services described in clause 7(1) shall be charged to and paid for by the Customer at the Supplier's standard scale of charges for such services in force from time to time (which shall be supplied to the Customer on request) [less a discount of X per cent]. Unless otherwise agreed with the Supplier, training shall take place at the premises of the Supplier. Access to the Supplier's help line for assistance in relation to a particular item of Software shall be restricted to those employees of the Users who have first successfully completed a training course in respect of that Software in accordance with the Supplier's current minimum recommendations or who can demonstrate to the Supplier's reasonable satisfaction that they are competent in the use of that Software.

8 Audits

(1) The Users shall keep and shall make available to the Supplier on request accurate records to enable the Supplier to verify all payments due to it under this Agreement.

(2) During the term of this Agreement and for the period of 6 months after its termination and upon 5 business days' prior written notice to the Customer, the Supplier shall have the right at any time and from time to time (subject as provided in clause 8(4)), during the Customer's normal business hours, to send an independent accountant (not generally providing services to the Supplier except in respect of payment audits) to audit the records of the Users and the use of the Software by the Users and to verify the payments due to the Supplier under this Agreement. The Users shall give such accountant full access to their premises, computers, employees and relevant records to the extent reasonably required for such purpose. Any such audit shall be conducted in such a manner as to endeavour not to interfere with the Users' normal business activities and will not include access to the Users' cost or profit information. Each such audit shall cover the period since the last most recent audit or, if none, the date of this Agreement down to the business day immediately preceding the commencement of the audit ("Audit Period").

(3) The Supplier shall procure that such accountant shall keep confidential the information which comes to his knowledge as a consequence of his audit and shall require that it enters into any confidentiality undertaking reasonably requested by the Customer in respect thereof prior to any disclosure, except that the accountant shall be entitled to reveal to the Supplier any information necessary to provide the Supplier with confirmation of the accuracy of any Customer Reports, the payment remittances made to the Supplier or any deviations therefrom. Upon written request, the Supplier agrees to make available to the Customer, in the event the Supplier makes any claim with respect to an audit, a copy of the records and reports pertaining to the audit.

(4) The Supplier agrees not to cause such audits to be carried out more frequently than *twice* a year, except where the Supplier has reasonable cause to believe that correct Customer Reports or payments are not being tendered by the Customer, in which case the Supplier may cause any number of audits to be carried out until such time as the Supplier is reasonably satisfied that the position has been corrected.

(5) Each such audit shall be carried out at the Supplier's expense unless it reveals a deficiency of 5 per cent or more of the payment remittances for the relevant Audit Period in which event the Customer shall pay the costs thereof. Payment of such costs and any payment deficiency shall be made within 7 days after the Customer shall have received written notice thereof from the Supplier together with a copy of the accountant's report and, if applicable, fee note showing the amount(s) due. Any such deficiency shall carry interest in accordance with clause 5(5)(b) from the date it was originally due.

9 Limited warranty

(1) The Supplier warrants to the Customer that each of the Products provided to the Customer hereunder will, at the time of delivery and for 90 days thereafter (or the warranty period specified in the relevant End User Licence Agreement, if longer), be free from defects in materials and will conform to the [Supplier's] [Owner's] applicable standard written specifications. The Customer's remedy and the Supplier's obligations under this limited warranty shall be limited to, at the Supplier's election, return of the Product in question for a refund of amounts paid to the Supplier hereunder for each copy of the Product or replacement of any defective Product. Any replacement shall not extend the original warranty period. This limited warranty shall not apply to Products which the Supplier reasonably determines have been subject to misuse, neglect, improper installation, repair, alteration or damage by any of the Users.

(2) The Supplier does not warrant that the Products will meet the Users' requirements or that the operation of the Products will be uninterrupted or error-free or that defects in the Products will be corrected.

(3) The express terms of this Agreement are in lieu of all warranties, conditions, terms and obligations implied by statute, common law, custom, trade usage, course of dealing or otherwise, all of which are hereby excluded to the fullest extent permitted by law.

(4) Each of the Users hereby warrants to the Supplier that such User has not been induced to enter into this Agreement by any prior representations whether oral or in writing except as specifically mentioned in this Agreement and each of the Users hereby waives any claim for breach of any such representations which are not so specifically mentioned.

10 Liability

(1) The Supplier shall indemnify the Customer and keep the Customer fully and effectively indemnified on demand against any loss of or damage to any property or injury to or death of any person caused by any negligent act or omission or wilful misconduct of the Supplier, its employees, agents or subcontractors.

(2) The Customer shall indemnify the Supplier and keep the Supplier fully and effectively indemnified on demand against any loss of or damage to any property or injury to or death of any person caused by any negligent act or omission or wilful misconduct of the Customer, its employees, agents or subcontractors.

(3) Except in respect of injury to or death of any person (for which no limit applies), the respective liabilities of the Supplier and the Customer under clauses 10(1) and

10(2) above in respect of each event or series of connected events shall not exceed £500,000.

[Note: some contracts specifically require the parties to back up their indemnities and/or prospective liabilities. Others seek to link the limit of liability with the value of the contract, although the effectiveness of this approach for the purposes of the Unfair Contract Terms Act is uncertain.]

(4) Notwithstanding anything else contained in this Agreement, the Supplier shall not be liable to the Customer and/or any User for loss of profits or contracts or other indirect or consequential loss whether arising from negligence, breach of contract or howsoever.

(5) The Supplier shall not be liable to the Customer for any loss arising out of any failure by the Customer and/or any User to keep full and up to date security copies of the computer programs and data it uses in accordance with best computing practice.

11 Warranty of authority and indemnity

(1) The Supplier warrants to each of the Users that it has the right to grant the rights and comply with its obligations contained in this Agreement

(2) The Supplier agrees to indemnify, hold harmless and defend each of the Users from and against any and all damages, costs and expenses, including reasonable legal fees, incurred in connection with any claim that the Supplier does not have the necessary authority to enter into this Agreement, or that a Product infringes the [U.K.] intellectual property rights of any third party, provided that the Supplier is notified promptly in writing of any claim, that the Supplier is given immediate and complete control of such claim, that at the Supplier's request and expense each of the Users gives the Supplier all reasonable assistance with such claim, and that none of the Users prejudices the Supplier's defence of such claim.

(3) Following notice of a claim the Supplier shall at its option and at its expense, either procure for the Users the right to continue to use the alleged infringing Product or replace or modify the Product to make it non-infringing. If the Supplier elects to replace or modify that Product, such replacement shall meet substantially the [Owner's] [Supplier's] current written specifications for that Product. If the Supplier is unable to replace or modify the Product, the Customer shall be entitled to a refund of amounts paid to the Supplier hereunder for each copy of that Product.

(4) The Supplier shall have no liability for any claim under this clause 11 in respect of the Supplier's lack of authority in respect of a Product or any claim of infringement of any intellectual property rights based on a User's (i) use or reproduction of the Product after the Supplier's notice to the Customer that the Users should cease use or reproduction of such Product due to an infringement claim, or of other than the then current release of a Product received from the Supplier if such claim would have been avoided by the use of the then current release, and/or (ii) the combination of a Product with a program or data not supplied by the Supplier if such claim would have been avoided by the exclusive use of the Product.

(5) The foregoing states the entire liability of the Supplier to the Users in respect of any lack of authority or any infringement of the intellectual property rights of any third party.

12 Termination

Notwithstanding anything else contained herein, this Agreement may be terminated:

(1) by the Supplier forthwith on giving notice in writing to the Customer if:

    (a) the control (as defined for the purposes of section 416 of the Income and Corporation Taxes Act 1988) of the Customer shall be transferred to any person or persons other than the person or persons in control of the Customer at the date hereof (but the Supplier shall only be entitled to terminate within the period of *60* days after the Customer shall have been notified in writing of the change in control); or

    (b) any audit carried out pursuant to clause 8 shall reveal a deficiency of *10* per cent or more in the payment remittances which should have been made in the period covered by the audit.

(2) by either the Supplier or the Customer forthwith on giving notice in writing to the other if:

    (a) the other (and the Customer shall be deemed to be in breach if any of the Users is in breach) commits any breach of any term of this Agreement and (in the case of a breach capable of being remedied) shall have failed, within *30* days after the receipt of a request in writing from the first party so to do, to remedy the breach (such request to contain a warning of such party's intention to terminate); or

    (b) the other (which in the case of the Customer shall mean any of the Users) shall have a receiver or administrative receiver appointed of it or over any part of its undertaking or assets or shall pass a resolution for winding-up (otherwise than for the purpose of a bona fide scheme of solvent amalgamation or reconstruction) or a court of competent jurisdiction shall make an order to that effect or if the other (with the meaning aforesaid) shall enter into any voluntary arrangement with its creditors or shall become subject to an administration order.

13 Effect of termination

(1) In the event that this Agreement is terminated by either the Supplier or the Customer pursuant to clause 4 or is terminated by the Supplier pursuant to clause 12(1)(a) or by the Customer pursuant to clause 12(2), the Users may continue to use and possess those copies of the Products which they use and possess on the date of such termination subject to the terms and conditions of the End User Licence Agreements applicable to such Products which shall thereafter apply to such use and possession to the exclusion of this Agreement (and which such Users hereby covenant and agree with the Supplier to observe, perform and be bound by) but no other use may be made of such Products by such Users and, in particular, no copying or reproduction of the Software shall thereafter be permitted (save for back-up copies permitted by law or by the terms of an End User Licence Agreement).

(2) In the event that this Agreement is terminated by the Supplier pursuant to clause 12(1)(b) or clause 12(2) the Users shall immediately cease using the Products

and copying and reproducing the Software and shall forthwith return the Products and all copies thereof in the possession of the Users to the Supplier or, at the option of the Supplier, shall destroy the same and certify to the Supplier that they have been so destroyed. The Users shall also cause the Software to be erased from all Authorised Computers and all other computers in their possession or under their control and shall certify to the Supplier that the same has been done.

(3) On the termination of this Agreement all the rights and obligations of the parties under this Agreement shall automatically terminate except for such rights of action as shall have accrued prior to such termination and any obligations and rights which expressly or by implication are intended to come into or continue in force on or after such termination.

14 Associates

(1) Associates who make use of the Software pursuant to this Agreement shall be bound by and required to comply with the terms of this Agreement as a User, and shall be entitled to the rights and benefits conferred on a User by this Agreement.

(2) Upon an Associate ceasing to be an Associate because the requisite control described in the definition of "Associate" in clause 1 no longer exists, such former Associate shall forthwith and automatically cease to be a beneficiary under this Agreement and all its rights and obligations under this Agreement (including any rights which it may have had pursuant to the Contracts (Rights of Third Parties) Act 1999) shall automatically terminate save for any provision hereof which in relation to such former Associate is expressly or by implication intended to come into force on or to continue in force after cessation and without prejudice to the due performance by such former Associate of all its obligations up to the date of such cessation and the remedies of any of the other parties hereto in respect of a breach thereof.

(3) If an Associate ceases to be a party to this Agreement in the circumstances mentioned in clause 14(2), such former Associate may continue to use and possess those copies of the Products which it uses and possesses on the date of such cessation subject to the terms and conditions of the End User Licence Agreements applicable to such Products and subsisting on the date of such cessation which shall thereafter apply to such use and possession to the exclusion of this Agreement but no other use may be made of such Products by such former Associate and, in particular, no copying or reproduction of the Software shall thereafter be permitted (save for back-up copies permitted by law or by the terms of an End User Licence Agreement). Upon such cessation all Authorised Computers owned or lawfully used immediately prior to such cessation by such former Associate shall immediately cease to be Authorised Computers for the purposes of this Agreement. Notwithstanding the foregoing, clause 2(10) shall continue to apply to such Products such that, except in respect of Stand Alone Products, all copies of such Products shall remain the property of the Supplier and may not be sold or otherwise disposed of by such former Associate to any third party. If such former Associate fails to abide by any of its obligations under this clause 14(3) the Supplier may by notice in writing to such former Associate terminate forthwith the rights of such former Associate under this clause 14(3) whereupon such former Associate shall forthwith return the Products and all copies thereof in its possession to the Supplier or, at the option of the Supplier, shall destroy the same and certify to the Supplier that they have been so destroyed and shall also cause the Software to be erased from all

computers in its possession or under its control and shall certify to the Supplier that the same has been done.

(4) If an Associate ceases to be a party to this Agreement in the circumstances mentioned in clause 14(2):

(a) such former Associate shall continue to be liable in respect of any claim made by the Supplier against such former Associate under clause 3 of this Agreement which is notified to such former Associate prior to such cessation but shall not otherwise have any liability under clause 3 following such cessation;

(b) the Users shall continue to be liable in respect of any claim made by the Supplier against them or any of them under clause 3 of this Agreement in relation to any breach by such former Associate of any of its obligations under this Agreement which is notified to them prior to such cessation but shall not otherwise be liable under clause 3 in relation to any breach by such former Associate of any of its obligations under this Agreement.

(5) The Customer undertakes to notify the Supplier in writing immediately upon any of its Associates ceasing to be such for the purposes of this Agreement and also to report that fact in its next Customer Report and to include therein details of the copies of the Products which that former Associate will be entitled to use pursuant to clause 14(3) and the computers on which they will be used following such cessation.

15 Confidentiality

See clause 21 of Precedent A.

16 *Force majeure*

See clause 15 of Precedent A.

17 Waiver of remedies

See clause 28 of Precedent A.

18 Entire agreement

This Agreement supersedes all prior agreements, arrangements and understandings between the parties and constitutes the entire agreement between the parties relating to the subject matter hereof (save that neither party seeks to exclude liability for any fraudulent precontractual misrepresentations on which the other party can be shown to have relied). No addition to or modification of any provision of this Agreement shall be binding upon the parties unless made by a written instrument signed by a duly authorised representative of each of the parties. Any addition to or modification of this Agreement agreed to by the Customer shall be binding on all the Users at that time or thereafter to become Users.

19 Notices

All notices which are required to be given hereunder shall be in writing and shall be sent to the address of the recipient set out in this Agreement or such other address in England as the recipient may designate by notice given in accordance with the provisions of this clause. Any such notice may be delivered personally or by first class pre-paid letter or facsimile transmission and shall be deemed to have been served if by hand when delivered, if by first class post 48 hours after posting and if by facsimile transmission when despatched. Any notice served on the Customer shall be deemed to have been served simultaneously on all the Users at that time.

20 Severability

See clause 36 of Precedent A.

21 Interpretation

See clause 33 of Precedent A.

22 Law

See clause 34 of Precedent A.

23 Disputes

See clause 35 of Precedent A or clause 37 of Precedent D.

24 Third Parties

The parties confirm their intent not to confer any rights on any third parties except the Users by virtue of this Agreement, and accordingly the Contracts (Rights of Third Parties) Act 1999 shall not apply to this Agreement except in respect of the Users.

EXECUTED under hand in two originals the day and year first before written

SIGNED for and on behalf of
SUPPLIER [LIMITED] [PLC]

By

Signature

Title

Witness

SIGNED for and on behalf of
CUSTOMER [LIMITED] [PLC]

By

Signature

Title

Witness

SCHEDULE 1

DESCRIPTION OF THE ORIGINAL SOFTWARE

SCHEDULE 2

DESCRIPTION OF THE INITIAL AUTHORISED COMPUTERS AND PREMISES

1. HOSTS:

    Item   Serial Number   User   [Premises at which item located
                                                  (*Street, Town, Postcode*)])

2. PERSONAL COMPUTERS/WORKSTATIONS ON WHICH ELECTRONIC COPIES WILL BE LOADED

    Item   Serial Number   User   [Premises at which item located
                                                  (*Street, Town, Postcode*)]

3. PERSONAL COMPUTERS ON WHICH STAND ALONE COPIES WILL BE LOADED:

    Item   Serial Number   User   [Premises at which item located
                                                  (*Street, Town, Postcode*)]

SCHEDULE 3

CHARGES

1. The total price for the supply of the master copies of the Original Software shall be as follows:

    Item of Original Software   Price
                                                                           ———

                                              Total £   ——

2. It is recorded that the Users wish to make the following numbers of Electronic Copies of the Original Software immediately, the total price for which shall be as follows:

Item of Number of	Aggregate		
Original Software	Electronic Copies	Unit Price	Price
	Total £		

[**Note**: It is assumed that the supplier will wish to offer an extra discount at this stage to encourage the customer to commit to the greatest possible number of copies. If no such incentive is offered, the customer may defer its commitment in order to take advantage of the credit period built into the customer reporting procedure. The customer's initial order may also affect the future discount levels which the supplier is willing to provide.]

3. The Customer requires immediately the following number of copies of the Software Documentation in respect of the Original Software, the total price for which shall be as follows:

Item of	Number of Copies	Unit Price	Aggregate
Original Software	of Software		Price
	Documentation		
	Total £		

4. The Customer requires immediately the following numbers of copies of the Stand Alone Products in respect of the Original Software, the total price for which shall be as follows:

Item of	Number of Copies	Unit Price	Aggregate
Original Software	of Stand alone	Price	
	Products		
	Total £		

5. The price for each Electronic Copy made by Users in addition to those mentioned in paragraph 2 above shall be a sum equal to the price of the relative item of Software appearing in the Supplier's standard retail price list in force at the time the Electronic Copy is made [less a discount of X per cent].

Where the relative Software is Supplemental Software the previous version of which is already used by Users and the Supplier generally offers in its standard retail price list a more favourable price (including nil) to an existing user of the previous version in question then the price of each Electronic Copy thereof (up to an aggregate number equal to the total number of Electronic Copies of such previous version used by Users prior to such Supplemental Software being made available to the Customer) shall be calculated as aforesaid using such more favourable price.

6. The price for each of the master copies of any Supplemental Software shall be a sum equal to the price of a single copy of such Supplemental Software appearing in the Supplier's standard retail price list in force from time to time. Where the previous version of such Supplemental Software is already used by Users and the Supplier generally offers in its standard retail price list a more favourable price (including nil) to an existing user of the previous version in question then the price payable by the Customer shall be that more favourable price.

7. The price for any new or additional copies of the Software Documentation and Stand Alone Products shall be a sum equal to the price therefor appearing in the Supplier's standard retail price list in force from time to time less a discount of *Y* per cent.

[**Note**: Documentation may be listed separately from the software if (as is increasingly the case) the documentation is not automatically provided with the software but has to be ordered separately. The same may go for such items as templates and even training courses.]

8. All prices quoted or referred to above are exclusive of Value Added Tax.

SCHEDULE 4

CUSTOMER REPORT

Customer:

For the calendar month ending:

[Words and expressions defined in the Multiple Copy Software Licence Agreement made between [NAME OF SUPPLIER] and the Customer dated [   ] shall have the same meanings in this Customer Report Form]

[If the Customer has no information to report under a particular section of this Customer Report Form then the relevant section should be completed "none" or "not applicable" as appropriate]

A   NEW AUTHORISED COMPUTERS BROUGHT INTO USE DURING THE CALENDAR MONTH:

(1) HOSTS:

Item	Serial Number	User	[Premises at which item located (*Street, Town, Postcode*)]

(2) PERSONAL COMPUTERS/WORKSTATIONS ON WHICH ELEC-TRONIC COPIES WILL BE LOADED:

Item	Serial Number	User	[Premises at which item located (*Street, Town, Postcode*)]

B   AUTHORISED COMPUTERS NO LONGER USED FOR RUNNING ANY SOFTWARE AND FROM WHICH ALL SOFTWARE HAS BEEN ERASED DURING THE CALENDAR MONTH:

Item	Serial Number	User	[Premises at which item located (*Street, Town, Postcode*)]

C ELECTRONIC COPIES NO LONGER USED ON, AND WHICH HAVE
   BEEN ERASED FROM, AUTHORISED COMPUTERS DURING THE
   CALENDAR MONTH AND FOR WHICH CREDITS NOW ARISE:

Item of Software (*Description and version number*)	Authorised Computer on which previously used (*Description and serial number*)	User	Premises at which which Authorised Computer located (*Street, Town, Postcode*)

D NUMBERS OF UNUSED CREDITS CARRIED FORWARD FROM PRE-
   VIOUS CALENDAR MONTHS:

Item of Software (*Description and version number*)	Number of Credits

E TOTAL NUMBERS OF UNUSED CREDITS NOW AVAILABLE (*i.e.* C +
   D):

Item of Software (*Description and version number*)	Number of Credits

F NUMBERS OF NEW ELECTRONIC COPIES MADE DURING THE
   CALENDAR MONTH AND THE CHARGES PAYABLE:

   (1) NEW ELECTRONIC COPIES:

Item of Software (*Description and version number*)	Authorised Computer on which loaded (*Description and serial number*)	User	[Premises at which Authorised Computer located (*Street, Town, Postcode*)]

   (2) CHARGES:

Item of Software (*Description and version number*)	Number of Electronic Copies made	Number of Credits available (*as per E above*)	Net number of Electronic Copies for which payment is required	Total price payable (*Supplier's retail price per copy less X per cent discount multiplied by number of copies*)

Grand Total Due this month   £[_____]

Remittance attached   £[_____]
(*including VAT*)

G   NUMBER OF UNUSED CREDITS CARRIED FORWARD TO FUTURE CALENDAR MONTHS (*i.e.* E LESS CREDITS UTILISED IN F):

Item of Software (*Description and version number*)	Number of Credits

H   IDENTITY OF ANY USER WHICH CEASED TO BE AN ASSOCIATE DURING THE CALENDAR MONTH TOGETHER WITH DETAILS OF THOSE PRODUCTS WHICH IT IS ENTITLED TO CONTINUE TO USE SUBJECT TO THE TERMS AND CONDITIONS OF APPLICABLE END USER LICENCE AGREEMENTS:

User (*Name and address*)	Products which it will continue to use (*Description and version number*)	Number of copies	Computer on which used (*Description and serial number*)

I certify on behalf of [CUSTOMER] that the information set out in this Customer Report is true and complete

Name (Please print or type)

Title

Signature

Date:

This Customer Report and the enclosed payment should be sent to:

[NAME OF SUPPLIER]

[ADDRESS]

Attention: [_____]

[**Note:** the End User Licence Agreement also requires attachment: this could match that set out as Precedent C or possibly Precedent E, as adapted]

EXCLUSIVE DISTRIBUTORSHIP AGREEMENT

THIS AGREEMENT is made the   day of   20

PARTIES:

(1) COMPANY [LIMITED] [PLC] whose registered office is at

("the Company")

(2) DISTRIBUTOR [LIMITED] [PLC] whose registered office is at

("the Distributor")

RECITALS:

(A) The Company is the manufacturer and producer of various computer products

(B) The Company has agreed to appoint the Distributor as its exclusive distributor in the Territory (as hereinafter defined) for certain of its products on the terms and conditions hereinafter contained

NOW IT IS HEREBY AGREED as follows:

1 Definitions

In this Agreement (which expression shall be deemed to include the Schedules hereto), unless the context otherwise requires, the following expressions have the following meanings:

"Confidential Information"	means this Agreement and all information obtained by one party from the other pursuant to this Agreement which is expressly marked as confidential or which is manifestly confidential or which is confirmed in writing to be confidential within 7 days of its disclosure.
"Hardware Products"	means those of the Products which are computer hardware.
"Initial Order"	means the Distributor's initial order for the Products [and spare parts] as set out in the Company's invoice delivered to the Distributor on the execution hereof and signed by the Distributor for the purpose of identification.
"intellectual property rights"	means patents, trade marks, Internet domain names, service marks, registered designs, applications for any of the foregoing, copyright, design rights, trade and business names and any other similar protected rights in any country.

"Invoice Price"	means, in relation to the purchase of any of the Products, the amount invoiced by the Company to the Distributor excluding Value Added Tax and any other taxes, duties or levies and any transport and insurance charges included in such invoice.
"Products"	means the products described in Schedule 1 (including both the Hardware Products and/or the Software Products) and such other products as the parties may agree in writing from time to time.
"Product Documentation"	means the operating manuals and other literature accompanying the Products for use by customers.
"Shrink Wrap Licence"	means the licence agreement accompanying each of the Software Products and contained within its packaging expressed to be made between the Company and the end-user of such product.
"Software Products"	means those of the Products which are computer software.
"Territory"	means *the United Kingdom of Great Britain and Northern Ireland.*
"Year"	means any period of 12 months commencing on [the date hereof] or any anniversary of [the date hereof].

2 Appointment [5.0.2, 5.3.2]

(1) The Company hereby appoints the Distributor and the Distributor hereby agrees to act as the [exclusive] distributor of the Company for the resale of the Products in the Territory.

(2) The Company shall not during the continuance of this Agreement appoint any other person to act as its distributor or agent in the Territory for the Products [save that the Company reserves the right to market the Products on its own behalf.

[Note: The Company may want expressly to reserve the right to market its products in the territory itself, in which case an express caveat to the distribution rights may be required.]

(3) The Distributor shall not be entitled to assign or sub-contract any of its rights or obligations under this Agreement or appoint any sub-distributor or agent to perform such obligations.

(4) The Distributor shall not be entitled to any priority of supply of the Products over the Company's customers outside the Territory and the Company may allocate production and delivery among its customers as it sees fit.

(5) The Distributor represents and warrants to the Company that it has the necessary ability and experience to carry out the obligations assumed by it under

this Agreement and that by virtue of entering into this Agreement it is not and will not be in breach of any express or implied obligation to any third party binding upon it.

3 Duration [5.4]

EITHER (VERSION A Fixed Term):

[This Agreement shall commence on the [date hereof] for an initial period of 2 years and shall continue thereafter [unless or] until terminated by either party giving to the other not less than 6 months' written notice [expiring] [given] on the last day of the said initial period or at any time thereafter, but shall be subject to earlier termination as hereinafter provided.]

OR (VERSION B Indefinite Term):

[This Agreement shall commence on the date hereof and shall continue thereafter until termination in accordance with clause 15 or 16.]

4 Sale and purchase of the products [5.2]

(1) [The Company shall sell and the Distributor shall purchase the Products in accordance with the provisions of Schedule 2.] [The sale and purchase of the Products as between the Company and the Distributor shall be governed by the Company's standard conditions of sale in force at the date hereof, a copy of which is annexed hereto for the purpose of identification as Schedule 2.]

[**Note**: The distributor will want to know in advance what terms will apply to its purchases, so that it knows what terms to pass on to its customers.]

(2) If there shall be any inconsistency between the provisions of [Schedule 2] [the said conditions of sale] and the [other] provisions of this Agreement, then the latter shall prevail.

(3) On the execution of this Agreement the Distributor shall deliver a [cheque] [banker's draft] to the Company in full payment for the Initial Order.

5 Demonstration versions [5.3.6.3]

(1) The Company shall provide the Distributor with a reasonable number of demonstration versions of the Products which shall be and shall remain the property of the Company. The Distributor shall not make any copies of such demonstration versions.

(2) The Distributor shall not remove or interfere with any notices on such demonstration versions indicating that they are the property of the Company.

(3) The Distributor shall not copy such demonstration versions without the Company's prior written permission.

(4) The Company shall promptly replace such demonstration versions with an equivalent number of any new versions of the Products which the Company may produce from time to time, subject to all previous demonstration versions (whether provided by the Company or copied with the prior written permission of the

Company in accordance with clause 5(3) hereof) being delivered up to the Company.

(5) The Distributor shall use such demonstration versions for the purpose of demonstrating the Products to bona fide prospective customers only and for no other purpose.

(6) The Distributor shall at all times keep such demonstration versions properly stored, protected and insured and under its exclusive control and shall return them to the Company free from any lien, restriction or encumbrance or otherwise dispose of them as the Company may from time to time direct.

6 Training [5.3.6.6]

(1) The Company shall provide training in the use, installation and maintenance of the Products for the Distributor's personnel as specified in Schedule 3, free of charge.

[**Note:** Clause 6(1) presupposes a minimum period of free training, to assist the distributor in the marketing of the products.]

(2) Any additional training required by the Distributor shall be provided by the Company (within a reasonable period of time from the Distributor's request for such additional trading) in accordance with its standard scale of charges in force from time to time.

EITHER: (VERSION A Training by Distributor):

[(3) The Distributor shall offer training in the use of the Products to all its customers on commercially reasonable terms and shall use its reasonable endeavours to persuade them to complete training courses in accordance with the Company's minimum recommendations from time to time in force.]

OR (VERSION B Training by Company):

[(3) All training to customers of the Distributor in relation to the use of the Products shall be provided by the Company at its direction. The Distributor shall refer all requests for such training to the Company.]

7 Distributor's obligations [5.1, 5.6]

The Distributor shall:

(1) use all reasonable endeavours to promote and extend the sale of the Products throughout the Territory;

(2) perform its obligations hereunder in accordance with all reasonable instructions which the Company may give the Distributor from time to time;

(3) promptly inform the Company of any opportunities of which the Distributor becomes aware and which are likely to be relevant in relation to the commercial exploitation of the Products in the Territory and which are advantageous or disadvantageous to the interests of the Company;

(4) at all times conduct its business in a manner that will reflect favourably on the Products and on the good name and reputation of the Company;

(5) not by itself or with others participate in any illegal, deceptive, misleading or unethical practices including, but not limited to, disparagement of the Products or the Company or other practices which may be detrimental to the Products or the Company;

(6) not during the continuance of this Agreement [and for the period of *1 year(s)* after its termination] (whether alone or jointly and whether directly or indirectly) be concerned or interested in the manufacture, marketing, distribution or sale of any products in the Territory which are similar to or competitive with any of the Products or which perform the same or similar functions;

[**Note**: The parties should consider the application of U.K. and E.U. competition law to such restrictive arrangements. In practice, many sellers structure such restrictions so as to fall within applicable E.U. block exemptions. In general, distributors will object to post-termination restrictions of more than one year, although in practice, it is likely that restrictions on manufacturing, purchasing selling or reselling goods which are greater than a year will not be enforceable under current E.U. regulations.]

(7) if any dispute shall arise between the Distributor and any of its customers in respect of the Products (or their installation or maintenance), promptly inform the Company and comply with all reasonable directions of the Company in relation thereto;

(8) at all times employ a sufficient number of full-time technical support and sales staff having sufficient training and expertise properly to display, demonstrate, sell and instruct customers in the installation and use of the Products and address customer enquiries and needs regarding the Products;

[**Note**: On occasion, minimum numbers of trained staff may be specified or else specific training and qualifications may be identified as being required.]

(9) at all times maintain adequate demonstration facilities for the Products;

(10) supply to the Company such reports, returns and other information relating to orders and projected orders for the Products as the Company may from time to time reasonably require;

(11) provide the Company with quarterly stock reports showing the Distributor's stock of each of the Products at the beginning and end of each quarter [and the movement of stocks during the quarter];

(12) provide the Company with such financial information relating to the Distributor's business as may be necessary for the Company to establish and maintain a credit limit for the Distributor from time to time;

(13) not make any promises or representations or give any warranties or guarantees in respect of the Products except such as are consistent with those which accompany the Products or as expressly authorised by the Company in writing;

(14) use the Company's trade marks and trade names relating to the Products only in the registered or agreed style in connection with the marketing and sale of the Products and shall not use such trade marks or trade names in connection with any other products or services or as part of the corporate or any trade name of the Distributor;

(15) not alter, obscure, remove, interfere with or add to any of the trade marks, trade names, markings or notices affixed to or contained in the Products or the Product Documentation at the time when they are delivered to the Distributor;

(16) not alter or interfere with the Products or the Product Documentation;

(17) ensure that it sells only the latest versions of the [Software] Products and that on receipt of the latest versions of the [Software] Products from the Company, all earlier versions of the [Software] Products are surrendered to the Company or otherwise disposed of in accordance with the Company's instructions;

[**Note**: if the software products have been pre-installed, this obligation may require some re-installation of the new software on the hardware products.]

(18) keep sufficient stocks of the Products to satisfy customer demand;

[**Note**: This depends on the method of distribution; sometimes, the supplier will only ship the products on receipt of an order for products and payment thereafter.]

(19) be responsible for the proper installation of the Products, save where installation can readily and easily be undertaken by the customer in accordance with the instructions set out in the Product Documentation and the customer indicates that he wishes to undertake installation himself;

[(20) offer training courses in respect of the then current version of each of the [Software] Products to its customers on commercially reasonable terms and shall undertake its obligations thereunder to standards generally observable in the industry;]

(21) ensure that it sells only the latest version of the [Software] Products and that on the receipt of the latest versions of each of the same [Software] Products from the Company all earlier versions of each of the same [Software] Products are surrendered to the Company or otherwise disposed of in accordance with the Company's written instructions;

[(22) ensure that it sells only the latest version of the Software Products on the Hardware Products and that on receipt of a new version of any one or more of the Software Products where any earlier version of any such of the Software Products has been pre-installed on any one of the Hardware Products it will erase it from the Hardware Product and substitute it for the latest version of the Software Products;]

[**Note**: This last sub-clause will only be required where the software is pre-installed on the hardware. If the software is not pre-installed on the hardware from the company, this sub-clause will need further adaptation.]

(23) offer maintenance contracts in respect of the [Hardware] Products to its customers on commercially reasonable terms and shall undertake its obligations thereunder to the standards generally observed in the industry;

[**Note**: In appropriate circumstances, software support may also be offered.]

(24) purchase and maintain an inventory of spare parts for the [Hardware] Products in accordance with the Company's minimum recommendations from time to time (such spare parts to be purchased on the same terms as the Products (so far as the same are applicable));

(25) not offer or undertake any maintenance services in respect of the Software Products;

[Note: See comments above; the distributor may in certain circumstances also be the support services provider.]

(26) provide an efficient after sales service in respect of the Products;

(27) observe all applicable laws and regulations in respect of and obtain all necessary licences, consents and permissions required for the storage, marketing and sale of the Products and for the maintenance of the [Hardware] Products in the Territory;

(28) provide the Company with all information necessary to enable the Company to ensure that the Products comply with local laws and regulations and promptly advise the Company of any change or proposed change thereto;

(29) co-operate with the Company in the recall of any of the Products for safety checks or modifications;

(30) not at any time represent itself as the agent of the Company; and

(31) permit the Company and its authorised agents at all reasonable times to enter any of the Distributor's premises for the purpose of ascertaining that the Distributor is complying with its obligations under this Agreement.

[Note: Disclosures of books of account, etc., may be required if the distributor's payments are linked to volumes of sales and/or percentages of revenues resulting from sales of the products.]

8 Company's obligations [5.1, 5.3.6.6, 5.5, 5.7]

The Company shall:

(1) provide the Distributor with such marketing and technical assistance [as is reasonably necessary] [as the Company may in its discretion consider necessary] to assist the Distributor with the promotion of the Products;

(2) endeavour to answer as soon as reasonably possible all technical queries raised by the Distributor [or its customers] concerning the use or application of the Products;

(3) provide the Distributor with adequate quantities of Product Documentation and promotional literature and other information relating to the Products to enable the Distributor to fulfill its obligations under this Agreement;

(4) subject to the Distributor complying with its obligations under clause 7(27), ensure that the Products comply with local laws and regulations relating to their [manufacture,]sale, maintenance and use in the Territory;

[Note: Manufacturing responsibility will depend on whether the distributor is supplied with the products by the company, or is also charged with manufacturing them.]

(5) promptly provide the Distributor with the newest commercially available versions of the [Software] Products and, where necessary, revised Product Documentation relating to such [Software] Products;

(6) give the Distributor reasonable advance written notice of any significant change to any of the Products or of the Company's intention to discontinue selling any of the Products to the Distributor;

(7) offer to the Distributor for inclusion in the Products any product of the Company which can reasonably be regarded as a replacement for or successor to any Product which the Company discontinues selling pursuant to clause 12(2); and

(8) provide the Distributor with all information and assistance reasonably necessary to enable the Distributor properly to perform its obligations hereunder in respect of any modified or enhanced versions of the Products.

9 Intellectual property rights [2.8, 3.8]

(1) All intellectual property rights in or relating to the Products and the Product Documentation are and shall remain the property of the Company [or its licensors].

(2) The Distributor shall notify the Company immediately if the Distributor becomes aware of any illegal or unauthorised use of any of the Products or the Product Documentation or any of the intellectual property rights therein or relating thereto and will assist the Company (at the Company's expense) in taking all steps necessary to defend the Company's rights therein.

(3) The provisions of this clause shall survive the termination of this Agreement.

10 Software Products [5.3.6, 5.3.6.4, E]

(1) The Distributor shall ensure that:

EITHER (VERSION A):

[the Company is named as a beneficiary in any contract for sale of Software Products between the Distributor and its customers, such as to confer on the Company rights and obligations as a named third party pursuant to the Contracts (Rights of Third Parties) Act 1999.]

OR (VERSION B):

[all copies of the Software Products which are sold to its customers shall be accompanied by a Shrink-Wrap Licence together with the following sticker (which will appear on the front of the packaging for the Software Products):

"IMPORTANT NOTICE: This software and its associated documentation is the copyright of [   ]. The use of this software is governed by the Licence Agreement accompanying this package."]

(2) If any of the Distributor's customers shall return any Software Product to the Distributor within the time period permitted by its accompanying Shrink-Wrap Licence on the ground that he does not agree to the terms of such licence, the Distributor shall promptly refund the purchase price to that customer and return the relevant Software Product to the Company (whereupon the Company will give the Distributor a new copy of the Software Product in exchange for the returned copy).

11 Confidentiality

Each party shall treat as confidential all Confidential Information obtained form the other pursuant to this Agreement and shall not divulge any such Confidential

Information to any person (except to such party's own employees and then only to those employees who need to know the same) without the other party's prior written consent provided that this clause 11 shall not extend to information which was rightfully in the possession of such party prior to the commencement of the negotiations leading to this Agreement, which is already public knowledge or becomes so at a future date (otherwise than as a result of a breach of this clause 11) or which is trivial or obvious. Each party shall ensure that its employees are aware of and comply with the provisions of this clause 11. The foregoing obligations as to confidentiality shall survive any termination of this Agreement.

12 Reservation of rights

The Company reserves the right:

(1) to make modifications or additions to the Products or the packaging or finish thereof in any way whatsoever as the Company may in its discretion determine;

(2) to discontinue selling any of the Products to the Distributor;

(3) to require the Distributor to substitute for any of the Products or Product Documentation a new version of such Product or Product Documentation; and

(4) to require the Distributor either not to use or to cease to use any advertising or promotional materials in respect of the Products which the Company considers not to be in the Company's best interests.

13 The Territory [5.3.1]

(1) The Company shall not during the continuance of this Agreement sell or supply any of the Products (including any products which it has discontinued selling to the Distributor pursuant to clause 12(2)) to any third party situated in the Territory.

(2) The Company shall promptly forward to the Distributor any enquiries it may receive for any of the Products from persons situated in the Territory.

[Note: The company may wish to reserve the right to continue with its own marketing; subclause (1) and (2) would then need to be deleted.]

(3) The Company shall have no liability to the Distributor in the event that any of the Company's distributors appointed in other territories import any of the Products into the Territory for sale therein.

(4) The Distributor shall not advertise or maintain stocks of the Products outside the Territory or otherwise actively solicit orders for the Products from persons who are situated outside the Territory but the Distributor shall not be prohibited from fulfilling any unsolicited orders actually placed by such persons.

14 Legal relationship [5.0.2]

(1) During the continuance of this Agreement the Distributor shall be entitled to use the title "[   ] AUTHORISED DISTRIBUTOR" but such use shall be in accordance with the Company's policies in effect from time to time and before using such title (whether on the Distributor's business stationery, advertising material or elsewhere) the Distributor shall submit to the Company proof prints and

such other details as the Company may require and the Company may in its discretion grant or withhold permission for such proposed use.

(2) The relationship of the parties is that of seller and buyer and nothing in this Agreement shall render the Distributor a partner or agent of the Company. The Distributor is an independent contractor buying and selling in its own name and at its own risk. The Distributor shall not bind or purport to bind the Company to any obligation nor expose the Company to any liability nor pledge or purport to pledge the Company's credit.

15 Termination [5.4]

(1) Notwithstanding anything else contained herein, this Agreement may be terminated:

> (a) by the Company forthwith on giving notice in writing to the Distributor if:
>
> > (i) the Distributor shall [(or shall threaten to)] sell, assign, part with or cease to carry on its business or that part of its business relating to the distribution of the Products; or
> >
> > (ii) the control (as defined for the purposes of section 416 of the Income and Corporation Taxes Act 1988) of the Distributor shall be transferred to any person or persons other than the person or persons in control of the Distributor at the date hereof (but the Company shall only be entitled to terminate within the period of *60* days after the Company shall have been notified in writing of the change in control).
>
> (b) by either party forthwith on giving notice in writing to the other if:
>
> > (i) the other party commits any material [or persistent] breach of any term of this Agreement and (in the case of a breach capable of being remedied) shall have failed, within *30* days after the receipt of a request in writing from the other party so to do, to remedy the breach (such request to contain a warning of such party's intention to terminate);

[**Note**: Allowing termination for "persistent" breaches can be problematic, as they can on occasion be used to engineer terminations for convenience.]

> > [(ii) diplomatic relations between the respective countries of the parties makes the continuance of this Agreement unduly difficult;]
> >
> > (iii) the other party shall have been unable to perform its obligations hereunder for a period of *90* consecutive days or for periods aggregating *180* days in any Year (but the party entitled to terminate may only terminate within the period of *60* days after the expiration of the said consecutive period or Year); or
> >
> > (iv) the other party shall have a receiver or administrative receiver appointed of it or over any part of its undertaking or assets or shall pass a resolution for winding up (otherwise than for the purpose of a bona fide scheme of solvent amalgamation or reconstruction) or a court of competent jurisdiction shall make an order to that effect or if the other party shall enter into any voluntary arrangement with its creditors or shall become subject to an administration order.

(2) The Distributor shall not be entitled to any compensation or indemnity (whether for loss of distribution rights, goodwill or otherwise) as a result of the termination of this Agreement in accordance with its terms.

[(3) Each delivery of a consignment of the Products shall be regarded as a separate contract of sale and, notwithstanding the foregoing provisions of this clause 15, no one default in a delivery shall be cause for terminating this Agreement.]

[**Note**: This clause favours the company, whose obligation it is to deliver consignments of the Products.]

16 Sales coverage [5.2]

If the Distributor shall fail to submit orders to the Company for the Products having (or, in the event of any failure to respond to such orders by the Company, which would have had if fulfilled by the Company) an aggregate Invoice Price of £*1,000,000* in any Year the Company may within *60* days after the expiration of such Year forthwith by notice in writing to the Distributor:

(1) vary the extent of the distributorship either by reducing the extent of the Territory or by converting the exclusive distributorship into a non-exclusive distributorship (in which latter event clauses 2(2), 13(1) and 13(2) hereof shall cease to have effect); or (and whether or not the Company has previously taken any action pursuant to this sub-clause (1) in relation to any prior Year); or

(2) terminate this Agreement.

[Notes:

(1) A more sophisticated clause might provide for a scale of sales targets in respect of successive years automatically adjusted for inflation against an appropriate index. Such clauses are not without their problems however as it may be difficult to assess in advance what the targets should be and actual sales may dip in any year for a whole number of legitimate reasons (*e.g.* the obsolescence of the products coupled with a time lag in introducing a new range).

(2) The stance of the parties on this Clause will depend on its objectives. In some cases it will be a genuine minimum requirement with actual sales expected to be much greater; in others the sales target will be aggressively pitched to ensure maximum sales effort (although in achieving this the distributor may spend less effort on training, maintenance and after sales support).

(3) The Clause attempts to deal with the problem of the company failing to supply due to *force majeure*, by referring to orders submitted rather than actual sales. However, this does not deal with the *force majeure* of the distributor; in that case it might be appropriate to take the period of *force majeure* out of account in the relative year and adjust the sales target for that year pro-rata. Again, it depends whether the sales target is an aggressive one or not.]

(4) This Clause is of particular relevance if clause 3 has been structured so as to allow the Agreement to continue for an indefinite term.]

17 Effect of termination [5.4]

On the termination of this Agreement:

(1) all the rights and obligations of the parties under this Agreement shall automatically terminate except:

(a) for such rights of action as shall have accrued prior to such termination and any obligations which expressly or by implication are intended to come into or continue in force on or after such termination;

(b) the Distributor shall be entitled to sell any of its stocks of the Products which have been fully paid for and which are required to fulfil any unperformed contracts of the Distributor outstanding at the date of termination (and to that extent and for that purpose the provisions of this Agreement shall continue in effect);

(2) the Distributor shall immediately eliminate from all its literature, business stationery, publications, notices and advertisements all references to the title "[   ] AUTHORISED DISTRIBUTOR" and all other representations of the Distributor's appointment hereunder;

(3) the Distributor shall at its own expense forthwith return to the Company or otherwise dispose of as the Company may instruct all Confidential Information belonging to the Company and all technical and promotional materials and other documents and papers whatsoever sent to the Distributor and relating to the Products or the business of the Company (other than correspondence between the parties) and all property of the Company being in each case in the Distributor's possession or under its control;

(4) the Distributor shall cause the Software Products to be erased from all computers of or under the control of the Distributor and shall certify to the Company that the same has been done;

(5) save where required for the purposes of fulfilling unperformed contracts, all orders for undelivered Products shall be automatically cancelled;

(6) all outstanding unpaid invoices in respect of the Products shall become immediately payable in place of the payment terms previously agreed between the parties;

(7) the Company shall forthwith pay to the Distributor any amount standing to the credit of the Distributor's account with the Company (less any moneys then owed by the Distributor to the Company);

(8) the Company shall be entitled to repossess any of the Products which have not been paid for against cancellation of the relevant invoices (and so that the Distributor hereby irrevocably licenses the Company, its employees and agents to enter any of the premises of the Distributor for such purpose);

(9) the Company shall be entitled (but not obliged) to purchase all or any unsold Products in the possession or under the control of the Distributor which have been paid for by the Distributor (and which are not required to fulfil any unperformed contracts of the Distributor outstanding at the date of termination) at the Invoice Price (or, if lower, the written down value of the Products appearing in the accounting records of the Distributor at the date of termination), subject to the Company paying all necessary Value Added Tax and other taxes, duties or levies, and paying the cost of and arranging transport and insurance and to notifying the Distributor in writing of its requirements within *14* days of the date of termination. The Distributor shall give the Company all necessary assistance and co-operation for the purpose of giving effect to the provisions of this sub-clause and of delivering the Products to the Company but, subject thereto, any Products which are not purchased by the Company within *30* days of its notice may be sold by the Distributor (the Distributor using its best endeavours to sell the same within *3* months thereafter) in accordance with the terms of this Agreement (and to that extent and for that purpose such terms shall continue in effect); and

(10) the Distributor shall give the Company details of all outstanding maintenance contracts which it has entered into in respect of the Hardware [and/ or Software] Products [and subject thereto and to the Distributor forthwith

taking all necessary steps to determine the same at the earliest possible date (without causing the Distributor to incur any additional liability thereby) the Company shall continue to supply the Distributor on the terms of this Agreement (which to that extent and for that purpose shall continue in effect) with all spare parts necessary for the Distributor properly to perform its remaining obligations under such maintenance contracts but for a period of no longer than 2 years after the date of termination]; Provided that the provisions of this sub-clause shall apply only where this Agreement has been terminated by notice given in accordance with clause 3 or by the Distributor under clause 15 or by the Company under clause 16.

18 Liability [5.8]

(1) The Company warrants to the Distributor that the Products sold to the Distributor hereunder will comply with the relevant specifications published by the Company, including without limitation, the Product Documentation and will be of [satisfactory] quality.

(2) If the Company shall be in breach of the said warranty in clause 18(1) above its liability shall be limited to replacing the Products concerned (at the Company's risk and expense) or, at its option, refunding the price paid by the Distributor (subject to the Distributor returning the defective Products to the Company at the Company's risk and expense) or (if an abatement of the price is agreed with the Distributor) refunding to the Distributor the appropriate part of the price paid.

(3) The Company shall have no liability to the Distributor under sub-clauses (1) and (2) above:

(a) for any damage to or defects in any of the Products caused by fair wear and tear, improper use, maintenance or repair, negligent handling, failure to observe the instructions accompanying the Products or any alterations thereto;

(b) unless, in the case of any damage to or defect in the Products which would have been apparent on reasonable inspection, the Distributor notifies the Company of the same in writing within 14 days after the date of delivery thereof or, in any other case, the Company receives written notice thereof within 2 years after the date of delivery, and if no such notification is given (in either case) within the requisite period the Distributor shall not be entitled to reject the Products concerned and shall be obliged to pay the price therefor in full.

(4) Notwithstanding anything else contained in this Agreement but subject to sub-clause (5) below, the Company shall not be liable to the Distributor for loss of profits or contracts or other indirect or consequential loss or damage whether arising from negligence, breach of contract or any other cause of action arising out of the subject matter of this Agreement.

(5) Neither party excludes liability for death or personal injury caused by that party's breach of contract or negligence.

(6) The express terms of this Agreement are in lieu of all warranties, conditions, terms, undertakings and obligations implied by statute, common law, custom, trade

usage, course of dealing or otherwise, all of which are hereby excluded to the fullest extent permitted by law.

19 Waiver of remedies

See clause 28 of Precedent A.

20 Indemnities

(1) The Company shall indemnify the Distributor and keep the Distributor fully and effectively indemnified against any and all losses, claims, damages, costs, charges, expenses, liabilities, demands, proceedings and actions which the Distributor may sustain or incur or which may be brought or established against it by any person and which in any case arise out of or in relation to or by reason of:

  (a) any claim or allegation that any of the Products infringes any [U.K.] intellectual property rights of any unaffiliated third party;

  (b) any claim that the Products do not comply with local laws and regulations relating to their sale and use in the Territory;

and which are not due to the Distributor's negligence, recklessness or wilful misconduct or any breach of its obligations under this Agreement.

(2) The Distributor shall indemnify the Company and keep the Company fully and effectively indemnified against any and all losses, claims, damages, costs, charges, expenses, liabilities, demands, proceedings and actions which the Company may sustain or incur, or which may be brought or established against it by any person and which in any case arise out of or in relation to or by reason of:

  (a) the negligence, recklessness or wilful misconduct of the Distributor in the performance of any of its obligations in connection with the installation and maintenance of the Products;

  (b) any unauthorised action or omission of the Distributor or its employees;

  (c) the manner in which the Distributor markets and sells the Products;

  (d) the independent supply by the Distributor of any products or services for use in conjunction with or in relation to the Products; or

  (e) any breach or alleged breach of any applicable laws or regulations relating to the storage, marketing or sale by the Distributor of the Products in the Territory.

(3) If any claim is made against either party for which indemnification is sought under this clause, the indemnified party shall notify the indemnifying party and shall allow the indemnifying party sole conduct of the defence or settlement of such claim. The indemnified party shall co-operate with the indemnifying party in relation to any reasonable request made by the indemnifying party in respect of such claim, at the cost of the indemnifying party. The indemnified party shall not prejudice the defence of such claim.

21 *Force majeure*

See clause 15 of Precedent A.

22 Notices

See clause 32 of Precedent A.

[**Note**: This clause will require modification if the parties are situated in different countries.]

23 Interpretation

See clause 33 of Precedent A.

24 General

This Agreement constitutes the entire understanding between the parties concerning the subject matter of this Agreement and shall be governed by and construed in accordance with the laws of England. No waiver or amendment of any provision of this Agreement shall be effective unless made by a written instrument signed by both parties. Each provision of this Agreement shall be construed separately and notwithstanding that the whole or any part of any such provision may prove to be illegal or unenforceable the other provisions of this Agreement and the remainder of the provision in question shall continue in full force and effect. The parties submit to the exclusive jurisdiction of the English Courts [but without prejudice to either party's rights to bring proceedings in any other jurisdiction where the other party is incorporated or has assets to enforce any ruling made in the English Courts.]

25 Third Parties [1.3]

See clause 37 of Precedent A.

EXECUTED under hand in two originals the day and year first before written

SIGNED for and on behalf of
COMPANY [LIMITED] [PLC]

By

Signature

Title

Witness

SIGNED for and on behalf of
DISTRIBUTOR [LIMITED] [PLC]

By

Signature

Title

Witness

SCHEDULE 1

PRODUCTS

[HARDWARE PRODUCTS]

[SOFTWARE PRODUCTS]

[TRAINING/TECHNICAL MATERIALS]

[PRODUCT DOCUMENTATION]

[SPARE PARTS]

SCHEDULE 2

[SALES TERMS] or [COMPANY STANDARD TERMS
& CONDITIONS OF SALE]

[1. Orders

(1) Each order for the Products submitted by the Distributor to the Company shall be in writing and shall stipulate the type and quantity of the Products ordered and the requested delivery date and delivery destination.

(2) The Distributor may cancel any order [(whether or not accepted)] or reduce the quantity of any of the Products ordered by submitting to the Company a written notice that specifically refers to the relevant order, stipulates the change and is actually received by the Company not less than *14* days prior to the requested delivery date or, if later, the estimated delivery date notified to the Distributor pursuant to paragraph 3(2) below.

[**Note**: delete the square-bracketed phase if sub-paragraph (4) is omitted.]

(3) The Distributor shall be responsible for ensuring the accuracy of its orders.

[(4) Each order shall be subject to acceptance by the Company which may be made either by depositing an acknowledgement card in the [United Kingdom] mail, postage prepaid and addressed to the Distributor or by delivering the Products ordered or any part thereof].

[**Note**: If the company reserves the right to refuse to accept orders the distributor will be less inclined to agree to sales targets or any other obligation which could be affected by the company's refusal to supply.]

2. Price and payment

(1) Subject as hereinafter provided, the price for each of the Products (including packaging) to be paid by the Distributor shall be the Company's published ex-factory price (in *pounds sterling*) in effect on the date of delivery ("the Ex-Factory Price") less a discount of *15* per cent ("the Basic Price").

(2) The Company reserves the right to change the Ex-Factory Price at any time and from time to time but shall give the Distributor not less than *60* days' prior written notice ("Price Change Notice Period") of the effective date of any change.

(3) In the case of an increase in the Ex-Factory Price, the price for any of the Products ordered under a purchase order submitted to the Company prior to the commencement of a Price Change Notice Period requesting delivery during the Price Change Notice Period shall be based on the Ex-Factory Price in effect prior to the effective date of such price increase whether or not delivered prior to that effective date.

(4) In the case of a decrease in the Ex-Factory Price, the price for any of the Products delivered within the Price Change Notice Period shall be based on the Ex-Factory Price as decreased.

(5) All prices for the Products are exclusive of Value Added Tax or other applicable sales tax which shall be paid by the Distributor at the appropriate rate.

(6) Payment for the Products shall be made no later than the last day of the calendar month next following the date of the Company's invoice therefor.

(7) The Company may sue for the price of the Products notwithstanding that delivery has not occurred or property in them not passed to the Distributor.

(8) The Distributor shall be entitled to a pre-payment discount of 3 per cent of the Ex-Factory Price in addition to the discount referred to in sub-paragraph (1) above. To take advantage of the pre-payment discount the Distributor must remit the price for the Products (less the pre-payment discount) to the Company at the same time as it submits its order therefor and contemporaneously notify the Company in writing of its decision. If payment is not received by the Company in cleared funds within 7 days after receiving the Distributor's order, the Distributor shall not be entitled to the pre-payment discount and sub-paragraph (6) above shall apply.

(9) The Distributor shall be entitled to an additional volume discount on the Ex-Factory Price (before the discounts referred to in sub-paragraphs (1) and (8) above are applied) calculated by reference to its purchase of the Products in any Year in accordance with the following table:

[Sterling] Volume Purchased in Year (calculated on the Basic Price before any pre-payment discount)	*Discount*
Up to £299,999	Nil
£300,000 to £499,999	*[ ]%*
£500,000 to £699,999	*[ ]%*
£700,000 to £899,999	*[ ]%*
£900,000 and above	*[ ]%*

If the Distributor is entitled to any such additional discount in respect of its purchase of the Products in any Year the Company shall within 30 days after the end of that Year credit to the Distributor's account the amount of the additional discount to which it is entitled. Purchases in a Year shall be calculated by reference to the date on which the Company receives payment in cleared funds.

(10) Payment for the Products shall be made in *pounds sterling* and by bank transfer to such bank account(s) as the Company shall notify in writing to the Distributor from time to time

(11) If payment for any of the Products is not received by the due date then (without prejudice to the Company's other rights and remedies) the Company shall be entitled to:

(a) suspend all further deliveries of the Products until payment is received; and

(b) charge the Distributor interest on the unpaid sum on a day to day basis (as well after as before judgment) from the date or last date for payment thereof to the date of actual payment (both dates inclusive) at the rate of 3 per cent above the base rate of [   ] Bank plc (or such other London Clearing Bank as the Company may nominate) from time to time in force compounded quarterly. Such interest shall be paid on demand by the Company.

(12) The Company reserves the right to suspend deliveries of the Products while the aggregate amount of outstanding unpaid invoices exceeds the Company's credit limit for the Distributor from time to time as notified to the Distributor in writing.

3. Deliveries

(1) The Company shall use all reasonable endeavours to meet the delivery dates requested by the Distributor [(subject to acceptance of the relative order)], but time of delivery shall not be of the essence and the Company shall have no liability to the Distributor if it fails to meet any requested or estimated date for delivery.

[Note: delete the square bracketed phrase if paragraph 1(4) is omitted.]

(2) If the Company is unable to meet any requested delivery date it shall as soon as practicable notify the Distributor of its estimated date for delivery.

(3) Appropriation of the Products to any order of the Distributor shall occur when the Products are delivered to the Distributor.

(4) Delivery of the Products will be ex the Company's main distribution centre at [   ] [or such other place in *the United Kingdom* as the Company shall notify the Distributor from time to time] ("the Delivery Point").

(5) The Company shall bear the expense of putting the Products in the possession of the carrier at the Delivery Point but the Distributor shall pay all other costs of transport and insurance.

(6) If requested in the Distributor's order, the Company shall arrange (as agent for the Distributor) transport and insurance of the Products to the destination designated in the Distributor's order and shall obtain and promptly deliver to the Distributor the documents, if any, necessary for the Distributor or the Distributor's customer (as the case may be) to obtain possession of the Products. The Distributor shall reimburse the Company for all costs incurred by the Company in respect of the foregoing and all applicable provisions of this Schedule shall apply, mutatis mutandis, to the payment of such costs as they apply to the payment of the price for the Products.

(7) The Company reserves the right to make partial deliveries of any consignment of the Products ordered but, unless otherwise agreed, no delivery of the whole or

any part of a consignment shall be made before the delivery date requested by the Distributor.

(8) The Company will pack the Products suitably for delivery to the destinations requested by the Distributor and each consignment shall be accompanied by a delivery note in such form as may be agreed between the parties.

[(9) The Distributor shall be responsible for obtaining, prior to delivery, all necessary licences, certificates of origin and other documents for the importation of the Products into the Territory and for paying all applicable import duties and other levies.]

(10) The Distributor shall notify the Company in writing of any Products delivered in excess of the quantities ordered within *14* days after delivery. The Distributor reserves the right to return such surpluses to the Company at the Company's risk and expense. Alternatively, the Distributor shall have the right to retain such surpluses upon payment therefor at the price which the Distributor would have paid if it had ordered the same.

(11) The Distributor shall notify the Company within *14* days after the delivery of any consignment of the Products of any shortage in the quantity ordered. The Company shall make good any such shortage as soon as reasonably practicable after written notice is received from the Distributor in compliance with this paragraph but otherwise the Company shall have no liability to make good such shortage.

4. Risk and property

(1) Risk in each consignment of the Products shall pass to the Distributor at the Delivery Point upon placement of that consignment into the carrier's possession by the Company.

(2) Legal and beneficial ownership of any consignment of the Products shall not pass to the Distributor until payment in full and in cleared funds has been received by the Company in respect of the price for that consignment and for all other consignments of the Products for which payment is then due.

Schedule 3

TRAINING

[**Note**: This Schedule should identify:

    (1) How many staff are to be trained in total?

    (2) How many can be trained at one time?

    (3) How many days' training is required for each person?

    (4) Where and when training is to take place?

    (5) Who is to be responsible for subsistence and travelling expenses?]

[SCHEDULE 4

THIRD-PARTY RIGHTS]

SOFTWARE MARKETING AGREEMENT

[**Note**: Schedule 1 contains a software licence agreement to be used by the dealer in procuring contracts with end-users (licensees).]

THIS AGREEMENT is made the   day of   20

PARTIES:

(1) COMPANY [LIMITED] [PLC] whose registered office is at

("the Company")

(2) DEALER [LIMITED] [PLC] whose registered office is at

("the Dealer")

RECITALS:

(A) The Company is the proprietor of certain computer software known as
["   "]

[**Note**: If the agreement relates to more than one piece of software from the company rather than a particular package then the agreement will need to be modified accordingly with reference to a schedule listing the relevant software.]

(B) The Company has agreed to appoint the Dealer as its non-exclusive marketing agent for the purpose of securing licence and support agreements for such software with end-users situated in the Territory (as hereinafter defined) on the terms and conditions hereinafter contained.

NOW IT IS HEREBY AGREED as follows:

1 Definitions

In this Agreement, unless the context otherwise requires, the following expressions shall have the following meanings:

"Confidential Information"	means this Agreement and all information obtained by one party from the other pursuant to this Agreement which is expressly marked as confidential or which is manifestly confidential or which is confirmed in writing to be confidential within 7 days of its disclosure.
"End-User Agreement"	means a software licence and support agreement in the form set out in Schedule 1 as amended from time to time or in such other form as the Company may from time to time direct or approve in writing.

"intellectual property rights"	means patents, trade marks, Internet domain names, service marks, registered designs, applications for any of the foregoing, copyright, design rights, trade and business names and any other similar protected rights in any country.
"licensee"	means a person situated in the Territory who is a party to an End-User Agreement with the Company in respect of the Software and who was introduced (or deemed to be introduced) by the Dealer pursuant to this Agreement.
"Net Licence Fee" [5.2]	means the fee paid by a licensee to use the Software excluding (i) support charges, (ii) any charges payable in respect of modifications, additions, installation or training made or provided by the Company in respect of the Software and (iii) Value Added Tax.
"Product Description"	means the product description of the Software describing the facilities and functions thereof as supplied to the Dealer by the Company from time to time.
"Recommended Compatible Hardware List"	means a list of computer hardware, provided by the Company to the Dealer from time to time, setting out computer hardware products which the Company recommends as being compatible with the Software.
"Software"	means [the Company's "[ ]" software] [the Company's proprietary software set out in Schedule [ ] hereto] including all demonstration versions as described in clause 5 and all modifications, enhancements and replacements thereof and additions thereto [which result in a generally available new release or version of such software] produced by the Company from time to time [together with any patches or other supplementary software as may be issued by the Company to the Dealer from time to time].
"Software Documentation"	means the operating manuals and other literature provided by the Company from time to time to end-users for use in conjunction with the Software.
"Software Materials"	means the Software, the Product Description and the Software Documentation.
"Territory" [5.3.1]	means *the United Kingdom of Great Britain and Northern Ireland*.

"Year"   means any period of 12 months commencing on *the date hereof* or any anniversary of *the date hereof*.

2 Appointment [5.0.2, 5.3.3]

(1) The Company hereby appoints the Dealer and the Dealer hereby agrees to act as the non-exclusive marketing agent of the Company for the purpose of securing End-User Agreements with prospective licensees situated in the Territory.

(2) The Dealer shall secure End-User Agreements in accordance with the licence and support fees specified by the Company from time to time and in accordance with the terms of this Agreement and otherwise in accordance with any reasonable instructions which the Company may give the Dealer from time to time.

(3) The Dealer shall not be entitled to assign or sub-contract any of its rights or obligations under this Agreement or appoint any agent to perform such obligations.

(4) The Dealer represents and warrants to the Company that it has the ability and experience to carry out the obligations assumed by it under this Agreement and that by virtue of entering into this Agreement it is not and will not be in breach of any express or implied obligation to any third party binding upon it.

[**Note**: The dealer may be appointed as exclusive marketing agent for the company in which case the following additional clause should be inserted:

"(5) The Company shall not during the continuance of this Agreement in respect of the Software and in the Territory:

(a)   appoint any other person to act as its marketing agent; and/or

(b)   grant to any party, without the Dealer's prior consent (not to be unreasonably withheld), any rights similar in scope or nature to the rights granted to the Dealer under this Agreement."

The dealer may also be appointed as "sole" marketing agent in which case the company will itself also be prevented from carrying out any marketing activities in relation to the software.]

3 Duration

This Agreement shall commence on the *date hereof* for an initial period of *2* years and shall continue thereafter [unless or] until terminated by either party giving to the other not less than *6* months' written notice [expiring] [given] on the last day of the said initial period or at any time thereafter, but shall be subject to earlier termination as hereinafter provided.

4 Licensing [5.3.6]

(1) The Dealer shall ensure that any prospective licensee who wishes to obtain a licence of and support for the Software shall execute an End-User Agreement in duplicate which shall then be submitted to the Company for approval

(2) The Dealer shall take reasonable steps to ensure that only bona fide prospective licensees are invited to enter into End-User Agreements.

(3) The Dealer shall be responsible for ensuring that all particulars required by each End-User Agreement are fully completed prior to its submission to the Company

(except the agreement number which shall be allocated by the Company) and for remitting to the Company [within 7 days of receipt from the licensee] the licence and support charges payable by the licensee on signature of the End-User Agreement.

(4) The Company shall not be bound to enter into any End-User Agreement, but in the event of a refusal to enter into an End User Agreement submitted by the Dealer, it shall notify the Dealer of such refusal promptly.

(5) No End-User Agreement shall become effective unless and until it is executed by the Company.

(6) The Dealer shall have no authority to enter into any End-User Agreement on behalf of the Company. The Dealer shall not purport to any prospective licensee that it has such authority.

(7) The Dealer shall use its reasonable endeavours to persuade each prospective licensee to pay the full licence fee and the first year's support charge immediately upon the prospective licensee's signature of an End-User Agreement but if this is not acceptable the Dealer shall be entitled to invite the prospective licensee to agree to instalment payments no less favourable to the Company than the following:

   (a) *30* per cent of the licence fee (by way of a refundable deposit) on the prospective licensee's signature of the End-User Agreement;

   (b) *50* per cent of the licence fee at the time of installation of the Software at the licensee's site; and

   (c) *20* per cent of the licence fee and the full amount of the first year's support charge within *30* days after installation at the licensee's site.

(8) After the Company's acceptance of a licensee and signature of an End-User Agreement, the Company shall deliver to the Dealer, as soon as reasonably practicable, one copy of the current version of the Software and the Software Documentation together with an original of the End-User Agreement duly executed by the Company, whereupon the Dealer shall be responsible for the following (which shall be undertaken as soon as reasonably possible):

   (a) delivery of the Software Materials and the executed End-User Agreement to the licensee;

   (b) successful installation and implementation of the Software on one or more (as specified in the End-User Agreement) of the licensee's computers;

   (c) demonstrating to the licensee that the Software is in accordance with the Product Description and the Software Documentation by the use of test data [as [set out] [recommended] in the Software Documentation];

   (d) obtaining the licensee's acceptance of the Software by returning to the Company a completed acceptance certificate in a form approved by the Company and signed by the licensee;

   (e) where applicable, obtaining the balance of the licence fee and the full amount of the first year's support charge in accordance with the payment dates agreed with the licensee.

(9) If the Dealer fails to comply with any of its obligations under clause 4 (8) above the Company may effect compliance on behalf of the Dealer whereupon the Dealer shall forthwith become liable to pay to the Company all reasonable costs and expenses incurred by the Company as a result.

(10) The Dealer shall ensure that only the current versions of the Software and the Software Documentation supplied to the Dealer from time to time are delivered to licensees.

(11) All copies of the Software and the Software Documentation shall remain at the risk of the Company until delivered to a licensee but the Dealer shall at all times take proper care of any copies which are from time to time in its possession or under its control.

(12) The Dealer shall be entitled in its discretion to negotiate and to charge a licensee reasonable additional fees for services provided by it to the licensee in relation to delivery, implementation, training or any of these in respect of the Software, but such additional fees shall be charged only after payment in full of the licence fee and the first year's support charge due to the Company and until payment is made in full as aforesaid any additional fees received by the Dealer shall be held in trust for the Company and may be appropriated by the Company in payment of all outstanding charges due to the Company from the licensee.

5 Demonstration [copies] [versions] [4.3.2, 5.3.6.4]

(1) The Company shall provide the Dealer with *10* demonstration [copies] [versions] of the Software and the Software Documentation which shall be and shall remain the property of the Company.

[**Note**: Instead of demonstration software in its "full" form (*i.e.* with access to its entire functionality), it is quite common for a demonstration version of software to be produced which lacks many of the main features but enables a prospective customer to get an idea of its capabilities; see 4.3.2.]

(2) Such demonstration [copies] [versions] shall be promptly replaced with an equivalent number of any new releases of the Software and the Software Documentation which the Company may produce from time to time, subject to all copies of the previous releases being delivered up to the Company.

(3) The Dealer shall use such demonstration [copies] [versions] for the purpose of demonstrating the Software to bona fide prospective licensees only and for no other purpose.

(4) The Dealer shall at all times keep such demonstration [copies] [versions] properly stored and protected and under its exclusive control.

6 Training [5.3.6.6]

(1) The Company shall provide training in the installation, implementation and use of the Software for the Dealer's personnel as specified in Schedule 2.

(2) Any additional training required by the Dealer shall be provided by the Company (within a reasonable period of time from the Dealer's request for such additional training) in accordance with its standard scale of charges in force from time to time.

(3) The Company shall offer training courses for licensees at its standard rates in force from time to time and the Dealer shall use its reasonable endeavours to persuade all licensees to complete training courses in accordance with the Company's minimum recommendations from time to time.

(4) The Dealer may apply to the Company to become an authorised trainer for the Software and if so appointed shall be entitled during such appointment to train licensees [at the Company's standard rates in force from time to time].

[Note: The dealer may want to profit (or at least avoid making a direct loss) from providing training courses for licensees. However, the ability to offer training courses itself (which presumably will be more convenient for licensees than making arrangements directly with the company) may be crucial to the dealer in order to attract prospective licensees.]

(5) The Dealer's appointment as an authorised trainer may be revoked at any time or in a particular case by notice of not less than 3 months in writing given by the Company and shall automatically be revoked by the termination (for whatever reason) of this Agreement.

[Note: The dealer may also consider limiting the company's termination rights to, for example, cases where the dealer has failed to meet the appropriate training standards, and even then, perhaps only after repeated failures.]

7 Dealer's obligations [5.1, 5.6]

The Dealer shall:

(1) use its reasonable endeavours to secure End-User Agreements with prospective licensees situated in the Territory and to promote and extend the licensing of the Software throughout the Territory;

(2) promptly inform the Company of any opportunities of which the Dealer becomes aware and which are likely to be relevant in relation to the commercial exploitation of the Software and which are advantageous or disadvantageous to the interests of the Company;

(3) at all times conduct its business in a manner that will reflect favourably on the Software and on the good name and reputation of the Company;

(4) not by itself or with others participate in any illegal, deceptive, misleading or unethical practices including, but not limited to, disparagement of the Software or the Company or other practices which may be detrimental to the Software or the Company;

EITHER:

[(5) not during the continuance of this Agreement [and for the period of *1* year(s) after its termination] (whether alone or jointly and whether directly or indirectly) be concerned or interested in the marketing, distribution or sale of any software products which are similar to or competitive with the Software or which perform the same or similar functions];

[Note: The parties should consider the application of U.K. and E.U. competition law to such restrictive arrangements. In addition, the Commercial Agents (Council Directive) Regulations 1993 (the "Regulations") require post-termination restrictive covenants in agreements falling within the Regulations to be "concluded in writing" in order to be effective.]

OR:

[(5) at all times display, demonstrate and otherwise represent the Software fairly in comparison with competitive products from other suppliers];

(6) at all times employ a sufficient number of full-time staff [and in any event not less than 5 such staff] who are capable of competently demonstrating the Software to prospective licensees;

(7) at all times maintain adequate demonstration facilities for the Software;

(8) supply to the Company such reports, returns and other information relating to orders and projected orders for the Software and regarding prospective licensees as the Company may from time to time reasonably require;

(9) not make any promises or representations or give any warranties or guarantees in respect of the Software except such as are contained in the Product Specification or the Software Documentation or as expressly authorised by the Company in writing;

(10) use the Company's trade marks and trade names relating to the Software only in the registered or agreed style in connection with the marketing of the Software and shall not use such trade marks or trade names in connection with any other products or services or as part of the corporate or any trade name of the Dealer;

(11) deliver copies of the Product Description [or demonstration versions of the Software in accordance with clause 6 hereof] only to prospective licensees it reasonably believes to be bona fide;

(12) not alter, obscure, remove, interfere with or add to any of the trade marks, trade names, markings or notices affixed to or contained in the Software Materials at the time when they are delivered to the Dealer;

(13) not supply or recommend any computer equipment to a licensee for use in conjunction with the Software save for that equipment which is contained in the Company's current Recommended Compatible Hardware List supplied to the Dealer from time to time; and

(14) permit the Company and its authorised agents at all reasonable times to enter any of the Dealer's premises for the purpose of ascertaining that the Dealer is complying with its obligations under this Agreement (and so that the Dealer hereby irrevocably licenses the Company, its employees and agents to enter any such premises for such purpose).

[Note: One sometimes also sees dealers made subject to minimum sales targets, failing which their commission entitlements may be reduced and/or their distribution rights revoked.]

8 Company's obligations [5.1, 5.3.6.6, 5.5, 5.7]

The Company shall:

(1) provide the Dealer with such marketing and technical assistance [as the Company may in its discretion consider necessary] [as is reasonably necessary] to assist the Dealer with the promotion of the Software;

(2) provide the Dealer with an adequate number of copies of the Product Description [or demonstration versions of the Software in accordance with clause 6 hereof] and such other promotional literature relating to the Software which the Company may produce from time to time in order to enable the Dealer to fulfill its obligations under the Agreement;

(3) notify the Dealer from time to time of any change in the Net Licence Fee or in the Company's charges for the support of the Software;

(4) give the Dealer reasonable advance written notice of any change in the Software (including in particular any new releases or versions thereof) or of the Company's intention to discontinue licensing the Software in the Territory; and

(5) provide the Dealer promptly with all information and assistance reasonably necessary to enable the Dealer properly to perform its obligations hereunder in respect of any modified, enhanced or replacement version of or addition to the Software [subject to payment in respect of its time spent in providing such assistance at its standard rates then in force].

9 Commission [5.2]

(1) The Company shall pay the Dealer a commission at the rate of *30* per cent on the Net Licence Fee for copies of the Software licensed to and paid for by licensees.

(2) The said rate of commission shall be exclusive of Value Added Tax which shall be paid by the Company at the appropriate rate and the Dealer shall be responsible for delivering a VAT invoice to the Company at the same time as its commission accrues. No commission shall be paid except against receipt of such invoice.

(3) No commission shall be payable in respect of an End-User Agreement submitted by the Dealer and not accepted and signed by the Company.

(4) The Dealer's commission shall accrue on the execution by the Company of an End-User Agreement but, where the Net Licence Fee is payable in instalments, commission on the first instalment shall accrue on a pro rata basis and on each subsequent instalment shall accrue when the instalment is received by the Company.

(5) Within 7 days of receipt by the Company of the Net Licence Fee (or an instalment thereof) the Company shall send to the Dealer a remittance advice showing particulars of the amount due to the Dealer by way of commission accompanied by a remittance for the commission due.

(6) The Dealer shall receive all payments of licence fees and support charges as agent for the Company, shall hold such payments separate from its own moneys and shall remit such payments to the Company within 7 days of the receipt of such payments from prospective licensees.

10 Property rights [5.3.6.2]

(1) The Software Materials and the intellectual property rights therein or relating thereto are and shall remain the property of the Company and all copies thereof in the Dealer's possession, custody or control shall (to the extent that they are not exhausted by proper use) be returned to the Company or otherwise disposed of by the Dealer as the Company may from time to time direct.

(2) The Dealer shall notify the Company immediately if the Dealer becomes aware of any unauthorised use of any of the Software Materials or any of the intellectual property rights therein or relating thereto and will assist the Company (at the Company's expense) in taking all steps to defend the Company's rights therein.

(3) The Dealer shall not use, reproduce or deal in the Software Materials or any copies thereof except as expressly permitted by the terms of this Agreement.

(4) The provisions of this Clause shall survive the termination of this Agreement.

11 Confidentiality

See clause 21 of Precedent A.

[**Note**: The reference, in clause 21 of Precedent A, to the appointment of sub-contractors will not be relevant in this instance as the distributor is prohibited from sub-contracting its obligations under this agreement. Such reference should therefore not be incorporated.]

12 Reservation of rights [5.3.1]

The Company reserves the right:

(1) [to exploit the Software itself in the Territory by such means as it may think fit [including, without limitation, by the appointment of other agents, distributors and dealers];]

[**Note**: The first part of this clause (but not the second) will apply where the dealer is exclusive agent.]

(2) to modify, enhance, replace or make additions to the Software in any way whatsoever as the Company may in its discretion determine (whether for a particular licensee or generally) and to charge additional fees therefor;

(3) to discontinue licensing the Software in the Territory (whereupon this Agreement shall automatically terminate); and

(4) to require the Dealer either not to use or to cease to use any advertising or promotional materials in respect of the Software which the Company considers not to be in the Company's best interests.

13 Customer enquiries [5.3.1]

(1) The Dealer shall promptly forward to the Company any enquiries it may receive for the Software from persons situated outside the Territory.

(2) During the continuance of this Agreement the Company shall not enter into any agreement for the licensing and support of the Software with any prospective licensee situated in the Territory in which the Dealer has established and recorded his interest pursuant to clause 4(1) unless the Dealer fails to secure the execution of an End-User Agreement (other than by reason of a refusal by the Company to enter into such agreement) with that prospective licensee within a reasonable time thereafter.

(3) The Company may if it wishes (but without being under any obligation so to do) refer to the Dealer any enquiry for the Software it may receive direct from a potential licensee situated in the Territory and if the Dealer shall secure an End-User Agreement with that person the Dealer shall be deemed to have introduced that person pursuant to this Agreement and shall be entitled to its commission in the usual way.

14 Legal relationship [5.0.2]

(1) During the continuance of this Agreement the Dealer shall be entitled to use the title "AUTHORISED [   ] DEALER" but such use shall be in accordance with the Company's policies in effect from time to time and before using such title (whether on the Dealer's business stationery, advertising material, website or

elsewhere) the Dealer shall submit to the Company proof prints and such other details as the Company may require and the Company may in its discretion grant or withhold permission for such proposed use.

(2) Nothing in this Agreement shall render the Dealer a partner or (except for the purpose of securing End-User Agreements in the manner permitted by this Agreement) an agent of the Company and the Dealer shall not (except as expressly permitted or contemplated by this Agreement) purport to undertake any obligation on the Company's behalf nor expose the Company to any liability nor pledge or purport to pledge the Company's credit, nor agree to any variation of the terms of any End-User Agreement.

15 Termination [5.4]

(1) Notwithstanding anything else contained herein, this Agreement may be terminated:

   (a) by the Company forthwith on giving notice in writing to the Dealer if:

      (i) the Dealer shall (or shall threaten to) sell, assign, part with or cease to carry on its business or that part of its business relating to the marketing of the Software; or

      (ii) the control (as defined for the purposes of section 416 of the Income and Corporation Taxes Act 1988) of the Dealer shall be transferred to any person or persons other than the person or persons in control of the Dealer at the date hereof (but the Company shall only be entitled to terminate within the period of *60* days after the Company shall have been notified in writing of the change in control); or

      (iii) the Dealer shall fail to submit *10* End-User Agreements to the Company pursuant to clause 4 (1) in any Year].

   (b) by either party forthwith on giving notice in writing to the other if:

      (i) the other commits any material [or persistent] breach of any term of this Agreement and (in the case of a breach capable of being remedied) shall have failed, within *30* days after the receipt of a request in writing from the other party so to do, to remedy the breach (such request to contain a warning of such party's intention to terminate);

[**Note**: Allowing termination for "persistent" breaches can be problematic, as they can on occasion be used to engineer terminations "for convenience". However, it can be useful for a company which is concerned about the potential effect a series of minor but repeated problems may have upon its ultimate customer base.]

      (ii) the other party shall have been unable to perform its obligations hereunder by reason of an event of *force majeure* for a period of *90* consecutive days or for periods aggregating *180* days in any Year (but the party entitled to terminate may only terminate within the period of *60* days after the expiration of the said consecutive period or Year); or

      (iii) the other party shall have a receiver or administrative receiver appointed of it or over any part of its undertaking or assets or shall pass a resolution for winding up (otherwise than for the purpose of a bona fide scheme of solvent amalgamation or reconstruction) or a court of competent jurisdiction shall make an order to that effect or if the other party shall enter into any voluntary arrangement with its creditors or shall become subject to an administration order.

(2) The Dealer shall not be entitled to any compensation or indemnity (whether for loss of agency rights, goodwill or otherwise) as a result of the termination of this Agreement in accordance with its terms.

[Note: The parties should consider the provisions of the Regulations which, in relation to commercial agency agreements to which it applies, provides agents with a mandatory right to compensation or indemnity upon the termination of an agency agreement for specified reasons.]

16 Effect of termination [5.4]

On the termination of this Agreement:

(1) all rights and obligations of the parties under this Agreement shall automatically terminate except:

(a) for such rights of action as shall have accrued prior to such termination and any obligations which expressly or by implication are intended to come into or continue in force on or after such termination;

(b) that the terms of this Agreement shall remain in full force and effect in respect of any obligations to be performed hereunder by the parties in respect of an execution of End-User Agreement which remain unperformed at the time of termination (and the Dealer's obligations under sub-clauses (3) and (4) below shall be deferred insofar as may be necessary for the Dealer to perform its outstanding obligations but only until they are so performed).

(2) the Dealer shall immediately eliminate from all its literature, business stationery, publications, website, notices and advertisements all references to the title "AUTHORISED [   ] DEALER" and all other representations of the Dealer's appointment hereunder;

(3) the Dealer shall at its own expense forthwith return to the Company or otherwise dispose of as the Company may instruct all Confidential Information belonging to the Company and all promotional materials and other documents and papers whatsoever sent to the Dealer and relating to the business of the Company (other than correspondence between the parties), all property of the Company and all copies of the Software Materials, being in each case in the Dealer's possession or under its control; and

(4) the Dealer shall cause the Software [and Software Materials] to be erased from all computers of or under the control of the Dealer and shall certify to the Company that the same has been done.

17 Waiver of remedies

See clause 20 of Precedent A.

18 Indemnities

(1) The Company shall indemnify the Dealer and keep the Dealer fully and effectively indemnified against any and all losses, claims, damages, costs, charges,

expenses, liabilities, demands, proceedings and actions which the Dealer may sustain or incur or which may be brought or established against it by any person and which in any case arise out of or in relation to or by reason of:

(a) any claim or allegation that any of the Software Materials infringes any intellectual property rights of any third party;

(b) any breach or alleged breach by the Company of any of the terms (whether express or implied) of any End-User Agreement; or

(c) any breach or alleged breach by the Company of any applicable laws or regulations relating to the licensing or support of the Software in the Territory,

and which are not in any such case due to the Dealer's negligence, recklessness or wilful misconduct or any breach of its obligations under this Agreement.

(2) The Dealer shall indemnify the Company and keep the Company fully and effectively indemnified against any and all losses, claims, damages, costs, charges, expenses, liabilities, demands, proceedings and actions which the Company may sustain or incur, or which may be brought or established against it by any person and which in any case arise out of or in relation to or by reason of:

(a) any breach by the Dealer of its obligations under this Agreement;

(b) the negligence, recklessness or wilful misconduct of the Dealer in the performance of its obligations under clause 4(8);

(c) any unauthorised act or omission of the Dealer or its employees;

(d) the manner in which the Dealer markets the Software; or

(e) the independent supply by the Dealer of any products or services for use in conjunction with or in relation to the Software.

(3) If any claim is made against either party for which indemnification is sought under this Clause, the indemnified party shall promptly notify the indemnifying party and allow it sole control of the defence of the claim (provided always that the indemnifying party shall not settle or compromise the claim without the prior written consent of the indemnified party, such consent not to be unreasonably withheld or delayed). The indemnified party shall not do anything which may prejudice the defence of the claim and shall provide all reasonable assistance required by the indemnifying party in defending the claim, at the indemnifying party's cost and expense.

[Note: Owing to their commercial interests in their respective abilities to continue to market the software, both parties may have an interest in the proceedings, hence the need for each to consent to any proposed settlement.]

19 *Force majeure*

See clause 15 of Precedent A.

20 Notices

See clause 32 of Precedent A.

21 Interpretation

See clause 32 of Precedent A.

22 General

This Agreement constitutes the entire understanding between the parties concerning the subject matter of this Agreement and shall be governed by and construed in accordance with the laws of England. No waiver or amendment of any provision of this Agreement shall be effective unless made by a written instrument signed by both parties. Each provision of this Agreement shall be construed separately and notwithstanding that the whole or any part of any such provision may prove to be illegal or unenforceable the other provisions of this Agreement and the remainder of the provision in question shall continue in full force and effect. [The parties submit to the exclusive jurisdiction of the English Courts [but without prejudice to either party's rights to bring proceedings in any other jurisdiction where the other party is incorporated or has assets to enforce any ruling made in the English Courts.]]

23 Third Parties [1.3]

See clause 37 of Precedent A.

EXECUTED under hand in two originals the day and year first before written

SIGNED for and on behalf of
COMPANY [LIMITED] [PLC]

By

Signature

Title

Witness

SIGNED for and on behalf of
DEALER [LIMITED] [PLC]

By

Signature

Title

Witness

SCHEDULE 1

SOFTWARE LICENCE AND SUPPORT AGREEMENT [5.3.6.5]

Agreement No.:
(to be completed by [*Insert the name of the Company*])

Dealer's Name and Address:

Licensee's Name and Address:

Licensee's Business:

Designated Equipment:

(to be specified by type and serial number)

Installation Address:

Delivery Date:

We request the grant of a licence and the provision of support services in accordance with the above particulars and on the terms and conditions of this Agreement, which we undertake to observe.

Date:_____
for and on behalf of the
prospective licensee
("the Licensee")

Name and Title of signatory:

We approve the above prospective licensee and agree to grant and provide the requested licence and support services on the terms and conditions of this Agreement.

Date:_____
for and on behalf of
Company [Limited] [plc]
("the Company")

Name and Title of signatory:

1 Definitions

In this Agreement, unless the context otherwise requires, the following expressions have the following meanings:

"Acceptance"	means the Licensee's acceptance of the Licensed Programs pursuant to clause 5(3);
"the Delivery Date"	means the delivery date specified on the face of this agreement;
"the Designated Equipment"	means the Licensee's computer hardware and associated peripherals in respect of which the Licence is granted, specified by type and serial number on the face page of this Agreement or in a notice given to the Company in accordance with clause 4 (12)(b) [and using the *XYZ* operating system];

"intellectual property rights"	means patents, trade marks, Internet domain names, service marks, registered designs, applications for any of the foregoing, copyright, design rights, know-how, confidential information, trade and business names and other similar protected rights in any country;
"the Licensed Programs"	means the applications computer programs known as [insert a description of the programs] in object code form including any modified or enhanced versions thereof which may be supplied by the Company to the Licensee from time to time;
"the Licensed Program Materials"	means the Licensed Programs, the Program Documentation and the Media;
"the Licence"	means the licence to Use the Licensed Program Materials granted by the Company pursuant to clause 4;
"the Media"	means the media on which the Licensed Programs and the Program Documentation are recorded or printed as provided to the Licensee by the Company;
"the Premises"	means the Licensee's premises [at];
"the Product Description"	means the product description of the Licensed Programs describing the functions and facilities thereof as supplied to the Licensee by the Company;
"the Program Documentation"	means the operating manuals, user instructions, technical literature [on-line help] and other documentation and other related materials [in eye-readable form] supplied to the Licensee by the Company for aiding the use and application of the Licensed Programs by the Licensee;
"Recommended Equipment"	means any computer equipment which the Company may recommend for use with the Licensed Programs from time to time;
"the Specification"	means the specification of the Licensed Programs describing the facilities and functions thereof, a copy of which is [annexed hereto] [contained in the Program Documentation];

[**Note**: where the licensed programs are applications programs intended for use with the licensee's existing systems programs, this should be made clear in the specification. It should also be made clear that such use will not affect the company's obligations and liabilities under this agreement.]

"the Support Period"	means the period during which the Support Services shall be provided determined in accordance with clause 8(5);

"the Support Services"	means the software support services to be provided by the Company pursuant to Clause 8(1);
"Use the Licensed Programs"	means to load and subsequently to process the Licensed Programs on the Designated Equipment in accordance with the terms of this Agreement; and
"Use the Licensed Program Materials"	means to Use the Licensed Programs, to read and possess the Program Documentation in conjunction with the use of the Licensed Programs and to possess the Media in accordance with the terms of this Agreement.

2 Effective date

This Agreement shall come into effect on the date on which it is executed by the Company but unless so executed shall never become effective.

3 Products and services to be provided

The Company hereby agrees to:

[(1) make the agreed modifications to the Licensed Programs;]

(2) deliver the Licensed Programs to the Licensee and to install them on the Designated Equipment;

(3) license the Licensee to Use the Licensed Program Materials;

(4) provide training in the use of the Licensed Programs for the staff of the Licensee; and

(5) provide software support services in respect of the Licensed Programs, upon the terms and conditions hereinafter contained.

4 Licence

(1) The Company hereby grants to the Licensee (with effect from the date of Acceptance) a non-exclusive and non-transferable licence to Use the Licensed Program Materials subject to the terms and conditions hereinafter contained.

(2) The Licensee hereby acknowledges that it is licensed to Use the Licensed Program Materials in accordance with the express terms of this Agreement but not further or otherwise.

(3) In consideration of the grant of the Licence, the Licensee shall pay to the Company the single licence fee specified in the Schedule hereto in accordance with the payment terms set out therein.

(4) The Licensed Program Materials (and the intellectual property rights therein or relating thereto) are and shall remain the property of the Company.

(5) The Licensee shall Use the Licensed Program Materials for processing its own data for its own internal purposes only. The Licensee shall not permit any third party to use the Licensed Program Materials in any way whatsoever nor use the

Licensed Program Materials on behalf of or for the benefit of any third party in any way whatsoever (including, without limitation, using the Licensed Program Materials for the purpose of operating a bureau service).

[**Note**: Sub-clause (5) will have to be altered if mutual back-up arrangements with another user are envisaged.]

(6) The Licensee shall treat the Licensed Program Materials as strictly confidential and shall not divulge the whole or any part thereof to any third party provided that this sub-clause shall not extend to information which was rightfully in the possession of the Licensee prior to commencement of this Licence which is already public knowledge or becomes so at a future date (otherwise than as a result of a breach of this sub-clause). The Licensee shall ensure that its employees comply with such confidentiality and non-disclosure obligations. The foregoing obligations shall survive any termination of the Licence.

(7) The Licensee shall keep exclusive possession of and control over the copies of the Licensed Program Materials in its possession and shall effect and maintain adequate security measures to safeguard the Licensed Program Materials from access or use by any unauthorised person.

[(8) The Licensee shall not without the prior written consent of the Company Use the Licensed Program Materials at any location other than the [Premises][installation address specified on the face page of this Agreement]].

[**Note**: Some licences restrict use to a designated location, particularly if there are any applicable export restrictions.]

(9) Except to the extent and in the circumstances expressly required to be permitted by law, the Licensee shall not alter, modify, adapt or translate the whole or any part of the Licensed Program Materials in any way whatsoever nor permit the whole or any part of the Licensed Programs to be combined with or to become incorporated in any other programs nor to decompile, disassemble or reverse engineer the Licensed programs or any part thereof nor attempt to do any of such things. To the extent that local law grants to the Licensee the right to decompile the Licensed Programs in order to obtain information necessary to render the Licensed Programs interoperable with other computer programs used by the Licensee, the Company hereby undertakes to make that information readily available to the Licensee and the Licensee agrees to make such requests of the Licensor before attempting to decompile the Licensed Programs. The Company shall have the right to impose reasonable conditions such as a reasonable fee for doing so. In order to ensure that the Licensee receives the appropriate information, the Licensee must first give the Company sufficient details of the Licensee's objectives and the other software concerned. Requests for the appropriate information should be made to [*contact name and address*].

(10) The Licensee may make up to 3 copies of the Licensed Programs for operational security and back-up purposes but shall make no other copies thereof. Such copies and the media on which they are stored shall be the property of the Company and the Licensee shall ensure that all such copies bear the same proprietary notices as the original. The provisions of this Agreement shall apply to all such copies as they apply to the Licensed Programs. No copies may be made of the Program Documentation without the prior written consent of the Company.

(11) The following termination provisions shall apply:

(a) the Licensee may terminate the Licence at any time by giving at least *30* days' prior written notice to the Company.

(b) the Company may terminate the Licence forthwith by notice in writing to the Licensee if

   (i) the Licensee commits any material breach of the terms of this Agreement and (in the case of a breach capable of remedy) shall have failed within *30* days after the receipt of a request from the Company to do so, to remedy the breach; or

  (ii) the Licensee shall become insolvent or shall have a liquidator, receiver, administrator or administrative receiver appointed or any part of its undertaking or assets or shall pass a Resolution for winding up (otherwise than for the purpose of a bona fide scheme of solvent amalgamation) or a court of competent jurisdiction shall made an order to that effect.

(c) forthwith upon termination of the Licence the Licensee will return the Licensed Program Materials [including modifications thereof made by the Licensee] and all copies of the whole or any part thereof to the Company or, at the option of the Company, shall destroy the same and certify to the Company that they have been so destroyed. The Licensee shall also cause the Licensed Programs to be erased from the Designated Equipment and shall certify to the Company that the same has been done. Termination of the Licence shall not affect any accrued rights or liabilities of the either party. For the avoidance of doubt, there shall be no refund of any element of the Licence Fee by reason of termination by the Licensee.

(12) The use of the Licensed Program Materials is restricted to use on and in conjunction with the Designated Equipment save that:

(a) if the Licensed Program Materials cannot be used with the Designated Equipment because it is inoperable for any reason then the Licence shall be temporarily extended without additional charge to use with any other item of Recommended Equipment at any one time until such failure has been remedied[, provided such item is under the direct control of the Licensee];

[Note: the bracketed words at the end should not be used if the licensee has a mutual back-up arrangement with another user and has agreed this with the company.]

(b) the Licensee may use the Licensed Program Materials on and in conjunction with any replacement equipment (which is Recommended Equipment) if the use of the Licensed Program Materials on and in conjunction with the Designated Equipment is permanently discontinued and provided such replacement equipment does not comprise more than one [processor] [personal computer]. Upon such discontinuance the Licensee shall forthwith give the Company written notice of the type and serial number of the replacement equipment whereupon the replacement equipment shall become the Designated Equipment for all the purposes of the Licence.

(13) The Licensee hereby acknowledges that the Licence is limited to the use of the Licensed Program Materials with Designated Equipment which comprises one

[processor] [personal computer] only and that an additional licence fee is payable for each additional [processor] [personal computer] which the Licensee wishes to use with the Licensed Program Materials.

(14) Risk in the Media shall pass to the Licensee on delivery of the same to the Licensee. If any part of the Media shall thereafter be lost, destroyed or damaged the Company shall replace the same promptly (embodying the relevant part of the Licensed Programs or Program Documentation) subject to the Licensee paying the [Company's standard charge for such replacement] [the reasonable cost of such replacement].

(15) In the event that any enhancement or modification of the Licensed Program Materials is made or evolves in the performance of or as a result of this Agreement the Licensee agrees that the same (and all intellectual property rights therein) shall be the exclusive property of the Company unless otherwise agreed in writing by the Company.

(16)(a) The Company warrants to the Licensee that the Licensed Programs, when delivered to the Licensee, shall provide the facilities and functions described in the Product Description and the Program Documentation. The Licensee acknowledges that the Licensed Programs are of such complexity that they may have certain defects when delivered, and the Licensee agrees that the Company's sole liability and the Licensee's sole remedy in respect of a defect shall be for the Company to provide correction of documented program errors which the Company's investigation indicates are caused by a defect in an unaltered version of the Licensed Programs, and are not due to a defect or deficiency in, or a failure of, the equipment upon which the Licensed Programs are operated or hardware or software not recommended or approved by the Company, or incorrect handling or employment of the Licensed Programs by the Licensee. All warranties hereunder extend only to and are for the benefit only of the Licensee. The Company's obligation to correct any such program errors shall cease at the end of the Support Period.

(b) The Company makes no warranties or representations concerning the Designated Equipment used in conjunction with the Licensed Program Materials.

(17) The Company shall indemnify the Licensee against any claim that the normal use or possession of the Licensed Program Materials infringes the intellectual property rights of any third party provided that the Company is given immediate and complete control of such claim, that the Licensee does not prejudice the Company's defence of such claim, that the Licensee gives the Company all reasonable assistance with such claim and that the claim does not arise as a result of the use of the Licensed Program Materials otherwise than in accordance with the terms of this Agreement or in combination with any equipment (other than the Designated Equipment) or programs not supplied or approved by the Company. The Company shall have the right to replace or change all or any part of the Licensed Program Materials in order to avoid any infringement. The foregoing states the entire liability of the Company to the Licensee in respect of the infringement of the intellectual property rights of any third party.

(18) The Licensee shall notify the Company if the Licensee becomes aware of any unauthorised use of the whole or any part of the Licensed Program Materials by any person.

(19) The Licensee will permit the Company to check the use of the Licensed Program Materials by the Licensee at all reasonable times and for that purpose and the purpose of verifying the discharge of the Licensee's obligations under sub-clause (11) the Company shall be entitled to enter the Premises (and so that the Licensee hereby irrevocably licenses the Company, its employees and agents to enter the Premises for such purpose).

5 Installation and acceptance

EITHER: (VERSION A Time of the Essence):

[(1) On the Delivery Date the Company shall deliver the Licensed Program Materials to the Licensee and install the same on the Designated Equipment at the Location. Time shall be of the essence in this regard]

OR (VERSION B Time Not of the Essence):

[The Company shall use all reasonable endeavours to deliver the Licensed Program Materials to the Licensee [and to install them on the Designated Equipment at the Premises] on or before the Delivery Date. [Time shall not be of the essence in this regard, [save that if delivery [and installation] of the Licensed Programs has not taken place within 7 days of the Delivery Date, the Licensee may serve written notice on the Company requiring delivery [and installation] to be completed within a further 7 days, in respect of which time shall be of the essence.]]]

EITHER (VERSION A Capacity to Acceptance Test):

[(2A) The Licensee shall supply to the Company [as soon as reasonably possible after installation of the Licensed Programs] test data which in the reasonable opinion of the Licensee is suitable to test whether the Licensed Programs are in accordance with the Specification together with the results expected to be achieved by processing such test data using the Licensed Programs. The Company shall not be entitled to object to such test data or expected results unless the Company can demonstrate to the Licensee that they are not suitable for testing the Licensed Programs as aforesaid, in which event the Licensee shall make any reasonable amendments to such test data and expected results as the Company may request. Subject to the receipt of such test data and expected results, the Company shall process such data, in the presence of the Licensee or its authorised representative, on the Equipment using the Licensed Programs by way of acceptance testing within 7 days after such receipt at a time mutually convenient to both parties.

[**Note**: This clause is less likely to be applicable to lower value package software.]

(3A) The Licensee shall accept the Licensed Programs immediately after the Company has demonstrated that the Licensed Programs have correctly processed the test data by achieving the expected results. The Licensee shall not unreasonably withhold or delay its acceptance. The Licensee shall, if required by the Company, sign an acceptance certificate in the form annexed hereto acknowledging such acceptance. If the Licensed Programs shall fail to correctly process the test data so as to achieve the expected results, [the Licensee shall be entitled to reject the Licensed Programs and to be repaid all sums paid by it to the Company] [the Company shall, within a period of 14 days of the completion of the acceptance tests, correct the Licensed Programs so as to enable them to correctly process the test data and achieve the expected results].

[**Note**: the second option is only likely to be applicable where there has been an element of bespoke programming; licensors of package software are unlikely to make amendments to reflect the requirements of individual licensees.]

(4A) If the Licensee shall not supply any test data as aforesaid or shall fail to make itself available to attend acceptance tests within the said period of 7 days then the Licensee shall be deemed to have accepted the Licensed Programs.]

OR (VERSION B No Detailed Acceptance Tests):

[(2B) The Licensed Programs shall be deemed to be accepted when they have been installed on the Designated Equipment and the Company has successfully carried out acceptance tests and the Licensee has accepted the same. Such acceptance shall not be unreasonably withheld by the Licensee.]

[**Note**: This second alternative is more appropriate for lower-value software.]

(5) The Licensed Programs shall not be deemed to have incorrectly processed such test data by reason of any failure to provide any facility or function not specified in the Specification.

6 Training

Upon request, the Company undertakes to provide training in the use of the Licensed Programs for the staff of the Licensee in accordance with the Company's standard scale of charges in force from time to time. Such training shall take place at the premises of the Company or its appointed agent.

[7 Modifications

(1) Before delivery of the Licensed Programs, the Company shall make the modifications to the Licensed Programs described in the Schedule hereto.

(2) An additional charge shall be made for such modifications at the hourly rate(s) specified in the Schedule hereto. Such additional charge shall be paid to the Company on the date of Acceptance.

(3) The Licensee shall indemnify the Company against all liabilities, costs and expenses which the Company may incur as a result of any such modifications which are made in accordance with the Licensee's requirements or specifications and which give rise to an infringement of any intellectual property rights of any third party.]

8 Support services [5.7]

(1) Subject to compliance by the Licensee with its responsibilities as specified in sub-clause (2), the Company shall during the Support Period:

> (a) use its reasonable endeavours to correct any faults in the Licensed Programs notified to it by the Licensee (but not to recover or reconstruct the Licensee's own computer records corrupted or lost as a result of such faults);

> (b) deliver to the Licensee from time to time such enhanced versions of the Licensed Programs as the Company shall release to its licensees generally and which are compatible with the version installed for the Licensee;

(c) provide the Licensee with all documentation which the Company reasonably deems necessary for the utilisation of any modified, enhanced or replacement versions of or additions to the Licensed Programs delivered to the Licensee by the Company from time to time;

(d) provide the Licensee with such technical advice by telephone, facsimile transmission or mail as shall be necessary to resolve the Licensee's difficulties and queries in using the current version of the Licensed Programs; Provided that the provision of this service shall be conditional upon the relevant member of the Licensee's staff having first successfully completed a training course in accordance with the Company's current minimum recommendations; and

(e) make visits to the Licensee's premises at the request of the Licensee to test the functions of the Licensed Programs and make such adjustments and modifications as shall be necessary to ensure that the Licensed Programs continue to operate correctly.

(2) The Licensee shall:

(a) use only the current version of the Licensed Programs made available to it from time to time by the Company;

(b) ensure that the Licensed Programs are used on the Designated Equipment in a proper manner by competent trained employees only or by persons under their supervision;

(c) notify each software fault to the Company as it arises and shall supply the Company with a documented example of such fault;

(d) co-operate fully with the Company in diagnosing any software fault;

(e) make available to the Company free of charge all reasonable facilities and services which are required by the Company to enable it to provide the Support Services including, without limitation, computer runs, memory dumps, telecommunications facilities, printouts, data preparation, office accommodation, typing and photocopying;

(f) not request, permit or authorise anyone other than the Company to provide any support services in respect of the Licensed Programs; and

(g) keep full security copies of the Licensed Programs and other computer programs it uses in accordance with best computing practice.

(3) The Support Services do not include:

(a) attendance to faults caused by using the Licensed Programs otherwise than in accordance with the Program Documentation;

(b) support or maintenance of software, accessories, attachments, computer hardware, systems or other devices not supplied by the Company;

(c) diagnosis and/or rectification of problems not attributable to the Licensed Programs; or

(d) loss or damage caused directly or indirectly by operator error or omission,

and any service which is provided by the Company as a result of any of the foregoing shall be charged extra at the Company's standard rates from time to time in force.

(4) (a) In consideration of the Support Services the Licensee shall pay the annual support charge specified in the Schedule hereto. The first such charge shall be paid on the date specified in the Schedule and then annually in advance on each subsequent anniversary. No support services shall be provided while the Licensee is in default of its payment obligations;

   (b) The Company shall be entitled at any time and from time to time after the payment of the first support charge to make reasonable increases thereto to accord with any change in the Company's standard scale of charges by giving to the Licensee not less than *30* days' written notice expiring on the date for payment of the next support charge from time to time.

(5) The Support Period shall commence on the date of Acceptance, shall continue for an initial period of *1* year and shall remain in force thereafter unless and until terminated by either party giving to the other not less than *3* months' written notice of termination expiring on the last day of the said initial period or on any subsequent anniversary of such day, but shall automatically terminate on the termination of the Licence. No refund of any part of the support charge shall be made on the termination of the Licence.

9 Assignment

This Agreement is personal to the Licensee and the Licensee shall not assign, sub-license or otherwise transfer this Agreement or any of its rights or obligations hereunder whether in whole or in part without the prior written consent of the Company.

10 *Force majeure*

See clause 15 of Precedent A.

11 Liability

(1) The Company shall not be liable for any loss or damage sustained or incurred by the Licensee or any third party resulting from any defect or error in the Licensed Programs except to the extent that such loss or damage arises from any unreasonable delay by the Company in providing the Support Services.

(2) The Company shall not be responsible for the maintenance, accuracy or good running of any version of the Licensed Programs except the latest version thereof supplied to the Licensee for the time being.

(3) Notwithstanding anything else contained in this Agreement but subject to sub-clause (4) below, the Company shall not be liable to the Licensee for loss (whether direct or indirect) of profits, business or anticipated savings or for any indirect or consequential loss or damage whatsoever even if the Company shall have been advised of the possibility thereof and whether arising from negligence, breach of contract or howsoever.

(4) The Company does not exclude liability for death or personal injury caused by the Company's negligence.

(5) Where the Company is liable to the Licensee for negligence, breach of contract or any other cause of action arising out of this Agreement such liability shall not exceed a sum equal to the licence fee (exclusive of VAT) referred to in clause 4(3).

(6) The Company will not be liable for any loss arising out of any failure by the Licensee to keep full and up-to-date security copies of its data and the computer programs it uses in accordance with best computing practice.

(7) The express terms of this Agreement are in lieu of all warranties, conditions, terms, undertakings and obligations implied by statute, common law, custom, trade usage, course of dealing or otherwise all of which are hereby excluded to the fullest extent permitted by law.

12 General

(1) This Agreement constitutes the entire understanding between the parties concerning the subject matter of this Agreement and the Licensee warrants to the Company that in entering into this Agreement it has not relied on any warranty, representation or undertaking save as expressly set out in this Agreement. No waiver or amendment of any provision of this Agreement shall be effective unless made by a written instrument signed by both parties. Each provision of this Agreement shall be construed separately and notwithstanding that the whole or any part of any such provision may prove to be illegal or unenforceable the other provisions of this Agreement and the remainder of the provision in question shall continue in full force and effect.

(2) No forbearance, delay or indulgence by either party in enforcing the provisions of this Agreement shall prejudice or restrict the rights of that party nor shall any waiver of its rights operate as a waiver of any subsequent breach and no right, power or remedy herein conferred upon or reserved for either party is exclusive of any other right, power or remedy available to that party and each such right, power or remedy shall be cumulative.

(3) All notices which are required to be given hereunder shall be in writing and shall be sent to the address of the recipient set out in this Agreement or such other address in England as the recipient may designate by notice given in accordance with the provisions of this clause. Any such notice may be delivered personally or by first class pre-paid letter or facsimile transmission and shall be deemed to have been served if by hand when delivered, if by first class post 48 hours after posting and if by facsimile transmission when despatched.

(4) Save as expressly provided in the attached Schedule, all payments shall be made within 30 days after the date of the Company's invoice therefor.

(5) All sums payable under this Agreement are exclusive of Value Added Tax which the Licensee shall be additionally liable to pay to the Company.

(6) If any sum payable under this Agreement is not paid within 7 days after the due date then (without prejudice to the Company's other rights and remedies) the Company reserves the right to charge interest on such sum on a day to day basis (as well after as before any judgment) from the date or last date for payment thereof to the date of actual payment (both dates inclusive) at the rate of 2 per cent above the base rate of ABC Bank plc (or such other London Clearing Bank as the Company may nominate) from time to time in force compounded quarterly. Such interest shall be paid on demand by the Company. For the avoidance of doubt, any failure to make payment within 7 days after the due date shall constitute a material breach of contract for the purposes of clause 4(11).

(7) In this Agreement:

[(a) reference to any statute or statutory provision includes a reference to that statute or statutory provision as from time to time amended, extended or re-enacted;]

(b) words importing the singular include the plural, words importing any gender include every gender and words importing persons include bodies corporate and unincorporate; and (in each case) vice versa;

(c) any reference to a party to this Agreement includes a reference to his successors in title and permitted assigns;

(d) the headings to the Clauses are for ease of reference only and shall not affect the interpretation or construction of this Agreement.

(8) This Agreement shall be governed by and construed in accordance with the laws of England

[**Note:** If the governing law is changed to that of any of the States of the U.S., the Choice of Law clause should expressly exclude the application of the Uniform Computer Information Transactions Act.]

(9) The Company shall be entitled to engage the services of sub-contractors or agents to perform any of its obligations hereunder.

[(10) This Agreement is subject to the special conditions (if any) contained in the Schedule hereto. In the event of any inconsistency between such special conditions and the other terms of this Agreement such special conditions shall prevail.]

(11) Third Parties

See clause 37 of Precedent A.

SCHEDULE 1

(to the Software Licence and Support Agreement)

A   LICENCE FEE: £[   ] plus VAT

B   PAYMENT TERMS

C   MODIFICATIONS

(1) [*insert a description of the modifications*]

(2) [*insert hourly charge out rates*] plus VAT

D   SUPPORT CHARGE

£[   ] plus VAT payable on [   ]

and then annually on each subsequent anniversary

E   SPECIAL CONDITIONS

[F THIRD-PARTY RIGHTS]

[ACCEPTANCE CERTIFICATE]

[**Note**: See clause 5(3A).]

[**Note**: Schedules 2 and 3 belong to the Software Marketing Agreement.

SCHEDULE 2

TRAINING

[**Note**: This Schedule should identify:

   (1) How many staff are to be trained in total?

   (2) How many can be trained at one time?

   (3) How many days' training is required for each person?

   (4) Where and when training is to take place?

   (5) Who is to be responsible for subsistence and travelling expenses?]

[SCHEDULE 3

THIRD-PARTY RIGHTS]

SOFTWARE DISTRIBUTION AGREEMENT

[**Note**: Schedule 1 contains a software licence and support agreement to be used by the distributor in entering into contracts with end-users (licensees).]

THIS AGREEMENT is made   the day   of 20

PARTIES:

(1) COMPANY [LIMITED] [PLC] whose registered office is at

("the Company")

(2) DISTRIBUTOR [LIMITED] [PLC] whose registered office is at

("the Distributor")

RECITALS:

(A) The Company is the proprietor of certain computer software known as
["   "]

[**Note**: If the agreement relates to all software from the company rather than a particular package then the agreement will need to be modified accordingly.]

(B) The Company has agreed to appoint the Distributor as its non-exclusive distributor to distribute and sub-license such software and its associated documentation in the Territory (as hereinafter defined) on the terms and conditions hereinafter contained

NOW IT IS HEREBY AGREED as follows:

1 Definitions

In this Agreement, unless the context otherwise requires, the following expressions have the following meanings:

"Business Day"	means a day other than a Saturday, Sunday or a public holiday.
"Confidential Information"	means this Agreement and all information obtained by one party from the other pursuant to this Agreement which is expressly marked as confidential or which is manifestly of a confidential nature or which is confirmed in writing to be confidential within 7 days of its disclosure.
["Distributor Modifications"	means all modifications and enhancements of the Software made by the Distributor pursuant to clause 7(4) but excluding any such modifications or enhancements which are adopted by the Company and embodied in the Software from time to time.]

"End-User Agreement"	means a software licence and support agreement in the form set out in Schedule 1 or in such other form as the Company may from time to time direct or approve in writing and as the same may be amended by agreement with the Company from time to time.
"Intellectual Property Rights"	means patents, trademarks, Internet domain names, service marks, registered designs, applications for any of the foregoing, copyright, design rights, trade and business names and any other similar protected rights in any country.
"licensee"	means a person situated in the Territory who is a party to an End-User Agreement with the Distributor in respect of the Software.
"the Product Description"	means the product description as modified, enhanced or altered by the Company from time to time of the Software describing the facilities and functions thereof as supplied to the Distributor by the Company from time to time.
"the Software"	means the Company's [" "] software and all modifications, enhancements, versions and replacements thereof and additions thereto provided by the Company and made available to the Distributor from time to time pursuant to this Agreement [but excluding Distributor Modifications].
"the Software Documentation"	means the operating manuals and other literature provided by the Company to the Distributor from time to time for use by end-users in conjunction with the Software.
"the Software Materials"	means the Software, the Product Description and the Software Documentation.
"the Source Materials"	means all logic, logic diagrams, flowcharts, orthographic representations, algorithms, routines, sub-routines, utilities, modules, file structures, coding sheets, coding, source codes listings, functional specifications, program specifications and all other materials and documents necessary to enable a reasonably skilled programmer to maintain, amend and enhance the software in question without reference to any other person or documentation and whether in eye-readable or machine-readable form.
"the Support Services"	means the software support services provided or to be provided by the Distributor pursuant to each End-User Agreement.

"the Territory"   means *the United Kingdom of Great Britain and Northern Ireland*.

"Year"   means any period of 12 months commencing on *the date hereof* or any anniversary of *the date hereof*.

2 Appointment [5.0.2, 5.3.3]

(1) The Company hereby appoints the Distributor and the Distributor hereby agrees to act as the non-exclusive distributor of the Company to distribute and sub-license the Software Materials in the Territory.

(2) The Distributor shall not be entitled to assign or sub-contract any of its rights or obligations under this Agreement or appoint any agent to perform such obligations.

(3) The Distributor represents and warrants to the Company that it has the ability and experience to carry out the obligations assumed by it under this Agreement and that by virtue of entering into this Agreement it is not and will not be in breach of any express or implied obligation to any third party binding upon it.

3 Duration

This Agreement shall commence on the [date hereof] for an initial period of 2 years and shall continue thereafter [unless or] until terminated by either party giving to the other not less than 6 months' written notice [expiring] [given] on the last day of the said initial period or at any time thereafter, but shall be subject to earlier termination as hereinafter provided.

[Note: occasionally, the agreement is expressed as continuing in perpetuity, so long as minimum sales targets are achieved.]

4 Distribution and sub-licensing [5.2.7, 5.3.6]

(1) The Company hereby grants to the Distributor a non-exclusive licence to reproduce, distribute and sub-license the Software and the Software Documentation and provide the Support Services on the terms and conditions set out in this Agreement.

(2) Save as contemplated by clause 6(2)(c), the Distributor will make the Software available to licensees in object code form only.

(3) The Software and the Software Documentation shall not be made available without the Support Services and both shall be made available to end-users by the Distributor only on the terms of an End-User Agreement which all parties thereto have executed.

[Note: the company will often wish to ensure that support services are offered so as to maintain a good public perception of the amount of back-up available for its products.]

(4) Except as provided in clause 5(2), the Distributor shall not deliver possession of any copies of the Software or the Software Documentation to any third party unless that person has first executed an End-User Agreement and paid the relevant licence fee.

(5) The Distributor shall enter into End-User Agreements only with persons situated in the Territory [and whereby the Software is to be used only in the Territory].

[**Note**: the second qualification is increasingly irrelevant for organisations operating across national boundaries.]

[(6) Within *14* days after the execution of this Agreement, the Company shall provide the Distributor with a master copy of the Software (in machine-readable form), the Software Documentation and the Product Description suitable for reproduction of multiple copies by the Distributor. Thereafter, the Company will provide the Distributor promptly with master copies, suitable for reproduction, of any new versions of the Software Materials in the event that the Company releases any modifications, enhancements or replacements of or additions to any of the Software Materials.

(7) The Distributor shall reproduce the Software Materials only in identical form to the master copies provided by the Company (and in particular shall reproduce the Company's copyright and proprietary notices on every such reproduction) and shall only make such number of copies as are necessary to satisfy the Distributor's obligations pursuant to End-User Agreements together with a reasonable number of copies for demonstration, support and training purposes.]

[**Note**: sub-clauses (6) and (7) will only be appropriate if the distributor is to be entrusted with a master copy of the software; alternatively, it may be obliged to pass orders for software on to the company, who will then supply the media on which the software is loaded in order to enable it to be passed to the end user.]

(8) The Distributor shall enter into End-User Agreements only with prospective licensees whom the Distributor reasonably believes are responsible and likely to comply with their obligations under an End-User Agreement.

(9) The Distributor undertakes to the Company to comply with and perform its obligations under each End-User Agreement fully and promptly.

(10) If the Distributor fails to comply with any of its obligations under an End-User Agreement the Company may effect compliance on behalf of the Distributor whereupon the Distributor shall forthwith become liable to pay to the Company all reasonable costs and expenses incurred by the Company as a result.

[**Note**: this provision may be an important safeguard if the company is to preserve goodwill with its ultimate customer base.]

(11) The Distributor shall ensure that only the current versions of the Software and the Software Documentation supplied to the Distributor from time to time are delivered to licensees and shall make any new or modified versions available to licensees promptly.

(12) The Distributor shall at all times take proper care of any copies of the Software and the Software Documentation which are from time to time in its possession or under its control.

(13) The Distributor shall deliver copies of the Product Description to bona fide prospective licensees only.

(14) If any licensee breaches the terms of his End-User Agreement, the Distributor shall use all reasonable endeavours to procure that the breach is remedied but if the

Distributor is unsuccessful or the breach is incapable of remedy the Distributor shall (if it is entitled so to do) terminate the End-User Agreement in accordance with its terms and exercise its rights to recover the Software Materials from the licensee or procure that they are destroyed.

5 Demonstrations

See clause 5 of Precedent G.

6 Source materials [5.3.6.6]

(1) Within *14* days after the execution of this Agreement, the Company shall provide the Distributor with one copy of the Source Materials relating to the Software. At the same time as any modified, enhanced or replacement version of or addition to the Software is delivered to the Distributor pursuant to clause 4(6), the Company shall provide the Distributor with one copy of any modified version of the Source Materials relating thereto.

(2) The Distributor shall use the Source Materials relating to the Software solely for the purposes of:

(a) providing the Support Services;

[(b) analysis to determine the correct interfaces between any other programs supplied by the Distributor and the Software;] and

(c) depositing copies of the same pursuant to source code escrow arrangements requested by licensees,

and shall only make such number of copies as is reasonably necessary for those purposes.

(3) Any source code escrow arrangements to be entered into by the Distributor with licensees shall be subject to the prior written approval of the Company and no copies of the Source Materials relating to the Software shall be delivered to any escrow agent without such approval.

[**Note**: The company may wish to set up an escrow scheme for the whole territory and negotiate a standard agreement to be used by the distributor. In particular, it may wish to be a party to the agreement and provide that if the distributor becomes insolvent or defaults but the company assumes its support obligations or cures the default the source codes will not be released.]

(4) Save as permitted by clauses 6(2)(c) and 6(3), no copy of the Source Materials or any part thereof shall be made available to any third party by the Distributor.

7 Corrections [and modifications] [5.3.6.6, 5.5]

(1) The Distributor shall promptly notify the Company of any error or defect in the Software Materials of which it becomes aware and give the Company documented examples of such errors or defects.

(2) The Company shall within *5* business days of receipt of such notification evaluate the notified error or defect and provide to the Distributor an estimate of the length of time it will take to issue a [new version] [master copy of a] correction under clause 6(1). The Company will use its reasonable endeavours to provide such [new version] [master copy] [correction] within the estimated timescale.

(3) Pending the delivery of the said [new version] [master copy] [correction] the Distributor shall be entitled to take, with the prior approval of the Company (such approval not to be unreasonably withheld or delayed), such measures and give such advice as may be necessary to provide a temporary solution to the fault for licensees.

EITHER:

[(4) The Distributor may modify or enhance the Software for the purposes of [fulfilling any requirements of licensees] [improving the overall functionality of the combination of the Software with any other computer programs with which it may be supplied by the Distributor]. The Distributor shall promptly provide the Company with a copy of all such Distributor Modifications and the Source Materials relating thereto and details of any licensees to whom such modifications or enhancements have been provided. The Distributor Modifications and the Source Materials relating thereto and the intellectual property rights therein or relating thereto shall be the absolute property of the Company, and the Distributor hereby, with full title guarantee, assigns (by way of present and future assignment) to the Company all such property and intellectual property rights free from any encumbrance. The Distributor shall assume full responsibility for any errors or defects in Distributor Modifications (including any infringements of any third party intellectual property rights occasioned by the Distributor Modifications). The Company may but shall have no obligation to make any corrections to Distributor Modifications pursuant to clause 7(2) and any warranties, indemnities and other obligations given or assumed by the Company in respect of the Software shall be void as to Distributor Modifications. In the event that the Company agrees to support any Distributor Modifications such support shall be provided to the Distributor on a time and materials basis at the Company's standard rates in force from time to time. Save as provided above, all the provisions of this Agreement shall apply to Distributor Modifications and the Source Materials relating thereto, mutatis mutandis, as they apply to the Software and the Source materials relating to the Software.]

OR:

[(4) Save as permitted by sub-clause (3), the Distributor shall not alter or modify the whole or any part of the Software in any way whatever nor permit the whole or any part of the Software to be combined with, or become incorporated in, any other programs.]

[Note: if the distributor has not been granted the right to utilise a master copy for the purposes of sublicensing, the company's obligation may need to be revised to an obligation to provide patches/new releases to/of the sublicensed software.]

8 Training [5.3.6.6]

(1) The Company shall provide training in the installation, implementation and use of the Software for the Distributor's personnel as specified in Schedule 2, free of charge.

[Note: Clause 8(1) presupposes a minimum period of free training, to assist the distributor in the marketing of the software. Further training may be required in the event of substantial changes to the software. Training may need to be repeated—still free of charge—if the changes in a new version of the software are substantial.]

(2) Any additional training required by the Distributor shall be provided by the Company (within a reasonable period of time from the Distributor's request for

such additional training) in accordance with its standard scale of charges in force from time to time

(3) The Distributor shall offer training courses for licensees at its standard rates in force from time to time and the Distributor shall use its reasonable endeavours to persuade all licensees to complete training courses in accordance with the Company's minimum recommendations from time to time.

[**Note**: one needs to consider whether the distributor is itself to be authorised to offer training services, or whether the company will reserve this right to itself.]

9 Distributor's obligations [5.1, 5.6]

The Distributor shall:

(1) use all reasonable endeavours to promote and extend the licensing of the Software throughout the Territory;

(2) perform its obligations hereunder in accordance with all reasonable instructions which the Company may give the Distributor from time to time;

(3) promptly inform the Company of any opportunities of which the Distributor becomes aware and which are likely to be relevant in relation to the commercial exploitation of the Software and which are advantageous or disadvantageous to the interests of the Company;

(4) at all times conduct its business in a manner that will reflect favourably on the Software and on the good name and reputation of the Company;

(5) not by itself or with others participate in any illegal, deceptive, misleading or unethical practices including, but not limited to, disparagement of the Software or the Company or other practices which may be detrimental to the Software, the Company or the public interest;

EITHER:

[(6) not during the continuance of this Agreement (whether alone or jointly and whether directly or indirectly) be concerned or interested in the marketing, distribution, licensing or sale of any software products in the Territory which are similar to or competitive with the Software or which perform the same or similar functions;]

[**Note**: the parties should consider the application of U.K. and E.U. competition law to such restrictive arrangements. In practice, many licensors structure such restrictions so to fall within the applicable E.U. block exemptions.]

OR:

[(6) at all times display, demonstrate and otherwise represent the Software fairly in comparison with competitive products from other suppliers;]

(7) at all times employ a sufficient number of full-time staff who are capable of competently demonstrating the Software to prospective licensees;

(8) at all times maintain adequate demonstration facilities for the Software;

(9) supply to the Company such reports, returns and other information relating to orders and projected orders for the Software and regarding licensees as the Company may from time to time reasonably require;

(10) not make any promises or representations or give any warranties, guarantees or indemnities in respect of the Software Materials except such as are contained in an End-User Agreement or as expressly authorised by the Company in writing and shall not supply the Software to any person knowing that it does not meet that person's specified requirements;

(11) use the Company's trade marks and trade names relating to the Software only in the registered or agreed style in connection with the distribution and sub-licensing of the Software and shall not use such trade marks or trade names in connection with any other products or services or as part of the corporate or any trade name of the Distributor;

(12) not alter, obscure, remove, interfere with or add to any of the trade marks, trade names, markings or notices affixed to or contained in the Software Materials delivered to the Distributor;

(13) not supply or recommend any computer equipment to a licensee for use in conjunction with the Software save for that equipment which is contained in the Company's current Recommended Compatible Hardware List supplied to the Distributor from time to time;

(14) permit the Company and its authorised agents at all reasonable times to enter any of the Distributor's premises for the purpose of ascertaining that the Distributor is complying with its obligations under this Agreement (and so that the Distributor hereby irrevocably licenses the Company, its employees and agents to enter any such premises for such purpose);

(15) comply with the provisions of each End User Agreement entered into with a licensee of the Software.

10 Company's obligations [5.1, 5.7]

The Company shall:

(1) provide the Distributor with such marketing and technical assistance [as is reasonably necessary] [as the Company may in its discretion consider necessary] to assist the Distributor with the promotion of the Software;

(2) endeavour to answer as soon as reasonably possible all technical queries raised by the Distributor or licensees concerning the use or application of the Software;

[Note: such obligations may be better set out in the Licence and Support Agreement, in Schedule 1.]

(3) provide the Distributor with a reasonable number of copies of any promotional literature relating to the Software which the Company may produce from time to time;

(4) give the Distributor reasonable advance written notice of any material changes in or modifications of the Software or of the Company's intention to discontinue licensing or sub-licensing the Software in the Territory;

(5) provide the Distributor with all information and assistance reasonably necessary to enable the Distributor properly to perform its obligations hereunder in respect of any modified, enhanced or replacement version of or addition to the Software;

(6) provide the Distributor with not less than 2 months notice of any proposed price changes in relation to the Software.

[**Note**: It is in the Company's interests that the amount of notice of such changes should be commensurate with the price payable for the software, so as to enable the distributor to amend its marketing practices accordingly.]

11 Royalties and payments [5.2]

(1) The Distributor agrees to pay to the Company royalties in respect of each End-User Agreement entered into by the Distributor with a licensee of the Software.

(2) The royalty amount shall be *50* per cent of the Company's standard price for the Software ("Licence Royalty") for each licence fee levied by the Distributor under an End-User Agreement and *30* per cent of the Company's standard annual support charge for the Software ("Support Royalty") for each annual support charge levied by the Distributor under an End-User Agreement, both as shown on the Company's [United Kingdom] domestic price list in force from time to time. The Company shall give the Distributor at least *60* days' advance notice of any change to such price list. The current price list is set out in Schedule 3.

[**Note**: If the domestic price list is in a currency different from that charged by the distributor an appropriate clause to fix the exchange rate should be included.]

(3) The Licence Royalty and the Support Royalty shall be payable by the Distributor to the Company in cleared funds not later than the *14th* day of the calendar month following receipt of the relevant licence fee or annual support charge from a licensee by the Distributor. If for any reason the Distributor receives payment in part only then part payment proportional thereto shall likewise be made by the Distributor to the Company. All payments shall be made in *pounds sterling*.

[**Note**: the company may also want to impose an obligation upon the distributor actually to collect the sums due, so that it does not suffer cash flow problems due to the distributor's inefficiencies or inclination to indulge delays in payments by licensees.]

(4) The Distributor shall be free to fix its own licence fees and annual support charges with licensees in respect of each End-User Agreement and any additional delivery, implementation and training fees, provided always that the royalties payable to the Company shall remain calculated in accordance with clause 11(2).

(5) At the time of each payment of the Licence Royalty the Distributor shall supply the Company with one executed original of each of the End-User Agreements to which the payment relates.

(6) The Distributor shall keep and shall make available to the Company on request accurate records to enable the Company to verify all royalty payments due to it.

(7) During the term of this Agreement and for any period thereafter during which royalties shall continue to accrue and upon *5* business days' prior written notice to the Distributor, the Company shall have the right at any time and from time to time (subject as provided below), during the Distributor's normal business hours, to send an independent accountant (not generally providing services to the Company except in respect of other royalty audits) to audit the records of the Distributor relating to the sub-licensing and support of the Software and to verify the royalty payments due to the Company under this Agreement. The Distributor shall give such accountant full access to its premises, computers, employees and relevant records for such purpose. Any such audit shall be conducted in such a manner as to minimise any interference with the Distributor's normal business activities and will not include

access to the Distributor's cost or profit information. Each such audit shall cover the period since the last most recent audit or, if none, the date of this Agreement down to the business day immediately preceding the commencement of the audit ("Audit Period"). The Company shall use its reasonable endeavours to procure that such accountant shall keep confidential the information which comes to his knowledge as a consequence of his audit (and to enter into any confidentiality undertaking reasonably requested by the Distributor in respect thereof prior to any disclosure) except that the accountant shall be entitled to reveal to the Company any information necessary to provide the Company with confirmation of the accuracy of the Distributor's royalty remittances or any deviations therefrom. Upon written request, the Company agrees to make available to the Distributor, in the event the Company makes any claim with respect to an audit, a copy of the records and reports pertaining to the audit. The Company agrees not to cause such audits to be carried out more frequently than *twice* a year, except where the Company has reasonable cause to believe that correct payments are not being tendered by the Distributor in which case the Company may cause any number of audits to be carried out until such time as the Company is reasonably satisfied that the position has been corrected. Each such audit shall be carried out at the Company's expense unless it reveals a deficiency of 5 per cent or more of the royalties remitted for the relevant Audit Period, in which event the Distributor shall pay the costs thereof. Payment of such costs and any royalty deficiency shall be made by the Distributor within 7 days after the Distributor shall have received written notice thereof from the Company together with a copy of the accountant's report and, if applicable, fee note showing the amount(s) due. Any such deficiency shall carry interest in accordance with clause 11(8)(c) from the date it was originally due.

(8) If the Distributor fails to make any payment to the Company under this Agreement on the due date then, without prejudice to any other right or remedy available to the Company, the Company shall be entitled to:

(a) suspend the performance or further performance of its obligations under this Agreement without liability to the Distributor;

(b) suspend (by notice in writing) the Distributor's right to enter into any further End-User Agreements until payment in full is made (and the Distributor shall so comply with such suspension); and

(c) charge the Distributor interest (both before and after any judgment) on the amount outstanding on a daily basis at the rate of 2 per cent per annum above the base rate of *ABC* Bank plc (or such other London Clearing Bank as the Company may nominate) from time to time in force, such interest to be calculated from the date or last date for payment thereof to the date of actual payment (both dates inclusive) compounded quarterly. Such interest shall be payable on demand by the Company.

(9) All royalties payable under this Agreement are exclusive of any Value Added Tax and other applicable sales taxes, which the Customer shall be additionally liable to pay to the Company.

(10) The provisions of this Clause shall survive the termination of this Agreement.

12 Property rights [5.3.6.2]

(1) The Software Materials and the Source Materials relating to the Software and the intellectual property rights therein or relating thereto are and shall remain the

property of the Company and all copies thereof in the Distributor's possession, custody or control shall (to the extent that they are not exhausted by proper use) be returned to the Company or otherwise disposed of by the Distributor as the Company may from time to time direct.

(2) The Distributor shall notify the Company immediately if the Distributor becomes aware of any unauthorised use of any of the Software Materials or the Source Materials relating to the Software or any of the intellectual property rights therein or relating thereto and will assist the Company (at the Company's expense) in taking all reasonable steps to defend the Company's rights therein.

(3) The Distributor shall not use, reproduce or deal in the Software Materials or the Source Materials relating to the Software or any copies thereof except as expressly permitted by this Agreement.

(4) The provisions of this Clause shall survive the termination of this Agreement.

13 Confidentiality

(1) The Distributor shall not use or divulge or communicate to any person (other than as permitted by this Agreement or with the written authority of the Company):

   (a) any of the Company's Confidential Information which may come to the Distributor's knowledge during the continuance of this Agreement;

   (b) the Software Materials or any information concerning the same;

   (c) the Source Materials relating to the Software; or

   (d) any of the terms of this Agreement,

and the Distributor shall use all reasonable endeavours to prevent the unauthorised publication or disclosure of any such information, materials or documents.

(2) The Distributor shall ensure that its employees are aware of and comply with the confidentiality and non-disclosure provisions contained in this Clause and the Distributor shall indemnify the Company against any loss or damage which the Company may sustain or incur as a result of any breach of confidence by any of its employees.

(3) If the Distributor becomes aware of any breach of confidence by any of its employees it shall promptly notify the Company and give the Company all reasonable assistance in connection with any proceedings which the Company may institute against any such employees.

(4) The provisions of this clause shall survive the termination of this Agreement but the restrictions contained in clause 13(1) shall cease to apply to any information which may come into the public domain otherwise than through unauthorised disclosure by the Distributor or its employees, which is received by the Distributor from a third party who does not breach a duty of confidence in disclosing it, or which is required to be disclosed by law, by any court of competent jurisdiction or any administrative or regulatory authority.

14 Reservation of rights [5.3.1]

The Company reserves the right:

(1) to exploit the Software itself in the Territory by such means as it may think fit including, without limitation, by the appointment of other distributors;

(2) to modify, enhance, replace or make additions to the Software in any way whatsoever as the Company may in its discretion determine;

(3) to discontinue licensing or sub-licensing the Software in the Territory (whereupon this Agreement shall automatically terminate); and

(4) to require the Distributor either not to use or to cease to use any advertising or promotional materials in respect of the Software which the Company reasonably considers not to be in the Company's best interests.

15 Customer enquiries [5.3.1]

(1) The Distributor shall promptly forward to the Company any enquiries it may receive for the Software from persons situated outside the Territory.

(2) The Company shall not enter into any agreement for the licensing and support of the Software with any prospective licensee situated in the Territory in which the Distributor has established and recorded its interest unless the Distributor fails to enter into an End-User Agreement with that prospective licensee within a reasonable time thereafter.

[Note: if such a provision is to be adopted, there needs to be a clear mechanism for distributor to register its interests, and for the company to confirm that they are not simply speculative.]

(3) The Company may if it wishes (but without being under any obligation so to do) refer to the Distributor any enquiry for the Software it may receive direct from a potential licensee situated in the Territory.

16 Legal relationship [5.0.2]

(1) During the continuance of this Agreement the Distributor shall be entitled to use the title "AUTHORISED [   ] SOFTWARE DISTRIBUTOR" but such use shall be in accordance with the Company's policies in effect from time to time and before using such title (whether on the Distributor's business stationery, advertising material, website or elsewhere) the Distributor shall submit to the Company proof prints and such other details as the Company may require and the Company may in its discretion grant or withhold permission for such proposed use.

(2) Nothing in this Agreement shall render the Distributor a partner or (except as expressly permitted by this Agreement) an agent of the Company and the Distributor shall not (except as expressly permitted or contemplated by this Agreement) purport to undertake any obligation on the Company's behalf nor expose the Company to any liability nor pledge or purport to pledge the Company's credit.

17 Termination [5.4]

(1) Notwithstanding anything else contained herein, this Agreement may be terminated:

(a) by the Company forthwith on giving notice in writing to the Distributor if:
    (i) the Distributor shall [(or shall threaten to)] sell, assign, part with or cease to carry on its business or that part of its business relating to the distribution of the Software;

(ii) the control (as defined for the purposes of section 416 of the Income and Corporation Taxes Act 1988) of the Distributor shall be transferred to any person or persons other than the person or persons in control of the Distributor at the date hereof (but the Company shall only be entitled to terminate within the period of *60* days after the Company shall have been notified in writing of the change in control);

(iii) the Distributor shall fail to remit to the Company in any Year royalties equal to or in excess of the royalty targets set out in Schedule 4 or such other targets as may be agreed between the Company and the Distributor from time to time; or

(iv) any audit carried out pursuant to clause 11(7) shall reveal a deficiency of *10* per cent or more in the relevant Audit Period.

(b) by either party forthwith on giving notice in writing to the other if:

(i) the other commits any material [or persistent] breach of any term of this Agreement and (in the case of a breach capable of being remedied) shall have failed, within *30* days after the receipt of a request in writing from the other party so to do, to remedy the breach (such request to contain a warning of such party's intention to terminate);

[**Note**: allowing termination for "persistent" breaches can be problematic as they can on occasion be used to engineer terminations for convenience.]

(ii) the other party shall have been unable to perform its obligations hereunder for a period of *90* consecutive days or for periods aggregating *180* days in any Year (but the party entitled to terminate may only terminate within the period of *60* days after the expiration of the said consecutive period or Year); or

(iii) the other party shall have a receiver or administrative receiver appointed of it or over any part of its undertaking or assets or shall pass a resolution for winding up (otherwise than for the purpose of a bona fide scheme of solvent amalgamation or reconstruction) or a court of competent jurisdiction shall make an order to that effect or if the other party shall enter into any voluntary arrangement with its creditors or shall become subject to an administration order.

(2) The Distributor shall not be entitled to any compensation or indemnity (whether for loss of distribution rights, goodwill or otherwise) as a result of the termination of this Agreement in accordance with its terms.

18 Effect of termination [5.4]

On the termination of this Agreement:

(1) all rights and obligations of the parties under this Agreement shall automatically terminate except:

(a) for such rights of action as shall have accrued prior to such termination and any obligations which expressly or by implication are intended to come into or continue in force on or after such termination;

(b) that the terms of this Agreement shall remain in full force and effect to the extent and for the period necessary to permit the Distributor properly to perform its continuing obligations under each End-User Agreement subsisting at the date of termination (and the Distributor's obligations under sub-clauses (3) and (4) below shall be deferred during such period as those continuing obligations subsist);

(c) that the obligations of the parties contained in clauses 4(9), 4(10) and 4(14) shall continue in respect of each End-User Agreement subsisting at the date of termination.

(2) the Distributor shall immediately eliminate from all its literature, business stationery, publications, websites, notices and advertisements all references to the title "AUTHORISED [   ] SOFTWARE DISTRIBUTOR" and all other representations of the Distributor's appointment hereunder.

(3) the Distributor shall at its own expense forthwith return to the Company or otherwise dispose of as the Company may instruct all promotional materials and other documents and papers whatsoever sent to the Distributor and relating to the business of the Company (other than correspondence between the parties), all property of the Company and all copies of the Software Materials and the Source Materials relating to the Software, being in each case in the Distributor's possession or under its control.

(4) the Distributor shall cause the Software to be erased from all computers of or under the control of the Distributor and shall certify to the Company that the same has been done.

(5) each End-User Agreement then subsisting shall continue in effect and shall survive the termination of this Agreement.

19 Novation of end-user agreements

In the event of a termination of this Agreement by the Company, the Company shall have the right to require the Distributor to novate all subsisting End User Agreements to it or to an alternative distributor nominated by it, pursuant to clause 11 of the End User Agreement in Schedule 1. If the Company novates an End-User Agreement in favour of itself or another distributor in accordance with its entitlement hereunder, the Distributor shall:

(1) give the Company or such distributor, at the Company's request, all reasonable cooperation in transferring the Distributor's obligations under such End-User Agreement to the Company or such distributor; and

(2) forthwith pay to the Company or as it shall direct a proportionate part of any annual support fee (including VAT) paid in advance by the licensee thereunder apportioned from the effective date of the novation down to the expiry of the year to which the payment relates.

20 Waiver of remedies

See clause 28 of Precedent A.

21 Indemnities

(1) The Company shall indemnify the Distributor against any claim (or claim for indemnity from any licensee against a claim) that the normal use or possession of the Software Materials infringes the U.K. intellectual property rights of any

unaffiliated third party provided that the Company is given immediate and complete control of such claim, that the Distributor does not prejudice the Company's defence of such claim, that the Distributor gives the Company all reasonable assistance with such claim (at the Company's expense) and that the claim does not arise as a result of the use of the Software Materials otherwise than in accordance with the terms of this Agreement or an End-User Agreement or with any equipment or programs not approved by the Company. The Company shall have the right to replace or change all or any part of the Software Materials in order to avoid any infringement. The foregoing states the entire liability of the Company to the Distributor in respect of the infringement of the intellectual property rights of any unaffiliated third party.

(2) The Company shall indemnify the Distributor against any claim, loss, liability, damage or expense resulting from or due to a claim for breach of warranty, design defect, negligence or product liability or any similar claim directly attributable to the Software Materials save to the extent that such claim arises as a result of the Distributor's negligence, recklessness or wilful misconduct or any breach of its obligations under this Agreement or any End-User Agreement and provided that the Company is given immediate and complete control of such claim, that the Distributor does not prejudice the Company's defence of such claim and that the Distributor gives the Company all reasonable assistance with such claim (at the Company's expense).

[**Note**: the company may well wish to place a limit on its liability under this indemnity.]

(3) The Distributor shall indemnify the Company and keep the Company fully and effectively indemnified on demand from and against any and all losses, claims, damages, costs, charges, expenses, liabilities, demands, proceedings and actions which the Company may sustain or incur, or which may be brought or established against it by any person and which in any case arise out of or in relation to or by reason of:

(a) any breach by the Distributor of its obligations under this Agreement; or

(b) any unauthorised action or omission of the Distributor or its employees; or

(c) the manner in which the Distributor markets the Software; or

(d) the independent supply by the Distributor of any products or services for use in conjunction with or in relation to the Software; [or

(e) any Distributor Modifications].

If any claim is made against the Company for which indemnification is sought under this clause 21(3), the Company shall consult with the Distributor and, subject to being secured to its reasonable satisfaction, shall co-operate with the Distributor in relation to any reasonable request made by the Distributor in respect of such claim.

[**Note**: although the general approach to the giving of indemnities is that the indemnifying party will have conduct of the defence of claim, in the circumstances above the company's need to protect the goodwill associated with the software may justify it retaining control of any litigation.]

22 Warranties and liability [5.8]

(1) The Company warrants to the Distributor that the Software, when delivered to the Distributor, shall provide, if properly used by the Distributor and licensees, the

facilities and functions described in the Product Description and the Program Documentation. The Distributor acknowledges that the Software is of such complexity that it may have certain defects when delivered, and the Distributor agrees that the Company's sole liability and the Distributor's sole remedy in respect of any breach of the said warranty shall be for the Company to provide corrections of documented program errors in accordance with clause 7(2). If the Company fails (other than through the act or default of the Distributor) within a reasonable time to correct non-conforming Software as aforesaid its liability therefor shall be limited to a sum equal to the total royalties received by the Company from the Distributor pursuant to this Agreement.

(2) The express terms of this Agreement are in lieu of all warranties, conditions, terms, undertakings and obligations implied by statute, common law, custom, trade usage, course of dealing or otherwise, all of which are hereby excluded to the fullest extent permitted by law.

(3) Notwithstanding anything else contained in this Agreement but subject to clause 22(4), the Company shall not be liable to the Distributor for loss of profits, goodwill, business or anticipated savings or for any indirect or consequential loss or damage whatsoever even if the Company shall have been advised of the possibility thereof and whether arising from negligence, breach of contract or howsoever.

(4) The Company does not exclude liability for death or personal injury caused by the Company's negligence, or for any other form of liability which cannot be excluded or restricted by law.

[(5) The Company shall have no liability or responsibility whatsoever under clauses 21(1) or 21(2) or clause 22(1) or otherwise under this Agreement for any claims, loss or expenses arising from Distributor Modifications.]

23 *Force majeure*

See clause 15 of Precedent A.

24 Notices

See clause 32 of Precedent A.

25 Interpretation

See clause 33 of Precedent A.

26 General

See clause 24 of Precedent G.

27 Third parties

See clause 37 of Precedent A.

EXECUTED under hand in two originals the day and year first before written

SIGNED for and on behalf of
COMPANY [LIMITED] [PLC]

By

Signature

Title

Witness

SIGNED for and on behalf of
DISTRIBUTOR [LIMITED] [PLC]

By

Signature

Title

Witness

SCHEDULE 1

SOFTWARE LICENCE AND SUPPORT AGREEMENT

THIS AGREEMENT is made the   day of   20

PARTIES:

(1) DISTRIBUTOR [LIMITED] [PLC] whose registered office is at

(“the Distributor”)

(2) LICENSEE [LIMITED] [PLC] whose registered office is at

(“the Licensee”)

RECITALS:

(A) [Company] [Limited] [Plc] (“the Owner”) is the proprietor of certain computer software known as [“   ”]

(B) By a distribution agreement made between the Distributor and the Owner, the Distributor has been appointed as a distributor of the Owner to distribute and sub-license such software and its associated documentation in the Territory (as hereinafter defined) and to provide support services therefor on the terms and conditions of agreements in the form of this Agreement.

(C) The Distributor has agreed to sub-license such software and documentation and provide support services to the Licensee on the terms and conditions hereinafter contained.

NOW IT IS HEREBY AGREED as follows:

1 Definitions

In this Agreement, unless the context otherwise requires, the following expressions have the following meanings:

“Acceptance”	means the Licensee's acceptance of the Licensed Programs pursuant to clause 4(2).
“Designated Processors”	means the computer processors designated by type and serial number in the Schedule hereto.
“the Designated System”	means the Licensee's computer system comprising the Designated Processors and the peripheral equipment listed in the Schedule.
“the Distributor”	means the Distributor named in this Agreement and includes any successor to the Distributor pursuant to a novation under clause 11(3).
“the Distribution Agreement”	means the distribution agreement in force between the Owner and the Distributor from time to time relating to the Licensed Programs.

"intellectual property rights"	means patents, trade marks, service marks, registered designs, applications for any of the foregoing, copyright, design rights, trade and business names and other similar protected rights in any country.
"the Licensed Programs"	means the applications computer programs known as [insert a description of the programs] in object code form including any modified, enhanced or replacement versions thereof or additions thereto which may be supplied by the Distributor to the Licensee from time to time.
"the Licensed Program Materials"	means the Licensed Programs, the Program Documentation and the Media.
"the Licence"	means the licence to Use the Licensed Program Materials granted hereunder.

[**Note**: The licence is drafted as a site licence for a computer network, alternative forms of licensing will require corresponding amendments.]

"the Media"	means the media on which the Licensed Programs and the Program Documentation are recorded or printed as provided to the Licensee by the Distributor.
"the Product Description"	means the product description of the Licensed Programs describing the functions and facilities thereof as supplied to the Licensee by the Distributor.
"the Program Documentation"	means the operating manuals, user instructions, technical literature and other related materials supplied to the Licensee by the Distributor for aiding the use and application of the Licensed Programs.
"Recommended Equipment"	means any computer equipment which the Distributor may recommend for use with the Licensed Programs from time to time.

[**Note**: Both the owner and the distributor will wish to guard against degradation of performance of the software because of undersized equipment. The recommendations from the distributor should therefore include recommendations as to size and capacity.]

"the Support Period"	means the period during which the Support Services shall be provided determined in accordance with clause 7(5).
"the Support Services"	means the software support services to be provided by the Distributor pursuant to clause 7(1).
"the Territory"	means *the United Kingdom of Great Britain and Northern Ireland.*
"User"	means any employee of the Licensee accessing the Licensed Programs from a single processor keyboard terminal or peripheral device.

"Use the Licensed Programs"	means to load the object code form of the Licensed Programs into and store and run them on the Designated Processors in accordance with the terms of this Agreement.
"Use the Licensed Program Materials"	means to Use the Licensed Programs, to read and possess the Program Documentation in conjunction with the use of the Licensed Programs and to possess the Media.

2 Services to be provided

The Distributor hereby agrees to:

[(1) make the agreed modifications to the Licensed Programs;]

[**Note**: only required if there are to be customisations of the software, as opposed to simply the creation of interfaces, etc.]

(2) deliver the Licensed Programs to the Licensee and to install them on the Designated Processors;

(3) license the Licensee to Use the Licensed Program Materials;

(4) provide training in the use of the Licensed Programs for the staff of the Licensee; and

(5) provide software support services to the Licensee in respect of the Licensed Programs, in each case upon the terms and conditions hereinafter contained.

3 Licence

(1) The Distributor hereby grants to the Licensee a non-exclusive and non-transferable licence to Use the Licensed Program Materials subject to the terms and conditions hereinafter contained.

(2) The Licensee hereby acknowledges that it is licensed to Use the Licensed Program Materials in accordance with the express terms of this Agreement but not further or otherwise.

(3) In consideration of the grant of the Licence, the Licensee shall pay to the Distributor the single licence fee specified in the Schedule in accordance with the payment terms set out therein.

(4) The Licensed Program Materials (and the intellectual property rights therein or relating thereto) are and shall remain the property of the Owner.

(5) The Licensee shall Use the Licensed Program Materials for processing its own data for its own internal purposes only. The Licensee shall not permit any third party to use the Licensed Program Materials in any way whatever nor use the Licensed Program Materials on behalf of or for the benefit of any third party in any way whatever (including, without limitation, using the Licensed Program Materials for the purpose of operating a bureau service).

(6) The Licensee shall treat the Licensed Program Materials as strictly confidential and shall not divulge the whole or any part thereof to any third party. The Licensee

shall ensure that its employees comply with such confidentiality and non-disclosure obligations.

[**Note**: the licensee may wish to qualify its confidentiality obligations; see for example clause 11 of precedent G.]

(7) The Licensee shall keep exclusive possession of and control over the copies of the Licensed Program Materials in its possession and shall effect and maintain adequate security measures to safeguard the Licensed Program Materials from access or use by any unauthorised person.

(8) The Licensee shall not without the prior written consent of the Distributor use the Licensed Program Materials at any location other than the installation address specified in the Schedule. In any event, the use of the Licensed Program Materials is limited to use in the Territory only.

[**Note**: the suitability on territorial restrictions may increasingly be in doubt as a result of the general globalisation of business.]

(9) Except to the extent and in the circumstances expressly required to be permitted by law, the Licensee shall not alter, modify, adapt or translate the whole or any part of the Licensed Program Materials in any way whatever nor permit the whole or any part of the Licensed Programs to be combined with or to become incorporated in any other programs nor to decompile, disassemble or reverse engineer the Licensed Programs or any part thereof nor attempt to do any of such things. To the extent that local law grants to the Licensee the right to decompile the Licensed Programs in order to obtain information necessary to render the Licensed Programs inter-operable with other computer programs used by the Licensee, the Distributor shall use all reasonable endeavours to procure that the Owner makes that information readily available to the Licensee, on the basis that the Owner shall have the right to impose reasonable conditions such as a reasonable fee for doing so. In order to ensure that the Licensee receives the appropriate information, the Licensee must first give the Owner sufficient details of the Licensee's objectives and the other software concerned. Requests for the appropriate information should be made to [*contact name and address*].

(10) The Distributor shall supply the number of copies of the Licensed Programs and Program Documentation specified in the Schedule. In addition, the Licensee may make up to *3* copies of the Licensed Programs for operational security and back-up purposes but shall make no other copies thereof. All copies and the media on which they are stored shall be property of the Owner and the Licensee shall ensure that all such copies bear the same proprietary notices as the original. The provisions of this Agreement shall apply to all such copies as they apply to the originals. No copies may be made of the Program Documentation without the prior written consent of the Owner.

(11) The Distributor shall be entitled to terminate the Licence forthwith by notice in writing to the Licensee if the Licensee shall commit any [material] breach of the terms of this Agreement or shall become insolvent or shall have a liquidator, receiver, administrator or administrative receiver appointed or if the Licensee permanently ceases to use the Licensed Program Materials. Upon such termination the Licensee shall return the Licensed Program Materials and all copies thereof to the Distributor or, at the option of the Distributor, shall destroy the same and

certify to the Distributor that they have been so destroyed. The Licensee shall also cause the Licensed Programs to be erased from the Designated Processors and shall certify to the Distributor that the same has been done.

(12) The use of the Licensed Program Materials is restricted to use on the Designated Processors save that:

(a) if the Licensed Program Materials cannot be used on any one Designated Processor because it is inoperable for any reason then the Licence shall be temporarily extended without additional charge to use on a single back-up or substitute processor (which is Recommended Equipment) until the Designated Processor is operable again, provided such substitute processor is under the direct control of the Licensee; and/or

(b) the Licensee may use the Licensed Program Materials on and in conjunction with a single replacement processor (which is Recommended Equipment) if the use of the Licensed Program Materials on and in conjunction with any one Designated Processor is permanently discontinued. Upon such discontinuance the Licensee shall forthwith give the Distributor written notice of the type and serial number of the replacement processor whereupon the replacement processor shall become a Designated Processor for all the purposes of the Licence.

(13) The Licence is limited to the use of the Licensed Program Materials with the Designated System and by the maximum number of concurrent Users specified in the Schedule. The Licensee acknowledges that an additional licence fee is payable for each additional processor on which the Licensed Programs are to be used or additional concurrent User which is to have access to the Licensed Programs.

(14) Risk in the Media shall pass to the Licensee on delivery of the same to the Licensee. If any part of the Media shall thereafter be lost, destroyed or damaged the Distributor shall replace the same (embodying the relevant part of the Licensed Programs or Program Documentation) subject to the Licensee paying the Distributor's standard charge for replacement.

(15) In the event that any enhancement or modification of the Licensed Program Materials is made or evolves in the performance of or as a result of this Agreement the Licensee agrees that the same (and all intellectual property rights therein) shall be the exclusive property of the Owner unless otherwise agreed in writing by the Owner.

(16)(a) The Distributor warrants to the Licensee that the Licensed Programs, when delivered to the Licensee, shall provide the facilities and functions described in the Product Description and the Program Documentation. The Licensee acknowledges that the Licensed Programs are of such complexity that they may have certain defects when delivered, and the Licensee agrees that the Distributor's sole liability and the Licensee's sole remedy in respect of a defect shall be for the Distributor to provide correction of documented program errors which the Distributor's investigation indicates are caused by a defect in an unaltered version of the Licensed Programs, and are not due to a defect or deficiency in, or a failure of, the equipment upon which the Licensed Programs are operated or hardware or software not recommended or approved by the Distributor, or incorrect handling or employment of the Licensed Programs by the Licensee. All warranties hereunder extend only to the Licensee and are for the benefit only of the Licensee. The Distributor's obligation to correct any such program errors shall cease at the end of the Support Period.

(b) The Distributor makes no warranties or representations concerning the computer equipment used in conjunction with the Licensed Program Materials.

(17) The Distributor shall indemnify the Licensee against any claim that the normal use or possession of the Licensed Program Materials infringes the [U.K.] intellectual property rights of any unaffiliated third party provided that the Distributor is given immediate and complete control of such claim, that the Licensee does not prejudice the Distributor's defence of such claim, that the Licensee gives the Distributor all reasonable assistance with such claim (at the Distributor's expense) and that the claim does not arise as a result of the use of the Licensed Program Materials otherwise than in accordance with the terms of this Agreement or in combination with any equipment (other than the Designated System) or programs not supplied or approved by the Distributor. The Distributor shall have the right to replace or change all or any part of the Licensed Program Materials in order to avoid any infringement. The foregoing states the entire liability of the Distributor to the Licensee in respect of the infringement of the intellectual property rights of any unaffiliated third party.

(18) The Licensee shall notify the Distributor if the Licensee becomes aware of any unauthorised use of the whole or any part of the Licensed Program Materials by any person.

(19) The Licensee will permit the Distributor to check the use of the Licensed Program Materials by the Licensee at all reasonable times and for that purpose and the purpose of verifying the discharge of the Licensee's obligations under clause 3(11) the Distributor shall be entitled to enter any of the Licensee's premises (and so that the Licensee hereby irrevocably licenses the Distributor, its employees and agents to enter any such premises for any such purpose).

4 Installation and acceptance

(1) The Distributor shall deliver the Licensed Programs to the Licensee and install them on the Designated Processors at a time mutually convenient to both parties. The Licensee shall pay to the Distributor the delivery and installation charge specified in the Schedule on the payment terms set out therein.

(2) The Licensed Programs shall be deemed to be accepted when they have been installed and the Distributor has successfully carried out appropriate acceptance tests and the Licensee has accepted the same. Such acceptance shall not be unreasonably withheld by the Licensee.

[Note: "appropriate" acceptance tests will usually be the standard installation tests as designated by the owner.]

5 Training

Upon request, the Distributor undertakes to provide training in the use of the Licensed Programs for the staff of the Licensee in accordance with the Distributor's standard scale of charges in force from time to time. Such training shall take place at the premises of the Distributor, and shall be subject to the availability of the Distributor's training personnel.

[6 Modifications

(1) Before delivery of the Licensed Programs, the Distributor shall make the modifications thereto as described in the Schedule.

[(2) An additional charge shall be made for such modifications at the hourly rate(s) specified in the Schedule. Such additional charge shall be paid to the Distributor on the date of Acceptance.]

(3) The Licensee shall indemnify the Distributor against all liabilities, costs and expenses which the Distributor may incur as a result of any such modifications which are made in accordance with the Licensee's requirements or specifications and which give rise to an infringement of any intellectual property rights of any unaffiliated third party.]

7 Support services

(1) Subject to compliance by the Licensee with its obligations under clause 7(2), the Distributor shall during the Support Period:

(a) use its reasonable endeavours to correct any faults in the Licensed Programs notified to it by the Licensee (but shall not be required to recover or reconstruct the Licensee's own computer records corrupted or lost as a result of such faults);

(b) deliver to the Licensee from time to time and install such new versions of the Licensed Programs as the Owner shall deliver to its distributors for general release to licensees from time to time and which are compatible with the Licensee's version;

(c) provide the Licensee with all documentation which the Distributor reasonably deems necessary for the utilisation of any modified, enhanced or replacement versions of or additions to the Licensed Programs delivered to the Licensee by the Distributor from time to time;

(d) provide the Licensee with remote telephone diagnostic assistance during the hours specified in the Schedule to help resolve the Licensee's difficulties and queries in using the current version of the Licensed Programs; Provided that the Licensee has first successfully completed a training course in accordance with the Distributor's current minimum recommendations; and

[Note: the provision of telephone assistance is often specifically limited to those of the licensee's staff who have attended the requisite training courses.]

(e) make visits to the Licensee's premises at the reasonable request of the Licensee to test the functions of the Licensed Programs (such requests not to exceed 2 in any twelve month period] and make such adjustments and modifications as shall be reasonably necessary to ensure that the Licensed Programs continue to operate correctly.

(2) The Licensee shall:

(a) use only the current version of the Licensed Programs made available to it from time to time by the Distributor;

(b) ensure that the Licensed Programs are used on the Designated Equipment in a proper manner by competent trained employees only or by persons under their supervision;

(c) notify each software fault to the Distributor as it arises and shall supply the Distributor with a documented example of such fault;

(d) co-operate fully with the Distributor in diagnosing any software fault;

(e) make available to the Distributor free of charge all reasonable facilities and services which are required by the Distributor to enable it to provide the Support Services including, without limitation, computer runs, memory dumps, telecommunications facilities, printouts, data preparation, office accommodation, typing and photocopying;

(f) not request, permit or authorise anyone other than the Distributor or the Owner or the Owner's authorised representatives to provide any support services in respect of the Licensed Programs; and

(g) keep full security copies of the Licensed Programs and of the Licensee's data and other computer programs it uses in accordance with best computing practice.

(3) The Support Services do not include:

(a) attendance to faults caused by using the Licensed Programs otherwise than in accordance with the Program Documentation;

(b) support or maintenance of software, accessories, attachments, computer hardware, systems or other devices not supplied by the Distributor;

(c) diagnosis or rectification of problems not attributable to the Licensed Programs; or

(d) loss or damage caused directly or indirectly by operator error or omission,

and any service which is provided by the Distributor as a result of any of the foregoing shall be charged extra at the Distributor's standard rates in force from time to time.

(4) (a) In consideration of the provision of the Support Services, the Licensee shall pay the annual support charge specified in the Schedule. The first such charge shall be paid on the date specified in the Schedule and then annually in advance on each subsequent anniversary. Interest shall accrue on any later payments at the rate of 2 per cent above the base rate for the time being of the *ABC* Bank, and the Distributor reserves the right to suspend the provision of the Support Services while the Licensee is in default of its payment obligations.

(b) The Distributor shall be entitled at any time and from time to time after the payment of the first support charge to make reasonable increases thereto to accord with any change in the Distributor's standard scale of charges by giving to the Licensee not less than *30* days' written notice expiring on the date for payment of the the next annual support charge.

(5) The Support Period shall commence on the date of Acceptance, shall continue for an initial period of *one year* and shall remain in force thereafter unless and until terminated by either party giving to the other not less than 3 months' written notice of termination expiring on the last day of the said initial period or on any subsequent anniversary of such day, but shall automatically terminate on the termination of the Licence. No refund of any part of the annual support charge shall be made on termination of the Support Services.

8 Assignment

This Agreement is personal to the Licensee and the Licensee shall not assign, sub-license or otherwise transfer this Agreement or any of its rights or obligations hereunder whether in whole or in part.

9 *Force majeure*

No party shall be liable for any delay in performing any of its obligations hereunder if such delay is caused by circumstances beyond the reasonable control of the party so delaying and such party shall be entitled to a reasonable extension of time for the performance of such obligations.

10 Liability

[(1) The Distributor shall not be liable for any loss or damage sustained or incurred by the Licensee or any third party resulting from any defect or error in the Licensed Programs except to the extent that such loss or damage arises from any unreasonable delay by the Distributor in providing the Support Services.]

[Note: the enforceability of this sub-clause (1) may be open to question under the provisions of the Unfair Contract Terms Act 1977.]

(2) The Distributor shall not be responsible for the maintenance, accuracy or good running of any version of the Licensed Programs except the latest version thereof supplied to the Licensee from time to time

(3) Notwithstanding anything else contained in this Agreement but subject to clause 10(4) below, the Distributor shall not be liable to the Licensee for loss of profits, business or anticipated savings or for any indirect or consequential loss or damage whatsoever even if the Distributor shall have been advised of the possibility thereof and whether arising from negligence, breach of contract or howsoever.

(4) The Distributor does not exclude liability for death or personal injury caused by the Distributor's negligence.

(5) Where the Distributor is liable to the Licensee for negligence, breach of contract or any other cause of action arising out of this Agreement such liability shall not exceed a sum equal to the licence fee (exclusive of VAT) referred to in clause 3(3).

[Note: if the licence fee is relatively modest, it may be wise to include any support fees paid to date and/or a de minimis cap, so as to guard against the possibility of the limitation being ruled unenforceable under the Unfair Contract Terms Act 1977.]

(6) The Distributor will not be liable for any loss arising out of any failure by the Licensee to keep full and up-to-date security copies of its data and the computer programs it uses in accordance with best computing practice.

(7) The express terms of this Agreement are in lieu of all warranties, conditions, terms, undertakings and obligations implied by statute, common law, custom, trade usage, course of dealing or otherwise all of which are hereby excluded to the fullest extent permitted by law.

11 The owner

(1) The Distributor enters into this Agreement for itself and with the intent that the restrictions on the use to be made of the Software Materials shall extend to the benefit of the Owner.

(2) The Licensee undertakes to comply with and perform its obligations under this Agreement fully and promptly so as not to infringe the rights of the Owner in respect of the Software Materials.

(3) This Agreement shall continue in effect notwithstanding any termination of the Distribution Agreement but at any time after such termination the Owner shall be entitled to serve notice ("Novation Notice") on the Licensee (with a copy to the Distributor) requesting the Licensee to convert this Agreement into a direct agreement between the Owner or another distributor of the Owner as specified in such notice who has entered into a direct covenant with the Licensee to be bound by the terms of this Agreement (the Owner or such distributor being hereinafter referred to as "the Replacement") (1) and the Licensee (2). The Licensee shall have a period of *30* days from the date of service of the Novation Notice to serve notice ("Acceptance Notice") on the Owner accepting such novation.

(4) If an Acceptance Notice is served on the Owner within the said period of *30* days then this Agreement shall be novated as follows:

(a) the Licence shall thereby take effect on the date of such service ("the Transfer Date") as a licence from the Replacement to the Licensee;

(b) this Agreement shall thereby be novated on the Transfer Date by the substitution of the Replacement for the Distributor as the Distributor under this Agreement;

(c) the Replacement shall thereby undertake, and shall be deemed to have so undertaken with effect from the Transfer Date, to observe and perform all the terms and conditions of this Agreement as if it had been a party hereto and named herein instead of the Distributor but the Replacement shall not be liable for any antecedent breach of this Agreement by the Distributor;

(d) the Licensee and the Distributor shall thereby release and discharge each other with effect from the Transfer Date from all obligations, responsibilities and liabilities in respect of this Agreement but not in respect of any liabilities arising out of any antecedent breach of this Agreement;

(e) the Licensee shall thereby undertake, and shall be deemed to have undertaken with effect from the Transfer Date, to observe and perform all the terms and conditions of this Agreement as if the Replacement were a party hereto and named herein instead of the Distributor;

[(f) the Owner may exclude from the scope of the Support Services and from any warranties and any other liability hereunder such part of the Licensed

Programs as it may specify in this Novation Notice (not being any part of the Licensed Programs which the Owner has released generally to end-users) and any such exclusion shall thereafter take effect from the Transfer Date onwards];

[**Note**: for example, the owner may wish to exclude responsibility for distributor modifications.]

(g) the parties hereto and the Replacement shall execute and do and/or procure the execution and doing of all such further deeds, documents and acts as may be necessary to carry the provisions of this Clause 11(4) into full force and effect.

(5) If an Acceptance Notice is not served by the Licensee within the said period of *30* days then the provisions of clause 11(4) shall have effect on the day following the expiry of the said period of *30* days save that:

(a) the Support Period shall be deemed to have terminated by mutual agreement at the expiry of the said period of *30* days; and

(b) the Owner shall be deemed to be the Replacement.

[**Note**: if the licensee is to effectively be compelled to accept such novations, it may insist upon the deletion of clause 11(4)(f) above, so as to be sure of at least having the benefit of all of its previously agreed licence terms.]

(6) The Owner does not warrant to the Licensee that the Licensed Programs will meet the requirements of the Licensee or that the operation of the Licensed Programs will be uninterrupted or error-free or that defects in the Licensed Software will be corrected. In no event will the Owner be liable to the Licensee for any loss or damage of any kind (except personal injury or death resulting from the Owner's negligence) including lost profits or other consequential loss arising from the Licensee's use of or inability to use the Licensed Programs or from errors or deficiencies in it whether caused by negligence or otherwise howsoever. Nothing in this sub-clause shall affect any obligations assumed by the Owner pursuant to a novation of this Agreement under clause 11(3).

12 General

(1) This Agreement constitutes the entire understanding between the parties concerning the subject matter of this Agreement and the Licensee warrants to the Distributor and the Owner that in entering into this Agreement it has not relied on any warranty, representation or undertaking save as expressly set out in this Agreement (save that neither party seeks to exclude liability for any fraudulent precontractual misrepresentation upon which the other party can be shown to have relied). No waiver or amendment of any provision of this Agreement shall be effective unless made by a written instrument signed by all the parties. Each provision of this Agreement shall be construed separately and notwithstanding that the whole or any part of any such provision may prove to be illegal or unenforceable the other provisions of this Agreement and the remainder of the provision in question shall continue in full force and effect.

(2) No forbearance, delay or indulgence by either party in enforcing the provisions of this Agreement shall prejudice or restrict the rights of that party nor shall any waiver of its rights operate as a waiver of any subsequent breach and no right,

power or remedy herein conferred upon or reserved for either party is exclusive of any other right, power or remedy available to that party and each such right, power or remedy shall be cumulative

(3) All notices which are required to be given hereunder shall be in writing and shall be sent to the address of the recipient set out in this Agreement or such other address in England as the recipient may designate by notice given in accordance with the provisions of this Clause. Any such notice may be delivered personally or by first class pre-paid letter or facsimile transmission and shall be deemed to have been served if by hand when delivered, if by first class post *48* hours after posting and if by facsimile transmission when despatched.

(4) If any sum payable under this Agreement is not paid within *7* days after the due date then (without prejudice to the Distributor's other rights and remedies) the Distributor reserves the right to suspend the provision of any services being rendered to the Licensee and/or to charge interest on such sum on a day to day basis (as well after as before any judgment) from the date or last date for payment thereof to the date of actual payment (both dates inclusive) at the rate of *2* per cent above the base rate of *ABC* Bank plc (or such other London Clearing Bank as the Supplier may nominate) from time to time in force compounded quarterly. Such interest shall be paid on demand by the Distributor.

(5) Save as expressly provided herein, all payments shall be made within *30* days after the date of the Distributor's invoice therefor.

(6) All sums payable under this Agreement are exclusive of Value Added Tax which the Licensee shall be additionally liable to pay to the Distributor.

(7) In this Agreement:

[(a) reference to any statute or statutory provision includes a reference to that statute or statutory provision as from time to time amended, extended or re-enacted;]

(b) words importing the singular include the plural, words importing any gender include every gender and words importing persons include bodies corporate and unincorporate; and (in each case) vice versa;

(c) any reference to a party to this Agreement includes a reference to his successors in title and permitted assigns;

(d) the headings to the Clauses are for ease of reference only and shall not affect the interpretation or construction of this Agreement.

(8) This Agreement shall be governed by and construed in accordance with the laws of England and the parties agree that any dispute relating to its terms or subject matter shall be subject to the exclusive jurisdiction of the English courts.

[**Note**: If the governing law is changed to that of any of the States of the U.S., the Choice of Law clause should expressly exclude the application of the Uniform Computer Information Transactions Act.]

EXECUTED under hand in three originals the day and year first before written

SIGNED by a duly authorised
officer on behalf of THE
DISTRIBUTOR in the presence
of:

SIGNED by a duly authorised
officer on behalf of THE
LICENSEE in the presence
of:

SIGNED by a duly authorised
officer on behalf of the
Distributor as agent for THE
OWNER in the presence of:

SCHEDULE 1

(to the Software Licence and Support Agreement)

A   DESIGNATED PROCESSORS

[Type:]

[Serial No.:]

B   PERIPHERAL EQUIPMENT

C   INSTALLATION ADDRESS

D   LICENCE FEE

£[   ] plus VAT

Payment Terms:

E   NUMBER OF COPIES TO BE SUPPLIED

Licensed Programs:

Program Documentation:

F   MAXIMUM NUMBER OF CONCURRENT USERS

G   DELIVERY AND INSTALLATION CHARGE

£[   ] plus VAT

Payment Terms:

[H   MODIFICATIONS

(1) [insert a description of the modifications]

(2) [insert hourly charge-out rates] plus VAT]

I   HOURS FOR REMOTE TELEPHONE DIAGNOSTIC ASSISTANCE

J   SUPPORT CHARGE

£[   ] plus VAT payable on [   ]

and then annually on each subsequent anniversary

[**Note**: Schedules 2 to 5 belong to the Software Distribution Agreement.]

Schedule 2

TRAINING

[**Note**: This Schedule should identify:

(1) How many staff are to be trained in total?

(2) How many can be trained at one time?

(3) How many days' training is required for each person?

(4) Where and when training is to take place?

(5) Who is to be responsible for subsistence and travelling expenses?]

Schedule 3

CURRENT [UNITED KINGDOM] DOMESTIC PRICE LIST OF THE COMPANY

Schedule 4

ROYALTY TARGETS

Schedule 5

THIRD-PARTY RIGHTS

BETA TEST AGREEMENT

THIS AGREEMENT is made the   day of   20

PARTIES:

(1) COMPUTER COMPANY [LIMITED] [PLC] whose registered office is at

("the Supplier")

(2) COMPANY [LIMITED] [PLC] whose registered office is at

("the Customer")

RECITALS:

(A) The Supplier has developed the computer [hardware] [software] product specified in the Schedule hereto in a pre-production form ("the Product").

(B) The Supplier has agreed to deliver the Product and its associated documentation ("the Documentation") to the Customer and to grant the Customer a licence to evaluate the Product and the Documentation upon the terms and conditions hereinafter contained.

NOW IT IS HEREBY AGREED as follows:

1 Consideration [6.2]

In consideration of the agreements and undertakings set out in this Agreement, the parties have granted the rights and accepted the obligations hereinafter appearing.

2 Delivery and installation [6.3, 6.7]

(1) The Supplier shall deliver and install the Product in accordance with the delivery instructions and at the installation site ("the Installation Site") specified in the Schedule.

(2) Such delivery and installation shall take place at a time and on a date mutually convenient to both parties [but in any event before [   ].

3 Evaluation [6.2]

(1) The Supplier hereby grants to the Customer a licence to evaluate the Product and the Documentation on the terms and subject to the conditions of this Agreement.

(2) During the term of this Agreement the Customer shall evaluate the Product and the Documentation diligently, shall report promptly to the Supplier's evaluation personnel all faults and problems with the Product and the Documentation which it

discovers and shall co-operate with such personnel in diagnosing and correcting such faults and problems.

(3) In the course of evaluating the Product and the Documentation, the Customer may process its own data and retain the benefit of such processing but subject to clause 9(3) the Supplier shall have no liability whatsoever for any errors or defects therein.

(4) The Company shall during the continuance of this Agreement provide to the Customer the Support Services in respect of the Product set out in the Schedule.

[(5) In consideration of the Customer entering into this Agreement to evaluate the Product and Documentation, within *one* year of the Product becoming available on the open market in the U.K. the Customer shall be entitled to a discount of *20* per cent upon entering into its first contract with the Supplier for the supply of the Product or multiples thereof, provided that pursuant to this Agreement:

(a) the Customer has taken reasonable care to complete and return to the Supplier the evaluation forms provided with the Product by the date specified on such evaluation forms; and

(b) the Customer has complied with its other obligations under this Agreement.]

4 Title and risk [6.3]

(1) The Product and the Documentation are confidential and proprietary to the Supplier and title to both shall remain with the Supplier at all times.

(2) Risk in the Product and the Documentation shall remain with the Supplier but the Customer shall take all reasonable steps to safeguard the Product and the Documentation from loss or damage.

5 The customer's obligations [6.6]

The Customer shall:

(1) keep the Product and the Documentation at the Installation Site unless the Supplier consents in writing to the Customer moving the Product and the Documentation to alternative premises;

(2) keep confidential and not disclose the existence, features, capabilities or contents of the Product or the Documentation or the results of the Customer's evaluation thereof or the contents of this Agreement to any third party except to the Customer's employees who are directly involved in the evaluation and have a specific need to know the information concerned (such confidentiality and non-disclosure obligations to survive the termination of this Agreement), provided that this clause shall not extend to information which was rightfully in the possession of the Customer prior to the negotiations leading to this Agreement, which is already public knowledge or becomes so at a future date(otherwise than as a result of a breach of this clause) or which is trivial or obvious;

(3) ensure that its employees observe the confidentiality and non-disclosure obligations contained in clause 5(2);

(4) allow the Supplier access to the Installation Site to inspect and make modifications to the Product and the Documentation at all convenient times during the continuance of this Agreement;

[(5) indemnify the Supplier against any loss of or damage to the Product arising as a result of the wilful misconduct, recklessness or gross negligence of the Customer or its employees;]

(6) except as expressly provided in this Agreement, not use, reproduce, dispose of, deal with, rent, lease, [sub-license], loan, modify, adapt, [reverse engineer, decompile] or disassemble the whole or any part of the Product or the Documentation;

(7) keep the Product and the Documentation in its exclusive possession and control and safeguard them from access by any unauthorised person;

(8) not incorporate the Product or the Documentation or allow them to be incorporated in any other product or documentation; and

(9) not change, remove or obscure any labels, plates, notices, insignia, lettering or other markings which are on or embodied in the Product or the Documentation at the time of delivery thereof to the Customer.

6 Term and termination [6.4]

(1) This Agreement shall continue for an initial period of *3* months and shall remain in force thereafter unless or until terminated by either party giving to the other not less than *14* days' notice in writing expiring at the end of the said initial period or at any time thereafter, but shall be subject to earlier termination as hereinafter provided.

(2) This Agreement may be terminated forthwith by either party on giving notice in writing to the other if the other shall have a receiver or administrative receiver appointed or shall pass a resolution for winding-up (otherwise than for the purpose of a bona fide scheme of solvent amalgamation or reconstruction) or a court of competent jurisdiction shall make an order to that effect or if the other party shall become subject to an administration order or shall enter into any voluntary arrangement with its creditors or shall cease or threaten to cease to carry on business or shall commit any breach of this Agreement.

(3) Any termination of this Agreement (howsoever occasioned) shall not affect any accrued rights or liabilities of either party nor shall it affect the coming into force or the continuance in force of any provision hereof which is expressly or by implication intended to come into or continue in force on or after such termination.

EITHER:

[(4) Upon termination of this Agreement the Customer shall surrender up to the Supplier the Product and the Documentation and all copies of the whole or any part thereof and for that purpose the Customer hereby irrevocably licenses the Supplier, its employees and agents to enter the Customer's premises to repossess the same.]

OR:

[(4) The Supplier advises the Customer that at the time of delivery the Product will contain special software which will deny the Customer the use of the Product after *3* months from the date hereof. In the event that this Agreement continues in force for more than *3* months from the date hereof and the Customer is not in breach of any of the provisions of this Agreement the Supplier undertakes to amend or remove the said special software so as to allow the Customer to continue to use the Product under the terms of this Agreement.]

[**Note:** for the validity of so-called logic bombs for non-payment see 3.2.2.]

7 Reservation of rights [6.5]

The Supplier reserves the right to:

(1) recall the Product and the Documentation forthwith (by giving no less than *14* days' notice in writing to the Customer) up to *60* days before the release by the Supplier of the Product for supply to the [U.K.] market, whereupon this Agreement shall automatically terminate; and

(2) recall the Product or the Documentation and replace it with another version at any time during the term of this Agreement.

8 Intellectual property rights indemnity [6.7]

The Supplier shall indemnify the Customer against any claim that the Customer's use or possession of the Product and the Documentation infringes the intellectual property rights of any third party provided that the Supplier is given immediate and complete control of such claim, that the Customer does not prejudice the Supplier's defence of such claim, that the Customer gives the Supplier all reasonable assistance with such claim (at the cost of the Supplier) and that the claim does not arise as a result of the use of the Product or the Documentation in combination with any equipment or programs not supplied or approved by the Supplier or by reason of any alteration or modification which was not made by the Supplier or with the Supplier's prior written consent or which arises as a result of the use of the Product or the Documentation otherwise than in accordance with the terms of this Agreement. The Supplier shall have the right to replace or change all or any part of the Product or the Documentation or to terminate this Agreement forthwith by notice in writing to the Customer in order to avoid any infringement. The foregoing states the entire liability of the Supplier to the Customer in respect of the infringement of the intellectual property rights of any third party.

9 Liability [6.3]

(1) Because of the experimental nature of the Product and the Documentation, the Supplier does not warrant to the Customer that either is free from faults or defects.

(2) Subject to clause 9(3) the Customer shall use the Product and the Documentation at its own risk and in no event shall the Supplier be liable to the Customer for any loss or damage of any kind (except personal injury or death resulting from the Supplier's negligence) arising from the Customer's use of or inability to use the Product or the Documentation or from faults or defects in either whether caused by negligence or otherwise.

(3) If the Customer is required by the Supplier to use its live data in order to evaluate the Product and/or the Documentation, the Supplier will accept liability to pay damages in respect of loss or damage (including consequential loss) suffered by the Customer as a direct result of using the Product and/or the Documentation where this arises as a result of the Supplier's negligence. In such circumstances, the Supplier's entire and collective liability to the Customer arising out of or relating to this Agreement will not exceed [   ].

(4) The express terms of this Agreement are in lieu of all warranties, conditions, undertakings, terms and obligations implied by statute, common law, trade usage, course of dealing or otherwise all of which are hereby excluded to the fullest extent permitted by law.

10 Interpretation

In this Agreement the expressions "the Product" and "the Documentation" include any modified or replacement versions thereof made available pursuant to clause 5(4) or clause 7(2) and, where the context so requires, any other version supplied by the Supplier to the [United Kingdom] market from time to time.

11 Waiver of remedies

See clause 28 of Precedent A.

12 Entire agreement

This Agreement supersedes all prior agreements, arrangements and understandings between the parties and constitutes the entire agreement between the parties relating to the subject matter hereof(save that neither party seeks to exclude liability for any fraudulent precontractual misrepresentation upon which the other party can be shown to have relied). No addition to or modification of any provision of this Agreement (including for the avoidance of doubt any substitution of the Product or Documentation or any part of it pursuant to clauses 5(4) or 7(2)) shall be binding upon the parties unless made by a written instrument signed by a duly authorised representative of each of the parties.

[Note: This clause may have to be amended in the light of any side letters or collateral agreements.]

13 Assignment

See clause 30 of Precedent A.

14 Notices

See clause 32 of Precedent A.

[15 Sub-contracts

The Customer shall not enter into any sub-contract with any person for the performance of any part of this Agreement.]

[Note: this may seem harsh and it may even cause difficulties for the customer in employing temporary staff, but the secrecy requirements of the project may on occasions make such a clause necessary.]

16 Law

See clause 34 of Precedent A.

17 Disputes

See clause 35 of Precedent A.

18 Severability

See clause 36 of Precedent A.

19 Third parties

See clause 37 of Precedent A.

EXECUTED under hand the day and year first before written

SIGNED for and on behalf of
COMPUTER COMPANY [LIMITED] [PLC]

By

Signature

Title

Witness

SIGNED for and on behalf of
COMPANY [LIMITED] [PLC]

By

Signature

Title

Witness

THE SCHEDULE

A   THE PRODUCT

B   DELIVERY AND INSTALLATION INSTRUCTIONS

C   INSTALLATION SITE

D   SUPPORT SERVICES

[E THIRD-PARTY RIGHTS]

HARDWARE MAINTENANCE AGREEMENT

THIS AGREEMENT is made the   day of   20

PARTIES:

(1) COMPUTER COMPANY [LIMITED] [PLC] whose registered office is at

("the Supplier")

(2) CUSTOMER [LIMITED] [PLC] whose registered office is at

("the Customer")

RECITAL:

The Supplier has agreed to maintain the Customer's computer equipment hereinafter described upon the terms and conditions hereinafter contained.

NOW IT IS HEREBY AGREED as follows:

1 Definitions

In this Agreement, unless the context otherwise requires, the following expressions have the following meanings:

"the Additional Equipment"	has the meaning attributed thereto in clause 4(3).
"the Commencement Date"	means the date on which this Agreement shall become effective as specified in the Schedule.
"the Confidential Information"	means all information obtained by one party from the other pursuant to this Agreement which is expressly marked as confidential or which is manifestly of a confidential nature or which is confirmed in writing to be confidential within 7 days of its disclosure.
"the Emergency Maintenance Services"	means the emergency maintenance services to be provided by the Supplier pursuant to clause 3.
"the Equipment" [8.1.1, 8.5.1]	means the computer equipment specified in the Schedule and the Additional Equipment and such additions and changes thereto as shall from time to time be agreed in writing between the parties.
"the Initial Period"	means the initial period of this Agreement as specified in the Schedule.

"the Location" [8.1.1]	means the Customer's premises in which the Equipment is installed as specified in the Schedule.
"the Maintenance Charge"	means the periodic charge for the Scheduled Maintenance Services specified in the Schedule as varied from time to time pursuant to Clause 4 or as shall from time to time be agreed in writing between the parties.
"Maintenance Hours"	means the hours between 9.00 a.m. and 5.00 p.m. each day excluding Saturdays, Sundays and public holidays [in the United Kingdom].
"the Maintenance Services"	means the Scheduled Maintenance Services and the Emergency Maintenance Services.
"the Scheduled Maintenance Services"	means the maintenance services to be provided by the Supplier pursuant to clause 2.

2 Scheduled maintenance services [8.1.2]

During the continuance of this Agreement the Supplier shall provide the following maintenance services in respect of the Equipment:

(1) *Preventive maintenance*

The Supplier shall make visits to the Location [at such intervals as the Supplier shall reasonably determine to be required for the Equipment] [every 6 months] to test the functions of the Equipment and make such adjustments as shall be necessary to keep the Equipment [in good working order] [in working order in accordance with its specification]. Such visits shall be made during Maintenance Hours by prior appointment with the Customer. If it is expedient in the opinion of the Supplier so to do, such maintenance may be carried out at the same time as corrective maintenance.

(2) *Corrective maintenance*

Upon receipt of notification from the Customer that the Equipment has failed or is malfunctioning, the Supplier shall during Maintenance Hours make such repairs and adjustments to and replace such parts of the Equipment as may be necessary to restore the Equipment to its proper operating condition.

(3) *Response time*

On receipt of a request for corrective maintenance the Supplier undertakes [to use its reasonable endeavours] to despatch a suitably qualified service engineer to the Location within 4 Maintenance Hours [but such response time is an estimate only and shall not be binding on the Supplier].

[Note: The time of arrival of the service engineer at the location will depend upon how far he has to travel and on whether there are financial penalties imposed whenever the supplier fails to respond within the anticipated timeframe in accordance with clause 13.]

(4) *Escalation*

In the event that any such notified failure or malfunction shall not have been corrected within 3 hours of such an engineer arriving at the Location, the Supplier hereby undertakes to fulfil the escalation procedures set out in the Schedule.]

[**Note**: If this sub-clause is to be used the words bracketed at the end of sub-clause (3) should be omitted.]

3 Emergency maintenance services [8.3.2]

In addition to the Scheduled Maintenance Services the Supplier shall provide during the continuance of this Agreement an emergency corrective maintenance service outside Maintenance Hours as soon as practicable after the receipt of a request by the Customer therefor [(such request to be made during Maintenance Hours)] at the Supplier's standard scale of charges for such service from time to time in force. Such charges shall be calculated from the first arrival of the Supplier's service engineer at the Location to his final departure therefrom.

4 Charges [8.2, 8.5.1, 8.5.2]

(1) In consideration of the Scheduled Maintenance Services the Customer shall pay the Maintenance Charge periodically in advance as specified in the Schedule. The Maintenance Charge shall be paid without prior demand and no payment shall be considered made until it is received by the Supplier in cleared funds. All payments shall be made in the manner specified in the Schedule.

(2) Any charges payable by the Customer hereunder in addition to the Maintenance Charge shall be paid (unless otherwise provided elsewhere in this Agreement) within *14* days after receipt of the Supplier's invoice therefor.

(3) Where the Supplier becomes aware of equipment [supplied by the Supplier] at the Location which is not included in the Equipment and in respect of which the Customer requests any maintenance services ("Additional Equipment") the Supplier will provide the Maintenance Services in respect of the Additional Equipment in the same way as in respect of the Equipment and charge for it according to the rate set out in the Schedule such charge backdated to the date when the Additional Equipment was installed at the Location and to be added to the Maintenance Charge in respect of future payments.

EITHER (VERSION A Discretion to Increase Charges):

[(4) The Supplier shall be entitled at any time and from time to time after the expiry of the [Initial Period] [the period of *one year* after the Commencement Date] to increase the Maintenance Charge to accord with any change in the Supplier's standard scale of charges by giving to the Customer not less than *90* days' prior written notice. Where and whenever such notice is given, the Customer shall have the right to terminate this Agreement as from the date on which such notice expires by giving to the Supplier written notice of termination not less than *30* days before such date.]

OR (VERSION B Indexed Increases in Charges):

[(4) The Supplier shall be entitled at any time and from time to time (subject as mentioned below) after the expiry of the [Initial Period] [the period of *one* year after the Commencement Date] to increase the Maintenance Charge by giving to the Customer not less than *90* days' prior written notice provided that any such increase shall not exceed a percentage equal to *the percentage increase in the Retail Prices Index published by the Central Statistical Office* for the period from the

Commencement Date (in the case of the first such increase) or the date on which the immediately preceding increase came into effect pursuant to this sub-clause (in the case of the second or subsequent increase) up to the date of such notice plus 2 per cent provided further that no increase may be made pursuant to this sub-clause until a period of at least *one* year has elapsed since the date on which the immediately preceding increase came into effect pursuant to this sub-clause.]

(5) The Maintenance Charge and any additional charges payable under this Agreement are exclusive of Value Added Tax which shall be paid by the Customer at the rate and in the manner for the time being prescribed by law.

(6) If any sum payable under this Agreement is not paid within 7 days after the due date then (without prejudice to the Supplier's other rights and remedies) the Supplier reserves the right to charge interest on such sum on a day to day basis (as well after as before any judgment) from the date or last date for payment thereof to the date of actual payment (both dates inclusive) at the rate of 2 per cent above the base rate of *ABC* Bank plc (or such other London Clearing Bank as the Supplier may nominate) from time to time in force compounded quarterly. Such interest shall be paid on demand by the Supplier. In addition or in the alternative (at the option of the Supplier), the Supplier may suspend the provision the Maintenance Services until such time as the payment is made.

5 Exceptions [8.3]

(1) The Maintenance Services exclude any maintenance of the Equipment which is necessitated as a result of any cause other than fair wear and tear or the Supplier's neglect or fault, including without limitation:

(a) failure or fluctuation of electric power, air conditioning, humidity control or other environmental conditions; or

(b) accident, transportation, neglect, misuse, or default of the Customer, its employees or agents or any third party; or

(c) any fault in any attachments or associated equipment (whether or not supplied by the Supplier) which do not form part of the Equipment; or

[**Note**: it may be appropriate for (c) above to be deleted in relation to other peripherals supplied by the same supplier if it purports to offer support services in relation to them as well.]

(d) act of God, fire, flood, war, act of violence, or any other similar occurrence; or

(e) any attempt by any person other than the Supplier's personnel to adjust, repair or maintain the Equipment; or

(f) any head crash or failure of fixed or removable storage media.

(2) The Supplier will (if it is reasonably able to do so) at the request and expense of the Customer repair or replace any part of the Equipment which has failed due to a cause other than fair wear and tear or due to the Supplier's neglect or fault subject to the Customer accepting the Supplier's written quotation therefor prior to the commencement of work.

(3) The Maintenance Services also exclude:

(a) the provision of services other than at the Location (or such other location as the Supplier shall have approved in writing);

(b) repair or renewal of tapes, disk packs, printing cartridges or other consumable supplies;

[(c) maintenance or support of the operating system of any computer;]

(d) electrical or other environmental work external to the Equipment;

[(e) maintenance of any attachments or associated equipment not supplied by the Supplier which do not form part of the Equipment;] or

(f) recovery or reconstruction of any data or programs lost or spoiled as a result of any breakdown of or fault in the Equipment.

[Note: (c) and/or (e) may be excluded, depending on the scope of support services offered; for example, if the support provider is the OEM, it should usually be in a position to offer combined support for both the hardware and its operating software.]

6 Replacement [8.5.1, 8.6.5]

(1) The Supplier reserves the right to replace the whole of the Equipment or any part or parts thereof which may be found to be faulty or in need of investigation as to whether faults may exist in their operation.

(2) The Supplier, in effecting any such replacement, shall not remove the Equipment or any part or parts thereof ("the Removed Equipment") until he is ready to install equipment to replace it ("the Replacement Equipment").

(3) The Supplier shall at the time of any such replacement notify the Customer in writing of the serial numbers of the Replacement Equipment.

(4) If the Replacement Equipment is not equipment which is identical in all respects to the Removed Equipment the Supplier shall inform the Customer in writing at the time of replacement. The Replacement Equipment shall not in any event provide less than an equivalent level of performance and functionality to the Removed Equipment.

(5) Within 2 weeks of being informed of replacement of non-identical equipment the Customer shall have the right to request that the Replacement Equipment or any part or parts thereof be removed and either the Removed Equipment be put back or other equipment identical to the Removed Equipment be installed and the Supplier shall comply with such request forthwith.

(6) The Replacement Equipment shall become the property of the [Customer] [owner of the Equipment]. The Removed Equipment removed pursuant to this clause 6 shall become the property of the Supplier

[Note: The phrase "owner of the Equipment" will be appropriate when the customer is not the owner— e.g. when the equipment is leased.]

(7) The provisions of this Agreement shall apply to all replacements and renewals of any part or parts of the Equipment made by the Supplier during the continuance of this Agreement.

(8) In removing any Equipment or part thereof, the Supplier undertakes (provided the condition of the Removed Equipment reasonably allows) to copy and provide

such copy to the Customer or to allow the Customer first to copy any information or data which may be stored on the Removed Equipment. The Supplier thereafter undertakes not to disclose any such information or data but to expunge it forthwith from the Removed Equipment and to certify to the Customer that it has done so.

7 Service visits outside the maintenance services [8.3.1, 8.3.2]

The Supplier shall make an additional charge, in accordance with its standard scale of charges from time to time in force, for service visits:

(1) made at the request of the Customer by reason of any fault in the Equipment due to causes not covered by the Maintenance Services; or

(2) made at the request of the Customer but which the Supplier finds are frivolous or not necessary.

8 Duration

This Agreement shall commence on the Commencement Date, shall continue for the Initial Period and shall remain in force thereafter [unless or] until terminated by either party giving to the other not less than 6 months' written notice of termination [given on] [expiring on] the last day of the Initial Period or at any time thereafter but shall be subject to earlier termination as provided elsewhere in this Agreement.

[Note: Delete the first and third bracketed phrases if the agreement is to be for a minimum period equal to the Initial Period plus the notice period. Delete the second bracketed phrase if the agreement is to be for a minimum period equal to the Initial Period.]

9 Customer's obligations [8.5.1, 8.6]

During the continuance of this Agreement the Customer shall:

Use and care of the Equipment [8.6.1]

(1) ensure that proper environmental conditions are maintained for the Equipment and shall maintain in good condition the accommodation of the Equipment, the cables and fittings associated therewith and the electricity supply thereto;

(2) not make any modification to the Equipment without the Supplier's prior written consent;

(3) keep and operate the Equipment in a proper and prudent manner in accordance with [the manufacturer's] [the Supplier's] operating instructions and ensure that only competent trained employees (or persons under their supervision) are allowed to operate the Equipment;

(4) ensure that the external surfaces of the Equipment are kept clean and in good condition and shall carry out any minor maintenance recommended by [the manufacturer] [the Supplier] from time to time;

(5) save as aforesaid, not attempt to adjust, repair or maintain the Equipment and shall not request, permit or authorise anyone other than the Supplier to carry out any adjustments, repairs or maintenance of the Equipment;

(6) use on the Equipment only such operating supplies as [the manufacturer] [the Supplier] shall recommend in writing;

(7) not to make any movement of those items of the Equipment specified as not to be moved in the Schedule, nor to remove any of the Equipment from the Location without the Supplier's prior written consent;

[**Note**: Older contracts had a blanket prohibition against moving the equipment. If the equipment includes (say) PCs this seems a little harsh. The proposed wording allows some items to be moved and others not as set out in A of the Schedule. It must also be construed by reference to clause 5(1)(b) which covers the case of a customer who moves equipment and in doing so damages it.]

(8) not use in conjunction with the Equipment any accessory, attachment or additional equipment other than that which has been supplied by or approved in writing by the Supplier;

Access [8.6.2]

(9) upon reasonable notice, provide the Supplier with full and safe access to the Equipment for the purposes of this Agreement;

(10) provide adequate working space around the Equipment for the use of the Supplier's personnel [and shall make available such reasonable facilities as may be requested from time to time by the Supplier for the storage and safekeeping of test equipment and spare parts];

[(11) provide a suitable vehicle parking facility for use by the Supplier's personnel which is free from any legal restrictions and immediately close to the Location [and the place where spares are held in accordance with clause 10 hereof];]

[**Note**: As response time is specified as the time when the engineer arrives at the location (clause 2(3)), it is in both supplier's and customer's interest that the engineer's proceeding from arrival at the premises ("Location") to the actual room where the equipment is kept should be as rapid as possible. By the same token if the spares are distant from the location this will also delay the engineer's ability to get on with his job.]

(12) ensure in the interests of health and safety that the Supplier's personnel, while on the Customer's premises for the purposes of this Agreement, are at all times accompanied by a member of the Customer's staff familiar with the Customer's premises and safety procedures;

Notification and information [8.6.3]

(13) promptly notify the Supplier if the Equipment needs maintenance or is not operating correctly. [Failure by the Customer so to notify the Supplier within 2 months of the Customer first becoming aware of such failure or incorrect operation shall free the Supplier from all obligations to investigate or correct such failure or incorrect operation];

(14) subject to clause 15, make available to the Supplier access to such of its programs, operating manuals and information as may be reasonably necessary to enable the Supplier to perform its obligations hereunder and shall if requested by the Supplier provide staff familiar with the Customer's programs and operations, which staff shall co-operate fully with the Supplier's personnel in the diagnosis of any failure or incorrect operation of the Equipment;

(15) make available to the Supplier free of charge all facilities and services reasonably required by the Supplier to enable the Supplier to perform the Maintenance Services including without limitation computer runs, memory dumps, print-outs, data preparation, office accommodation, typing and photocopying;

(16) at all times keep a record of the use of the Equipment in a form to be approved by the Supplier and at the Supplier's request provide the Supplier with copies of the entries and allow the Supplier to inspect such record at all reasonable times;

(17) in the event that the Supplier is requested to supply any Maintenance Services in respect of any Additional Equipment, advise the Supplier forthwith of the date of installation of such item of Additional Equipment at the Location;

Miscellaneous [8.6.5]

(18) provide such telecommunication facilities as are reasonably required by the Supplier for testing and diagnostic purposes at the Customer's expense;

(19) keep full security copies of the Customer's programs, data bases and computer records in accordance with best computing practice.

[10 Spare parts [8.6.4]

(1) The Customer shall purchase from the Supplier such spare parts as the Supplier shall recommend, which shall be supplied at the Supplier's list prices from time to time in force.

(2) The Customer shall keep such spare parts at the Location or at a place immediately close thereto [such place to be subject to the Supplier's prior written approval]. The Supplier may draw on this stock of spare parts for the maintenance and repair of the Equipment.

(3) The Supplier shall not be liable for any delay in performing its obligations hereunder if any recommended spare parts are not available (otherwise than due to the fault of the Supplier) and shall be entitled to charge the Customer for all additional expenses and costs incurred by the Supplier as a result of such delay.

(4) Any spare parts which are not included in the Supplier's recommendations shall be supplied by the Supplier at its list prices from time to time in force.]

[**Note**: this clause will only be necessary in relatively rare cases, *e.g.* where the equipment being supported consists of large quantities of replaceable parts, or the location is in a remote place.]

[11 Electromagnetic compatibility [2.7.2]

(1) In this clause the expression "Electromagnetic Equipment" means any part or parts of the Equipment which are electric or electronic and covered by the Electromagnetic Compatibility Regulations 1992, as amended.

(2) The Supplier warrants to the Customer that at the date hereof all the Electromagnetic Equipment complies fully with the Electromagnetic Compatibility Regulations 1992, as amended.

(3) The Customer undertakes to the Supplier that it will not make any modification to the Electromagnetic Equipment without the prior written consent of the Supplier.]

[12 Telecommunications [2.7.4]

(1) In this clause the expression "Relevant Equipment" means any part of the Equipment which is intended to be connected to any telecommunication system which is, or is to be connected to, a public telecommunication system.

(2) If after the date hereof the Secretary of State for Trade and Industry or any person to whom he has delegated his powers requires the Relevant Equipment or any part thereof to be modified as a condition of the continuance of his approval the Supplier reserves the right to make such modification at the Customer's expense.

(3) If the Customer connects the Relevant Equipment to any telecommunication system the Customer shall be responsible for obtaining the consent of the owner of that system (if necessary) to such connection and for complying with all conditions relating thereto.]

[13 Downtime

(1) In this clause:

"Effectiveness Level"	means in relation to each Month (Available Time less Downtime) divided by Available Time and then multiplied by 100.
"Available Time"	means the number of Maintenance Hours in the Month in question.
"Downtime"	means those complete hours of Available Time during which the Equipment is unusable or substantially unusable, other than where such circumstances have arisen as a result of any of the matters set out in clause 5.
"Month"	means any complete calendar month during which this Agreement continues.

(2) Without prejudice to any of the Customer's other rights and remedies, if the Effectiveness Level for any Month falls below 95 the Customer shall be entitled to a credit against the Maintenance Charge for such Month calculated as follows:

$$\text{Credit} = \frac{(95 - \text{Effectiveness Level for such Month})}{100} \times M$$

where "M" is the Maintenance Charge for such Month.

(3) The amount of such credit shall be set against the Maintenance Charge for the Month immediately following the Month in respect of which the credit is given.]

[Notes:

(1) Where reliability is an important factor the customer may ask for a clause such as this to enable him to obtain a credit against maintenance charges if "downtime" exceeds a certain level. The effectiveness of the clause will depend on the customer keeping an accurate record of downtime.

(2) This clause assumes that the maintenance charge is payable monthly.

(3) There may in addition need to be a number of express assumptions made vis à vis the applications being run on the equipment, the technical infrastructure with which it is connected, etc.]

14 Termination [8.4]

(1) Notwithstanding anything else contained herein, this Agreement may be terminated:

(a) forthwith by the Supplier on giving notice in writing to the Customer if the Customer fails to pay any sum due under the terms of this Agreement (otherwise than as a consequence of any default on the part of the Supplier) and such sum remains unpaid for *14* days after written notice from the Supplier requiring such sum to be paid and referring to this clause 14(1)(a); or

(b) by the Customer forthwith on giving notice in writing to the Supplier if the Equipment or a material part thereof is lost, stolen or destroyed or damaged beyond economic repair; or

(c) forthwith by either party on giving notice in writing to the other if the other party is in material breach of any term of this Agreement (other than any failure by the Customer to make any payment hereunder in which event the provisions of paragraph (a) above shall apply) and (in the case of a breach capable of being remedied) shall have failed to have remedied, within *30* days of receiving a written notice requiring it to do so; or

(d) forthwith by either party on giving notice in writing to the other if the other party shall have a receiver or administrative receiver appointed or assets or shall pass a resolution for winding-up (otherwise than for the purpose of a bona fide scheme of solvent amalgamation or reconstruction) or a court of competent jurisdiction shall make an order to that effect or if the other party shall become subject to an administration order or shall enter into any voluntary arrangement with its creditors or shall cease or threaten to cease to carry on business.

(2) Any termination of this Agreement howsoever occasioned shall not affect any accrued rights or liabilities of either party nor shall it affect the coming into force or the continuance in force of any provision hereof which is expressly or by implication intended to come into or continue in force on or after such termination

(3) On the termination of this Agreement the Customer shall be entitled to reimbursement of such aspects of the Maintenance Charge as have been paid in advance and relate to Maintenance Services which will not now be provided, calculated on a pro rata basis.

15 Confidentiality [8.7.2]

(1) *See clause 21 of Precedent A.*

(2) In performing its Services under this Agreement the Supplier may process (albeit for diagnostic or investigative purposes only) personal data belonging to the Customer. The Supplier hereby warrants to the Customer that in such circumstances it will in respect of such personal data observe all the obligations pertaining to a data processor under the Data Protection Act 1998 and will indemnify the Customer against all breaches of the said Act by the Supplier in respect of the Customer's data.

16 *Force majeure*

See clause 15 of Precedent A.

17 Customer's warranty

The Customer hereby warrants to the Supplier that the Customer has not been induced to enter into this Agreement by any prior representations or warranties, whether oral or in writing, except as specifically contained in this Agreement and the Customer hereby irrevocably and unconditionally waives any right it may have to claim damages for any misrepresentation not contained in this Agreement or for breach of any warranty not contained herein (unless such misrepresentation or warranty was made fraudulently) and/or to rescind this Agreement.

[Note: At first sight this may appear harsh on the customer, but it will be in the best interests of the customer to incorporate important representations into the agreement by specific reference, rather than rely on oral promises or general descriptions. It will probably not be possible to bind the customer to waive damages for fraudulent misrepresentation, nor reasonable to try to do so.]

18 Liability [8.3.4]

(1) Subject to the provisions of clause 15(2) [and clause 13] the Supplier shall not be liable for any loss or damage sustained or incurred by the Customer or any third party (including without limitation any loss of use of the Equipment or loss or corruption of the Customer's programs or data) resulting from any breakdown of or fault in the Equipment unless such breakdown or fault is caused by the negligence or wilful misconduct of the Supplier, its employees, agents or sub-contractors, or to the extent that such loss or damage arises from any unreasonable delay by the Supplier in providing the Maintenance Services and then only to the extent not excluded by this Agreement.

[Note: if the supplier is not also the manufacturer or OEM, it may wish expressly to exclude liability for inherent or pre-existing defects in the equipment. The supplier will in such case wish to satisfy itself as to the condition of the equipment before entering into the agreement.]

(2) The Supplier shall indemnify the Customer and keep the Customer fully and effectively indemnified on demand against any loss of or damage to any property or injury to or death of any person caused by any negligent act or omission or wilful misconduct of the Supplier, its employees, agents or sub-contractors.

(3) The Customer shall indemnify the Supplier and keep the Supplier fully and effectively indemnified on demand against any loss of or damage to any property or injury to or death of any person caused by any negligent act or omission or wilful misconduct of the Customer, its employees, agents or sub-contractors.

(4) Except in respect of injury to or death of any person (for which no limit applies) the respective liability of the Supplier and the Customer under sub-clauses (2) and (3) in respect of each event or series of connected events shall not exceed £500,000.

[Note: Some contracts specifically require the parties to back up their indemnities with insurance. It is also common to see suppliers link their liability limits to some multiple of the maintenance charge, although it is not certain that this would be accepted as reasonable in a contract written on standard terms for the purposes of the Unfair Contract Terms Act 1977.]

[(5) Notwithstanding anything else contained in this Agreement the Supplier shall not be liable to the Customer for loss of profits or contracts or other indirect or consequential loss whether arising from negligence, breach of contract or howsoever.]

(6) The Supplier shall not be liable to the Customer for any loss arising out of any failure by the Customer to keep full and up-to-date security copies of the computer programs and data it uses in accordance with best computing practice.

19 Waiver of remedies

See clause 28 of Precedent A.

20 Entire agreement

This Agreement supersedes all prior agreements, arrangements and understandings between the parties and constitutes the entire agreement between the parties relating to the subject matter hereof (save that neither party seeks to exclude liability for any fraudulent precontractual misrepresentations upon which the other party can be shown to have relied). No addition to or modification of any provision of this Agreement shall be binding upon the parties unless made by a written instrument signed by a duly authorised representative of each of the parties.

[**Note**: This clause may have to be amended in the light of any side letters or collateral agreements.]

21 Assignment

See clause 30 of Precedent A.

22 Sub-contracts

See clause 31 of Precedent A.

23 Notices

See clause 32 of Precedent A.

24 Interpretation

See clause 33 of Precedent A.

25 Law

See clause 34 of Precedent A.

26 Disputes

See clause 35 of Precedent A.

27 Severability

See clause 36 of Precedent A.

28 Third parties

See clause 37 of Precedent A.

EXECUTED under hand the day and year first before written

SIGNED for and on behalf of
COMPUTER COMPANY [LIMITED] [PLC]

By

Signature

Title

Witness

SIGNED for and on behalf of
CUSTOMER [LIMITED] [PLC]

By

Signature

Title

Witness

The Schedule

A   THE EQUIPMENT

[**Note**: Whether any items can be moved in accordance with clause 9(7) should also be included here.]

B   THE LOCATION

C   THE COMMENCEMENT DATE

either:

(a) the date of this Agreement; or

(b) *December 31, 2005*; or

(c) the date on which the Equipment is accepted by the Customer under the terms of a sale agreement made between the Customer and [the Supplier] dated [   ]. If the Equipment is not accepted by the Customer as aforesaid then this Agreement shall never become effective.

D   THE INITIAL PERIOD

E   THE MAINTENANCE CHARGE

£[   ] for each [month] [quarter] [year], payable in advance

First charge payable on: [the Commencement Date]

Subsequent charges payable on the first working day of each [month] [quarter] [year] thereafter.

F   CHARGING RATE FOR ADDITIONAL EQUIPMENT

G   METHOD OF PAYMENT

By standing order to [   ] Bank PLC

(Supplier's Account No. [   ])

[H   SUB-CONTRACTS]

[I   ESCALATION [8.7.1]

(1) (a) In the event that any notified failure or malfunction shall not have been corrected within *3* hours of the Supplier's engineer arriving at the Location in response to a call from the Customer to correct such failure or malfunction, the Supplier hereby undertakes that the Supplier's *Services*

Supervisor shall notify the Customer's *Operations Supervisor* by telephone or otherwise and discuss with him the failure or malfunction and the Supplier's ability to solve it.

(b) In the event that any such failure or malfunction shall not have been corrected within *24* hours of such engineer first arriving at the Location in response to a call about such failure or malfunction, the Supplier hereby undertakes that the Supplier's *Head of Maintenance Services* shall notify the Customer's *Head of Operational Services* by telephone or otherwise and discuss with him the failure or malfunction and the Supplier's ability to solve it.

(c) In the event that any such failure or malfunction shall not have been corrected within *48* hours of such engineer first arriving at the Location in response to a call about such failure or malfunction, the Supplier hereby undertakes that the Supplier's *Managing Director* shall notify the Customer's *Managing Director* by telephone or otherwise and discuss with him the failure or malfunction and the Supplier's ability to solve it.

(2) In the event that any such escalation as is described in the preceding sub-clause (1) shall become due and that any of the [Supplier's and] Customer's officers named in the sub-clause are unavailable, the provisions of sub-clause (1) shall be fulfilled by the next higher officer being available].

[J THIRD-PARTY RIGHTS]

SOFTWARE MAINTENANCE AGREEMENT: LICENCE

THIS AGREEMENT is made the   day of   20

PARTIES:

(1) COMPUTER COMPANY [LIMITED] [PLC] whose registered office is at

("the Licensor")

(2) CUSTOMER [LIMITED] [PLC] whose registered office is at

("the Licensee")

RECITALS:

(A) By a licence agreement dated [   ] made between the Licensor and the Licensee ("the Licence Agreement") the Licensor granted to the Licensee a non-exclusive and non-transferable licence to use the Licensor's computer programs and associated documentation more particularly described therein. A copy of the Licence Agreement is attached

(B) [By clause 17 of the Licence Agreement it was agreed that the parties would enter into a maintenance agreement in respect of the said programs and documentation in the form of this Agreement] [The Licensor has agreed to maintain the said programs and documentation upon the terms and conditions hereinafter contained]

NOW IT IS HEREBY AGREED as follows:

1 Definitions

In this Agreement unless the context otherwise requires, the following expressions have the following meanings:

"the Commencement Date"	means the date on which this Agreement shall become effective as specified in the Schedule.
"Confidential Information"	means all information obtained by one party from the other pursuant to this Agreement which is expressly marked as confidential or which is manifestly of a confidential nature or which is confirmed in writing to be confidential within 7 days of its disclosure.
"the Current Release"	means the most recent Release accepted by the Licensee under this Agreement or if no Release has been accepted the Licensed Programs.

"the Initial Period"	means the initial period of this Agreement as specified in the Schedule.
"the Licensed Programs" "the Licensed Program Materials" and "the Equipment"	have the meanings respectively given to them in the Licence Agreement.
"the Maintenance Charge"	means the charges payable for the Maintenance Services specified in the Schedule as may be amended from time to time pursuant to clause 3.
"the Maintenance Services"	means the maintenance services to be provided by the Licensor pursuant to clause 5.
"New Release"	means any new Release made available to the Licensee by the Licensor pursuant to clause 5(2).
"the Program Documentation"	means the operating manuals, user instructions, online help material, technical literature and all other related materials in either printed form or machine readable form supplied by the Licensor to the Licensee for aiding the use and application of the Current Release.
"Release"	means a version of the Licensed Programs (defined by reference to variations in version numbers, *e.g.* v. 1, v. 2, etc.)
"the Specification"	means the specification of the Current Release describing the facilities and functions thereof.

2 Services to be performed [9.1.1, 9.1.2]

The Licensor hereby agrees to provide the Maintenance Services to the Licensee upon the terms and conditions hereinafter contained.

3 Charges and payment [9.2]

(1) In consideration of the Maintenance Services the Licensee shall pay the Maintenance Charge periodically in advance as specified in the Schedule. The Maintenance Charge shall become due and payable without prior demand on the dates specified in the Schedule and no payment shall be considered made until it is received by the Licensor in cleared funds. All payments shall be made in the manner specified in the Schedule.

(2) Any charges payable by the Licensee hereunder in addition to the Maintenance Charge shall be paid by the Licensee within *30* days after the receipt of the Licensor's invoice therefor.

EITHER (VERSION A Unfettered right to increase charges):

[(3) The Licensor shall be entitled at any time and from time to time after the expiry of the [Initial Period] [the period of *one year* after the Commencement Date] to increase the Maintenance Charge to accord with any change in the Licensor's standard scale of charges by giving to the Licensee not less than *90* days' prior written notice. Where and whenever such notice is given, the Licensee shall have the right to terminate this Agreement as from the date on which such notice expires by giving to the Licensor written notice of termination not less than *30* days before such date.]

OR (VERSION B Inflation-linked right to increase charges):

[(3) The Licensor shall be entitled at any time and from time to time (subject as mentioned below) after the expiry of the [Initial Period] [the period of *one* year after the Commencement Date] to increase the Maintenance Charge by giving to the Licensee not less than *90* days' prior written notice provided that any such increase shall not exceed a percentage equal to the percentage increase in *the Retail Prices Index published by the Central Statistical Office* for the period from the Commencement Date (in the case of the first such increase) or the date on which the immediately preceding increase came into effect pursuant to this sub-clause (in the case of the second or subsequent increase) up to the date of such notice plus *2* per cent provided further that no increase may be made pursuant to this sub-clause until a period of at least *one* year has elapsed since the date on which the immediately preceding increase came into effect pursuant to this sub-clause.]

(4) The Maintenance Charge and any additional charges payable under this Agreement are exclusive of Value Added Tax which shall be paid by the Licensee at the rate and in the manner for the time being prescribed by law.

(5) If any sum payable under this Agreement is not paid within *7* days after the due date then (without prejudice to the Licensor's other rights and remedies) the Licensor reserves the right to charge interest on such sum on a day to day basis (as well after as before any judgment) from the date or last date for payment thereof to the date of actual payment (both dates inclusive) at the rate of *2* per cent above the base rate of *ABC* Bank plc (or such other London Clearing Bank as the Supplier may nominate) from time to time in force compounded quarterly. Such interest shall be paid on demand by the Licensor. In addition or in the alternative (at the option of the Licensor), the Licensor may suspend the provision of the Maintenance Services until such time as the payment is made.

4 Duration

This Agreement shall commence on the Commencement Date and shall continue for the Initial Period and remain in force thereafter [unless or] until terminated by either party giving to the other party not less than *12* months' written notice of termination [given on] [expiring on] the last day of the Initial Period or at any time thereafter but shall be subject to earlier termination as provided elsewhere in this Agreement.

[**Notes:**

    (1) Delete the first and third bracketed phrases if the agreement is to be for a minimum period equal to the Initial Period plus the notice period. Delete the second bracketed phrase if the agreement is to be for a minimum period equal to the Initial Period.

(2) A short initial period will give the licensee little protection and he should therefore look to the licensor for a realistic initial commitment. In a long term arrangement an index-linked charges review clause will be preferable from the licensee's point of view.]

5 Maintenance services [9.1.3, 9.3.1]

Subject to the payment by the Licensee of the Maintenance Charge the Licensor shall provide the Licensee with the following maintenance services:

(1) *Error correction*

(a) If the Licensee shall discover that the Current Release fails to conform with any part of the Specification then the Licensee shall within *14* days after such discovery notify the Licensor in writing of the defect or error in question and if reasonably practicable provide the Licensor with a documented example of such defect or error.

(b) The Licensor shall thereupon promptly investigate the reported defect or error and thereafter use its reasonable endeavours to correct promptly such defect or error. Provided the Licensor has in its reasonable opinion been able to rectify the defect or error, it shall, forthwith upon such correction being completed, deliver to the Licensee the corrected version of the object code of the Current Release in machine readable form together with appropriate amendments to the Program Documentation specifying the nature of the correction and providing instructions for the proper use of the corrected version of the Current Release. The Licensor shall provide the Licensee with all assistance reasonably required by the Licensee to enable the Licensee to implement the use of the corrected version of the Current Release.

(c) If, for any reason, the Licensor has not in its reasonable opinion been able to rectify the defect or error, it shall immediately notify the Licensee and provided the failure substantially hinders or prevents the Licensee from using a material part of the functionality of the Licensed Programs, the Licensee shall be entitled to terminate this Agreement forthwith by giving written notice to the Licensor.

[Notes:

(1) Depending on the value and complexity of the software, more sophisticated clauses may be required. For example, the agreement could categorise reported failures into different degrees of seriousness each with its own required response time and deadlines for resolution for the business critical application. In particular, lengthy response times may be unacceptable.

(2) If the agreement is to be terminated under clause 5(1)(c), one needs to consider what remedies are to be available to the licensee, *e.g.* repayment of the support fee?

(3) As speed is important for providing these rectifications they are likely to fall well short of being new releases and will probably be "patches" [9.0].]

(d) The foregoing error correction service shall not include the provision of services in respect of:

　(i) defects or errors resulting from any modifications of the Current Release made by any person other than the Licensor without the Licensor's prior written consent;

　(ii) any version of the Licensed Programs other than the Current Release [and/or the immediately preceding Release];

　(iii) use of the Current Release other than in accordance with the Program Documentation or operator error;

(iv) any defect or error in the Equipment or in any programs used in conjunction with the Current Release [and/or the immediately preceding Release];

(v) defects or errors caused by the use of the Current Release [and/or the immediately preceding Release] on or with equipment (other than the Equipment) [or programs] not supplied by or approved in writing by the Licensor [provided that for this purpose any programs designated for use with the Current Release [and/or the immediately preceding Release] in the Specification shall be deemed to have the written approval of the Licensor];

(vi) act of God, fire, flood, war, act of violence or any other similar occurrence;

(vii) any modification or enhancement of the Current Release if such modification or enhancement results in a departure from the Specification.

(e) The Licensor shall make an additional charge in accordance with its standard scale of charges from time to time in force for any services provided by the Licensor:

(i) at the request of the Licensee but which do not qualify under the aforesaid error correction service by virtue of any of the exclusions referred to in paragraph (d) above; or

(ii) at the request of the Licensee but which the Licensor finds are not necessary.

For the avoidance of doubt nothing in this paragraph shall impose any obligation on the Licensor to provide services in respect of any defect, error or circumstance arising due to any of the exclusions referred to in paragraph (d).

(f) If the Licensee shall discover that the Program Documentation does not provide adequate or correct instruction for the proper use of any facility or function set out in the Specification then the Licensee shall notify the Licensor in writing of the fault in question within *14* days after such discovery. The Licensor shall thereupon promptly correct the fault and provide the Licensee with appropriate amendments to the Program Documentation.

(2) Releases [9.1.2, 9.1.5]

EITHER (VERSION A Licensee's option whether or not to accept new Releases):

[(a) The Licensor shall promptly notify the Licensee of any new Release of the Licensed Programs which the Licensor shall from time to time make generally available to its licensees. The Licensor shall provide with such notification an explanatory memorandum specifying not only the nature of the improvements but also any adverse effects which the new Release may be expected to have including in particular any expected degradation in the performance of the Licensed Programs. While it is acknowledged by the Licensee that the explanatory memorandum may not be equivalent to a detailed specification of the New Release it shall contain sufficient information to enable the Licensee to judge whether the New Release will be appropriate to the Licensee's requirements.

[**Note**: To talk of an improved version having adverse effects may appear to be strange at first sight. However, while an improved version may provide a host of additional facilities and functions (none or all of which may be required by the licensee) it may also (for example) affect memory capacity or response times which would result in a degradation in performance criteria and this might outweigh the advantages.]

(b) If the Licensee shall wish to evaluate the new Release then the Licensee shall notify the Licensor in writing accordingly. Upon receipt of such notification, the Licensor shall deliver to the Licensee as soon as reasonably practicable (having regard to the number of other users requiring the new Release) the object code of the New Release in machine-readable form together with any amendments to the Specification and the Program Documentation which shall be necessary to describe and enable proper use of the improved facilities and functions of the New Release. The Licensee's use of such New Release shall be governed by the provisions of the Licence Agreement.

(c) The Licensee shall be responsible for evaluating the new Release during the period of 3 months after its delivery to the Licensee pursuant to clause 5(2)(b). On the expiry of such period the Licensee shall notify the Licensor whether or not it wishes to accept the New Release. If the Licensor does not receive any such notification then the Licensee shall be deemed to have rejected the New Release in which case the provisions of paragraph (f) below shall apply.

(d) If requested by the Licensee, the Licensor shall provide training for the Licensee's staff in the use of the New Release at the Licensor's standard scale of charges from time to time in force as soon as reasonably practicable after the delivery of the New Release.

(e) If the Licensee accepts the New Release then the New Release shall thereby become the Current Release and the provisions of this Agreement shall apply accordingly. Upon such acceptance the Licensee shall [if requested by the Licensor] return to the Licensor the Licensed Programs or the previous Current Release (as the case may be) and any part of the Program Documentation or the Specification which has been superseded and all copies of the whole or any part thereof, or, if required by the Licensor, shall destroy the same and certify in writing to the Licensor that they have been destroyed.

(f) If the Licensee shall not accept the New Release then the Licensee shall immediately return to the Licensor the New Release and the amendments to the Specification and the Program Documentation insofar as they relate solely to the New Release and all copies of the whole or any part thereof or, if required by the Licensor, shall destroy the same and certify in writing to the Licensor that they have been destroyed. This Agreement shall automatically terminate on receipt of such notice.

(g) The Licensor shall not be relieved of its obligations to provide the Maintenance Services for the Current Release during the period of 3 months referred to in paragraph (d) above.]

[**Note**: the above wording would require amendment in the event that the licensor is willing and able to provide support for more than one Release (*e.g.* the Current Release and the preceding version). If there is to be an additional charge for the provision and/or installation of the New Release, this should also be set out.]

OR (VERSION B Licensee contractually bound to accept new Releases – subject to safeguards):

[(a) The Licensor shall deliver to the Licensee any new version of the Licensed Programs which the Licensor shall from time to time make generally available to its licensees and the Licensee shall be responsible for using such Release subject to the conditions set out below.

(b) In reasonable time prior to the delivery of a new Release the Licensor shall make available to the Licensee all amendments to the Specification which shall be necessary to properly describe the facilities and functions of the new Release.

(c) Notwithstanding anything else contained herein, the Licensee shall not be obliged to accept or use the new Release if its use would result in any of the facilities and functions set out in the Specification being [materially] diminished or curtailed.

(d) The Licensor shall deliver to the Licensee the object code of the New Release in machine-readable form together with any amendments to the Program Documentation which shall be necessary to enable proper use of the improved facilities and functions of the New Release. The Licensee's use of the New Release shall be governed by the provisions of the Licence Agreement.

(e) If requested by the Licensee, the Licensor shall provide training for the Licensee's staff in the use of the New Release as soon as reasonably practicable after the delivery of the New Release at the Licensor's standard scale of charges from time to time in force.

(f) Within 3 months of the Licensee receiving the New Release the Licensee shall test the New Release and shall notify the Licensor of any failure of the New Release to fulfil the amended Specification as delivered to the Licensee pursuant to paragraph (b).

(g) If within 3 months after such delivery no such notification shall have been received by the Licensor then, subject to the Licensor having complied with its foregoing obligations, the Licensee shall be deemed to have accepted the New Release which shall then become the Current Release and the provisions of this Agreement shall apply accordingly.

(h) If the Licensee shall have notified the Licensor of any failure of the New Release to fulfil any part of the amended Specification within the said period of 3 months then the Licensor shall either correct the New Release and re-issue it in accordance with this clause (as if it were a New Release) within a reasonable period of time, or withdraw it, in which event it shall remain obliged to provide the Maintenance Services in respect of the Current Release.

(i) Upon acceptance under paragraph (g) above, the Licensee shall return to the Licensor [if required by the Licensor] the previous Current Release and any part of the Program Documentation which has been superseded and all copies of the whole or any part thereof, or, if required by the Licensor, shall destroy the same and certify in writing to the Licensor that they have been destroyed.

(j) The Licensor shall not be relieved of its obligations to maintain the Current Release and the Program Documentation under sub-clause (1) during the period of 3 months referred to in paragraph (d) above and any extended period during which corrections are carried out pursuant to paragraph (h) above].

[**Note**: the above wording would require amendment in the event that the licensor is willing and able to provide support for more than just the latest release. If there is to be an additional charge for the provision and/or installation of the new release, this should also be set out—this is of particular importance if the licensee is to be obliged to take on new releases.]

(3) *Advice* [9.1.4]

The Licensor shall provide the Licensee between the hours of *0830 to 1800, Monday* to *Friday (excluding public holidays in England and Wales)* with such technical advice by any of the telecommunications (including but not limited to electronic mail) telephone calls facsimile transmission postal mail or visits by staff of the Licensor as shall be reasonably necessary to resolve the Licensee's difficulties and queries in using the Current Release. For the avoidance of doubt, the Licensor shall not be obliged to provide such technical advice in respect of any difficulties or queries which arise by reason of any of the matters described in clause 5(1)(d).

[(4) *Changes in law* [9.1.2]

The Licensor shall from time to time make such modifications to the Current Release as shall ensure that the Current Release conforms to any change of legislation or new legal requirements which affect the application of any function or facility described in the Specification. The Licensor shall promptly notify the Licensee in writing of all such changes and new requirements and shall implement the modifications to the Current Release (and all consequential amendments to the Program Documentation and the Specification which may be necessary to enable proper use of such modifications) as soon as reasonably practicable thereafter.]

[**Note**: it may be preferable from the licensor's point of view to provide that such modifications will be dealt with in the next New Release, with a possible "long stop" date as to when such New Release will be made available.]

(5) *The Euro*

(a) As soon as HM Government announce that the United Kingdom is to use the Euro as its currency, the Licensor undertakes to commence work on a modification to the Licensed Programs to allow use of the Euro and any conversion from the Pound Sterling [and other currencies] to the Euro in conformance with the applicable conversion and rounding requirements of E.C. Regulation 1103/97.

(b) The Licensor undertakes to make such modification to the Licensed Programs available to the Licensee as soon as practicable thereafter, whether in a new Release or otherwise, as part of the Licensed Programs.]

6 Licensee's obligations [9.6]

During the continuance of this Agreement the Licensee shall:

(1) use only the Current Release;

(2) ensure that the Current Release and the Equipment are used only in accordance with the Program Documentation or advice from the Licensor under clause 5(3) hereof by competent trained employees only or by persons under their supervision;

(3) make 2 back-up copies of the Current Release and so many back-up copies of the Licensee's data bases and computer records as may be necessary in accordance with best computing practice;

(4) not alter or modify the Current Release or the Program Documentation in any way whatever nor permit the Current Release to be combined with any other programs to form a combined work;

(5) not request, permit or authorise anyone other than the Licensor to provide any maintenance services in respect of the Current Release or the Program Documentation;

(6) co-operate fully with the Licensor's personnel in the diagnosis of any error or defect in the Current Release or the Program Documentation;

(7) make available to the Licensor free of charge all information facilities and services reasonably required by the Licensor to enable the Licensor to perform the Maintenance Services including without limitation computer runs, on-line access, memory dumps, printouts, [data preparation], [office accommodation], [typing] and photocopying;

(8) provide such telecommunication facilities as are reasonably required by the Licensor for testing and diagnostic purposes at the Licensee's expense;

[(9) provide a suitable vehicle parking facility for use by the Licensor's personnel when visiting the Licensee's premises which is free from any legal restrictions;] and

(10) ensure in the interests of health and safety that the Licensor's personnel, while on the Licensee's premises for the purposes of this Agreement, are at all times accompanied by a member of the Licensee's staff familiar with the Licensee's premises and safety procedures.

7 Proprietary rights and licence [3.8.1]

EITHER (VERSION A Licensor owns all intellectual property rights):

[(1) The Current Release (and all corrected versions thereof and all other Releases), the Program Documentation and the Specification and all parts thereof and the copyright and other intellectual property rights of whatever nature therein are and shall remain the property of the Licensor.]

OR (VERSION B Licensor does not own all intellectual property rights):

[(1) The Current Release (and all corrected versions thereof and all other Releases), the Program Documentation and the Specification and all parts thereof and the copyright and other intellectual property rights of whatever nature therein are and shall remain the property of the Licensor except for third-party software set out in the Schedule ("the Third-Party Software") whose copyright and other intellectual property rights are and shall remain the property of the copyright owners specified in the Schedule ("the Third-Party Copyright Owners") and the Licensor hereby warrants to the Licensee that it has full authority from the Third-Party Copyright Owners to grant to the Licensee a sub-licence to use the Third-Party Software and it will indemnify the Licensee against any claim by the Third-Party Copyright Owners.]

(2) The provisions of the Licence Agreement shall apply to the Current Release, any New Release, the Program Documentation, and the Specification as such provisions are expressed to apply to the Licensed Program Materials and to the specification referred to in the Licence Agreement mutatis mutandis and the parties hereby undertake to be bound by and comply with the terms of the Licence Agreement accordingly.

8 Confidentiality [3.7.2, 9.7, 10.3.3]

(1) *See clause 21 of Precedent A.*

(2) The Licensor shall establish and maintain such security measures and procedures as are reasonably practicable to provide for the safe custody of the Licensee's information and data in its possession and to prevent unauthorised access thereto or use thereof.

9 Data protection [3.7.2, 9.7, 10.3.3]

EITHER (VERSION A The Act does not apply to the Licensee's data):

[The Licensee hereby warrants and undertakes to the Licensor that the Licensee's data will not contain any personal data as defined in section 1(1) of the Data Protection Act 1998 or that if it does the processing (if any) of such data by the Licensor under this Agreement will not be processing as defined in section 1(1) and paragraph 5 of Schedule 8 of that Act or that the Licensee will be exempt from notifying in respect of the Licensee's data under the said Act by reason of one or more of the provisions for exemption in Part IV of the said Act and the Licensee shall indemnify the Licensor against all or any damages, losses, claims, costs and expenses sustained or incurred by the Licensor in connection with any prosecution of the Licensor under the said Act or any civil action brought by any person or persons under the said Act against the Licensor in so far as any such prosecution or civil action may be in respect of the Licensee's data.]

OR (VERSION B The Act does apply to the Licensee's data):

[(1) The Licensee hereby notifies the Licensor that the Licensee's data contains personal data as defined in section 1(1) of the Data Protection Act 1998 ("the Licensee's Personal Data") and warrants to the Licensor that the Licensee has notified under the said Act in respect of the Licensee's Personal Data.

(2) The Licensee warrants and undertakes to the Licensor that:

(a) The Licensee's Personal Data has been obtained and processed (in so far as the Licensee's Personal Data has been processed) lawfully;

(b) The services to be provided by the Licensor under this Agreement will be entirely consistent with and appropriate to the specified and lawful purposes for which the Licensee has notified under the said Act in respect of the Licensee's Personal Data ("the Notified Purposes");

(c) The Licensee has not hitherto and will not during the continuance of this Agreement use or disclose the Licensee's Personal Data or any part thereof in a manner incompatible with the Notified Purposes;

(d) The Licensee's Personal Data is adequate, relevant and not excessive in relation to the Notified Purposes; and

(e) The Licensee's Personal Data is accurate and the Licensee shall keep the Licensee's Personal Data fully up to date at all times during the continuance of this Agreement.

(3) The Licensee shall indemnify the Licensor against any loss or damage which the Licensor may sustain or incur as a result of any breach by the Licensee of the provisions of this clause.

[(4) *See sub-clause 15(2) of Precedent K.*]]

10 Termination [9.4]

(1) Notwithstanding anything else contained herein, this Agreement may be terminated:

(a) forthwith by the Licensor on giving notice in writing to the Licensee if the Licensee fails to pay any sum due under the terms of this Agreement (otherwise than as a consequence of any default on the part of the Licensor) and such sum remains unpaid for *14* days after written notice from the Licensor requiring such sum to be paid and referring to this clause 10(1)(a); or

(b) forthwith by either party on giving notice in writing to the other if the other party is in material breach of any term of this Agreement (other than any failure by the Licensee to make any payment hereunder in which event the provisions of paragraph (a) above shall apply) and (in the case of a breach capable of being remedied) shall have failed to have remedied within *30* days of receiving a written notice requiring it to do so; or

(c) forthwith by either party on giving notice in writing to the other if the other party shall have a receiver or administrative receiver appointed or shall pass a resolution for winding-up (otherwise than for the purpose of a bona fide scheme of solvent amalgamation or reconstruction) or a court of competent jurisdiction shall make an order to that effect or if the other party shall become subject to an administration order or shall enter into any voluntary arrangement with its creditors or shall cease or threaten to cease to carry on business.

(2) Any termination of this Agreement (howsoever occasioned) shall not affect any accrued rights or liabilities of either party nor shall it affect the coming into force or the continuance in force of any provision hereof which is expressly or by implication intended to come into or continue in force on or after such termination.

(3) Any termination of this Agreement (howsoever occasioned) shall not of itself affect the Licensee's right to continue to use the Current Release and the Program Documentation in accordance with the provisions of the Licence Agreement.

11 Assignment

See clause 30 of Precedent A.

12 *Force majeure*

See clause 36 of Precedent B.

13 Licensee's warranty

See clause 20 of Precedent A.

14 Liability [9.3.3]

(1) The Licensor shall not be liable for any loss or damage sustained or incurred by the Licensee or any third party (including without limitation any loss of use of the Current Release or loss of or spoiling of the Licensee's data) resulting from any defect or error in the Current Release or the Program Documentation except to the extent that such loss or damage arises from any unreasonable delay by the Licensor in providing the Maintenance Services and then only to the extent not excluded by this Agreement.

(2) The Licensor shall not be responsible for the maintenance, accuracy or good running of any version of the Licensed Programs except the Current Release.

(3) The Licensor shall indemnify the Licensee and keep the Licensee fully and effectively indemnified on demand against any loss of or damage to any property or injury to or death of any person caused by any negligent act or omission or wilful misconduct of the Licensor, its employees, agents or sub-contractors.

(4) The Licensee shall indemnify the Licensor and keep the Licensor fully and effectively indemnified on demand against any loss of or damage to any property or injury to or death of any person caused by any negligent act or omission or wilful misconduct of the Licensee, its employees, agents or sub-contractors.

(5) Except in respect of injury to or death of any person (for which no limit applies) the respective liability of the Licensor and the Licensee under sub-clauses (3) and (4) in respect of each event or series of connected events shall not exceed £*500,000.*

[**Note**: Some contracts specifically require the parties to back up their indemnities with insurance. It is also common to see licensors link their liability limits to some multiple of the maintenance charge, although it is not certain that this would be accepted as reasonable in a contract written on standard terms for the purposes of the Unfair Contract Terms Act 1977.]

[(6) Notwithstanding anything else contained in this Agreement the Licensor shall not be liable to the Licensee for loss of profits or contracts or other indirect or consequential loss whether arising from negligence, breach of contract or howsoever.]

(7) The Licensor shall not be liable to the Licensee for any loss arising out of any failure by the Licensee to keep full and up-to-date security copies of the computer programs and data it uses in accordance with best computing practice.

15 Waiver of remedies

See clause 28 of Precedent A.

16 Entire agreement

This Agreement is made pursuant to the Licence Agreement and supersedes all prior agreements, arrangements and understandings between the parties other than the Licence Agreement and constitutes with the Licence Agreement the entire agreement between the parties relating to the subject matter of the Licence

Agreement and this Agreement (save that neither party seeks to exclude liability for any fraudulent precontractual misrepresentation upon which the other party can be shown to have relied). No addition to or modification of any provision of this Agreement shall be binding upon the parties unless made by a written instrument signed by a duly authorised representative of each of the parties

[Note: this clause may have to be amended in the light of any side letters of collateral agreements.]

17 Notices

See clause 32 of Precedent A.

18 Interpretation

See clause 33 of Precedent A.

19 Law

See clause 34 of Precedent A.

20 Disputes

See clause 35 of Precedent A.

21 Severability

See clause 36 of Precedent A.

22 Third parties

See clause 37 of Precedent A.

[Note: Use Version B if Version B of clause 7(1) has been used.]

EXECUTED under hand the day and year first before written

SIGNED for and on behalf of
COMPUTER COMPANY [LIMITED] [PLC]

By

Signature

Title

Witness

SIGNED for and on behalf of
CUSTOMER [LIMITED] [PLC]

By

Signature

Title

Witness

The Schedule

A   THE COMMENCEMENT DATE

either:

(a) The date of this Agreement; or

(b) *December 31, 2005*; or

(c) The date on which the Licensed Programs are accepted by the Licensee under the terms of the Licence Agreement. If the Licensed Programs are not accepted by the Licensee as aforesaid then this Agreement shall never become effective.

B   THE INITIAL PERIOD

C   THE MAINTENANCE CHARGE

£[   ] for each [month] [quarter] [year] payable in advance

First charge payable on: [the Commencement Date]

Subsequent charges payable on the first working day of each [month] [quarter] [year] thereafter.

D   METHOD OF PAYMENT

By standing order to [   ] Bank PLC

(Licensor's Account No. [   ])

[E   [THIRD PARTY RIGHTS]

F   THE LICENCE AGREEMENT

[G   THIRD-PARTY SOFTWARE]

[**Note**: insert terms of third party software pursuant to clause 7(1), if relevant.]

SOFTWARE MAINTENANCE AGREEMENT: COMMISSIONED

THIS AGREEMENT is made the   day of 20

PARTIES:

(1) SYSTEMS HOUSE [LIMITED] [PLC] whose registered office is at

("the Systems House")

(2) CLIENT [LIMITED] [PLC] whose registered office is at

("the Client")

RECITALS:

(A) Pursuant to an agreement dated [ ] made between the Systems House and the Client ("the Programming Agreement" a copy of which is annexed hereto) the Systems House prepared and wrote certain computer programs and operating manuals for the Client

[Note: See Precedent D for programming agreements.]

(B) [By clause 16 of the Programming Agreement it was agreed that the parties would enter into a maintenance agreement in respect of the said programs and operating manuals in the form of this Agreement] [The Systems House has agreed to maintain the said programs and operating manuals upon the terms and conditions hereinafter contained]

NOW IT IS HEREBY AGREED as follows:

1 Definitions

In this Agreement (which expression includes the Schedule), unless the context otherwise requires, the following expressions have the following meanings:

"Confidential Information"	means all information obtained by one party from the other pursuant to this Agreement which is expressly marked as confidential or which is manifestly of a confidential nature or which is confirmed in writing to be confidential within 7 days of its disclosure.
"the Commencement Date"	means the date on which this Agreement shall become effective as specified in the Schedule.
"the Equipment"	has the meaning attributed thereto in the Programming Agreement.

"the Functional Specification"	means the functional specification of the Programs describing the facilities and functions thereof (a copy of which is annexed hereto) as modified from time to time pursuant to any provision of this Agreement.
"the Initial Period"	means the initial period of this Agreement as specified in the Schedule.
"the Operating Manuals"	means the operating manuals prepared by the Systems House pursuant to the Programming Agreement for aiding the use and application of the Programs as corrected or modified from time to time pursuant to any provision of this Agreement.
["the Performance Criteria"	means the performance criteria which the Programs have been designed to fulfil as specified in the Functional Specification subject to the tolerances, limitations and exceptions stated therein.]
"the Programs"	means the computer programs written by the Systems House pursuant to the Programming Agreement as corrected or modified from time to time pursuant to this Agreement.
"the Maintenance Charge"	means the periodic charge for the Maintenance Services specified in the Schedule as increased from time to time pursuant to clause 3.
"the Maintenance Services"	means the maintenance services to be provided by the Systems House pursuant to clause 5 of this Agreement.
"the Program Materials"	means the Programs, the Functional Specification and the Operating Manuals.

2 Services to be performed [9.1.3]

The Systems House shall provide the Maintenance Services upon the terms and conditions hereinafter contained.

3 Payment [9.2]

See clause 3 of Precedent L.

4 Duration

See clause 4 of Precedent L.

5 Maintenance services

(1) *Error correction* [9.1.3, 9.3.1]

(a) If the Client shall discover that any of the Programs fails to conform with any part of the Functional Specification [or the Performance Criteria] then the Client shall within *14* days after such discovery notify the Systems House in writing of the failure and if necessary and practicable provide the Systems House with a documented example of the failure. The Client undertakes to provide the Systems House promptly with any information which the Systems House may reasonably require from time to time to enable the Systems House to proceed with investigating and correcting the failure without undue delay or impediment.

(b) Upon receipt of such notification from the Client the Systems House shall (subject to its then current commitments) normally begin work on investigating and correcting the failure not later than the first working day thereafter and shall diligently continue the work during normal working hours or at such other times as may be mutually agreed between the parties until the work is accepted by the Client as completed satisfactorily. If the Client requests support in an emergency the Systems House shall use all reasonable efforts to respond to the request as quickly as possible.

(c) Forthwith upon such correction being completed the Systems House shall deliver to the Client the corrected version of the object code of the Programs or the part of the Programs in which the failure lay in machine-readable form for loading on to the Equipment together with any appropriate amendments to the Operating Manuals specifying the nature of the correction and providing instructions for the proper use of the corrected version of the Programs on the Equipment.

(d) The Systems House shall as soon as reasonably practicable after such delivery provide for the number and category of the Client's staff specified in the Schedule any such additional training as may be necessary to enable the Client to make proper use of the corrected version of the Programs. The Systems House shall in addition provide the Client with all other assistance reasonably required by the Client to enable the Client to implement the use of the corrected version of the Programs.

(e) The foregoing error correction service shall not include service in respect of:

    (i) defects or errors resulting from any modifications of the Programs made by any person other than the Systems House;

    (ii) use of the Programs other than in accordance with the Operating Manuals;

    (iii) defects or errors in the Equipment or in the *XYZ* operating system referred to in the Functional Specification or in any other programs used by the Client in conjunction with the Programs; or

    (iv) any modification or enhancement of the Programs if such modification or enhancement would result in a departure from the Functional Specification.

(f) The Systems House shall make an additional charge in accordance with its standard scale of charges from time to time in force for any services provided by the Systems House:

    (i) at the request of the Client but which do not qualify under the aforesaid error correction service by virtue of any of the exclusions referred to in sub-clause (e) above;

(ii) at the request of the Client but which the Systems House finds are not necessary.

For the avoidance of doubt nothing in this sub-clause shall impose any obligation on the Systems House to provide services in respect of any of the exclusions referred to in sub-clause (5) above.

(g) If the Client shall discover that the Operating Manuals do not provide adequate or correct instruction to enable the Client to make proper use of any facility or function set out in the Functional Specification then the Client shall notify the Systems House in writing of the fault in question within *14* days after such discovery. The Systems House shall thereupon promptly correct the fault and provide the Client with appropriate amendments to the Operating Manuals.

(2) *Changes in law* [9.1.2]

EITHER (VERSION A Client identifies change in law):

[(a) The Client shall notify the Systems House at the earliest opportunity of any change of legislation or new legal requirements which affect the application of any function or facility described in the Functional Specification ("Change in Law").

(b) Upon receipt of such notification by the Client of a Change in Law the Systems House shall forthwith [(at no further cost to the Client)] make such modifications to the Programs as shall ensure that the Programs conform to such Change in Law ("Change in Law Modifications").

(c) The Systems House shall also provide [at no further cost to the Client] such amendments to the Functional Specification or the Operating Manuals as may be necessary to describe or enable the Client to make proper use of the Change in Law Modifications.

(d) The Systems House shall use its best endeavours expeditiously to complete the implementation of any Change in Law Modification but nothing in this Agreement shall oblige the Systems House to complete the implementation of such Change in Law Modification in time for the coming into force of the change of legislation or new legal requirement which gave rise to such Change in Law.

[**Note:** This clause puts the onus of recognising an impending change in law on the client. This may be appropriate if the software deals with some specialised function. Omit the bracketed words in (b) or (c) if this is to be charged under clause 5(3).
Sub-Clause (d) may seem harsh but legislation rarely seems to take account of how long systems houses have to implement changes.]

OR (VERSION B Systems House identifies change in law):

(a) The Systems House shall from time to time make such modifications to the Programs as shall ensure that the Programs conform to any change of legislation or new legal requirements which affect the application of any function or facility described in the Functional Specification ("Change in Law").

(b) The Systems House shall promptly notify the Client in writing of all such Changes in Law and forthwith [(at no further cost to the Client)] make such modifications to the Programs as shall ensure that the Programs conform to such Change in Law ("Change in Law Modifications").

(c) The Systems House shall also provide [at no further cost to the Client] such amendments to the Functional Specification or the Operating Manuals as may be necessary to describe or enable the Client to make proper use of the Change in Law Modifications.

(d) The Systems House shall use its best endeavours expeditiously to complete the implementation of any Change in Law Modification but nothing in this Agreement shall obligate the Systems House to complete the implementation of such Change in Law Modification in time for the coming into force of the change of legislation or new legal requirement which gave rise to such Change in Law.]

[**Note:** This version will be more appropriate for less specialised software where the systems house can reasonably be expected to be aware of impending changes. Omit the bracketed words in (b) and (c) if this is to be charged under clause 5(3).

Sub-Clause (d) may seem harsh but legislation rarely seems to take account of how long systems houses have to implement changes.]

(3) *Advice and enhancements* [9.1.4, 9.1.5]

(a) The Systems House shall provide to the Client up to *10* man-days per annum of advice, consultancy, systems analysis and design about the work undertaken pursuant to the Programming Agreement at no further cost to the Client [save for all reasonable travelling and subsistence expenses incurred by the Systems House in so doing].

(b) The Systems House shall provide to the Client up to *20* man-days per annum of programming effort in connection with the work undertaken pursuant to the Programming Agreement at no further cost to the Client [save for all reasonable travelling and subsistence expenses incurred by the Systems House in so doing].

(c) The Client shall not be entitled to carry forward any time unused under sub-clauses (a) and (b) in any year to any succeeding year. For these purposes "year" shall mean any year commencing on the Commencement Date or on any subsequent anniversary of the Commencement Date.

(d) All other advice, consultancy, systems analysis, design or programming services shall be provided by the Systems House to the Client at the Systems House's standard scale of charges from time to time in force.

[(e) Apart from minor out-of-pocket expenses all claims by the Systems House for reimbursement of expenses shall be accompanied by the relevant receipts.]

[(4) *The Euro*

See clause 5(5) of Precedent L.]

6 Client's obligations

See clause 6 of Precedent L.

7 Proprietary rights [3.8.2]

EITHER (VERSION A Proprietary Rights vested in the Systems House):

[(1) The copyright and all other intellectual property rights of whatever nature in any corrected or modified versions of the Program Materials made pursuant to this Agreement shall be and shall remain vested in the Systems House.

(2) The provisions of Clauses 14(2) and 14(4) of the Programming Agreement shall apply to all corrected and modified versions of the Program Materials as such provisions are expressed to apply to the Program Materials mutatis mutandis and the parties hereby undertake to be bound by and to comply with the terms thereof accordingly.

(3) Any termination of this Agreement (howsoever occasioned) shall not of itself affect the Client's right to continue to use the then current versions of the Program Materials in accordance with the provisions of the licence granted by the Systems House pursuant to clause 14(2) of the Programming Agreement.]

OR (VERSION B Proprietary Rights vested in the Client):

[(1) The copyright and all other intellectual property rights of whatever nature in any corrected or modified versions of the Program Materials made pursuant to this Agreement shall belong to the Client and the Systems House with full title guarantee hereby assigns (by way of future assignment) all such rights to the Client.

(2) Notwithstanding sub-clause (1), the Systems House reserves the right to use in any way it thinks fit any programming tools, skills and techniques acquired or used by the Systems House in the performance of this Agreement.

(3) The provisions of clause 14(3) of the Programming Agreement shall apply to all corrected and modified versions of the Program Materials as those provisions are expressed to apply to the Program Materials mutatis mutandis and the Systems House hereby undertakes to be bound by and to comply with the terms thereof accordingly.

(4) The Systems House shall be entitled during the continuance of this Agreement to retain a copy of the Program Materials and of the source code of the Programs and all other materials necessary for the proper maintenance of the Programs. Such copies of the Program Materials and source code and other materials shall be held in confidence, shall only be used by the Systems House for the purposes of this Agreement and shall be delivered up (together with all copies thereof) to the Client forthwith upon the termination of this Agreement (howsoever occasioned).

(5) If any corrected or modified version of the Program Materials shall be made by the Systems House pursuant to this Agreement then the Systems House shall promptly deliver to the Client copies thereof together with:

(a) the source code of the corrected or modified version of the Programs in the form both of printed listings and magnetic disk; and

(b) all other materials necessary to enable a reasonably skilled programmer to correct, modify and enhance the corrected or modified version of the Programs without reference to any other person or document.]

8 Confidentiality

See clause 21 of Precedent A.

9 Data protection [3.7.2, 10.3.3]

See clause 9 of Precedent L.

[10 Poaching staff

See clause 25 of Precedent D.]

11 Termination [9.4]

(1) Notwithstanding anything else contained herein, this Agreement may be terminated:

(a) forthwith by the Systems House on giving notice in writing to the Client if the Client shall fail to pay any sum due under the terms of this Agreement (otherwise than as a consequence of any default on the part of the Systems House) and such sum remains unpaid for *14* days after written notice from the Systems House requiring such sum to be paid; or

(b) forthwith by either party on giving notice in writing to the other if the other party is in material breach of any term of this Agreement (other than any failure by the Client to make any payment hereunder in which event the provisions of paragraph (a) above shall apply) and (in the case of a breach capable of being remedied) shall have failed to have remedied such, within *30* days of receiving a written notice requiring it to do so; or

(c) forthwith by either party on giving notice in writing to the other if the other party shall have a receiver or administrative receiver appointed or shall pass a resolution for winding-up (otherwise than for the purpose of a bona fide scheme of solvent amalgamation or reconstruction) or a court of competent jurisdiction shall make an order to that effect or if the other party shall become subject to an administration order or shall enter into any voluntary arrangement with its creditors or shall cease or threaten to cease to carry on business.

(2) Any termination of this Agreement (howsoever occasioned) shall not affect any accrued rights or liabilities of either party nor shall it affect the coming into force or the continuance in force of any provision hereof which is expressly or by implication intended to come into or continue in force on or after such termination.

12 Assignment

See clause 30 of Precedent A.

13 *Force majeure*

See clause 36 of Precedent B.

14 Liability [9.3.3]

(1) The Systems House shall not be liable for any loss or damage sustained or incurred by the Client or any third party (including without limitation any loss of

use of the Programs or loss of or spoiling of the Client's data) as a result of any defect or error in the Programs or the Operating Manuals except to the extent that such loss or damage arises from any unreasonable delay by the Systems House in providing the Maintenance Services and then only to the extent not excluded by this Agreement.

(2) to (6) *See sub-clauses 18(2) to 18(6) of Precedent K.*

[15 Minor amendments

The Systems House may at its own discretion introduce into the Programs such minor amendments as it shall from time to time consider necessary provided that such amendments shall not result in a departure from the Functional Specification [or the Performance Criteria]. In such event the Systems House shall deliver to the Client the amended version of the object code of the Programs or any part thereof together with any consequential amendments to the Operating Manuals.]

16 Waiver of remedies

See clause 28 of Precedent A.

17 Entire agreement

This Agreement is made pursuant to the Programming Agreement and supersedes all prior agreements, arrangements and understandings between the parties other than the Programming Agreement and constitutes with the Programming Agreement the entire agreement between the parties relating to the subject matter of the Programming Agreement and this Agreement (save that neither party seeks to exclude liability for any fraudulent precontractual misrepresentation upon which the other party can be shown to have relied). No addition to or modification of this Agreement shall be binding upon the parties unless made by a written instrument signed by a duly authorised representative of each of the parties.

18 Client's warranty

See clause 20 of Precedent A.

19 Notices

See clause 32 of Precedent A.

20 Interpretation

See clause 33 of Precedent A.

21 Law

See clause 34 of Precedent A.

22 Disputes

See clause 35 of Precedent A.

23 Severability

See clause 36 of Precedent A.

24 Third parties [1.3]

See clause 37 of Precedent A.

[Note: if the software contains any embedded software from third parties this clause could be very relevant.]

EXECUTED under hand in two originals the day and year first before written

SIGNED for and on behalf of
SYSTEMS HOUSE [LIMITED] [PLC]

By

Signature

Title

Witness

SIGNED for and on behalf of
CLIENT [LIMITED] [PLC]

By

Signature

Title

Witness

THE SCHEDULE

A   THE MAINTENANCE CHARGE

£[   ] for each [month] [quarter] [year] payable in advance

First charge payable on: [the Commencement Date]

Subsequent charges payable on the first working day of each [month] [quarter] [year] thereafter.

B   METHOD OF PAYMENT

By standing order to [   ] Bank PLC

(Systems House's Account No. [   ])

C   THE COMMENCEMENT DATE

D   THE INITIAL PERIOD

E   TRAINING (Client's staff)

[F   THIRD-PARTY RIGHTS]

[**Note:** This agreement requires to be annexed to it:

    (a) the Programming Agreement [D] by Recital A;

    (b) the Functional specification [including the Performance Criteria] by clause 1.]

SOURCE CODE DEPOSIT AGREEMENT [9.0]

THIS AGREEMENT is made the   day of   20

PARTIES:

(1) OWNER [LIMITED] [PLC] whose registered office is at

("the Owner")

(2) CUSTODIAN [LIMITED] [PLC] whose registered office is at

("the Custodian")

RECITALS:

(A) The Owner [has granted and] is proposing to grant to its customers non-exclusive, non-transferable licences to use the object code version of the Owner's computer programs hereinafter described

(B) The Owner wishes to establish for the benefit of its customers a facility for the safe custody of the source codes of the said programs and for the release of the same to its customers upon the occurrence of certain pre-defined events

(C) The Owner and the Custodian have agreed to enter into this Agreement for the purpose of implementing such a facility

[Note: This agreement envisages that the software is a package to be licensed to a number of end-users. It can be easily adapted where the software is bespoke and there is only one user.]

NOW IT IS HEREBY AGREED as follows:

1 Definitions

In this Agreement, unless the context otherwise requires, the following expressions have the following meanings:

"Additional Deposit"	means a deposit of Source Materials pursuant to clause 4(2).
"Business Day"	means a day other than a Saturday, Sunday or a public holiday.
"the Facility"	means the source code deposit facility hereby established.
"Initial Deposit"	means a deposit of the Source Codes pursuant to clause 4(1).
"the Licensed Programs"	means the Owner's computer programs described in Schedule 1 in object code form and all modifications, enhancements and replacements thereof and additions thereto used by the relevant User from time to time.

"Licence Agreement" [C, D]	means any agreement between the Owner and the User whereby the Owner has granted to the User a licence to use some or all of the Licensed Programs.
"Maintenance Agreement"	means any agreement between the Owner and a User for the maintenance of the Licensed Programs.
"the Register"	means the register to be kept in compliance with clause 2.
"the Source Codes"	means the Source Materials relating to the Licensed Programs.
"Source Materials"	means all logic, logic diagrams, flowcharts, orthographic representations, algorithms, routines, sub-routines, utilities, modules, file structures, coding sheets, coding, source codes, listings, functional specifications and program specifications and all other materials and documents necessary to enable a reasonably skilled programmer to maintain, amend and enhance the software in question without reference to any other person or document and whether in eye-readable or machine-readable form.
"User"	means any person who is licensed by the Owner to use the Licensed Programs and who is a party to this Agreement from time to time.

2 The register

(1) The Custodian shall forthwith establish and thereafter maintain a full and accurate register of Users.

(2) A person shall be entitled to have his name entered in the Register (and the Custodian shall enter it therein promptly) if he has been licensed to use the Licensed Programs by the Owner, has signed an undertaking in the form set out in Schedule 2 which has been countersigned by the Owner and has paid the Owner and the Custodian the currently applicable fees for the use of the Facility.

(3) Each User shall become a party to this Agreement on being entered in the Register and shall remain a party until he ceases to be such in accordance with the terms of this Agreement or this Agreement is terminated.

(4) The Register shall contain the name and address of each User together with his telephone and facsimile numbers and the name(s) of his representative(s) authorised to act on his behalf for the purposes of this Agreement. The Register shall also contain details of the current version of the Licensed Programs being used by each User.

(5) The Owner shall promptly notify the Custodian of all new Users and their particulars.

(6) Each User undertakes promptly to notify the Custodian of any change in his registered particulars. The Custodian shall record the same in the Register accordingly.

(7) Each User shall be entitled to a copy of the Register free of charge on request to the Custodian at any time.

(8) If a User shall cease to be a party to this Agreement the Custodian shall delete his name and other details from the Register forthwith.

3 The custodian's obligations

The Custodian shall:

(1) accept as a new party to this Agreement each new User notified to it by the Owner;

(2) provide for the safe custody of the copies of the Source Codes deposited with it;

(3) release the Source Codes in the circumstances hereinafter described;

(4) not itself inspect in detail or use any part of the Source Codes or allow any of its employees to do so;

(5) notify the Owner and User if it becomes aware at any time during the term of this Agreement that the copy of the Source Materials held by it has been lost, damaged or destroyed other than when withdrawn or renewed under clause 4(2) and (3) of this Agreement;

(6) not subject the Source Codes or allow them to be subjected to any charge, lien or encumbrance or deal in the Source Codes in any way (whether as a means of satisfying any unpaid charges under this Agreement or otherwise) unless as directed by [the Owner or] any court of competent jurisdiction, save that the Custodian may take copies of the Source Codes for distribution to the User(s) in the event of the occurrence of any of the events contained in clause 9 below provided that the Custodian does not keep a copy for his own purposes; and

(7) upon the Owner replacing the Source Code or Source Materials pursuant to clauses 4(1) and 4(2) below, return to the Owner or destroy as the Owner shall direct any previous editions of the Source Code except that edition being immediately replaced.

4 Deposit of source codes

(1) The Owner undertakes with each User that within *10* business days after the User has been entered in the Register the Owner will deposit with the Custodian, in a container marked with the User's name, one copy of all the Source Codes relevant to the Licence Agreement entered into between the Owner and that User.

(2) The Owner shall deposit with the Custodian in the manner provided in sub-clause (1) the Source Materials relating to any modification, enhancement or replacement of or addition to the Licensed Programs made available to each User by the Owner from time to time (whether pursuant to a Maintenance Agreement or

otherwise) within *10* business days after the same has been made so available and shall at the same time withdraw any Source Materials previously deposited which have been superseded by the new deposit, save that the immediately superseded Source Materials shall remain deposited.

(3) The Owner shall renew the copy of the Source Codes deposited with the Custodian in respect of each User not less frequently than *one year* after the immediately preceding delivery thereof. The Custodian shall not be responsible for ensuring that the Owner complies with this Clause 4(3).

[**Note**: This is to protect against natural degeneration of the source codes on magnetic media. See also Clause 6(4).]

(4) Contemporaneously with the delivery to the Custodian of the Initial Deposit and any Additional Deposit and any deposit pursuant to sub-clause (3), the Owner shall deliver to the User concerned and the Custodian a certificate in the form set out in Schedule 3 signed by *a director* of the Owner.

(5) All items deposited under this Agreement by the Owner shall be packaged in a manner suitable for archive storage of [magnetic] [electronic] media.

(6) The Custodian will place the items deposited hereunder in a secure place [in a climate-controlled environment] and will be responsible for their safekeeping.

(7) The Custodian shall notify the Owner and the relevant User promptly in writing of the receipt of any deposit of Source Materials pursuant to this Agreement.

(8) (a) Each User shall be entitled at any time and from time to time while it is a party to this Agreement to require an independent expert ("the Expert") to verify whether the items deposited hereunder in the name of that User are the relevant Source Codes, deposited in conformity with this Agreement.

(b) The Expert shall be appointed by agreement between the Owner and such User or, failing such agreement within *14* days after the request of such User therefor, nominated at the request of such User by the President from time to time of the *British Computer Society*. The Expert shall act as an expert and not an arbitrator and his decision shall (in the absence of clerical or manifest error) be final and binding on the Owner and such User.

(c) For the purpose of his determination the Expert shall be given full access to the items deposited in the User's name hereunder and to all other information and facilities which he may reasonably require (which the parties hereby undertake promptly to make available).

(d) The Expert shall keep all information disclosed to him for the purpose of his determination strictly confidential and will not divulge the same to the User or any third party. It shall be a condition of any disclosure to the Expert that he enters into a binding undertaking with the Owner to observe such confidentiality and non-disclosure obligations, such undertaking to be on terms reasonably acceptable to the Owner.

(e) If the Expert decides that a default has occurred then the Owner shall cure the default to the Expert's reasonable satisfaction within *30* days after receiving the Expert's determination.

(f) The fees and expenses of the Expert in making his determination and of his appointment shall be borne by the User unless the Expert determines that the Owner has defaulted to a material extent in its obligations in respect of the Source Codes in which event such fees and expenses shall be paid by the Owner.

(g) In the case of default by the Owner in paying any fees or expenses it is liable to pay hereunder, the User may pay such sums in its stead and any payment made in so doing shall be recoverable from the Owner as a debt payable on demand.

(h) Any reasonable expenses of the Custodian incurred in complying with this Clause 4(8) shall be borne in the same manner as the fees of the Expert.

[Note: A source code deposit arrangement relies heavily on the integrity of the owner in depositing complete and accurate copies of the source codes. To encourage compliance Clause 4(4) requires a director of the owner to give a personal certificate each time a deposit occurs (which usually concentrates the mind wonderfully) and clause 4(8) gives each user a right to have an independent expert verify compliance. It is worth verifying the initial deposit as a matter of course as this will give clause 9(1)(e) teeth in respect of a default in relation to an additional deposit.]

[(9) Each time the Owner deposits a copy of the Source Codes ("the Original") hereunder it will at the same time deposit a duplicate copy thereof ("the Duplicate") with the Custodian. The Duplicate shall be stored by the Custodian in a separate building from the Original [located not less than *1 mile* from the place where the Original is stored] but subject thereto all the provisions of this Agreement shall apply, mutatis mutandis, to the Duplicate as they apply to the Original].

[Note: This considerably reduces the risk of total loss of the source codes through fire or other disasters but depends on the custodian being able to offer the facility of separate storage.]

5 Owner's undertakings

The Owner hereby undertakes with and warrants to each User that:

(1) each copy of the Source Codes deposited by the Owner in respect of such User with the Custodian from time to time will contain everything reasonably necessary (including but not limited to the provision of information in human-readable form and on suitable media) to enable a reasonably skilled programmer to maintain, amend and enhance the Licensed Programs without the necessity for reference to any other person or document;

(2) it will promptly cure any default under sub-clause (1);

(3) the Owner is the owner of the intellectual property rights in the Source Codes and is legally entitled to enter into this Agreement and to perform its obligations hereunder and that by virtue of entering into this Agreement it is not and will not be in breach of any express or implied obligation to any third party binding upon it; and

(4) it will not assign or otherwise transfer the intellectual property rights in the Source Codes without first procuring a novation of this Agreement with the substitution of the assignee or transferee for the Owner hereunder.

6 The custodian's liability

(1) If any copy of the Source Codes or any part thereof deposited in respect of any User shall be lost, destroyed or damaged then the Owner shall replace promptly the

copy or part so lost, destroyed or damaged provided however that if such loss, destruction or damage is caused by the negligence, wilful misconduct or recklessness of the Custodian or any of its employees then the cost of such replacement shall be paid by the Custodian. The foregoing states the entire liability of the Custodian for any loss, destruction or damage of or to any of the Source Codes. The Custodian shall promptly notify the Owner and each relevant User of any such loss, destruction or damage. The Custodian's liability under this Agreement shall not in any event exceed £[   ].

(2) Notwithstanding anything else contained in this Agreement, the Custodian shall not be liable to any of the other parties hereto for loss (whether direct or indirect) of profits, business or anticipated savings or for any indirect or consequential loss or damage whatsoever (except in respect of personal injury or death caused by the Custodian's negligence) even if the Custodian shall have been advised of the possibility thereof and whether arising from negligence, breach of contract or howsoever.

(3) The Custodian shall have in place for the duration of this Agreement an adequate insurance policy to cover any liabilities that might arise under this Agreement.

(4) The Custodian shall have no liability to the Owner or any User for any natural degeneration or loss of quality of any of the Source Codes deposited with it which arises as a result of the passage of time alone.

(5) The Custodian shall not be responsible for determining whether any items deposited with it pursuant to this Agreement are in conformity with this Agreement or for ensuring the Owner's compliance with any other of its obligations hereunder.

(6) If any dispute shall arise between any of the parties to this Agreement relating to the release or non-release of the Source Codes and the Custodian shall be uncertain of its obligations or rights hereunder then the Custodian shall be entitled, without liability to any other party hereto, to refrain from taking any action to release the Source Codes until the Custodian shall be directed otherwise by a court of competent jurisdiction, or by agreement with both the Owner and the relevant User.

(7) The Custodian shall bear no obligation or responsibility to any person, firm, company or entity whatsoever to determine the existence, relevance, completeness, accuracy, effectiveness or any other aspect of the Source Codes.

7 Charges

(1) In consideration of the use of the Facility, each User shall pay to the Owner and the Custodian the annual charges in force from time to time hereunder. The annual charges in force at the date hereof are those specified in Schedule 4. Such charges shall be paid in advance on the date on which such User shall be entered in the Register and on each subsequent anniversary of such date.

(2) The Owner and the Custodian shall each be entitled to increase the annual charge payable to it by giving written notice to the Users affected by such increase not less than *30* days' prior to the anniversary of the User having been entered into

the Register provided that any such increase shall not exceed a percentage equal to the percentage increase in the *Retail Prices Index published by the Central Statistical Office* during the previous 12 months, plus *2* per cent.

[**Note**: if there are large numbers of users, it may be preferable for the owner to have a mechanism whereby the annual charge increases automatically for all users as from a certain date, but with the increase only coming in to effect for each user as at the anniversary of the date it was entered on to the register.]

(3) The charges payable under this Agreement are exclusive of Value Added Tax which shall be paid by the User at the rate and in the manner for the time being prescribed by law.

(4) If any sum payable under this Agreement is not paid within 7 days after the due date then (without prejudice to the other rights and remedies of the person entitled to payment) the person entitled to payment reserves the right to charge interest on such sum on a day to day basis (as well after as before any judgment) from the date or last date for payment thereof to the date of actual payment (both dates inclusive) at the rate of *2* per cent above the base rate of *ABC* Bank plc (or such other London Clearing Bank as the person entitled to payment may nominate) from time to time in force compounded quarterly. Such interest shall be paid on demand by the person entitled to payment.

(5) No refund of any part of the annual charges shall be made upon a User ceasing to be a party to this Agreement or this Agreement being terminated.

8 Cessation of a user's participation

A User shall cease to be a party to this Agreement forthwith in the event that:

(1) the Licence Agreement under which such User is from time to time entitled to use the Licensed Programs is properly terminated in accordance with its terms and is not replaced by a new or novated licence;

(2) such User shall fail to pay any sum due to the Owner or the Custodian under the terms of this Agreement (otherwise than as a consequence of any default on the part of the person entitled to payment) and such sum remains unpaid for *30* days after written notice from the person entitled to payment that such sum has not been paid (such notice to contain a warning of that party's intention to terminate) and while such default continues thereafter the person entitled to payment serves written notice of termination on the User;

(3) such User at any time gives 60 days' notice in writing to that effect to the Owner and the Custodian; or

(4) such User receives the Source Codes deposited in his name pursuant to one of the events described in clauses 9(1)(e), 9(1)(f) or 9(1)(i).

The accrued rights and liabilities of a User shall not be affected by his ceasing to be a party to this Agreement.

9 Release of the source codes

(1) If the Owner shall:

(a) pass a resolution for winding-up (otherwise than for the purpose of a bona fide scheme of solvent amalgamation or reconstruction) or a court of competent jurisdiction shall make an order to that effect; or

(b) have a receiver or administrative receiver appointed of it or over the whole or any part of its undertaking or assets; or

(c) cease to carry on business; or

(d) enter into any voluntary arrangement with its creditors or become subject to an administration order; or

(e) fail to remedy a material default in any obligation imposed upon it from time to time to provide corrections to or maintenance or enhancements of the Licensed Programs under any Maintenance Agreement or any other agreement between the Owner and a User from time to time after having been given not less than *30* days' notice in writing from the User concerned requiring such remedy (such notice to contain a warning of the User's intention to invoke this Clause); or

[**Note**: The owner may be required to provide error correction under a licence agreement as well as a maintenance agreement.]

(f) voluntarily terminate a Maintenance Agreement without cause by giving notice in writing to the relevant User; or

[**Note**: This would cover the situation where the owner simply ceases to support the software and terminates the maintenance agreement by notice.]

(g) fail to comply with any of its obligations under clauses 4(2), 4(3), 5(2) or 5(4) after having been given not less than *30* days' notice in writing from the User concerned requiring such failure to be remedied (such notice to contain a warning of the User's intention to invoke this Clause); or

(h) fail to cure a default to an expert's reasonable satisfaction within *30* days as required by clause 4(8); or

(i) be ordered by a court of competent jurisdiction to release the Source Codes to a User or be requested by a direction in writing signed by or on behalf of the Owner and a User to release the Source Codes to that User,

then, and in any such event (but not otherwise) each User (or in the case of paragraphs (e) to (i), the User or each User affected) shall be entitled (subject to the terms of sub-clause (2) below) to have delivered to him the copy of the Source Codes deposited in his name with the Custodian free of charge and from any encumbrance (subject to the provisions of clause 10 below).

[**Note**: Another option would be to provide for a release fee to be paid to the owner. If this is significant it will discourage spurious demands for a release of the source codes.]

(2) The Custodian shall upon receipt from a User of:

(i) a statutory declaration confirming that one or more of the events set out in sub-clause (1) has or have occurred or, if such be the case, to the best of the User's knowledge, information and belief the same has or have occurred; and

(ii) evidence that the License Agreement was still valid and effective up to the occurrence of such event:

EITHER (VERSION A Statutory declaration sent to owner):

[(a) forthwith deliver a copy of the statutory declaration to the Owner; and

(b) on the *20th* business day after the Custodian's receipt of the statutory declaration (unless directed otherwise by a court of competent jurisdiction) deliver to that User the copy of the Source Codes deposited in his name.

Subject as provided in sub-clause (5), the Custodian shall not deliver to any User (and such User shall not be entitled to delivery of) a copy of the Source Codes unless the Custodian has first received a statutory declaration as aforesaid. The receipt by the Custodian of a statutory declaration shall be conclusive evidence to the Custodian of the facts stated therein and the Custodian shall not be required or entitled to make any enquiry regarding their accuracy. The Custodian shall be under no liability to the Owner for any loss or damage suffered by the Owner as a result of any copy of the Source Codes being released by the Custodian in accordance with the foregoing provisions of this clause.]

[**Note**: The custodian will not wish to become embroiled in arguments over whether users are entitled to the source codes; hence the reason for this procedure. The delay of 20 business days should give the owner sufficient time to seek an injunction if it considers that a user's demand is unjustified.]

OR (VERSION B Intervention of Qualified Person):

[(a) release to the User a copy of the Source Code provided that the User has undertaken to pay to the Owner compensation in the sum of £[   ] if the event, in the view of an independent qualified person ("Qualified Person"), has not in fact taken place.

(b) it shall be the Owner's obligation to instruct the Qualified Person to determine whether the event has in fact taken place.

(c) if the Qualified Person determines the event has taken place, the User shall be entitled to keep the Source Code and this Agreement will terminate forthwith. The Owner shall pay the costs of the Qualified Person.

(d) if the Qualified Person determines the event has not in fact taken place the User shall return the Source Code to the Custodian and pay the compensation to the Owner as set out in Sub-clause 9(2)(a) above. The User shall pay the costs of the Qualified Person.

(e) the Custodian shall be entitled to payment of its reasonable costs incurred in complying with this sub-clause 9(2).]

(3) Any dispute arising out of the operation of this clause 9 shall be referred to the procedure contained in clause 21 below.

(4) Upon the termination of this Agreement pursuant to clause 13(1), (2) or (3) the Custodian shall deliver to the Owner forthwith all copies of the Source Codes then in its possession.

(5) Upon a User ceasing to be party to this Agreement pursuant to clause 8(1), (2) or (3) the Custodian shall deliver to the Owner forthwith the copy of the Source Codes deposited with the Custodian in that User's name.

(6) If the Source Codes deposited in a User's name shall be released to him by reason of any event mentioned in paragraphs (a) to (d) of sub-clause (1) then the

Custodian shall forthwith release to all the other Users the copies of the Source Codes deposited in their names.

10 User's undertakings

Each User undertakes with the Owner that if a copy of the Source Codes is delivered to him pursuant to this Agreement he will:

(1) use the Source Codes only for the purpose of correcting, modifying and/or enhancing the Licensed Programs and the Source Codes and for no other purpose whatsoever (and the licence governing the use of the Licensed Programs by the User shall be extended automatically to permit the User to use the object code form of any such corrections, modifications and enhancements in accordance with that licence);

(2) treat the Source Codes as confidential and will not divulge the whole or any part thereof to any third party except any person whom the User has appointed from time to time to maintain the Licensed Programs on the User's behalf but the User shall ensure that such person is aware of and shall comply with these obligations as to confidentiality and non-disclosure;

(3) keep the Source Codes in a secure place and safeguard them from access by any unauthorised person;

(4) not deface or remove any proprietary notices affixed to or contained in the Source Codes;

(5) forthwith upon the proper termination (in accordance with its terms) of the licence under which the User is entitled to use the Licensed Programs deliver to the Owner all copies of the Source Codes under the User's control or, if required by the Owner, destroy the same and certify to the Owner that they have been destroyed.

11 Property rights

(1) The copyright and all other intellectual property rights of whatever nature in the Source Codes shall remain the property of the Owner.

(2) If, after the release of a copy of the Source Codes to a User, such User shall correct, modify or enhance the Licensed Programs or the Source Codes the copyright and other intellectual property rights in such corrections, modifications and enhancements shall vest in the Owner and the User hereby assigns (by way of future assignment) with full title guarantee all such copyright and other intellectual property rights to the Owner.

(3) The Owner shall not after the release of the Source Codes to a User under clause 9 be able to charge such User for the use of the Source Codes so released.

[Note: Without this clause an unscrupulous owner might wilfully refuse to maintain the licensed programs, trigger a release under clause 9(1)(f), and still charge the user.]

12 Assignment

Save as expressly provided in this Agreement, none of the parties shall assign or otherwise transfer this Agreement or any of its rights and obligations hereunder whether in whole or in part without the prior written consent of the other parties.

13 Termination of agreement

(1) The Owner or the Custodian shall be entitled to terminate this Agreement forthwith by notice in writing to the other party or parties hereto in the event that:

    (a) no Users are from time to time party to this Agreement; or

    (b) all the Users from time to time shall have given their prior written consent to such termination.

(2) (a) The Custodian may at any time during the continuance of this Agreement serve on the other parties hereto a written request for a new custodian to be appointed. The Owner and the Users shall thereupon use their respective reasonable endeavours to appoint a mutually acceptable new custodian on terms similar to this Agreement (subject to such modifications as the proposed parties may reasonably require) within *90* days of such written request.

    (b) If a new agreement is not entered into within the said period of *90* days then the matter shall be referred to an independent expert to appoint an appropriate new custodian on such terms as he shall think fit. Such expert shall be appointed by agreement between the parties hereto or, failing such agreement within *14* days after the request of any of the parties hereto to the others therefor, nominated at the request of any of the parties hereto by the President from time to time of the *British Computer Society*. Such expert shall act as an expert and not an arbitrator and his decision shall be final and binding on the parties hereto.

    (c) The fees and expenses of the expert in making his determination and of his appointment shall be borne as to *one-third* by the Users (pro-rata according to the number of them), *one-third* by the Owner and *one-third* by the Custodian. In the case of default by any party in paying his due proportion of such fees and expenses any of the other parties hereto may pay such sum in his stead and any payment made in so doing shall be recoverable from the defaulter as a debt payable on demand. If any User shall fail to pay his due proportion within *30* days after being requested so to do in writing by any of the other parties hereto then that User shall not be entitled to benefit under the arrangement with the new custodian and shall be excluded from the facility thereby established.

    (d) The parties hereto shall do everything within their power which the expert shall consider necessary or desirable in order to give effect to his decision (including, in the case of the Owner, depositing fresh copies of the Source Codes with the new custodian).

    (e) This Agreement shall automatically terminate on the appointment of a new custodian pursuant to this sub-clause (2).

(3) (a) If any of the events referred to below occurs the Owner or any of the Users may serve on the other parties hereto a written request for a new custodian to be appointed and the provisions of sub-clause (2) shall apply mutatis mutandis save that the costs of any expert shall be borne as to *one half* by the Users (pro-rata according to the number of them) and the *other half* by the Owner.

(b) The events referred to above are the Custodian passing a resolution for winding-up (otherwise than for the purpose of a bona fide scheme of solvent amalgamation or reconstruction) or a court of competent jurisdiction making an order to that effect or having a receiver or administrative receiver appointed of it or over the whole or any part of its undertaking or assets or ceasing to carry on business or entering into a voluntary arrangement with its creditors or becoming subject to an administration order or failing to cure any breach by it of this Agreement within *30* days of being requested so to do by notice in writing from the Owner or any of the Users (such notice to contain a warning of that party's intention to invoke this sub-clause).

(4) This Agreement shall automatically terminate upon the release to all Users of the copies of the Source Codes deposited in their names pursuant to clause 9.

(5) This Agreement shall not terminate except in accordance with the express terms of this Agreement.

(6) Any termination of this Agreement (howsoever occasioned) shall not affect any accrued rights or liabilities of any of the parties hereto nor shall it affect the coming into force or the continuance in force of any provision hereof which is expressly or by implication intended to come into or continue in force on or after such termination.

14 Confidentiality

(1) The Custodian shall:

(a) keep the Source Codes and the other information, documentation and materials coming into its possession or to its knowledge under this Agreement strictly confidential and shall not divulge the whole or any part thereof to any third party except in accordance with the terms of this Agreement or except to the Custodian's employees who are directly involved with the Facility and have a specific need to know the information concerned;

(b) not release the Source Codes to any person except in accordance with the terms of this Agreement;

(c) ensure that its employees observe the confidentiality, non-disclosure and non-release obligations contained in sub-clauses (a) and (b); and

(d) keep the items deposited with it in its exclusive possession and control and safeguard them from access by any unauthorised person.

(2) The provisions of this clause shall survive the termination of this Agreement.

15 Relationship of the parties

The Custodian is an independent contractor and nothing contained in this Agreement shall constitute the Custodian an agent or partner of the Owner or any User.

16 Waiver of remedies

See clause 28 of Precedent A.

17 Entire agreement

See clause 29 of Precedent A.

18 Notices

See clause 32 of Precedent A.

19 Interpretation

See clause 33 of Precedent A.

20 Law

See clause 34 of Precedent A.

21 Disputes

See clause 35 of Precedent A.

22 Severability

See clause 36 of Precedent A.

23 Third parties

See clause 37 of Precedent A.

EXECUTED under hand in two originals the day and year first before written

SIGNED for and on behalf of
OWNER [LIMITED] [PLC]

By

Signature

Title

Witness

SIGNED for and on behalf of
CUSTODIAN [LIMITED] [PLC]

By

Signature

Title

Witness

Schedule 1

LICENSED PROGRAMS

Schedule 2

USER'S UNDERTAKING

TO: OWNER [LIMITED] [PLC]

FROM: USER [LIMITED] [PLC]

Date: 20

1. We refer to the Agreement ("the Agreement") dated [   ] made between yourselves and Custodian [Limited] [PLC] ("the Custodian") relating to the establishment of a facility for the safe custody of the source codes of your computer programs which we have been licensed to use by virtue of a Licence Agreement dated [   ].

2. We wish to take advantage of the said facility and to become a party to the Agreement and we set out below the details required by clause 2(4) thereof:

(a) Name:

(b) Address:

(c) Telephone and fax numbers:

(d) Authorised representative(s):

(e) Identity of the Licensed Programs:

(f) Version of the Licensed Programs used:

3. We enclose our cheques for £[   ] (in your favour) and £[   ] (in favour of the Custodian) being the currently applicable fees for the use of such facility for the first year.

4. We confirm that we have been supplied with a copy of the Agreement, have full knowledge of its terms and conditions and undertake to you and the Custodian to comply with and be bound thereby as a User.

SIGNED for and on behalf of
USER [LIMITED] [PLC]

Signature

Name

Title

COUNTERSIGNED for and on
behalf of OWNER [LIMITED]

[PLC]

Signature

Name

Title

SCHEDULE 3

DEPOSIT CERTIFICATE

TO   :   USER [LIMITED] [PLC]

       — and —

       CUSTODIAN [LIMITED] [PLC]

Date: 20

Items deposited:

[Items withdrawn:]

I certify that on [   ] Owner [Limited] [plc] deposited with [and withdrew from] Custodian [Limited] [plc] for the benefit of User [Limited] [plc] the source code items specified above. Those items have been inspected by me and I certify that they are the items they purport to be and are complete and that Owner [Limited] [plc] has complied in all respects with its obligations in respect thereof under the Source Code Deposit Agreement dated [   ] made initially between Owner [Limited] [plc] and Custodian [Limited] [plc].

Director of
Owner [Limited] [plc]

Schedule 4

ANNUAL CHARGES

Payable by each User to the Owner:

£[   ] plus VAT

Payable by each User to the Custodian:

£[   ] plus VAT

[Schedule 5

THIRD-PARTY RIGHTS]

TURNKEY AGREEMENT

THIS AGREEMENT is made the   day of   20

PARTIES:

(1) COMPUTER COMPANY [LIMITED] [PLC] whose registered office is at

("the Supplier")

(2) CUSTOMER [LIMITED] [PLC] whose registered office is at

("the Customer")

RECITAL:

The Supplier has agreed to supply and install a fully operational computer system for the Customer and thereafter to maintain the same upon the terms and conditions hereinafter contained

NOW IT IS HEREBY AGREED as follows:

1 Definitions

In this Agreement, unless the context otherwise requires, the following expressions have the following meanings:

"the Acceptance Date" [2.3.4]	means the date on which the System is accepted (or deemed to be accepted) by the Customer pursuant to clause 15.
"the Completion Date"	means the date specified in the Implementation Plan by which the Supplier is to provide the System Ready for Use or such extended date as may be granted pursuant to clause 15.

[Note: When fixing the Completion Date the parties should allow sufficient time for acceptance testing. The definition of a specific completion date may also be linked to penalties for late completion if the project is time-critical.]

"Confidential Information"	means all information obtained by one party from the other pursuant to this Agreement which is expressly marked as confidential or which is manifestly of a confidential nature or which is confirmed in writing to be confidential within 7 days of its disclosure.
"the Equipment" [2.1]	means the computer equipment specified in Schedule 1 and any replacement equipment and/or parts provided pursuant to the maintenance agreements referred to in clauses 21 and 22 [and the Integral Software] as the context admits or the case may require.

466

["the Equipment Price"	means that part of the Price payable in respect of the Equipment as specified in Schedule 1.]
"the Implementation Plan"	means the estimated time schedule and sequence of events for the performance of this Agreement (the details of which are set out in Schedule 2) as the same may be amended from time to time pursuant to clause 15.
["the Integral Software" [2.8.3]	means the computer software embedded in or forming an integral part of the Equipment as specified in Schedule 1.]
"the Licensed Programs"	means the computer programs of the Supplier specified in Schedule 1.
"the Premises" [2.1.2]	means the Customer's premises in which the System is to be installed as specified in Schedule 1.
"the Off-Loading Point"	means the Customer's off-loading point specified in Schedule 1.
"the Operating Manuals"	means the operating manuals to be provided by the Supplier pursuant to clause 23.
["the Performance Criteria"	means the performance criteria which it is intended the System shall fulfil as specified in the Specification subject to the tolerances, limitations and exceptions stated therein.]
"the Price"	means the price for the System and the services to be provided hereunder as specified in Schedule 1.
"the Project"	means the implementation of a fully operational and integrated System in compliance with the requirements of the Specification.
"Ready for Use"	means fully installed, tested and accepted in accordance with clause 15.
"the Specification"	means the specification of the System [dated *July 31, 2000*] describing the intended facilities and functions thereof, [a copy of which is annexed hereto].
"the System"	means the Equipment and the Licensed Programs in combination with each other.
"the Training Plan"	means the training in the use of the System to be provided by the Supplier for the Customer's staff, the details of which are set out in Schedule 3.

2 Products and services to be provided [2.1.1, 3.0.2]

(1) The Supplier hereby agrees to:

(a) sell the Equipment to the Customer free from any encumbrance;

(b) grant to the Customer a non-exclusive licence to use the Licensed Programs and the Operating Manuals on the terms of the agreement referred to in clause 20;

(c) deliver the System to and install it at the Premises;

[(d) provide the System Ready for Use by the Completion Date;]

(e) provide the Operating Manuals;

(f) provide training in accordance with the Training Plan;

(g) provide maintenance for the System after the Acceptance Date,

upon the terms and conditions hereinafter contained.

(2) Operating supplies such as disk packs, stationery, printing cartridges and similar accessories are not supplied as part of the Equipment.

[Note: (d) above suggests a binding time-related obligation; the parties should consider whether this is appropriate in the knowledge that the supplier will charge a premium to reflect the risk of being seen to be in breach of contract for a "late" delivery. It may be preferable to rely primarily on the liquidated damages provision—see clause 16(1).]

3 Implementation plan

The Supplier undertakes to perform its obligations under this Agreement in accordance with the Implementation Plan but time shall not be of the essence in relation to the performance of such obligations.

[Note: This agreement provides for liquidated damages to be paid in the event of a delay by the supplier—see clause 16(1).]

4 Price and payment [2.2.1]

(1) The Price shall be paid by the Customer as to *15* per cent upon the signing of this Agreement [(by way of a deposit)] [(by way of a part payment)] and as to the balance upon the Acceptance Date.

[Note: more detailed payment plans may be appropriate for larger projects, involving the splitting of payments across a greater number of milestones [1.12.]

[*Currency rate*

(2) (a) The Equipment Price is based on an exchange rate between the United States dollar and the United Kingdom pound sterling of *$1.61* to *£1* ("the Contract Rate"). If on the date on which the Supplier pays its supplier for the Equipment ("the Payment Date") the dollar value of the pound shall have fallen by *2* cents or more below the Contract Rate then the Supplier shall be entitled to increase proportionately the Equipment Price to compensate the Supplier for such fall in the dollar value of the pound but not further or otherwise. The amount of such increase shall be paid by the Customer on the Acceptance Date.

(b) For the purposes of paragraph (a) above the value of the pound on the Payment Date shall be taken as [the arithmetic average of the buying and selling dollar prices of the pound quoted by *ABC* Bank plc as their closing prices on the business day immediately preceding the Payment Date.]

[**Notes**: The use of sub-clause (2) should be examined critically by the customer who should consider the following:

(1) The clause assumes that the supplier will be purchasing with dollars and selling in pounds. If the supplier is purchasing in pounds then the clause is unnecessary.

(2) Strictly speaking, any adjustment to the price should be crystallised on the date on which the supplier buys his dollars not when he pays for the equipment. However, if a supplier is constantly purchasing dollars this date might be difficult to establish. It is therefore suggested that the date of payment be used; although this does to some extent leave the situation open to manipulation by the supplier who could choose a payment date (within the constraints of its contractual arrangements with its own supplier) when the dollar value of the pound is low and then pay with dollars already purchased at a more favourable rate.

(3) It should be noted that the clause does not provide for the price to be reduced in the event of a rise in the value of the pound. Also, some of the equipment may not be purchased in the U.S. (or not in dollars) in which case any increase should only apply to the equipment which is.

(4) There may be more than one U.S. manufacturer delivering to the supplier on different dates.]

(3) The Price and any additional charges payable under this Agreement are exclusive of Value Added Tax which shall be paid by the Customer at the rate and in the manner for the time being prescribed by law.

(4) Any charges payable by the Customer under this Agreement in addition to the Price shall be paid on the Acceptance Date.

(5) If any sum payable under this Agreement is not paid within 7 days after the due date then (without prejudice to the Supplier's other rights and remedies) the Supplier reserves the right to charge interest on such sum on a day to day basis (as well after as before any judgment) from the date or last date for payment thereof to the date of actual payment (both dates inclusive) at the rate of 2 per cent above the base rate of *ABC* Bank plc (or such other London Clearing Bank as the Supplier may nominate) from time to time in force compounded quarterly. Such interest shall be paid by the Customer on demand by the Supplier.

[**Note**: this clause presupposes that the parties have agreed a fixed price in relation to the delivery of the System; if the parties have instead agreed upon a time and materials payment scheme, the customer should obtain a commitment from the supplier to provide regular updates of progress, to include any variations to the original budget as soon as they become apparent.]

5 Title to and risk in the equipment [2.8.1]

(1) The legal and beneficial ownership of the Equipment shall pass to the Customer on payment in full and in cleared funds of the Price and any other sums which may then be due under this Agreement.

[**Note**: the customer may object to this clause as it prevents it from obtaining title to any of the equipment until the very last payment has been made.]

(2) Risk in the Equipment shall pass to the Customer on delivery of the Equipment to [the Off-Loading Point] [the Premises] and accordingly the Customer shall be responsible for insuring the Equipment against all normal risks with effect from the time risk passes.

(3) In relation to each item of Integral Software the copyright, design right or other intellectual property rights in which are owned by a third party ("the software owner") as identified in the Schedule:

(a) the performance by the Supplier of its obligations under this Agreement is in all respects conditional upon the Customer entering into on the date of this Agreement an end-user licence agreement with the software owner or (as the case may be) a sub-licence agreement with the Supplier (in either case a "Licence Agreement") governing the use by the Customer of that item of Integral Software as may be required by the software owner in the form annexed to this Agreement; and

(b) the Customer agrees with the Supplier as a term of this Agreement to be bound and abide by the terms and conditions of each such Licence Agreement.

[(4) In relation to each item of Integral Software the copyright, design right or other intellectual property rights in which are owned by the Supplier as identified in the Schedule:

(a) the Customer is purchasing the media and/or the Equipment on which such Integral Software is recorded or embedded only;

(b) nothing contained in this Agreement shall be construed as an assignment or transfer of any copyright, design right or other intellectual property rights in such Integral Software, all of which rights are reserved by the Supplier;

(c) the Supplier hereby grants to the Customer a non-exclusive and (except as provided in paragraph (e) below) non-transferable licence to use such Integral Software in the form in which it is embedded in or integrated into the Equipment at the time of delivery to the Customer as an integral part of the Equipment for use in conjunction with the remainder of the Equipment but subject to the condition that the Equipment is used only for its intended purpose and for the Customer's internal business purposes only;

(d) except as expressly permitted by this sub-clause (4) and save to the extent and in the circumstances expressly required to be permitted by law, the Customer shall not rent, lease, sub-license, loan, copy, modify, adapt, merge, translate, reverse engineer, decompile, disassemble or create derivative works based on the whole or any part of such Integral Software or use, reproduce or deal in such Integral Software or any part thereof in any way, or interface the Integral Software with any other Software. In respect of any such activities claimed to be made permissible by law, the Customer undertakes first to make a prior written statement to the Supplier identifying the activity and stating why the Customer believes it to be permissible, and to refrain from commencing any such activity until the Supplier shall have had a reasonable opportunity to consider and thereafter give a response to the Customer in respect of each such statement;

(e) the Customer shall be entitled to transfer the benefit of the licence granted pursuant to paragraph (c) ("the Licence") and the right to transfer the Licence in terms of this paragraph (e) to any purchaser of the Equipment provided the purchaser agrees before making such purchase to be bound by the terms of this sub-clause (4) including the provisions of this paragraph (e), with such agreement including a recognition that the provisions of this sub-clause (4) are intended to benefit and shall so benefit the Supplier for the purposes of the Contracts (Rights of Third Parties) Act 1999. If the purchaser does not accept such terms then the Licence shall automatically and immediately terminate;

(f) the Licence shall remain effective without limit in time until it is terminated in accordance with paragraph (e) or until the Customer shall terminate it by erasing or destroying such Integral Software. The Licence shall also terminate automatically and immediately if the Customer shall fail to abide by the terms of this sub-clause (4). Upon termination of the Licence, for whatever reason, the Customer shall deliver up to the Supplier the media on which such Integral Software is recorded or embedded (and all copies thereof (if any) in the Customer's possession) or, at the Supplier's option, shall erase or otherwise destroy such Integral Software (and all copies thereof (if any) in the Customer's possession) and shall certify to the Supplier that the same has been done.

(5) The Price includes the right for the Customer to use the Integral Software in terms of sub-clauses (3) and (4).]

6 Premises preparation [2.6.3]

The Supplier shall supply to the Customer in reasonable time before delivery of the System such information and assistance as may be necessary to enable the Customer to prepare the Premises for the installation of the System and to provide proper environmental and operational conditions for the efficient working and mainte-nance of the System [and for this purpose the Supplier will make available to the Customer free of charge the advice of a suitably qualified engineer]. The Customer shall at its own expense prepare the Premises and provide such environmental and operational conditions prior to delivery.

[Note: It will be in the interests of the customer to require the supplier to provide the necessary advice in writing. This may avoid arguments at a later stage if it is alleged that the customer failed to prepare the location properly.]

7 Customer's obligations [2.6.1]

(1) The Customer undertakes to provide the Supplier promptly with any informa-tion which the Supplier may reasonably require from time to time to enable the Supplier to perform its obligations under this Agreement.

(2) The Customer shall, for the purposes of this Agreement, afford to the authorised personnel of the Supplier during normal working hours full and safe access to the Premises and shall provide adequate free working space and such other facilities as may be necessary for the installation of the System.

[Note: If the proposed location is particularly sensitive then the customer may wish to restrict access to the supplier's named personnel only. The customer may also wish to reserve a right to refuse to admit persons who are in its reasonable opinion unfit to be on its premises.]

(3) The Customer shall make available to the Supplier such office, telecommunica-tions, [computer], and secretarial services as may be reasonably necessary for its work under this Agreement.

(4) The Customer shall ensure that its employees and/or subcontractors will co-operate fully with the Supplier and that such employees and/or subcontractors will be qualified to carry out any tasks which they may be assigned in relation to the Project.

(5) The Customer shall put in place adequate security and virus checking pro-cedures in relation to any computer facilities to which it provides the Supplier with access.

8 Personnel

(1) The parties shall each appoint a representative who shall have full authority to take all necessary decisions regarding the Project [including the variation of this Agreement].

(2) The parties shall procure that their representatives shall meet at [regular intervals] [at least once a *week*] during the continuance of this Agreement to discuss and minute the progress of the Project.

(3) The Customer shall be entitled to request and obtain, at its discretion, the removal and replacement of any of the Supplier's personnel assigned to work on the Project who are not providing their services with the requisite degree of skill and care, provided that the Customer shall not exercise such right unreasonably, frivolously or vexatiously.

[Note: the supplier may resist such a right if the Project is being performed for a fixed price, in which event it will be essential for the supplier to retain control of the make-up of its project team.]

(4) The Supplier shall ensure that while any of its personnel are on the Customer's premises, they will conform to the Customer's normal codes of staff and security practice [of which the Supplier is notified in writing by the Customer.]

[9 Pre-delivery tests [2.3.2]

(1) The Supplier shall submit the Equipment to its standard works tests ("the Works Tests") before delivery to the Customer. The Supplier shall promptly supply to the Customer on request copies of the specification of the Works Tests and a certificate that the Equipment has passed the same.

(2) The Customer or its authorised representative may attend the Works Tests. If the Works Tests are held in the presence of the Customer or its authorised representative, the Supplier will charge the Customer its standard fee therefor. The Supplier shall give the Customer at least 7 days' written notice of the date and time at which the Supplier proposes to carry out the Works Tests. In the event of any delay or failure by the Customer or its authorised representative in attending the Works Tests at such time, the Supplier reserves the right to proceed with the Works Tests without the Customer.]

[Note: the parties will need to agree whether the customer should pay for the carrying out of the Works Test.]

10 Delivery of the equipment [2.1.1, 3.0.2]

EITHER (VERSION A Customer Transports):

[(1) On the date specified in the Implementation Plan the Supplier shall deliver the Equipment to the Off-Loading Point but shall not be responsible for off-loading the Equipment or moving it to the Premises which shall be undertaken by the Customer at its own expense].

OR (VERSION B Supplier Transports):

[(1) (a) On the date specified in the Implementation Plan the Supplier shall deliver the Equipment to the Off-Loading Point and then be responsible for its transportation thereafter to the Premises.]

(b) The Supplier shall not carry out or be responsible for the removal of doors, widening of entrances or any other structural work of any description for the purpose of moving the Equipment from the Off-Loading Point to the Premises, which work shall be undertaken by the Customer at its own expense prior to delivery.

(c) The Customer shall be responsible for all reasonable costs incurred by the Supplier in providing any special equipment, personnel or works reasonably necessary to move the Equipment from the Off-Loading Point to the Premises. Such costs shall be paid by the Customer in addition to the Price.]

EITHER (VERSION A Transportation costs included):

[(2) [Save for the special delivery costs referred to in sub-clause (1)(c)] the Price includes the cost of delivery of the Equipment to the [Off-Loading Point] [the Premises] by any method of transport selected by the Supplier]

OR (VERSION B Transportation costs not included):

[(2) The Price does not include the cost of transportation of the Equipment [from the Supplier's premises] [within the United Kingdom] or any other delivery costs, which shall be paid by the Customer in addition to the Price.]

[(3) All packing cases, skids, drums and other packing materials used for delivery of the Equipment to the Premises must be returned by the Customer to the Supplier in good condition and at the Customer's expense. The Supplier reserves the right to charge for any such cases and materials not so returned.]

11 Installation of the equipment [2.3.3]

(1) The Supplier shall install the Equipment at the Premises on the date specified in the Implementation Plan.

(2) If in the reasonable opinion of the Supplier it is reasonably necessary to remove or otherwise disconnect any of the Customer's existing equipment at the Premises in order to carry out the installation of the Equipment, then the Customer shall permit, and obtain all necessary consents for, such removal and/or disconnection and shall give the Supplier all necessary assistance to enable such work to be carried out.

12 Installation tests [2.3.4]

(1) The Supplier shall, [on or before the date] [within *14* days of the date] specified in the Implementation Plan, submit the Equipment to the Supplier's standard installation tests ("the Installation Tests") to ensure that the Equipment and every part thereof is in full working order. The Supplier shall supply the Customer with copies of the Installation Test scripts applicable to the Equipment and results of the Installation Tests.

(2) The Customer shall attend the Installation Tests on the said date and shall provide all necessary facilities to enable the Installation Tests to be carried out.

(3) If the Equipment or any part thereof shall fail to pass the Installation Tests then, if requested by the Customer, the Installation Test or Tests for the Equipment or

for such part or parts of the Equipment as have failed the Installation Test or Tests, shall be repeated within a reasonable time thereafter but in any event no later than *14* days thereafter up to a maximum of three such tests for the Equipment as a whole or any one part of it. If the Equipment or any part thereof shall fail such repeat tests then the Customer may by written notice to the Supplier elect at its sole option:

    (a) to require (without prejudice to its other rights and remedies) the Supplier to provide such replacement equipment as will enable the Equipment to pass the Installation Tests; or

    (b) to accept the Equipment subject to an abatement of the Price such abatement to be such amount as, taking into account the circumstances, is reasonable. In the absence of written agreement as to abatement within *14* days after the date of such notice the Customer shall be entitled to reject the Equipment in accordance with paragraph (c) below; or

    (c) to reject the Equipment as not being in conformity with this Agreement in which event this Agreement shall automatically terminate and the Supplier shall (without prejudice to the Customer's other rights and remedies) forthwith refund to the Customer all sums previously paid to the Supplier under this Agreement. Upon rejection as aforesaid the risk in the Equipment shall forthwith pass to the Supplier.

(4) Once the Equipment and every part thereof has successfully passed the Installation Tests then the Equipment shall be accepted by the Customer.

(5) Any acceptance of the Equipment by the Customer pursuant to this clause shall be without prejudice to the Customer's right to reject the System pursuant to clause 15.

13 Delivery and installation of the licensed programs [3.3]

The Supplier shall, within *7* days after the Customer's acceptance of the Equipment, deliver the Licensed Programs to the Customer and install the same on the Equipment at the Location. The Licensed Programs so delivered shall consist of one copy of the object code of the Licensed Programs in machine-readable form only, on the storage media specified in Schedule 1.

14 Risk in the licensed programs

Risk in the media on which the Licensed Programs are recorded shall pass to the Customer on installation. If any part of such media shall thereafter be lost, destroyed or damaged the Supplier shall promptly replace the same (embodying the relevant part of the Licensed Programs) subject to the Customer paying the cost of such replacement media. The Supplier shall not make any further or additional charge for the replacement of the Licensed Programs.

15 Testing and acceptance of the system [2.3.4, 2.3.6, 3.3.1]

(1) [On or before] [Within *14* days of] the applicable date specified in the Implementation Plan, the Customer shall submit to the Supplier test data which in the reasonable opinion of the Customer is suitable to test whether the System is in accordance with the Specification [and the Performance Criteria] together with the

results expected to be achieved by processing such test data on the System. The Supplier shall not be entitled to object to such test data or expected results unless the Supplier can demonstrate to the Customer that they are not in accordance with the Specification [and/or the Performance Criteria], in which event the Customer shall make such amendments to such test data and expected results as may be necessary for them to conform to the Specification [and/or the Performance Criteria].

(2) After the Licensed Programs have been fully installed on the Equipment pursuant to clause 13, the Supplier shall give to the Customer at least 7 days' prior written notice (or such shorter notice as may be agreed between the parties) of the date ("the Testing Date") on which the Supplier will be ready to attend acceptance tests at the Customer's premises. The Customer and the Supplier shall attend such tests on the Testing Date and the Customer shall provide all necessary facilities to enable such tests to be carried out.

(3) On the Testing Date the Customer shall process, in the presence of the authorised representatives of the Supplier, the test data agreed in accordance with sub-clause (1) on the System. The Supplier shall if required by the Customer give the Customer's personnel all reasonable assistance in processing such test data.

(4) The Customer shall accept the System immediately after the System has correctly processed such test data by achieving the expected results. The Customer shall, if required by the Supplier, sign an acceptance certificate in the form annexed hereto acknowledging such acceptance.

[Note: See Precedents A and C for specimen forms of acceptance certificate.]

(5) The System shall not be deemed to have incorrectly processed such test data by reason of any failure to provide any facility or function not specified in the Specification.

(6) If the System shall fail to process the test data correctly then repeat tests shall be carried out on the same terms and conditions within a reasonable time thereafter up to a maximum of 3 such repeated tests for the System as a whole or for any one part of the System but in any event no later than 14 days thereafter.

(7) If such repeat tests demonstrate that the System is not in accordance with the Specification [or the Performance Criteria] then the Customer may by written notice to the Supplier elect at its sole option:

(a) to fix (without prejudice to its other rights and remedies) a new date for carrying out further tests on the System on the same terms and conditions (save that all costs which the Customer may incur as a result of carrying out such tests shall be reimbursed by the Supplier). If the System shall fail such further tests then the Customer shall be entitled to proceed under paragraph (b) or (c) below; or

(b) to accept the System subject to an abatement of the Price, such abatement to be such amount as, taking into account the circumstances, is reasonable. In the absence of written agreement as to abatement within 14 days after the date of such notice the Customer shall be entitled to reject the System in accordance with paragraph (c) below; or

(c) to reject the System as not being in conformity with this Agreement in which event this Agreement shall automatically terminate [and the Supplier shall (without prejudice to the Customer's other rights and remedies) forthwith refund to the Customer all sums previously paid to the Supplier under this Agreement]. Upon rejection as aforesaid the risk in the System shall forthwith pass to the Supplier.

[**Note**: the right to repayment of all sums previously paid is a potentially onerous one, if the customer can fairly be said to have derived value from the services provided up to the final acceptance tests. However, it may well be appropriate if the system genuinely has no use other than as an integrated whole.]

(8) Notwithstanding anything else contained in this Clause the Supplier shall be entitled (provided it has complied with its obligations under this Clause) at any time and from time to time after the Testing Date to serve written notice on the Customer requiring the Customer to identify any part of the Specification [or the Performance Criteria] which the System does not fulfil. If the Customer shall fail to identify in writing to the Supplier within *14* days after the receipt of such notice any part of the Specification [or the Performance Criteria] which the System does not fulfil then the Customer shall be deemed to have accepted the System.

(9) If at any time the Customer shall commence live running of the whole or any part of the System (as distinct from acceptance testing) then the Customer shall be deemed to have accepted the System.

[**Note**: this clause provides a relatively straightforward acceptance test procedure; more detailed provisions may be required for larger implementations, e.g. so as to categorise reported faults into different categories of severity, with less serious errors able to be addressed during a subsequent warranty or support services period.]

16 Delays [2.3.7]

Supplier's default

(1) (a) The Supplier shall provide the System Ready for Use on or before the Completion Date.

(b) If the Supplier shall fail to provide the System Ready for Use by the Completion Date then the Supplier shall pay to the Customer as and by way of liquidated damages for any loss or damage sustained by the Customer resulting from delay during the period from the Completion Date to the date on which the Supplier provides the System Ready for Use the sum of £*500* for each week of such delay and pro rata for parts of a week up to a total maximum of *ten weeks*. Subject to the provisions of paragraph (c) below, the payment of such sums shall be in full satisfaction of the Supplier's liability for any loss suffered by the Customer during the period of such delay. The payment of liquidated damages shall not relieve the Supplier from its obligation to provide the System Ready for Use or from any other liability or obligation under this Agreement.

(c) If the Supplier shall fail to provide the System Ready for Use within *10* weeks after the Completion Date then notwithstanding anything else contained in this Agreement the Customer shall be entitled to terminate this Agreement forthwith on giving written notice to the Supplier and to recover from the Supplier the amount of all [direct] damages and loss suffered by the Customer resulting from such failure. [Upon such termination the Supplier shall (without prejudice to the Customer's right to recover the amount of such damages and loss as aforesaid) forthwith refund to the Customer all moneys previously paid to the Supplier under this Agreement. Upon such termination the risk in the System shall forthwith pass to the Supplier.]

[**Note**: see earlier comment regarding return of all monies paid. Note also that the amount of any liquidated damages set must be a genuine pre-estimate of likely losses, and not simply an arbitrary penalty.]

Customer's default

(2) If the Supplier is prevented or delayed from performing its obligations under this Agreement by reason of any act or omission of the Customer (other than a delay by the Customer for which the Customer is excused under clause 17) then the Customer will pay to the Supplier all reasonable costs, charges and losses sustained or incurred by the Supplier as a result. The Supplier shall promptly notify the Customer in writing of any claim which it may have under this sub-clause giving such particulars thereof as it is then able to provide.

[**Note**: this clause pre-supposes that the completion of the project is time-critical.]

17 *Force majeure*

(1) Notwithstanding anything else contained in this Agreement, neither party shall be liable for any delay in performing its obligations hereunder if such delay is caused by circumstances beyond its reasonable control (including without limitation any delay caused by any act or omission of the other party) provided however that any delay by a sub-contractor or supplier of the party so delaying shall not relieve that party from liability for delay except where such delay is beyond the reasonable control of the sub-contractor or supplier concerned. Subject to the party so delaying promptly notifying the other party in writing of the reasons for the delay (and the likely duration of the delay), the performance of such party's obligations shall be suspended during the period that the said circumstances persist and such party shall be granted an extension of time for performance equal to the period of the delay. Save where such delay is caused by the act or omission of the other party (in which event the rights, remedies and liabilities of the parties shall be those conferred and imposed by the other terms of this Agreement and by law):

(a) any costs arising from such delay shall be borne by the party incurring the same;

(b) either party may, if such delay continues for more than 5 weeks, terminate this Agreement forthwith on giving notice in writing to the other in which event neither party shall be liable to the other by reason of such termination [save that the Customer shall pay the Supplier a reasonable sum in respect of any work carried out by it prior to such termination and for that purpose the Supplier may deduct such sum from any amounts previously paid by the Customer under this Agreement (the balance (if any) of which shall be refunded to the Customer whether paid by way of a deposit or otherwise)].

[**Notes**:

(1) Even if time is made of the essence in relation to a particular obligation this clause will override that provision to give the delaying party an extension of time for performance without incurring any liability for the delay.

(2) A frequent problem with a clause of this nature is that the delaying party is inclined to seek its protection even if the delay is due to its own default. This can be avoided to some extent by requiring the delaying party promptly to notify the reason for the delay (which can then be investigated) and by providing the other party with an opportunity to terminate the agreement if the delay continues for an unreasonable period.

(3) Many customers will refuse to entertain a clause of this nature if it excuses defaults by sub-contractors or suppliers. Customers will argue, perhaps rightly so, that it is up to the supplier to ensure that his sub-contractors and suppliers are reliable.

(4) Where a delay does occur it will be in the interests of both parties to ensure that a proper record of the period of the delay is kept and that the extended date for performance is confirmed in writing.]

(2) In the event of any extension of time being granted pursuant to sub-clause (1) the Implementation Plan shall be amended accordingly.

18 Electromagnetic compatibility [2.7.3]

See clause 13 of Precedent A.

19 Telecommunications [2.7.4]

See clause 14 of Precedent A.

20 Licence to use [2.6.4]

The parties undertake to enter into a licence agreement on the Acceptance Date in respect of the use of the Licensed Programs and the Operating Manuals in the form of the Licence Agreement annexed hereto in Schedule 4, marked "A".

[Notes:

(1) Adapt Precedent C.

(2) Alternatively, the parties could undertake to enter into the licence agreement immediately after the signature of this Agreement in which event the licence agreement should be expressed to become effective on the Acceptance Date. The same point applies to clauses 21 and 22 below.]

21 Maintenance of the equipment

The parties undertake to enter into a maintenance agreement on the Acceptance Date in respect of the Equipment in the form of the Maintenance Agreement annexed hereto in Schedule 4, marked "B".

[Note: See Precedent K.]

22 Maintenance of the licensed programs

The parties undertake to enter into a maintenance agreement on the Acceptance Date in respect of the Licensed Programs and the Operating Manuals in the form of the Maintenance Agreement annexed hereto in Schedule 4, marked "C".

[Note: See Precedent L.]

23 Operating manuals [3.7.3]

See clause 22 of Precedent A.

24 Training [3.7.3]

(1) The Supplier shall provide training in the use of the System for the Customer's staff in accordance with the Training Plan.

(2) Any additional training required by the Customer shall be provided by the Supplier in accordance with its standard scale of charges from time to time in force.

25 Warranties [2.3.8, 3.3.3]

(1) The Supplier warrants that:

    (a) the System will after acceptance by the Customer:

        (i) provide the facilities and functions set out in the Specification [and will fulfil the Performance Criteria];

        (ii) be free from substantial defects in materials, workmanship and installation.

    (b) the Operating Manuals will provide adequate instruction to enable the Customer to make full and proper use of the System.

[Note: a performance warranty may need to be made subject to a series of assumptions/dependencies, as the performance levels required will often be impacted by matters outside the control of the supplier.]

(2) The Supplier shall have no liability or obligations under the said warranties other than to remedy breaches thereof by the provision of maintenance services in accordance with the maintenance agreements referred to in clauses 21 and 22, save that if the Supplier shall fail to remedy any breach of the said warranties as aforesaid then the Supplier shall be liable to the Customer for all [direct] loss and damage suffered by the Customer as a result of such failure (subject always to the limitations in clause 32) provided that the Customer shall have given the Supplier written notice of the breach in question no later than the expiration or termination of the relevant maintenance agreement.

[Note: if the supplier is not the originator of the hardware/software being provided, it will need to ensure that the scope of the warranties it is providing reflects those which it is able to obtain from the third-party manufacturer/licensor.]

(3) The Supplier warrants to the Customer that the Equipment complies fully as to noise heat radiation and all other characteristics with the requirements in the Health and Safety (Display Screen Equipment) Regulations 1992 and in particular that the display screens and keyboards comply fully with the said Regulations.

(4) The express terms of this Agreement are in lieu of all warranties, conditions, terms, undertakings and obligations implied by statute, common law, custom, trade usage, course of dealing or otherwise, all of which are hereby excluded to the fullest extent permitted by law.

26 Customer's warranty

See clause 20 of Precedent A.

27 Confidentiality [2.6.2, 2.7.1]

See clause 21 of Precedent A.

28 Removal of labels [2.6.5]

See clause 23 of Precedent A.

[29 Export control [2.9.1]

See clause 25 of Precedent A.

30 Intellectual property rights indemnity [2.8.1, 3.8.1]

See clause 26 of Precedent A.

[Note: if the supplier is also relying upon and/or receiving materials provided by the client, it may be appropriate to make the Intellectual Property Rights indemnity reciprocal.]

31 Termination [2.4.1]

See clause 18 of Precedent A.

32 Liability

See clause 27 of Precedent A.

33 Waiver of remedies

See clause 28 of Precedent A.

34 Entire agreement [2.6.5]

See clause 29 of Precedent A.

35 Assignment

See clause 30 of Precedent A.

36 Sub-contracts

See clause 31 of Precedent A.

37 Notices

See clause 32 of Precedent A.

38 Interpretation

See clause 33 of Precedent A.

39 Law

See clause 34 of Precedent A.

40 Disputes

See clause 35 of Precedent A.

41 Severability

See clause 36 of Precedent A.

42 Third parties [1.3]

See clause 37 of Precedent A.

EXECUTED under hand in two originals the day and year first before written

SIGNED for and on behalf of

COMPUTER COMPANY [LIMITED] [PLC]

By

Signature

Title

Witness

SIGNED for and on behalf of
CUSTOMER [LIMITED] [PLC]

By

Signature

Title

Witness

SCHEDULE 1

A THE EQUIPMENT

[B THE INTEGRAL SOFTWARE

Owned by third parties:

Owned by the Supplier:]

C THE LICENSED PROGRAMS

D THE PRICE

E THE EQUIPMENT PRICE

F THE OFF-LOADING POINT

G THE PREMISES

H STORAGE MEDIA

I SUB-CONTRACTS]

SCHEDULE 2

THE IMPLEMENTATION PLAN

SCHEDULE 3

THE TRAINING PLAN

SCHEDULE 4

ASSOCIATED AGREEMENTS

A SOFTWARE LICENCE AGREEMENT

B MAINTENANCE AGREEMENT: EQUIPMENT

C MAINTENANCE AGREEMENT: LICENSED PROGRAMS

[D THIRD-PARTY RIGHTS]

BUREAU SERVICE: GENERAL ON-LINE

THIS AGREEMENT is made the   day of   20

PARTIES:

(1) COMPUTER BUREAU COMPANY [LIMITED] [PLC] whose registered office is at

("the Bureau")

(2) CUSTOMER [LIMITED] [PLC] whose registered office is at

("the Customer")

RECITALS:

(A) The Bureau carries on the business of providing the shared use of a computer by means of [the supply of] on-line terminals through which its customers can obtain direct access to the Bureau's computer for the purpose of running their programs and the processing of their data

(B) The Bureau has agreed to permit the Customer to share the use of its computer and certain of its programs upon the terms and conditions hereinafter contained

NOW IT IS HEREBY AGREED as follows:

1 Definitions

In this Agreement, unless the context otherwise requires, the following expressions have the following meanings:

"business day"	means a day other than a Saturday, Sunday or a public holiday [in England and Wales].
"the Bureau's Premises"	means the Bureau's premises at [ ].
"the Commencement Date"	means the date on which this Agreement shall become effective as specified in Schedule 1.
"Confidential Information"	means all information which is expressly marked as confidential or which is manifestly of a confidential nature or which is confirmed in writing to be confidential within 7 days of its disclosure.
"the Equipment"	means the Bureau's computer equipment specified in Schedule 1 (situate at the Bureau's Premises) or such other equipment as shall be agreed between the parties.

"the Initial Period"	means the initial period of this Agreement as specified in Schedule 1.
"the Licensed Programs"	means the programs specified in Schedule 1 which are to be made available by the Bureau for use by the Customer under this Agreement.
"the Customer's Premises"	means the Customer's premises as specified in Schedule 1.
"the Printer"	means the Bureau's *XYZ* [laser] printer[s] situate at the Bureau's Premises.
"the Services"	means the services to be provided by the Bureau pursuant to this Agreement, as provided in clause 2.
"the Specification"	means the specification of the Equipment and the Licensed Programs describing the facilities and functions thereof, a copy of which is annexed hereto.
"the Terminal"	*EITHER:*
	[means the [visual display] [terminal] [personal computer] [and its associated [serial] printer] specified in Schedule 1 which [is][are] to be let on hire to the Customer under this Agreement.]
	OR:
	[means any suitable terminal or personal computer of the Customer [installed at the Customer's Premises].]

[**Note**: The customer might provide his own terminal in which case the second alternative should be used.]

2 Services to be provided [10.1.2]

Subject to the provisions of this Agreement, the Bureau hereby agrees to:

(1) permit the Customer to use the Equipment and the Licensed Programs by means of the Terminal for the storage and processing of the Customer's programs and data;

[(2) install the Terminal and let the same on hire to the Customer for the purpose of obtaining access to the Equipment and the Licensed Programs;]

(3) print, copy and download the Customer's programs and data or any part or parts thereof as reasonably required by the Customer from time to time;

(4) provide the other services hereinafter described,

upon the terms and conditions hereinafter contained.

3 Access and use

(1) On or before the Commencement Date, the Bureau shall supply the Customer with:

(a) a set of operating instructions containing sufficient information to enable the Customer to make full and proper use of the Equipment and the Licensed Programs [and the Terminal];

(b) details of the Bureau's security procedures and a security password to enable the Customer to obtain access to the Equipment and the Licensed Programs.

(2) The Bureau shall periodically change the Customer's standard security procedures or password and shall notify the Customer accordingly. If the Bureau shall become aware, or shall suspect, that any unauthorised person has obtained or has attempted to obtain access to the Customer's programs or data then the Bureau shall promptly notify the Customer and shall forthwith change the Customer's security password. The Customer shall likewise notify the Bureau if it becomes aware, or shall suspect, that any unauthorised person has obtained or has attempted to obtain access to the Customer's programs or data, and the Bureau shall forthwith change the Customer's security password.

[Note: The customer may have its own password which it can change without reference to the Bureau, in which case this clause will need to be modified.]

(3) The Bureau shall make the Equipment and the Licensed Programs available to the Customer [for use by means of the Terminal] during the hours of 8.00 am to 7.00 pm each business day.

(5) The Bureau hereby grants to the Customer all necessary rights by way of licence to use the Licensed Programs in accordance with the terms of this Agreement but not further or otherwise.

[Note: if the Licensed Programs include application software as well as simply the software required to enable the customer to access the bureau's systems, separate licence terms are likely to be required]

(6) The Customer undertakes not to attempt to obtain access to, use or interfere with any programs or data of the Bureau (other than access to and use of the Licensed Programs in accordance with this Agreement) or of any other customer of the Bureau and shall indemnify the Bureau against any loss, damage or liability which the Bureau may sustain or incur as a consequence of the Customer failing to comply with such undertaking.

4 Charges and payment [10.2.2, 10.5.1]

(1) The Customer shall pay the following charges for the services to be provided by the Bureau hereunder:

[(a) for the use of the Equipment and the Licensed Programs—the hourly connect time rate set out in Part A of Schedule 2 and the on-line storage rate per Gigabyte per [business] day set out in Part B of Schedule 2;

(b) for downloading any of the Customer's programs and/or data on to magnetic media and for loading any of such programs or data back on to the Equipment—at the rate per Gigabyte set out in Part C of Schedule 2;

(c) for off-line storage of the Customer's programs and/or data—at the rate per magnetic [tape] [disk] per business day set out in Part D of Schedule 2;

(d) for print-outs from the Printer—at the rate per page set out in Part E of Schedule 2;

[(e) for the hire of the Terminal—at the monthly rate set out in Part F of Schedule 2];

(f) for installing the Terminal—at the rate set out in Part F of Schedule 2.

(2) The Bureau shall invoice the Customer monthly in arrears for the charges referred to in clause 4(1). Each invoice will be paid by the Customer within *30* days after the Customer's receipt of such invoice.

[(3) Notwithstanding the provisions of clause 4(1)(a), the use of the Equipment and the Licensed Programs shall be subject to the minimum charge per month specified in Part G of Schedule 2 which charge shall be payable whether or not the Equipment and the Licensed Programs are actually used during the month in question.]

EITHER (VERSION A Discretion to Increase Charges):

[(4) The Bureau shall be entitled at any time and from time to time after the expiry of the [Initial Period] [the period of *one year* after the Commencement Date] to increase all or any of the charges referred to in clauses 4(1) and 4(3) to accord with any change in the Bureau's standard scale of charges by giving to the Customer not less than *90* days' prior written notice. Where and whenever such notice is given, the Customer shall have the right to terminate this Agreement as from the date on which such notice expires by giving to the Bureau written notice of termination not less than *30* days before such date.]

OR (VERSION B Indexed Increase in Charges):

[(4) The Bureau shall be entitled at any time and from time to time (subject as mentioned below) after the expiry of the [Initial Period] [the period of *one year* after the Commencement Date] to increase the charges referred to in sub-clauses (1) and (3) by giving to the Customer not less than *90* days' prior written notice, provided that any such increase shall not exceed a percentage equal to the percentage increase in the *Retail Prices Index published by the Central Statistical Office* for the period from the Commencement Date (in the case of the first such increase) or the date on which the immediately preceding increase came into effect pursuant to this sub-clause (in the case of the second or subsequent increase) up to the date of such notice, plus *2* per cent, provided further that no increase may be made pursuant to clause 4(4) until a period of at least *one year* has elapsed since the date on which the immediately preceding increase came into effect pursuant to this sub-clause].

(5) The charges payable under this Agreement are exclusive of Value Added Tax which shall be paid by the Customer at the rate and in the manner for the time being prescribed by law.

(6) If any sum payable under this Agreement is not paid within *7* days after the due date then (without prejudice to the Bureau's other rights and remedies) the Bureau

reserves the right to charge interest on such sum on a day to day basis (as well after as before any judgment) from the date or last date for payment thereof to the date of actual payment (both dates inclusive) at the rate of 2 per cent above the base rate of *ABC* Bank plc (or such other London Clearing Bank as the Supplier may nominate) from time to time in force compounded quarterly. Such interest shall be paid on demand by the Bureau. The Bureau shall, in addition, be entitled to suspend the provision of the Services pending payment of all sums due.

5 Duration

This Agreement shall commence on the Commencement Date, shall continue for the Initial Period and shall remain in force thereafter [unless or] until terminated by either party giving to the other not less than 6 months' written notice of termination [given on] [expiring on] the last day of the Initial Period or at any time thereafter but shall be subject to earlier termination as provided elsewhere in this Agreement.

[**Note**: Delete the first and third bracketed phrases if the agreement is to be for a minimum period equal to the Initial Period plus the notice period. Delete the second bracketed phrase if the agreement is to be for a minimum period equal to the Initial Period.]

[6 The terminal [10.1.2, 10.6]

(1) The Bureau shall let and the Customer shall take on hire the Terminal for the duration of this Agreement.

(2) The Customer shall be responsible for providing proper accommodation and operating conditions for the Terminal in accordance with the Bureau's instructions before the delivery of the Terminal.

(3) The Bureau shall deliver the Terminal to the Customer's Premises and shall install the same at the Customer's Premises on or before the Commencement Date.

(4) Prior to the delivery of the Terminal the Customer shall:

(a) arrange for the provision of a telephone line and appropriate modem to connect the Terminal to the Equipment; and

(b) obtain and produce to the Bureau any necessary consents for such connection.

[**Note**: details of the modem and/or other communications links may need to be set out in detail as part of the specification for the services to be provided.]

(5) The Terminal shall at all times remain the sole and exclusive property of the Bureau and the Customer shall have no right or interest therein except for quiet possession and the right to use the same upon the terms and conditions contained in this Agreement.

(6) The Terminal shall be at the risk of the Bureau which shall be responsible for insuring the same against all normal risks. The Customer shall notify the Bureau immediately of any loss of or damage to the Terminal and shall give all necessary information and assistance to the Bureau in connection with any such loss or damage.

(7) The Customer shall not create or suffer to exist over the Terminal any mortgage, charge, lien or other encumbrance.

(8) The Customer shall not utilise or attempt to utilise any equipment other than the Terminal for the purpose of obtaining access to the Equipment and the Licensed Programs.

(9) The Customer shall use the Terminal only for the purpose of obtaining access to the Equipment and the Licensed Programs in accordance with the terms of this Agreement.

(10) The Customer shall use the Terminal only for inputting and processing its own programs, the Licensed Programs and its own data for its own internal business purposes and shall not make the use of the Terminal available to any third party nor use the Terminal on behalf of or for the benefit of any third party.

(11) The Customer shall operate the Terminal in a proper and prudent manner in accordance with the Bureau's operating instructions and ensure that only competent trained employees (or persons under their supervision) are allowed to operate the same.

[(12) The Customer shall be responsible for obtaining at its own expense all consumable supplies for use on the Terminal. The Customer shall only use such consumable supplies as the Bureau shall recommend.]

(13) The Bureau shall provide preventive and corrective maintenance for the Terminal during the hours of 8.00 a.m. to 7.00 p.m. on business days ("Working Hours").

(14) Preventive maintenance shall be performed by the Bureau during Working Hours at such intervals as the Bureau shall reasonably determine to be necessary for the Terminal.

(15) Corrective maintenance shall be performed by the Bureau during Working Hours as soon as possible after the Customer's request therefor on the basis of a response time of 8 Working Hours but such response time is an estimate only and shall not be binding on the Bureau.

[Note: the maintenance provisions outlined above are of a de minimis nature; more detailed support and maintenance provisions are likely to be required in the case of complex/larger contracts.]

(16) The Customer shall not without the prior written consent of the Bureau permit any person, firm or company other than the Bureau (or a person appointed for such purpose by the Bureau) to carry out or attempt to carry out any maintenance, adjustment, replacement or repair of the Terminal or any part thereof.

(17) The Customer shall ensure that the Terminal is not moved from the Customer's Premises except with the prior written consent of the Bureau.

(18) Upon termination of the Customer's right to hire the Terminal (for any reason) the Customer shall forthwith redeliver possession of the Terminal to the Bureau in a condition consistent with the proper performance by the Customer of its obligations under this Clause and the Bureau shall for the purpose have access to the Customer's Premises.]

7 Preparation of programs and data

The Customer shall have sole responsibility for the preparation of its programs and data and for the scheduling and control of the running and processing thereof. The

Bureau shall not be responsible for any fault or error in the Customer's programs or data.

8 On-line storage [10.3.1]

The Customer shall be entitled to store on-line on the Equipment such programs and data as it shall require provided that the total storage volume for all such programs and data at any one time shall not exceed *100* Gigabytes and provided also that the total volume of such programs and data resident in the main memory of the Equipment at any one time shall not exceed *500* Gigabytes.

9 Off-line storage

(1) The Bureau shall at the request of the Customer download on to [magnetic] [electronic] storage media all or any part of the Customer's programs and/or data from time to time stored on-line on the Equipment subject to the Customer giving to the Bureau at least [2] business days' notice in writing.

(2) Upon receiving such a request the Bureau shall take two copies of the programs or data in question, one of which shall be kept by the Bureau and one of which shall be delivered to the Customer at the Customer's expense.

(3) The Bureau shall keep the media to be held by it [in its fireproof safe] at the Bureau's Premises.

[**Note**: for larger projects, it may be appropriate to require the Bureau to utilise a separate disaster recovery facility.]

(4) The Bureau shall not be liable to the Customer for any loss or damage sustained or incurred by the Customer resulting from any loss or destruction of or damage to any of the media held by the Bureau unless such loss, destruction or damage is caused by the wilful misconduct of the Bureau, its employees, agents or sub-contractors provided however that nothing in this clause 9 (4) shall affect the Bureau's liability under clause 13(5).

(5) If any of the media held by the Bureau shall be lost, destroyed or damaged then the Bureau shall forthwith make duplicates of such media and for this purpose the Customer shall promptly make available to the Bureau the copies of such media held by the Customer. Where any media held by the Bureau is lost, destroyed or damaged due to the negligence or wilful misconduct of the Bureau, its employees, agents or sub-contractors then the cost of making such duplicates shall be borne by the Bureau, subject always to the limitations on liability contained in clause 23.

[(6) The Bureau shall not be responsible for the loss or spoiling of any of the Customer's programs or data stored on magnetic media if such programs or data were downloaded on to that media more than *3* months previously. The Bureau will at the request of the Customer take duplicates of any of the Customer's programs or data stored off-line on magnetic media subject to the Customer giving to the Bureau at least *2* business days' notice in writing. Where any of the Customer's programs or data are lost or spoiled by reason of their deterioration on magnetic media within the said period of *3* months then the Bureau will forthwith make duplicates of such media free of charge and for this purpose the Customer will promptly make available the copies of such media held by it. The foregoing states the entire liability of the Bureau for the loss or spoiling of any of the Customer's programs or data by reason of their deterioration on magnetic media.]

[**Note:** If the downloading is onto non-magnetic media omit this clause.]

(7) Subject to the provisions of clause 8, the Bureau shall at the request of the Customer load on to the Equipment all or any part of the Customer's programs and/or data from time to time stored off-line on magnetic media subject to the Customer giving to the Bureau at least 2 business days' notice in writing.

10 Security copies

The Bureau shall take each business day a single security copy of all the Customer's data and programs stored on-line on the Equipment at that time and shall keep such security copies for a period of *one week* after copying. The Bureau shall not charge for making such security copies but their storage and use (subject to the other provisions of this Agreement) shall be subject to such conditions as the Bureau may from time to time impose.

11 Maintenance of the equipment and licensed programs [10.7.3]

(1) (a) The Bureau shall be responsible for maintaining the Equipment in good working order and condition.

    (b) If the Equipment shall fail or breakdown the Bureau shall use its reasonable endeavours promptly to restore the Equipment to its proper operating condition [and shall in the meantime whenever possible provide suitable alternative equipment for the Customer's use].

[**Note:** The customer may require a more positive commitment to provide back-up equipment in the event of a breakdown. The position is usually clear cut—either the bureau will have a back-up machine or it will not. The imposition of service credits linked to defined minimum levels of availability is also increasingly common.]

(2) If the Customer shall become aware of any fault in the Licensed Programs then the Customer shall promptly notify the Bureau. Upon receipt of such notification (or upon receipt of a similar notification from one of the Bureau's other customers) the Bureau shall forthwith use its reasonable endeavours to procure that such fault is corrected as quickly as possible.

[**Note:** This clause assumes that the bureau does not own the licensed programs and that the bureau would have to arrange for the proprietor to correct the fault.]

(3) (a) In the event of any failure or breakdown of the Equipment or any fault in the Licensed Programs with consequent loss or spoiling of the Customer's data and/or programs or any part thereof the Bureau shall use such security copies as described in clause 10 to reconstitute the Customer's programs and data free of charge as soon as reasonably practicable after the Equipment and the Licensed Programs are available for use again (in accordance with known priorities).

    (b) The Bureau shall notify the Customer of any such failure of the Equipment or the Licensed Programs and reconstitution of the Customer's data and programs from such security copies within *24* hours of such reconstitution.

(4) Clause 11 (3) states the entire liability of the Bureau for any loss or spoiling of the Customer's programs and/or data caused by any failure or breakdown of the

Equipment or fault in the Licensed Programs. The Bureau shall not be liable for any other loss or damage sustained or incurred by the Customer as a result of any failure or breakdown of the Equipment or fault in the Licensed Programs except to the extent that such loss or damage arises from any unreasonable delay by the Bureau in performing its obligations under clauses 11(1) and 11(2) above, in which event the limitations of liability in clause 23 shall apply.

12 Print-outs

(1) The Bureau shall at the Customer's request make such print-outs of the Customer's data using the Printer as the Customer shall from time to time reasonably require.

(2) The Bureau shall not be responsible for the delivery of such print-outs but shall make them available for collection by the Customer at the Bureau's Premises within 2 business days after the Customer's request therefor.

13 Ownership of programs and data [10.6.3]

(1) The Customer's programs and data shall be and shall remain the property of the Customer.

(2) The Bureau shall ensure that all copies of the Customer's programs and data in the Bureau's possession shall bear a notice that such programs and data are the property and confidential information of the Customer.

(3) The Bureau shall assist in the protection and defence of the Customer's title to its programs and data against all persons claiming against or through the Bureau and shall use its reasonable endeavours to keep such programs and data free from any distress, execution or other legal process.

(4) (a) The Bureau undertakes to treat as confidential and keep secret all Confidential Information of the Customer as contained or embodied in the Customer's programs and data.

(b) The Bureau shall not without the prior written consent of the Customer divulge the whole or any part of the Confidential Information to any person except the Bureau's own employees and then only to those employees who need to know the same, and to the extent necessary, for the proper performance of this Agreement.

(c) The Bureau undertakes to ensure that its employees are made aware that the Confidential Information is confidential and that such employees owe a duty of confidence to the Customer. The Bureau shall indemnify the Customer against any loss or damage which the Customer may sustain or incur as a result of the Bureau failing to comply with such undertaking.

(d) The Bureau shall notify the Customer promptly if the Bureau becomes aware of any breach of confidence by any of the Bureau's employees and shall give the Customer all reasonable assistance in connection with any legal proceedings which the Customer may bring against any such employees or any other person for breach of confidence.

(e) The foregoing obligations as to confidentiality shall remain in full force and effect notwithstanding any termination of this Agreement (howsoever occasioned), but shall not extend to any information which was rightfully in the possession of the Bureau prior to the commencement of negotiations leading to this Agreement or which is otherwise public knowledge or becomes so at a future date (other than as a result of a breach of this clause).

(5) The Bureau will establish and maintain adequate security measures and procedures to provide for the safe custody of the Customer's programs and data and to prevent unauthorised access thereto or use thereof. The Bureau shall indemnify the Customer against any loss or damage which the Customer may sustain or incur consequent upon any of the Customer's programs or data coming into the possession of any unauthorised person as a result of any negligent act or omission or wilful misconduct of the Bureau, its employees, agents or sub-contractors [provided that the Bureau's liability therefor shall not in any circumstances whatsoever exceed £100,000 in respect of each event or series of connected events].

(6) (a) Upon any termination of this Agreement (howsoever occasioned) the Customer shall have the right to require the Bureau to do any one or more of the following:

    (i) to deliver up to the Customer all or any off-line storage and security copies of the Customer's programs and data then in the Bureau's possession subject to the Customer reimbursing the Bureau for the cost of the magnetic media on which they are stored;

    (ii) to download on to magnetic media all or any of the Customer's programs and data then stored on-line on the Equipment and to deliver up such media to the Customer subject to the Customer paying the charges for such downloading at the applicable rate for the time being payable hereunder and to reimbursing the Bureau for the cost of such magnetic media;

    (iii) to erase all or any of the Customer's programs and data then in the Bureau's possession from the magnetic media on which they are stored;

    (iv) to make and deliver up to the Customer such print-outs of the Customer's data using the Printer as the Customer may require subject to the Customer paying the charges for such print-outs at the applicable rate from time to time payable hereunder.

(b) If upon any termination of this Agreement the Customer shall require the Bureau to deliver up any of its programs and/or data on magnetic media then the Bureau shall:

    (i) deliver up such programs and/or data on industry compatible magnetic or other electronic media; and

    (ii) supply to the Customer free of charge all information necessary to enable such magnetic media to be read on another computer.

(c) Except where this Agreement is properly terminated by the Customer as a result of any breach by the Bureau of its obligations under this Agreement, the Bureau's obligations under paragraphs (a) and (b) of this clause 13(6) shall be conditional upon the Customer having paid all charges then due to the Bureau under the terms of this Agreement.

14 Content of customer's data

The Customer undertakes that the Customer's data (whether stored on-line or off-line) will not contain anything obscene, offensive or defamatory. The Customer will indemnify the Bureau and keep the Bureau fully and effectively indemnified against all actions, proceedings, claims, demands, damages and costs (including legal costs on a full indemnity basis) occasioned to the Bureau as a result of any breach of the said undertaking.

15 Data protection [10.3.3]

See clause 9 of Precedent L.

16 Intellectual property rights indemnities [2.8, 3.8]

(1) The Bureau shall indemnify the Customer against any claim by any third party for alleged infringement of any [U.K.] copyright or other [U.K.] intellectual property rights which arises as a result of the use of the Equipment or the Licensed Programs [or the Terminal] in accordance with the terms of this Agreement provided that the Bureau is notified promptly in writing of any claim, that the Bureau is given immediate and complete control of any such claim, that the Customer does not prejudice the Bureau's defence of such claim, that the Customer gives the Bureau all reasonable assistance with such claim (at the cost of the Bureau).

(2) The Customer shall indemnify the Bureau against any claim by any third party for alleged infringement of any [U.K.] copyright or other [U.K.] intellectual property rights which arises as a result of the storage or processing of any of the Customer's programs or data on the Equipment provided that the Customer is notified promptly in writing of any claim, that the Customer is given immediate and complete control of any such claim, that the Bureau does not prejudice the Customer's defence of such claim and that the Bureau gives the Customer all reasonable assistance with such claim (at the cost of the Customer).

17 Bureau's confidential information

The Customer shall treat as confidential all Confidential Information supplied to it by the Bureau. Such information shall only be disclosed to those employees of the Customer who need to know the same and the Customer undertakes to ensure that such employees are made aware of its confidential nature prior to such disclosure. These obligations shall not extend to any information which was rightfully in the possession of the Customer prior to the commencement of negotiations leading to this Agreement or which is otherwise public knowledge or becomes so at a future date (other than as a result of a breach of this clause).

18 Warranties [10.7.5]

(1) The Bureau warrants that the Licensed Programs will provide the facilities and functions described in the Specification when used in conjunction with the Equipment. The Customer acknowledges however that the Equipment and the Licensed Programs are not being made available to the Customer to meet the Customer's individual requirements and that it is therefore the responsibility of the Customer to ensure that the facilities and functions described in the Specification meet the Customer's requirements. The Bureau shall not be liable for any failure of the Licensed Programs to provide any facility or function not specified in the Specification. The Bureau's entire liability for any fault in the Licensed Programs is as stated in clause 11.

[(2) The Bureau warrants that the terminal response times for the interactive processing of the Customer's programs and data shall be those specified in Schedule 3 subject to the tolerances, limitations and exceptions stated therein.]

19 Termination [10.4]

(1) Notwithstanding anything else contained herein, this Agreement may be terminated:

(a) by the Bureau forthwith on giving notice in writing to the Customer if the Customer shall fail to pay any sum due under the terms of this Agreement (otherwise than as a consequence of any default on the part of the Bureau) and such sum remains unpaid for *14* days after written notice from the Bureau that such sum has not been paid (such notice to contain a warning of the Bureau's intention to terminate); or

(b) by either party forthwith on giving notice in writing to the other if the other commits any [material] [serious] breach of any term of this Agreement (other than any failure by the Customer to make any payment hereunder in which event the provisions of paragraph (a) above shall apply) and (in the case of a breach capable of being remedied) shall have failed, within *30* days after the receipt of a request in writing from the other party so to do, to remedy the breach (such request to contain a warning of such party's intention to terminate); or

(c) by either party forthwith on giving notice in writing to the other if the other party shall have a receiver or administrative receiver appointed over it or over any part of its undertaking or assets or shall pass a resolution for winding-up (otherwise than for the purpose of a bona fide scheme of solvent amalgamation or reconstruction) or a court of competent jurisdiction shall make an order to that effect or if the other party shall become subject to an administration order or shall enter into any voluntary arrangement with its creditors or shall cease or threaten to cease to carry on business.

(2) Any termination of this Agreement (howsoever occasioned) shall not affect any accrued rights or liabilities of either party nor shall it affect the coming into force or the continuance in force of any provision hereof which is expressly or by implication intended to come into or continue in force on or after such termination.

[(3) On the termination of this Agreement the Customer shall no longer be in possession of the Terminal with the Bureau's consent who may without notice repossess the Terminal and may for that purpose without notice enter any of the Customer's premises in which the Terminal is or is reasonably believed by the Bureau to be situated (and so that the Customer hereby irrevocably licenses the Bureau, its employees and agents to enter upon any such premises for such purpose).]

20 Assignment

Save as expressly provided in this Agreement, neither party shall assign or otherwise transfer this Agreement or any of its rights and obligations hereunder whether in whole or in part without the prior written consent of the other, such consent not to be unreasonably withheld or delayed.

21 *Force majeure*

See clause 15 of Precedent A.

22 Customer's warranty

See clause 20 of Precedent A.

23 Liability

See clause 27 of Precedent A.

24 Waiver of remedies

See clause 28 of Precedent A.

25 Entire agreement

See clause 29 of Precedent A.

26 Notices

See clause 32 of Precedent A.

27 Interpretation

See clause 33 of Precedent A.

28 Law

See clause 34 of Precedent A.

29 Disputes

See clause 35 of Precedent A or clause 37 of Precedent D.

30 Severability

See clause 36 of Precedent A.

31 Third Parties

See clause 37 of Precedent A.

EXECUTED under hand in two originals the day and year first before written

SIGNED for and on behalf of
COMPUTER BUREAU COMPANY [LIMITED] [PLC]

By

Signature

Title

Witness

SIGNED for and on behalf of
CUSTOMER [LIMITED] [PLC]

By

Signature

Title

Witness

Schedule 1

A   THE EQUIPMENT

B   THE LICENSED PROGRAMS

[C   THE TERMINAL]

D   THE CUSTOMER'S PREMISES

E   THE COMMENCEMENT DATE

F   THE INITIAL PERIOD

[G   THIRD-PARTY RIGHTS]

Schedule 2

CHARGES

A   HOURLY CONNECT TIME RATE

B   ON-LINE STORAGE RATE PER GIGABYTE PER [BUSINESS DAY]

C   DOWNLOADING/LOADING RATE PER GIGABYTE

D   OFF-LINE STORAGE RATE PER GIGABYTE PER [BUSINESS] DAY

E   PRINTER RATE PER PAGE

[F   TERMINAL HIRE PER MONTH
     INSTALLATION CHARGE FOR THE TERMINAL]

[G   MINIMUM MONTHLY CHARGE]

[SCHEDULE 3

TERMINAL RESPONSE TIMES]

[**Note**: this Agreement requires to be annexed to it:

(a) Specification of the Equipment and Licensed Programs describing the facilities and functions thereof—by clause 1.

(b) Specifications to include details of the modem and/or telecommunications links—see note to clause 6(4).]

BUREAU SERVICE: BATCH

[**Note**: This precedent is intended to form a general framework. For specialised services, arrangements can vary considerably and it will be up to the parties to specify the exact service to be provided. This precedent can be used for data conversion since the input does not have to be in eye-readable form and the output does not have to be a print-out, but either or both of these can be in machine-readable (electronic) form.]

THIS AGREEMENT is made the   day of   20

PARTIES:

(1) COMPUTER BUREAU COMPANY [LIMITED] [PLC] whose registered office is at

("the Bureau")

(2) CUSTOMER [LIMITED] [PLC] whose registered office is at

("the Customer")

RECITALS:

(A) The Bureau carries on the business of providing the shared use of a computer by means of receiving and inputting its customers' input data, processing such data and then delivering to them the resulting output

(B) The Bureau has agreed to process the Customer's data upon the terms and conditions hereinafter contained

NOW IT IS HEREBY AGREED as follows:

1 Definitions

In this Agreement, unless the context otherwise requires, the following expressions have the following meanings:

"the Bureau's Premises"	means the Bureau's premises at [ ].
"business day"	means a day other than a Saturday, Sunday or a public holiday in England and Wales.
"the Commencement Date"	means the date on which this Agreement shall become effective as specified in Schedule 1.
"the Data"	means the Customer's computer records from time to time stored on the System in machine-readable form.
"the Equipment"	means the Bureau's computer equipment specified in Schedule 1 (situate at the Bureau's Premises) or such other equipment as shall be agreed between the parties.

"the Initial Period"   means the initial period of this Agreement as spec-
                          ified in Schedule 1.

"the Input"   means the data [in eye-readable form] from time to
                          time submitted to the Bureau by the Customer for
                          inputting on the System.

[**Note**: For data to be converted which is already in electronic form omit the words in square brackets.]

"the Licensed Programs"   means the computer programs specified in Schedule
                          1 which are to be made available by the Bureau
                          under this Agreement.

"the Output"   means the [print-outs] [outputs] resulting from pro-
                          cessing the Data on the System.

[**Note**: The output to be produced will of course vary with the type of service being offered. In the case of
a payroll service one would expect payslips, P60s, etc., the precise form and content of which should be
described in the Specification. For data conversion, the outputs may simply be processed data,
transmitted back to the customer.]

"the Services"   means the services to be provided by the Bureau
                          under this Agreement.

"the Specification"   means the specification of the Services describing
                          inter alia the facilities and functions of the System
                          and the form, content and layout of the Input and
                          the Output a copy of which is annexed hereto.

"the System"   means the Equipment and the Licensed Programs
                          in combination one with the other.

"the Timetable"   means the timing and sequence of events for the
                          delivery of the Input, the processing of the Data
                          and the return of the Output as set out in Schedule
                          2.

[**Note**: Again, the timetable will vary considerably with the type of service being offered. It is essential
that the parties define exactly what their respective responsibilities are. Time limits will usually be
expressed as maxima.]

2 Services to be provided [10.1.1]

The Bureau hereby agrees to:

    (a) provide the use of the System to accept the Input, process the Data and
        produce the Output in accordance with the Timetable;

    (b) provide the other Services hereinafter described,

upon the terms and conditions hereinafter contained.

3 Charges and payment [10.2.1]

(1) The Customer shall pay the following charges for the Services:

    (a) for inputting the Input and processing the Data—[at the rate per *1000
        postings*] as set out in Part A of Schedule 3;

(b) for the storage of the Data—[at the rate per *1000 records* per [business] day] as set out in Part B of Schedule 3;

(c) for outputting the Output [in print form—at the rate per *1,000* lines] [onto [magnetic] [electronic] media—at the rate per Megabyte] as set out in Part C of Schedule 3;

(d) for delivering the Output to the Customer at the rate set out in Part D of Schedule 3.

[**Note**: the precise charging structure will obviously depend upon the nature of the services being provided, and also whether Schedule 3 will include a regime of service credits, which will reduce payments in the event of poor performance.]

(2) The Bureau shall invoice the Customer monthly in arrears for the charges referred to in clause 3(1). Each invoice will be paid by the Customer within *30* days after the Customer's receipt of such invoice. The first month for payment shall commence on the date on which the Customer's initial data records are set-up on the System pursuant to clause 6(1).

[(3) Notwithstanding the foregoing the Services shall be subject to the payment of the minimum charge per month specified in Part F of Schedule 3 which charge shall be payable whether or not the Services are actually used by the Customer during the month in question.]

(4) The Bureau shall be entitled at any time and from time to time (subject as mentioned below) after the expiry of the [Initial Period] [the period of *one year* after the Commencement Date] to increase all or any of the charges referred to in clause 4(1) by giving to the Customer not less than *90* days' prior written notice provided that any such increase shall not exceed a percentage equal to the percentage increase in the *Retail Prices Index published by the Central Statistical Office* for the period from the Commencement Date (in the case of the first such increase) or the date on which the immediately preceding increase came into effect pursuant to this sub-clause (in the case of the second or subsequent increase) up to the date of such notice plus *2* per cent and provided further that no increase may be made pursuant to this sub-clause until a period of at least *one* year has elapsed since the date on which the immediately preceding increase came into effect pursuant to this sub-clause.

[**Note**: If a minimum charge is provided for then the bureau may also wish to reserve a right to increase that minimum charge from time to time.]

(5) The charges payable under this Agreement are exclusive of Value Added Tax which shall be paid by the Customer at the rate and in the manner for the time being prescribed by law.

(6) If any sum payable under this Agreement is not paid within *7* days after the due date then (without prejudice to the Bureau's other rights and remedies) the Bureau reserves the right to suspend the provision of the Services and/or to charge interest on such sum on a day to day basis (as well after as before any judgment) from the date or last date for payment thereof to the date of actual payment (both dates inclusive) at the rate of *2* per cent above the base rate of *ABC* Bank plc (or such other London Clearing Bank as the Bureau may nominate) from time to time in force compounded quarterly. Such interest shall be paid on demand by the Bureau.

4 Duration

This Agreement shall commence on the Commencement Date, shall continue for the Initial Period and shall remain in force thereafter [unless or] until terminated by either party giving to the other not less than *6* months' written notice of termination [given on] [expiring on] the last day of the Initial Period or at any time thereafter but shall be subject to earlier termination as provided elsewhere in this Agreement.

[**Note:** Delete the first and third bracketed phrases if the agreement is to be for a minimum period equal to the Initial Period plus the notice period. Delete the second bracketed phrase if the agreement is to be for a minimum period equal to the Initial Period.]

5 Warranty

The Bureau warrants and undertakes that the Services will be provided in accordance with the Specification but not further or otherwise. The Customer acknowledges that the Services are not being provided to the Customer to meet the Customer's individual requirements and that it is therefore the responsibility of the Customer to ensure that the services described in the Specification meet the Customer's requirements. The Bureau shall not be responsible for providing any service not described in the Specification.

6 Set-up of customer's records [10.3.1]

(1) The Customer shall be responsible for delivering to the Bureau within *7* days after the Commencement Date the Customer's initial data records described in the Specification. The Bureau shall be responsible for setting-up such records on the System within *one* week after such delivery.

(2) The Customer shall pay the Bureau the sum of £*500* for setting-up its data records in accordance with clause 6(1), which sum shall be paid on the execution of this Agreement.

7 Preparation of the input [10.1.1, 10.3.1, 10.3.2, 10.6]

(1) The Customer shall be responsible for preparing the Input in the form and layout described in the Specification.

EITHER (VERSION A Eye-readable data):

[(2) The Bureau does not accept responsibility for any loss or damage sustained or incurred by the Customer as a result of the Input being incorrect, illegible or not being prepared in accordance with the Specification. The Bureau shall not however input or attempt to input on to the System any part of the Input which it becomes aware is illegible or otherwise faulty but shall instead request the Customer to correct the fault in question. The Bureau reserves the right to charge for any additional work required as a result of any element the Input being incorrect, illegible or not being prepared in accordance with the Specification.]

OR (VERSION B Electronic input):

[(2) The Bureau does not accept any loss or damage sustained or incurred by the Customer as a result of the Input not being in accordance with the Specification. The Bureau shall not however input or attempt to input on to the System any part of the Input which it becomes aware is not in accordance with the Specification but instead shall ask the Customer to correct the data to make it conform to the Specification. The Bureau reserves the right to charge for any additional work required as a result of any element of the Input not being in accordance with the Specification.]

(3) The Customer shall deliver the Input to the Bureau at the Bureau's Premises in accordance with the Timetable. The cost of such delivery shall be borne by the Customer. The Bureau reserves the right to make a charge for any additional costs incurred by the Bureau as a result of the late arrival or non-arrival of the Input.

[**Note**: This clause assumes that there will be a regular delivery of data. Where data is to be provided by the customer on an irregular basis it will be necessary to establish a procedure for booking time on the computer. The timetable will then come into effect once time has been booked.]

(4) The Customer shall be responsible for keeping a duplicate of the Input as delivered to the Bureau for a period of at least *14* days after such delivery.

8 Processing of the data and delivery of the output [10.3.1]

(1) Following receipt of the Input from the Customer the Bureau shall input the same on the System, process the Data as required by the Specification and deliver the Output to the Customer in accordance with the Timetable.

(2) The Bureau shall produce the Output in the form specified in the Specification.

9 On-line storage of the data

The Customer shall be entitled to store on-line on the Equipment such programs and data as it shall require provided that the total storage volume for all such programs and data at any one time shall not exceed *100* Gigabytes and provided also that the total volume of such programs and data resident in the main memory of the Equipment at any one time shall not exceed *200* Gigabytes.

10 Off-line storage of the data

(1) The Bureau shall at the request of the Customer write to [magnetic] [electronic] storage media all or any part of the Customer's programs and/or data from time to time stored on-line on the Equipment subject to the Customer giving to the Bureau at least *2* business days' notice in writing.

(2) Upon receiving such a request the Bureau shall take two copies of the programs or data in question, one of which shall be kept by the Bureau and one of which shall be delivered to the Customer at the Customer's expense.

(3) The Bureau shall keep the media to be held by it [in its fireproof safe] at the Bureau's Premises.

(4) The Bureau shall not be liable to the Customer for any loss or damage sustained or incurred by the Customer resulting from any loss or destruction of or damage to any of the media held by the Bureau unless such loss, destruction or damage is caused by the wilful misconduct of the Bureau, its employees, agents or sub-contractors provided however that nothing in this sub-clause shall affect the Bureau's liability under clause 17(4).

(5) If any of the media held by the Bureau shall be lost, destroyed or damaged then the Bureau shall forthwith make duplicates of such media and for this purpose the Customer shall promptly make available to the Bureau the copies of such media held by the Customer. Where any media held by the Bureau is lost, destroyed or damaged due to the negligence or wilful misconduct of the Bureau, its employees,

agents or sub-contractors then the cost of making such duplicates shall be borne by the Bureau.

(6) The Bureau shall not be responsible for the loss or spoiling of any of the Customer's programs or data stored on [magnetic] [electronic] media if such programs or data were dumped on to that media more than 3 months previously. The Bureau will at the request of the Customer take duplicates of any of the Customer's programs or data stored off-line on [magnetic] [electronic] media subject to the Customer giving to the Bureau at least 2 business days' notice in writing. Where any of the Customer's programs or data are lost or spoiled by reason of their deterioration on [magnetic] [electronic] media within the said period of 3 months then the Bureau will forthwith make duplicates of such media free of charge and for this purpose the Customer will promptly make available the copies of such media held by it. The foregoing states the entire liability of the Bureau for the loss or spoiling of any of the Customer's programs or data by reason of their deterioration on [magnetic] [electronic] media.

(7) Subject to the provisions of clause 9, the Bureau shall at the request of the Customer load on to the Equipment all or any part of the Customer's programs and/or data from time to time stored off-line on magnetic media subject to the Customer giving to the Bureau at least 2 business days' notice in writing.

11 Security copies

The Bureau shall take each business day a single security copy of the Data and shall keep such security copies for a period of *one week* after copying. The Bureau shall not charge for making such security copies but their storage and use (subject to the other provisions of this Agreement) shall be subject to such conditions as the Bureau may from time to time impose.

12 Maintenance of the system

(1) (a) The Bureau shall be responsible for maintaining the Equipment in good working order and condition.

    (b) If the Equipment shall fail or breakdown the Bureau shall use its reasonable endeavours promptly to restore the Equipment to its proper operating condition [and shall in the meantime whenever possible provide suitable alternative equipment for the Customer's use].

[Note: The customer may require a more positive commitment to provide back-up equipment in the event of a breakdown. The position is usually clear cut—either the Bureau will have a back-up machine or it will not. The unavailability of the Equipment will also impact upon any service credit regime set out in Schedule 3.]

(2) If the Customer shall become aware of any fault in the Licensed Programs then the Customer shall promptly notify the Bureau. Upon receipt of such notification (or upon receipt of a similar notification from one of the Bureau's other customers) the Bureau shall forthwith use its reasonable endeavours to procure that such fault is corrected as quickly as possible.

[Note: This Clause assumes that the bureau does not own the licensed programs and that the bureau would have to arrange for the proprietor to correct the fault.]

(3) (a) In the event of any breakdown of or fault in the System with consequent loss or spoiling of the Data or any part thereof the Bureau shall use such

security copies as described in clause 11 to reconstitute the Data free of charge as soon as reasonably practicable after the System is available for use again (in accordance with known priorities).

(b) The Bureau shall notify the Customer of any such breakdown or fault and of such reconstitution of the Data from such security copies within *24* hours after such reconstitution.

(4) Clause 12(3) states the entire liability of the Bureau for any loss or spoiling of the Data caused by any breakdown of or fault in the System. The Bureau shall not be liable for any other loss or damage sustained or incurred by the Customer as a result of any breakdown of or fault in the System except to the extent that such loss or damage arises from any unreasonable delay by the Bureau in performing its obligations under Clauses 12(1) and 12(2) above.

[13 Changes in law [9.1.2]

The Bureau will from time to time make (or procure the making of such modifications to the Licensed Programs as shall ensure that the Licensed Programs conform to any change of legislation or new legal requirements which materially affect the application of any function or facility described in the Specification. The Bureau shall promptly notify the Customer in writing of all such changes and new requirements and shall implement the modifications to the Licensed Programs (and all consequential amendments to the Specification which may be necessary to describe and enable proper use of such modifications) as soon as reasonably practicable thereafter.]

[14 Loss of the input or output [10.7.3]

(1) If the Input or any part thereof shall be lost, destroyed or damaged prior to the inputting thereof whilst in the Bureau's possession then the Bureau shall forthwith notify the Customer who shall promptly supply the Bureau with the copy of the Input retained by the Customer pursuant to clause 7(4). The Bureau shall thereupon use such copy for inputting the Input. The cost of delivering such copy shall be borne by the Customer unless such loss, damage or destruction of the Input is caused by any negligent act or omission or breach of this Agreement by the Bureau, its employees, agents or sub-contractors.

(2) If the Output or any part thereof shall be lost, damaged or destroyed prior to the delivery thereof to the Customer then the Bureau shall produce a further copy as soon as possible thereafter. The cost of producing such further copy shall be borne by the Customer unless such loss, damage or destruction of the Output is caused by any negligent act or omission or breach of this Agreement by the Bureau, its employees, agents or sub-contractors.]

[**Note:** Clause 14 is likely to become less common as on-line inputting and outputting of data becomes the norm.]

15 Volumes [10.1.4]

The Services shall be performed in accordance with the Timetable unless the volume of the Input shall exceed the maximum specified volumes as set out in the Specification. Any work in excess of the said maximum volumes shall be performed by the Bureau as soon as reasonably practicable having regard to the Bureau's other commitments.

16 Rectification of errors [10.7.3]

If the Output or any part thereof is incorrect by reason of a breakdown of or a fault in the System or of a mistake due to the negligence or inadvertence of the Bureau, its employees, agents or sub-contractors then the Bureau shall promptly correct and reprocess the Data free of charge to produce the Output in the correct form provided that the error in question is notified to the Bureau in writing within *14* days after the [Customer's receipt of the Output]. [Customer became owner of the inaccuracy.] [The foregoing states the entire liability of the Bureau for errors in the Output.]

[**Note**: the extent of the bureau's liability under this clause is likely to be subject to debate; the customer will be concerned about the potential damage to its business which could result from incorrect data, but the bureau will likewise be concerned to restrict its exposure to such losses. Ultimately, much will depend on whether it will practically be possible to redress any damage caused by reprocessing the data concerned.]

17 Ownership of the input, data and output [10.7.1]

(1) The Input, the Data and the Output (hereinafter collectively referred to as "the Customer's Data") shall be and shall remain the property of the Customer.

(2) The Bureau shall protect and defend the Customer's title to the Customer's Data against all persons claiming against or through the Bureau and shall use its reasonable endeavours to keep the same free from any distress, execution or other legal process.

(3) (a) The Bureau shall treat as confidential information and shall keep secret the Customer's Data. The Bureau shall not without the prior written consent of the Customer divulge the whole or any part of the Customer's Data to any person except the Bureau's own employees and then only to those employees who need to know the same, and only to the extent necessary for the proper performance of this Agreement.

(b) The Bureau undertakes to ensure that its employees are made aware that the Customer's Data is confidential and that such employees owe a duty of confidence to the Customer. The Bureau shall indemnify the Customer against any loss or damage which the Customer may sustain or incur as a result of the Bureau failing to comply with such undertaking.

(c) The Bureau shall promptly notify the Customer if the Bureau becomes aware of any breach of confidence by any of the Bureau's employees and shall give the Customer all reasonable assistance in connection with any legal proceedings which the Customer may bring against any such employees or any other person for breach of confidence.

(d) The foregoing obligations as to confidentiality shall remain in full force and effect notwithstanding any termination of this Agreement (howsoever occasioned) but shall not apply to any information which:

(i) comes into the public domain other than by way of a breach of this Agreement by the Bureau;

(ii) is received by the Bureau from a third party who does not breach any duty of confidence in disclosing it; or

(iii) is required to be disclosed by law, by any court of competent jurisdiction or by any regulatory or administrative body.

(4) The Bureau will establish and maintain proper security measures and procedures to provide for the safe custody of the Customer's Data and to prevent unauthorised access thereto or use thereof. The Bureau shall indemnify the Customer against any loss or damage which the Customer may sustain or incur consequent upon the Customer's Data or any part thereof coming into the possession of any unauthorised person as a direct result of any negligent act or omission or breach of this Agreement by the Bureau, its employees, agents or sub-contractors [provided that notwithstanding anything to the contrary in clause 27, the total liability of the Bureau therefor shall not in any event exceed £100,000 in respect of each event or series of connected events, or £500,000 in the aggregate.

(5) (a) Upon any termination of this Agreement (howsoever occasioned) the Customer shall have the right to require the Bureau to do any one or more of the following:

(i) to deliver up to the Customer all or any off-line storage and security copies of the Data then in the Bureau's possession subject to the Customer reimbursing the Bureau for the cost of the [magnetic] media on which they are stored;

(ii) to write on to [magnetic] [electronic] media (or such other media as the Customer may reasonably specify) the Data or any part thereof and to deliver up such media to the Customer subject to the Customer paying the charges for such dumping at the applicable rate from time to time payable hereunder and to reimbursing the Bureau for the cost of such media;

(iii) to erase all or any of the Data from the media then in the Bureau's possession on which it is stored.

(iv) to deliver up to the Customer all copies of the Input and the Output then in the possession of the Bureau or to destroy the same;

(v) to make and deliver up to the Customer such print-outs of the Data as the Customer may require subject to the Customer paying the charges for such print-outs at the applicable rate from time to time payable hereunder.

(b) If upon any termination of this Agreement the Customer shall require the Bureau to deliver up any of the Data on [magnetic] [electronic] media then the Bureau shall:

(i) deliver up such data on industry compatible [magnetic] [electronic] media;

(ii) supply to the Customer free of charge all information necessary to enable such [magnetic] [electronic] media to be read on another computer;

(c) Except where this Agreement is properly terminated by the Customer as a result of any breach by the Bureau of any term hereof, the Bureau's obligations under paragraphs (a) and (b) of this clause 17(5) shall be conditional upon the Customer having paid all charges then due to the Bureau under the terms of this Agreement.

18 Intellectual property rights indemnities [2.8; 3.8]

(1) The Bureau shall indemnify the Customer against any claim by any third party for alleged infringement of any copyright or other intellectual property rights which

arises as a result of the use of the Equipment or the Licensed Programs in accordance with the terms of this Agreement provided that the Bureau is given immediate and complete control of any such claim, that the Customer does not prejudice the Bureau's defence of such claim and that the Customer gives the Bureau all reasonable assistance with such claim (at the Bureau's expense).

(2) The Customer shall indemnify the Bureau against any claim by any third party for alleged infringement of any copyright or other intellectual property rights which arises as a result of the storage or processing of any of the Customer's programs or data on the Equipment provided that the Customer is given immediate and complete control of any such claim, that the Bureau does not prejudice the Customer's defence of such claim and that the Bureau gives the Customer all reasonable assistance with such claim (at the Customer's expense).

19 Bureau's confidential information [10.6.3]

(1) The Customer shall treat as confidential and shall keep secret all information obtained by it under this Agreement concerning the Services and the System provided that such obligation shall not extend to information which:

(a) comes into the public domain other than by way of a breach of this Agreement by the Customer;

(b) is received by the Customer from a third party who does not breach of any duty of confidence in disclosing it; or

(c) is required to be disclosed by law, by any court of competent jurisdiction or by any regulatory or administrative body.

(2) The Customer shall not without the prior written consent of the Bureau divulge any of such confidential information to any person except:

(a) the Customer's own employees and then only to those employees who need to know the same; or

(b) the Customer's auditors, HM Inspector of Taxes, Customs & Excise and any other persons or bodies having a right, duty or obligation to know the business of the Customer and then only in pursuance of such right, duty or obligation.

The Customer shall be responsible for ensuring that the persons and bodies mentioned in paragraphs (a) and (b) are made aware prior to the disclosure of any such confidential information that the same is confidential and that they owe a duty of confidence to the Bureau. The Customer shall promptly notify the Bureau if it becomes aware of any breach of confidence by any such person or body and shall give the Bureau all reasonable assistance in connection with any legal proceedings which the Bureau may bring against any such person or body or any other person for breach of confidence.

20 Use of the services

Except as may be otherwise agreed by the Bureau the Customer shall use the Services only for [inputting] [converting] its own data for its own internal business purposes and shall not use the Services on behalf of or for the benefit of any third party.

21 Contents of the data
See clause 14 of Precedent P.

22 Data protection [10.3.3]
See clause 9 of Precedent L.

23 Termination
See clause 10 of Precedent L.

24 Customer's warranty
See clause 20 of Precedent A.

25 Assignment
See clause 30 of Precedent A.

26 Force majeure
See clause 16 of Precedent K.

27 Liability
See clause 27 of Precedent A.

28 Waiver of remedies
See clause 28 of Precedent A.

29 Entire agreement
See clause 29 of Precedent A.

30 Notices
See clause 32 of Precedent A.

31 Interpretation
See clause 33 of Precedent A.

32 Law
See clause 34 of Precedent A.

33 Disputes
Any dispute which may arise between the parties concerning this Agreement shall be determined by the English Courts and the parties hereby submit to the exclusive jurisdiction of the English Courts for such purpose.

[Note: An alternative is to provide for an expert or an arbitrator to resolve disputes—see Clause 37 of Precedent D—or use the British Computer Society Recommended clause [15.1.1].]

34 Severability
See clause 36 of Precedent A.

35 Third Parties

See clause 37 of Precedent A.

EXECUTED under hand in two originals the day and year first before written

SIGNED for and on behalf of
COMPUTER BUREAU COMPANY [LIMITED] [PLC]

By

Signature

Title

Witness

SIGNED for and on behalf of
CUSTOMER [LIMITED] [PLC]

By

Signature

Title

Witness

SCHEDULE 1

A   THE EQUIPMENT

B   THE LICENSED PROGRAMS

C   THE COMMENCEMENT DATE

D   THE INITIAL PERIOD

SCHEDULE 2

THE TIMETABLE

SCHEDULE 3

CHARGES

A   INPUT RATE

B   STORAGE RATE

C   OUTPUT RATE

D   DELIVERY RATE

[E   SERVICE CREDITS]

[F   MINIMUM CHARGE]

[SCHEDULE 4

THIRD-PARTY RIGHTS]

[**Note**: This agreement requires to be annexed to it. The specification of the Services (clause 1):

    (a) the facilities and functions of the System;

    (b) form, content and layout of the Input;

    (c) form, content and layout of the Output;

    (d) maximum volume (clause 15).

NETWORK SERVICE LEVEL AGREEMENT

THIS AGREEMENT is made the　　　　day of　　　20

PARTIES:

(1) SERVICE COMPANY [LIMITED] [PLC] whose registered office is at

("the Service Provider")

(2) CUSTOMER [LIMITED] [PLC] whose registered office is at

("the Customer")

RECITALS:

(A) The Service Provider carries on the business of providing information technology services for customers

(B) The Service Provider has agreed to permit the Customer to use its Network and Services upon the terms and conditions hereinafter contained

1 Definitions

In this Agreement, unless the context otherwise requires, the following expressions have the following meanings:

"business day"	means a day other than a Saturday, Sunday or a public holiday in England and Wales.
"the Commencement Date"	means the date on which this Agreement shall become effective as specified in Schedule 1.
"the Customer's Data"	means any data input onto the Network by the Customer.
"the Customer's Equipment"	means the Customer's computer[s] as specified in Schedule 1.
"the Customer's Staff"	means the Customer's staff specified in Schedule 1 and such other members of the Customer's staff as may be agreed in writing between the Service Provider and the Customer from time to time.
"the Documentation"	means the documentation specified in Schedule 1.
"the Helpdesk Services"	means the helpdesk services included in the Services as specified in Schedule 1.

"the Initial Period"	means the initial period of this Agreement as specified in Schedule 1.
"the Management Personnel"	means the senior and/or administrative personnel named or filling the positions in Schedule 1 who shall be authorised to make general mailings of email for the purposes of clause 3(9).
["the Modem"	means [the modem specified in Schedule 1 which is to be let on hire to the Customer under this Agreement] [any suitable modem of the Customer [installed as part of the Customer's Equipment].]

[**Note:** the customer may provide his own modem in which case the second alternative may be used.]

"the Network"	means the cabling, equipment and software by which the Service Provider provides the Services as specified in Schedule 1.
["the Network Area"	means the area covered by the Network as specified in Schedule 1.]

[**Note:** If this agreement is between different divisions of the same company or different companies in the same group, the network area may be defined as the company's building or buildings in a particular place.]

["the Network Card"	means the network card specified in Schedule 1 which is provided to the Customer by the Service Provider and installed in the Customer's Equipment by the Service Provider.]
"the Security Procedures"	means the security procedures specified in Schedule 1.
"the Security Passwords"	has the meaning attributed thereto in clause 3(1)(c).
"the Services"	means the services specified in Schedule 1.
["the Software"	means the programs specified in Schedule 1 which are to be made available by the Service Provider for use by the Customer to gain access to the Network and the Services.]
"the Training"	means the training specified in Schedule 1.

2 Services to be provided [10.1.3, 10.7.1]

The Service Provider hereby agrees to:

(1) permit the Customer to use the Services [and the Software] over the Network [within the Network Area] [by means of [the Network Card] [and] [the Modem];]

(2) provide the Customer with the Helpdesk Services;

(3) comply with the service quality criteria set out in Schedule 3, upon the terms and conditions hereinafter contained.

3 Access and use

(1) On or before the Commencement Date the Service Provider shall provide the Customer with:

(a) the Training;

(b) the Documentation;

(c) security passwords ("the Security Passwords") to enable the Customer and each of the Customer's [authorised] Staff to obtain access to the Network and the Services;

(d) the telephone number of and access to the Helpdesk Services;

[(e) the Software;]

[(f) the Modem;]

[(g) the Network Card.]

[(2) Subject to clause 6, the Customer shall be entitled to use [the Network Card] [and] [the Modem] for the purposes of gaining access to the Network and the Services thereon.

(3) The Customer shall use the [Network Card and] [Modem and] [Software and] Network only for access to and use of the Services for its own internal business purposes and shall not make the use of the [Network Card] [and] [Modem or] [Software or] Network available to any third party nor use the [Network Card] [and] [Modem or] Network on behalf of or for the benefit of any third party.

(4) The Service Provider shall make the Network and Services available to the Customer [by means of the Modem] [during the hours of *8.00 a.m.* to *7.00 p.m.* each business day.]

[Note: There may well be no restriction on the hours when the Network is actually available though there is likely to be a restriction on the hours when the Helpdesk is available.]

(5) The Service Provider shall provide the Helpdesk Services to the Customer during the hours of *8.00 a.m* to *7.00 p.m.* each business day.

[(6) The Service Provider hereby grants the Customer a licence to use the Software to the extent required in connection with the receipt of the Services and in accordance with the terms of this Agreement but not further or otherwise.]

(7) Except as expressly permitted by this Agreement, the Customer shall not attempt to obtain access to or interfere with any programs or data of the Service Provider or of any other customer of the Service Provider and shall indemnify the Service Provider against any loss, damage or liability which the Service Provider may sustain or incur as a consequence of the Customer failing to comply with such undertaking.

[Note: Breach of this is also likely to be an offence under section 1(1) of the Computer Misuse Act 1990.]

(8) The Service Provider shall have the right upon giving to the Customer not less than 2 weeks' notice in writing to take the Network down and deny the Customer

the use of the Network and the Services [and the Software] on a Saturday, Sunday or public holiday in England and Wales for a maximum of *88 hours* in any one calendar year.

[**Note**: The Network downtime in the above example amounts to only about 1 per cent of the total availability time during the course of the year. The service provider will probably also wish to retain some leeway in terms of unplanned downtime/unavailability, which would ordinarily be addressed by the setting of the service levels in Schedule 3.]

(9) The Customer shall not and shall procure that the Customer's Staff shall not without the Service Provider's prior written consent send messages using the electronic mail service comprised in the Services to all other users over the Network simultaneously, save as required by the Management Personnel.

[**Note**: Unacceptably heavy traffic may be generated by mass mailing over a network and the irritation among users can be considerable, eg in relation to "spamming". In most systems there is a bulletin board service which provides the mechanism whereby general messages can be posted to all users and the purpose of this Clause is to encourage the users to use the bulletin board service rather than sending generally addressed e-mails. However, the need for organisation-wide mailings by senior and/or administrative personnel means that limited authorisation to make general mailings may be required, e.g. for heads of personnel, security managers, department heads etc.]

4 Charges and payment

(1) The Customer shall pay the following charges for the services to be provided by the Service Provider hereunder:

(a) for the Training at the rates set out in Part A of Schedule 2;

(b) for the Documentation at the rates set out in Part B of Schedule 2;

(c) for the use of the Network and the provision of the Services [including the Software] at the rate set out in Part C of Schedule 2;

[(d) for the use of the Modem at the monthly rate set out in Part D of Schedule 2;]

[(e) for the use of the Network Card at the monthly rate set out in Part E of Schedule 2.]

(2) The Service Provider shall invoice the Customer monthly in arrears for the charges referred to clause 4(1). Each invoice will be paid by the Customer within *30* days after the Customer's receipt of such invoice.

(3) The Service Provider shall be entitled at any time and from time to time (subject as mentioned below) after the expiry of the [Initial Period] [the period of *one year* after the Commencement Date] to increase all or any of the charges referred to in clause 4 (1) by giving to the Customer not less than *90* days' prior written notice provided that any such increase shall not exceed a percentage equal to the percentage increase in the *Retail Prices Index published by the Central Statistical Office* for the period from the Commencement Date (in the case of the first such increase) or the date on which the immediately preceding increase came into effect pursuant to this sub-clause (in the case of the second or subsequent increase) up to the date of such notice plus *2* per cent and provided further that no increase may be made pursuant to this sub-clause until a period of at least *one* year has elapsed since the date on which the immediately preceding increase came into effect pursuant to this sub-clause.

(4) The charges payable under this Agreement are exclusive of Value Added Tax which shall be paid by the Customer at the rate and in the manner for the time being prescribed by law.

(5) If any sum payable under this Agreement is not paid within 7 days after the due date then (without prejudice to the Service Provider's other rights and remedies) the Service Provider reserves the right to suspend the provision of the Services and/ or to charge interest on such sum on a day to day basis (as well after as before any judgment) from the date or last date for payment thereof to the date of actual payment (both dates inclusive) at the rate of 2 per cent above the base rate of *ABC* Bank plc (or such other London Clearing Bank as the Service Provider may nominate) from time to time in force compounded quarterly. Such interest shall be paid on demand by the Service Provider.

[**Note**: it is also common to find that the service levels set in Schedule 3 are linked with service credits, *i.e.* pre-set reductions in the charges which might be set out in Schedule 2 and accrue whenever a required service level has not been met, and which are deducted from the sums otherwise payable to the service provider.]

5 Duration

This Agreement shall commence on the Commencement Date, shall continue for the Initial Period and shall remain in force thereafter [unless or] until terminated by either party giving to the other not less than 6 months' written notice of termination [given on] [expiring on] the last day of the Initial Period or at any time thereafter but shall be subject to earlier termination as provided elsewhere in this Agreement.

[**Note**: Delete the first and third bracketed phrases if the agreement is to be for a minimum period equal to the Initial Period plus the notice period. Delete the second bracketed phrase if the agreement is to be for a minimum period equal to the Initial Period.]

[6 The modem and network card [10.6.2]

(1) The Service Provider shall let and the Customer shall take on hire [the Network Card] [and] [the Modem] for the duration of this Agreement.

(2) The Customer shall be responsible for providing proper operating conditions for the [the Network Card] [and] [Modem] in accordance with the Service Provider's instructions before the delivery of the [the Network Card] [and] [Modem].

(3) The Service Provider shall deliver the [the Network Card] [and] [Modem] to the Customer on or before the Commencement Date.

[(4) The Service Provider shall install the Network Card in the Customer's Equipment.]

(5) Prior to the delivery of [the Network Card] [and] [Modem]the Customer shall:

   (a) arrange for the provision of a telephone line to connect the Modem to the Network; and

   (b) obtain and produce to the Service Provider any necessary consents for such connection.

(6) The [Network Card] [and] Modem shall at all times remain the sole and exclusive property of the Service Provider and the Customer shall have no right or interest therein except for quiet possession and the right to use the same during the term of this Agreement and upon the terms and conditions contained in this Agreement.

(7) [The Network Card] [and] [Modem]shall be at the risk of the Service Provider which shall be responsible for insuring the same against all normal risks. The

Customer shall notify the Service Provider immediately of any loss or damage to [the Network Card] [and] [Modem]and shall give all necessary information and assistance to the Service Provider in connection with any such loss or damage.

(8) The Customer shall not create or suffer to exist over the [the Network Card] [and] [Modem] any mortgage, charge, lien or other encumbrance.

(9) The Customer shall not utilise or attempt to utilise any modem other than the Modem for the purpose of obtaining access to the Network and the Services.

(10) The Customer shall use [the Network Card] [and] [Modem] only for the purpose of obtaining access to the Network [and the Software] in accordance with the terms of this Agreement.

(11) The Service Provider shall provide preventive and corrective maintenance for [the Network Card] [and] [Modem] during the hours of *8.00 a.m.* to *7.00 p.m.* on business days ("Working Hours").

(12) Corrective maintenance shall be performed by the Service Provider during Working Hours as soon as possible after the Customer's request therefor on the basis of a response time of *8* Working Hours but such response time is an estimate only and shall not be binding on the Service Provider.

(13) The Customer shall not without the prior written consent of the Service Provider permit any person, firm or company other than the Service Provider (or a person appointed for such purpose by the Service Provider) to carry out or attempt to carry out maintenance, adjustment replacement or repair of [the Network Card] [and] [Modem]or any part thereof.

(14) Save for the purposes of preventative and corrective maintenance as set out in clauses 6 (11) and (12) above the Customer shall ensure that [the Network Card] [and] [Modem] be not moved from connection with the Customer's Equipment except with the prior written consent of the Service Provider.

(15) Upon termination of the Customer's right to hire [the Network Card] [and] [Modem] (for any reason) the Customer shall forthwith redeliver possession of [the Network Card] [and] [Modem] to the Service Provider in a condition consistent with the proper performance by the Customer of its obligations under this clause and the Service Provider shall for the purpose have access to the Customer's premises (or any other place where [the Network Card] [and] [Modem] may be situated).]

7 Security

(1) The Service Provider shall periodically require the Customer to change the Security Passwords in accordance with the Security Procedures and shall notify the Customer accordingly. If either party becomes aware, or shall suspect, that any unauthorised person has obtained or has attempted to obtain access to the Services or the Network by means of any of the Security Passwords, then they shall promptly notify the other party and the Service Provider shall forthwith cancel such of the Security Passwords as are thought to have been affected by the breach of security and, if necessary, issue the Customer with replacement Security Passwords.

(2) The Customer shall and the Customer shall procure that each member of the Customer's Staff shall at all times comply with all the Security Procedures. If the Service Provider shall become aware that the Customer or any of the Customer's staff has failed to comply with the Security Procedures the Service Provider shall notify the Customer and have the right to exclude the Customer or such of the Customer's Staff as it suspects to have failed to comply with the Security Procedures from all use of the Network and the Services forthwith until such time as the Customer or such of the Customer's Staff as have been so excluded shall have complied with the Security Procedures.

[Note: the security procedures (Schedule 1 J) may well include a requirement that the customer's users obtain and keep up to date a specific virus-protection software and use it to test all data and software input by them.]

8 Maintenance of the network [and the Software]

(1) (a) The Service Provider shall be responsible for maintaining the Network in good working order and condition.

(b) If the Network shall fail or break down the Service Provider shall use its reasonable endeavours promptly to restore the Network to its proper operating condition and shall notify the Customer when this is the case.

[Note: the customer may require a more positive commitment to appropriate measures in the event of a breakdown. The position is usually clear cut: either the Service Provider will have back-up servers and gateways or alternative cabling routes, or it will not. What constitutes "proper operating condition" may also need to be defined, *e.g.* by reference to availability and response times.]

[(2) If the Customer should become aware of any fault in the Software then the Customer shall promptly notify the Service Provider and shall provide the Service Provider with such information as it is reasonably able to in order to assist the Service Provider in the diagnosis and correction of the fault. Upon receipt of such notification (or upon receipt of a similar notification from one of the Service Provider's other customers) the Service Provider shall forthwith use its reasonable endeavours to procure that such fault is corrected as quickly as possible and shall notify the Customer when this has been done.]

[Note: This Clause assumes that the service provider does not own the software and that the service provider would have to arrange for the proprietor to correct the fault.]

(3) In the event of any failure or breakdown of the Network [or any fault in the Software] with the consequent loss of spoiling or the Customer's Data or any part thereof the Service Provider shall notify the Customer as soon as reasonably practicable after the Network [and the Software] are available for use again.

(4) The Service Provider shall not be liable for any loss or damage sustained or incurred by the Customer as a result of any failure or breakdown of the Network [or fault in the Software] except to the extent that such loss or damage arises from any unreasonable delay by the Service Provider in performing its obligations under sub-clauses (1) [and (2)] above.

[Note: If there is no software provided by the service provider all the bracketed phrases in the above clause must be omitted.]

9 Ownership of data

(1) The Customer's Data shall be and shall remain the property of the Customer.

(2) (a) The Service Provider undertakes to treat as confidential and keep secret all information ("the Information") contained or embodied in the Customer's Data.

(b) The Service Provider shall not without the prior written consent of the Customer divulge the whole or any part of the Information to any person except those to whom the Customer shall direct, the Service Provider's employees (and then only to those employees who need to know the same), and/or to the extent necessary for the proper performance of this Agreement.

(c) The Service Provider undertakes to ensure that its employees are made aware that the Information is confidential and that such employees owe a duty of confidence to the Customer. The Service Provider shall indemnify the Customer against any loss or damage which the Customer may sustain or incur as a result of the Service Provider failing to comply with such undertaking.

(d) The Service Provider shall notify the Customer promptly if the Service Provider becomes aware of any breach of confidence by any of the Service Provider's employees and shall give the Customer all reasonable assistance in connection with any legal proceedings which the Customer may bring against any such employees or any other person for breach of confidence.

(e) The foregoing obligations as to confidentiality shall remain in full force and effect notwithstanding any termination of this Agreement (howsoever occasioned), but shall not apply to any information which:

    (i) comes into the public domain other than by way of a breach of this Agreement by the Service Provider;

    (ii) is received by the Service Provider from a third party who does not breach any duty of confidence in disclosing it; or

    (iii) is required to be disclosed by law, by any court of competent jurisdiction or by any regulatory or administrative body.

(3) The Service Provider will establish and maintain proper security measures and procedures to provide for the safe custody of the Customer's Data and to prevent unauthorised access thereto or use thereof. The Service Provider shall indemnify the Customer against any loss or damage which the Customer may sustain or incur consequent upon any of the Customer's Data coming into the possession of any unauthorised person as a result of any negligent act or omission or breach of this Agreement by the Service Provider, its employees, agents or sub-contractors [provided that the Service Provider's liability therefor shall not in any circumstances whatsoever exceed £*100,000* in respect of each event or series of connected events, or £500,000 in the aggregate].

(4) (a) Upon the termination of this Agreement (howsoever occasioned) the Customer shall have the right to require the Service Provider to do one or more of the following:

    (i) to dump on to magnetic media all or any of the Customer's programs and the Customer's Data then stored on-line on the Network and to deliver up such media to the Customer subject to the Customer paying the charges for such dumping and to reimbursing the Service Provider for the cost of such magnetic media;

    (ii) to erase all or any of the Customer's Data then in the Service Provider's possession from the Network on which they are stored;

    (iii) to make and deliver up to the Customer such print-outs of the Customer's Data as the Customer may require subject to the Customer paying the charges for such print-outs at the applicable rate from time to time payable hereunder.

(b) If upon termination of this Agreement the Customer shall require the Service Provider to deliver up any of the Customer's Data on magnetic media then the Service Provider shall:

  (i) deliver up such data on industry compatible magnetic media; and
  (ii) supply to the Customer free of charge all information necessary to enable such magnetic media to be read on another computer.

(c) Except where this Agreement is properly terminated by the Customer as a result of any breach by the Service Provider of its obligations under this Agreement, the Service Provider's obligations under paragraphs (a) and (b) of this clause 9(4) shall be conditional upon the Customer having paid all charges then due to the Service Provider under the terms of this Agreement.

10 Content of the customer's data

The Customer undertakes that the Customer's Data (whether stored on or sent over the Network) will not contain anything obscene, offensive or defamatory, or which is in breach of any laws on regulations. The Customer will indemnify the Service Provider and keep the Service Provider fully and effectively indemnified against all actions, proceedings, claims, demands, damages and costs (including legal costs on a full indemnity basis) occasioned to the Service Provider as a result of any breach of the said undertaking, provided that the Service Provider promptly notifies any such claim to the Customer, does nothing to prejudice the defence of the claim and allows the Customer immediate and complete control of the defence and settlement of the claim. The Service Provider shall provide the Customer with all reasonable assistance required by it in relation to the defence of the claim, at the Customer's expense.

11 Data protection [10.6.3]

See clause 9 of Precedent L.

12 Intellectual property rights indemnities [3.8.1]

See clause 18 of Precedent M.

13 The service provider's confidential information [10.7.1]

See clause 19 of Precedent M.

[14 Warranties

The Service Provider warrants that the Software will provide the facilities and functions necessary to enable the Customer to gain access to the Network and the Services. The Customer acknowledges that the Network and the Software are not being made available to the Customer to meet the Customer's other individual requirements. The Service Provider shall not be liable for any failure of the Software to provide any facility or function other than access to the Network and the Services. The Service Provider's entire liability for any fault in the Software is as stated in clause 8.]

15 Termination [10.4]

(1) See clause 10(1) of Precedent L.

(2) *See clause 10(2) of Precedent L* [(3) In the event of a termination by the Service Provider pursuant to clause 15(1):

(a) the Customer shall no longer be entitled to possession of the [Network Card] [and] [the Modem] and the Service Provider and may without notice repossess the [Network Card] [and] [the Modem] and may for that purpose without notice enter any of the Customer's premises in which the [Network Card] [and] [the Modem] is or are situated or may be reasonably believed by the Service Provider to be situated (and so that the Customer hereby irrevocably licenses the Service Provider, its employees and agents to enter upon any such premises for such purpose);

(b) the Customer shall not be entitled to the repayment of any sums previously paid by it to the Service Provider under the terms of this Agreement nor to any credit or allowance in respect of any such payments].

16 Assignment

See clause 30 of Precedent A.

17 *Force majeure*

See clause 15 of Precedent A.

18 Customer's warranty

See clause 20 of Precedent A.

19 Liability

See clause 27 of Precedent A.

20 Waiver of remedies

See clause 28 of Precedent A.

21 Entire agreement

See clause 29 of Precedent A.

22 Notices

See clause 32 of Precedent A.

23 Interpretation

See clause 33 of Precedent A.

24 Law

See clause 34 of Precedent A.

25 Disputes

Any dispute which may arise between the parties concerning this Agreement shall be determined by the English Courts and the parties hereby submit to the exclusive jurisdiction of the English Courts for such purpose.

[**Note:** An alternative is to provide for an expert or an arbitrator to resolve disputes—see clause 37 of Precedent D—or use the British Computer Society Recommended clause [15.1.1].]

26 Severability

See clause 36 of Precedent A.

27 Third Parties

See clause 37 of Precedent A.

EXECUTED under hand in two originals the day and year first before written

SIGNED for and on behalf of
SERVICE COMPANY [LIMITED] [PLC]

By

Signature

Title

Witness

SIGNED for and on behalf of
CUSTOMER [LIMITED] [PLC]

By

Signature

Title

Witness

SCHEDULE 1

A   THE SERVICES

[**Note**: this will include the Helpdesk Services.]

B   THE NETWORK

[C   THE NETWORK AREA]

D   THE CUSTOMER'S EQUIPMENT

E   THE CUSTOMER'S STAFF

F   THE TRAINING

G   THE DOCUMENTATION

H   THE COMMENCEMENT DATE

I   THE INITIAL PERIOD

J   THE SECURITY PROCEDURES

[K   THE MODEM]

[L   THE NETWORK CARD]

[M   THE SOFTWARE]

[N   THIRD-PARTY RIGHTS]

O   MANAGEMENT PERSONNEL

Schedule 2

CHARGES

A   TRAINING

B   DOCUMENTATION

C   THE NETWORK AND SERVICES

[D THE MODEM]

[E THE NETWORK CARD]

[F SERVICE CREDITS]

Schedule 3

SERVICE QUALITY CRITERIA

[**Note 1**: These will involve such criteria as may be appropriate, *e.g.*:

(a) 95 per cent of all electronic mail of less than two pages in length will be despatched over the Network to be received within 5 minutes of despatch;

(b) 95 per cent of all Helpdesk calls will be answered within 2 minutes;

(c) The Network will be available for 95 per cent of the time in any one calendar year;

etc.]

[**Note 2**: Service levels/requirements will frequently be linked with defined service credits, *i.e.* such that the charges payable to the service provider are automatically reduced if the service levels/requirements are not met.]

OUTSOURCE AGREEMENT

[**Note**: Outsource agreements are inevitably complex documents, which may differ significantly depending on the nature of the business functions being assigned to the service provider. However, this precedent endeavours to provide a basis for the population of such agreements.]

THIS AGREEMENT is made   the   day of   20

PARTIES:

(1) OUTSOURCE PROVIDER [LIMITED[[PLC] whose registered office is at

("the Supplier")

(2) CUSTOMER [LIMITED] [PLC] whose registered office is at

("the Customer")

RECITALS:

(A) The Customer wishes to outsource certain of its [business] [IT] [administrative] functions to the Supplier such that the Supplier will carry out such functions on the Customer's behalf during the term of this Agreement

(B) The Supplier has agreed to provide the services related to such functions upon the terms and conditions hereafter contained

(C) By an Agreement dated [20   ] the Customer has transferred to the Supplier certain [premises] [hardware] [etc.]

NOW IT IS HEREBY AGREED as follows:

1 Definitions

In this Agreement, unless the context otherwise requires, the following expressions have the following meanings:

"Change Control Note"	means the note submitted to the Customer by the Supplier pursuant to clause 3(2).
"Change Request"	means a request by made either Party pursuant to clause 3.
"the Charges"	means the charges payable by the Customer to the Supplier as set out in Schedule 2.
["Commencement of Service Date"	means the date specified for the Supplier's commencement of the provision of the Services to the Customer, as set out in Schedule 7.]

"Contract Manager"	means the individual appointed by the Customer pursuant to clause 8.
"Existing Software"	means the software identified in Schedule 8A which is at present used by the Customer for its operations which are to be the subject of the Services; and which will be required by the Supplier to enable it to provide the Services under this Agreement.
"the Expert"	means the independent expert as defined in clause 28(3).
"Faults"	means significant interruptions to the Services or the Service Levels.
"the Helpdesk"	means the Supplier's help desk in place to respond to reports of faults, problems and enquiries by Users.
"the Implementation Plan"	means the implementation plan as set out at Schedule 7.
"Intellectual Property Rights"	means the copyright and all other intellectual property rights (including, without limitation, in patents, trademarks, service marks, domain names, database rights, and design rights, (whether registered or unregistered)) arising from the provision of the Services.
"Key Milestone"	means the milestone dates/events as identified in the Implementation Plan.
"Key Personnel"	means the Supplier personnel as set out in Schedule 6.
"London Clearing Bank"	means the bank nominated by the Supplier pursuant to clause 4(5).
"Project Manager"	means the individual appointed by the Supplier pursuant to clause 8.
"Service Credits"	means the credits which become payable to the Customer by way of a reduction in the Charges where the Service Levels are not achieved, and as set out in Schedule 4.
"Service Levels"	means the levels of service required of the Supplier as set out in Schedule 3.
"the Services"	means the services to be provided by the Supplier to the Customer as set out in Schedule 1.

"Steering Committee"   means the committee comprising [   ] individ-
                             uals appointed by [   ].

"Transfer Payment"   means the sum to be paid to the Customer by the
                             Supplier in consideration of the transfer to the Sup-
                             plier of the assets specified in Schedule 8.

[**Note**: such transfer payments may simply be nominal or may reflect a genuine pre-estimate of value; in
either event, the effect will be costed in to the supplier's charges.]

2 Services to be provided [11.1]

(1) The Supplier agrees to provide the Services during the term of this Agreement.

(2) The Supplier undertakes to provide the Services with reasonable skill and care
in accordance with relevant industry best practice.

(3) In providing the Services, the Supplier shall take account and comply with all
reasonable directions provided by the Customer's Contract Manager.

(4) The Services shall be provided in accordance with the Implementation Plan,
such that the Supplier is able to achieve the Key Milestones set out therein,
provided always that the Key Milestones shall be amended to the extent reasonably
necessary in order to reflect:

(a) any breach of any obligations of the Customer under this Agreement and/
    or negligence by it; and/or

(b) any cause of delay which was beyond the reasonable control of the
    Supplier.

(5) In the event that a Key Milestone is not achieved other than by reason of a
matter falling within clause 2(4)(a) or (b), the Supplier shall compensate the
Customer for its losses resulting from such delay in the sum of £500 for each day of
delay beyond the relevant Key Milestone, such sums being agreed by the parties to
represent a genuine pre-estimate of the Customer's likely loss resulting from such
delay. Such compensation shall be payable for a maximum of 50 days following each
Key Milestone and shall represent the Supplier's sole liability for any loss suffered
by the Customer by reason of the delay during the relevant 50 day period, provided
always that the Customer shall not be constrained by this clause 2(5) from seeking
any remedy or enforcing any right available to it during such period arising from
any other provision of this Agreement.

[**Note**: this provision would be appropriate when the initiation of the outsourced services is time critical,
i.e. so as to commence in line with the expiry of an existing arrangement in order to ensure continuity of
service etc.]

3 Changes to the services [11.5]

(1) Either Party may submit a Change Request in respect of the Services and/or to
this Agreement. Such Change Requests shall contain sufficient detail to enable the
other party adequately to assess the likely impact of the requested change upon the
other aspects of this Agreement, including but not limited to the Service Levels and
the Charges.

(2) In the event a Change Request is submitted by the Customer, the Supplier shall as soon as reasonably possible and in any event within *14* days prepare and submit to the Customer a Change Control Note, setting out:

  (i) the identity of the person(s) submitting the Change Request;

  (ii) the justification provided for the Change Request;

  (iii) the nature of the change to the Services and/or the provisions of this Agreement which has been proposed;

  (iv) where relevant, the Supplier's estimate of the effort which would be required to implement any alteration to the Services proposed by the Change Request;

  (v) the estimated cost of implementing the Change Request, together with a breakdown of any estimates of man days of effort required on other supporting information upon which the Supplier's estimate has been based;

  (vi) the likely impact of the Change Request on the Service Levels; and

  (vii) the impact of the Change Request on any other aspect of this Agreement.

(3) In the event a Change Request is submitted by the Supplier, a Change Control Note containing the information set out in clause 3(2) shall be submitted at the same time as the Change Request or within *5* business days thereafter.

(4) Change Control Notes shall thereafter be considered by the Customer and, where agreed, returned with written confirmation that each has been approved, in which event this Agreement shall be deemed to have been amended accordingly. Change Control Notes affecting only the nature or extent of the Services and involving a variation in the Charges of less than *£5,000* may be approved by *the Customer's Contract Manager*. All other Change Control Notes and in particular any Change Control Notes involving any amendment to the terms and conditions of this Agreement require the approval of *the Customer's Project Directors.*

(5) Until a Change Control note has been approved in writing in accordance with clause 3(4), each party shall continue to perform their respective obligations in accordance with the latest agreed version of this Agreement.

[**Note**: In long-term outsource arrangements, the customer will often be concerned about the risk of being "held to ransom" in relation to the change requests which will inevitably arise over time; a frequently used means of combating this threat is to have pre-set man day rates (usually discounted) in relation to the effort required from the supplier in respect of change requests, allied with a cap on the profit margin to be made by the supplier in respect of any change which is implemented.]

4 Payment [11.2]

(1) In consideration of the provision of the Services, the Customer agrees to pay the Supplier the Charges, as set out in Schedule 2.

(2) The Charges shall be invoiced to the Customer monthly in arrears. Each invoice will be paid by the Customer within *30* days of the Customer's receipt of such invoice.

(3) The Charges are exclusive of Value Added Tax which shall be paid by the Customer at the rate and in the manner for the time being prescribed by law.

(4) The Charges are [inclusive of expenses] [exclusive of the Supplier's reasonable expenses incurred in connection with the provision of the Services, which shall be payable by the Customer in addition].

(5) If any sum payable under this Agreement which is not the subject of a bona fide dispute is not paid within 7 days after the due date then (without prejudice to the Supplier's other rights or remedies), the Supplier reserves the right to suspend the provision of the Services (provided that it shall first have given the Customer not less than 7 days' prior written notice of its intention to do so) and/or to charge interest on such sum on a day to day basis (after as well as before any judgment) from the date or last date for payment thereof to the date of actual payment (both dates inclusive) at the rate of 2 per cent above the base rate of *ABC* Bank plc (or such other London Clearing Bank as the Supplier may nominate) from time to time in force, compounded quarterly. Such interest shall be paid on demand by the Supplier.

[Note: The right to suspend the provision of the services is a particularly onerous one in the context of an outsource agreement, owing to the degree of reliance that the customer will have upon the Supplier. It is accordingly essential that it should not become exercisable if there is a bona fide dispute as to the Services provided, and/or without a warning to the customer to enable it to break any logjam in its accounts department.]

5 Duration

This Agreement shall commence on the date of execution hereof and shall thereafter remain in force [for a period of *10* years from the Commencement of Service Date] [until terminated by either party in accordance with its terms].

[Note: Outsource agreements are most commonly subject to a fixed term of years, albeit sometimes extendable for a further period at the option of the customer]

6 Acceptance

(1) All software to be provided by the Supplier pursuant to this Agreement shall be subject to acceptance by the Customer, pursuant to this clause 6.

(2) The parties shall agree upon the criteria to be applied to any software produced by the Supplier, and in default of agreement they shall be determined in accordance with clause 28.

(3) Acceptance testing will be carried out by the Customer as soon as reasonably possible after the Supplier has notified it that the software ready for testing [and in any event within 7 days of such notification].

[Note: A definite time limit may be required if the supplier is to have time-related obligations, such as those in clause 2(5), which may be impacted by a delay by the customer in carrying out the relevant tests.]

(4) The Supplier shall provide the Customer with such assistance as it may reasonably require in connection with the conduct of the acceptance tests. The Customer shall not unreasonably withhold or delay any confirmation that the software has passed such acceptance tests.

(5) If the software fails to pass the relevant acceptance tests, the tests shall be repeated within a reasonable period thereafter, up to a maximum of 3 such repeated tests for such software. In the event that the software has still failed to pass

the relevant acceptance test following such repeat tests, the Customer may reject the software and/or terminate this Agreement pursuant to clause 14(2).

[**Note:** Acceptance procedures will rarely be relevant once the outsourced services are up and running, but may well be necessary during the initial transfer/transition phase, when the supplier will need to demonstrate that it has been able to put in place the necessary infrastructure to take on the provision of the outsourced functions.]

(6) In the case of non-software deliverables to be produced by the Supplier, the deliverables will be deemed to have been accepted by the Customer unless it notifies the Supplier of any reason for the withholding of its acceptance within 5 working days of delivery. The Customer's acceptance shall not be unreasonably withheld.

7 Intellectual property rights [11.6.3, 11.7.3]

(1) Save in relation to any materials created by or licensed to the Supplier prior to or outside the scope of this Agreement (the ownership of which shall be unaffected by any provision in this Agreement), the Customer shall own all Intellectual Property Rights in all software and other materials produced for the Customer by the Supplier pursuant to this Agreement.

(2) Ownership of all Intellectual Property Rights in any information, materials or assets supplied to the Supplier by the Customer other than the Existing Software and the Transferred Assets shall remain vested in the Customer or its third-party licensors. The Customer shall grant or procure the grant of a licence to the Supplier to utilise such information, materials or assets to the extent required for the provision of the Services.

(3) Prior to or upon the date of this Agreement, the Customer shall procure either:-

    (a) the assignment of its licences in respect of the Existing Software to the Supplier; or

    (b) the extension of its licence rights in respect of the Existing Software (if required) so as to ensure that the Supplier has the right to utilise the Existing Software for the purposes of providing the Services.

(4) The Customer shall indemnify the Supplier against any claim by any third party for alleged infringement of any U.K. copyright or other U.K. intellectual property rights which arises as a result of the storage or processing of any of the Customer's programs or data on the Supplier's systems and/or the provision of any information, materials or other assets to the Supplier by the Customer provided that the Customer is notified promptly in writing of any claim, that the Customer is given immediate and complete control of any such claim, that the Supplier does not prejudice the Customer's defence of such claim and that the Supplier gives the Customer all reasonable assistance with such claim (at the cost of the Customer).

(5) The Supplier shall indemnify the Customer against any claim by any third party for alleged infringement of any U.K. copyright or other U.K. intellectual property rights which arises as a result of the use of any deliverables provided by it and/or the provisions of the Services in accordance with the terms of this Agreement provided that the Supplier is notified promptly in writing of any claim, that the Supplier is given immediate and complete control of any such claim, that the Customer does not prejudice the Supplier's defence of such claim and that the Customer gives the Supplier all reasonable assistance with such claim (at the cost of the Supplier).

8 Project management [11.7.4]

(1) The Supplier shall forthwith appoint a Project Manager who shall act as the main point of contact for the Supplier in respect of all day to day matters relating to the supply of the Services and/or this Agreement

(2) The Customer shall forthwith appoint a Contract Manager who shall act as the main point of contact for the Customer in respect of all day to day matters relating to the supply of the Services and/or this Agreement.

(3) The Project Manager and the Contract Manager shall meet at least *weekly* or at such other intervals as the Steering Committee shall determine in order to discuss the progress being made in relation to the provision of the Services and any disputes or disagreements which may have arisen (which shall, if necessary, be escalated for resolution pursuant to clause 28).

(4) The Project Manager shall also, on a *monthly* basis, provide a status report for submission to the Steering Committee. Such status report shall contain such matters as the Steering Committee shall appoint and as a minimum contain:

(a) details of progress made against the Implementation Plan;

(b) details of progress made in meeting any forthcoming Key Milestones;

(c) details of any Change Requests made and any Change Control Notes agreed;

(d) details of the success or failure of the Supplier in meeting the Service Levels, and of any Service Credits incurred.

9 Supplier warranties

(1) The Supplier warrants that:

(a) it has obtained all permissions and consents required by it to enter into this Agreement and to provide the Services;

(b) it shall, during the terms of this Agreement, assign personnel to provide the Services who possess the requisite degrees of skill, qualification and experience required to fulfil the tasks assigned to them;

(c) it shall comply with all statutes, laws, regulations, and bye-laws as are applicable to it and/or the provision of the Services including (but not limited to) the Transfer of Undertakings (Protection of Employees) Regulations 1981 as amended in respect of the employees listed in Schedule 9;

(d) it shall maintain adequate insurance cover to enable it to comply with its obligations and meet its potential liabilities under this Agreement, and produce reasonable evidence of such insurance cover and the payment of premiums to the Customer upon request;

(e) it shall comply with the Customer's IT security, premises and health and safety policies as notified to it from time to time;

[Note: The supplier may wish to reserve a right for further payment if any changes to such policies have a material impact upon the provision of the services.]

(f) use all reasonable endeavours to ensure that the Key Personnel involved in the provision of the Services remain in their respective positions until at least *12* months after the Commencement of Service Date.

10 Customer warranties [11.3, 11.6]

(1) The Customer warrants that:

(a) it has obtained all permissions and consents required by it to enter into this Agreement and to provide the Services;

(b) it shall provide the Supplier with all assistance, materials and accurate information reasonably required by the Supplier for the purposes of enabling it to provide the Services;

(c) it shall ensure that all personnel assigned by it to provide assistance to the Supplier shall have the requisite skill, qualification and experience to perform the tasks assigned to them;

(d) it shall provide the Supplier with such access to its premises as may be reasonably required for the purposes of providing the Services, provided that the Supplier shall first have provided the Customer with details of the personnel who are to provide Services at the Customer's premises and obtained authorisation from the Customer (such authorisation not to be unreasonably withheld or delayed);

(e) the assets, licences and agreements currently utilised by the Customer in the provision of the internal support services equivalent to the Services to be provided by the Supplier are as specified in Schedule 8;

(f) the employee details contained in Schedule 9 are, to the best of the Customer's knowledge and belief, true and accurate.

(g) all data or other information provided by it shall not be obscene or defamatory, or likely to result in any claim being made against the Supplier by any third party.

[**Note**: Occasionally, responsibility for ascertaining the nature and extent of transferring assets and agreements etc is assigned to the supplier as part of the "due diligence' process. However, in reality this should at the very least be a joint effort.]

11 Asset Transfer [11.6]

(1) In consideration of the payment of the Transfer Payment by the Supplier upon the execution of this Agreement, the Customer agrees to:

(a) transfer to the Supplier the assets listed in Part B of Schedule 8; and

(b) grant or procure the grant of a licence to the Supplier in respect of the software listed in Part A of Schedule for the duration of his Agreement; and

(c) assign or procure the assignment to the Supplier of the licences and agreements listed in Part B of Schedule 8.

[**Note**: It will be essential for the Supplier to either ensure that it is able to take the benefit of all such agreements and/or acquire use of all of the assets, or else price into its charges the likely cost of acquiring replacement assets and software, etc.]

(2) The Customer shall ensure that all assets transferred to the Supplier pursuant to this clause 11 are in good condition at the date of transfer and are suitable for the purposes for which they are being applied immediately prior to such date. Title and risk to the assets shall pass to the Supplier upon payment of the Transfer Payment.

(3) The Customer shall be responsible for and shall indemnify the Supplier in respect of all claims and liabilities in relation to any use of the assets and/or any matter relating to the licences and agreements assigned or granted to the Supplier pursuant to this clause 11 which relate to acts or omissions of the Customer prior to the date of execution of this Agreement. The Supplier shall likewise be liable for and shall indemnify the Customer in respect of all such claims and liabilities in relation to any use of the assets and/or any matter relating to the licences and agreement assigned or granted to the Supplier pursuant to this clause 11 which arise from any acts or omissions of the Supplier subsequent to the date of execution of this Agreement.

[Note: major assets such as premises may have been transferred under a collateral agreement [Recital C].]

12 Employee provisions [11.6.4]

(1) The Customer warrants that the details of all of the employees whose contracts of employment or to transfer across to the Supplier upon the commencement of the Services are as specified in Schedule 9, and that it has complied with the provisions of their employment contracts and all applicable legal requirements in relation both to their employment and the transfer of their contracts to the Supplier pursuant to this Agreement.

(2) The Customer shall be responsible for any arrears of wages, accrued holiday pay, taxes, penalties, social security payments, contributions to pensions or unemployment funds incurred prior to the date of this Agreement. The Supplier shall be responsible for all such liabilities which accrue after the date of this Agreement.

(3) The Customer warrants that it is not aware of any current or threatened labour dispute or other claim relating to any of the employees named in Schedule 9, and that none of the said employees have in the previous *12 months* been subject to any disciplinary or grievance procedure, save as expressly disclosed to the Supplier.

(4) The Customer agrees to indemnify the Supplier against any liabilities which it may incur by reason of a breach by the Customer of the warranties contained in this clause 12.

[Note: the above provisions are very much a minimal set of employee-related terms; if there are large numbers of employees to transfer across, more details wording is likely to be required. See 11.6.4 for TUPE and its impact on agreements of this sort.]

13 Service levels [11.1, 11.2, 10.1.3]

(1) The Supplier shall provide the Services so as to achieve or exceed the Service Levels set out in Schedule 3.

(2) In the event that the Service Levels are not achieved, the Supplier shall incur Service Credits as set out in Schedule 4. Such Service Credits shall be calculated monthly and applied as a deduction to any Charges payable pursuant to clause 4.

(3) The Supplier shall not be liable for any failure to achieve the required Service Levels and shall not incur Service Credits to the extent that such failure results from:

(a) a breach by the Customer of any of its obligations under this Agreement;

(b) a failure attributable solely to the use of public telecommunications links between the Supplier and the Customer; or

(c) an event of *force majeure* falling within the scope of clause 29.

(4) In the event that the failure to achieve the required Service Levels is only partially the result of any matter falling within clause 12(3)(a) or (b) the actual performance of the Supplier in relation to the required Service Levels shall be adjusted to such levels as the parties agree would have been achieved, but for the impact of such matters. In the event that the parties are unable to agree upon the appropriate adjustment, the matter shall be reverted to an expert for determination pursuant to clause 28.

14 Termination [11.4]

(1) This Agreement may be terminated forthwith by either party on giving notice in writing to the other if the other party shall have a liquidator, receiver, administrative receiver or administrator appointed or shall pass a resolution for winding-up (otherwise than for the purpose of a bona fide scheme of solvent amalgamation or reconstruction) or a court of competent jurisdiction shall make an order to that effect or if the other party shall become subject to an administration order or shall enter into any voluntary arrangement with its creditors or shall cease or threaten to cease to carry on business.

(2) This Agreement may also be terminated forthwith by either party on giving notice to the other if the other party is in material breach of the terms of this Agreement and has failed to rectify such breach (in the case of a breach capable of being remedied) within *30* days of receiving a written notice requiring it to do so.

(3) Any termination under clauses 14(1) or (2) shall discharge the parties from any liability for further performance of this Agreement (save in the case of the Supplier as may be required pursuant to Schedule 5) and in the case of a termination by the Supplier shall entitle the Supplier to enter any of the Customer's premises and recover any equipment and materials which are the property of the Supplier (and the Customer hereby irrevocably licenses the Supplier, its employees and agents to enter any such premises for that purpose upon being given reasonable prior notice) and also to be paid a reasonable sum for any work carried out by it prior to such termination.

(4) Any termination of this Agreement (howsoever occasioned) shall not affect any accrued rights or liabilities of either party nor shall it affect the coming into force or the continuance in force of any provision hereof which is expressly or by implication intended to come into or continue in force on or after such termination.

(5) If this Agreement is terminated for any reason, the Exit Provisions contained in Schedule 5 shall apply and the Supplier shall co-operate with the Customer to enable the transfer of the responsibility for the provision of the Services to the Customer or, at the Customer's request, to another supplier.

[15 Technology upgrade [11.7.3]

(1) In the *fourth* year of this Agreement (unless this Agreement shall have been terminated earlier or there shall be a notice to terminate in existence in accordance

with clause 14 of this Agreement), the Supplier agrees to upgrade the hardware used by it for the Services so as to use then current technology and best computer practice to continue to provide the Services to the Customer at at least equal to or better Service Levels.

(2) From time to time the Supplier agrees to install and use for the Services later releases of the software listed in Schedule 8 or replacement software for such software, but so that the Services and the Service Levels to the Customer are maintained or improved.]

16 Data protection [11.3.1]

See clause 9 of Precedent L.

17 Liability

See clause 27 of Precedent A.

18 Confidentiality

See clause 21 of Precedent A.

19 Waiver

See clause 28 of Precedent A.

20 Assignment

See clause 30 of Precedent A.

21 Subcontracts

See clause 31 of Precedent A.

22 Notices

See clause 32 of Precedent A.

23 Severability

See clause 36 of Precedent A.

24 Third parties [1.3]

See clause 37 of Precedent A.

25 Interpretation

See clause 33 of Precedent A.

26 Entire agreement

See clause 29 of Precedent A.

27 Law

See clause 34 of Precedent A.

28 Disputes [11.4]

(1) In the event of any disagreement or dispute between the parties arising out of any matter relating to or arising out of this Agreement, the parties shall in the first instance seek to resolve the matter by discussions between *the Customer's Contracts Manager* and *the Supplier's Project Manager*. In the event that they are unable to resolve the disagreement or dispute within *2* business days, it shall be escalated for resolution to *the parties' senior representatives*.

(2) If the disagreement or dispute is not resolved pursuant to either clause 28 (1) above or if either party believes that it is unlikely to be resolved in this matter, the matter may by agreement between the parties be referred to mediation.

(3) If the disagreement or dispute is not resolved pursuant to either clause 28(1) or (2) above and is of a technical nature, either party may by written notice to the other require that the matter be referred to a technical expert ("the Expert") for resolution. The Expert shall be appointed by agreement between the parties or, in default of agreement, by the President for the time being of the *British Computer Society* and both parties shall at their own cost afford the Expert with such assistance as he/she may reasonably request in connection with the resolution of the disagreement or dispute. The Expert shall be instructed to provide his/her decision as soon as reasonably possible. Unless otherwise directed by the Expert in the context of his/her decision, the costs of the Expert shall be borne equally by the parties.

(4) In all other circumstances all disputes arising under or in relation to this Agreement shall be the subject to the exclusive jurisdiction of the English courts.

29 *Force majeure*

See clause 15 of Precedent A.

EXECUTED under hand in two originals the day and year first before written

SIGNED for and on behalf of
OUTSOURCE PROVIDER [LIMITED] [PLC]

By

Signature

Title

Witness

SIGNED for and on behalf of
CUSTOMER [LIMITED] [PLC]

By

Signature

Title

Witness

SCHEDULE 1

SERVICES TO BE PROVIDED

[**Note**: the detail of the services will need to be set out here, possibly including provision for the Euro [LS(5)].]

SCHEDULE 2

PAYMENT PROVISIONS

SCHEDULE 3

SERVICE LEVELS

[**Note**: The details of the Service Levels will obviously depend upon the nature of the Services being provided; the details below are provided as an indicative basis only, so as to give an idea of what such a schedule could look like.]

The Service Levels to be achieved by the supplier in the provision of the Services are a follows:

Details of Service	Service Level (measured monthly)
Response to on-line accounts enquiry initiated by user	*95%* to be responded to within *10* seconds
Number of budgetary reports produced on time	*90%* to produced in line with deadlines set out Schedule 1
Response to Faults reported by Users	*95%* to be responded to within *2* hours of notification to Help Desk

SCHEDULE 4

SERVICE CREDITS

[**Note**: again, the Service Credit regime will need to reflect the nature of the Service Levels set; ambitious Service Level targets may justify less onerous Service Credits (at least the Services to be provided and for relatively small shortfalls in performance), whereas if the Service Levels are themselves generous to the supplier, it may be appropriate to impose Service Credits which quickly mount up.]

1. The value of the Service Credit shall be calculated by reference to the amount of the Charges for the month in question, according to the following calculation:

Amount of Service Credit = *1%* of the Charges for the month in question.

[**Note**: There are various means of setting the value for an individual Service Credit; the example given above is a fairly common one, *i.e.* one which links it to the value of the fees.]

2. Service Credits will accrue on the following basis:

Service Level	Accrued of Service Credits
Response to on-line accounts enquiry initiated by user	*x* for each *y%* of accounts enquiries not responded to within the required service level
Number of budgetary reports produced on time	*x* for each *y%* of reports not produced in time within the required service level
Response to Faults reported by Users	*x* for each *y%* not responded to within the required service level

SCHEDULE 5

EXIT PROVISIONS

1. General obligation

On termination of this Agreement for any reason, the Supplier will provide all reasonable assistance to the Customer to facilitate the orderly transfer of the Services back to the Customer or to enable another party chosen by the Customer to take over the provision of all or part of the Services.

2. Plans and procedures

Upon receiving a written request from the Customer to do so, the Supplier shall, within *one month* of such request, deliver to the Customer written plans demonstrating the procedures by which it will fulfil its obligations under this Schedule, such plans and procedures to be subject to the approval of the Customer, such approval not to be unreasonably withheld or delayed.

3. Continuation of the provision of services

If, in the reasonable opinion of the Customer, the orderly transfer of the Services to the Customer or a new supplier can only be effected if the Supplier continues to provide the Services for a limited period of time, the Customer can require the Supplier to continue to provide the Services for [*specify period*].

4. Assets

4.1 Transfer

On ceasing to provide the Services hereunder and in consideration of the payment of their net book value, the Supplier shall transfer to the Customer, or deliver as the

Customer shall specify, all the assets listed in [Part A of] Schedule 8. Any dispute as to the net book value of such assets shall be determined pursuant to clause 28.

[Note: if the supplier only paid a nominal sum for the original transfer of such assets, a nominal re-transfer fee is also likely to be appropriate. The customer may, however, wish to extend the transfer obligation to cover all additional assets required by the supplier for the purposes of providing the services over the course of the agreement.]

4.2 Shared equipment

Where the Services provided to the Customer are dependent on equipment which is not used exclusively for the provision of the Services to the Customer (and which is not owned by the Customer) the Supplier will ensure that all programs, data and other materials held or stored thereon are moved from such equipment to similar equipment owned by the Customer or a new supplier.

[Note: the parties may wish to consider specifying who should bear the cost of dealing with any compatibility issues; the supplier is unlikely to accept the burden of such costs.]

5. Contracts, software, and know-how

5.1 Upon the Supplier ceasing to provide the Services, it will, at the request of the Customer, do everything necessary so as to notify the other parties to any contracts entered into by it with third parties in respect of the supply of goods or services to the Customer that this Agreement has come to an end.

5.2 The Customer shall be entitled to use (and to authorise any new supplier to use), free of charge but on a non-exclusive basis, all know-how and other information acquired by the Supplier in the course of providing the Services or otherwise used by the Supplier in the provision of the Services, whether or not such know-how or information was produced specifically or used exclusively to provide the Services.

6 Premises

6.1 The Customer will be entitled upon reasonable prior written notice to enter the Supplier's premises in order to take back any of its assets which have been kept on the Supplier's premises.

[Note: This assumes that the equipment is at the supplier's premises. Otherwise, if the equipment remains with the customer, this clause should state that the supplier's rights of access, etc., will cease.]

7 Personnel

7.1 The Supplier will procure that the provision of the Services is managed so that there is no undertaking or part of an undertaking (within the meaning of the Transfer of Undertakings (Protection of Employment) Regulations 1981, (as amended), the business of which is the provision of the Services.

7.2 If, notwithstanding such obligations, the Regulations apply to transfer the employment of any person employed by the Supplier to the Customer or any new supplier then if the Customer or such new supplier shall serve a notice terminating the employment of such person within *six months* of the date of such transfer, the Supplier shall pay to the Customer, as liquidated damages, a sum equal *to any sum payable to the person in question as damages for unfair and/or wrongful dismissal or as a reasonable settlement of a claim for such damages*.

[Note: the wording above presupposes that the customer will not wish to be impacted by TUPE upon the termination or expiry of this Agreement. If, on the other hand, employees are to be either re-transferred to the customer or passed to a new supplier, more extensive employee provisions will be required here, along the lines of those set out in clause 12.]

SCHEDULE 6

KEY PERSONNEL

SCHEDULE 7

IMPLEMENTATION PLAN

SCHEDULE 8

EXISTING ASSETS

A   Existing Software

[**Note**: List all software to be assigned/made available to the supplier pursuant to clause 7(3).]

B   Assets, Licences and Agreements

[**Note 1**: list all key assets and agreements to be transferred to the supplier, pursuant to clause 11.]

[**Note 2**: This version assumes that the transfer of any premises, hardware and other physical assets has taken place under a separate collateral agreement [11.6.1].]

SCHEDULE 9

EMPLOYEE DETAILS

[SCHEDULE 10

THIRD-PARTY RIGHTS]

WEBSITE HOSTING/COMMERCIAL ISP AGREEMENT

THIS AGREEMENT is made the   day of   20

PARTIES:

(1) WEBSITE HOST [LIMITED] [PLC] whose registered office is at [   ]

(the "Host")

and

(2) CUSTOMER [LIMITED][PLC] whose registered office is at [   ]

(the "Customer").

RECITAL:

(A) The Host is a provider of website hosting services with a dedicated system providing a link to the world-wide web via the Internet

(B) The Customer wishes to appoint the Host to host its website on this system and to provide the services upon the terms and conditions hereinafter contained

NOW IT IS HEREBY AGREED as follows:

1 Definitions

In this Agreement, unless the context otherwise requires, the following expressions have the following meanings:

"Confidential Information"	means this Agreement and all information obtained by one party from the other pursuant to this Agreement which is expressly marked as confidential or which is manifestly confidential or which is confirmed in writing to be confidential within 7 days of its disclosure.
"Customer's Material"	means the Customer's [software and] data loaded, received, maintained or transmitted by the Host on the System for the Customer under this Agreement.
"Customer's Personnel"	means such authorised personnel of the Customer who shall, on behalf of the Customer, be responsible for managing all issues relating to the performance of this Agreement and shall be notified to the Host in writing from time to time.
"Domain Name"	means the domain name www.*xxxxxxxxx.xxx*.

"Effective Date"	means the effective date specified in Schedule 1.
"System"	means the equipment [and telecommunications equipment] (as enhanced from time to time) belonging to or used by the Host and which provides a link to the world wide web via the Internet.
"the Services"	means the services identified in Schedule 1.
"the Third Party Property"	means any graphics, screen designs, audio-visual effects, pictures, software and other proprietary material belonging to a third party and which form part of the Website.
"Web Pages"	means the Internet pages whether they contain or comprise text, graphics, pictures, screen designs, screen layouts, sound, audio-visual material, film or software.
"Website"	means the Customer's existing Internet Web Pages and the Web Pages to be constructed, maintained and transmitted by the Host for the Customer under this Agreement.

2 Host's responsibilities [12.1.2, 12.7.2]

(1) The Customer appoints the Host to host the Website on its behalf and to provide the Services in accordance with the provisions contained in this Agreement.

(2) The Host shall exercise such reasonable skill, care and diligence as expected of an experienced provider of website hosting services.

(3) The Host shall store the Website on the System and make available the Website for access by users of the Internet from and including the Effective Date.

[Note: if the host is also to accommodate communications or other equipment provided by the customer, terms may also be required in relation to the amount of space at the host's premises to be provided for this purpose.]

(4) The Host undertakes to maintain certain service levels as set out in Schedule 2.

(5) The Host agrees to perform such maintenance and other actions as are reasonably required to maintain the System in full working order.

(6) The Host undertakes that whenever possible, any significant maintenance of the hardware and software infrastructure on which the Website is located shall be undertaken outside of the hours of *8 a.m. to 6 p.m.* However, the Host reserves the right to carry out any emergency maintenance work at any time, giving to the Customer as much warning as reasonably possible.

[Note: the Customer may also require notice to be given to it of scheduled maintenance tasks.]

(7) The Host shall, on request by the Customer's Personnel, immediately suspend availability of the Website over the Internet. The Host shall likewise, on request by

the Customer's Personnel, immediately resume the provision of access to the Website following such suspensions.

(8) The Host undertakes to establish and maintain reasonable safeguards against the destruction, loss or unauthorised alteration of the Customer's Material, and shall institute reasonable security procedures to restrict the destruction, corruption or unauthorised access to the Website, data and data files, including back up material.

(9) The Host will at all times during the continuance of this Agreement maintain and use appropriate virus-protection procedures and software on the Customer's Material.

3 Ownership of the website and domain name [12.1.2]

The Host acknowledges and agrees that the copyright, trademarks, trade names, patents and all other intellectual property rights subsisting in the Website and the right to the Domain Name shall vest and remain vested in the Customer and its licensors and nothing in this Agreement shall operate as an assignment to the Host of such intellectual property rights and/or right to the Domain Name.

4 Licence

The Customer grants to the Host, for the duration of this Agreement, a non-exclusive, non-transferrable licence to host the Website on the System in accordance with the provisions of this Agreement, solely for the purposes of providing the Services and availability of the Website over the Internet.

5 Modifications to the website [12.1.2]

(1) Subject to clause 5(2) below, the Host shall, as soon as reasonably possible, amend, modify or replace any of the Web Pages with such new material or replacement pages as may from time to time be supplied by the Customer to the Host.

[Note: compatibility of formats will need to be spelled out in Schedule 1.]

(2) The Host reserves the right to refuse to carry out such amendments, modifications or replacements where, in its reasonable opinion such amendments, modifications or replacements are or are likely to be construed as being illegal, obscene, threatening, defamatory, discriminatory, promoting illegal or unlawful activity, or are otherwise actionable or in violation of any rules, regulations or laws to which the Website is subject. The Host shall immediately notify the Customer in writing and state in reasonable detail, the reason for such refusal, and the Host shall immediately at the request of the Customer attend a meeting for the purpose of discussing the matter further. In the event of a continued disagreement between the parties, the dispute resolution procedure in clause 19 shall apply.

(3) Save as provided in sub clause 5(1), the Host shall not amend, modify or replace or alter in any way any of the Web Pages at any time without the prior written approval of the Customer.

(4) The Host shall indemnify the Customer against any claims, proceedings, losses, liabilities, damages (including reasonable costs), charges and expenses of whatever

nature arising out of or in connection with any claim or action relating to an infringement of any third party patent, copyright, registered or unregistered design right, trademark or of any other intellectual property right in the Third Party Property, which arises out of any change, amendment or modification made to such Third Party Property by the Host, save where the claim or action arises solely by reason of the Customer's specific directions as to how any such amendment, modification or replacement was to be effected.

6 Customer obligations, undertakings and indemnities [12.6.1]

(1) The Customer shall provide the Host with a copy of the Website [electronically] [on CD-ROM] at least *3 months* prior to the Effective Date.

(2) The Customer acknowledges that the Host does not operate or exercise control over, and accepts no responsibility for the content of the Website or the Customer's Materials received on the System.

(3) The Customer warrants that any material contained in or linked to the Website and (if applicable) contained in any discussion group, chat room or bulletin board which forms part of the Website will not be illegal, obscene, threatening, defamatory, discriminatory, promote illegal or unlawful activity, or be otherwise actionable or in violation of any rules, regulations or laws to which the Website is subject. The Customer shall be solely responsible for the accuracy, legality, and compliance with the relevant rules and regulations of the Web Pages.

[Note: the customer should be wary of its potential liability to the host by reason of third party materials posted to discussion groups, etc.]

(4) The Customer warrants that it has obtained all necessary consents, approvals and licences for the use of Third Party Property and the use of such Third Party Property will not violate any intellectual property rights belonging to any third party.

(5) In the event of allegations of an infringement of clause 6(3) and/or clause 6(4) above, or if the Host reasonably suspects such an infringement has occurred, the Host may, without giving notice to the Customer and without liability, suspend availability of the Website or any Web Pages over the Internet or remove the Website or any Web Pages from the System, pending clarification of such allegations or suspicion.

(6) The parties shall notify each other as soon as reasonably possible after becoming aware of any third party allegation of a breach of the provisions of clause 6(3) and/ or clause 6(4) above.

(7) Save as provided in clause 5(4) above, the Customer shall indemnify the Host against any claims, proceedings, losses, liabilities, damages (including reasonable costs), charges and expenses of whatever nature arising out of or in connection with any claim or action made against the Host relating to a breach of clause 6(3) and clause 6(4) above, provided that the Host will not make any admissions without the Customer's prior written consent not take any step (or omit to take any step) which would prejudice the Customer's defence of the claim, and shall allow the Customer to conduct and/or settle all negotiations and litigation resulting from such claim. The Host shall, at the request of the Customer, afford all reasonable assistance with such negotiations or litigation and shall be reimbursed by Customer for any reasonable out of pocket expenses incurred in so doing.

7 Payment [12.2.1]

(1) The Customer shall pay the Host for the hosting of the Website and the provision of the Services in Schedule 1.

(2) All charges payable by the Customer shall be payable within *14* days after the receipt by the Customer of the Host's invoice therefor.

(3) The charges payable under this Agreement are exclusive of Value Added Tax which shall be paid by the Customer at the rate and in the manner for the time being prescribed by law

(4) If any sum payable under this Agreement is not paid within *7* days after the due date then (without prejudice to the Host's other rights and remedies) the Host reserves the right to charge interest on such sum on a day to day basis (as well after as before any judgment) from the date or last date for payment thereof to the date of actual payment (both dates inclusive) at the rate of *2* per cent above the base rate of *ABC* Bank plc (or such other London Clearing Bank as the Host may nominate) from time to time in force compounded quarterly. Such interest shall be paid on demand by the Host.

8 Reports

The Host shall provide to the Customer on a [monthly][quarterly] basis, a report containing statistical information which shall include the following:

    (a) the number of visitors to the Website.

    (b) a break down of the most popular sections of the Website.

    (c) a breakdown of the times at which visitors access the Website and the duration of their visit; and

    (d) such other information as the Customer may reasonably request from time to time.

9 Meetings

The Host shall, at the reasonable request of the Customer and at no additional cost to the Customer, attend *quarterly* meetings with the Customer, for the purpose of discussing matters relating to the Website.

10 Data protection [12.3.1, 12.7.1]

(1) to (4)

See clause 9 of Precedent L.

[**Note**: if e-mail forms part of the services it will be inevitable that personal data will be transmitted and version B of Clause 9 of Precedent L should be used.]

[(5) to enable the Customer to defend any action in defamation, obscenity or other illegal activity arising from electronic mail in the Services, the Host agrees to keep for a period of *5 years* copies of all electronic mail sent by the Customer as part of the Services and shall from time to time at the [written] request of the Customer make available to the Customer but shall not otherwise divulge them to any other person save as required by law. At the end of the *5 years* the copies so kept will be destroyed by the Host and the Host hereby warrants to the Customer that it will do so. The Host acknowledges that it shall have no intellectual property or other rights over any electronic mail so stored.]

[Note: This clause will not be needed if there is no e-mail service. To safeguard as far as possible the customer's position under the Data Protection Act 1998, all users of the e-mail service in the customer's organisation should be told that this storage for these purposes is a deliberate policy of the company, that the customer's e-mail should not be used for non-business purposes, that each member of staff is responsible for his own e-mails, and that any misuse is a disciplinary offence. The copyright of this material will presumably lie with the customer.]

11 Confidentiality [12.7.1]

See clause 21 of Precedent A.

12 Commencement and termination [12.4.1]

(1) This Agreement shall commence on the Effective Date and continue for a period of *5 years*, and thereafter on an annual basis unless terminated by one of the parties on giving to the other party at least *12 months'* written notice.

(2) This Agreement may be terminated forthwith by either party on giving notice in writing to the other if the other party shall have a receiver or administrative receiver appointed or shall pass a resolution for winding-up (otherwise than for the purpose of a bona fide scheme of solvent amalgamation or reconstruction) or a court of competent jurisdiction shall make an order to that effect or if the other party shall become subject to an administration order or shall enter into any voluntary arrangement with its creditors or shall cease or threaten to cease to carry on business.

(3) This Agreement may also be terminated forthwith by either party on giving notice to the other if the other party is in material breach of the terms of this Agreement and has failed to rectify such breach (in the case of a breach capable of being remedied) within *30* days of receiving a written notice requiring it to do so.

(4) Any termination under clauses 12(2) or 12(3) shall discharge the parties from any liability for further performance of this Agreement and in the case of a termination by the Customer shall entitle the Customer to receive at no further cost from the Host a copy in any reasonable electronic form of all the Customer's Material as at that time and to enter any of the Host's premises and recover any equipment, information and materials the property of the Customer (and so that the Supplier hereby irrevocably licenses the Customer, its employees and agents to enter any such premises for that purpose) shall entitle the Customer to be repaid forthwith any sums previously paid under this Agreement (whether paid by way of a deposit or otherwise) and to recover from the Host the amount of any direct loss or damage sustained or incurred by the Customer as a consequence of such termina-tion. In the case of a termination under clause 12(2) or (3) by the Host, the Host shall in addition to any claim for damages be entitled to be paid a reasonable sum of any work carried by it prior to such termination.

13 Liability

See clause 27 of Precedent A.

14 Entire agreement

See clause 29 of Precedent A.

15 *Force majeure*

See clause 15 of Precedent A.

16 Amendments

No variation to the provisions of this Agreement shall be of any effect unless made in writing and agreed and signed by both parties.

17 Waiver of remedies

See clause 28 of Precedent A.

18 Law

See clause 34 of Precedent A.

19 Disputes

See clause 35 of Precedent A.

20 Severability

See clause 36 of Precedent A.

21 Third parties

See clause 37 of Precedent A.

EXECUTED under hand in two originals the day and year first before written

Signed for and on behalf of
WEBSITE HOST[LIMITED][PLC]

By

Signature

Title

Witness

Signed for and on behalf of
CUSTOMER [LIMITED] [PLC]

By

Signature

Title

Witness

SCHEDULE 1

SERVICES

[**Note**: This Schedule will contain details of the services to be provided, including any website design related services, although it may be more appropriate to have such design work carried out as a distinct project, pursuant to a consultancy agreement: see Precedent X. It will also contain the Effective Date (clause 1) and format of pages (Note to clause 5(1)).]

PAYMENT

[**Note**: relevant provisions are likely to include a one-off set-up charge, a recurring hosting fee based on the amount of space the web pages and e-mails require, a variable fee depending on bandwidth (see Note on Schedule 2), a fee for progressive destruction of e-mails and any charges for any additional services.]

SCHEDULE 2

SERVICE LEVELS

[**Note**: The essence of the hosting services is that the host must provide an adequate telephone link to an existing point on the Internet which is capable of handling the traffic to and from the system. This capability is known as the bandwidth and its size will depend on how many sites the host is hosting on the system and the popularity of these websites. If the host provides inadequate bandwidth, visitors to the website will experience delays in accessing the pages of the website which may be detrimental to business.

To circumvent this issue, a possibility is to require the host to provide a minimum bandwidth. However, while this approach is straightforward, a bandwidth which may be adequate today may become inadequate in the near future as demand for Internet services increase.

A more sophisticated approach is to require the host to comply with a service level obligation, which seeks to define not only the maximum permitted levels of system's downtime but also the speed, and quality with which a system responds to a request for access to a particular website. This is likely to be difficult to define and if any delays are caused between the system and the visitor's computer (*e.g.* by reason of problems in relation to transmissions across the Internet in general) then the host will require this to be at the risk of the website owner. The advantage of such an approach is that the website owner does not need to be concerned with how the host meets its service level obligation and therefore maintenance provisions can be kept to a minimum.]

1. Availability

(1) The Host shall ensure that the System on which the Website is based and the Website itself shall remain continuously available to third party users via the Internet.

(2) (a) In the event of the Website's becoming unavailable over the Internet for reasons other than *Force Majeure* as defined in clause 15 or by the default or action of the Customer the Host shall credit the Customer with *1* per cent of any charges payable during the month for each *hour* or part *hour* during which the Website is unavailable.

[(b) In the event of the System's becoming unavailable for electronic mail alone for reasons other than *Force Majeure* as defined in clause 15 or be default or action of the Customer, the Host shall credit the Customer with *1* per cent of any charges payable during the month for each *hour* or part *hour* during which the System is unavailable for electronic mail.]

[**Note**: The customer is getting two basic services: website hosting and e-mail. This clause allows for either to be down without the other. If the target level of availability is set at 100 per cent, as above, the host may also need to allow for scheduled maintenance tasks.]

2. Performance

(1) The expected usage of the Website is up to *2,000* hits per hour and the Host undertakes to provide sufficient bandwidth to enable the Website to be accessible to this number of hits.

[SCHEDULE 3

THIRD-PARTY RIGHTS]

INTERNET SERVICE PROVIDER AGREEMENT (CONSUMER) [12.1]

LICENCE AGREEMENT

[Note: On the sleeve of the CD will be instructions as to loading and installation. The following will then be displayed as a Click-wrap agreement [4.3.1] as the user attempts to load the necessary software from the CD.]

This agreement will govern your use of [The Company] ("the Company") as an Internet service provider. It describes the services we offer, the conditions under which we offer them and your obligations. The copyright and other intellectual property rights in this software ("the Software") and its associated documentation are owned by the Company [and   ]. Please read through the following conditions. If you agree to be bound by them please click YES at the end of the conditions at which point the software will be loaded onto your computer and you will be enabled to use the services. If you do not agree to be bound by these terms the software will not be loaded onto your computer.

1. The services [12.1.1, 12.7.1]

(1) If you agree to be bound by these conditions and have the necessary system requirements set out in clause 2, the Company will provide you with access to the Internet. The Company's services will continue so long as you continue to observe these conditions, maintain the necessary system requirements and this Agreement is not terminated under the provisions of clause 6.

(2) The Company will subject to these conditions provide you with the Services as follows:

- a licence to use the Company's access software for the Internet;
- access thereby to the Internet;
- the use of *the Company's* search engine on the Internet;
- access to certain free data on the Company's web pages;
- the ability for you to download and/or print results of searches and other data from the Internet;
- space for storing your messages, "favourites" etc.;
- an Internet and e-mail address;
- automated notification to you when e-mail addressed to you has been received;

- an address book for e-mail;
- [a virus protection service on incoming e-mails;]
- [a screening system for you to exclude certain types of data;]
- a telephone helpdesk service available 24 hours a day every day.

[**Note**: Only those services from the above list which are actually relevant should be included.]

(3) The Company shall use all reasonable endeavours to provide the Services on a continuous basis. However, the Company shall not be responsible for any failure to provide the Services which is due to problems with any aspects of your system or the Internet (to the extent that it is outside of the Company's control).

(4) The Company undertakes to keep your data confidential and to run a security system to prevent it being divulged to any third party without your authorisation.

2. System requirements

To use the Services your computer must be of the following minimum specification or Better:

- *IBM PC or any other fully compatible computer;*
- *Intel Pentium (I) Processor or better;*
- *Windows 95, 98, 2000 or NT 4.0;*
- *100Mb of free space on your hard disk;*
- *16Mb RAM;*
- *CD-Rom drive;*
- *256-colour SVGA display or better;*
- *Mouse;*
- *14,000 bps modem or faster.*

3. Registration [12.4.1, 12.7.1]

(1) When you install the software, you will be asked to register with the Company and choose a unique user name, password and e-mail address.

- The user name will be in the form. *Company*.co.uk
- The password will consist of up to 10 characters.
- The e-mail address will in part depend on your User name and will be in the form   @*user name.Company*.co.uk

Please note that all these items are case-sensitive.

You are responsible for keeping a secure record of these items. You must keep your password confidential.

(2) You must at the time of registration provide your full postal address and telephone number. If you fail to provide these you will not be granted access to the

Services. This is to protect the Company and all users of the Services against anonymous users. We reserve the right immediately to terminate this Agreement if any details provided by you are found to be false.

[(3) The Company may pass your e-mail address to selected third parties for marketing and related purposes. If you do not want this please click No on the relevant box at the end of this Agreement.]

4. Your responsibilities [12.3.1, 12.4.1, 12.6.1]

(1) You are responsible for everything you put onto the Internet or send as e-mail.

(2) You must not send anything which is defamatory, obscene, contrary to the provisions of the Data Protection Act 1998 or in breach of any other legal right or duty. In the event that you do any of these things, the Company will forthwith delete all your data, terminate the Services and you will be fully responsible for the consequences and the Company will bear no responsibility. The Company reserves the right to seek compensation from you for any charges or liabilities the Company may incur as a result of your doing any of these things. The Company reserves the right to suspend the Services in the event that it reasonably suspects you of doing any of these things.

(3) You must not use the Services to send a computer virus.

(4) You must not use any of the Services for any illegal purpose.

[**Note**: This would include not only fraud but also hacking which is an offence under the Computer Misuse Act 1990.]

(5) You must not send any single e-mail to more than *20* persons simultaneously.

[**Note**: this "anti-spamming" provision may be problematic if the threshold is set too low, as it is quite common for groups of friends/family to create address lists which can be quite lengthy, but do not relate to spamming, *per se*.]

(6) You will not copy or seek to e-mail any of the Company's software including but not limited to installation software, access software [, search engine] [, virus-protection software] [, filtering software].

[**Note**: A copy for the client's security purposes is already provided by the CD.]

5. Charges [12.2.1, 12.6.1]

[(1) The Company will charge you a flat rate of £[ ] per month or part of a month for the Services.]

(2) You are responsible for paying all the Company's charges for the Services.

(3) You are responsible for paying for all your telephone calls for access to the Services.

(4) These telephone calls may include any use by you of the telephone helpdesk service which will be charged at a premium rate of *50p per minute* or part thereof or at such other rate as the Company may from time to time determine and advise you of.

[Note: Clause 5 (1) will not be used for a free service.]

6. Termination [12.4.1]

(1) If you fail to use any of the Services for a period of *3 months* or more this Agreement will terminate immediately.

(2) If you are in breach of any of the conditions of this Agreement this Agreement will terminate immediately.

(3) This Agreement may be terminated by either party giving to the other not less than *one month's* written notice.

(4) On any termination of this Agreement, however caused, all outstanding charges will become due and the Company will erase all your data including any e-mails from the space allocated to you under this Agreement.

7. Alteration [12.5.1]

(1) The Company reserves the right to vary any of the terms of this Agreement upon giving to you not less than *one month's* notice by e-mail or post. If you do not agree to the change you may then forthwith terminate this Agreement.

[Note: This may seem harsh but there is no shortage of alternative suppliers if the client disagrees.]

8. Liability

(1) Our liability to you shall be limited to [the amount of the Company's Charges] [£x], except that no limit shall apply for any loss or damage which cannot be excluded or restricted by law.

[Note: linking the limit to the amounts paid may not be applicable to free Internet services and will in any event be a low amount which may accordingly be open to challenge under the Unfair Contract Terms Act 1977. A preferable approach may accordingly be to set a minimal limit of liability.]

[9. Rights of third parties [1.3]

(1) Rights in the[   ] software belong to [   ] and you must not copy or seek to e-mail any of the [   ] software. In return for the legitimate use of the [   ] software your obligations in this respect shall be with [   ] under the Contracts (Rights of Third Parties) Act 1999.]

10. Law

(1) This Agreement and your receipt of the Services shall be subject to English law. Any dispute relating to it shall be dealt with exclusively in the English courts.

If you agree to be bound by the above conditions please click YES at which point the software will be loaded onto your computer and Registration can begin. If you do not agree click NO. The software will then not be loaded onto your computer and no Registration can take place.

I agree to be bound by the above conditions for the use of the services and the software.	**YES**	**NO**

[If you are content to receive e-mails from selected third parties in accordance with 3(3) above please click YES. If you do not wish to receive such mailings please click NO here.

I agree to allow my e-mail address to be divulged to selected third parties for marketing and related purposes.]	**YES**	**NO**

AGREEMENT FOR ACCESSING A SPECIFIC WEBSITE (BUSINESS)

[**Note:** These terms will appear on the user's screen as soon as he gains access to the website.]

Important Notice

The following terms and conditions will apply to any order you place with us and if you find yourself unable to agree to them, then you must not use our ordering service and should click on the "NO button" at the end of this document. If however, you agree to these terms and conditions unconditionally, you should click on the "YES button" which also appears at the end of this document, and you will then be able to place an order with us to which these terms and conditions will apply.

PART A

General information

For your convenience, we have listed below some general information about ourselves:

- "We" are [*insert the full name of the supplier*] and our business address is [*insert details of address*].
- If you have an order related query, you may contact us as follows:

  Writing
  Phone
  Fax
  E-mail
- Our VAT number is [*insert details of VAT number*].

PART B

Contract information

(1) We do not offer to sell any of the goods appearing in this website to you. Instead, we are inviting you to place an offer with us and we reserve the right to reject any such offer received from you. We may choose to exercise this right if, for example, [*insert non-exhaustive list, e.g., unable to fulfil order, unsatisfactory credit rating, incomplete or inaccurate details given, price change*].

(2) If we accept your order, we will notify you and a legally binding contract will be formed between us at the time of sending such notification to you.

(3) You agree to be bound by the terms and conditions set out below. We may vary such terms and conditions at any time.

PART C

Terms of sale

Outline here the standard conditions for the supply of goods or services to business customers. Some useful headings are listed below.

1 Description and pricing

2 Delivery and risk

3 Title

Title to the goods ordered remains with us until such time as payment in cleared funds has been received from you.

4 Payment

5 Returns policy

6 Warranties and liability

7 Termination

8 *Force majeure*

We do not take responsibility for any event which is outside our reasonable control nor for any consequential loss arising from such an event.

9 Entire agreement

This agreement supersedes any prior agreements or arrangements which may have subsisted between us, provided the information you have given to us is not incorrect or fraudulent.

10 Interpretation

See clause 33 of Precedent A.

11 Law

See clause 34 of Precedent A.

12 Severability

See clause 36 of Precedent A.

If you agree to be bound by the above conditions please click YES at which point the software will make available to your computer our Order Form. If you do not agree click NO. The Order Form will not then be made available on your computer and no ordering can take place.

I agree to be bound by the above conditions for the use of the services and the software.	**YES**	**NO**

AGREEMENT FOR ACCESSING A SPECIFIC WEBSITE (CONSUMER)—TERMS AND CONDITIONS

[**Note**: These terms will appear on the user's screen as soon as he gains access to the website.]

Important Notice

These terms and conditions will apply when you access our website and use our on-line ordering service. Before proceeding to place an order, we ask that you read these terms and conditions carefully. You will also find that they contain some useful advice on how to use our on-line ordering service.

If you find yourself unable to agree to these terms and conditions, then you must not use our ordering service and we ask that you click on the "NO button" which shall appear at the end of this document. By doing so, you will return to our home page. If however, you agree to them unconditionally, you will be given the opportunity to click on the "YES button" which also appears at the end of this document, and you will then be able to place an order with us to which these terms and conditions will apply.

PART A

1 General information

For your convenience, we have listed below some general information about ourselves:

- "We" are [*insert the full name of the supplier*] and our address of establishment is at [*insert details of address*];

- Our e-mail address is [*insert details of e-mail address*];

- Our VAT number is [*insert details of VAT number*];

- We subscribe to the following codes of conduct [*insert details and address at which a copy of such codes can be obtained*].

2 Formation of contract

(1) Set out below is a useful summary of the steps which you must follow in order to conclude a legally binding contract with us:

(a) *Step 1*: Provided that you agree unconditionally to these terms and conditions, you will be given the opportunity at the end of this document to click on the "accept" button. The next page to appear on your screen will be our standard order form which contains information on price together with a description of the products and services which are available, and an explanation of any promotional offers and methods of payment.

(b) *Step 2*: On completing the order form you will be given the opportunity to submit an order to us by clicking on the "order" button which appears at the end of the form. On receipt, we will send to you notification by electronic mail that your order has been processed. Upon receipt of such notification and provided that you are able to access it, a legally binding contract will have been formed between us. We reserve the right not to process your order and accordingly, we will notify you immediately by electronic mail if this is the case.

If you do not wish to submit an order to us, you should click on the "escape" button and you will return to our home page.

(2) Please note that while we guarantee to send to you a notification of every valid order we receive from you, you will understand that we cannot equally guarantee that the notification we send will be received by you, nor that, if it is received by you, it is legible and uncorrupted.

(3) These terms and conditions shall override any contrary terms or conditions published by us or appearing on this website in relation to any order placed by you with us.

(4) [*Insert here, details as to whether the contract concluded will be filed and whether it will be accessible.*]

(5) [*Insert here, the steps which the customer must take to rectify any handling errors.*]

3 Conditions of use of this website and the on-line ordering service

(1) There are some situations where we cannot accept an order, and in the order form, you will be asked to identify if any of these are applicable to you by either clicking on a "YES" or "NO" box. You will ensure that your responses are not misleading or inaccurate, and accordingly you acknowledge that we are reliant upon you to complete the order form accurately.

(2) You agree not to post or transfer to our website (nor include in any message) any material which is obscene, misleading, inaccurate, defamatory, illegal, in breach of any copyright or other intellectual property right, or damaging to data, software or the performance of our or any other parties' computer system. You agree to indemnify us in respect of any liabilities, losses, expenses, or other costs whatsoever incurred as a result of a breach of your obligation under this condition 3(2), including, but not limited to, any claims made against us by any third party.

(3) The Data Protection Act 19998 is designed to protect individuals about whom information is entered and stored on computer and other systems. Accordingly, it lays down strict standards of accuracy, relevance and care of such data including how it may be divulged. Any data about individuals you enter onto our website directly or include in any message to us will be subject to the Act and you are

responsible for its accuracy and relevance and must have the authority to disclose it and for us to utilise it for the purposes of any transaction concluded for or by you through this website. If you are in any doubt about any data please feel free to e-mail us with details of the problem first.

(4) In consideration of agreeing to your use of this website, you acknowledge that the ownership in any intellectual property rights (including, for the avoidance of doubt, copyright) in this website belongs to us. Accordingly, any part of this website (or its source HTML code) may not be used, transferred, copied or reproduced in whole or in part in any manner other than for the purposes of utilizing this website meaning that you may only display it on your computer screen and print it out on your printer for the sole purpose of viewing its content.

(5) You may only use the trademarks featured in our website for the purpose of displaying this website on your computer screen or printing out this website on your printer in accordance with Condition 2(3) above.

(6) You may not link this website to any other website. Furthermore, we do not make any warranties, representations or undertakings about the content of any other website which may be referred to or accessed by hypertext link with this website, and we do not endorse or approve the content of such third party websites.

(7) We will collate the information which you give to us in the order form to provide you with our on line ordering service. By giving us this information, you consent to our use of it in order to process your order.

[*Alternative additional wording if disclosure required for the purposes of the Data Protection Acts:*

"In addition, we may provide this information to other companies who may be interested in sending you details of the goods or service which they would be able to offer to you. If you do not wish to have your details passed to such companies, please click NO on the relevant button at the end of the order form".]

(8) Please be aware that to the extent permitted by law and except as expressly provided for in part B of these terms and conditions, we do not accept liability in respect of this website, your use of it or our on-line ordering service.

(9) Use of this website is subject to the laws of England and Wales, and the exclusive jurisdiction of the English Courts.

PART B

Outline here the standard conditions for the supply of goods or services to consumers. Some useful headings are listed below.

1 Description and pricing

2 Delivery and risk

3 Title

See clause 3 of Precedent V.

4 Payment

5 Right to withdraw

(1) In certain circumstances, you may have the right to withdraw from the contract without penalty and without the need to give us any reason, at any time during a period of seven working days (Monday to Friday inclusive) which in the case of goods shall begin from the day after the day of receipt of the goods by you and in the case of services, from the day after the day of conclusion of the contract.

(2) For your convenience, we will notify you as to whether you have a right to withdraw in respect of any of the products on the order form which will appear on the screen if you click the "YES" button at the bottom of this document.

(3) We agree to reimburse you, free of charge, within 30 days of notification of withdrawal, the purchase price you paid for the goods or services, although we do reserve the right to charge you for the cost of returning any goods (which shall be by deduction from the purchase price).

(4) This right of withdrawal shall not apply, in any event, in the following circumstances:

- to services if performance of the contract has begun with your agreement, before the end of the seven working day period; or
- to any goods made to your specification or personalised at your request.

[Note: other exceptions may apply depending upon nature of goods/services being supplied—see The Consumer Protection (Distance Selling) Regulations 2000 (S.I. 2000 No. 2334), reg. 13.]

6 Returns policy

7 Warranties and liability

See clause 6 of Precedent V.

8 Termination

[Note: Include a right to terminate the contract in the event the consumer acts in breach of their obligation under Part 1, section 3, Conditions 2 and 3.]

Part C

1 Complaints

We aim to provide you with a quality service. If, however, you feel that you have cause to complain, you can contact us at the address given in section 1 of Part A above. We will try to do our best to solve any problems that arise.

2 *Force majeure*

See clause 8 of Precedent V.

3 Entire agreement

See clause 9 of Precedent V.

4 Interpretation

See clause 33 of Precedent A.

5 Law

See clause 34 of Precedent A.

6 Severability

See clause 36 of Precedent A.

If you agree to be bound by the above conditions please click YES at which point the software will make available to your computer our Order Form. If you do not agree click NO. The Order Form will not then be made available on your computer and no ordering can take place.

I agree to be bound by the above conditions for the use of the services and the software.	**YES**	**NO**

If you are content to receive e-mails from selected third parties in accordance with A3(7) above please click YES. If you do not wish to receive such mailings, please click NO here.

I agree to allow my e-mail address to be divulged to selected third parties for marketing and related purposes.	**YES**	**NO**

PRECEDENT X

CONSULTANCY AGREEMENT

THIS AGREEMENT is made the   day of   20

PARTIES:

(1) CONSULTANT [LIMITED] [PLC] whose registered office is at

("the Consultant")

(2) CLIENT [LIMITED] [PLC] whose registered office is at

("the Client")

RECITALS:

(A) The Client wishes to acquire a computer system to meet its requirements as hereinafter mentioned

(B) The Client has agreed to engage the Consultant to provide certain consultancy services in connection with the proposed acquisition of such computer system and the Consultant has agreed to accept such engagement on the terms and conditions hereinafter contained

NOW IT IS HEREBY AGREED as follows:

1 Definitions

In this Agreement, unless the context otherwise requires, the following expressions have the following meanings:

"Acceptance Tests"	means the agreed tests carried out on Project Materials to confirm that they are in conformance with the requirements of this Agreement.
"Completion of the Project"	means the acceptance by the Client of the System in accordance with the contract(s) for its supply.
"Confidential Information"	means this Agreement and all information obtained by one party from the other pursuant to this Agreement which is expressly marked as confidential or which is manifestly confidential or which is confirmed in writing to be confidential within 7 days of its disclosure.
"the Consulting Services"	means the consulting services to be provided by the Consultant pursuant to this Agreement.
"the Project"	means the acquisition by the Client of a fully operational computer system to meet the Client's requirements described in Schedule 1.

"the Project Materials"	means any and all works of authorship and materials developed, written or prepared by the Consultant, its employees, agents or sub-contractors in relation to the Project (whether individually, collectively or jointly with the Client and on whatever media) including, without limitation, any and all reports, studies, data, diagrams, charts, specifications, pre- contractual and contractual documents and all drafts thereof and working papers relating thereto, but excluding ordinary correspondence passing between the Consultant and the Client.
"the Project Participants"	means those employees and permitted sub-contractors of the Consultant engaged from time to time in providing the Consulting Services and any employees of any such sub-contractors who are so engaged.

2 Engagement

(1) The Client hereby agrees to engage the Consultant and the Consultant hereby agrees to provide the Consulting Services to the Client in relation to the Project.

(2) The Consultant represents and warrants to the Client that by virtue of entering into this Agreement it is not and will not be in breach of any express or implied obligation to any third party binding upon it.

3 Term [13.3, 13.4]

(1) This Agreement shall commence on *the date hereof* and shall continue until Completion of the Project, subject to any prior termination pursuant to clause 14.

[(2) In addition to the provision on termination in clause 14, the Client shall be entitled to terminate this Agreement forthwith by notice in writing to the Consultant given at any time, provided that it pays the Consultant for all the Consulting Services provided up to the date of termination and for all reasonable costs and expenses incurred by it by reason of such early termination including but not limited to *20 days'* fees for each of the Project Participants working on the Consulting Services at the time of such termination.

[Note: The reason for the 20 days' payment is to recognise that the consultant cannot instantaneously redeploy the project participants on receipt of a notice of termination which is not the consultant's fault. In this example, 20 working days represents (approximately) one month's work. For a large consultancy project which represents a sizeable part of the consultant's work force the charge might be even larger. Alternatively the agreement could provide for a period of notice to be given to the consultant, but with immediate termination on the occurrence of certain pre-defined events such as those specified in clause 14. If the consultant has incurred significant costs in bidding for the project or gearing up for the provision of the services, it may also expect to recover a proportion of its lost profit in such circumstances.]

4 Duties [13.1, 13.5, 13.7.1]

(1) The Consultant shall:

(a) review the requirements of the Client and advise it on the most appropriate type of computer system to fulfil such requirements [and whether the Client should rent, lease or buy such system];

(b) assist the Client with the preparation of a detailed requirements specification and a standard form of invitation to tender to be sent to potential suppliers;

(c) recommend a short-list of potential suppliers;

(d) review the tenders received from potential suppliers and assist the Client in choosing the most suitable contractor(s);

(e) assist the Client and its solicitors in the negotiation of the contract(s) for the supply of a computer system;

(f) assist the Client with the recruitment of appropriate personnel to operate and supervise the running of such computer system;

(g) supervise the installation of such system and conduct appropriate acceptance tests on behalf of the Client and advise it on the issue of any necessary acceptance certificates;

(h) *[Here set out any other specific duties of the consultant]*;

(i) perform such other duties in relation to the Project as may be mutually agreed from time to time.

[Note: These duties are given by way of example only and will vary according to the particular nature of the consultancy.]

(2) The Consultant shall devote to its obligations hereunder such of its time, attention and skill as may be necessary for the proper performance of those obligations.

(3) While the Consultant's method of work is its own, the Consultant shall comply with the reasonable requests of the Client and shall use all reasonable endeavours to promote the interests of the Client in relation to the Project.

(4) In the event that any change to the nature or scope of the Consultancy Services is identified as being desirable by either the Consultant or the Client, a request may be submitted to the other party to effect such change. Any such request shall be sufficiently detailed to enable the other party to assess the impact of the proposed change. No such change will become effective until agreed in writing between the parties.

[Note: this is a very simple change control procedure; for larger projects, a more formal approach may be required, eg with pro forma change request forms, identified reviewing and authorising points of contact, etc. [3.5.2, D7].]

5 Consultant's undertakings [13.0.3, 13.7.2]

The Consultant warrants and undertakes to the Client that:

(1) the Consultant and the Project Participants will have the necessary skill and expertise to provide the Consulting Services on the terms set out in this Agreement and for the avoidance of doubt agrees that the warranty in this subclause does not negative or vary its obligations to the Client under the Supply of Goods and Services Act 1982;

[Note: In *Salvage Association v. CAP*, the defendant argued (unsuccessfully) that its own wording of its warranty as to the quality of its services negatived its obligations under the Act.]

(2) the Consultant will provide independent and unbiased advice to the Client in relation to the Project;

(3) the Consultant will make available (amongst others) those employees of the Consultant named in Schedule 2 to perform the duties of the Consultant hereunder or such replacements of equivalent status as may be approved by the Client (such approval not to be unreasonably withheld or delayed) and will use all reasonable endeavours to ensure that they remain available to the extent necessary to perform their allotted tasks until the Completion of the Project;

(4) the Project Materials will, so far as they do not comprise pre-existing material originating from the Client, its employees, agents or contractors, be original works of authorship and the use or possession thereof by the Client or the Consultant will not subject the Client or the Consultant to any claim for infringement of any proprietary rights of any third party;

(5) the Consulting Services will be provided in a timely and professional manner and in accordance with the time schedules reasonably stipulated by the Client [provided always that time shall not be of the essence in this regard], will conform to the standards generally observed in the industry for similar services and will be provided with reasonable skill and care;

(6) the Consultant will not, without the prior written consent of the Client, accept any commission or gift or other financial benefit or inducement from any supplier or potential supplier of the whole or any part of the System and will ensure that its employees, agents and sub-contractors will not accept any such and will forthwith give the Client details of any such commission, gift, benefit or inducement which may be offered;

(7) no announcement or publicity concerning this Agreement or the Project or any matter ancillary thereto shall be made by the Consultant without the prior written consent of the Client;

[(8) the Consultant has in effect and will maintain in effect during the continuance of this Agreement professional indemnity insurance on the terms set out in Schedule 3 and will not do or omit to do anything whereby such insurance may be vitiated either in whole or in part;]

[(9) the fees to be charged to the Client for the Consulting Services will be no greater than the lowest rates charged by the Consultant from time to time to its other clients requiring similar services.]

[Note: sub-clause (9) will only be appropriate in rare circumstances,, such as where it has a preferential rate for (for example) charities or educational trusts, and will almost certainly be contested by the larger IT and management consultancy organisations, for whom it would be almost impossible to police.]

6 Client's obligations [3.6.1, 13.6]

In addition to its obligations set out elsewhere in this Agreement the Client shall:

(1) make available to the Consultant such office, [computer] and secretarial services as may be necessary for its work under this Agreement;

(2) ensure that its employees and any sub-contractors co-operate fully with the Consultant and the Project Participants in relation to the provision of the Consulting Services and that such employees and any such sub-contractors will be qualified to carry out any tasks which they may be assigned in relation to the Project;

(3) promptly furnish the Consultant with such information and documents as it may reasonably request for the proper performance of its obligations

hereunder and be responsible for ensuring that such information is true, accurate, complete and not misleading in any material respect;

(4) obtain all third party consents, licences and rights reasonably required in order to allow the Consultant and the Project Participants to perform the Consulting Services; and

(5) put in place adequate security and virus checking procedures in relation to any computer facilities to which it provides the Consultant with access.

Should the Client fail to perform any of its obligations under this Agreement then the Consultant will not be responsible for any delay, cost increase or other consequences arising from such failure, and the Client shall reimburse the Consultant for any costs or expenses incurred due to such failure.

7 Personnel [3.6.1, 3.7.1]

(1) The parties shall each appoint a representative who shall have full authority to take all necessary decisions regarding the Project and the provision of the Consulting Services [including the written variation of this Agreement].

(2) The parties shall procure that their representatives shall meet at [regular intervals] [at least once a *week*] during the continuance of this Agreement to discuss and minute the progress of the Project and the Consulting Services.

(3) The Client shall be entitled to request and obtain, at its discretion, the removal and replacement of any of the Project Participants which it may designate, provided that the Client shall not exercise such right unreasonably, frivolously or vexatiously.
[**Note:** the Consultant may resist such a right if the work is being performed for a fixed price, in which event it will be essential for the Consultant to retain control of the make-up of its project team.]

(4) The Consultant shall ensure that while any of the Project Participants are on the Client's premises they will conform to the Client's normal codes of staff and security practice [of which the Consultant is notified in writing by the Client].

8 Ownership of project materials [3.8, 13.4]

(1) Subject to the rights of the Consultant and/or its third party licensors in respect of any pre-existing materials which are supplied in conjunction with the Project Materials (which shall remain unaffected), the Client shall be entitled to all property, copyright and other intellectual property rights in the Project Materials, which property, copyright and other intellectual property rights the Consultant hereby, with full title guarantee, assigns to the Client.

(2) At the request and expense of the Client, the Consultant shall do all such things and sign all documents or instruments reasonably necessary to enable the Client to obtain, defend and enforce its rights in the Project Materials.

(3) Upon request by the Client, and in any event upon the expiration or termination of this Agreement, the Consultant shall at its expense promptly deliver to the Client all copies of the Project Materials then in the Consultant's custody, control or possession.

(4) Notwithstanding the above, the Consultant reserves the right to use in any way it sees fit any programming tools, skills and techniques acquired or used by it in the performance of the Consulting Services.

(5) The provisions of this Clause shall survive the expiration or termination of this Agreement.

9 Fees and expenses [3.0.3, 3.2, 13.2, D5]

(1) The Client shall pay the Consultant for the time properly spent by the Project Participants in providing the Consulting Services at the [hourly] [daily] charge-out rates specified in Schedule 2.

(2) The [hourly] [daily] charge-out rates of any new Project Participants which the Consultant wishes to use from time to time shall be agreed in writing with the Client, such agreement not to be unreasonably withheld or delayed.

[(3) The Consultant shall be entitled at any time and from time to time to vary any or all of such [hourly] [daily] charge-out rates to accord with its or its permitted sub-contractors' standard scale rates in force from time to time, provided that no such variation shall have effect unless and until written notice thereof is given to the Client.]

(4) The Consultant shall maintain full and accurate records of the time spent by the Project Participants in providing the Consulting Services and shall produce such records to the Client for inspection at all reasonable times on request.

(5) The Consultant shall render monthly itemised invoices to the Client in respect of the said charges and shall show any Value Added Tax separately on such invoices. The Client shall not account to the Consultant for any charges save on receipt of such invoice. Each invoice shall be accompanied by a statement specifying the time spent by each of the Project Participants in providing the Consulting Services during the period covered by the invoice.

(6) All charges payable by the Client shall, subject as aforesaid, be paid within *14* days after the receipt by the Client of the Consultant's invoice therefor.

(7) If it shall be necessary for any of the Project Participants to visit the Client's premises or make any other journeys in the course of providing the Consulting Services then the Client shall reimburse the Consultant for all reasonable travelling and subsistence expenses properly incurred in so doing [((and for the avoidance of doubt time spent travelling in this manner shall be included within the time spent by the Project Participants in providing the Consulting Services)]. Apart from minor out-of-pocket expenses, claims for reimbursement of expenses shall be paid by the Client only if accompanied by the relevant receipts.

(8) The charges payable under this Agreement are exclusive of Value Added Tax which shall be paid by the Client at the rate and in the manner for the time being prescribed by law

(9) If any sum payable under this Agreement is not paid within *7* days after the due date then (without prejudice to the Consultant's other rights and remedies) the Consultant reserves the right to charge interest on such sum on a day to day basis (as well after as before any judgment) from the date or last date for payment thereof to the date of actual payment (both dates inclusive) at the rate of *2* per cent above the base rate of *ABC* Bank plc (or such other London Clearing Bank as the

Consultant may nominate) from time to time in force compounded quarterly. Such interest shall be paid by the Client on demand by the Consultant.

[**Note**: this clause pre-supposes that the Consultant is to be paid on a time and materials basis; different wording would be required if there is to be either a fixed fee or a cap on the amount of time and materials fees which can be charged.]

10 Acceptance [13.3, 13.7.1]

(1) All Project Materials shall be deemed to have been accepted by the Client if no issues concerning their quality and/or contents have been raised by the Client within 5 *working days* of their delivery by the Consultant. The Client shall not in any event unreasonably withhold or delay its acceptance.

(2) Completion of the Project shall be deemed to have occurred when all Project Materials which are subject to acceptance by the Client have been so accepted.

[**Note**: this clause provides a simple acceptance procedure; (*e.g.* in relation to documentary deliverables such as reports, specifications and so on); more detailed provisions may be required, particularly if there is software/hardware involved—see for example clause 10 of Precedent D.]

11 Confidential information [13.7.2]

(1) The Consultant shall not use or divulge or communicate to any person (other than those whose province it is to know the same or with the authority of the Client) any Confidential Information of the Client [and its subsidiaries] which may come to the Consultant's knowledge in the course of providing the Consulting Services, including any information concerning the Project.

(2) The Consultant shall use its best endeavours to prevent the unauthorised publication or disclosure of any such Confidential Information.

(3) The Consultant shall ensure that its employees, agents and sub-contractors are aware of and comply with the confidentiality and non-disclosure provisions contained in this Clause and the Consultant shall be responsible to the Client in respect of any loss or damage which the Client may sustain or incur as a result of any breach of confidence by any of such persons

(4) If the Consultant becomes aware of any breach of confidence by any of its employees, agents or sub-contractors it shall promptly notify the Client and give the Client all reasonable assistance in connection with any proceedings which the Client may institute against any such persons.

(5) The provisions of this clause shall survive the expiration or termination of this Agreement but the restrictions contained in sub-clause (1) shall not apply to any Confidential Information which:

(a) comes into the public domain otherwise than through unauthorised disclosure by the Consultant, its employees, agents or sub-contractors;

(b) is already known to the Consultant prior to the commencement of the Consulting Services;

(c) is independently developed by the Consultant;

(d) is lawfully acquired from a third party who owes no duty of confidence to the Client; or

(e) is required by any court of competent jurisdiction or by a governmental or regulatory authority to be disclosed or where there is a legal right, duty or requirement to disclose, provided that where possible and without breaching any such requirements, 2 days' notice is given to the Client of any such disclosure.

[Note: it may be that the consultant will also disclose confidential material of its own to the Client, in which case it may be appropriate for the obligations of confidentiality to be made mutual.]

[12 Restrictions [13.0.2, 13.7.2]

(1) The Consultant shall not [and will procure that none of the Project Participants shall] (whether directly or indirectly or whether on its [or their] own account or for the account of any other person, firm or company, or as agent, director, partner, manager, employee, consultant or shareholder of or in any other person, firm or company) at any time during the period from the date hereof to the expiry of *one year* after the date of expiration or termination of this Agreement for any reason and in any manner whatsoever work on any project similar to the Project for any person, firm or company which is engaged in or conducts a business [in the United Kingdom] the same as or similar to or competitive with the business of the Client as carried on at the date hereof.

[Note: Consider whether any such restrictions might infringe the Competition Act 1998; in general, the scope of any restriction must be closely related to the nature of the work carried out under the Agreement, and many consultants will in any event be reluctant to accept such restrictions.]

[(2) Neither party shall (whether directly or indirectly or whether on its [or their] own account or for the account of any other person, firm or company, or as agent, director, partner, manager, employee, consultant or shareholder of or in any other person, firm or company) at any time during the period from the date hereof to the expiry of *one year* after the date of expiration or termination of this Agreement solicit any person then employed by the other party who has been involved in the Project without the prior written consent of that other party.]

13 Assignment

(1) Save as provided in sub-clause (2) below, the Consultant shall not be entitled to assign or sub-contract any of its rights or obligations under this Agreement.

(2) The Consultant shall be entitled (subject to the prior written approval of the Client, which shall not be unreasonably withheld or delayed) to engage the services of independent contractors of its own to assist it with its duties hereunder, provided that the Consultant:

(a) shall not be relieved from any of its obligations hereunder by engaging any such independent contractor;

(b) shall secure binding obligations from any such independent contractor so as to ensure that the Consultant can comply with its obligations under this Agreement including, in particular, its obligations under clauses 8, 11 hereof; and

(c) shall, upon request by the Client, first procure that any such independent contractor enters into direct covenants with the Client in terms similar to and covering the provisions of clauses 8, 11 hereof.

14 Termination

See clause 18 of Precedent A.

15 Effect of termination

On the expiration or termination of this Agreement:

(1) all rights and obligations of the parties under this Agreement shall automatically terminate except for such rights of action as shall have accrued prior thereto and any obligations which expressly or by implication are intended to come into or continue in force on or after such expiration or termination;

(2) the Client shall pay the Consultant for all unpaid charges and reimbursable expenses accrued up to the date of expiration or termination;

(3) the Consultant shall give the Client, at its request, all reasonable co-operation in transferring all sub-contracts made by the Consultant here-under to the extent that sub-contractors approve and provided that the Consultant is fully released from its obligations in relation thereto;

(4) each party will return to the other any property of the other that it then has in its possession or control.

16 Liability

See clause 27 of Precedent A.

17 Interpretation

See clause 33 of Precedent A.

18 Notices

See clause 32 of Precedent A.

19 *Force majeure*

See clause 15 of Precedent A.

20 Disputes

See clause 35 of Precedent A.

21 General [13.0.2]

The Consultant is an independent contractor and nothing in this Agreement shall render it an agent or partner of the Client and the Consultant shall not hold itself out as such. The Consultant shall not have any right or power to bind the Client to any obligation. This Agreement constitutes the entire understanding between the parties concerning the subject matter hereof and shall be governed by and construed in accordance with the laws of England. No waiver or amendment of any provision of this Agreement shall be effective unless made by a written instrument signed by both parties. Each provision of this Agreement shall be construed separately and notwithstanding that the whole or any part of any such provision may prove to be illegal or unenforceable the other provisions of this Agreement and the remainder of the provision in question shall continue in full force and effect.

22 Third parties [1.3]

See clause 37 of Precedent A.

EXECUTED under hand in two originals the day and year first before written

SIGNED for and on behalf of
CONSULTANT [LIMITED] [PLC]

By

Signature

Title

Witness

SIGNED for and on behalf of
CLIENT [LIMITED] [PLC]

By

Signature

Title

Witness

Schedule 1

CLIENT'S REQUIREMENTS FOR THE PROPOSED COMPUTER SYSTEM

Schedule 2

CONSULTANT'S EMPLOYEES TO BE MADE AVAILABLE TO THE CLIENT FOR THE PURPOSES OF THE PROJECT

[HOURLY] [DAILY] CHARGE OUT RATES OF PROJECT PARTICIPANTS.

[Note: this will probably be expressed by identifying a particular grade or position for each project participant and then giving rates for all participants at a particular grade or position.]

Schedule 3

DETAILS OF CONSULTANT'S PROFESSIONAL INDEMNITY INSURANCE

[Schedule 4

THIRD-PARTY RIGHTS]

MASTER AGREEMENT FOR PROGRAMMING SERVICES

THIS AGREEMENT is made the   day of   20

PARTIES:

(1) CLIENT [LIMITED] [PLC] whose registered office is at

("the Company")

(2) . . .   of

("the Contractor")

RECITALS:

(A) The Contractor is a self employed computer programmer [13.0.2]

(B) The Company has agreed to engage the Contractor to provide computer programming and related services from time to time and the Contractor has agreed to accept such engagement on the terms and conditions hereinafter contained

NOW IT IS HEREBY AGREED as follows:

1 Definitions

In this Agreement, unless the context otherwise requires, the following expressions have the following meanings:

"this Agreement"	means this *Master Agreement* and the Subsidiary Agreements both collectively and individually.
"Confidential Information"	means this Agreement and all information obtained by one party from the other pursuant to this Agreement which is expressly marked as confidential or which is manifestly confidential or which is confirmed in writing to be confidential within 7 days of its disclosure.
"Equipment"	means the Company's computer hardware [network] and associated peripherals equipment specified in any subsidiary Agreement or such other equipment as may be agreed between the parties.

[Note: If performance criteria are relevant then any change in the configuration of the equipment ought to be agreed between the parties.]

"intellectual property rights"	means patents, trade marks, Internet domain names, service marks, registered designs, applications for any of the foregoing, copyright, design rights, know-how, confidential information, databases, trade and business names and any other similar protected rights in any country.

"Programs"	means the [applications] computer programs to be written by the Contractor as part of any project.
"Project"	means the work undertaken pursuant to any Subsidiary Agreement.
"Project Materials"	means any and all works of authorship, products and materials developed, written or prepared by the Contractor in relation to the Projects (whether alone or jointly with the Company or any other independent contractor of the Company and on whatever media) including, without limitation, any and all computer programs, data, diagrams, charts, reports, specifications, studies and inventions and all drafts thereof and working papers relating thereto.
"Subsidiary Agreement"	has the meaning attributed thereto in clause 4(2).
"the Services"	means [the computer programming and related] services to be provided by the Contractor pursuant to this Agreement.

2 Engagement [13.0.2]

(1) The Company hereby agrees to engage the Contractor and the Contractor hereby agrees to provide the Services as an independent contractor on the terms and conditions set out in this Agreement.

(2) The Contractor represents and warrants to the Company that by virtue of entering into this Agreement he is not and will not be in breach of any express or implied obligation to any third party binding upon him.

3 Term

(1) This Master Agreement shall commence on *the date hereof*, shall continue for an initial period of *one year* and shall remain in force thereafter [unless or] until terminated by either party giving to the other not less than 6 months' written notice of termination [given on] [expiring on] the last day of the said initial period or at any time thereafter but shall be subject to any prior termination pursuant to clause 13.

[(2) In addition to the provisions on termination in clause 13, in the event that the Contractor is unable to carry out his obligations under this Agreement due to illness or accident and such incapacity continues for a period of more than 3 months the Company shall be entitled to terminate this Master Agreement forthwith by notice in writing to the Contractor given at any time while such incapacity continues.]

4 Duties

(1) Any work to be undertaken by the Contractor pursuant to this Agreement shall be jointly agreed between the parties and shall be set out in a written proposal describing:

(a) the nature of such work;

(b) the time schedules pursuant to which such work will be undertaken and completed;

(c) the time and other resources which the Contractor will devote to such work; and

(d) the amount and/or method of calculation of the fees of the Contractor for such work.

(2) Each proposal will be incorporated into a subsidiary agreement ("Subsidiary Agreement") between the parties substantially in the form of the letter agreement set out in Schedule 1 hereto.

(3) The Contractor is not authorised to undertake any work for the Company which is not the subject of a duly executed Subsidiary Agreement.

[(4) If the Contractor shall undertake any work at the Company's request which is not the subject of a Subsidiary Agreement then, unless the parties otherwise agree in writing, the provisions of this Master Agreement shall apply thereto (so far as the same are capable of applying) and if no fee is agreed for such work the Contractor shall be paid on a quantum meruit basis.]

[Note: Sub-clause (4) is a safety clause to cover the situation where the company requests the contractor to undertake some programming work but forgets to sign up a Subsidiary Agreement.]

(5) This Agreement is personal to the Contractor and he shall not be entitled to assign or sub-contract any of his rights or obligations under this Agreement.

(6) Subject to the restrictions on disclosure of information contained in Clause 10 and to the other obligations of the Contractor contained in this Agreement, nothing in this Agreement shall prevent the Contractor from engaging in other activities on a self-employed basis or in part time employment.

5 Contractor's undertakings

The Contractor warrants and undertakes to the Company that:

(1) he will have the necessary skill and expertise to provide the Services on the terms set out in this Agreement and for the avoidance of doubt agrees that the warranty in this subclause does not negative or vary his obligations to the Company under the Supply of Goods and Services Act 1982;

[Note: In *Salvage Association v. CAP*, the defendant argued (unsuccessfully) that its own wording of its warranty as to the quality of its services negatived its obligations under the Act.]

(2) the Project Materials will, so far as they do not comprise existing materials originating from the Company, its employees, agents or contractors, be original works of authorship and the use or possession thereof by the Company or the Contractor will not subject the Company or the Contractor to any claim for infringement of any intellectual property rights of any third party;

(3) the Services will be provided in a timely and professional manner and in accordance with the time schedules stipulated in each Subsidiary Agreement [provided always that time shall not be of the essence in this regard],

will conform to the standards generally observed in the industry for similar services and will be provided with reasonable skill and care;

(4) no announcement or publicity concerning this Agreement or any Project or any matter ancillary thereto shall be made by the Contractor without the prior written consent of the Company;

(5) he will conform to the Company's normal codes of staff and security practice while he is on the Company's premises;

[(6) he has in effect and will maintain in effect during the continuance of this Agreement professional indemnity insurance on the terms set out in Schedule 2 and will not do or omit to do anything whereby such insurance may be vitiated either in whole or in part;]

[(7) in the event that the Contractor is unable to work as a result of either illness or injury, he shall immediately inform the Company and provide an estimate of the likely period of absence;]

[(8) he will notify as far as possible in advance of any periods during which he will be unable to provide the Services due to holiday, sickness or third party commitments [and he further agrees not to arrange holidays which would impact upon the provision of services by the Company to any end-client without the prior written consent of the Company];]

[(9) he will comply with the requirements of all relevant U.K. legislation and agreements, including those relating to Value Added Tax, income and other taxes and charges in respect of the provision of the Services and the fees payable to him under this Agreement.]

6 Company's obligations

In addition to its obligations set out elsewhere in this Agreement the Company shall:

(1) make available to the Contractor such office [, computer] and secretarial services as may be necessary for his work under this Agreement, provided that the Contractor shall not be obliged to make use of such facilities and services if, in his view, to do so would not be the most effective method of carrying out his obligations;

(2) ensure that its employees and any sub-contractors and other independent contractors co-operate fully with the Contractor in relation to the provision of the Services and that such employees and any such sub-contractors will be qualified to carry out any tasks which they may be assigned in relation to the Project;

(3) promptly furnish the Contractor with such information and documents as he may reasonably request for the proper performance of his obligations under this Agreement and be responsible for ensuring that such information is true, accurate, complete and not misleading in any material respect;

(4) obtain all third party consents, licenses and rights reasonably required in order to allow the Contractor to perform the Services; and

(5) put in place adequate security and virus checking procedures in relation to any computer facilities to which it provides the Contractor with access.

Should the Company fail to perform any of its obligations under this Agreement then the Contractor will not be responsible for any delay, cost increase or other consequences arising from such failure, and the Company shall reimburse the Contractor for any costs or expenses incurred due to such failure.

7 Supervision

(1) The Company shall appoint a representative who shall have full authority to take all necessary decisions regarding the Project and the provision of the Services [including the variation of this Agreement].

(2) The Contractor and the Company's representative shall meet at [regular intervals] [at least once a *week*] during the continuance of each Project to discuss and minute the progress of such Project.

(3) While the Contractor's method of work is his own, the Contractor shall comply with the reasonable requests of the Company and shall use all reasonable endeavours to promote the interests of the Company in relation to each Project.

(4) In the event that any change to the nature or scope of the Services being performed under the Master Agreement or any Subsidiary Agreement is identified as being desirable by either the Contractor or the Company, a request may be submitted to the other party to effect such change. Any such request shall be sufficiently detailed to enable the other party to assess the impact of the proposed change. No such change will become effective until agreed in writing between the parties.

[**Note:** this is a very simple change control procedure; for larger projects, a more formal approach may be required, e.g. with pro forma change request forms, identified reviewing and authorising points of contacts, etc.]

8 Ownership of project materials

(1) Subject to the rights of the Contractor and/or its third party licensors in respect of any pre-existing materials which are supplied in conjunction with the Project Materials (which will remain unaffected) the Company shall be entitled to all property, copyright and other intellectual property rights in the Project Materials which property, copyright and other intellectual property rights the Contractor hereby, with full title guarantee, assigns to the Company.

(2) At the request and expense of the Company, the Contractor shall do all such things and sign all documents or instruments reasonably necessary to enable the Company to obtain, defend and enforce its rights in the Project Materials.

(3) Upon request by the Company, and in any event upon the expiration or termination of this Master Agreement, the Contractor shall promptly deliver to the Company all copies of the Project Materials then in the Contractor's custody, control or possession.

(4) Notwithstanding the above, the Contractor reserves the right to use in any way it sees fit any programming tools, skills and techniques acquired or used by it in the performance of the Services.

(5) The provisions of this Clause shall survive the expiration or termination of this Agreement.

9 Fees and expenses

(1) In consideration of the services rendered by the Contractor pursuant to each Subsidiary Agreement the Company shall pay to the Contractor fees in the amounts and at the rates set out in such Subsidiary Agreement (plus Value Added Tax, if applicable) and, where appropriate, the Contractor shall submit time sheets in respect of work carried out under any Subsidiary Agreement.

(2) Unless otherwise agreed in a Subsidiary Agreement, such fees shall accrue *monthly* and the Contractor shall render *monthly* invoices to the Company in respect of such fees and, where he is registered for Value Added Tax, shall show any Value Added Tax separately on such invoices. The Company shall not account to the Contractor for any fees save on receipt of such invoice.

(3) All fees shall be payable to the Contractor without deductions of any kind save in respect of monies owed by the Contractor to the Company. The Contractor shall account for his Income Tax, Value Added Tax and Class 2 and 4 Social Security contributions to the appropriate authorities.

(4) [The Contractor shall be responsible for all out-of-pocket expenses incurred by him in the performance of his duties under this Agreement] [The Company shall pay or reimburse to the Contractor (on production of such vouchers and/or other evidence as it may require) all reasonable and proper expenses incurred in connection with his duties under this Agreement].

(5) All charges payable by the Company shall, subject as aforesaid, be paid within *14* days after the receipt by the Company of the Contractor's invoice therefor.

(6) If any sum payable under this Agreement is not paid within *7* days after the due date then (without prejudice to the Contractor's other rights and remedies) the Contractor reserves the right to charge interest on such sum on a day to day basis (as well after as before any judgment) from the date or last date for payment thereof to the date of actual payment (both dates inclusive) at the rate of *2* per cent above the base rate of *ABC* Bank plc (or such other London Clearing Bank as the Contractor may nominate) from time to time in force compounded quarterly. Such interest shall be paid on demand by the Contractor.

[**Note:** this clause pre-supposes that the contractor is to be paid on a time and materials basis; different wording would be required if there was to be either a fixed fee or a cap on the amount of time and materials fees which can be charged.]

10 Testing and acceptance [3.3.1]

(1) On or before the completion of a Project the Company shall submit to the Contractor test data which in the reasonable opinion of the Company is suitable to test whether the Programs are in accordance with the specifications and/or performance criteria outlined in the Proposal attached to the relevant Subsidiary Agreement ("the Specification") together with the results expected to be achieved by processing such test data on the Equipment using the Programs and the *XYZ* operating system. The Contractor shall not be entitled to object to such test data or expected results unless the Contractor can demonstrate to the Company that they are not in accordance with the Specification, in which event the Company shall make such amendments to such test data and expected results as may be necessary for them to conform to the Specification.

(2) After the Programs have been successfully installed on the Equipment, the Contractor shall give to the Company at least 7 days' prior written notice (or such shorter notice as may be agreed between the parties) of the date ("the Testing Date") on which the Contractor will be ready to attend acceptance tests at the Company's premises. The Company and the Contractor shall attend such tests on the Testing Date and shall provide all necessary facilities to enable such tests to be carried out.

(3) On the Testing Date the Company shall process, in the presence of the Contractor, the said test data on the Equipment using the Programs and the said *XYZ* operating system. The Contractor shall if required by the Company give the Company's personnel all reasonable assistance in processing such test data.

(4) The Company shall accept the Programs immediately after the Programs have correctly processed such test data by achieving the expected results.

(5) The Programs shall not be deemed to have incorrectly processed such test data by reason of any failure to provide any facility or function not specified in the Specification.

(6) If the Programs shall fail to process such test data correctly then repeat tests shall be carried out on the same terms and conditions within a reasonable time thereafter but in any event no later than *14* days thereafter. [The Contractor shall not be entitled to make any charge for attending such repeat test.]

[Note: The words in brackets will be needed only in the case of a time and materials contract.]

(7) If such repeat tests demonstrate that the Programs are still not in accordance with the Specification then the Company may by written notice to the Contractor elect at its sole option:

(a) to fix (without prejudice to its other rights and remedies) a new date for carrying out further tests on the Programs on the same terms and conditions as the repeat tests (save that all reasonable costs which the Company may incur as a result of carrying out such tests shall be reimbursed by the Contractor. If the Programs shall fail such further tests then the Company shall be entitled to proceed under paragraph (b) or (c) below; or

(b) to accept the Programs subject to an abatement of the total consideration payable hereunder such abatement to be such amount as, taking into account the circumstances, is reasonable. In the absence of written agreement as to abatement within *14* days after the date of such notice the Company shall be entitled to reject the Programs in accordance with paragraph (c) below; or

(c) to reject the Programs as not being in conformity with the relevant Subsidiary Agreement in which event that Subsidiary Agreement shall automatically terminate [and the Contractor shall (without prejudice to the Company's other rights and remedies) forthwith refund to the Company all sums previously paid to the Contractor under this Subsidiary Agreement.]

[Note: A refund of all monies paid may not be appropriate if, notwithstanding termination, the client has acquired benefit from the services previously provided.]

(8) Notwithstanding anything else contained in this Clause, the Contractor shall be entitled (provided it has complied with its obligations under this Clause) at any time and from time to time after the Testing Date to serve written notice on the Company requiring the Company to identify any part of the Specification which the Programs do not fulfil. If the Company shall fail to identify in writing to the Contractor within *14* days after the receipt of such notice any part of the Specification which the Programs do not fulfil then the Company shall be deemed to have accepted the Programs.

(9) If at any time the Company shall commence live running of the whole or any part of the Programs (as distinct from acceptance testing) then the Company shall be deemed to have accepted the Programs.

(10) For the avoidance of doubt, "acceptance" shall denote that, at the relevant date, the Programs were in apparent compliance with the Specification but shall not operate as a form of waiver of any claim which either party may have against the other.

[Notes:

(1) Sub-clauses (8) and (9) are designed to protect the contractor in the event that the company unreasonably refuses to accept the programs.

(2) In a complicated development, testing and acceptance will be undertaken in stages with a final contractual acceptance at the end.

(3) The contractor may seek relief in relation to failures of acceptance tests which can be shown to result directly from user input in relation to the interpretation of functional or user requirements. Such instances however, will be rare, and the company will usually resist such a clause on the basis that the contractor may seek to use it as a general "get out".]

11 Confidential information [3.7.2, 13.7.2]

(1) The Contractor shall not use or divulge or communicate to any person (other than to those whose province it is to know the same or with the authority of the Company) any of the Confidential Information of the Company [and its subsidiaries] which may come to the Contractor's knowledge in the course of providing the Services, includingany information concerning any Project.

(2) The Contractor shall use his best endeavours to prevent the unauthorised publication or disclosure of any such Confidential Information.

(3) The provisions of this Clause shall survive the termination of this Master Agreement but the restrictions contained in sub-clause (1) shall not apply to any Confidential Information which:

(a) comes into the public domain otherwise than through unauthorised disclosure by the Contractor or anyone on his behalf;

(b) is already known to the Contractor prior to the commencement of the Services;

(c) is independently developed by the Contractor;

(d) is lawfully acquired from a third party who owes no duty of confidence to the Company; or

(e) is required by any court of competent jurisdiction or by a governmental or regulatory authority to be disclosed or where there is a legal right, duty or requirement to disclose, provided that where possible and without breaching any such requirements 2 days notice are given to the Company of any such disclosure.

[Note: it may be that the contractor will also disclose confidential material of its own to the company, in which case it may be appropriate for the obligations of confidentiality to be made mutual.]

[12 Restriction

If stipulated in any Subsidiary Agreement the Contractor shall not (whether directly or indirectly or whether on his own account or for the account of any other person, firm or company, or as agent, director, partner, manager, employee, consultant or shareholder of or in any other person, firm or company) at any time during the period from the commencement of the Project specified in such Subsidiary Agreement to the expiry of *one year* after the completion of such Project for any reason and in manner whatsoever work on any project similar to such Project for any other person, firm or company.]

[Note: Consider whether any such restrictions might infringe the Competition Act 1998; in general the scope of any restriction must be closely related to the nature of the work carried out under the contract, and many contractors will in any event be reluctant to accept such restrictions.]

13 Termination

See clause 18 of Precedent A.

14 Effect of termination

On the termination of this Master Agreement:

(1) all rights and obligations of the parties under this Master Agreement and each Subsidiary Agreement shall automatically terminate except:

(a) for such rights of action as shall have accrued prior to such termination and any obligations which expressly or by implication are intended to come into or continue in force on or after such termination including, in particular the provisions of clauses 8 and 11 hereof;

(b) that, in the event that this Master Agreement has been terminated by notice given by the Contractor pursuant to clause 3(1), the Contractor shall, at the request of the Company, complete any work to be performed under any existing Subsidiary Agreement and to that extent and for that purpose the provisions of this Master Agreement shall continue in effect until the Project under such Subsidiary Agreement has been completed.

(2) the Company shall pay the Contractor for all unpaid fees [and reimbursable expenses] accrued up to the date of termination;

(3) each party shall return to the other any property of the other that it has in its possession or control.

15 Indemnity

See clause 27 of Precedent A.

16 Interpretation

See clause 33 of Precedent A.

17 Notices

See clause 32 of Precedent A.

18 Inconsistency

Unless otherwise expressly provided in a Subsidiary Agreement by specific reference to this clause, if there shall be any inconsistency between the provisions of this Master Agreement and any Subsidiary Agreement the provisions of this Master Agreement shall prevail.

19 *Force majeure*

See clause 15 of Precedent A.

20 Disputes

See clause 35 of Precedent A.

21 General

The Contractor is an independent contractor and nothing in this Agreement shall render him an employee, agent or partner of the Company and the Contractor shall not hold himself out as such. The Contractor shall not have any right or power to bind the Company to any obligation. This Agreement constitutes the entire understanding between the parties concerning the subject matter of this Agreement and shall be governed by and construed in accordance with the laws of England. No waiver or amendment of any provision of this Agreement shall be effective unless made by a written instrument signed by both parties. Each provision of this Agreement shall be construed separately and notwithstanding that the whole or any part of any such provision may prove to be illegal or unenforceable the other provisions of this Agreement and the remainder of the provision in question shall continue in full force and effect.

22 Third parties [1.3]

See clause 37 of Precedent A.

EXECUTED under hand the day and year first before written

SIGNED for and on behalf of
CLIENT [LIMITED] [PLC]

By

Signature

Title

Witness

SIGNED for and on behalf of
[THE CONTRACTOR]

Signature

Witness

SCHEDULE 1

[To be typed on the Company's headed notepaper]

Dated: 20

Dear [   ]

We refer to the Master Agreement for programming services dated [   ] ("the Master Agreement") between Client [Limited] [PLC] ("the Company") and yourself pursuant to which you have agreed to perform certain services for and on behalf of the Company subject to the terms and conditions set out in the Master Agreement.

In consideration of the mutual covenants and agreements contained in this Subsidiary Agreement and in the Master Agreement, we agree as follows:

(1) *Nature of Work.* The nature and object of each task to be performed by you under this Subsidiary Agreement and the products that will be delivered by you to the Company in connection with such tasks are set out in the Proposal attached hereto ("the Proposal").

(2) *Timing.* You will perform the services in accordance with the time schedules contained in the Proposal.

(3) *Resources.* You will devote to the performance of such services the time and other resources described in the Proposal and such additional resources as may be necessary diligently to perform such services in a timely and efficient manner in accordance with the Proposal.

(4) *Fees.* In consideration of the services to be performed by you pursuant to this Subsidiary Agreement the Company will pay to you the fees set out in the Proposal.

(5) *Confirmation of Master Agreement.* You agree to perform the services described in this Subsidiary Agreement subject to the terms and conditions of the Master Agreement.

[(6) *Restriction.* The provisions of clause 12 of the Master Agreement shall apply in relation to the work to be undertaken pursuant to this Subsidiary Agreement.]

Please indicate your agreement to these terms and conditions by signing the enclosed copy of this Subsidiary Agreement and returning it to the undersigned.

Yours sincerely

Director
CLIENT [LIMITED] [PLC]

On the copy:

I agree the above terms and conditions

Dated: 20

[SCHEDULE 2

DETAILS OF CONTRACTOR'S PROFESSIONAL INDEMNITY INSURANCE]

[SCHEDULE 3

THIRD-PARTY RIGHTS]

NON-DISCLOSURE AGREEMENT

[Note: This is a practical way of reminding a supplier/contractor of his duty of confidence in respect of the customer/client's data. The danger arises not only from a negligent contractor or supplier, but also from negligence or worse on the part of his individual employees, even after they have left his service. The agreement is therefore in two parts: a corporate agreement to be signed by a representative of the supplier/contractor, and individual agreements to be signed by each of the employees reminding them of their duty of confidence both during the contractor's service and after they have left it [1.1, 3.7.2].]

For Company:

To: [*Insert name and address of disclosing party*]

In consideration of your agreeing to disclose to us information and documents in connection with studies [for the computerisation] of [   ] ("the Project") we [   ] of [   ] hereby agree that, save as hereinafter provided, such information and documents shall be treated by us as confidential and that we shall be subject to the following obligations:

(1) We will not without your prior written consent disclose any such information or documents to any third party and will use our best endeavours to prevent the unauthorised publication or disclosure of the same;

(2) We will divulge such information and documents only to those of our employees who are directly concerned with the Project [and who have been named by us to you in writing on or before the signing hereof] [and who have a legitimate need to know or see such information and/or documents for the purposes of fulfilling our responsibilities to you under this agreement];

(3) We will ensure that our employees are aware of and comply with the confidentiality and non-disclosure obligations contained herein and we will indemnify you against any loss or damage which you may sustain or incur as a result of any breach of confidence by any of our employees;

(4) We will not use such information or documents for any purpose other than for the Project;

(5) All papers furnished to us by you will be returned or otherwise disposed of as you may from time to time direct.

The foregoing obligations shall not extend to any such information or documents which were rightfully in our possession prior to the date hereof, which are already public knowledge or become so at a future date (otherwise than through unauthorised disclosure by us or our employees) or which are trivial or obvious. Nor shall such obligations apply to any disclosure which is required by law, by any court of competent jurisdiction or any regulatory body, provided that we give you as much notice of such impending disclosure as is reasonably possible.

The said obligations shall continue in full force and effect notwithstanding the completion of the Project, or the termination of our involvement with it.

This agreement shall be governed by the laws of England and subject to the exclusive jurisdiction of the English Courts.

Signed:

for and on behalf of [*receiving party*]

Position:

Date: 20

For Individual:

To: [*insert name and address of disclosing party*]

In consideration of your disclosing to me (whether directly or through my employer) information and documents in connection with studies [for the computerisation] of [   ] ("the Project") I [   ] of [   ] hereby agree that, save as hereinafter provided, such information and documents shall be treated by me as confidential and that I will be subject to the following obligations:

(1) I will not without your prior written consent disclose any such information or documents to any third party and will use my best endeavours to prevent the unauthorised publication or disclosure of the same;

(2) I will divulge such information and documents only to those of my fellow employees who are directly concerned with the Project [and who have a legitimate need to know or use such information or documents for the purposes of fulfilling their responsibilities] and who have prior to such disclosure entered into an agreement with you in the same form, *mutatis mutandis*, as this agreement or in such other form as may be approved by you;

(3) I will ensure that any such employees to whom I divulge any such information or documents are aware that the same is confidential to you;

(4) I will indemnify you against any loss or damage which you may sustain or incur as a result of any breach of confidence on my part;

(5) I will not use such information and documents for any purpose other than for the Project;

(6) All papers furnished to me by you (whether directly or through my employer) will be returned or otherwise disposed of as you may from time to time direct.

The foregoing obligations shall not extend to any such information or documents which were rightfully in my possession or that of my employer prior to the date hereof, which are already public knowledge or become so at a further date (otherwise than through unauthorised disclosure by me or by my employer or fellow employees) or which are trivial or obvious. Nor shall such obligations apply to any disclosure which is required by law, by any court of competent jurisdiction or any regulatory body, provided that I give you as much notice of such impending disclosure as reasonably possible.

The said obligations shall continue in full force and effect notwithstanding the completion of the Project, and/or the termination of my involvement with it.

This agreement shall be governed by the laws of England and subject to the exclusive jurisdiction of the English courts.

Signed:

[*receiving individual*]

Date: 20

UNSOLICITED DISCLOSURE AGREEMENT [4.3.3]

[**Note**: This is to be used by a company receiving an unsolicited offer of disclosure of new software/ business idea.]

Dear [   ]

Thank you for your letter of [   ] giving details of your [ideas] [programs] relating to [   ] ("the Work").

It is our policy to act fairly towards anyone who submits new ideas to us, but we are unable to accept any disclosure of new ideas unless it is governed by an agreement between us which clearly establishes our respective rights and obligations.

As I am sure you will appreciate, we are actively involved in many areas of research in the high technology field and we often receive disclosures from third parties. It would clearly be unfair to us if we were to be restrained from or otherwise penalised for making use of an idea or invention which has already been developed by us or is already rightfully in our possession merely because it is similar to your own work.

For this reason I must ask you to confirm that you will agree to submit details of the Work to us on the following basis:

(1) Acceptance of your disclosures will not, except as provided in this letter, place us under any obligation towards you.

(2) We will treat as confidential all information and documents disclosed by you which are clearly designated as such and which are not already public knowledge ("Confidential Information"), but this obligation shall not prevent us from making use of any information and documents already rightfully in our possession (except where such use would infringe any patent rights belonging to you) and shall cease to apply to any Confidential Information supplied by you which may come into the public domain otherwise than through unauthorised disclosure by us or our employees. In addition, this obligation shall not apply where we are required by a court of competent jurisdiction or by a governmental or regulatory authority or where we are subject to a legal right, duty or requirement to disclose any Confidential Information. However, provided that such requirements would not be breached we will give you 2 days' notice of any such disclosure.

(3) If our negotiations fail then we shall promptly return all written material supplied by you together with our certificate that no copies have been retained by us and that no unauthorised use has been made thereof.

(4) You warrant to us that:

    (a) the Work has not been written, prepared or developed in the course of your carrying out your duties on behalf of any other person, firm or company and that you are the exclusive owner thereof free from any encumbrances; and

    (b) you have not disclosed the Work to any third party with a view to its exploitation or acquisition and undertake that you will not do so for a period of *30* days after submitting the Work to us pursuant to the terms set out in this letter.

(5) Prior to the end of that period of *30* days we shall notify you either that we do wish to commence negotiations with you or that we do not, in which latter case paragraph (3) above will apply.

(6) If we inform you that we wish to proceed with negotiations then we shall endeavour to reach a formal agreement with you for the exploitation or acquisition of the Work but in the event that a formal agreement is not signed within *60* days after the commencement of negotiations we reserve the right to withdraw therefrom. While negotiations are proceeding with us you undertake not to approach any third party with a view to offering the Work to that third party. You will notify us if you decide to withdraw from negotiations.

(7) If we consider that the Work is similar to any which we have already developed or had submitted to us by a third party we will inform you accordingly and, if we decide to proceed with that work but not to enter into a contractual relationship with you for the commercial exploitation or acquisition of the Work you will be entitled (at any time during the period of *one month* after we notify you in writing (which we undertake to do) that we are in a position to proceed with the commercial exploitation of our own work), to appoint an independent expert to report to you as to whether our work impinges on your own and, if so, whether it is based solely on information already rightfully in our possession or whether it makes use of any of the information disclosed by you. The following provisions shall govern the appointment of the expert:

    (a) he will be appointed by agreement between us, failing which, by the President from time to time of the *British Computer Society* on the application of either of us;

    (b) he will be given full access to all relevant documents and information subject to his entering into a confidentiality undertaking in a form acceptable to us;

    (c) he will use the information and documents disclosed to him only for the purpose of reporting to you as aforesaid and in particular he will not be entitled to make any disclosure of such information or documents to you;

    (d) he will supply one copy of his report to us;

    (e) the conclusions set out in his report will (save in the case of clerical or manifest error) be final and binding on both of us and if the report concludes that we have not made use of any information received from you, you agree that you will have no claim against us in respect thereof except for any infringement of any patent rights belonging to you resulting from our activities;

(f) he will act as an expert and not an arbitrator and his fees for so acting shall be borne [[as to *one half*] by you [and the *other half* by us]]. [as he may direct upon making his ruling]

If you agree the above terms please indicate your agreement by signing and returning to me the enclosed copy of this letter together with all the material which you wish to disclose to us.

I return with this letter you letter of [   ] [together with its enclosures] and I confirm that no copies have been taken or other use made thereof except for the purpose of writing this letter.

I look forward to hearing from you.

Yours, etc.

On the copy:

I agree the terms of the above

Signed:

Dated: 20

INDEX

THE COMPANION DISK

Instructions for Use

Introduction

These notes are provided for guidance only. They should be read and interpreted in the context of your own computer system and operational procedures. It is assumed that you have a basic knowledge of WINDOWS. However, if there is any problem please contact our help line on 020 7393 7266 who will be happy to help you.

Diskette Format and Contents

The diskette, which accompanies this book, is suitable for WINDOWS 95 computers that can read *high density* (1.44 Mbytes) 3.5 inch diskettes.

The diskette contains data files covering the *precedent* section of this book. It does not contain software, or other text or commentary.

Please refer to the "**Contents List**" document for the numbering of Appendices.

Installation

Please note that the documents on this diskette are stored in compressed form and *cannot be used directly*. Be sure to install the documents to your hard disk as described below.

The following instructions make the assumption that you will copy the data files to a single directory on your hard disk (e.g. C:\Morgan), and that your diskette drive is called A:\.

1. Insert the diskette into the A drive of your computer. From your **Start** button, choose **Run**. Type **A:\Morgan.exe** and click on the **OK** button. Follow the instructions on the screen.

Using the materials with Microsoft Word

N.B. for other versions of Word, and other Windows word processors in general, the instructions will be similar, but if you are not sure refer to the documentation that came with your word processor.

1. To open a Morgan document in Word, select **File, Open** from the menu. Highlight the Morgan directory in the **Directories** list box. Select the desired document, e.g. "PrecA" from the list and press OK.

2. You may wish to save the document to your working folder: select **File Save As** from the menu. In the **Directories** list box, highlight your working folder. In the **File Name** list box type a suitable name such as "**newdoc**". Press **OK**.

Any other amendments can now be dealt with.

LICENCE AGREEMENT

Definitions

1. The following terms will have the following meanings:

"The PUBLISHERS" means Sweet & Maxwell of 100 Avenue Road, London NW3 3PF (which expression shall, where the context admits, include the PUBLISHERS' assigns or successors in business as the case may be) of the other part on behalf of Thomson Books Limited of Cheriton House, North Way, Andover SP10 5BE.

"The LICENSEE" means the purchaser of the title containing the Licensed Material.

"Licenced Material" means the data included on the disk;

"Licence" means a single user licence;

"Computer" means an IBM-PC compatible computer.

Grant of Licence; Back-up Copies

2.(1) The PUBLISHERS hereby grant to the LICENSEE, a non-exclusive, non-transferable licence to use the Licensed Material in accordance with these terms and conditions.

(2) The LICENSEE may install the Licensed Material for use on one computer only at any one time.

(3) The LICENSEE may make one back-up copy of the Licensed Material only, to be kept in the LICENSEE's control and possession.

Proprietary Rights

3.(1) All rights not expressly granted herein are reserved.

(2) The Licensed Material is not sold to the LICENSEE who shall not acquire any right, title or interest in the Licensed Material or in the media upon which the Licensed Material is supplied.

(3) The LICENSEE shall not erase remove, deface or cover any trademark, copyright notice, guarantee or other statement on any media containing the Licensed Material.

(4) The LICENSEE shall only use the Licensed Material in the normal course of its business and shall not use the Licensed Material for the purpose of operating a bureau or similar service or any online service whatsoever.

(5) Permission is hereby granted to LICENSEES who are members of the legal profession (which expression does not include individuals or organisations engaged in the supply of services to the legal profession) to reproduce, transmit and store small quantities of text for the purpose of enabling them to provide legal advice to or to draft documents or conduct proceedings on behalf of their clients.

(6) The LICENSEE shall not sublicence the Licensed Material to others and this Licence Agreement may not be transferred, sublicensed, assigned or otherwise disposed of in whole or in part.

(7) The LICENSEE shall inform the PUBLISHERS on becoming aware of any unauthorised use of the Licensed Material.

Warranties

4.(1) The PUBLISHERS warrant that they have obtained all necessary rights to grant this licence.

(2) Whilst reasonable care is taken to ensure the accuracy and completeness of the Licensed Material supplied, the PUBLISHERS make no representations or warranties, express or implied, that the Licensed Material is free from errors or omissions.

(3) The Licensed Material is supplied to the LICENSEE on an "as is" basis and has not been supplied to meet the LICENSEE's individual requirements. It is the sole responsibility of the LICENSEE to satisfy itself prior to entering this Licence Agreement that the Licensed Material will meet the LICENSEE's requirements and be compatible with the LICENSEE's hardware/software configuration. No failure of any part of the Licensed Material to be suitable for the LICENSEE's requirements will give rise to any claim against the PUBLISHERS.

(4) In the event of any material inherent defects in the physical media on which the licensed material may be supplied, other than caused by accident abuse or misuse by the LICENSEE, the PUBLISHERS will replace the defective original media free of charge provided it is returned to the place of purchase within 90 days of the purchase date. The PUBLISHERS' entire liability and the LICENSEE's exclusive remedy shall be the replacement of such defective media.

(5) Whilst all reasonable care has been taken to exclude computer viruses, no warranty is made that the Licensed Material is virus free. The LICENSEE shall be responsible to ensure that no virus is introduced to any computer or network and shall not hold the PUBLISHERS responsible.

(6) The warranties set out herein are exclusive of and in lieu of all other conditions and warranties, either express or implied, statutory or otherwise.

(7) All other conditions and warranties, either express or implied, statutory or otherwise, which relate to the condition and fitness for any purpose of the Licensed Material are hereby excluded and the PUBLISHERS shall not be liable in contract or in tort for any loss of any kind suffered by reason of any defect in the Licensed Material (whether or not caused by the negligence of the PUBLISHERS).

Limitation of Liability and Indemnity

5.(1) The LICENSEE shall accept sole responsibility for and the PUBLISHERS shall not be liable for the use of the Licensed Material by the LICENSEE, its agents and employees and the LICENSEE shall hold the PUBLISHERS harmless and fully indemnified against any claims, costs, damages, loss and liabilities arising out of any such use.

(2) The PUBLISHERS shall not be liable for any indirect or consequential loss suffered by the LICENSEE (including without limitation loss of profits, goodwill or data) in connection with the Licensed Material howsoever arising.

(3) The PUBLISHERS will have no liability whatsoever for any liability of the LICENSEE to any third party which might arise.

(4) The LICENSEE hereby agrees that

(a) the LICENSEE is best placed to foresee and evaluate any loss that might be suffered in connection with this Licence Agreement,

(b) that the cost of supply of the Licensed Material has been calculated on the basis of the limitations and exclusions contained herein; and

(c) the LICENSEE will effect such insurance as is suitable having regard to the LICENSEE's circumstances.

(5) The aggregate maximum liability of the PUBLISHERS in respect of any direct loss or any other loss (to the extent that such loss is not excluded by this Licence Agreement or otherwise) whether such a claim arises is contract or tort shall not exceed a sum equal to that paid as the price for the title containing the Licensed Material.

Termination

6.(1) In the event of any breach of this Agreement including any violation of any copyright in the Licensed Material, whether held by the PUBLISHERS or others in the Licensed Material, the Licence Agreement shall automatically terminate immediately, without notice and without prejudice to any claim which the PUBLISHERS may have either for moneys due and/or damages and/or otherwise.

(2) Clauses 3 to 5 shall survive the termination for whatsoever reason of this Licence Agreement.

(3) In the event of termination of this Licence Agreement the LICENSEE will remove the Licensed Material.

Miscellaneous

7.(1) Any delay or forbearance by the PUBLISHERS in enforcing any provisions of this Licence Agreement shall not be construed as a waiver of such provision or an agreement thereafter not to enforce the said provision.

(2) This Licence Agreement shall be governed by the laws of England and Wales. If any difference shall arise between the Parties touching the meaning of this Licence Agreement or the rights and liabilities of the parties thereto, the same shall be referred to arbitration in accordance with the provisions of the Arbitration Act 1996, or any amending or substituting statute for the time being in force.